TARA
A MAHRATTA TALE

"Now listen, all ye Brahmuns; I am true and pure, and I am Sutee henceforth."

P. 401

TARA
A MAHRATTA TALE

MEADOWS TAYLOR

GYAN

Published by

GYAN

Gyan Publishing House
5, Ansari Road
Daryaganj, New Delhi-110002
Phone: 011-47034999, 9811692060
E-mail: books@gyanbooks.com

Distribution Network
gyanbooks.com
India, USA, Canada, UK, Australia, France

ISBN : 978-81-212-4091-8 (PB)
First Published, 1863

2nd Impression 2020

Printed at: Gyan Press, Delhi.

TARA A Mahratta Tale
Author: Meadows Taylor

To

HIS EXCELLENCY

THE EARL OF CARLISLE, K. G.,

VICEROY OF IRELAND,

ETC. ETC. ETC.

MY LORD,

THE SCENES AND CHARACTERS WHICH I HAVE ENDEAVOURED TO DEPICT IN THESE VOLUMES WILL BE NECESSARILY NEW AND STRANGE TO YOU; BUT IF THEY EXCITE INTEREST IN THE NATIVE ANNALS OF A COUNTRY OF WHICH I FIND BUT LITTLE REAL KNOWLEDGE EXISTING, THE OBJECT OF THE WORK WILL HAVE BEEN ATTAINED; WHILE, BY THE KIND COURTESY WHICH PERMITS ME TO DEDICATE IT TO YOU, YOUR EXCELLENCY CONFERS UPON ME A VERY SINCERE GRATIFICATION.

I HAVE THE HONOUR TO BE,

YOUR LORDSHIP'S VERY FAITHFUL SERVANT,

MEADOWS TAYLOR.

OLD COURT,
HAROLD'S CROSS, NEAR DUBLIN,
August, 1863.

PROLOGUE.

In the year 1839, I became acquainted with the late Professor Wilson; and in course of conversation on the possibility of illustrating events in Indian history by works of fiction, the details of the present story, among other subjects, were slightly sketched out by me. He was interested in them, and suggested my writing the tale for "Blackwood's Magazine." I could not, however, then commence it, and deferred doing so till my return to India; but, falling into political and civil employment there, was never able to continue what I had begun, till my return home.

The history of the period of this tale, A.D. 1657, will be found at length in Scott's "Ferishta," and vol. i. of Grant Duff's "History of the Mahrattas;" and to these works I beg to refer such of my readers as may be curious in regard to its particulars, of which a slight sketch may not, perhaps, be altogether out of place.

In A.D. 1347, a great portion of the Dekhan was consolidated into a kingdom by Sultan Alla-oo-deen, who founded the Bahmuni dynasty. It was divided into three great provinces, Dowlatabad, Beejapoor, and Golconda, which, on the decay of the royal house, became separate kingdoms under their several viceroys, who successively declared their independence. Of these, Beejapoor was the largest, and became by far the most important and powerful. Yoosuf Adil Shah, a Turk of European descent, believed, indeed, to have been the son of a Sultan of Constantinople, threw off his allegiance to the Bahmuni dynasty in A.D. 1489, and established himself at Beejapoor, which afterwards rose to be the greatest, as it was the most magnificent, city of the Dekhan.

The prosperity of the Dekhan kingdoms excited the jealousy of the Moghul Emperors of Dehli, and their subjugation was projected by the Emperor Akbur; but it had made little progress at his death in A.D. 1605. In the reign of his grandson Shah Jehán, the State of Ahmednugger, or Dowlatabad, was finally subdued about 1630, and the Moghul power so far established in the Dekhan. His son, Aurungzeeb, pursued the reduction of the two remaining kingdoms, Beejapoor and Golconda, with varying success, but untiring pertinacity; and, before his death in 1707, they had succumbed to him. Beejapoor fell on the 15th October, 1686; Golconda in September, 1687.

Amidst the struggles of the Mahomedans, the predatory power of the Mahratta people arose under Sivaji, and assumed a more definite form than it had ever before possessed; and, as the author of the Mahratta History observes, "stirred those latent embers till, like "the parched grass kindled amidst the forests of the Syhadree "mountains, they burst forth in spreading flame, and men afar "wondered at the conflagration."

Of the many remarkable and romantic events connected with the rise of the Mahratta power, those which form the subject of the present tale are, of all, the most cherished by the people; and they are recited, or sung in ballads, with an interest which time does not diminish, and which has exalted the national hero, Sivaji Rajah, to the distinction almost of a demigod.

At the period of the tale, 1657, though the political foundations of Beejapoor were shaking, nothing had affected its material prosperity; and the palaces, mosques, mausoleums, and other public buildings of the capital, were in their greatest magnificence. The city itself, except its vast fortifications, which are still perfect, has now, for the most part, disappeared; and long lines of shapeless mounds, covering an immense area, mark where its streets existed. In some quarters there are villages, widely separated, which once formed part of the general masses of habitations; and there are everywhere remains of mosques, tombs, and palaces, which convey a true estimate of the wealth of those for whom they were constructed, and the taste and skill of the architects.

The citadel is still perfect as to walls, towers, and ditch, and is a very complete and picturesque specimen of Puthán fortification. The royal palaces situated in it, are, however, roofless, much ruined, and advancing to destruction; and the gardens and terraces, with their fountains, are covered by brushwood and tangled creepers. It is a happy thing, however, that the liberality of the Indian Government has arrested decay, wherever practicable, and that all the most beautiful buildings have been restored, while repairs continue to be made as needful.

The buildings so restored are—

> The Mausoleum of Ibrahim Adil Shah, called the Ibrahim Roza;
> The Mausoleum of Mahmood Adil Shah;
> The Méhturi Mahal;
> The Jumma Mosque;
> The Assar Shureef;
> The Royal Well, with its cloisters; and some others.

Of the above, the Assar Shureef is one of the ancient royal palaces, which contains some sacred relics; and, being in the actual condition in which it was left, is perhaps the most interesting of all.

By orders of Government also, drawings from actual measurement were made a few years ago by a clever civil engineer and architect, of all the principal buildings. These are now in the India Library in London; and, to any one curious on the subject, will give a far better idea of the superb Saracenic architecture of the Adil Shahy dynasty, than any description. Mahomedan architecture in India is always beautiful; but there is a combination of grandeur and grace about that of Beejapoor which is not approached elsewhere, and a beauty of ornament and execution nowhere exceeded. The Jumma Mosque, with its side aisles, was constructed for the accommodation of eight thousand persons at prayer; and the superb dome of the Mausoleum of Sultan Mahmood Adil Shah, built of hewn stone, is the largest in its outward diameter in the world.

With these noble remains, the country around them, and its population of all classes, I have been familiar for many years past; and such descriptions of scenery and character as may be found in these volumes, are the result of personal knowledge. The actors in my story are Hindus and Mahomedans; but the same passions and affections exist among them as among ourselves, and thus the motives and deeds of my characters may, at least, be intelligible. I can only hope they may prove of interest.

It was very strange, twenty-five years ago, to observe the remarkable interval of exactly one hundred years, between the attack of

Sivaji on the Beejapoor Mahomedans in 1657, and the victory of Lord Clive over those of Bengal at Plassey in 1757. Both results led directly to the establishment of powers widely differing in their aims and characters, but not the less irresistible by the Mahomedans; and the victory at Pertabgurh was as directly conducive to the establishment and extension of the Mahratta authority, and the decadence of the Mahomedan, as that of Plassey has been to our own sovereignty, and to the political extinction of both. But this curious accordance of dates becomes still more interesting, when we observe that, on the anniversary of a third century, June, 1857, the heads of Mahomedan and Mahratta power were leagued against that which had subdued both; and know that their combined efforts however desperate, and their intrigues however virulent, proved alike futile.

TARA: A MAHRATTA TALE.

CHAPTER I.

"TARA, O Tara! where art thou?"

"Mother, I am here. Is it time?"

"Yes; we should go with the offerings to the temple. Come, thy father hath long been gone, and it will be broad day ere we can reach it. Come," said her mother, entering a small open verandah which skirted the inner court of the house, where the girl sat reading by the light of a lamp, now paling before the dawn which was fast spreading over the sky.

She shut her book with a reverential gesture, laid it aside in its quilted cover, and stood up. How beautiful she was! Let us describe this Brahmun girl to you, O reader! if we can, and tell you a little concerning her.

There were many fair women of her sect in Tooljapoor, and they are always the most remarkable of their country-women, but none so fair as Tara, the daughter of Vyas Shastree.* From her earliest childhood she had given promise of grace and beauty, and since that period—from the time when, hanging shyly to the skirt of her mother's garment, she passed daily through the crowded bazaar and street which led to the upper gate of the temple—to the present, she had ever been an object of remark and admiration; while the rank and learning of her father, and his position as chief priest, had maintained for her a continued and increasing interest as she grew up. None who had the privilege of addressing her ever omitted a loving greeting or respectful salutation: the public flower-sellers intrusted her with their choicest garlands or nosegays to offer up at the shrine—the confectioners had ever a delicate sweetmeat with which to tempt the child—and even the rudest peasant or soldier looked at her, as she passed him, in wonder, stretched out his hands to her, and kissed the tips of his fingers in a worshipful salutation and benediction.

* For explanation of Oriental words, see Glossary.

The promise of the child was more than fulfilled in the girl now budding into early womanhood; and her appearance was so remarkable that, while many of her old friends in the bazaar now rarely ventured to accost her, and even turned aside their heads reverently as she passed, she could not traverse the crowded street which led from her house to the temple, or, indeed, move anywhere during the day without attracting admiration from the crowds of strangers who, from all parts of India, visited that renowned shrine of which her father was the chief priest and manager. Many a pilgrim and worshipper gazed wonderingly upon the calm, gentle face which met him at the earliest dawn in its devotional perambulation round the temple, or followed with his eye the graceful figure which, carrying the daily sacrificial offerings, descended the flights of steps by which the shrine was approached; and, far away in his native village, under the snows of Himalaya, the burning sands of Raméshwur, or the green plains of Bengal, told of the beautiful vision, and never forgot it.

Tara has been up since before the false dawn. She has assisted her father with water to bathe, and in his private worship of the household gods. She has bathed herself, and is now dressed in the simple saree, or robe of all Hindu females. It is of dark blue silk, striped with a fainter blue, and has a broad border of a light but rich pattern harmonizing with the colours of the garment which, consisting of one long piece only, is wound round her several times to form a skirt, then passed about her body and over her head on the left side, whence the end, which is of rich gold tissue interwoven with crimson flowers and green leaves, hangs heavily over her right shoulder and back. Below the garment is a closely-fitting bodice of striped orange silk only; but no portion of it is visible except a little of the sleeve above the elbow. Tara is holding the border of her dress close to her cheek, as if to conceal it even from her mother; and the graceful outline of her arm may be followed, from the tips of the taper fingers past the wrist partly covered with purple bangles and a massive gold ring, along the soft round arm to the dimpled elbow, whence it is lost among the folds of the saree which falls over it.

Do you expect that her complexion will be fair like that of our own northern girls? Ah, no! that would not harmonize with the dress or the country; and yet it is very fair. Not a deep rich olive, but what seems at a first glance pale and colourless; yet the skin is so glossy and transparent that the warm glow of her blood is suffused under it with the least passing emotion or excitement, which, as it fades, leaves, as you think, a more beautiful tint behind.

And the features harmonized with the colour. To a casual observer their expression was almost one of habitual sadness, yet it was not so in reality: there was calm, which as yet had known no rude ruffling—a sweetness that was index to a simple, loving, trustful mind. True, she had cares beyond those of ordinary household occurrences, and these had no doubt increased the pensive expression always remarkable. So her countenance was not easy to describe: nor could you account very well for the patient, care-enduring look which met you from one so young. What every one saw first, were the soft brown eyes, shaded with long eyelashes which rested upon the cheek. Ordinarily perhaps, or if seen when cast down, these eyes appeared nowise remarkable; yet if passing emotions were noticed, they closed when she was merry, till only a bright spark of light remained glistening through the long lashes; and again, if surprise, wonder, or admiration were excited, they suddenly expanded, so that one looked into a depth of clear glowing colour, violet and brown, the expression of which could not be fathomed. But habitually they were modest, pensive, and gentle—full of intelligence, and seemed to correspond with a low musical cadence of voice perfectly natural, yet assisted, perhaps, by the habit of reading and studying aloud, which she had learned from her father. In those calm eyes there was as yet no passion of any kind. Some suffering, perhaps, but no rough awakening to the reality of life.

The rest of her face left nothing to be desired. The Brahmuns of Western India usually possess features more European in their character than those of the same sect in other parts of the country, and in this respect the women share them with the men, if they do not, indeed, exceed them. So Tara had a soft oval face, with small full lips and mouth, a thin straight nose with nostrils almost transparent, which seemed to obey the passing emotions of her countenance. Though the features were soft, they were neither insipid nor weak in character; on the contrary, they appeared full of a woman's best strength—endurance and patience; while, in the full glossy chin and throat, enough of determination was expressed to show firmness and consistency of no common order. Except the eyes, perhaps, there was no feature of the face which could be called exactly beautiful, yet the whole combined to create an expression which was irresistibly interesting and charming; and where all harmonized, separate portions were not remarked.

Every movement of her lithe form was displayed by the soft silk drapery which fell over it in those graceful folds which we see expressed in ancient statues, and it was cast in those full yet delicately rounded proportions which sculptors have best loved to imitate. Standing as she was, the girl had fallen into an attitude which was most expressive: her head raised and turned to meet her mother's entrance: a delicate naked foot, with a chain anklet of gold resting on it, put out from beneath her robe: her eyes open, yet not to their full width: and her lips apart, disclosing the even glistening teeth: —she appeared, in her arrested movement, as if she waited some further communication from her mother, or had herself one to make before she stirred.

No wonder that, as each morning she left the house with her mother to pay her devotions at the temple, and passed along with downcast eyes, her graceful figure attracted increased attention day by day. Many a good wish followed her—many a benediction from the aged poor of the town, to whom her charities were liberally dispensed; and it might be, too, that other admiration, less pure in its character, also rested upon her, and often, unknown to her, dogged her steps.

The contrast between Tara and her mother was in most respects a striking one. No one could deny that Anunda Bye was a handsome woman; her neighbours and gossips told her so, and she quite believed it. She looked, too, very young of her age; and as she sailed down or up the street leading to the temple, and received the humble salutations of shopkeepers, flower-sellers, and all the tradesmen of that busy quarter, with an air which plainly showed how much she considered it due to her rank and station—it would have been difficult to say whether the timid girl following her, and screening her face from the gaze of the people as she moved along, was her daughter or youngest sister. Either she might be, and it seemed more probable the latter, than the former.

Taller than her daughter as yet, Anunda Bye was not without much of the same grace of figure; but it was cast on a bolder scale. The features were more decided and prominent, the colour several shades darker. The face, handsome as it was, had little of the softening element of intellectuality in it; and Anunda was ignorant of everything but household management, in which she excelled, in all departments, to a degree that made her the envy of her female acquaintance, and her husband the envied of his male associates whose domestic affairs were not conducted with the same regularity, and whose cookery was not so good.

Enter the Shastree's house at any time, and you were at once struck with its great neatness. The floor was always plastered with liquid clay by the women-servants when he was absent at the temple for morning worship, and retained a cool freshness while it dried, and, indeed, during the day. It was generally decorated by pretty designs in white and red chalk powder dropped between the finger and thumb, in the execution of which both mother and daughter were very expert and accomplished. The Shastree's seat, which was, in fact, a small raised dais at one side of the large room, was usually decked with flowers, while upon the floor before it, the greatest artistic skill was expended in ornament by Tara and her mother. Above it were pictures of favourite divinities, painted in distemper colour: the amorous blue-throated Krishna playing to the damsels of Muttra; the solemn four-armed Ganésha, sitting with a grave elephant's head on his shoulders; the beautiful Lakshmee and Suruswuti, the goddesses of wealth and learning, the objects of household adoration: and the terrible six-armed Bhowani in her contest with the demon Mahéshwur, in commemoration of which the temple had been erected—all surrounded by wreaths of flowers interwoven with delicate border patterns;—had been partly executed by the Shastree himself, and partly by Tara, who followed his tastes and accomplishments after a pretty fashion. Thus decorated, the dais had a cheerful effect in the room: and choice and intimate friends only were admitted to the privilege of sitting upon it.

The house itself was perhaps in no degree remarkable. Outside, facing the street, was a high wall, with a large door within a projecting porch or archway, which had a seat on either hand as you entered. The door-frame was richly carved, and on each side a horse's head projected from the upper corner. Above the door, in a space left for the purpose, was written in red Sanscrit letters, "Sree Martund Prussunn," "The holy Martund protects;" and Martund was one of the appellations of Siva. This legend was surrounded by wreaths of flowers in the same colour; and across the whole was a garland of mango leaves now withered, which had hung there since the last festival.

As you entered the court, the principal room was before you, on the basement of the house, which you ascended by three steps. It was a wide open verandah, extending the width of the court, supported upon seven wooden pillars, also richly carved, on which crossed square capitals were fixed, and from these, beams were laid to form the roof. This verandah was double; the inner portion being raised a step above the other to form a dais, and at each end of the inner portion were two small rooms in the corners, one of which was the Shastree's library. The whole of these verandahs could be shut in closely by heavy curtains of quilted cotton, neatly ornamented by devices of birds and flowers, which hung between the pillars; but usually all was open, or closed only by transparent blinds of split cane suspended outside.

Having a northern aspect, this room was always cool, and was the ordinary resort of the Shastree. Here he received his friends and neighbours, held disputations, and instructed his pupils. The women seldom entered it except in the evenings when undisturbed; for, though unsecluded from men, a certain degree of reserve and retirement is always observable in the women of Hindu families. There was no ornament about the main apartment except the

Shastree's dais, and the borders painted about the niches and architraves of the doors; but it was kept a pure white, and was scrupulously clean.

In the centre of the back wall of the inner verandah was a door which opened into a second court, round which was a verandah also open, and, leading from it on three sides, sleeping chambers and a bath-room. In this verandah there was nothing but a few spinning-wheels and their low stools; for Anunda Bye had no idea of allowing women-servants to be idle, and when they were not working otherwise, they were spinning cotton yarn for their own clothes. Anunda herself had her wheel, and Tara hers, and sometimes they spun yarn fine enough for the Shastree's waist-cloths.

On the fourth side of the court was the kitchen, and, passing by it, a door led into a third court, more private, though not so large as the second. In the centre of it was an altar painted in distemper, on which grew a bush of toolsee or sweet basil, grateful to the gods; and in the verandah, another altar, similar in form, on which burned the sacred fire never extinguished. Close to it was the door of the private temple of the house, which contained the household gods of the family. Here it was that Tara best loved to sit when her share of domestic affairs was completed. Here she tended the sacred fire, and offered worship, such as a woman could perform, in the temple. She had a small garden in one corner of the court, which contained a few jessamine bushes, marigolds, and other common flowers, which she cultivated for offerings to the household gods in the daily worship. Here she could study undisturbed, and did so with all her heart—here, too, it was that her mother found her.

There was no decoration about the house, except, as we have already mentioned, border patterns and quaintly designed birds and flowers upon the walls. Furniture, such as we need, was unknown. A small cotton or woollen carpet laid down here and there, with a heavy cotton pillow covered with white calico, sufficed for sitting or reclining; and as the goddess Bhowani, in her incarnation at Tooljapoor, does not choose, as is believed, that any one in the town should lie upon a bed except herself, a cotton mattress on the floor, or a cool mat, sufficed for sleeping.

The house, therefore, would have appeared bare in any of my readers' eyes; but it was neat and pleasant to look at: and one can imagine, though decorated in a higher style of art, the Roman houses at Pompeii to have been similar in most respects of plan and domestic arrangement.

There was no evidence of wealth, yet the Shastree was a prosperous man; and could you have seen Anunda Bye's stores of copper and brass utensils—large vessels for boiling vast quantities of rice on festivals and household ceremonies—her brass lamps and candelabra, her silver plates for eating from, and silver drinking vessels;—could you have seen the contents of her private room, in which were sundry large chests, full of sarees, or women's garments, of great value; some heir-looms, woven with gold and silver thread, each having its peculiar history; the shawls which belonged to her husband, the gifts of princes and nobles, tributes to his learning, of which she was very proud;—could you have seen, too, the strong box that lay hidden among the clothes in the largest chest, full of family jewels and ornaments, among which were two necklaces of fine pearls, massive gold ornaments for ankles and wrists, for neck and ears;—could you have seen all these, and the heavy gold cinctures round Anunda's and Tara's trim waists, and their massive gold bracelets and anklets,—you would have been envious, my dear reader, of considerable wealth in this particular.

Otherwise, indeed, the Shastree was a man of substance. Being an only son, with no other sharers, at his father's death, he had inherited a considerable property. He had himself earned, by his scholarly abilities, a small estate in a neighbouring province, the rent of which was punctually paid, and was improving, for he was a good landlord. He derived a handsome income from the temple service, and from the offerings made to him as head of the establishment. He farmed some land, too, near the town, on the bank of the small river Boree, and had an excellent garden near the village of Sindphul, in the plain below the hills, the daily supply of vegetables from which was very profitable from the large and constant consumption in the town. Finally, as one of the most learned Sanscrit scholars of the Dekhan, his instruction was held in deserved repute, and his classes were attended by young Brahmuns from all parts of the country, from whom he received fees according to their means.

CHAPTER II.

In many respects Vyas Shastree was a remarkable man, and, very deservedly, he was held in great respect throughout the country. No one could look on him without being conscious of his extreme good breeding and intellectuality. Well made, there was no appearance of great strength, though in the town gymnasium, as a youth, he had held his own among the wrestlers, and had even been famous as a sword-player. Those were troubled times, when a knowledge of weapons was needed by all men, and even peaceful merchants and priests did not neglect the use of them; but, as he grew older, the Shastree had laid aside these exercises, and spare, strong, muscular arms were perhaps the only evidence of them that remained. Certainly the head and face were fine. The forehead was high and broad, slightly wrinkled now, and furrowed by parallel lines. The head was shaved, except the lock behind, and its intellectual organs were prominent. The eyebrows, strongly marked, but not bushy, projected boldly over expressive eyes of a deep steel grey, which were very bright and clear, and a prominent nose of Roman character, which corresponded with a well-shaped mouth and chin. Certainly it was a handsome face—pale, sallow perhaps in colour, yet healthy, and which occasionally assumed a noble and even haughty expression; but, ordinarily, it was good-humoured: and evidently elevated and purified in character by intellectual pursuits.

The Shastree was a man of note, as we have said, as to learning and accomplishments. He was a profound Sanscrit scholar; and in law, grammar, and logic, with the deep metaphysics of the Vedas, and their commentators, he had few superiors. With mathematics and astronomy to calculate eclipses and positions of planets, he had sufficient acquaintance to assist an old friend, who was infirm, in the arrangement of the "Tooljapoor Almanac," a task by no means easy, as it included calculation of the eclipses of the year, and astrological tables. Of the popular Poorans he had less knowledge, or perhaps did not believe them; and, as many do now in these later days, held more to the ancient Vedantic theism than to the modern idolatry of the Pooranic worship. The Shastree, as a devout Brahmun, had made pilgrimages, being accompanied by his wife; and in disputations at Benares, Nuddea in Bengal, and Gya—as well as at Madura and Conjevaram, in the south of India—had gained credit, if not renown.

In lighter accomplishments, too, such as music, he had a fair amount of knowledge, and sang sweetly the various Rāgs, Droopuds, and other measures of the classic styles. He considered, perhaps, ordinary songs below notice; yet when he relaxed, and was prevailed upon to sing some of the plaintive ballads of his own Mahratta country, to his own Vina accompaniment, or any of his own compositions, the effect was very charming. Tara had been carefully taught by him, and the neighbours often listened to her sweet voice in the morning and evening hymns, and chants of the service, in the little temple of the house. Yet with all this wealth, which he shared liberally with the poor—all this worldly good and honour—Vyas Shastree had two great cares which pressed upon him heavily, and were shared by his wife. The first was that he had no son; the second, that his beautiful daughter was already a virgin widow. And these were heavy griefs.

Annnda Bye had borne him two sons and a daughter, of which Tara was the first-born. The others had followed, and had died successively when giving promise of healthy childhood. In vain had the parents made pilgrimages to the shrines in the Dekhan after the death of the last son, and to Benares also, to propitiate Siva in his holiest of temples, and had from time to time remitted propitiatory gifts to his shrine—no further offspring followed. An heir was not only desirable for the property, which, in default of one, must devolve upon a very distant relative—but, in a higher degree, for the performance of those ceremonies for himself and his family after death, which could only be effectual from a son, real or adopted.

Often had Anunda urged him to marry again, and assured him of her love and protection to a young wife, as a mother or elder sister; and she had even named several parties of good family who would have considered an alliance with the Shastree a positive honour. Why should he not marry? He was yet comparatively young: men older than himself had married twice, nay thrice, or till the object of their desire was accomplished. Why should he not do the same? Was he too old at forty, nay, even less? So urged his wife and his best friends.

Yet the Shastree had not consented. The fact was, he loved Anunda very dearly; she had been a good and true wife to him. He feared, too, a certain imperious tone of temper which he could control, but which, in contact with a second and younger wife, might change to jealousy, and become, to say the least, inconvenient. Or, if he made new connections, there would be the usual tribe of new relations to provide for, or to trouble him with importunate demands. On the whole, it might be better to adopt a son of that distant cousin who lived at Nassuk, and bring him up as his own. In any form, his necessity was urgent, and Anunda grew more and more earnest about the matter, and had even induced Tara to join in it.

"If you had a son," she would say to her husband, "he would be a young man before you were old. Even if you died, the property would descend to him, and the ceremonies would be properly performed. If you grew old, and I were with you, he would take care of us and of Tara. Who will do this now?"

Yes, the echo in his heart was sad enough. Who would do so? There might be two widows, perhaps, mother and daughter, both left to the mercies of distant relatives who had no personal knowledge of them, and to whom they would be as ordinary widows only, no matter what amount of property they had brought with them—shaven, dressed in the coarsest and scanticst raiment, and used for menial offices—perhaps worse. Yes! the echo—"who would do so?"—often as the words were said, fell heavily on the Shastree's heart; and recently he had told his wife that—"he would think about it if his life were spared for another year; until after the next unfavourable conjunction of planets"—"he would think about it;" and so Anunda, without making any formal propositions, was yet collecting information as to the appearance, character, property, and accomplishments of many girls in the neighbourhood, and, in short, wherever she had any acquaintance.

Most heavily, however, of all domestic cares did the situation of his daughter oppress the Shastree. She was growing very beautiful; in his eyes supremely so. So kind, too, so loving, so thoughtful, so unselfish, so clever a scholar! She might have been a happy wife —ere this, perhaps, a happy mother—yet at sixteen she was a widow, with a gloomy future: not felt as yet; for the girl had grown up with him, had shared in his studies, and had in all respects so entirely enjoyed her young and peaceful life, that any thought of change had never occurred to her.

She had been married at an early age, according to the custom of her sect—when, indeed, she was little more than six years old—to a youth, the son of a friend, who was one of the chief priests of the temple of Punderpoor, a lucrative office, and one which would devolve upon his son by hereditary right. The family was opulent, and the young man gave promise of learning and of character. No matter now; he was dead. Three years after the marriage he had been cut off suddenly by a fever, to the grief of his family and to the extinction of the Shastree's hopes for his daughter. Since then, with no further worldly hope before her, Tara had betaken herself to the study of the holy books in which her father delighted; and, doomed as it were to a life of celibacy, had vowed it to the performance of religious exercises after the manner of her faith.

It was unusual then, that Brahmun girls were taught to read or write—more so than it is now; and in accordance with the rules of the sect and the customs of the country, Tara, had her husband lived, would ere now have joined him, and become mistress of his household—a sufficient distinction for a Brahmun girl; but before that event, the application of the child to such rudimental teaching as her father had given her was so remarkable, that in process of years the conventional rules of the caste had been set aside, and it was a loving and grateful task to the father to lead his widowed daughter through the difficult mazes of Sanscrit lore, and find in hers an intellect and comprehension little short of his own.

Many of his friends shrugged their shoulders at this strange innovation of ordinary custom, and argued astutely, that it was a dangerous thing to fill a girl's mind with learning. Others, his enemies, were loud in their condemnation of the precedent it would afford to many, and the bad uses it could be put to; and in disputes upon the subject, texts were hurled at the Shastree by angry parties, to be answered, however, by appeals to ancient times, as illustrated in holy books, when women were deep scholars and emulated the men; and so Tara's desultory education went on. "After all, what does it matter?" said her father very frequently, if hard pressed by caste clamour; "she does not belong to the world now: God has seen it good to cut off her hopes: she has devoted herself to a religious life, and I am teaching her and preparing her for it."

But this did not satisfy the adverse Pundits, still less the fact that Tara as yet wore ordinary clothes, and her head as yet had not been shaved. The degradation of Brahmun widowhood had not been put on her; and she was too beautiful to escape notice, or the envious comments of others, both male and female. The rites of widowhood must be performed some time or other. Her father and mother both knew that; they would have to take her to Punderpoor, or to Benares, or to Nassuk, or other holy city, and after ceremonials of purification, all that beautiful hair must be cut off and burned, the pretty chaste bodice discarded, and she must be wrapped, ever after, in a coarse white cotton—or silk—or woollen—sheet, and all other dresses of every kind or colour be unknown to her.

Ah! it seemed cruel to disfigure that sweet face which they had looked upon since she was a child, and had watched in all its growing beauty! Any other less pure, less powerful parents, would long ago have been obliged to comply with those cruel customs; and were they not performed every day at the temple itself? "Why should the rite be delayed?" said many; "the girl is too handsome; she will be a scandal to the caste. The excuses of going to Benares, or to Nassuk, are mere devices to gain time, and sinful." "The matter must be noticed to the Shastree himself, and he must be publicly urged and warned to remove the scandal from his house and from the sect, which had been growing worse day by day for the last three years."

Yes, it was true—quite true. Tara herself knew it to be true, and often urged it. What had she before her but a dreary widowhood? Why should she yet be as one who ostensibly lived in the world, and yet did not belong to it? For whom was she to dress herself and to braid her hair every day? For whom deck herself in jewels? She did not remember her husband so as to regret his memory. She had had no love for him. Married as a child, she had seen him but a few times afterwards, when he came to perform needful annual ceremonies in the house, and she had then looked up to him with awe. He had rarely spoken to her, for she was still a child when he died. Once she remembered, when he was on a visit, her father had made her recite Sanscrit verses to him, and read and expound portions of the Bhugwat Geeta, and had said in joke that she would be a better Pundit than he was.

She remembered this incident better than any other, and soon after its occurrence he had died. Now she felt that, had he lived, she might have loved him, and the reproach of widowhood would not have belonged to her. These thoughts welled up often from her heart with grief, and yearning only known to herself, and as yet only half admitted: yet which increased sensibly with time, and recurred, too, more frequently and painfully, as girls of her own age, honoured wives and happy mothers—girls who had already taken their places in life—met her at the temple with laughing crowing children on their hips, proud of their young maternity: or came to visit her, and spoke of domestic matters commonly—interests which she could never create or enjoy, and yet for which the natural yearning was ever present.

"Why did he go from me?" she would cry to herself, often with low moaning; "why leave me alone? Why did they not make me Sutee with him? Could I not even now be burned, and go to him?" And if these thoughts changed, it was to the idea of a new wife for her father, who, perhaps, would be as a sister. If a brother were born, what a new source of pleasant care and occupation! Yet this had its dark side also. "Would she be friendly to her and her mother? and if not——"

Her father and mother observed when gloomy thoughts beset her, and when she became excitable and nervous in her manner, and they did their best to cheer them away. "She might yet be happy in doing charitable acts," they said, "in reading holy books, in meditation, in pilgrimages; and they would go with her to Benares and live there." "Why not," the Shastree would say; "why not, daughter? We have but thee, and thou hast only us; it will be good to live and die in the holy city."

Well, it sufficed for the time, and there were intervals when people's tongues were quiet, and these were happy days because so tranquil, and Tara had given herself and her destiny into her father's hands.

"Do with me as thou wilt, O father," she said; "what is good to thee is best for me; but do not risk anything of thy honoured name for one so hopeless as I am. Why should I be a mockery to myself? It may cost me a pang to part with all these;" and she would pass her hand through those long, glossy, curling tresses; "and ye too will grieve to see them gone, and your poor Tara shaved and degraded; but there is no help for it, and the honour of your house is more to your daughter than these ornaments. Without them I should be a comfort to ye, and at peace with the world and with myself; with them, only a source of disgrace and calumny, and I were better dead. Yes, let us go to Benares, to Nassuk—anywhere—so that I leave my shame behind me."

If that poor struggling heart were laid open, was there nothing in its depths which, as she spoke it, combated this resolve fiercely and unremittingly? If it had not been so, she would have been more than human. There was the natural repugnant dread of this disfigurement and disgrace. Worse, far worse, the endurance of the after-life—the life of childless barren widowhood of which she knew and saw daily sad examples. She knew of the bitter experience of such widows, when all modest retirement, respect, and honour of virgin or married life was discarded with the ceremonial rites, and men's insult and women's contempt took their place: and that from this there was no refuge till death.

When she shuddered at these truths—they were no delusions, and her soul rebelled against them—some ideal being, mingling his life with hers, caressing the beauty she was conscious of possessing, would present himself in dreamy visions, waking or sleeping, and beset her in terribly seductive contrasts. The very books she read offered such to her imagination. There were no demigods now, no heroes fighting for the glory of Hinduism, as related in the Ramayun; but there were ideal examples of nobility—of bravery—of beauty, which enthralled her fancy, and led it to portray to her realities. Yet there was no reality, and could be none. She had not seen any one to love, and never could see any one. Who would care for her—a widow—who could love a widow? And yet the dreams came nevertheless, and her poor heart suffered terribly in these contests with its necessity. After all, it was more the calmness of despair than conviction of higher motive which brought to her lips words such as we have recorded:—"she would leave her shame behind her."

But her parents did not go, and the rites were deferred indefinitely. Last year they were to have gone to Nassuk for the purpose to their relatives; but the planets were not propitious, or the business of the temple and its ceremonies interfered. This year, when the cold season was nearly over, in the spring, at the Bussunt festival, if the conjunctions were favourable, "they would see about it." They did not get over the—"if."

So here were the two great cares of the household. Which was the heaviest? To the Shastree, certainly, Tara's ceremony of widowhood. His own marriage was a thing which concerned himself only, and, at the worst, he could adopt an heir; but that Tara should be a reproach to him, the revered Shastree and priest, and remain a reproach among women—it could not be. The caste were becoming urgent, and the Gooroo, or spiritual prince, the "Shunkar Bhartee Swâmi," whose agents travelled about enforcing discipline and reporting moral and ceremonial transgressions, sent him word, privately and kindly, that the matter should not be delayed. He quite approved of the ceremony being performed at Benares or at Nassuk, out of sight, for the old man knew Tara—knew her sad history, and admired her learning and perseverance in study. At his last visit, two years before, he had put up in the Shastree's house, and had treated the girl as his daughter; but the requirements of the caste were absolute, and were she his own daughter he dared not to have hesitated.

But we have made a long digression.

"Come, daughter," said Anunda, "cast that sheet about thy head. It strikes me that men look at thee too earnestly now as we pass the bazaar, and the morning air is chill from the night rain."

"Nay, dear mother, not so. Am I a Toorki woman to veil my face?" said Tara, quickly. "Am I ashamed of it? Art thou, mother?"

"If thou wert not so beautiful, Tara. I dread men's evil eyes on thee, my child, and I dread men's tongues more."

"Ah, mother! I dread neither," replied the girl. "They have done me no harm as yet, and if my heart is pure and 'sutee' before God and the Holy Mother, she will protect me. She has told me so often, and I believe it. Come—I think—I think," she added, with an excited manner, as she clasped her heavy gold zone about her waist, her bosom heaving rapidly beneath the silken folds over it, and her eyes glowing strangely, "I think, mother, she came to me last night in my dream. She was very beautiful, O, very beautiful! She took hold of my hair, and said, 'Serve me, Tara, I will keep it for thee.'"

"Tara! art thou dreaming still?" exclaimed Anunda. "Holy Mother! what light is in thine eyes? Put the thought far from thee, O dearest; it is but the echo of what thy father said last night when he comforted us both—it will pass away."

"Perhaps so, mother," answered the girl, abstractedly. "Yet it seemed so real, I think I feel the touch on my hair still. I looked at it when I rose, and combed it out, but I saw nothing. Yes, it will pass away—everything passes away."

"And what was she like, Tara?" asked her mother, unable to repress her curiosity.

"O mother, I was almost too dazzled to see. I am even now dazzled, and if I shut my eyes the vision is there. There!" cried the girl, closing her eyes and pointing forward, "there, as I saw it! The features are the same; she is small, shining like silver, and her eyes glowing, but not with red fire like those in the temple. O mother, she is gone!" she continued, after a pause, "she is gone, and I cannot describe her."

"Didst thou tell this to him—to thy father, Tara?" asked her mother, much excited.

"Yes, mother. I awoke before him and could not sleep again. I got up and drew water for him to bathe. I tended the fire, and sat down to read. Then he went and bathed; and when he had come out of the temple* and put on dry clothes, I read part of the 'Geeta' to him, but I was trembling, and he thought I was cold. Gradually I told him——"

"And what said he, daughter?" asked her mother, interrupting her.

"He seemed troubled, mother, and yet glad, I could not say which. He said he would ask 'the Mother' after the morning hymn was ended."

"Come then, Tara, we will go to him at once. Nay, girl, as thou art, thy words have given me strength, my pearl; come."

CHAPTER III.

THE Poorans relate that the goddess Doorga, Kalee, or Bhowani, the wife of Siva, once slew a frightful giant named Muhésha, having the head of a wild buffalo, to the great relief of the people who suffered from its existnce; and Hindus generally believe that this event took place at Tooljapoor in the Dekhan. Toolja is another name for Bhowani or Kalee, and hence Tooljapoor—the city of Toolja. After the monster was slain, and the presence of the goddess was no longer required on earth, she left the form she had appeared in as witness of what had been done, changed it to stone, and it was in after years discovered in the ravine where the monster had been slain.

The image still remains where it is alleged to have been first found, and where certain miraculous indications of its presence were made. A temple was built over it, and a town gradually gathered round the temple, which became famous throughout India, and is frequented by pilgrims from all quarters. It is now the idol worshipped there, and is a figure of black marble, or perhaps basalt, highly polished, small, but of elegant proportions, with features of the pure Hindu type. The eyes are composed of large

* Most Brahmuns perform their early morning worship after bathing in cold water, and with their garments still wet.

uncut rubies; and, as the image stands upon its altar, clothed in a woman's garment, in the small dark sanctum of the temple, they have always a strange, weird, and, to the worshippers, a fascinating appearance, glittering through the gloom, and smoke of lamps and incense always burning.

The temple is a very picturesque object, from its situation in a deep glen, the bottom of which is nearly filled by it. Pious worshippers, and votaries from time to time, have enriched it by buildings and courts surrounded by cloisters, ascending one above the other, connected by flights of steps: and in these courts are several cisterns, filled from springs in the sides of the hill. One of them, peculiarly sacred, as believed to come from the Ganges, gushes from a cow's mouth carved in the rock, and enters a large basin and reservoir: and in all these cisterns pilgrims to the shrine, both male and female, must bathe before they can worship the image. Crowded by these pilgrims from all parts of India, of various colours and physiognomies, languages and costumes, men and women,—bathing, ascending or descending the broad flights of steps, pouring into the lower courts in dense throngs, chanting mystic adorations, and singing hymns in different languages and accents; it is impossible to conceive a more picturesque or exciting scene than they present on occasions of particular festivals, or, in general, on the day of the full moon of every month.

The town of Tooljapoor adjoins the temple walls on three sides, and ascends from them—the terraced houses clinging, as it were, to ledges of the rugged glen—on the north and south. On the east, the ascent is more regular; and the principal street slopes from the crest of the table-land down to the first flight of steps leading to the first court, and thence down successive flights of steps, through other courts, to the lowest, which is the largest, and in which stands the principal shrine, surrounded by cloisters and other buildings. Large tamarind, peepul, and other trees, have grown accidentally among the cliffs around, or have been planted in the courts, and have flourished kindly, affording grateful shade; so the result, in the mingling of foliage and buildings of many styles in the temple—surrounded by the rugged sides of the ravine, occasionally precipitous:—and the terraced houses, temples, and other buildings of the town above them—is remarkably picturesque, and even beautiful.

The temple ravine opens into another of large dimensions, which, in the form of an irregular semicircle, is perhaps a mile long by nearly half of a mile at the broadest part of the diameter, narrowing to its mouth. It is called the Ram Durra, and opens gradually beyond the hills, upon one of the great undulating plains of the Dekhan. To the north, the large ravine presents the appearance of an amphitheatre with precipitous sides, from which, in rainy weather, a number of small but lofty cascades descend from the tableland above, and form the head of a small river which eventually falls into the Bheema.

The hills which bound the ravine are about four hundred feet high, and are, in fact, the edge of a very extensive plateau called the Bâlâ Ghaut, which extends nearly a hundred miles, with only a slight descent, towards the east; and, after ascending to the town of Toolja-poor from the ravine, a flat plain is reached, on which the greater portion of the town stands. One promontory of the entrance of the great ravine juts out past and bounds the temple on the left or south side, and along its face is the road by which the ascent is made from the plain below. The hill then turns round sharp to the east, with precipitous sides, leaving a level plain of a few hundred yards in width between the town and the declivity.

On the edge of this precipitous side, to the south, are two other temples, also holy. One, a tall octagon building, now covers the rock on which the goddess is stated to have alighted from heaven when she came to engage the monster who lived in the adjoining ravine; and the other, a little further on, and much more ancient, is situated at, and encloses the head of a spring which fills a cistern, as it trickles down the precipice at all seasons of the year. This is also a sacred place, and is called "Pâp-nâs," or "the sin destroyer;" and the legend says that the goddess bathed in this spring, and washed the monster's blood from her hands, after she had slain him; so it is held sacred.

Truly the whole corner of the plateau is very beautiful. The quaint old town hanging literally on the mountain edge: the deep gloomy ravine of the temple opening out to the larger one: the precipices and rugged hills to the west and north, and the beautiful undulating plain to the south, over which the eye wanders as over a map for fifty miles or more, checkered with thriving villages and their rich fields and gardens,—form a striking assemblage of objects. But the interest centres in the temple itself, with its gilded spires and picturesque groups of buildings, as well as its strange effect in the position in which it has been placed, attesting, no doubt, in the opinion of the people—if there were any question on the subject, the truth of the legend.

It will be understood from the foregoing, that the town is situated considerably above the temple, and part of it on the level ground of the plateau or plain. The Shastree's house was on the edge of the crest of the ground, looking to the south over the ravine of the temple, the cliffs, and a portion of the town beyond, across the small plain which lay between the edge of the temple ravine and the precipitous side of the mountain, and thence over the plain which, in the far distance, mingled with the sky. To the south-east the line of hills was rugged and broken, descending by steep spurs into the lower plain; but from its edge, all round to the north, the eye followed a fair, rich country, sloping eastwards, covered with grain-fields, through which the small river Boree, here only a brook, pursued a quiet course among the town gardens. Again, to the north and west, looking into and across the large wild ravine, were the precipices of the Ram Durra, and the rugged basalt hills beyond them. So, wherever you turned, it was a fair or wild scene alternately; and standing upon the terrace of the Shastree's house, or sitting in a small chamber which had been built over one of the corner rooms, you could see all that has been told; and very beautiful it was.

The Shastree had travelled in his pilgrimages all over India. He had seen wilder and grander scenes perhaps, but none pleasanter to live in, than this cool, breezy, healthful mountain town, enhanced by the presence of one of the holiest shrines in the country. Here he must bear his misfortune calmly; and though his necessity urged the change we have alluded to, he never issued from his door and looked over the fair prospect about him, or performed the sacrificial ceremonies at the temple, without being strengthened in his desire to live and die here; and therefore the struggle in regard to his daughter was the more bitter.

That morning he had risen unrefreshed—his sleep had been restless. Something in one of the books he had been explaining to Tara in the evening had brought up the subject of widowhood and its consequences and obligations, and the message of his spiritual prince had been discussed with much grief and misery to all. There seemed to be no evasion of them possible—the rites must be fulfilled; and he had again spoken of Benares, and Tara had simply and meekly given herself into his hands, and prostrated herself before him and her mother in submission. She was no doubt excited; and her first communication in the morning startled him exceedingly.

You, O Christian reader! must not try his feelings by your own standard. You live under a holier and simpler faith. If in the ordinary occurrences of life, and its joys and sorrows, there is little difference between you, it is very different in regard to faith. You have but one object of calm, loving, trustful, humble adoration. He, as all educated Hindus, believed in the same one God, but it was overlaid by a gorgeous and picturesque mythology, and two distinctions of—as he believed them to be—heavenly beings, to whom separately and collectively worship was due, and yet whose interests and designs were so different and apparently irreconcilable.

His household faith was for the most part a pure theism; but circumstances arising out of hereditary rights had placed him at the head of the local worship of the dread goddess, whom, either lovingly or in deprecation of her possible wrath, he worshipped daily. But the worship of Doorga or Bhowani, as the wife of the creating and preserving power in her beneficence, and of the same power in her destroying aspect—in her wrath terrible and unrelenting—is perhaps more fascinating to women than to men; and, alternating with both aspects, a woman, in all moods and in all necessities, may most naturally perhaps apply to another woman, in whose power she believes, for sympathy and assistance. Has it not ever been so? Greek, Roman, Egyptian, Indian—nay, even Christian?

Nevertheless the Shastree believed, not lovingly perhaps, but in deprecation of wrath; while his wife and daughter, unable to follow the mystically subtle metaphysical creeds of the Veds and Shastras, saw in their goddess enough to fill their hearts with practical faith in, and reliance upon, her power over their destinies. To her, both had addressed their vows and daily supplications, very simply and earnestly, for this devotion of their lives to her was all they could give, if their prayers were granted.

What wonder, then, that Tara's vision agitated him? The Shastree knew of many women on whom the spirit of the goddess in divine afflatus had descended. They were possessed by her: they spoke and prophesied when they were full of her presence: and he dreaded them while he worshipped the power displayed. As Tara told him her dream, and the service the goddess had asked, could it be real? Could his daughter, as an inspired priestess, ever speak before the image? That, however, must be tried without delay, and he hastened more rapidly than usual to the temple, having bid her follow when her mother was ready.

He arrived as the ceremonies of bathing and dressing the image were being performed by the inferior priesthood, and, these concluded, the morning service began. We need not detail it—the decking of the altar with flowers, the marking the forehead of the image with the sacred colours, the offerings of daily food and sacred elements with flowers, and the singing of mystic hymns. Vyas Shastree was speedily joined by other Brahmuns and priests, and bare-headed, naked to the waist, carrying the sacred fire and sacrificial offerings, and chanting hymns with the accompaniment of clashing cymbals and lutes. Thus the procession was passing round and round the temple, and the simple but strange melody rising and falling amidst the buildings, trees, and cliffs, and filling the ravine with sound, as Tara and her mother gained the outer gate, and began to descend the steps which led to the lower court.

Ordinarily they did not bathe in the sacred cistern where, from the carved stone cow's mouth, the stream of the holy spring gushed sparkling into the basin; but Tara paused as they passed it. She had felt more and more excited as she neared the temple, and the melody of the hymn and the clashing of the cymbals, as they came up together through the trees in the still air, had added to the effect already produced in her mind by her dream.

"Mother," she said, hesitatingly—"mother, ought I not to bathe here? Can I go into the presence, even with these garments on me, after what the Holy Mother said last night? They should be wet and pure."

"It is too cold for thee, my child," replied Anunda. "Come, Tara, come on; the hymn will be finished ere we can join—come."

"No, mother, I am hot—burning; something urges me to the well, and I cannot resist it. Mother, I must be pure before the shrine. May I go?"

"The spirit of the goddess is with her, truly," thought her mother. "Go, Tara, it may refresh thee," she said; "and there are dry clothes in the temple. Go, be quick, my child!"

The girl descended the steps into the basin, and, turning to the east, poured libations from her hands to the four quarters of the earth; then the three libations to the sun, saying a short hymn from the Veda. Then followed her prayer to the goddess. "Holy Mother, do what thou wilt with me; take me, leave me, or use me as thou wilt, but do not cast me away! Behold, I come!" Then she stepped forth from the basin, her silk garment clinging to her sweet form, and revealing its perfect proportions more than the innate modesty of her mind permitted; hastily, therefore, she shook it free from her limbs, while her mother wrung the water from the ends.

"I am ready now," she said, simply; "come, mother, I will go to her pure, and sit before her. If she wants Tara she will speak. Come!"

Her mother had observed her glistening eye and glowing cheek, which even the chill of the water did not subdue, and seeing the expression of her face, as she ascended from the basin, was changed from its habitual sadness to one of excited triumph, she caught the infection herself, and seized Tara by the hand. "Come," she cried, "Jey Kalee," "Victory to Kalee!" And so they descended the steps more rapidly, while the music of the hymn and the clash of the deep-toned cymbals resounded through the lower court, and seemed to be echoed and repeated in the cliffs and buildings above and around them.

The procession of Brahmuns and priests was turning the corner of the temple as Tara and her mother met it in the full swell of the music. Usually the girl and her mother fell in behind, reverentially and calmly, and followed it as it passed round. Now, however, the Shastree and his companions were amazed to see Tara separate herself from her mother, and put herself at the head of the party, toss her arms into the air, and join in the hymn they were singing—

leading them on more rapidly than they had moved before. The Shastree marked that she had bathed, and that her wet garments dripped as she went along. "She is pure," he thought; "she has prepared herself, and if the goddess will take her, it is her will. There is something in this that cannot be stayed."

The other Brahmuns stopped, still chanting, and looked to Vyas Shastree with wonder for some explanation, which was as quickly given. "The goddess spoke to her last night, and will not be repelled," he said. "Go on, do not stop her; let her do as she lists."

No one dared stop her, or touch Tara. The height of excitement, or, as they thought, inspiration, was in her eye, and that sweet face was lifted up with a holy rapture. She seemed to fly rather than to walk, so completely had her feelings carried her forward; and as she moved she looked behind to those following, still chanting with them, her arms waved above her head, and beckoning them onwards. They could not resist the influence. So they passed on, round and round the temple, still singing. Other morning worshippers, attracted by the strange sight, joined them, or stood by wondering till the hymn was finished. Then Tara, noticing no one, entered the porch of the temple rapidly, and advancing alone, knelt down before the door of the inner shrine in front of the image, and they watched her silently.

What did she see to cause that earnest look? The image was familiar to all. The light of the lamps within shone out strongly on the kneeling figure, shrouded in its wet clinging drapery, but hardly illuminated the gloomy space in the deep outer vestibule, around which the spectators arranged themselves reverentially. The ruby eyes of the goddess glittered with a weird brilliance from among the cloud of incense burning before her; and the fragrant smoke, issuing from the door, wreathed itself about her form and ascended to the roof, and hung about the pillars of the room.

Those looking on almost expected the image would move, or speak, in greeting or in reprehension of the young votary, and the silence was becoming almost oppressive when the girl's lips moved: "Mother," she cried, in her low musical voice—"Mother! O Holy Mother! Tara is here before thee. What wouldst thou of her?" And she leant forward, swinging her body to and fro restlessly, and stretching forth her hands. "Mother, take me or leave me, but do not cast me away!" She could only repeat this simple prayer, for the yearning at her heart could find no other words; but her bosom heaved as though it would burst the bodice, and her hands and arms, with her whole frame, trembled violently.

"She is possessed, brother," said another priest to her father. "What hath come to her? When did this happen?"

"Peace," said the father, in a hoarse whisper; "disturb her not:

let what will happen, even if she die. She is in hands more powerful than ours, and we are helpless. O Tara, my child! my child!"

"Mother, dost thou hear? I will do thy bidding," again murmured the girl. "Come, come! as thou wast in my dream. So come to Tara! Ah, yes, she comes to me! Yes, Holy Mother, I am with thee;" and, stretching forth her arms, she sank down on her face, shuddering.

"She is dying; my child! my pearl!" cried her mother, frantically, who had been with difficulty restrained and who rushed forward. "Will none of ye help?"

"Touch her not, Anunda," exclaimed her husband, holding her back; "this brooks no interference. Let her lie and do as the Mother would wish her; this will pass away." So they gathered round Tara and watched her. She was tranquil now, not shuddering: the fair round arms were stretched out towards the shrine, and the light fell on the rippled glossy hair, which had escaped from the knot behind, and hung over her face and neck, shrouding them in its heavy waves.

"Let us chant the hymn to the praise of Doorga," said the old Pundit who had before spoken; "brothers, this is no ordinary occurrence. Many come and feign the divine afflatus, but there hath been nothing so strange as this in my memory;" and, striking a few chords on the vina he held in his hand, the hymn—a strange wild cadence—was begun. The sound filled the vaulted chamber, and was taken up by those outside, who crowded the entrance. Still she moved not, but lay tranquilly; the full chorus of the men's voices and the clashing of the cymbals were not apparently heeded by her. As it died away, there was a faint movement of the arms, and gradually she raised herself to her knees, tossed back the hair from her face and neck, which fell over her shoulders and back, and looked around her wildly for a moment; then, seeing her mother, she leaned towards her as she advanced, and, stretching forth her arms and clasping her knees, hid her face in her garment, and sobbed convulsively.

"My child, I am here; I am with thee," said Anunda, supporting her, and herself sobbing hysterically. "Speak! what is it? What hast thou seen? My daughter, my sweet one, O speak to us!"

"Water, mother, water! my throat is parched! I cannot speak. Is she gone?"

"Who, Tara?"

"The Holy Mother; she was with me—she entered into me. O mother, what can I do? Where am I?"

"Here is water for thee, Tara; drink."

She tried to do so, but gasped at every attempt; at last she swallowed a little, and was relieved. "She was not angry, mother," she said, smiling. "Did you not hear her speak? What did I answer?"

"No, my child," said her father; "thou wert silent, and we feared the goddess had taken thy spirit; but thou livest, and we are grateful."

Tara turned to her father with an imploring look for silence, and again, but now calmly, prostrated herself before the image, while the brilliant ruby eyes seemed, to those who beheld them, to glow still more brightly through the smoke of the incense.

"Holy Mother of the gods," she said, in a low voice of prayer, "I am thy slave. I fear thee no longer. Blessed Mother, I will love thee, who art kind to Tara. . . . Here will I live and die with thee according to thy word." Then she arose and continued to him: "Come, father; behold, I am calm now."

"She is accepted, brethren," said the old priest, turning to the others; "let us do her honour. With no life for the world, let her widowhood remain in the Mother's keeping: she has chosen her, let no man gainsay it. Come, daughter, let me mark thee as she would have it done;" and, entering the shrine, he took several of the garlands from the neck of the image, and a small vessel containing water in which were the leaves of the sacred Toolsee; dipping his finger into which, he marked her gently on the forehead, sprinkling some on her head, on which he placed his hands as he said the incantation which denoted the presence of the divinity. Then he hung the garlands about her neck, and the fragrant red powder of the morning sacrifice being handed to him, he drew some gently across her forehead and bade her stand up.

"Jey Toolja!" "Victory to Toolja!" was shouted by the attendant priests and worshippers. "Victory to the Holy Mother!" "Victory to her votary!" "Let us take her in procession!" "Let us go with her!" cried all around.

"Ah, no, friends," said the girl, rising modestly; "ye see but a poor helpless child who was in grief, and whom the Mother has comforted. Leave me! let me go! I would go home. Mother, take me away! Father, do thou come with me!"

"It may not be, daughter," said the old priest, kindly; "we must neglect nothing, else it were dangerous for thee and for us. Bring a palkee," he shouted to the attendant priests, "and get the music ready, and flowers too, and offerings for the Pâp-nâs. Yes, brother," he continued to her father, "for once I usurp thy office; thou knowest what is needed. Come, let us not delay."

Tara looked imploringly at her father; she would fain have escaped the public procession if she could. She only wanted now to get home unperceived, and to hide herself in her chamber. What had she done to be so honoured—to be so noticed?

"It must be, my child," he said; "this cannot be begun and abandoned; let not thy heart fail thee, the Holy Mother will be with thee. Come!"

Tara yielded: she bent reverently before the old priest, and touched his feet, then her father's, and going round the Brahmuns assembled she did the same; last of all her mother's, who was sobbing, yet not in sorrow. "Come," she said. "I am ready; do with me as ye list. Ye are my elders, and I obey."

CHAPTER IV.

So they led Tara forth and placed her in the open palankeen, and, as they decked her with flowers, and strewed garlands over its canopy, the temple music struck up a joyous marriage measure. Then, as the bearers moved gently forward, her father and mother holding the sides of the litter, the priests arranged themselves on all sides of it, and began another solemn chant of victory to the goddess.

By this time, news of the event had passed on into the town, and it was the hour when all the people were astir. Men and women, collected in groups, heard strange tales of how the goddess had appeared to Tara and taken her away to heaven; again, that she had died before the shrine, and they were bringing away her body. The general conviction was, that she had died, and many women, collected in knots, were weeping bitterly and beating their breasts. But as the temple trumpets and conchs blew a sudden and quivering blast, and the glad music was heard with the chant, now rising, now falling, as the procession slowly ascended the steps, and traversed the court,—and at last, as it emerged from the gateway and entered the broad street which led to the centre of the town,—the popular enthusiasm knew no bounds. "Jey Toolja!" "Jey Kalee!" "Bome! Bome!" the cries of victory—were taken up from those who led the procession, leaping and shouting. Many ran for incense or for garlands: men and women thronged from street and alley and joined the procession as it moved up; others stood upon the terraces of their houses and waved garments or handkerchiefs, or hung out cloths from the balconies and windows. "Jey Toolja!" "Jey Bhowani!" shouted all who came. Pilgrims from the Ganges, Sunniasis holding aloft their withered arms; Gosaees with their orange clothes and matted locks, strange, wild, eerie folk,—issued from archways where they had slept, or vaults where they had lodged; and still the crowd swelled, and the shouting, and through all, and over all, the solemn chant and the hoarse and shrill quivering notes of the trumpets.

Few knew why this was, but the procession advanced out of the temple gate, so it belonged to it; and as the girl passed, seated calmly now in her litter, flowers were cast on her, incense was burned before her, and fragrant powder thrown over her, with blessings.

Her old friends, the flower-sellers, emptied their morning baskets of jessamine over her, and touched her feet reverentially; and the old confectioner, who had always kept a sweet morsel for his young friend, threw showers of comfits upon her litter, and in his excitement generously flung the contents of his baskets among the crowd.

So they passed on, through the eastern gate, and over the plain which led to the Pâp-nâs temple, and the sun was now rising over the distant purple hills in great glory among gorgeous golden clouds. As the first beams fell upon the procession, the priests changed their hymn to that in adoration of the Sun, from the Vedas, which we adopt from a free translation:—

"Risen in majestic blaze,
Lo, the Universe's eye,
Vast and wondrous host of rays,
Shineth brightly in the sky.

. . . . .

"See, he followeth the Dawn,
Brilliant in the path above,
As a youth by beauty drawn
Seeks the maiden of his love.

"Hear us, O ye gods, this day!
Hear us graciously, we pray;
As the Sun his state begins,
Free us from all heinous sins.

"Mitra, Varun, Aditi—
Hear, O hear us graciously!
Powers of Ocean, Earth, and Air,
Listen, listen, to our prayer."*

And the people still shouted the cry of the goddess, or joined in the hymn of the priests, till the small temple was reached.

The ceremonies there were brief and simple. Tara bathed in the sin-cleansing basin, but she would not change her wet garments, still resisting her mother. Once more were holy texts and incantations said over her by all the priests collectively; and for the last time they led her round and round the little shrine and court of the spring, chanting a hymn of praise; her father leading, but submitting to the old priest who has already been mentioned. It was finished, and her new life began. The excitement which had possessed her and carried her on was already passing away, and giving place to a sick weariness and irrepressible languor, which not only her face but her limbs expressed.

"She will need careful tending for a long time, brother," said the old priest to her father. "Give her a cooling drink of toolsee and

* "Specimens of Old Indian Poetry, translated from the original Sanskrit." By R. T. H. Griffith, A.M.

tamarinds, sweetened with honey; put her into dry clothes, and let her rest quietly; she may not even speak for many days; for so I have known it. Let us take her home."

"I am thankful to ye all, friends and brethren," said the Shastree, much affected. "This manifestation hath filled me with many cares, for we were not votaries of the goddess. Now she hath come into the house, and the service she exacts is rigid, yet we will obey and do her will. If ye will depart and leave us, take my blessing."

"Nay, say not so," cried all who were near. "Let us take her home; and in honour and duty let this rite be finished." So the procession was again formed, and in the same order that it had reached the temple, it again returned to the town-gate, and wound through the streets, thronged with curious gazers, to the door of the Shastree's dwelling, where the priest and Brahmuns were dismissed with thanks and those only remained who were specially bidden to do so.

Tara's exhaustion had been increasing since the ceremony was concluded; and the wet garments about her, which had not been felt while the excitement lasted, now struck a chill into her which even dry clothes, cast over her by her mother, did not remove. She could not speak, and could hardly move from the litter as it was set down; and when, supported by her mother and the servants, she reached the inner apartment, she sank helplessly in her mother's arms. But she was now in gentle, careful hands, and at rest; and though she did not speak as yet, her grateful looks ere long expressed all the consciousness her mother longed to see.

She had ever after only a confused recollection of what had occurred; and even as they came home there was a vacancy in her look which had seriously alarmed her parents. Her father could remember many such votaries, in whom the light of reason had been utterly quenched, and he trembled for his daughter. We can account for the occurrence by rational causes: a long-continued mental excitement and suppressed care brought on by the nature of her own belief in, to her, that goddess of dread power, yet of sympathy with human requirements,—and its hysterical effect; but to her father, and more so to her mother, as also to all the priests of the temple and people of the town, it was a manifestation of the divine interest, and a claiming of the girl for her own peculiar service.

We will not follow the conference between the Shastree and his friends, which related to ceremonies to be performed and sacrifices to be offered: nothing must be neglected. One of them was the resident agent of the spiritual prince before alluded to, who had only a few days before delivered the friendly warning, now unneeded. "The Mother hath settled this matter herself, friends," he said, "and no one can resist it; we will write collectively to the 'Swami,' and tell him of it; he, too, will be assured that this divine favour is the result of Vyas Shastree's piety, and his daughter's devotion to religious rites; better this than worldly allurements and ties, sweet as they are."

There was no dissentient voice. Nor in the town, nor among the caste, could any one impugn the act. It had been involuntary and public. Thousands had witnessed it, and they bore testimony of the holy fervour which had animated all who accompanied Tara from the temple. All seemed to have caught a portion of the divine manifestation and enthusiasm.

So every one said that the beautiful daughter of Vyas Shastree had become a Moorlee or priestess of the temple, and that the goddess herself had called her from her disgrace of widowhood to the glory of her own service. Was not this better than worldly ties? Now she was free!

Did Tara think so? It was many weeks ere the feverish excitement passed away, during which the loving eyes glowed with unnatural lustre, and a fierce fire seemed to possess her. It was to be expected; and she had skilful and tender attendance. With perfect rest and quiet, and simple remedies, it would pass away, they said, and it did so gradually, and Tara arose weaker, but calm. By-and-by she would be allowed to make her sacrificial offerings, but not yet; and till then her beloved books, the household worship, and occupation, were enough to occupy her.

"Time enough," said the old Pundit, who frequently visited her and had become interested in her, "with a life of service to be done. When you are strong you shall come to us, but not till then."

Was Tara satisfied? If the dread of her shame had been removed, the void in her heart had not as yet been filled; but the new life had to begin, and she would do her best, and so she comforted herself.

Were others satisfied? Yes. As we have said, most who knew her envied her lot, but some sneered, and already shook their heads.

One man had looked at the distraught girl, as she was placed in the litter and covered with garlands, who was satisfied, yet not as the rest. More beautiful in the unconsciousness of her excitement than he had ever seen her before,—far more so, to his sight, than she had ever appeared while ordinarily attending the temple worship with her mother, and where he had watched her for months past, Moro Trimmul had joined the throng in order to observe her better. Being a Brahmun, he had closed up to the edge of the litter bareheaded and unnoticed, singing the hymns as one of the attendant priests, and had thus been able to accompany the procession, gloating upon the girl's loveliness with an unholy desire. As the litter was taken up he fell out of the procession, and, watching it depart, sat down alone on the edge of the cliff looking over the plain, and by the side of the small stream which, issuing from the Pâp-nâs temple, fell down the face of the rock in a sheet of foam. A girl's voice aroused him from a reverie which we dare not follow.

"So the Pundit is not dancing back to the town as he came out, before the new Moorlee," she said ironically.

"Nor thou either, Gunga. Dost thou not welcome a new priestess?"

"I marvel at it," she continued, with a sneer; "thou wast looking enough at her. I dance before her? When she dances with us before the Mother, then she will be a true Moorlee—not else. Now I hate her; I shall always hate her."

"Ah! she will never join ye," he returned; "she is of another sort than the rest of ye: Gunga, thou art jealous of her beauty, girl."

"By the Holy Mother, she shall not remain so, Moro Trimmul. She—a widow—to think of setting herself above us! That cat-faced girl! If she has chosen to serve the Mother she must obey her rules, and be one of us. Think ye we will let her come there unless she is?"

The Brahmun shook his head. "I was thinking about her," he said, absently.

The girl sighed. "I thought so," she replied, "and thou wilt love me no more—no more now. Is it not so? say it, if it is to be so."

"Love thee!" returned the man, bitterly—"yes, as thou canst be loved—by gold. Hark ye, Gunga, make her as thou art; get her into my power, and I will give thee a waistbelt of gold."

"As heavy as hers?" cried the girl, excitedly.

"Thou shalt weigh the one against the other and thine shalt turn the scale—will that content thee?"

"Wilt thou?—shall it? Swear on my neck and my feet to give this, and I will do thy will. Yes, to humble her pride and her father's—who drove me from the temple one day, and I have hated him ever since. I shall hate thee too, afterwards; yet I will do it," cried the girl, excitedly, clapping her hands—"yet I will do it."

"I swear," said the man, touching her neck. "Come and sit here by me." She did so, but neither spoke for some time.

"Thou hast a sister, Moro Pundit, and she is beautiful. She ought to have been married ere this. A little more time, and can it be done?" she said, breaking the silence.

The Brahmun winced. "She was betrothed once," he said, "but the man died."

"Perhaps she was married," continued the girl, with a sneer, "and she is as Tara Bye, or worse. Is it not so?"

"No! by the Holy Mother, no!" cried the Pundit, sharply, and with flashing eyes. "Breathe such a thing and I will have thy life. Beware what thou sayest, even to me! A word more, and I fling thee down the precipice!"

"O, I fear not for my life," said the girl, carelessly, "the Mother takes care of that, and I will say nothing, lest I should lose my pretty gold zone. But what of thy sister? The Shastree wants a new wife, we hear; Anunda Bye wants a son to cheer her and him, and why should not thy sister be taken there? If I do not err, she can have her chance. She is of a good age—why not? Could she understand what to do? Could she be taught?"

"Ah!" said the Pundit, abstractedly, "I had thought of it too, but it seemed impossible. I do not know him—yes—if——"

"If?—why if? Art thou afraid? The girl is here—let me see her and know her, and leave the rest to us."

"Gunga," said the Brahmun, after a pause. "If thou canst bring this about—if thou canst get me speech of this Shastree——"

"Let me speak to the girl first. 'Radha,' that is her name, is it not? Let me see if she is resolute and as I hear of her. If she be, she shall have her desire; thou shalt have thine; and I—ah, yes! I will have more gold. Yes," she cried, clapping her hands again, "more gold! I will have gold anklets, like Tara's. Why should she wear gold anklets and mine be only silver? Wilt thou give them?—all I can hope, now she hath taken thy love from me——"

"When my sister is Vyas Shastree's wife thou mayst have what thou wilt, Gunga. I swear it to thee on thy neck and feet. Art thou content? Yes, thou shalt see her now. Manage the matter as ye will, women's wits are sharper than mine. Now follow me unobserved," he said, rising.

"Once more, Moro Pundit," continued Gunga, "tell me if the marriage can be performed now? Is there a fitting conjunction of planets?—within a month?"

"Yes; till the Now Ratree; after that not for a long time."

"Enough to do, enough to do, in the time," muttered the girl to herself. "Hast thou any women with thee—any relations?"

"Yes, her mother's sister—a widow; no more. Our mother is dead, my father is dead, and there are only ourselves left of a large family."

"Then the Shastree will like the connection all the better, and—ye are rich, they say. Yes, I will bring the widow and Anunda together."

"We have enough. In that respect I can satisfy the Shastree fully."

"Ah! he will ask no questions. His wife is shrewd and clever, and will guide him," she replied; "but he will be careful about the horoscope of thy sister, for he is a great astrologer."

"My aunt is wise, as you will find when you know her; and as for the rest, Gunga, it is in my hands. I, too, am an astrologer and can cast Radha's nativity as I please."

The girl laughed heartily. "Yes, it will answer," she said. "Now go by that path; we must not be seen together. I will come to thee before noon; we have no time to lose. Only remember thine oath, Moro Trimmul, and beware how thou triest to evade or deceive me. I would not hurt thee willingly; and for the sake of—— No matter now," she continued, gulping down what was rising in her throat, "no matter now. It is gone—I see no more of it in thine eyes."

"I am in thy hands, Gunga, and may be trusted," he replied; "nay, more, there may be better days for thee yet, girl——"

"No—no more. No more like the old ones," she said, shaking her head mournfully. "Only the gold now—only the gold!"

CHAPTER V.

"YES, surely it is strange that the two nativities should fit so exactly," said Vyas Shastree to himself, some days after the events recorded in the last chapter, as, seated by himself upon his dais, and having given orders not to be disturbed, he appeared absorbed in a table of nativity which lay before him; "yes, it is strange indeed. The date of birth, the signs under which she was born, and the few calculations which have been made by a master hand, all agree, as they ought to do; and the result, as I have worked it out, is clear enough. This girl, born at Wye, an utter stranger to me hitherto, and brought here by a chance pilgrimage, is proposed for me; and Anunda, Tara, and the old Josee will have it so. Yes, it is a curious coincidence indeed; but let me test these formulæ again; there may be error."

While the Shastree is busy with some curiously abstruse calculations upon his own and the other horoscope he is considering, we must digress a little, to show by what steps Gunga's plans, roughly shadowed out to Moro Trimmul, as we have recorded, were apparently fast approaching a satisfactory completion.

Negotiations had been satisfactorily opened by Anunda with Sukya Bye, the aunt of Moro Trimmul. This lady had, indeed, already become a great favourite with Anunda and Tara, and she had been guided in her intercourse with them by the directions of Gunga. Eventually, the question of marriage, or otherwise, having passed the ladies favourably, rested with the Shastree himself.

The contrivances by which this result had been brought about were apparently too simple to cause suspicion. Yet they had been produced by carefully designed arrangement. It was first of all necessary to get Sukya Bye and Anunda acquainted, and this was brought about at the temple on the night of the ceremonies of the last full moon. The wife of the chief priest had the power to render the performance of the necessary worship convenient to any one she pleased. She could direct special attendance by assistant priests on her friends, and could reserve seats for them, on which they could see and hear to the best advantage. So as Sukya Bye, whose figure and dress bespoke her rank and respectability, was apparently vainly endeavouring to reach the shrine to make her offerings with other women,—Gunga, seeing her hustled and pushed about, assisted her as far as possible; and, feigning to be unable to do more, appealed to Anunda, who had herself noticed the old lady's struggles, for assistance to her.

Sukya Bye was one with whom it was no degradation to be seen associating. Her tall figure, dressed in the richest of plain silk garments, and the heavy gold rings she wore round her arms, wrists, and ankles, betokened wealth, as did her shaved head that she was a widow; and the stout Mahratta serving-men, who, armed with sword and buckler, attended her, proved that she was of some rank, certainly of very respectable position.

Gunga had left her under Anunda's care, and ere the ceremony was concluded the ladies had become excellent friends. It will be remembered that Anunda herself was from the western provinces of the Dekhan, and the dialect and intonation of the lady Sukya sounded pleasantly in her ears. Questions were asked, some mutual acquaintances discovered, and a visit by Anunda soon followed.

Moro Trimmul, his aunt, and sister, lived or lodged but a short distance from the Shastree, and it soon came to pass that the ladies visited each other frequently. Sukya had a point to gain, so had her niece Radha, and both worked in concert with the girl Gunga, to whom whatever happened was related. Her fresh instructions from day to day guided them perfectly, not only to gaining the good will of mother and daughter, but of establishing a more affectionate interest in their concerns than would otherwise have arisen out of a common acquaintance.

Sukya, proud of her own birth and connections, found Anunda perfectly in accord with herself on that subject. She saw the wealth and comfort of the house, she led Anunda to detail their domestic cares, and offered her sympathy, which was accepted. "Ah, yes, if the Shastree would only marry again!" said Anunda to her in confidence, "and there should be a son born, they would take him to Benares and devote him to Siva. They had wealth; yet without this it was a weight and a care to them, which increased rather than diminished."

During these visits of confidence between the elders, Tara and Radha had their own pleasant time too, and Tara's trustful nature was easily won by the other. Radha was ignorant, it was true, but she was to all appearance open-hearted and simple, and she soon learned to feign that reverential yet intimate association with the beautiful widow and her mother, which Gunga counselled, and which was indeed necessary to the success of the whole scheme.

For some days Anunda made no communication to Sukya Bye of the subject nearest her heart; but as she saw the intimacy of the two girls increase, and that the intercourse had served to turn Tara's thoughts into new channels, and also that she herself, as she gradually gained strength, always found some pretext for a daily visit to her young friend, the thought gradually pressed the more upon her mind, that here was a connection which was most desirable for her husband; and, finally, the question alone remained, whether Radha's family would consent.

Tara had no objection either. Indeed, from the first sight of Radha's present extreme beauty, and promise of its development—from her respectful, nay reverential, demeanour to her mother, and her apparently loving trustfulness of herself—she, too, began to think that a better selection could not be made, if her father were willing to take a second wife, than this girl. So she grew to wish it.

Therefore, with much exhortation to privacy, and in the fullest assurance of confidence, Anunda had ventured to ask Sukya Bye, after all reserve had been broken down, whether the alliance might be hoped for. She dwelt at length upon her husband's accomplishments and his wealth. He was not old; many men married far beyond his age. Money was no object—it could be paid if necessary; and she herself would be as a mother, and Tara a sister, to the new wife. In short, Anunda opened her whole heart to her new friend, and in the end found the sympathy she had expected. Yes, the more Sukya Bye considered the matter, the more, as she told Anunda, was she convinced it would be an admirable arrangement. Radha had once been betrothed as a mere child; the person had died lately, else they were to have been married this year. Delay had occurred because the intended husband was poor. He had not sufficient to pay the expenses of the ceremonies. Then Radha's father had died, then her mother, when Moro Trimmul was as yet a youth. He had made no provision for his sister. How could he? So she remained unmarried. Another connection must have been sought for this year, and Anunda's proposal was admirably timed.

Now, all this was true enough in some respects, but not entirely. It was enough, however, for two persons to believe, whose affections were already enlisted in the progress of the matter; and such inquiries as they could make from people who knew Wye, confirmed what had been told them by their new acquaintance. Was the girl herself willing? Apparently she was. And she received, with all the bashfulness and interest necessary to the occasion, the proposal made to her by Tara on the part of her mother. Anunda had

had her fears on this subject, lest the young and beautiful girl should refuse to ratify what her aunt had proposed; but beyond a natural shyness there seemed no objection.

One doubt only remained,—were the horoscopes of the parties in good accordance? "Moro Trimmul," Sukya Bye said, "would never consent to give his sister where the planets did not provide good fortune—in short, till he was satisfied there was no ceremonial objection or direct hindrance. And before the proposition was made to the Shastree—before, in short, the men were to discuss the proposed arrangement, Moro Trimmul wished to see the Shastree's horoscope, in order that the last point of doubt should be removed." He also would give his sister's to the Shastree, if the proposal were to be persevered in.

Very unsuspectingly, therefore, did Anunda take the scheme of her husband's nativity, his "Junum Putr," from the casket in which it was kept, and, with many injunctions as to its safety, gave it to Sukya Bye. It was not long detained; and she was gratified by hearing that the Josee, seated in an adjoining apartment, considered it a most happy one. "Might he copy a few portions? they had been so admirably calculated." And the dame had no objection.

Certainly the plan had been well laid, and as yet well executed. No very deep persuasions were necessary with these simple unsuspecting people. The mother and daughter had yielded long ago; and the result of the examination of the Shastree's Junum Putr had removed the last obstacle which concerned him. The matter, as arranged, should be broken to him that evening on his return from the temple. And the lady Sukya suggested that he should examine her niece's horoscope as corroborative of his own.

So Moro Trimmul had that day put the finishing touch to his work. He had been concealed when the lady Anunda brought the paper we have mentioned; he had rapidly copied the principal points in the table, and noted all the most remarkable of the latter indications exhibited; and he knew that, before evening, he could prepare a corresponding document regarding his sister, which the Shastree himself could not detect. This was a branch of science which Moro Trimmul had studied deeply; and it was with perfect confidence that he followed the astrological combinations relating to the Shastree, and constructed, yet not with too minute detail, the table in his sister's name.

Few Hindu parents care to have the Junum Putr, or "birth letter," of their daughters worked out; but after Moro Trimmul had cast the table itself on an imaginary date of birth, two years later than the real age of his sister, and as if it had been done carelessly and then abandoned, he followed up several of the formulæ indicated, leaving the last incomplete. He felt assured, therefore, when the paper was submitted to the Shastree, that he would himself carry out the last calculation, which had been so arranged as to lead to the present time, and to a combination with his own.

All had been finished. The paper on which it was written was new, but it was not paper of that part of the country; it was from his own district. An ornamental border was quickly drawn round it, in red, black, and yellow lines; the signatures of the witnesses to his sister's original and true Junum Putr were carefully copied; finally, the whole document was held over wood-smoke till it was of a proper brown colour, then rubbed and frayed at the edges, and creased here and there as if it had been often examined; and, lastly, it was perfumed with camphor to remove the smell of wood-smoke, and with the odour of benzoin and sweet pastille. No one, without much difficulty, could have detected the forgery; and, without suspicion, the Shastree had set himself to work out the problem left unfinished—the occupation which we have already noted.

On leaving their friends, after this early visit, in which the Junum Putr was taken, Anunda and Tara had determined to lose no further time in breaking the matter to the Shastree. It was a fortunate day, as they had been told by the old astrologer, the Shastree's friend, whom they had consulted as they went home; whatever they did was sure to prosper. The Shastree was in good humour with himself, with them, and with the world generally, and for many reasons. His greatest care about Tara had been removed. She had been accepted as a votary of the goddess, and had already recovered from her excitement. He had written with others a joint petition to the "Swamî" on the subject, and she had been duly recognized by her spiritual prince. No fear of reproach now existed; and if the Shastree had at first winced at the idea of his daughter becoming a Moorlee, a public votary at the temple, the feeling was passing away. The gods forbid she should become as other girls, who were devoted to the temple service! No; she desired to be pure, and should continue so.

The long and expensive journey to Nassuk, or worse, to Benares, had been saved, and half a year's rent had just come in from his estate. The crops were fine; there were no remissions needed; prices were high, and the rent had been punctually paid. The produce of the gardens and farms was also good this year, and the fees and dues from pilgrims were abundant. This was a special year for pilgrimages to the shrine, and full moon after full moon the crowd would increase.

"What are we to do with it all?" Anunda would ask, as day after day the bag containing the Shastree's dues was brought from the temple by the attendant clerk, or as her husband gave over to her the liberal gifts presented to him by wealthy visitors to the shrine.

As she asked this question of him, the Shastree laughed, and told her it must increase, for the Now Ratree, or nine nights of the goddess, then coming on, were attended by a wonderful conjunction of planets foreboding marvellous events, and which could not indeed occur again in many years—indeed, not under less than a cycle. There would be thousands upon thousands of worshippers there, and the gain would be enormous. What, indeed, were they to do with it all? "We must spend it upon poor Brahmuns, dig wells in desert places, and give marriage portions—all good works, and pleasing to the gods: what have Brahmuns to do with wealth?" said the Shastree.

"Nay; but we will have a marriage at home," thought Anunda; and from the time the alliance was shaped into form she began to hoard every rupee she could get. Never had the gardeners found her so active in coming down to Sindphul to look after the fruit and vegetables in the garden there. Never had the sellers in the Bazar known her to be so keen after the returns of sale. As she said to herself, if there is a marriage, my lord shall have a good one.

This very plethora of wealth brought about the question with her husband. "What can we do with it?" he said one day, on receiving an unusually large gift.

"We will marry you," said the wife. "Tara and I have determined upon it in our own minds; and oh, my dear honoured husband, you are not to object! We have kept this from you as yet; but if you will agree, we have found a treasure, a jewel, such as we can give to you, and be proud and thankful to see you wear."

There was no circumlocution in the matter. Anunda, watching her opportunity, as a wife best knows how to do, had gone direct to the point, and, seconded by Tara, had smoothed away all difficulties and won the victory.

The Shastree made but one condition—that which Moro Trimmul had expected, and for which he had provided. "I care not for wealth or for beauty," he said to his wife. "We are rich—too rich; and thou, Anunda, art more beautiful than ever; but the 'birth letter' must accord; and she must be pure and high in blood."

So Anunda had told him that, as to the first, she would ask for the "birth letter," and hope it would be good; as to the second, what doubt at all? She could vouch for good birth, as good as their own, and for wealth if that were needed.

Now, therefore, that the matter all hinged upon the fitness or otherwise of Radha's "birth letter," and the last link in Anunda's chain was to be completed or for ever broken, it may be conceived that she awaited her husband's decision on the subject with much anxiety. He had requested not to be disturbed while he made the examination. So Anunda and Tara waited within. The outer door of the court had been fastened as well as that of the school, and he was, as we found him at the beginning of this chapter, alone on his dais, absorbed in the contents of the document before him.

"Yes," he said again aloud, "that it is strangely coincident, there can be no doubt. Again and again I have checked these formulæ, and they are right, and the abandoned calculation leads direct into my own. Ho, Tara! Anunda!" he cried, "bring my Junum Putr, quick; I need it." And Anunda took it, and, laying it before him, did not venture to stay or to speak; but she saw by the expression of his face that he was deeply interested, and she again withdrew.

He opened it, that strange shadowing of his life which, with a fascination he could not resist, he had occasionally examined, yet without daring to pry into the future. Enough that he could follow the past as nearly as might be from the fallible nature of the science. Now, he laid both papers together; and his eye passed from one to another rapidly, as his chest heaved and his pulses throbbed with an excitement to which he had long been a stranger, forcing from him the exclamations of wonder which we have recorded.

"Marvellous and mysterious agents in our existence," he continued, "who can withstand ye? who can refuse your directions? Here I bow before ye, O mystic fates, lead me as ye will; this happiness, aided by these heavenly indications, I dare not resist. Anunda! Tara! O wife! O child!" he continued as they entered, stretching out his hands towards them, "be it as ye will, beloved!"

That was a happy evening for the three. It was not too late to ratify the act, and then the preparations were soon made. A few lumps of sugar-candy and some spices were placed on a silver salver, and garlands of fresh flowers procured from the flower-sellers. Anunda dressed herself in one of her best suits, and Tara put on a simple new garment befitting her position. Several of the servants who had suspected the matter, poured forth their congratulations. A marriage, with all the new clothes, and feasting; oh, it would be delightful! And now the betrothal sugar was to be taken, so the matter was decided. Might they accompany the lady? Yes, they were all to come, and one was to go and prepare the lady Sukya; and so, finally, preceded by a pipe and tabor, the little procession went forth into the street.

No concealment now. As the neighbours gathered at their doors they knew why the lady Anunda and Tara went forth. Some wondered, some sneered; but the majority thought Anunda wise. The Shastree was to marry again, and there might again be a male child in the house.

The preparation by Sukya had been made, and the girl Radha, dressed by her aunt and Gunga, who was there, in a rich saree of orange and gold, with wreaths of flowers hanging about her, had been placed on the dais in the house where they lodged. She wore heavy ornaments of gold, and Anunda felt proud of her selection for her lord, as well for Radha's great beauty as for the wealth of which she had evidence. No, she was no common girl. Here were no crowds of poor relations; even money was needless; but they would be too well bred to refuse it.

So they were. The music continued to play a merry measure suited to the ceremony. The girl's forehead was marked with the sacred colours; a fragrant paste rubbed upon her hands and arms, neck and bosom, by Anunda and Tara. Rice and other grain, emblems of fertility, sprinkled over her head, money poured into her lap, and sugar put into her mouth; while the sacred hymn and incantation from the Veda was chanted by Tara and her mother, and joined in by those who had collected around.

Then all went into the household temple of the dwelling and paid their adoration to Bhowani and Lakshmee, and the rite was finished. Radha was the betrothed wife of Vyas Shastree.

"Mayst thou be happy, O my sister!" said Moro Trimmul, who, though present, had not interfered further than to direct the ceremonies. "Surely this is a fortunate day for us all. Now I go to the temple to lay my offerings before the Mother, and, with your permission, lady, I will visit the Shastree to-morrow. Long have I desired to know him, for the fame of his learning has gone far and wide; but who would make a stranger known to him? and surely it is providential that our houses have thus been united."

"You will be welcome, sir," said Anunda, as she rose to take her departure.

CHAPTER VI.

Anunda was not a person to allow useless time to elapse between the ascertained necessity of any act and its completion, and the preparation for the marriage went on merrily. What stores of flour, and rice and ghee, and condiments were laid in! What gorgeous dresses selected! Ah, young English ladies, and indeed I may include mothers also, who may read these pages, you are not to believe that wedding trousseaux are confined to your own country and society! Very far from it. A young Hindu lady, or Mahomedan either—there is not much to choose between them in this respect—is as full of hope of a liberal, a handsome, outfit on her marriage, as any fashionable young lady of Belgravia or Mayfair; and believe me, is as proportionably delighted if it be so.

There was much to spend, and no grudging. So one old cloth-seller had been dispatched to Sholapoor, and another to Wyrāg; one to Nuldroog also, then a large camp and emporium: and the result was, as we may say, an overplus of riches. It was hard to select from the bales on bales which were sent up from the shops; still, piece by piece, the dresses accumulated, and were indeed lovely. Silk and gold sarees; silk and cotton mixed; plain cotton with silk borders; bodice pieces, stiff with gold and brocade—all betokening wealth and comfort. No milliner required here. The garments of one piece, only remarkable for their richness and diversity of colour and pattern, were such as were, and are still, worn by the better classes of society. Annunda was determined that no fault could be found with her own and Tara's selection, and certainly it was better to be on the liberal side.

Then how busy the goldsmiths were! In the Shastree's school court, half-a-dozen men, sometimes more, were to be seen sitting over pans of charcoal, blowpipe in hand, beating silver or gold on small anvils, and fashioning them into massive and quaintly beautiful ornaments. Annunda had given some of her old things to be broken up and re-made. We will not say how many ounces of virgin gold were added, but here too the good lady was liberal—very liberal; and Tara, of her own accord, had added from her own store some valuable jewels. Yes, the arrangements for the marriage were to be pushed on; it must be completed within a month, for after that, there was a "gutt" or planetary conjunction averse to marriage, which was to last long. As yet the day had not been fixed, but it must soon be; and the Shastree was passive when it was mentioned. Not so those with whom he had now irrevocably connected himself.

On the other side, preparations had been as active, though simpler. Moro Trimmul's object was haste, and he had desired his aunt and sister to spare nothing within their means. Strangers as they were in the town, they found the girl Gunga, with whom, since the ceremony at the temple, Sukya Bye had become intimate, a very useful ally. She knew what Annunda was preparing. Her gossips—the flower-sellers, the cloth-merchants, and the goldsmiths—detailed all that was being done, and to aunt and niece they were amply satisfactory. They knew the Shastree was wealthy, but the profusion they heard of surprised them.

"The Shastree loves thee, girl," the lady Sukya would say. "He will spend his wealth on thee. What lucky chance brought us here, who can tell? else who would have cared for thee? To whom could we have given thee? Be content; he is not old; he will love thee, for thou art beautiful. Wait and see."

Truly she was so! Not Tara's tranquil, pensive beauty; not Annunda's even in her prime. This girl was very different from both. She was darker than either—a warm, richly-tinted, clear, golden brown, with a skin like velvet; a small head, oval face—perhaps more round than oval—and a mass of thick wavy hair, which, if loosened, fell far below her waist, curling at the ends; a low broad forehead, strongly marked arched eyebrows, and a nose straight and delicate in outline, were perhaps the ordinary possessions of a good-looking, well-bred Mahratta girl; but the eyes and mouth were more remarkable, because they gave an index to her character.

"We will not tell what she is like," Anunda said, as her husband frequently asked her of Radha, for as yet he had not seen her. Perhaps he was indifferent on the subject, yet hardly so; it would have been unnatural not to care at all. Certainly, as the days passed, the Shastree grew somewhat curious, and he had to wait many more ere he should see her.

"Content thyself, husband," Anunda would say, as he questioned her; "I have told thee she is beautiful, else I had not noticed her: she hath a shape like a nymph, eyes like a deer, and a mouth like that of Kāmdeo. What need to say more? Wait and see." So the Shastree waited patiently. Another would have followed the girl—contrived to see her by some means not perhaps over scrupulously; but the Shastree was very honourable, and such an alternative did not even suggest itself to him.

But they were right. What Anunda had noticed, and Tara too, were only the eyes and mouth and the figure. Who could pass them by unheeded? Such eyes—so large, so soft in their velvet blackness when at rest, yet if excited, how different! The long, thick lashes, which were positively heavy in character, shaded them ordinarily, and produced a soft, dreamy effect; but if the girl looked up, or was interested, or suddenly roused, these eyes seemed to glow internally, and to assume a character almost oppressively fascinating.

Radha well knew their power: since she was a child she had been told of the beauty of her eyes, and she believed it—nay, added to their expression by slightly staining the inner portion of her eyelids, which gave to the already heavy lashes a softer character if the eyes were at rest, or increased their effect if they were excited. Lately a habit had grown upon her of contracting her brows, and dilating her eyes till their effect was almost fierce, which both her brother and aunt had tried to check, but it did not leave her easily. Sometimes it gave place to a look of dreamy languor inexpressibly touching, and so sorrowful in character that, had the girl been older, it might have been attributed to some great grief lying at her heart, or some painful recollection. As it was, it was unsuspected, except by those who knew the cause.

The mouth followed the eyes. When they were excited by any emotion, the lips at once closed and were firmly compressed; but ordinarily they remained a little open in the centre, showing teeth white, pure, and glistening with a pearly lustre. The lips were full, red, and moist—the upper deeply arched and curved, with the corners falling back into deep dimples; yet the mouth was small and delicate, pouting, and decidedly voluptuous when at rest or smiling, yet capable of being hardened into an expression of self-will and obstinacy, which indicated an inflexible determination should there be occasion to exercise it. No wonder that, seeing her in her most placable moods—for the girl from the first had appeared charmed by the prospect of her marriage—Anunda and Tara had been captivated by beauty so remarkable. It would have been well, perhaps, could they have seen the face under other expressions, and so been saved from what, under different circumstances, had an irresistible fascination.

Need her figure be described? Being younger than Tara, there was not the same development of form. The arms and throat were less rounded, yet the lines were as graceful and full of promise of perfection as hers. Eventually they would be about the same height —Radha, perhaps, a shade taller, and both slighter than Anunda ever had been. Her hands and feet were small and beautifully formed, more so, perhaps, than Tara's; they were indeed, remarkable features in her figure—so much so that, as Tara was bathing her one day, and washing them, she had held them to her lips and kissed them in succession involuntarily.

It was difficult to tell her age. Her "birth letter" told the Shastree she was not yet twelve. Had she exceeded much that age, to their knowledge, Anunda would have objected to the marriage; indeed, she could not have been married at all. But she was in reality fourteen, nay more. Sometimes, when her features relaxed, her eyes soft and dreamy, her mouth smiling, and her whole face assuming a loving tenderness of expression, she appeared hardly the age she was said to be; but when there was any change, and the rigid look already noticed took its place, she appeared considerably older.

Now, Anunda was by no means desirous of a very young girl for her husband's new wife. Many had been offered of very tender age indeed, whom she had invariably declined. She could not be troubled with a child; and if a thought that Radha might be older than she was represented to be, ever crossed her mind, a bright smile, a tender caress from the girl at once removed the doubt, and restored confidence. As to her figure, it did but furnish earnest of mature development. And were not many girls precocious? She had been so herself. Yes, Radha was very beautiful; and, as day after day passed, Anunda longed the more for the time when she should be able to clothe her in one of those gorgeous dresses, to deck her with flowers and jewels, and to present her to her husband a bride worthy of him—worthy of her own affection—the most precious gift she could make to him.

We have said that Radha was older than she was represented—and perhaps a brief sketch of her previous history is needful. She had been an indulged and precocious child, of a vain, weak, but beautiful mother. Her father, one of the hereditary Josees, or astrologers, of Wye, had died some years before, and her mother shortly after him. Moro Trimmul, on succeeding to the care of the house, had given charge of his sister to his aunt, and betaken himself to the company of certain wild associates, with whom, from his powers of learning, he had become an especial favourite. The head of these was the Rajah Sivaji, whose rapid career to independence was one of the remarkable events of the times; and the wild exploits of the young prince, his raids against the Moghuls and Mahomedans in general, had long since enlisted the sympathies of the Mahratta people.

Sivaji's early career had been dissolute, but that was a venial fault among the people. His companions were the young Mahratta gentry,—yeomen, and farmers, whom he best loved to draw about him; above all, young Brahmuns who would join him, whether as priests or soldiers, or both, in his wild enterprises. Moro Trimmul was one of these—one who had grown into his deepest confidence. So long as Moro's father lived, he had in some degree restrained his son; but his private meetings with his prince were still frequent; and in the plays and recitations, of which Sivaji was passionately fond, Moro was generally an actor and reciter. Thus it was that Sivaji frequently came to Wye, and put up at the Josee's house; and so he came to know Radha—a beautiful child then, whom he could caress without hindrance. He a Mahratta, she a Brahmun—any union was impossible; and yet she grew to be more than interesting to him as she advanced in age.

Eventually Radha's betrothed husband died. Other offers were made for her, but were always refused, so peremptorily, that people believed the report designedly set afoot by her brother and Sukya Bye, that she was to be married to a distant relative who, now absent on pilgrimages, would return and claim her, or she would have to be taken to him. And so the girl grew, the time for marriage passed, and the Rajah's visits, often clandestine, were encouraged by aunt and nephew, with what ultimate hope of result might be imagined. Yet both were careful there should be no scandal.

Perhaps their scheme might have succeeded had not Sivaji himself, now feeling his way to power, seen the peril of the connection. Was she wife or widow, there might have been fewer scruples, but, an unmarried Brahmun girl would be a burden, a disgrace, which he dared not encounter—one that would not fail to be resented by the priests, whom it was his aim to gain. He could not spare one so devoted, so able, and so unscrupulous as Moro Trimmul, nor could he replace him; he needed many such, and he loved him too much to break with him on this point.

It was a hard struggle. But the young prince, whose firm will and self-control finally won him a kingdom, successfully resisted the opportunities deliberately offered. As the girl grew, as his intercourse with the house became more and more unreserved, it was clear to him that her love for him was growing as part of her existence. The girl, for whom he had always a kind word and free greeting, who claimed the privilege of serving "her Rajah," when he put up at their house, became by degrees shy and reserved; cried if he spoke kindly to her, and trembled if he approached her. He could not be mistaken in those eyes: they told their own story—love.

Under such circumstances, among such people, love is passion. It has no medium except in maturer age and constant association. The girl—still a child in years—loved deeply, passionately; and as she grew older, month by month, day by day, the news of her prince's exploits, now beginning to be sung in ballads through the country, excited her fearfully. Her aunt and brother had detected her in more than one attempt to escape to him, and, fearful of the result, had prevented it. Had he taken her away, would they have pursued? Surely not; but he was careful—he admitted his own danger to himself—and he gradually avoided the house, though he clung the more closely to Moro Trimmul. Radha found means to send occasional messages to him—a child's love, a child's yearning for him were told to him; and we know that, in some instances, a child's love—there and here the same—is more passionate, because more pure and more absorbing, than a woman's. What was marriage to her? If she could only be with her Rajah—to serve him, to live with him, to ride, nay, to fight with him—she would go, or die.

The last time Sivaji had seen her she had grown desperate. She had never spoken so to him before; but she had told him she must die if he did not take her away. "Nay, but I will come with thee," she cried, "even if thou cast me out among thy servants." And he confided this to her brother. "For my sake," he said, impressively, "if not for thine and hers, keep her safe; take her away and have her married; the farther away from hence the better. It is no use speaking to her. Moro Trimmul! save me from the temptation, thyself from the contumely this would bring upon us. I know what is in thy heart; but, beautiful as she is, it cannot be."

So a plan was quickly arranged between them. Moro had an intimate acquaintance with the Mahratta gentry of the Dekhan, and he was despatched to canvass them. This necessitated journeys from place to place. He was well provided with money, and he travelled, as one under vows of pilgrimage, to different shrines. Thus opportunity might occur for marrying Radha; and, leaving all servants behind him but a few men in whom he had perfect confidence, he took his aunt Sukya Bye with him as protection to his sister. No one cared to inquire who the young prince's envoy and counsellor was, or what his family affairs were. Enough that he had a sister and an aunt with him, and was conducting his secret mission with admirable policy and address.

Thus he at length arrived at Tooljapoor alone. The rainy season had set in, and travelling was no longer pleasant or easy. The town was a good position for his purpose, and there were many rich families and landholders in the "Bâlâ Ghaut" province to be brought over. For a time he secluded himself, and lived humbly in a hired lodging or in one of the courts of the temple. Here he had seen Gunga, and here also he daily watched Tara as she and her mother performed their worship. Even thus early the advantage of marrying his sister to the Shastree, of whose household circumstances Gunga had told him, had appeared most desirable; but as his passion for Tara grew, it was a thing to be accomplished at all hazards. Gunga did not appear able to help him, for it was clear that neither the Shastree nor his wife noticed the inferior priestesses of her class, and Tara never spoke to them. He therefore secured a good house for some months, and sent for his aunt and Radha from Punderpoor, where he had left them: and, till their arrival, had busied himself in obtaining local information for the furtherance of his future designs.

On leaving their home at Wye, and after Radha's first paroxysms of disappointment were past, Sukya Bye and Moro Trimmul had instructed the girl what to do. Perhaps, in despair of accomplishing her ends, or with the desire of all Hindu girls for an early settlement, she was an apt scholar. Radha was to deny all knowledge of her age, to assume a childish demeanour, to acquiesce modestly, and as she saw other girls do, if she were proposed for. She was assured she would be given to none but a man of wealth—her beauty would secure her this. If possible he should be young; but this was a difficult point, and what matter if he were old? She could have jewels, rich clothes, an establishment of her own—she would have all these secured to her, and afterwards would be her own mistress.

But if she refused, or opposed these efforts in her behalf, she would soon be too old to be assisted at all. As it was, few would believe her to be within the marriageable period for Brahmun girls. In a year, nay less, her marriage would be impossible, and she must be treated like a widow, shaven and degraded, or married to a dagger,* and turned into a temple to shift for herself.

* Female devotees are married to a sword or dagger, as emblematical of union to the divinity to which they have been devoted.

Was it wonderful that the girl submitted to, nay, even assisted in, their deceptions, or that those eyes looked dreamily after her own prince, while her spirit, chafing within, carried her, in those moments of abstraction, away into his glorious mountains, to be loved and caressed as she felt he, and, he only, could love and caress her if she were with him?

CHAPTER VII.

After preparations for the Shastree's marriage had been actively commenced on both sides, there was no further hindrance. Moro Trimmul having been made known to the Shastree by Anunda, as she had promised, the two men soon found a day in the calendar, so far unexceptionable as regarded planetary influences, that they at once fixed upon it; and the ladies, having been consulted, declared there were no objections or hindrances now, for on both sides of the houses everything was prepared.

Meanwhile his new acquaintance was a delightful addition to Vyas Shastree's circle of friends. Who more accomplished for his age than Moro Trimmul, more fascinating in manner, or astute in argument and judgment? He had not the refined beauty of his sister, except that his eyes were, like hers, large, soft, and very black, with the same habit of dilation, relaxing into an almost womanish tenderness: but when aroused, their excited expression was infinitely more fierce than Radha's, even to savage cruelty. The mouth was always coarse and sensual, but there was at least good-humour about it if he were not angered, and a strength of character in the countenance which could not be mistaken. Now, nothing occurred to cause even a passing cloud, and the days which intervened between the betrothal and the marriage were pleasantly spent by all. Even Radha was interested, and clung more closely to Tara than ever; for with Anunda, as with her aunt, she preserved the habitual reserve and respect required by their positions.

"I will go to the temple, daughter," said Anunda one evening, "and keep thy father there. Do thou bring Radha here, and let her look at the dresses and jewels: if there is anything she wants in addition, tell me, and we will get it." The good lady could not do too much.

Kind Anunda! it was so considerate. Could any doubt of her ultimate happiness remain in the girl's heart? What other "sister wife" would have cared so for her?

Oh, the girl's delight at those gorgeous clothes and jewels! She had heard of splendid gifts at marriages, and there was one at Wye in which she had helped to deck the bride; and when she had seen her—she was but a mere child—dressed in a brocade garment stiff with gold, she had wondered whether it would ever be possible to possess one like it. There were several—green and gold, crimson and gold, purple and gold. The most glossy of Pyetun silks, soft muslin sarees from Narrainpett and Dhunwar, of which she had heard, but had never seen; they did not come to her country: all were beautiful.

Then the ornaments. There were massive gold chain anklets, with small bells to them, armlets, bracelets, ear-rings, necklaces. There was the sacred "talee," which would be tied round her neck. Tara showed them all as they were laid out in cotton upon a tray covered with red muslin. How beautiful they were! and all would belong to her; they would be put on her the day of the ceremony, and her own taken off as she entered the house. Then the place where she was to be bathed and dressed was newly coloured and plastered, and the comfort of the house and its pretty decorations—all satisfied the girl's longing. It was what she had pictured to herself; and Tara said her father was kind, so kind—he would love his little wife after his quiet fashion, and deny her nothing.

So it was not to be wondered at if any repugnance which she had felt was fast passing away, and if, when her brother asked her whether she would be content, she told him she was grateful for what he had done; and for the time perhaps she was so.

Sukya Bye had told her nephew of Radha's visit to the Shastree's house by stealth with Tara: she was afraid he might hear of it otherwise, perhaps through the servants or Gunga, and was rejoiced that he considered it a happy circumstance. "She will be satisfied with the wealth," he said, "and all that she sees will excite the desire for more, and so, aunt, we shall best hold her to our purposes. She cannot recede now; and, while moulding the Shastree to her will, by-and-by she need not forget Sivaji Rajah." But he did not tell this to Radha; and neither by her brother, nor Sukya Bye, was any reference made to the past. When all was beyond chance of disturbance, he would set her to work to compass his own ends.

The Shastree and Pundit were of different schools of philosophy; the former, as we know, belonged to the ancient, and, as he considered, orthodox, Vedantic school of Veda Vasa; the Pundit to the more modern Mimansa school of Jomiai, and to the doctrines and mythological histories of the Poorans. So they had discussions, in which other Brahmuns of the town joined, while the ladies sat behind a screen and heard their disputations, and Tara explained to them what she could follow. Or the friends played at chess, both having excellent skill;—the Shastree calm and steady, the Pundit fiery and impetuous, as were their natures; and so they had many an earnest battle.

It was not long before the politics which then agitated the country began to be discussed between them. They lived under the same Mahomedan government, that of Beejapoor: but while Tooljapoor and the districts around it were as yet in entire subjection, those to the west—particularly the wild rugged country beyond Wye, the Mawuls or mountain-valleys of the Ghauts, stretching into the Dekhan—owed but a slight allegiance to the Mahomedan dynasty, and perhaps had never been completely subdued. Here it was that many of the oldest Mahratta families had taken refuge after the overthrow of the Hindu dynasty of Deogurh, the modern Dowlutabad, and the subsequent subjection of the country by the Mahomedan Emperors of Delhi; and it was among these families, the Bhoslays, Nimbalkurs, Morays, Ghoreparays, and others, that the germs of that combination to resist—to them an oppressive and corrupt government—existed, which was presently to be ripened into a successful revolution.

On the other hand, this dynasty of Beejapoor had already been attacked by the immense power of the Emperors of Delhi; and while the independent kingdom of Ahmednugger—itself at one period little inferior in splendour to that of Beejapoor—had been entirely subdued, and the princes of its house annihilated by the Moghuls, any combination to resist them by the two states had not only been rendered impossible, but it was clear that Beejapoor would follow its example: and those were not wanting who hoped, under a new power, to regain many privileges which hitherto had been withheld from them.

But it was in the antagonism of the two contending Mahomedan powers that the Hindu families of the Dekhan saw the means of emancipation from both. It might be a work of time, and of immense labour and skill: but the opportunity seemed to present itself; and while feigning submission alike to the Moghuls, as after the conquest of Ahmednugger their forces were poured into the provinces which had formed that kingdom, and, on the other hand, to the older-established dynasty of Beejapoor, a stirring spirit began to be aroused among the Mahrattas; and that secret combination silently progressed, of which Moro Pundit was one among many other agents employed by Sivaji, the prince to whom all now looked as the present head, if not the instigator, of the movement.

It had, in fact, already been some time covertly in progress. Shahji Bhoslay, the father of Sivaji, had commenced it in a series of wild irregular forays and raids from his patrimonial estate, which was situated among the Mawuls west of Poona, against the Mahomedan posts and garrisons of the western provinces of Beejapoor. For a time he was successful, but only as a mere freebooter; and in the end he was defeated, taken prisoner, and confined in a dungeon in Beejapoor for several years by the monarch Mahmood Adil Shah, the father of the king reigning at Beejapoor at the period of our tale. But Mahmood was not implacable. On the intercession of his mother, by whose wise counsels he had often been guided, Shahji was not only released but raised to a high command, and during the subsequent invasion of Beejapoor by the Moghuls did good service, and so the progress of the Mahratta power was stayed.

Of his two sons, Sivaji early took the lead, and, encouraged by his mother, a lady of high family and ambition, and admirable judgment, he aspired to be the head of a Mahratta confederacy. What progress he eventually made is already matter of history, which will have no record in these pages; but at the time of which we write, he was strengthening himself in his own wild country, collecting adherents, canvassing those who still held aloof, fortifying rugged and inaccessible strongholds, and, by the suddenness and successful issue of his continuous forays, was rendering himself famous in the eyes of the people. While he treated with both of the rival Mahomedan powers by turns, he took his own course; and yielding alternately to each whenever their force was locally in excess of his own, was in reality faithful to neither.

To Sivaji, also, belonged the prestige which none else had dared to assume—that of receiving aid from heavenly powers. The goddess Bhowani was the tutelar deity of his family; and it was the popular belief that she had chosen his father as the champion of her faith, but that he had transgressed warnings and visions, and, implacable as she was believed to be, she had cast him off. It was otherwise, however, with his second son Sivaji. She had chosen him to be the scourge of the cow-slaying, impure, and licentious Mahomedans. The cries of her votaries had arisen to her, and the land was to be purged of uncleanness. Temples would be again filled with Brahmuns, and the sweet incense of pure sacrifice would ascend to her. The mother of Sivaji, it was reported, saw and recorded visions, too glorious to relate, in which her son was a victorious conqueror, and the infidel Mahomedans were slain in tens of thousands by the Mahratta people in those great battles which were to ensue. And these visions were believed.

As yet these prophecies were circulated privately among the people, but there was not a Mahratta, far or near, who did not know of them. Ballads were written about them, and sung at fairs and markets. Women composed and chanted extempore verses as the household mills flew merrily round in the early morning. Men sang them to their oxen as they ploughed, or drew water from their wells; and so a spirit spread through the people which eventually became irresistibly powerful.

In this excitement, too, existed the incentive to the worship of Bhowani at all her most celebrated shrines; and everywhere—to gather her votaries together, to excite them to action, and to warn them to be ready when the time arrived—were agents such as Moro Trimmul, despatched by the young chieftain. Nothing appeared on the surface. Experience had taught extreme caution. There were no assemblies of armed men, no displays of force: an occasional successful raid or resistance by Sivaji kept up what might well be called the national spirit; but all delayed to strike, till, in the expressive Mahratta phrase, Dônguras, lavilé Déva, "the fire was on the hills."

Very dexterously, therefore, and after having prepared him for the communication, did Moro Trimmul confide to the Shastree some of the popularly-reported plans of his friend and prince, and sought his counsel and assistance, and partly also the purport of his own mission. He asked information as to the families of the Bâlâ Ghaut, the Nimbalkurs of Wasi, the Kallays of Nelinga, the Bhoslays and Ghoreparays of Akalkote, all neighbours; and also respecting the wealthy yeomen and farmers of the country. He did not mention Pahar Singh, with whom, through the Gosaees of Kullianee, and their agency at Tooljapoor, he had already opened negotiations, and found the robber chieftain fickle and undecided, extravagant in his demands for estates, for high command, and other rewards.

Nor did he disclose that weightier secret, known to his prince and himself, on which, for the present, the success of their enterprise rested. Khan Mahomed, the Wuzeer, or Prime Minister, of Beejapoor, might be detached, it was said, from the royal interest of his house; and he was then, with a large army, lying at and about Nuldroog, little more than twenty miles distant from Tooljapoor. To this man, at his own request, in phrases only to be interpreted by himself, a letter had been fowarded through the Gosaee banker's agent at Tooljapoor; but no reply had been received. Nor was Moro Trimmul sanguine on the subject, for reports of the Wuzeer's intrigues in other quarters were in men's mouths. No; it was from the Mahratta families alone that he had expectations; and he knew that at the ensuing festival, all or most of the province would assemble at Tooljapoor.

To say that he found a zealous coadjutor, or hoped for one, in the Shastree, would not be correct. The Shastree was not ambitious. He enjoyed already, as we know, a very lucrative and prominent position, in which he was honoured and respected. He avoided all Mahomedans upon principle; but the governors of the province often sought his advice and assistance in civil and judicial matters regarding Hindus, and he was not only never molested, but, on the contrary, respected and treated with consideration, and had even been invited to court. He had, therefore, no quarrel with the Mahomedans, and he well knew their power. He had watched Shahji's failures, and he had noted the effect of Sivaji's efforts; still he admitted there was more chance of success now than before; and he agreed to assist Moro Trimmul, by bringing him into communication with the gentry of the province, provided he were not required to take any prominent part in what should follow. To say that Vyas Shastree was indifferent in this matter, would be incorrect; but to anticipate enthusiasm or personal zeal would have been impossible from his character, and Moro Trimmul did not expect them.

"After the ceremony," he said to the Shastree, "Radha, of course, will remain with you. Sukya Bye will return to Wye with the servants. Give me, then, letters to the Nimbalkurs of Wasi, and to such others as you please, and I will go alone. Introduce me as a reciter of plays, and I will make my own way unnoticed and unsuspected. Here I can be of no use, and may even attract suspicion."

To this plan Vyas Shastree gave his cordial consent. Moro Trimmul would go before the Now Ratree, and return for the festival.

CHAPTER VIII.

I AM afraid it would take more time than the limits of this history will afford, were I to describe minutely all the festivities and observances of Radha's marriage. I assure you, dear readers, that a proper, orthodox Hindu marriage, is a very tiresome affair; and, like many other marriages, perhaps, everybody is glad when it is over. Very noisy, tediously minute in ceremonial, liable to interruption from disputes—it is often an arena for rival factions of families to fight out all the ill feeling, discontent, and jealousy which have accumulated for years. Sometimes the feasts provided are not eaten, and have to be thrown away or given to beggars. Musicians won't play, processions can't be formed, or are interrupted in progress: offence is taken at trifles, and the whole proceeding rocks to and fro as though it would tumble to pieces altogether, till it suddenly comes right, and affairs go on—to a happy conclusion, or otherwise, as it may be.

When all prospers, it is a right merry affair; but I am afraid you, dear young lady, would be very weary if you had to be married as Radha was. No such thing as going to church comfortably in a luxurious carriage, to be attended to the altar by six loving and lovely bridesmaids, to hear there a short, simple, affecting service and blessing, to sign your maiden name for the last time in the vestry, and to go home, having dried your eyes on the most delicate of lace-bordered cambric pocket-handkerchiefs, to a champagne breakfast, all the delicacies of the season, a carriage and four, and—unlimited bliss in prospect.

Ah, no! with Radha it was very different. Her marriage ceremonies—will you believe it?—occupied ten days of really very hard work. So many dressings and undressings; so many bathings; so many anointings; so many changes of ornaments; such smotherings in flowers, and in large sheets, lest her husband should see her; such being carried from place to place by the servants, lest her feet might touch the ground—once too by her husband, whom she could feel, but not see; and a rare strong arm and hand his was, taking her up, she felt, as if she were a child, and gently and respectfully too. Then worshippings at the great temple, where she had never been before, and where the priests put flowers on her and led her into the shrine where "the little Mother" sat, with her weird red eyes blinking through the smoke, and Radha was half frightened by them; greetings, too, from the people with whom the marriage was popular; and the flower-sellers and comfit-makers poured baskets of their stocks over her and her decorated litter, while she looked curiously about her from under the veil of jessamine flowers which covered her face, and acknowledged with shy timid gestures their hearty salutations. No doubt a great deal of this was excellent fun, and the girl's spirits rose with the genial joyousness; but at times she was very weary.

Seldom had there been a merrier wedding. What jokes were played off by her brother, who was a capital hand, as we know, at acting plays, disguising himself, and personating characters, with which he mercilessly interrupted the orthodox ceremonies. Now a Mahomedan mendicant, whose intrusion was resisted by the servants, and whose presence had polluted the food, proved to be he; or the pipers' instruments were filled with wax, and they blew discordant screeches, or could not blow at all; or a pertinacious begging Brahmun or Byragee pestered them when most engaged, insisted on seeing the bride, or threatened, otherwise, to cut himself and bring trouble on her. Now one thing, now another; teasing his sister, playing a sly joke with Anunda, tormenting the Shastree in all manner of ways, he was the life of the meeting, and always so disguised as to dress, figure, and even voice, that no one recognized him.

Then were there not all the pipers of the country? the temple musicians, and drums of all kinds, tenor and bass? Such crashes of noise! Village bands, the temple musicians, and the hired performers, and dancing women, all playing different tunes at the same moment. The horn-players and drums of half the country came in hopes of largess; and there was one burly fellow from Andoora, near Nuldroog, whose horn had wreaths of flowers tied to it, with gold and silver tinsel ribbon, the wild screams of whose instrument, and sometimes its mellow quivering notes, could be heard high above all the others.

And, to be sure, what feasting! The household cooking-pans were not half big enough, and those from the temple had to be borrowed: and the neighbours' kitchens, on both sides, were filled with cooks. Pecks and bushels of rice, butter, vegetable stews, and curries; sweet things, hot things, savoury things; and Anunda's famous "poorees," reserved for the choicest guests—some even made by herself and Tara.

There was no room in the house or in the courts for eating, so the street outside was swept and watered; and every day, early in the afternoon, you might see a posse of stout young Brahmuns laying down fresh green plantain-leaves in double rows on the ground, with broad alleys between them, and then long files of clean-shaven Brahmuns sit down behind them; and after them a procession of men bearing on their shoulders huge pans full of rice, hot from the kitchen, and slung on poles—baskets of hot bread, poorees, curries, stews, and the like, would march down the middle, ladling out portions of all to each, and helping liberally to melted butter, hot "chutnees," and other toothsome condiments.

And the men ate and ate till they could eat no more, and the crowds on the house-terraces above them watched the eating, cheered the eaters, and bandied free jokes from side to side of the street at themselves, the eaters, the carriers of the viands, or the passengers. So they ate and ate by hundreds and hundreds at a time; and many a hungry Brahmun, hardly knowing how to get a meal of coarse joware cakes in his own home, took his water-vessel and blanket, travelled from twenty to thirty miles round to the wedding, received a hearty welcome, and ate as he had perhaps never eaten before, and remembered it all his life afterwards.

Yes, it was a capital wedding; and the village and town gossips who criticised it at the time, and spoke of it afterwards, could actually find no fault. There was not a poor old hag in Tooljapoor or Sindphul, ay, and for the matter of that, in other villages further distant, who did not get a hearty meal; or if she were too infirm to stay and eat, a liberal dole of flour, or rice and butter, with salt and pepper. Not a family of Mahrattas in the town, nor, indeed, respectable Mahomedans either, who had not materials for a meal sent to them, accompanied by pipe and tabor, horn and drum, or band and trumpets, according to the scale of their rank. And from all friends, presents for the bride, in proportion to their means, from the richest silken and gold sarees, down to a humble cotton bodice, added to the stores with which Radha was already provided.

One by one the ceremonies were finished. The last—the solemn rite of actual marriage—as the bride and bridegroom sat side by side, when the consecrated thread was wound round them by the attendant Brahmuns, and the mystic hymns and invocations chanted; when their garments were tied together in the irrevocable knot, and they repeated the promises and vows, much like our own, to love and cherish each other—then Radha's veil was raised; and though he had seen her form for many days in succession, Vyas Shastree now saw his young wife's beautiful face for the first time.

It was a happy look, in one of her happy moods. Those glorious eyes were not excited, but soft, timid, and shyly raised to him in trust and confidence. Anunda and Tara had watched for the effect upon him with beating hearts and clasped hands. There could be no doubt of the expression of his face—wonder first, then gratification, perhaps love. "Thou wast right, wife," he said afterwards; "she hath a nymph's form, a deer's eyes, and a mouth like Kāmdeo."

So it was all finished at last; the guests departed, the courts were swept, and the house again cleaned out. The garlands of leaves and flowers still hung at the gate, and from pillar to pillar of the verandah; and certain post-nuptial ceremonies performed at the temple was all that remained of the outer show of the marriage. Within was the girl-bride, happy in being free from her brother, whom she feared though she loved him, and from her aunt, whom she disliked as well as feared; happy in her new sister-wife, to whom she felt like a daughter; happier in Tara, a sister in truth, and she never had known one before; content, too, to see the Shastree unreservedly, and to feel that her beauty grew on him—for as yet, beyond a few words, they had not spoken.

As Moro Trimmul had determined, Sukya Bye was despatched to their home a few days after the ceremony. She had pleaded hard to be allowed to stay over the Now Ratree, and Anunda had asked the favour at her instance; but her nephew was distinct in his refusal, yet not so as to display anger or vexation. It was simply impossible, he said; she had been too long absent from home, and he himself must go on his own affairs. So she received parting gifts of rich silk cloths from Radha, Anunda, and the Shastree, and departed to Wye.

. . . .

The last night that Moro Trimmul was to remain at Tooljapoor, he took an opportunity of telling Radha that he should pretend to go out, but conceal himself in the school court, which was not lighted, and that she was to come to him when all were asleep or retired; he should wait for her there, for he had much to say to her.

So he had. How he had restrained himself hitherto he knew not.

How, day by day, he had seen Tara, spoken to her, amused her, excited her, gloated over her beauty, which, if remarkable abroad where she was guarded, was in a thousand degrees more captivating and enthralling in the free household intercourse—and yet had done nothing towards possessing himself of her—was what he could neither understand nor endure any longer. Gunga could not help him; he saw clearly that Tara utterly refused communication with her: utterly refused to participate in the lower degrees of ceremonies and orgies at which Gunga assisted with a lower order of priests who officiated for the inferior castes of the people; and she refused the mystic marriage to the sword of the goddess, which the "Moorlees" performed in order to cloak their profligacy.

Gunga, therefore, baffled for a while, bided her time; but she and her sister priestesses had vowed revenge, and were all in Moro Trimmul's interest. Meanwhile his sister must help him; and this, with cruel perseverance, it was his object to effect through her at any risk.

He waited long, for the girl could not get away unobserved. At last she came, scared and terrified lest her absence should be detected; but all were asleep—Tara beside her in the verandah, the Shastree among his books in the book-room, Annda in her own sleeping-room within. She did not find her brother in better temper for his detention.

"Take this," he said to her, returning a gold anklet of Tara's, which Radha had borrowed from her to be copied; "for I go to-morrow early, and shall not see thee again till the Now Ratree; but thou hast kept me long, girl, and I had much to say to thee."

"The Shastree was awake reading: even till now I could not pass his door," she said; "be quick, brother."

"Ah, thou art trembling. Is this the girl who would have fled to Sivaji Rajah; and art thou changed already into a Shastree's wife?" he said, with a sneer.

The girl shivered. "Do not say such things, brother. I strive to put them away, and they will go, perhaps; yes, they will go, when no one tells me of him."

Her brother laughed. "No, they shall not go, Radha, if I can prevent it; but thou must be patient, girl. So much for thyself; now for me."

"What can I do, brother?"

"Thou canst gain Tara for me. Nay, Radha," he continued, as she trembled still more, and hung to the court door in terror, "none of this cowardice! I tell thee it must be, and thou must do it."

"Brother! brother!" gasped the girl, piteously. "Not I—not I! What can I do? O, not I! O, not I!"

"What canst thou do? Much," he returned, sharply; "listen,

Radha. Such things are no sin. She is a Brahmun, as I am; she is a widow. She is a Moorlee, as free as Gunga, or any of them, and she can please herself. I know she is not indifferent to me: it is for thee to improve this. Speak to her of me, lead her to think of me, tell her what deeds I have done with thy Rajah—I am with him in them—and sing her our country ballads. I tell thee, girl, if thou doest all this, it will gain her."

"Never, brother, never; she has no heart for thee. She shuddered yesterday when I spoke of thee. I saw her—I could not be mistaken. Her heart is with the gods, in her books, cold and dead. O brother, think not of her! What can I do?"

"Is it so, sister?" he said sneeringly. "Then she must be awakened, and that dead heart gain new life; Radha, thou must do it, thou!—else"—he felt the girl shivering as he grasped her arm, and shook her savagely—"else, wilt thou be long here? Would this Shastree keep thee one hour in his house if he thought, much less if he knew, thou hadst been married before, girl? Yes, married before! Ah, that touches thee! And listen more, if my affair is not furthered he shall know it. What if he cast thee out? Thou canst go to the temple like Tara; thou canst go to him—to Sivaji—but thou wilt be a reproach and an outcast. Choose!—to be happy as I have placed thee, or as I have said. One or other, girl! the last, and what I have risked for thee—what I have done for thee—will be repaid. O sister! what Sivaji Rajah is to thee, a burning thought day and night, so Tara is to me, and more. Dost thou hear?"

"I—I," gasped the terrified girl, "I hear—I hear. O brother, be not cruel, do not destroy me; or, if thou wilt, one blow of thy knife—now—now—here," and she bared her breast. "It will be mercy—strike!"

"Poor fool," said Moro Trimmul, "I would not harm thee. Go, remember what I have said, and do as I tell thee. If she be in the same mood when I return, why then—— Go," he continued, interrupting himself, "I can wait no longer. Fear not, my blessing is on thee," and he put his hands on her head. "For his sake, my lord, my prince and thine, thou shalt come to no harm. Go!" And saying this he put her gently away from him into the court, closed the door, and easily climbing the low wall, dropped into the street beyond.

"One thing more ere the night passes," he said, as he walked rapidly through the deserted streets to the house they had lived in, near the Shastree's: "if she is there, well; if not, I must seek her. What she wanted must have been brought ere this."

"She is within, master," said a man sitting at the gate, with a black blanket round him, who spoke ere Moro Trimmul could ask; "she has been here an hour or more; and here are some things the sonar brought this evening when you were absent."

"Good," said the Pundit, passing in; "see that no one enters."

The man laughed. "It is too late, master, now. No one will come. Are we to leave early?"

"Tell them to bring the horses at daylight," he replied; "we will get on to Darasew before noon. We must be at Thair before night. Is all prepared?"

"Yes, the saddle-bags are packed, and Bheema and myself remain; all the rest went with the lady Sukya."

"Then go and sleep, for we have a long journey to-morrow. I do not need thee. Give me the key of the court door. I can lock myself in, and I shall be awake long before you in the morning."

He entered the court and locked the gate behind him. A lamp was burning in a recess of the verandah, and its light fell upon the figure of the girl Gunga, who had covered herself with a sheet, and, most likely weary with waiting for him, had fallen asleep. She did not hear him; and as he had left his shoes by the side of the outer door, there was no noise whatever from his bare feet.

Moro Trimmul stood over her, and, as he did so, she moved uneasily in her sleep, turned and said something; he could not catch the words. Then some cruel thoughts passed suddenly through his mind. Gunga knew too much; a blow of his knife would silence for ever all chance of disclosure of what had been done for Radha; the gold he had to give her would be saved. There was a large well or cistern behind the house; the wall of the back-yard hung over it; it was a place where the women of the town washed their clothes, and was so held to be unclean. That would hide her. A Moorlee? What Moorlee had not jealousies and strifes? Who would care for her? And he drew the dagger and stood over her in an attitude to strike.

Why he hesitated he could never tell; certainly it was not from fear. Perhaps some lingering feeling of compassion for one so young—perhaps the memory of some caress—stayed the blow for an instant, for he did not strike. The light fell full on her eyes and face as she turned, and she smiled and awoke suddenly.

"I dreamed of thee, beloved," she said, stretching out her arms to him, "and thou art here—— But why the knife?" she continued, quickly sitting up, as the light gleamed on the blade. "Moro!—I—I—I fear thee; why dost thou look at me so? Ah!" and she covered her eyes with her hand, expecting death.

"Only to cut these strings," he said, with a hard laugh, recovering himself and dividing the cord which was tied round the paper containing the gold anklets. "Look, Gunga!" and he held them up to the light, and shook them till the little bells on them clashed gently.

"Thou art good," she said, looking up as he held them above her, still shaking them; "they are very, very beautiful, but thou wilt not give them to me, for thou hast not got Tara. Ah! thou hast just come from her, and wilt not give them. Go! go back to her."

"But my sister is her father's wife, and these are heavier than Tara's. I have not broken faith with thee, Gunga," he replied, "nor my oath at the Pâp-nâs temple. Take them—they are thine henceforth. And now wilt thou go with me, Gunga? I have prepared a horse for thee, and Bheema can walk."

"To the end of life," cried the girl, who had risen to her knees to put on the anklets, and who now clasped his feet,—"to the end of life! Kill me if thou wilt, Moro Trimmul, who would care? It would be no pain to Gunga."

CHAPTER IX.

A THICK heavy rain was falling, which had lasted nearly all day without intermission, and the afternoon was now advanced. The sky was one uniform tint of dark grey, in which, near the horizon, some yellowish, lurid colour occasionally appeared. Dark masses of cloud came up slowly from the south-west at times, causing a deeper gloom as they passed overhead, accompanied by bursts of rain, which sometimes fell in sheets, deluging the ground, and dashing up muddy spray from the soft earth. The air was stifling; and there was a strong sulphurous smell with the rain, which increased the disagreeable effect of the close, hot atmosphere. Sometimes a gentle breeze, hardly sufficient to give the rain a slanting direction, arose, and felt refreshing; but as the heavy clouds passed, it died away, and the rain fell perpendicularly again, with a constant monotonous plash, which, coming from a wide plain, sounded like a dull roar.

Little could be seen of the plain itself; for not only was the rain too thick to allow of any distance to appear definitely, but there was a steamy mist rising from the previously heated earth, which increased the already existing dimness and gloom. Sometimes a few trees in the vicinity, which appeared tall and ghostly in the grey light and thick air, stood out more in detail as the rain slackened for a while, and seemed to give promise of breaking; and on these occasions two villages became dimly visible; one of them nearly a mile distant, the other perhaps half a mile farther, situated to the right and left of what, in dry weather, was a well-beaten road-track, but which could only now be known as such, by being bare of grass, and by the slightly raised banks, covered here and there by low bushes, which bounded it.

The place we are about to describe occupied the summit of a small eminence, below which, in a valley watered by a rivulet, was a village surrounded by tall crops of grain, now coming into ear, mingled with fields of cotton, as yet very low, and pulse, and other cereals, generally about waist-high. This difference in the height of the crops left the valley comparatively open; and the road-track could be followed by the eye, whenever the mist and rain cleared a little—through the fields to the gate of the first village, before which there was an open piece of ground, past a small Hindu temple surrounded with trees, and up a slight ascent beyond, to a plain, along which it continued, till it disappeared among the tall jowaree fields and other cultivation of the next village. These two villages were called the greater and less Kinny.

The valley, or hollow, was little more than a descent in the undulation of the country; but, when the rain fell heavily at the nearer village, so as almost to conceal it, the effect from the eminence we describe was, as though it were actually deep and broad; and then also the farther village, with its trees, appeared distant, and sometimes was not visible at all. Thus alternating, as sometimes plainly in view, and at others not to be seen, these villages appeared to be objects of deep interest to three men, who occupied the spot we have just mentioned. Occasionally, and as the rain cleared a little, one or other of them would proceed to the top of a heap of stones near at hand, and look anxiously along the line of road, past the fields and the open space before the gate of the first Kinny, up the ascent beyond, and over the plain to the second; and there were moments when a man on horseback might easily have been descried even at the further village, certainly at the second, or between them, had such a person been upon the road; but no one appeared.

The spot was remarkable as the highest point for a long distance either way upon the road-track; and indeed, had the day been clear, a large extent of country could have been seen from it in all directions. Now, however, the view was very limited; and on the opposite sides from the two villages nothing could be seen but a plain, thinly covered with grass and bushes, and strewn thickly with black stones, which, uncultivated as it was for miles, looked doubly desolate through the misty air, being partially covered with pools of water of a yellowish brown colour, the result of the present rain. Over this plain, three roads or paths diverged from the place the men occupied. The main track, which had the appearance of being somewhat beaten, was broader than the others, and led westward to the town of Allund, about six miles distant,—the others to villages from two to four miles to the south and west.

The plain was, as we have said, very stony, and at the place we allude to, the heap of stones had been formed gradually by travellers who, coming from all sides, took up one from the path, and threw it, with a prayer to the local divinity, upon the pile. This had been done, no doubt, for centuries; still the stones upon the path appeared as thick as ever, and sorely impeded and harassed all travellers, whether on foot or horseback.

Over this heap of stones grew a large banian, and close to it several scraggy neem trees; a peepul, too, had once existed, but was dead. Part of the trunk and one large branch remained standing, white and dry, and a portion of another lay on the ground, from which chips of firewood had been cut from time to time. It looked as if it had been struck with lightning, which, indeed, was not improbable, as several branches of the banian were scathed and riven, probably from the same cause. Of all these trees, however, the banian or "burr," as it is called in the language of the country, was most remarkable.

Not possessed of the luxuriant foliage common to this tree in other places, probably because the soil was too poor and rocky, its huge gnarled boughs were bare of small branches and leaves; some were naked and actually withered, others apparently so, and all stretched their white gaunt arms into the sky, with a wild and ghastly effect against the leaden grey of the clouds. In process of the centuries of its existence, several boughs had become detached from the parent trunk, and were upheld by stems which had once been pendant roots, and had struck into the ground. These portions, if anything more bare, and more gnarled and twisted than the parent tree, rose loftily into the air, and with the same effect we have already noticed.

The larger boughs and stems were full of holes, which sheltered a numerous colony of small grey tree-owls, whose bright yellow eyes stared from behind large boughs, and out of crevices in the trunks, or from among the ornaments of the roof of the temple below; while they kept up a perpetual twittering, as if they conversed together, which indeed perhaps they did. On hot bright days lizards, large and small, crept out of crevices and basked in the sun; and among them a family of huge black ones, with bright eyes and scarlet throats, which they inflated as they appeared to swell with importance. Shepherd boys believed these to be evil spirits, and if they were brave, pelted them with stones, or if otherwise ran off, as one of them issued forth and looked about curiously.

Some large holes, too, near the top of the tree, contained great horned owls, which, if attracted by any noise, sat, with stupidly-grave aspect and wide saucer-eyes, looking down upon the road—the tufts of feathers over their ears alternately erected and depressed—till they flew out with a loud hoot to look for some more undisturbed retreat. These owls, great and small, with the lizards, had the tree, for the most part, to themselves. Probably there was not enough foliage to tempt other birds to rest there; for except an occasional wandering flock of chattering parroquets, mynas, or green pigeons, none frequented it by day. By night, however, it was otherwise: for it was then the roosting-place of the vultures, eagles, and other carrion birds of the district, with whom the owls did not apparently interfere.

At the back, partly behind the parent tree and the heap of stones, was a small and evidently ancient Hindu temple, consisting of one chamber and a porch. The chamber was not much larger than sufficed to contain the image, and allow a priest to officiate before it in case of necessity, and was too low to admit of a man's standing upright. The porch, which was supported in front by two roughly-hewn stone pillars, was somewhat larger; and the three men we have mentioned, were enabled to sit in it comfortably, protected from the rain. The doorway was narrow and low, and the inside of the chamber was dark; but a small Phallic emblem could be seen within set upon a low altar, and a rudely-sculptured stone bull, in a sitting posture, had originally been placed before the porch facing the image. The temple, image, and bull showed that the grove had been originally dedicated to Siva, or Mahadeo, in the form of that ancient "pillar and calf" worship so fatal to the Israelites of old, and which for them possessed so strange a fascination.

The temple was deserted, and, except on the annual festival of the god, when some priest from a neighbouring village swept out the chamber, brought a light to burn before the image, poured the usual libations, and hung a few garlands of jessamine and marigold flowers over it, no one ever came with intent to worship, and the place was utterly neglected. Last year's garlands were now but dry brown leaves hanging to a cotton thread; the chamber was dirty, and strewn with dead leaves; the stone bull in front was overthrown, and lying on its side, and even in bright sunshine the place presented a melancholy, deserted appearance. Sometimes, in the heat of the day, village lads, in charge of goats and cattle, would meet there, but only in lack of other shelter from the sun; for indeed the spot had an evil reputation, and not without reason.

It is not surprising that it was believed to be the resort of malignant spirits which love to dwell in such places, and of tricksy and mischievous sprites which inhabited the large holes in the old trunks, sharing them with the owls and lizards that lived there: vexed travellers' horses, causing them to cast shoes in the stones, or led wayfarers astray, especially at night, among the many paths over the stony plain—or bewitched cows and buffaloes, and dried up their milk. So, ofttimes, shepherds came with flowers, and poured libations of milk and curds, after a rude fashion, over a few large stones which lay among the gnarled roots of the great tree, and had been placed there as devoted to the local divinities—Fauns and Dryads—

and therefore held in rude reverence; and these, on such occasions, were smeared with red or black powder in a kind of deprecatory worship.

It was not for these reasons alone that the place was dreaded; it had, from other causes, even a worse reputation. It was notorious as the place of meeting for most of the gang robberies in the country; for assemblies of parties of highway robbers, and the distribution of stolen property. Watchmen on village towers at night, sometimes saw fires twinkling about the temple, and well knew the cause of them; and shepherd boys next day found rude clay crucibles and extinguished charcoal fires in one place where the trunk was hollow at the root of the tree, and thus knew that gold and silver had been melted there at night.

Murder, too, had been done there. On one occasion, not very long ago, several fresh corpses had been found in the old well barely concealed by leaves and bushes; and, more recently, a body found lying on the road had been dragged from the line of one village boundary to another—for several boundaries of village lands diverged from that spot—to escape the king's fine, till it was eaten by vultures and hyenas, and the bones lay and bleached under the great tree for many a day, to the terror of all wayfarers. In short, the place was thus esteemed evil for many reasons; and whether villagers or travellers came past it by any of the roads over the plain, or from the two Kinnys, alone or in company, they hurried past the temple, breathing a spell or prayer against the ghosts and spirits which dwelt in it, and heartily wishing themselves safe beyond its precincts.

CHAPTER X.

The three persons who were sheltering themselves in the porch of the temple had apparently no apprehensions. Each in turn, throwing a coarse black blanket about him, mounted the heap of stones and looked eagerly toward the villages and along the line of road. The others sat together, rolling up leaves of the banian tree from time to time, which they filled with tobacco from their pouches, and smoked as fast as made. All three were heavily armed with long straight swords with solid basket-handles, from which a spike projected below the hilt, enabling the wearer to use his weapon double-handed, as well as to protect the wrist; shields of stout hide, with brass bosses, hung at their backs, and daggers of different forms were in their girdles. In the chamber of the temple their three matchlocks leaned against the wall—two being ordinary ones with long bright barrels, the other short and handsomely inlaid with gold, evidently of superior value to the others. The men wore their large crooked powder-horns, and bullet-bags, with tinder-boxes, attached to soft leather waistbelts, and their priming-horns, hung to the breast-buckles of their sword-belts, of buff leather. The matchlocks were ready for instant use; for the matches were lighted, and the smoke, from the match-ends, and that of a small fire made of dried twigs, filled the chamber and issued from the door.

The two men who were sitting in the porch—one had just gone and taken post again upon the stones—were stout square-built fellows, of dark-brown complexion, with peculiarly round powerful shoulders, which gave them almost the appearance of deformity. They wore coarse cotton tunics and tight drawers, which reached to the knee, leaving the lower part of the legs bare, and showing them to be sinewy and well exercised by constant travel. They had not removed their sandals, which were strong and studded with large-headed nails, and, as they sat together, the resemblance in figure was very striking. They were, in fact, twin-brothers, and, being Mahrattas, had been named, as is usual, Rama and Lukshmun, after the popular heroes of the Mahabarut. Even in features there was a strong resemblance; but the expression of the elder, Rama, was as gloomy, if not savage, as that of the younger, Lukshmun, was cheerful and good-natured.

The brothers had been long silent, and the third person, who, with a heavy black blanket thrown over his head, had been sitting for some time upon the stones, got up and returned to the porch as a fresh cloud passed overhead, accompanied by heavier rain than before, which gradually shut out the village and road from his view, shook the wet from the blanket, and stood looking gloomily at the sky and the torrents of water which were running off the ground towards the declivity of the eminence. There was a great contrast between this person and the others in every respect, and he merits, perhaps, a separate description.

Though young, he was evidently the leader of the party, and his comparatively fair complexion and regular features, as well as the caste-mark on his forehead, showed him to be a Rajpoot, descended from those emigrants from Northern India whom military service, even at that period, had tempted from Oude and Delhi to the remote Dekhan. In stature, as in powerful make, he much exceeded his companions, and his carriage was soldierlike and graceful. He wore a quilted tunic of what had once been gay red "mushroo," the strong satin of the country, but now stained and frayed; long tight drawers, turned up to the calf; a dark red turban, of fine texture, jauntily cocked aside, its gold thread end being turned back over the top; and his powder-horn, bullet-bag, and shield, as well as a little gold embroidery upon his sword-belt, all of a better quality than the others, with a fine single pearl ear-ring—proved him to be as much superior to them in rank, as his expression and deportment were in intelligence.

Gopal Singh, for such was his name, was, in truth, decidedly good-looking. Large black eyes, full of light, a prominent nose, bushy whiskers, very neatly trimmed, and a small moustache twisted upwards into close curls at the corners of a mouth delicately formed and almost effeminate in character when relaxed, but which, when the lips were compressed, seemed full of deep expression both for good and evil,—the chin, clean-shaved and prominent, betokening firmness,—all combined to form a countenance in which decision and energy were evident; but, in spite of his good features, their general expression was repellant, expressing cruelty and lawlessness of no common order.

"He will never get across the Benathoora to-day, my friends," he said, stepping into a dry corner of the porch and sitting down; "and we have a weary journey to Itga before us in this mud; yet I dare not face the master, my uncle, without some news of him."

"Maharaj," replied Rama, respectfully, folding his hands—"Great prince"—by which title (an ordinary one of respect), or that of Jemadar, Gopal Singh was usually addressed by them—"I know the Benathoora, and she will not come down before night; and if it be true that the man left Kullianee yesterday, there is plenty of time for him to be here by sunset. Depend upon it, he will make for Allund to-day, and there will have been no deep mud for some hours after he left. Couldst thou see nothing on the road?"

"Nothing, Rama. At one time I thought I saw him at the gate of the village yonder, but as the rain cleared off, it was only some cattle going in; then the mist closed up the view, and I could see no more, and came away. By Krishna, but this rain is something to see! I question whether he could cross the nulla down there before Kinny, it seems filling so fast."

"Ah! he can ford it well enough if he is bent on coming," said Lukshmun, "and he could not stop at either village, for I told the Gowra this morning, if a stranger came, to send him on with a guide, and to shut the gate if he wanted to stop. So, if he left Kullianee yesterday, he ought to have come a good distance before night; and if he started again this morning, there is no river, or nulla, between to stop him but the Benathoora, and that will be fordable till midnight, even with heavier rain than this. He would not stay for the rain to clear?"

"He must have left it," returned the Jemadar; "he dared not stay there. One of old Lukmun Geer's disciples was to accompany him to a village half-way to Allund yesterday, and send him on from thence with guides from village to village. We offered escort, but he would take no one—the fellow was suspicious."

"Then he is quite safe, Maharaj. The guides may plague him; but if he started under injunctions from the old Bawa's disciple, he will be passed on carefully," returned Rama.

"I hope he is, brothers. I would not lose our chance of the gold he has for something—nor indeed of himself."

"Gold! Jemadar," cried both eagerly, in a breath.

"Yes, my friends; good royal mohurs, I know; for the day before yesterday he rested at the Gosai's Mutt, and had a Hoondee cashed in the shop. It was a goodly pouchful, I know, and it will come to us if we wait patiently."

Gopal Singh lighted some tinder with his flint and steel, and then a leaf cigarette, as we may call it, and began to smoke in silence which was only broken by the dripping of the rain from the porch of the temple and the tree, the general plash over the plain, and the loud and continuous croaking of the frogs in the pools and puddles.

The Jemadar first broke silence. "Some one must look again," he continued, after a while; "and it is brighter now. Go thou, Lukshmun, take the blanket and sit close."

"It is not weather to turn out a dog," muttered the man, sulkily, getting up and stepping down from the porch; "but I will go, Maharaj, if it is your order. Shall I go on to Kinny," he continued, "and see if I can get tidings of him? Better that than sitting up there like a drenched scarecrow in a field."

"Good, brother, go! Try the nulla before you venture into the middle of it, lest it be too strong for you," said Rama.

"And wait there for a time," added the Jemadar. "If he do not arrive before night thou canst bring some flour, ghee, and sugar from the Patel; for if we are to watch here all night we had need to eat, and I must make some bread; but if the man comes, bring him on—he will be well-mounted and will not fear the nulla, and thou canst invent something about going back to Allund on urgent business."

"Trust me for that, Jemadar. If I have an ugly face I can speak soft words when I choose, and I know enough of the camp language to make him understand. Now, I am going." So saying, he doubled the blanket in a peculiar manner, so as to form a cloak, threw it over his head and shoulders, and folded the sides tightly about him; then taking off his sandals, which he carried in his hand, he strode away in the rain, as rapidly as the mud would admit.

"Take care of the thorns in the lane near the village; put on your sandals there: we can't have you troubling us with a Babool thorn in your foot," shouted the Jemadar.

Lukshmun turned round and nodded his assent, and continued as before. They watched him silently till he disappeared over the brow of the eminence, when Rama said to his companion, "What if they have sent the man on by the other road, or warned him, Jemadar?"

There was another road which passed about half a mile to the south of where they sat.

"He dare not, Rama; by his soul he dare not," replied the Jemadar, with flashing eyes and distended nostrils. "Do you think he would dare my uncle's vengeance? does he wish his cattle to be harried by Pabar Singh, and his village burnt?"

"Perhaps not; and it would be likely enough to happen, Jemadar," said Rama, laughing; "and, I suppose, we should have to come to do it. But what is to be done with the man?—That?" and he pointed significantly to the old well with his thumb.

"O no, Rama," returned the other, laughing in his turn. "Nothing of that kind, now. The man himself is precious, why, the uncle knows, and some more of them, though they have not told me. I only hope he will not make a fight of it and get hurt."

"Then we could not help it, of course, Jemadar."

"No, indeed, friend. But we are three to one, and he is only a Mutsuddee after all—not a man of war—he will be quiet enough, I dare say."

"Well, if I am to say the truth, Maharaj, I am glad of it," returned Rama. "It is all very well to kill people in a fair foray, or if anybody will fight in a Durôra, one's blood is up, and it does not matter; but, somehow or other, the last affair here was not agreeable, and ever since I have not liked the place at night. We need not add to the people that lie yonder," and he pointed over his shoulder to a corner of the tree, "unless, indeed, it is to be, then of course we can't help it."

"Nor I either, Rama. It is only pleasant here when there are fifty or sixty good fellows assembled, and the gold and silver are boiling in the pots yonder. I don't like this new business as well as the old—— By Gunga, what a flash!"

Indeed the flash of lightning, which caused both to start to their feet, was nearly blinding. Without warning, except by the passage of another dark cloud above, it had fallen on part of the old tree which was separate from the rest—a branch supported by two roots which had struck into the ground—and had riven away part of it, which fell across the mound of stones with a loud and heavy crash, and was followed by a cracking peal of thunder, so loud and so near that the men involuntarily put their hands to their ears.

"It would have killed him if he had been on the stones," said Rama, who first spoke, as the peal, spreading itself over the heavens, was dying into deep growls in the distance. "By all the gods! was there ever such thunder?"

"It will break up the clouds, perhaps," returned the Jemadar, "and this rain will then stop. Yes, it was a narrow escape, indeed, and we may be thankful he went. It is a good omen for us, Rama!"

"I vow a rupee to be inlaid in the floor of the temple of Dévi, at Tooljapoor, and to feed twenty-four Brahmuns," said the man, reverently. "Yes," he added, looking up and over the plain, "I think it will break up before sunset."

But we must follow the spy on his double errand, while the pair, who still converse, speculate upon the probable issue of it, smoke by turns, and long for a break in the rain. And there is another person, too, who must needs be looked after on his journey hitherward.

CHAPTER XI.

A STOUT serving-man was holding a powerful grey horse, which, well, if not handsomely, caparisoned, stood neighing loudly before the door of an ordinary house in the main street of Surroori, a small village nearly midway between the towns of Kullianee and Allund, as a person within, evidently of a superior class, was girding up his waist with a shawl, and otherwise preparing himself for a day's journey. Of middle stature, thin but well-proportioned, with a light bamboo-coloured complexion of a pale cast, and a slight habitual stoop, the man seemed unaccustomed to rough exertion; and the sword he had just fastened into his waistbelt, along with an ivory-handled poniard and knife, was apparently more for ornament than for use —such a one as might be used at court, or by a boy,—not the weapon of a soldier.

The man's face was clean shaven, except a long moustache, which drooped very much at the corners, and the features were by no means ill-favoured. A first glance showed an expression of much intelligence, mingled, however, as you looked further, with much cunning. The eyes were small, deep-set under bushy eyebrows, and of a light grey; the nose high and aquiline, but broad across the nostrils, and hung over the moustache in a peculiar manner; the forehead was wrinkled into furrows by habitual elevation of the eyebrows; and, as far as the upper part of the face was concerned, it had an appearance of firmness, which the lower portion belied; for the mouth, drawn up at the corners in a constant and apparently hypocritical attempt to smile, was evidently performing an office foreign to its intention; and the chin, which suddenly retreated into a somewhat bony throat, had no character but decided weakness, if not, indeed, actual cowardice and deceit. Thus, the whole features wore a restless, suspicious, and hypocritical expression, which, most likely, was a true indication of the possessor's mind.

Lalla Toolsee Das was not a native of the Dekhan, but had served for the last two years, or nearly so, in the Dufter, or Record Office of the Emperor Aurungzeeb. The Lalla had been sent from Delhi to his uncle, who was in the Emperor's service: and, having given proofs of ability as a Persian scholar, he had been appointed to a confidential situation about the Emperor himself. What use the Lalla had made of his position will appear hereafter, as also why he now undertook a long journey alone, in a strange country, and at an inclement season of the year. Meanwhile we have only to describe his progress, which, so far as the weather is concerned, appears uncertain.

The Lalla had risen early, bathed, breakfasted, and packed his saddle-bags. He had looked out several times since morning, but always with the same result as to the sky, which continued of a dull, leaden grey, with occasional rain. There was no wind, it was close and hot, and his host, an old Byragee, who was a lay monk of the Mutt, or monastery, at Kullianee, which the Lalla had left the day before, was persuading him to remain. But the indifferent night's rest he had endured from the venomous mosquitoes, the moaning of a cow over a new-born calf, and other noises from cattle and goats, —from the women, who ground at the mill so early in the house, singing a discordant Canarese song—and, above all, his personal anxiety to proceed,—have weighed against the weather.

"Ah, my poor Mootee," said the Lalla, as he heard his horse neigh, "thou wilt have a hard day of it, I fear, in the mud. How far didst thou say it was, Bawa Sahib?" he continued to his host.

"It is six coss, by our reckoning here, by one road—seven or eight by the other," replied the Byragee, "which, in the coss you are accustomed to in Hindustan, will be ten one way, and thirteen the other."

"And you recommend the longest road, Bawajee?"

"Well, sir, it is as you please. You will have somewhat less mud and stones by the upper road than by the lower—that is all."

"Ah, friend," continued the Lalla, as we shall call him, "four coss more at the end of a hard day is not pleasant, and so the less the better. Let me see; here is my route. Ah, Kinny, little and great; I suppose I can rest at either if I like, though I should prefer getting on to the worthy Fathers' Mutt at Allund."

"Certainly," replied the old man; "but do not stop at Kinny, if you can help; and, above all, do not shelter yourself at the temple on the hill, under the 'Burr' tree. Ah, yes, there will be heavy rain to-day, Lallajee, for it is so hot," he continued, looking up at the clouds, now deepening into fringes of black here and there; "you had better stay."

"No, Bawa, I must go on; and if it rains I can't help it. But about the tree," the Lalla continued; "I suppose there are sprites and devils in it as usual; and, to say the truth, I am not afraid of them. A man that always lives among soldiers, you know, gets brave."

"Indeed," returned the Byragee dryly. "O, of course! But take my advice, and when you change guides at Kinny, ask them to send you by the south road; it's—it's the best, and some bad places are avoided. But here is the Patel," he added, as that functionary, emerging from his doorway opposite, with a striped blanket over his head and shoulders, saluted the Lalla with a loud "Numascar Maharaj!" "He will direct the guide himself, Lallajee, which will insure a speedy and safe journey."

They followed the Patel through the village, which, under the steadily increasing rain, looked sufficiently wretched to deter any one from staying, who had not urgent necessity for doing so. This was not the Lalla's predicament; and he now unfastened a large thick felt travelling-cloak from the pommel of his cloth saddle, put it over his head, and wrapped it around him so as to cover his legs, which were protected by long, soft, Persian riding-boots.

Few people were astir. Under shelter of the house-walls the dogs had assembled in groups, and, standing with their tails between their legs, barked at the stranger as he passed. Pigs and fowls, being disturbed by his horse, ran to and fro, with noisy grunt and cackle. Some cattle stood together in parties near their owners' houses, a heavy steam from their nostrils ascending into the thick air, and broke the silence by an occasional hoarse low. Here and there a stout motherly dame, with a child seated astride on her hip, and others hanging about her, stood, nothing abashed, at her house door, looking at the Lalla as he passed; or a farmer, with his blanket cast over his head, smoking his morning cigarette, lounged under shelter of his own eaves, and exchanged a morning greeting with the Patel. The spouts of terraced houses were beginning to run fast, and small streams of water were already making their way through the mud.

In the gateway were two or three "jowans," or young men, who watched and guarded it, and acted as messengers. One of these was sent for a guide, and the party stayed under shelter till he arrived, when the Lalla and his bundle were formally made over to him, to be delivered up at the next village, about two miles distant; and finally, the Lalla mounted.

"Don't forget the south road from Kinny," said the Byragee, wishing him a good journey, as the Lalla, making his parting salutation, rode out of the gateway.

"Who is that?" asked the Patel. "You kept him mighty close in your Mutt last night."

"I don't know," returned the other; "but he goes on the government business to Beejapoor, and you know the order which came with him. I suppose it is some secret matter, else he would have had an escort."

"Well, he is gone, whoever he is," said the Patel; "and I would rather he travelled than I, even on that good beast of his, to Allund, to-day. It is going to rain badly—but it will do the grain good." And so they fell to talking of their farms, and the prices of grain at the last market, while the Lalla and his guide proceeded onward.

If the Lalla could have understood his guide, the way might have been beguiled by pleasant gossip of the country round; but of the vernacular of that part of the country he was profoundly ignorant, and every attempt he made in the "Oordoo," or court language, was met with a curt "Tillid-illa"—"don't understand"—or an occasional very expressive pantomimic action on the part of the guide, who, looking back, sometimes pointed to the bundle on his head, then to the rain, and again tapped his own stomach, or stuffed his fingers into his mouth, conveying the intimation that he expected to be well rewarded, and was very hungry. Thus the next village was reached, the first guide was dismissed with a little extra gratuity, and the Lalla again proceeded with a fresh one.

The ranges of low hills crossed from time to time had been stony but firm ground, and as yet Motee had not suffered. The dreaded river, which might have cut him off from Allund, was now behind him; and, after ascending a small eminence, and a wide plain appeared before him, our traveller congratulated himself on a speedy arrival at his destination, having, as he considered, got over at least one half of his journey.

Very soon, however, the rough, stony path changed into one which at times was difficult to discern at all. The plain over which the road now lay was cultivated as far as could be seen, but the fields were as yet unsown. Step after step the mud appeared deeper, the stones in it more numerous and slippery; and, in fact, after about a mile, during which the rain had fallen more heavily than ever, the plain appeared covered with water, which could not run off, and the black soil of the road and fields to have turned into liquid mud, barely able to support the stones which lay so thickly upon it. So long, too, as the rain had not penetrated far below the surface, Motee's feet had at least the dry earth to rest upon; but now not even that remained, and yet the gallant horse struggled on, snorting, and occasionally plunging, but evidently becoming wearied by efforts which had no respite. Still the guide led on, sometimes by the road-track, sometimes by its grassy banks, and again leaving both, struck into other paths through the fields which promised firmer footing.

The rain continued to pour in torrents: indeed, it was more than ever violent: and a flash of blinding lightning, followed by a roar of thunder before them, promised worse weather. Poor Motee even

* Each village is obliged to furnish a guide to travellers on payment of a small gratuity, and these men relieve themselves at every village.

winced, evincing a strong determination to turn round and set his tail to it; but a few words of encouragement from his master, and being led a few paces by the guide, restored his temper, and he proceeded gallantly.

At the junction of two roads, the guide paused for a moment. One, it was clear, led to a village they had seen for some time past, the trees of which loomed large and heavy through the thick air, but it appeared out of direction of the path. The Lalla's stock of Canarese was simply nothing—of Mahratta not much more; but the name of his destination was, at least, intelligible. "Allund," he said, holding out a rupee between his finger and thumb, "Allund!"

The guide grinned as he took the coin. "Allund!" he returned affirmatively, and striking into a path to the right, the Lalla could see that, by avoiding the village to the left, the road led apparently in the direction of what looked like a clump of trees standing out against the sky. Was that the banian tree of which he had been warned by the old Byragee at Surroori? The Lalla's little stock of Mahratta was again put into requisition, and the guide seemed to understand it readily.

Yes, the village to the left was Little Kinny; that to the right, great Kinny, and that was the "Burr" tree beyond. Good; then he had only to avoid the tree, if that indeed were necessary. Since the peal of thunder the rain had decreased, and a breeze was springing up in his face, which was very refreshing. The clouds, too, were breaking, as appeared by patches of bright fringe in the south-west. The guide pointed to them cheerfully, as he moved on at a steady pace; for the plain, though muddy in parts, was now not so bad as what he had already passed. So, as our friend is likely to reach Kinny without farther trouble, let us see what Lukshmun has been doing since we left him.

The little rivulet in the valley was above his knees as he passed it, and, to any one who did not know it, the ford would have been dangerous; but Lukshmun waded through, without apprehension, and a few minutes after, as he entered the village gateway and shook the rain from his blanket, a group of people assembled there welcomed him with a hearty shout of greeting.

"We thought you would have given it up and departed," said the old Patel, who, with his son, a few of the village farmers, and the Putwari, or accountant, were sitting in an open chamber of the deep gateway, the usual place of business. "We thought you would have gone away, else I would have sent up some milk. Why did you not come and sit here, instead of in that ungodly place up yonder? Here, one of ye," he continued to a group of "jowans," who were sitting in the opposite chamber, "take his blanket and dry it. Hast thou eaten to-day, friend?"

"Nothing but a bit of stale cake I had in my waist-cloth," replied the man; "only that my teeth are strong, it would have broken them. The 'poor man's' bread in the Mutt at Kullianee is not dainty food, and the flour was musty, O Patel!"

"Take him away to the house, and let them feed him; the women will have something good, I dare say," replied the Patel. "Go and see."

"And no one has passed since morning?"

"Not a creature. It is not weather to send the dogs out; and the mud from Kulmus to Kinny and hitherwards will be hopeless. No, he won't come to-day; but go and eat, friend—go and eat."

"If I am wanted," said Lukshmun.

"Jee, jee! Ay, ay! I will not forget you. Go!"

"What does he want out such a day as this?" asked the Putwari. "What has Pahar Singh in hand just now?"

"What does it matter to us, Rao Sahib?" returned the Patel; "all we have to do is to keep his people in good humour, to save our cattle from being harried, our stacks from being burned, and our people," he added, looking round at the farmers and their wives, "from being robbed when they come from market? That is worth what we pay him. Should we have got the crops off that disputed land at Chitli if he had not sent those spearmen?"

"No, no; do not interfere," said a chorus of farmers' voices, who, in those unsettled times, might, unless their village were known to be under the protection of some local chieftain, at any time have their flocks and herds swept away by the people of a more powerful village, or by any of the independent gentry, or barons, as we may call them, of the country. "What have we to do with state affairs, or with Pahar Singh either?"

So the assembly having voted non-interference with whatever might be in hand, our friend Lukshmun was allowed to get his meal in peace. Smoking—the impossibility of getting anything—and a tight waistband, had kept appetite down as yet; but with the Patel's kitchen in prospect, it rose fiercely for the occasion as he approached the house.

Lukshmun washed his feet and hands before he entered and sat down. O, what a smell of fried onions there was! and, as a girl set before him a pile of hot, well-buttered jowaree cakes, a cup full of "char," or pepper-water with tamarind in it, a fresh leaf full of a savoury stew of vegetables of all kinds, and some *dall* or pease-pudding, well-seasoned with red pepper and garlic, Lukshmun's heart expanded, and he set to work with a good will. Every now and then a woman at the fireplace asked him if he would have more, and it was brought him from the pan, smoking hot. Lukshmun dallied with each morsel as he ate; and when even reduced by repletion to licking his fingers, grudged the summons brought by a man that he was to come.

"Couldst thou not give me a few cakes, O sweet one, and some dall?" he said to the good-natured looking wench who had been serving him. "I have a brother—hungry—all day in the rain—while I have eaten. Thou art like the moon, O beauty, and thy heart as soft as butter. Give me the cakes for a poor, weak, hungry brother."

"Was there ever such a tongue and such a face?" retorted the damsel, laughing. "Look, Rookmee!"

The cook turned round and looked, too, laughing heartily; for Lukshmun's attitude on one leg, with the sole of the other foot pressed against the calf of it, his hands joined and stretched out imploringly, and his seared face twisted into a grotesque expression of supplication, was not to be resisted.

"Give him these cakes," said the cook, handing two to the girl.

"By your antelope eyes, O sweet ones, more!" he said, not altering his posture. "Do you think two would fill a hungry man's belly? By your lotos feet——"

"There, begone!" said the cook, handing him a few more and some dall; "there is a meal for a Rajah. Go, if the mistress should hear you——"

"I am gone, O my beauties," continued Lukshmun, folding the cakes into his waist-cloth, and tying them behind, then washing his hands elaborately. "You have made my heart——"

"Come quickly, come," said a voice at the door; "they want thee. Wilt thou eat all day?"

"I worship you, lovely nymphs, even as Rama adored——"

"Begone!" cried both the girls in a breath. "Here is the mistress coming, and if she hear such nonsense thou wilt be whipped."

"Here is the man who will be your worship's guide," said the Patel deferentially to our friend the Lalla, who, having arrived safely, was now divested of his upper clothing, which some of the men were drying in the opposite chamber, and seated in the place of honour of the assembly; "but your worship should eat before you go on, and the Rao Sahib here will take you to his house—a Brahmun's house," he added, as the Lalla appeared to hesitate.

"Ah, no, sir," returned the traveller, who indeed was very hungry, "I could not eat without I bathed, and I had better wait till I get to Allund. Shookr, shookr! I should be too long about it, and my horse has had his feed, and is ready to go on. And this is the guide?—not beautiful exactly."

"No, Maharaj, I am not beautiful, truly," replied Lukshmun, with a deprecatory gesture to the Patel, "but I may be useful to this noble gentleman. You may trust me, my lord. The Patel knows me, and so do all these worthy gentlemen; and am I not come for you?"

"They expect me, then, good fellow," replied the Lalla, amused by the man's broken Oordoo, and his grotesque expression of face.

"Ah, yes, noble sir," answered the man, joining his hands, "ever since morning; and as I was coming here on business I was told to bring you on. And now let us proceed, else it will be night ere we reach Allund; and," he added, with a wink to the Patel, "it is not good to be out late on the roads."

"What, are they dangerous, then?" asked the Lalla, looking anxiously around him.

"O no," cried Lukshmun, interposing readily; "there is no trouble in the country, and my lord is armed, and so am I. O no, only in regard to the mud and the stones. My lord will not find the road long, for I can sing him Mahratta 'lownees' if he likes."

"There was a tree and a temple which I was told to avoid, and to ask to be sent by the south road," said the Lalla, preparing to mount.

Lukshmun exchanged glances with the Patel and the Putwari. "Could any one have warned the stranger?"

"A tree!" said the Patel, gravely. "What tree? dost thou know any, Lukshmun? And the south road? what road?"

"O, I suppose the noble gentleman means that by Navindgee, and Hoshully, and Chik-Wondully, and Hully Sullgarra," said Lukshmun, rolling out a volley of hard Canarese village names. "That road? Why, it is six coss further from here! They should have sent him by it from Surroori. No," he continued, dropping the Lalla's stirrup, which he had taken in his hand, "if the gentleman likes to go he can do so, of course, but his slave begs to be excused;" and he put his joined hands up to his nose.

"Very good," said the Lalla, "I don't know; only I was told——"

"By whom?" interrupted the Putwari.

"By Déo Bawa, the Byragee at Surroori."

"O, the old Bawa! said the Patel, laughing. "Curious, is it not, noble sir, that the old man thinks that there are devils in the tree? He tells me he was bewitched there once, and I ought to cut it down."

"And I told him I was not afraid of them, Patel; but he said there was something else," returned the Lalla.

"Robbers, I suppose," said Lukshmun, readily; "Pahar Singh's men, perhaps."

"Perhaps," added the Lalla, "but he did not say so."

"Well for him," thought the Putwari, "or his stacks would have been burnt to-morrow night."

"Ah! no fear of thieves when you have one of 'the hunchbacks' with you," said Lukshmun. "Come, mount, my lord. Salaam,

Maharaj," he continued, making a mock salutation to the sun, which was just struggling through a cloud. "Salaam! thou hast been moist to-day; come out and dry thyself and us too. Now, noble gentleman, mount, and you will see how fast the excellent dinner I have eaten in the Patel's kitchen will take my feet to Allund, and the good horse, too, looks as fresh as if he were but just starting," and he patted him. "Ah, well done, sir!" he continued, as the Lalla mounted not ungracefully; "we poor Dekhanies cannot compare ourselves on horseback with you northern cavaliers. Come, sir, the road waits for us."

And with a salutation all round, the Lalla rode out of the gate, and our friend Lukshmun, cutting a caper which showed his marvellous activity by way, as he said, of getting the dinner out of his legs, and calling to the guide who carried the bundle, they passed on over the village common.

The Putwari sighed as the party left the gate.

"I tell thee, Seeta Ram," said the Patel, "he will come to no harm, and he is gone away happy."

"I am glad he did not eat at my house; it is not pleasant feeding a man who has death in his throat," returned the Putwari.

"I tell thee he is safe," retorted the Patel; "and if he is killed, it is no affair of ours."

"No, it is no business of ours," said the Putwari, settling to his accounts with a sigh which vexed the Patel. "No, it is no business of ours," echoed the farmers.

At that time Rama, who was seated on the heap of stones, looking from the top of the hill, exclaimed, as the three persons emerged from a lane into a low field in which the road was distinctly visible,

"Jemadar! he is coming at last, and Lukshmun is with him; we must be ready. Look, they are there!" he continued, as Gopal Singh joined him, "between the village and the stream."

"Ah, I see them, Rama, and thy brother is as true as gold. We will join them as they go on; he must not suspect us yet."

CHAPTER XII.

Our friend the Lalla was soon at his ease with his new guide, whose injunctions to Motee, bidding him "take care," "mind a stone," "lift up his feet," and the like, encouraged the good beast, who now stepped out briskly, while the curious mixture of Oordoo and Mahratta, in which the small gossip and scandal of the neighbourhood was told him by Lukshmun, amused him much. The mile or so which intervened between the village and the temple was soon passed;

and as they began to ascend the short rising ground towards the temple and the tree, the latter could be seen in all its wild picturesque detail, and was indeed a striking object.

The sun had now broken forth, and its beams shone slantingly through its rugged trunks and gnarled branches, resting brightly upon the glossy foliage sparkling with raindrops, and lighting up every excrescence and furrow of the knotty bark, casting broad shadows on the road below: while a slight parting shower, the large drops of which flashed brightly in the air as they descended, pattered upon the leaves, and spread out into the valley in a silver rain. As the travellers gained the summit, the clear sky beyond to the west not only caused the tree to stand out boldly and grandly against it, but the brightness of the sun dispelled the gloomy associations which the appearance of the place had suggested during the rain. A slight breeze, which had hardly been felt in the hollow, rippled the little pools on the roadway and on the plain beyond the tree, which, level and stony, continued, apparently many miles, in the direction they had to go.

Motee paused at the summit of the eminence, and the Lalla could not help stopping him to look back upon the road by which he had come. The bright yellow gleams of the sun shone broadly upon the two villages, and upon the rich green masses of their corn-fields. In the distance both looked pretty and comfortable: and their terraced houses, several white temples, and the dome of a small village mosque shone brightly in the sun. Behind these, and to the south, the plain over which the Lalla had come stretched away for many miles, showing the trees of a village here and there, with the occasional sparkle of a white house or temple among them; and behind all, the great black cloud of the day's rain, upon which there was a rainbow forming of great beauty, and against which a flight of white storks flashed like silver in the sun. Away to the south, the eye followed hollow and rise, undulation after undulation, till they were lost in a farther distance, which melted tenderly into the sky.

"It is a fair country, friend, after all," said the Lalla, "though it did not look well in the rain. That plain yonder is in the direction of Beejapoor, perhaps?"

"It is, sir," returned Lukshmun; "that high land, near the sky yonder, is beyond the Bheema river, and, if we were there, we should see the tomb of the great Sultan Mahmood, now finished. It is very grand, sir, and shines like silver when the sun is on it; and when I go there," continued the man, "I stand like a fool, looking at the King's palace, the Ark fort, the great gun, and the 'Ibrahim Roza'—that's the place where Ibrahim Adil Shah was buried, you know, sir——"

"Numascar Maharaj," cried a clear manly voice, now beside the Lalla's horse, which appeared to him to rise out of the earth, for he had not observed the approach of Gopal Singh and Rama from the temple.

"Who are these?" exclaimed the Lalla, starting and beginning to tremble—"who are these?" and the warning of the old Byragee now came upon him, with the distressing conviction that he ought to have regarded it; but it was too late. "Who are ye?" he asked anxiously.

"O, this is my brother Rama," said Lukshmun, assuringly, "and that is our Jemadar Gopal Singh; they only waited here while I went to Kinny."

"Be assured, noble sir," added the Jemadar, laughing, and in good Oordoo, with a slight southern accent, which seemed to assure the Lalla, "there is nothing to fear. Your worship is from Kullianee, perhaps."

"Yes, from Kullianee yesterday."

"Ah, yes, I remember; you were at Poorungeer's Mutt. I was just about leaving when you arrived, and the old man offered you escort of my party, but you preferred staying."

"I—I—I—had business," replied the Lalla, stammering, not exactly relishing Gopal Singh's bold looks, and yet unable to object to him. "I was tired and needed rest, and you could not wait."

"You had come from the royal court, I think they said, and were going to Beejapoor with letters for the King—proposals for peace, perhaps."

"So they said—who?" Of all things, the Lalla supposed his destination and business were at least secret; yet they appeared known, and to a perfect stranger, too, by the wayside. He did not feel able to reply, and was almost inclined to trust to Motee's speed, and break through the men; but Lukshmun, on receiving his matchlock from his brother, fixed the match, which had been hanging loose upon the cock, in a very precise manner, pressing the trigger to see if the match descended upon the pan. The others, too, looked carelessly to the priming of their guns, but to the Lalla's idea ominously, and as if he should understand the action. Lukshmun's face, too, appeared changed—it was not so pleasant as it had been.

"Come," said the Jemadar, "we have far to go to-night—what kept thee so long, Lukshmun?"

"O, the Patel at Kinny said we were to escort this worthy gentleman, as government orders had come about him from Allund; so I waited, as the rain had delayed him."

The Lalla felt reassured; his arrival was no doubt expected. "Ah, yes, sir," continued Gopal Singh, "you had better have come on with us three days ago, but it does not matter now. That is a fine horse of yours," he added, patting Motee's neck, "and from Hindustan, I think, as my lord is. We, too—that is, my family—are also from thence, Kanouj Khutrees; so is this good gun, too;" and he held out his own. "Yes; one can hit a man on horseback at full speed half as far as to the stream yonder."

It appeared to the Lalla as if the Jemadar was reading his thoughts as clearly as if he were telling them himself.

"And if we were in battle," he continued, "and any one were trying to get away from me, he would be shot between the shoulders before he could even reach the tree yonder."

"I—I—have no doubt of it, Jemadar Sahib," returned the Lalla, —"no doubt: and your speech is pleasant to hear after the rough language hereabouts."

"Come, come," cried Lukshmun, with seeming impatience, "if you want to pay compliments, noble sir, wait till we get to the end of our journey. Come!" and as he spoke he touched Motee's rein. "Come on, my son!" he said, and the horse followed.

As they passed the little temple in its loneliness under the shadow of the huge tree, it looked a place for evil deeds. A large horned owl on the highest branch, now awakening for his evening flight, hooted loudly above them, and was answered by another. It seemed an evil omen, and struck to the Lalla's heart.

"Ah! we cannot pass you, my friend," said Gopal Singh. "Look, Lalla Sahib, what my gun can do."

As he spoke, he raised the piece and fired. The aim was true and deadly, and the huge bird fell down heavily close to Motee's feet with a rushing sound, causing the horse to start back.

"I never miss," said the man, decidedly, and reloading his piece. "Now come on."

"Shabash! Well shot," said the Lalla; but his heart was throbbing fast, and it was a positive relief to him when the dark grove was behind them, and they emerged upon the bare, wild, open plain beyond.

"A lonely place that, Jemadar," remarked the Lalla, turning to the man who walked behind him; "and the old Byragee, where I slept, advised me not to go by it; he said Pahar Singh's men might be about. Who is this Pahar Singh?"

"Pahar Singh?" returned the Jemadar. "O, a worthy gentleman who is quiet enough when not plagued. He is the lord of the marches hereabouts—a valiant man, and a good soldier; and in these troubled times, Lallajee, has his friends and his enemies, like most of us: 'tis the way of the world."

After another mile, during which none of the party spoke, the Jemadar proposed to the Lalla to dispense with the guide. "Evening was drawing on," he said; "they knew the country, and the contents of the bundle could be carried on the saddle or divided among them;" and, indeed, it appeared necessary, as the guide, limping, declared he could go no farther, and had a thorn in his foot. The necessary arrangements were soon completed; and, between the Lalla's saddle-bags and his saddle, the contents of the bundle were soon disposed of; the guide received a small gratuity, and retraced his steps at a far more rapid pace than he had advanced.

"He has no more a thorn in his foot than I have, Lalla Sahib," said the Jemadar, laughing. "Look how he goes! but Bheema there is no worse than his fellows, and does not like the idea of a night journey without change. Now we shall get on better. Let the horse walk out, Lukshmun; only keep by him."

Lukshmun let go the rein, but he did not leave his place, and though the rate at which the horse now proceeded kept the men at a rapid walk, and occasionally, indeed, at a trot, they preserved the positions they had taken up without alteration, speaking little among themselves, except occasionally in Mahratta or Canarese, with both of which languages they appeared familiar.

The sun was setting in great glory. After the heavy clouds had passed away to the eastward, a clear blue sky succeeded for a while; but as a gentle breeze arose, it had brought up with it light, fleecy vapours, which, as the wind again died away at sunset, became motionless, and, gradually attracted to each other, formed piles of white clouds edged with deep grey. As the sun declined, white became orange and gold and crimson: while the sky itself, of an intense purple above, faded into green, yellow, and rosy tints, on which the golden clouds seemed to float in soft but brilliant masses: and, as it dipped below the horizon, a flood of light suddenly shot up, tinging the lower edges of all the lighter portions with vivid scarlet, and mingling with the deep orange and purple hues above, gorgeously.

"The gods have a festival upon Mount Meru to-night, Lallajee. Does the sun go down in that fashion in your country?" said the Jemadar, pointing to the sky and breaking a long silence. "We have made good work of it since the guide left us. Come, here is a little stream, and you need a change of posture; dismount and rest, while I offer my evening libations to the four elements."

"No, I will not dismount, Jemadar," returned the Lalla; "you will not be long, and by all means let your men get a drink of water too, and wash their feet. I will stay here."

"He is not to be trusted," said the Jemadar to his men in Canarese; "I see it in his eyes. If he stirs, shoot him, and both of you stay by him."

Rama had fastened one of the horse's tether-ropes about his waist, and he now proceeded to tie the end of it to the cheek-strap of the bridle in a methodical manner.

"What are you doing?" cried the Lalla, alarmed at the action; "loose it!"

"O, my lord will dismount," said Lukshmun, "and who is to hold the horse?"

"I am not going to move: loose it, I say!" cried the Lalla, impatiently.

But Rama sat down doggedly at a little distance, holding the rope, and began deliberately to munch a cake his brother had unfastened from his back, resting his gun across his knees.

"Loose it!" again cried the Lalla, "Jemadar, why have I been tied like a thief?"

The Jemadar had divested himself of his upper clothing and stepped into the stream; he was taking up water in his hands and pouring it to the four quarters of the earth. His clothes and arms were on the river bank.

"There is no use in disturbing him, Maharaj," said Lukshmun, quietly; "he is at his prayers, and can't hear. My brother, you see, doesn't understand you, and he only does what the Jemadar told him; so get off and walk about a little. Come, I will hold the stirrup for you."

"No; loose the rope!" cried the Lalla again, eagerly, and reaching over to do so himself.

"Ah, Maharaj! you must not do that; you see my brother will be angry. I advise you to be quiet," said Lukshmun, putting back the Lalla's hand, and pulling the knot of the rope firmer.

But the Lalla could not now contain himself; his alarm was gradually increasing. He thought he could break away from the men, and dash through the stream ere they could fire at him. Touching Motee with the bridle and his heel at the same time, he aroused him from the sluggish position he had assumed, and moved him a little so as to face Rama, who still sat eating; and the Lalla was quietly gathering up the reins preparatory to urging the horse forward, when the keen practised eyes of the men detected the intention. Excited by his rider, the horse gathered himself on his haunches and made a bound; but Lukshmun, leaping at the bridle, hung on to it, jerking it back so violently that the horse reared, while the Lalla, whose right arm had been seized by Rama, lost his balance, and fell heavily to the ground.

Hearing the cries of the men, Gopal Singh had run from the stream hastily, taking up his sword, and reached the spot as the Lalla fell.

"Get up!" he cried, seizing his arm; "what folly is this? By the gods, he has fainted! Thou hast not used thy knife, Rama?"

"Not I, Jemadar; but he fell heavily. What could I do? He would have been off, for the horse is a strong beast, and I could hardly hold him—only for the old trick. Get some water, Jemadar, he will drink from thee. I will hold him up. Stay, here is his lota."

While the Jemadar ran for water, Rama knelt down and raised the Lalla's head, who now opened his eyes. "Speak to him, Lukshmun; tell him to get up and be quiet," said Rama to his brother.

"Do you hear, Maharaj? you are to get up and be quiet. Rama says so," cried Lukshmun, "and he is not a child."

"Nor I, Lalla," said the Jemadar, returning with the water. "By Krishna, what made thee vex the hunchbacks? they were likely to be rough enough if provoked. Art thou hurt?"

"No, my lord—that is, valiant sir—only a little," replied the Lalla, moving his body about to ascertain the fact. "No; but my life!—O spare my life!—do not kill me."

"I am more hurt than he is, Jemadar," said Rama, rubbing his arm, "for he fell on me. Ah, you rascal!" he continued with a Mahratta oath, "only for the Jemadar there I had settled accounts with thee; get up!"

"I petition," said Lukshmun, who led up Motee, now calmed, "as the Lalla broke faith with us, that he walks; and Rama rides, as he is hurt."

"Ah, by your heads, no!" exclaimed the Lalla; "I never could walk a coss in my life; and my feet would never go over these stones and briars. Kill me, if ye will, but walk I cannot."

"Tie him up," suggested Rama, "if he can't walk; we must not trust him in the dark on that good horse."

"A good thought," said the Jemadar; "give me his sheet from the saddle."

The Lalla guessed what had been said, and protested and resisted vehemently; but he was as a child in the hands of the men, and in a few moments his hands and arms were swathed to his body gently within the sheet, but so that he could not use them: and he was raised to his feet, trembling violently, while the bandage was fastened behind him.

"Ah, sir! do not shake so," said Lukshmun, smiling, and joining his own hands in mock supplication; "if you do, you will go to pieces, and there will be none of you left when we get to our uncle, Pahar Singh."

Pahar Singh! the Lalla's heart sank within him. But he had no time for remonstrance. He was lifted like a child into the saddle, the men resumed their arms and positions, and again set forward.

"Where are you going to take me, Jemadar?" asked the Lalla, trembling, as they crossed the stream. "Ah, be merciful to——"

"So you have got speech at last," returned Gopal Singh. "Listen, Lalla, if you had been quiet you should have ridden like a gentleman, now you go as a thief. Pahar Singh, my uncle, is lord of these marches, and knows what to do with you. One thing, however, I may tell you; if you make any further attempt to escape, I will shoot you. It is not your carcass that he wants, but what you have on it; the gold you got at Kullianee. Now, beware, for you know the worst."

Of what use was resistance, and the Lalla clung to life. They might take his gold. There remained, at least, the papers he possessed; and if he begged his way on foot to Beejapoor, what matter, so that he got there with them?

So they proceeded as rapidly as the ground would admit, still continuing to avoid all villages by paths through the fields, with which they seemed perfectly acquainted.

Before they reach their destination, which they will do in two or three hours more, we may describe the person to whom they are proceeding.

CHAPTER XIII.

As at the banian tree, when Lukshmun was guide, and the Lalla had ridden up the rising ground, the sun had shone out brightly with a broad gleam through its giant trunks and branches, and over the villages and corn-fields beyond; so about the same time the light, glittering through the watery particles which filled the air, spread over a rich landscape, as viewed from a height above the pretty village of Itga, whence, by a rough stony path, a company of horsemen were now proceeding to the village itself.

There might have been twenty-five to thirty men, from the youth yet unbearded to the grizzled trooper, whose swarthy sunburnt face, and large whiskers and moustaches touched with grey, wiry frame, and easy lounging seat on his saddle—as he balanced his heavy Mahratta spear across his shoulders—showed the years of service he had done. There was no richness of costume among the party; on the contrary, the dresses were worn and weather-stained, and of a motley character. Some wore thickly quilted white or chintz doublets, strong enough to turn a sword-cut; or ordinary white cotton clothes, with back and breast pieces of thick padded cloth, or light shirts of chain-mail, with a piece of the same, or twisted wire, folded into their turbans; and a few wore steel morions, with turbans tied round them, and steel gauntlets which reached to the elbows, inlaid with gold and silver in delicate arabesque patterns.

The caparisons of their horses were as shabby as the dresses; but some had once been handsome, with embroidered reins and cruppers, and gay muslin martingals. All were now, however, soiled by the wet and mud of the day. It was clear that this party had ridden far, and the horses, though excellent and in high condition, were, from their drooping crests and sluggish action, evidently weary. Four of the men had been wounded in some skirmish, for it was with difficulty they sat their horses: and the bandages about them, covered with blood, showed the wounds to have been severe. But the sight of the village appeared to have revived the party; the horses were neighing and tossing their heads, and the men, shifting their places in the saddles, pointed eagerly to it, or, brandishing their spears, shouted one to another, cheering up the wounded men.

Among these horsemen, as also over the valley below, the sun's gleams shone brightly, casting long irregular shadows over the ground as they moved, and, glinting from spear-head, morion, and steel armour as the men swayed in their saddles, lighted up faces of varied character, all now joyous, but wearing an expression of habitual recklessness and lawless excitement.

Below them, at less than half a mile's distance, was the village itself. In the centre of it, or rather more to the right hand, was a high square castle, with round bastions at the corners, having loopholed parapets, which, where it had not been wetted by the rain, was of a warm grey, the colour of the mud or clay of which it had been built. It was in perfect repair, and the close smooth plastering of the walls and parapets showed that the weather was not allowed to injure it.

Inside the castle walls were the white terraced roofs of a dwelling-house, and in the bastions in the east and north corners several windows and other perforations in the curtain walls, which showed that rooms were connected with them; but it was clear, from the height of the parapets above the ground, which might be sixty feet, that most of the inside must be a solid mass of earth, as indeed it was as far as the courtyard, around which were the houses already noticed. On one high bastion, in which several small cannon were placed, was a flag-staff, and a large white flag, bordered with green, which floated out lazily upon the evening breeze, showing the device—a figure cut out in red cloth and sewn upon the white—of the monkey god Hunooman, who might be supposed to be, as he was, the tutelary divinity of the castle.

To protect the gateway there was a double outwork with several narrow traverses and large flanking bastions, but otherwise no additional defence to the castle walls, which were quite inaccessible. Around their foot, separated only by an open courtyard, surrounded by a low wall with bastions at intervals, were the terraced houses of the place, thickly placed together, and filling up the space between the outer wall of the village and the castle itself. There was no doubt that the community living there was thriving, and better protected than those of the more open villages of the country. The houses, too, were of a superior and more substantial character, and gave assurance of habitual safety and wealth.

Outside all, ran a high wall, also of mud, with large round bastions at intervals, loopholed and mounted with jinjalls, and other wall-pieces, with two large gates, each defended by an outer work and traverse, and heavy bastions on each side; and there were several smaller wickets or posterns, each with a parapet wall before, and a tower beside it. The whole formed a very strong position, impregnable against any attack by marauding horse; and even in the event of a siege by a better organized force, it could have held out stoutly.

The ground for some distance round Itga formed a clear natural esplanade, over which it was impossible for anything to advance without being seen from the castle walls. This was now like a carpet of emerald green, on which fell the broad shadows of the tall trees near the gates and a grove round a small Hindu temple, and several large herds of cattle rested or browsed before entering the village walls for the night. Beyond the open ground the irrigated fields and gardens of the village commenced; and the bright yellow green of the sugar-cane, in large patches, catching the sun's rays, glowed among the darker colours of the grain crops and cotton, which spread up and down the valley as far as could be seen, and on both sides of the stream flowing in the centre.

Above the village the valley appeared to contract gradually, and the stream to disappear behind a projecting bluff. Below, it opened out considerably; and could be seen for several miles, showing other villages in the distance, with their ghurries, or castles, of the same character as that of Itga, but smaller, rising above the trees; while, here and there, the white dome of a mosque, or steeple of Hindu temple, with portions of the stream, sparkled in the evening sun.

A fair scene now when, over the rich crops and gardens, and spreading over the tender distance, the bright evening light threw a mellow radiance, resting with brilliant effect upon the projections and bastions of the castle, upon the terraces of the houses, the heavy gateways, the people passing to and fro, and the bright-coloured cattle upon the village green. A fair scene, truly, and in strong contrast with the character of the place, which, to say the truth, was evil enough in some respects.

The owner of this village, and of several adjoining villages, was the Pahar Singh, whom, casually, we have already had occasion to mention. Nominally a frontier officer of the Beejapoor State, "Hazaree," or commander of a thousand men, and holding the estate in maintenance of a troop of horse and a number of foot soldiers, which, though somewhat less, passed for a thousand in the royal musters of Beejapoor,—Pahar Singh had by no means followed his father's example of steady devotion to his duty, or confined his men to the purpose for which they were intended. During his father's lifetime he had engaged with the most dissolute and lawless of his father's retainers in border raids and forays without number, and had not unfrequently defied the troops of the State, bringing his father's good name into very questionable repute.

After the old man's death, wilder times ensued, when a bold stroke, here and there, decided a man's fortune; and proportionately as he was powerful or otherwise locally, his influence, both at court and in the provinces, extended. Pahar Singh had struck many such, with which, however, we have no concern. Following the example of the Beydur chief of Sugger, he had imposed a system of black-mail all over the frontier near his estate, which, if not regularly paid, was enforced roughly enough; while, on his part, his clients were protected from violence by other parties. The system, in fact, extended to the capital itself, and merchants and rich travellers paid Pahar Singh's dues as the best means of escaping outrage if they had to travel across his marches.

To others but his own people, Pahar Singh was a merciless savage, for the most part; and even his own relations, and those who knew him best, could hardly account for the variation of temper which could watch torture for the extortion of money—perhaps an agonized death—at one moment, and at the next listen to a tale of distress, or need, or sickness, and relieve it himself, or send it to his wife Rookminee, with a message which insured prompt attention from that kind lady.

It is perhaps unnecessary to go far back into history for illustrations of character like that of "the Hazaree." Such still exists among the native states of India, and even among our own subjects, restrained by the power of the paramount Government, if not by the spirit of the times—but still restrained—from lives as reckless and lawless, from savagery as deep and as unrelenting, as was that of Pahar Singh. With such characters, evil passions have taken the form of sensuality in its varied phases, which, as mostly concerning the individual himself, blunts the exercise of all finer feelings, but does not occasion the misery to others which would be the result of unfettered and misguided action.

The party we have mentioned had descended the small pass from the table-land above, and had pressed merrily on to the village gate, where they were met by friends, and welcomed by many a rough but kind greeting, and by a discharge of wall-pieces from the bastions, and shots from the castle, answered by the matchlocks of the party. Having entered the deep arched gateway, they were now emerging irregularly from its shadow into the main street, down which the sun streamed brightly. The terraced houses were covered with women and children waving cloths, or whatever they could catch up. The shopkeepers, for the most part, descended from their seats and exchanged respectful greetings with the leader; and as the small troop passed up towards the open space below the castle, still firing shots, it was plain that every one had forgotten the fatigue of the march in his safe return.

The horsemen remained mounted after the halt, and several stout serving-men took the heavy bags of money which each in succession loosed from his saddlebow, and carried them into the castle. This done, the leader dismounted, and the chief "Karkoon," or scribe, delivered a short but pleasant message from the chief, and dismissed the rest; and the men, wheeling round, discharged an irregular volley from their matchlocks, and, passing back round the foot of the outer bastion of the court, separated, each to his own house.

"He will not delay you long," said Amrut Rao, the Hazaree's chief Karkoon, or scribe, to the leader; "but you are not to go, he says, without seeing him."

"What temper is he in?" asked the person addressed.

"Not good—but no fear for you. He is angry at Gopal Singh's absence, that is all; so be careful, Maun Singh, and do not cross him to-day. Come, he has looked for you these many hours."

Maun Singh, an active, intelligent man, with a bright soldierly bearing, was a cousin of the chief, and a valuable and trusty leader of partisan expeditions. This foray had been remarkable for its success. A convoy of treasure, belonging to the neighbouring kingdom of Golconda, had been attacked on its way to the capital, its escort defeated, and the money for the most part secured and brought in. The largest portion of the force was returning by a different road; this, consisting of picked men and horses, had pressed on home with the booty.

Maun Singh entered the gate with his companions, and ascended an inclined plane leading to a court above, which, the outer one of the interior of the castle, was that to which men were alone allowed access. On two sides were open verandahs, consisting of double rows of wooden arches, supported upon carved pillars, the floor of the inner one being raised a little above that of the outer. On the east side, a large chamber of some pretension, ended in an oriel window, fitted with delicately carved shutters, which admitted light and air. This chamber was three arches in depth, and the woodwork of the pillars was carved in bold designs of flowers and leaves, the ends of the beams being fancifully cut into dragons' heads, the lines of which were carried gracefully into the general patterns of flowers and leaves. This was the chamber, or hall, of audience.

On the fourth side of the court was a stable, and a door which led to servants' rooms and offices, and there were folding-doors in the verandahs on both sides communicating with women's apartments, and stairs leading to the roofs of the buildings which formed the parapets for defence of the castle.

As he entered the court, Maun Singh greeted, and was saluted in turn by, those around; and a party of scribes, engaged in accounts at the entrance of the hall, rose at his approach. Passing these, he went on to his relative, who was sitting reclined against a large pillow in a recess of the window, and who half rose as he returned his salutation, but not courteously.

Pahar Singh was always remarkable—no one could look on him unmoved. He had a strong-featured hard face, prominent aquiline nose, deep-set black eyes, not so large, as penetrating in character, and covered by bushy eyelashes. The eyes were restless and unsettled in character, and, by this, and the general expression of his countenance, he was nicknamed the falcon. None of the hair on his face was shaved, and the whole was tied up in a knot and wound round his head in a thick heavy mass, while the thin grey and sandy-coloured beard and moustaches, divided in the centre, were usually passed over each ear, but could, if he pleased, be worn flowing down to the waist. The forehead was high and covered with deep wrinkles, and upon it the veins from the root of the nose stood out roughly and with a knotted appearance, apparently the result of habitual excitement. The mouth had hard cruel lines about it, and the sinewy throat tended to increase the rugged character of the whole countenance.

In age he appeared past forty. Naked to the waist, his figure was wiry, and showed great power, particularly in his arms. Pahar Singh's strength was proverbial in the country; and the large exercising clubs, standing in a corner, which he used several times during the day, could be wielded by none but himself.

"I received your letter, Maun Singh," he said, before that person was seated. "Why did you delay? Why did you let that boy leave you? By Gunga, if the boy dies, or comes to hurt, your life shall answer for it."

"Pahar Singh," replied the other, who always addressed his cousin by name if he were angry, and who had less fear of him than any one else, "I have done good work. There are more than twenty thousand rupees yonder, and I have only lost one man."

"True, true, brother," cried the chief, waving his hand; "there is no blame for that, only for the boy. What took him to Kullianee?"

"I sent him to Poorungeer, the banker, with the bills, to see if any were negotiable. There he heard of something; and when all was quiet at Muntalla, he departed at night without my knowledge. He only left word that he had gone after some good business, and was not to be followed."

"Wrong, Maun Singh. Thou wert wrong not to watch him—not to send men after him. If he dies, O Maun Singh, O brother, it were better thou wert never born!" and the chief smote his pillow angrily with his clenched fist.

"His fate is not in my hand, Pahar Singh," retorted the other; "and——"

"Do you answer me? do you answer me?" cried the chief, savagely grasping the pillow, the veins of his forehead swelling and his nostrils dilating as he spoke.

Amrut Rao knew the sign, and interposed. "Is this money to be counted?" he said, pointing to the bags; "if so, give me the key of the treasury, and let the Jemadar go home. He is tired, and you will like to see the coin. It shall be counted before you."

"Good! Go, Maun Singh. I shall be quieter when you return," replied the chief. "Ah, yes! we were once the same, brother. We could not be stopped either," he said more gently, "if we had anything to do."

"The hunchbacks are with him, and they are all on foot, brother," returned Maun Singh: "fear not; but if thou art restless, give me some fresh men and a fresh horse, and we will ride round the villages."

"No; go home—go home. No; let him hunt his own game," returned the chief.

"But about the money? Déo Rao wants to get home now, for he is starving," interposed the Karkoon.

"Let him go then!" exclaimed the chief tartly.

"No, he can't go till it is counted," retorted Amrut Rao.

"It need not be counted."

"It must be counted, Maharaj! If there is a rupee wrong we shall never hear the last of it. The bags have never been opened—who knows what is in them?"

"It may be gold, Amrut Rao. Come, who knows? yes, who knows? Come," exclaimed Pahar Singh excitedly.

Few could take the liberties in speech with the chief that were permitted to Amrut Rao, and even he was not always successful; but now the Suraffs, or money-changers, sent for had arrived, and Pahar Singh watched the opening of every bag with an almost childish curiosity. All anxiety for his nephew had departed before the sight of money. Yet Gopal Singh was the life and stay of the house; precious as Pahar Singh's heir, and more so as the husband of his daughter, who was as yet a child.

"Good coin, good coin!" cried the chief exultingly, as the contents of the bags passed through the experienced hands of the examiners without one being rejected. "Good coin! O Amrut Rao, I vow all the light weights to feed Brahmuns. Dost thou hear?"

"I am afraid their bellies will be empty enough," returned the Karkoon, laughing. "No, Maharaj! do better: send five hundred to Vyas Shastree to offer at the shrine of Sri Mata if Gopal Singh returns safe to-night. You cannot disappoint her and be secure."

"Well spoken! well spoken! Yes, put the money aside; yes, put all the light-weight coin and make it up; thou shalt have it—if—he comes. Holy Gunga! what is that?" he exclaimed, suddenly, as a separate bag rolled out of one then being emptied. "Gold, by all the gods! Give it me; I will count it myself."

CHAPTER XIV.

We must, however, return to our travellers, whose progress since night set in had been anything but agreeable, considering the state of the road; for though the light-footed men traversed it easily, poor Motee, weary enough, stopped fairly where the mud was deepest, and quivered in every limb in the intervals of stony ground. Indeed, he would have given up long ago but for Lukshmun, whose cheery voice and hand, now soothing, now encouraging, now remonstrating, urged him to put forth his whole power; and as if the promises of a good stable, the sweetest fodder, the best grain, which were repeated with every endearing variation that Mahratta and Canarese, oddly intermixed with scraps of Oordoo ballads, could supply, seemed to be understood by the gallant beast as he toiled on. His master, since he had been swathed up in the sheet, and had found it impossible to help himself, had fallen into what might be called a passive frame of mind. Nothing was clear to him, neither where he was, nor with whom or where he was going.

As before, villages were avoided, and it was evident that his guides knew the country perfectly—threading lanes, then emerging into open fields, again crossing waste ground, but still preserving, as nearly as possible, the same direction, as the Lalla could see by the moon which, struggling through masses of watery clouds that had risen since sunset, threw a misty and indistinct light upon the path and what lay in its immediate vicinity. Now and then they approached so near a village that the watch-dogs within its walls bayed and howled, and they could hear the hum of voices, or see lights high up in the ghurry, or the watch-towers at the gates; but they did not stop. All the Lalla asked occasionally was, "How far yet?" and received but one answer—"Coss bur." The trees of village after village, and the dark square forms of their ghurries, or castles, stood out against the moon in succession, and each one he hoped might be the last; but still they went on, through the same apparently endless succession of muddy lanes, and over open fields and waste lands,—faster if the ground were firm, slower if it were muddy.

Finding it of no use to speak to his companions, the Lalla's mind reverted naturally to his own condition, and was as busy now, though after a more dreamy fashion, than in the morning, when riches and honours seemed within his grasp. For after some misgivings he had argued himself into a belief of a positively agreeable reception by Pahar Singh. He would not at once admit his errand to the Beejapoor court, but reserve it for a confidential communication; and he would be able to tell Pahar Singh about their own country. Yes—the Lalla had framed, and was framing, many irresistibly polite speeches in his mind, recalling verses to quote from Persian poets, and the replies to his remarks would necessarily be in a similar strain. What else could be expected of one of his own countrymen? and he would make allowances for some omissions in strict etiquette and courtesy. Then what excellent cookery he should enjoy—what luxurious rest!

Alas! these were but the delusions of hunger, thirst, and weariness, and were but shortlived; for in their place would suddenly arise a ghastly anticipation of violence—a dungeon and chains—ending in a lingering or sudden death. Or, again, the loss of all his papers and his money—both as yet safe. Or, perhaps, of being again taken to the royal camp, and sold to the Emperor, a hasty doom following—an elephant's foot, or *that* executioner, always present, whom he so well remembered.

There was no denying that such thoughts would recur more vividly than the others, causing the Lalla to writhe in his bonds, and to break out into a cold sweat from head to foot, in, as it were, the very bitterness of death. This past, he would sink once more into apathy and weariness, while Motee groaned, trudged, and splashed, or Lukshmun cheered or warned him; and the two others, in their old places, their lighted matches glowing in the darkness, never varied in position or in pace.

It might have been the close of the first watch of the night, perhaps more, when the Lalla became sensible of a change in the demeanour of the men. They talked more among themselves, and laughed heartily. Gopal Singh even told him to be of good heart. The road, too, was more open and less muddy. Before him was a rising ground, and upon it a tree distinctly visible against the moon, to which they pointed, and stepped out at a better pace. As they neared the tree they halted for a moment, shook out their dresses, resettled their turbans, and rubbed up their moustaches. Yes, they were most likely near the end of their journey, but the Lalla dare not ask; his tongue was cleaving to his mouth with that peculiarly exhaustive thirst which is the effect of weariness and terror combined; and when all three men blew their matches, and shook fresh priming into the pans of their guns, the Lalla shut his eyes and expected death.

"Come, Lallajee," said Gopal Singh, in a cheery voice, "don't go to sleep, good man, we are near home now; no more 'coss burs,' you know. Ah, by-and-by, you will know what a Canarese coss is. Mind the horse as we go downhill," he continued to Lukshmun. "I must have that beast; he has done his work right well to-day."

Almost as the last word was spoken, they reached the brow of the ascent, and looked down upon Itga from the place we have already described. It appeared gloomy enough to the Lalla. The castle, or ghurry, stood out, a black mass, against the setting moon, and the men and horses were barely distinguishable in the faint light, while the towers at the gate, and round the outer walls, seemed to be exaggerated in height and dimensions. From the window over the castle gateway, a light twinkled brightly in the dark mass of the walls, and there was one also on a bastion of the gate, and a few here and there in the village. Around the fields and trees were in the deepest gloom, the upper portion of the trees, where the moon's rays caught the topmost branches only, being visible, and a sparkle here and there in the little river, as it brawled over the rocks and stones in its bed, its hoarse murmur being distinctly audible as though it were in flood.

"Cheer up, Lallajee! be comforted; our master never keeps any one in suspense very long," remarked Lukshmun pleasantly. "When he says ch-ck, ch-ck, as I do to Motee here, we know exactly what to do."

"Be quiet, for a prating fool, as thou art!" cried Gopal Singh, "and look after the horse. I would not have his knees broken for a thousand rupees. Sit square, O Lalla! lean back, good man, and ease him as you go down. Do not be afraid."

But for this assurance the Lalla had fainted. "Ah, Jemadar," he exclaimed, "by your mother, I am too poor to notice—a stranger in a strange land. I trust to you—pity me and be merciful, for the sake of my children."

"Bichara! poor fellow, he has children—so have I," interrupted Lukshmun; "and that makes it worse sometimes."

"Be silent, as you love your life," said the Jemadar, firing a shot over the Lalla's head, which caused him to start violently, and was followed by another each from the two men in succession; "be silent, and mind your seat downhill. If Maun Singh has not arrived," he continued to the men, "there will have been trouble enough by this time.'

"They have passed not long ago, Jemadar," said Rama; "look, here are the horses' footprints."

"That is good; and they see us now," continued Gopal Singh.

As he spoke, a vivid white flash, from the highest bastion turret of the castle, increased in brightness, as a large Bengal light was burned for an answering signal. The attitude of the signal-man, as he held an iron cresset high above his head, could be distinctly seen; and while the dazzling blaze continued, castle, and town, and village—even the open ground beyond, and the trees and temple upon it—were revealed in silvery brilliance. Then, as the first died out, another light took its place, and burned out, leaving the gloom more intense than before. Under any other circumstances, the effect would have been as surprising to the Lalla as it was really beautiful, but, under the circumstances, the sudden apparition of the castle, with its defences and outworks, struck an additional chill to his heart, and as the last gleam of the bright light went out, it seemed a type of the extinguishing of his own hopes.

CHAPTER XV.

PAHAR SINGH had been long watching from the window we have before mentioned. There were three descents from the plain above to the village, all within his view; and there were men on each of the bastions also, watching in all directions. He was very restless and moody; not even the gold found in several bags which he had taken to his private apartments—not even the large amount of booty, which had so few light coins in it—could dispel the gloom. He had ordered all about him to be silent, and even Amrut Rao had obeyed him as yet; and his little daughter, who was allowed to sit in the hall when no strangers were present, had nestled to his side, but was afraid to speak.

Amrut Rao knew, however, by experience, that the more his master was allowed to brood over anything in this manner, the harder it was to rally him; and as the account of the money had been made up, he took the paper, trimmed the lamp, and stood in an attitude to read, unchecked by the actual distortion of the chief's face in a repressed fury, at which even his daughter concealed herself, and cowered into a corner, and which soon broke out in violent oaths and abuse.

Amrut Rao bent to the storm, and did not reply. After an interval he read slowly :—

"Twenty-seven thousand two hundred and ninety-three rupees; and the five bags of ashruffees which you took inside—how many were in them?"

"What is that to you? do you want to steal them? By the gods! you are over-familiar to-night, Amrut Rao. Did I not bid ye all be silent, and dare you disobey? you—dare you?" cried the chief, raising himself, while the foam gathered upon his lips, and the veins swelled on his forehead. "Dare you?"

"My lord," replied Amrut Rao, joining his hands, "abuse of a Brahmun, out of a noble mouth, is sin—unfitting to hear. Be reasonable. This is the best booty which we have seen for many a day. If we knew the total of the ashruffees we could add it, and you could sign the day-book, and clear away all the bags. It is getting late."

"Let it be. No, I will not sign the paper," cried Pahar Singh, petulantly. "What need have I with wealth? he will not come now. I will go to Kasee, Jugunath, and Raméshwur; I will give up the world; I have committed much sin, and will have no more of it. I will—— Ha, by the gods! there is a shot on the road," he continued, as the sharp ring of Gopal Singh's matchlock broke the silence without: "another, and another! and a horse's neigh, too; and there were but the three. Can it be they, Maun Singh? speak! by your soul, speak: why are you silent?"

"Let the cloud pass from your spirit, brother: it is they, sure enough. I would swear to Gopal's gun by its ring anywhere."

"Burn a light from the upper bastion—two! it may cheer them down the pass. Quick!" cried the chief; "answer their signal. O Maun Singh! if I said anything bad, forgive me, brother; but I was distraught with care for that boy. Yes, they will see that," as the first blue light glittered over the village. "Burn another, Ranoba—a large one!" he called from the window to the men above; "we may even see them. By the gods! yes, Maun Singh, there they are: the three, and a man on horseback muffled up—a large grey horse—who can it be? Get hot water ready, and enough for all to eat. Bring a goat to kill before him. Tell thy mother, O daughter, to see to this; tell her they are come. How many short rupees were there, Amrut Rao?"

"My lord, it was as I said: the Brahmuns' bellies would be empty if we trusted to short rupees; all we could find were nine doubtful ones."

"Then, count out fifty more—stay, a hundred: will that feed them?"

"You have not told me how much gold there was, Maharaj," continued the Karkoon pertinaciously, not noticing the gift.

"Now, a plague on thee for an obstinate fool, Amrut Rao," replied the chief, laughing; "did I not tell thee not to speak about it?"

"The total of the silver is twenty-seven thousand two hundred and ninety-three rupees," returned the Karkoon; "and the gold must be added to complete the account before we retire."

"Well, then, there were five bags, and fifty Akburi mohurs in each: will that content you? or must you see them?"

"Why couldn't you tell me this at first?" continued Amrut Rao, writing in the account, which he spread on his left hand; "there, at twenty rupees each, another five thousand, that makes thirty-two thousand two hundred and ninety-three rupees. My lord ordered fifty rupees for the dole to-morrow; it might as well be the odd ninety-three."

"Ay, take that, and the two hundred over to boot, good fellow, if thou wilt. Here, some of you, stop him, stop my son, and kill a goat before him at the gate; see that lights are waved over him, and the evil eye is taken off him. Quick! there are the torches flashing in the bazar."

"I have deducted the sum, Maharaj," said the Karkoon deliberately; "now look at the total, and put your seal to it. Thirty-two thou——"

"By Krishna! thou wouldst leave me no peace, Amrut Rao," replied the chief; "here is the seal; seal the memorandum, and begone. Yet stay; thou art a good fellow after all; so take a handsome doopatta, or a pair of dhotees, out of that coin for thyself."

"Not out of the Brahmuns' bellies," retorted the Karkoon; "thank you. I shall have plenty of gifts by-and-by. Here is your seal."

The chief might have answered angrily, had his attention not been diverted at the moment. "Ah, here they are," he cried, looking from the window; "they have brought the man's horse up to the steps, and are taking him off—bound, too! Ai Purméshwar! but there must be much to hear. Why do they delay?"

In truth they had not delayed; for several torch-bearers, stationed at the gate, hearing the shots on the hill, had run forward in the direction of the pass, while the retainers and others from the bazar, crowded up to bid the young man welcome; for the anxiety in the castle had spread over the village. So Gopal Singh and his party entered the gates among many eager faces, lighted up by torches tossing above them, and were welcomed by noisy shouts as the men clustered round them. Then a bevy of village women awaited them, some bearing brass dishes filled with mustard-seed, and small lighted lamps, which were waved over him; others with jars of water, which were poured out before him; and, as others joined them, there was quite a procession up to the end of the second traverse.

Farther on, at the gate of the castle, stood a body of the household servants and retainers, one having a naked sword, and a goat before him bleating loudly. As Gopal Singh advanced, the sword flashed in the air, and the headless carcase struggled convulsively as the blood spouted over the sill and step, and trickled down towards the Lalla, who, lifted from his horse, shuddered as he was set down among it.

Again the ceremony of having lights waved over him by some of the women-servants was repeated; and Gopal Singh, bidding Lukshmun and the others search the Lalla carefully and keep what was found, ascended to the court, and was met in a warm embrace by his uncle, and led to the window, where, being seated, all present, including Maun Singh, advanced to salute him in turn.

"What did I say, brother?" cried Maun Singh joyfully. "I knew he would not disappoint us. Yet thou shouldst not have gone alone, Gopal."

"Nay, but I had the hunchbacks with me, and more would have spoiled my small hunt, which, if not so grand as thine, uncle, may yet be important," replied the young man.

"Ah, the boy, the boy!" exclaimed the chief, stroking the young man's face, and kissing the tips of his own fingers; "have I not brought him up since he was the height of my knee? And I thought him lost—Ai Bhugwân, Bhugwân! Ai Purméshwar! He is safe and well—safe and well, O Sri Mata! My heart swells. What did I say for the Brahmuns? Never mind now. Go, bathe and eat, my son, and we will see to everything afterwards."

"Not before that matter is settled, father—that is, about the man I brought with me."

"Yes, I had forgotten—certainly. Light the large lamps," cried the chief to the attendants at the lower end of the room; "let us see what manner of man he is. Who is he, Gopal?"

"That we have to find out, father. They thought him a spy of the Emperor's, and he came from Aurungabad, by Bheer, to Kullianee, to the Gosai's. He changed some bills for gold, and he has got it. I offered escort, but was refused; so I went from Muntalla to the Burr tree at Kinny, for we heard he was going to sleep in the Mutt at Surroori. They were sending him on privately, father."

"Shabash! well done, son. A spy? Well, if we are true to the King's salt, he goes no farther; and he was being sent privately! Ah, the old foxes! Here he is—what a sight!" cried the chief, breaking into uncontrollable laughter. "Who art thou? What have they done to thee? Speak."

In truth the poor Lalla was a show. The order to search him had been literally complied with, and while two stout fellows held his arms wide apart, he was helpless to struggle. Rama and Lukshmun, who would allow no one to touch him, had dived into every pocket, and felt every possible place of concealment, even to the Lalla's hair, which was loosened and hung about his shoulders. His turban had been removed and shaken out, while one end was now fastened to his right arm. The bag of gold, tied round his waist, his bundle of precious papers, his sword, dagger, and waist-shawl, had all been taken from him and made into a bundle, and the articles were deliberately counted by the hunchback as they were deposited, one by one, in the centre of the shawl spread out for the purpose. It was quite in vain that the Lalla entreated, besought, struggled, or resisted by turns; the place, the rough men around him, all forbade hope of pity, and he submitted. Finally, Lukshmun dragging him by the end of his turban, Rama pushing him behind, and several of the others assisting, the Lalla was brought into the presence of the chief, where he sank down, stupidly staring about him.

Where were all the fine speeches he had contrived, which should have carried the chief's heart at once? All the couplets, too, from the Bôstan that he was to have quoted?—All gone. His head was bare, his clothes untied and hanging loosely about him; his boots removed: and his appearance of utter helplessness, and the hopeless, piteous expression of despair in his face, might have excited compassion in any but the hardened men by whom he was surrounded and confronted.

"Who art thou, knave? Speak," cried the chief, sternly, again raising his voice and checking his laughter. "Who art thou?"

"There now, make a salaam to the 'Lion of the Jungle'" (as the chief was called among his people), said Lukshmun, raising the right hand of the Lalla to his head, which dropped helplessly. "Ah, I see he is ashamed, poor man, of his naked head. There, Lallajee," and he wound the turban round his head hastily, giving it a ludicrous cock to one side, increasing, if possible, the grotesque expression of the features—"there now, get up and make your Tusleemât, else my lord may be angry; and he is not exactly safe when he is," he added in a whisper. "Get up, and don't be afraid."

But the Lalla's terror was too great, his mouth too dry to speak. "Amān, amān!—Mercy, mercy!" was all he could gasp.

"Who art thou, knave?" cried Pahar Singh again. "Whence art thou come? Give a good account of thyself. Let go of him, rascals!" he continued to the men who held him; "begone all of ye."

"Maharaj," cried Lukshmun beseechingly to the chief, "here are the Lalla's things; who will take them? Look, Rao Sahib," he continued, to Amrut Rao, "here they are: count them. I have done with them—for the Lion is getting savage—let me go. Beware, O Lalla! take my advice, and tell all about yourself, else I shall have to kill you somehow. You don't know the Maharaj as I do."

This advice, and the diversion effected by the hunchback, afforded the Lalla a little time for the recovery of his senses; but who could have recognized the bland, accomplished Toolsee Das, in the abject figure before them? Hastily pressing the turban straight upon his brows, the Lalla arose, and, as well as he could, made the ordinary Tusleemât.

"Shabash!" cried the chief. "Well done, that was never learned in the jungle. Now speak truly, and at once, who art thou?"

"Noble sir," returned the Lalla, "I claim your protection. There has been a mistake about my treatment. My property has been taken, and I have been misused——"

"I misuse thee, knave?" cried Pahar Singh, his brow darkening; "who art thou to bandy words with Pahar Singh? I have never seen thee before."

"Beware, Lallajee," said Gopal Singh; "did I not warn thee? Say who thou art at once, or I will not answer for thee. Do not eat dirt."

"Peace, boy!" interrupted the chief angrily; "the fellow looks like a knave—a thief—his is no honest face. Speak; or, by the gods, there will be scant ceremony with thee!"

"My lord, my lord!" cried the Lalla piteously; "mercy, I am no thief; I am a poor Khayet of Delhi, travelling to Beejapoor, on business of my own—a stranger—a poor stranger."

"What business, Lalla?"

"My lord, we are merchants, and have dealings with people there for clothes and jewels. There is a dispute about the accounts, and I have come to settle them," said the Lalla glibly enough. It was one of the stories he had made up by the way.

"Who are the merchants?" asked the chief.

"The Gosais of the Mutt at Kullianee, where I was yesterday; they sent me on," replied the Lalla.

"O, hear!" cried Gopal Singh; "they knew nothing about thee, except that thou hadst a bill on them for a thousand rupees, and the money was given thee in gold. Is not this true? Did I not hear it myself?"

"Thou art no merchant, dog," exclaimed Pahar Singh. "Did ever merchant make an obeisance like that? Ah, we are true testers of gold here; the true and the false are soon found out. Who art thou? speak truly, and fear not."

"By the shrine at Muttra, by the Holy Mother, I am what I say, a poor Khayet, a Mutsuddee only. O noble sirs," continued the Lalla, "give me my property, and let me go. I will seek shelter in the bazar: let me go, for the love of your children."

"I beg to petition," interposed Lukshmun, joining his hands, "that, as I brought him, my share of the gold be given me before he goes. I took care of him on the road—did I not, master?"

"Silence!" roared the chief; "any one who speaks shall be flogged. Who art thou, O liar? Mutsuddee thou art, but whose? Thy speech betrays thee—beware!"

"I have told you, noble sir. Thakoor Das, Preym Das is the name of the firm; my name is Toolsee Das—Lalla Toolsee Das, your slave to command. Ask at Kullianee, and the house will be known there. I—I—am a poor man—a stranger; who knows me?" said the Lalla, now whimpering.

"A fool, a liar art thou, throwing away life," returned Gopal Singh. "This is the second time I have warned thee. We know thou art from the royal camp, and a spy to Beejapoor. Speak, else——"

"And the doom of a spy is death; and thou art a liar too, and a coward to boot. Look at him now, Gopala," said his uncle, interrupting and pointing to the man; "look at his coward face."

The Lalla was trembling violently. His knees shook, and his teeth chattered audibly as he shivered. He could not speak, but looked vacantly from one to another. "I am c-o-o-ld—c-o-o-o-ld," he said faintly; "the wet, sirs, and the long travel. Amān, amān! I am only a merchant, let me go."

"Thou art cold! then we will warm thee," cried the chief grimly. "Yet, speak, O Lalla, ere I give the order. We would not hurt thee without cause—otherwise——"

"Ai Narayun! Ai Ramchunder! believe me, I am no spy. I swear by God I am no spy," he replied earnestly.

"Bind him!" cried the chief furiously. "A liar and a spy. Make torches of his fingers! we will soon hear the truth."

CHAPTER XVI.

Ere he knew what to do or say, the Lalla was a second time bound with his own shawl; and Lukshmun, tearing a rag into strips, and soaking them in the oil of the lamp, was tying them coolly upon the ends of his fingers, one by one. "I told you, Lallajee," he said, "we are rough people here, and you should be careful. When I light these you will not like the pain, and if you bear that, he will do something worse. When he says 'ch-ck, ch-ck,' you know——"

"Silence, knave! thou art over-familiar," cried Maun Singh; "beware!"

"Nay, but if I can save him from the torches, uncle," returned the hunchback, with a grotesque grin, "he will perhaps be grateful, and give his wealth to me."

"Is it ready?" asked the chief.

"Quite ready, my lord," answered Lukshmun, taking one of the lighted wicks from the large lamp between his finger and thumb, "For your life, speak, good fellow," he said earnestly and under his breath to the Lalla, "and save yourself this torture. One word more from him, and I dare not disobey; few bear it—speak!"

"O, my lord! my lord!" shrieked the Lalla, now comprehending what was intended, and throwing himself prostrate on the ground, "do not burn me alive. I will speak the truth. Why should I tell lies?"

"Very well," returned the chief, on whose lips the ominous foam speckles were now visible. "Very well, get up; it is thine own business. Thou hast not heard of our Dekhan customs, perhaps, else I had not wasted words on thee. Speak, who sent thee? Alumgeer? He cannot help thee now."

"He would have no mercy on me if he knew—if he had me in his power," murmured the Lalla. "Loose me, my lord, I am faint, and cannot speak; yet I will speak the truth. And should all these hear? My lord knows best. Loose me, and have these rags taken from my fingers."

"When thou hast told the truth, Lalla; not till then," said Pahar Singh, slowly. "Dost thou hear? Away, all of ye!" he cried to the attendants, who had crowded round the Lalla. "Keep the torch alight. Now, Lalla," he continued, as the man stood alone below the dais, "speak. Once more, and this is my last warning; if I hear any more lies I will end that coward life of thine."

"Beware!" added Gopal Singh, "I would not be as thou art with that lying tongue of thine—ugh! no, not for lakhs. Remember that he, my uncle, never relents."

"I would rather speak to ye alone," said the Lalla.

"We three are as one. Yet stay," added the chief. "Go thou, Amrut Rao, let him have his own chance for life—but remain without."

"Do any of ye know the seal of the Wuzeer of Beejapoor," said the Lalla, when they were alone, "or do ye know the writing of Sivaji, the Mahratta Rajah?" He spoke with great difficulty, for his mouth was parched and clammy, and his lips white.

"Nay, but Sivaji cannot write, Lalla. This is some fool's story. Beware, too, how thou takest the name of my lord the Wuzeer," said the chief sternly.

"My lord, my lord, with death before me and one chance for life, I cannot lie," returned the Lalla, sadly shaking his head. "My hands are tied; but if one of you will open that bag, there will be truth enough found in it to save me. There, Jemadar," he continued, as Gopal Singh opened the bag, "in the side pocket are two Persian letters, fastened up; look at them first; look at the seals. If I am wrong I am wrong—I am helpless, do as ye like with me; I am helpless."

"It is the Wuzeer's seal, his private seal, uncle," said Gopal Singh excitedly. "Of this there is no doubt; look at it yourself."

"Ai Ram! Ai Seeta Ram! what have we here? It is the seal truly," said Pahar Singh, looking at the impressions on both letters, and rocking himself to and fro.

"Do any of ye read Persian?" asked the Lalla; "if so, read for yourselves. I need not speak; they will speak for me."

"I will try, uncle," said Gopal Singh; "give me the letters. By Krishna, father!" he continued, breaking the silence, and after his eye had glanced over a few lines, "I would rather go into the thickest fight than read treachery like this. Narayun, keep us!"

"Ay, may the gods be merciful, Gopala! But what is it?—what is it?" said the chief eagerly.

"He would sell our kingdom of Beejapoor to the Padshah of Delhi, uncle——"

"People said so—people said so," said Pahar Singh, interrupting; "but I did not believe it. What more, my son?"

"Nay, the style is too courtly for me to make much of it, but both the letters are to the same effect. Where didst thou get these letters, Lalla?"

"Noble gentlemen, if ye are true to your King's salt," exclaimed the Lalla, seeing that he had made an impression on his hearers, "then I deserve naught but good at your hands. I am in the royal service; I saw the papers; I read what danger threatened Ali Adil Shah; I took them; I escaped from the camp with them, to carry them to him, and I am here. O, noble sirs, put me not to loss and shame!"

On the next few words hung the Lalla's life. It were easy to kill him and secure the papers. The Wuzeer had sent several urgent messages to Pahar Singh lately. He had a matter of moment, attended with great profit, to communicate. Was it about these letters? The Wuzeer would give lakhs for them. The very threat of disclosure to the King would extort any terms. Again, if he denied them—and what more easy than to counterfeit his seal, or use it upon forged papers? If he took this course, they would be in a false position: false to the King and to the Wuzeer,—and the King's threats had of late been very menacing. So, as they deliberated, the Lalla's life hung in the balance, now ascending, now descending, in the eager consultation which the three men carried on in Canarese. The Lalla looked from one to another in piteous supplication, not daring to speak, his mouth parched, and trembling in every limb; for he felt this quick discussion, and the increasingly savage glances of the chief towards him, to be for life or for death.

"And this from Sivaji?" asked Gopal Singh, at length. "What of it, Lalla?"

"It was with the others, and there are some more of older date in the bag," he replied, "and of the Wuzeer's also. Sivaji's letters had to be translated to the Emperor: I had to copy the translations, and thus I came to know their contents. Noble sirs, I am telling no lies; look at the seal. They said in the Dufter it was Sivaji Bhóslay's. I do not know it myself."

"Keep the others close, and show this to Amrut Rao," said the chief. "Here," he continued, as the Karkoon, being called, advanced, "look at this; what dost thou make of it?"

The Karkoon looked at the seal and started. "May I open it?" he said.

"Yes, read it to us," said the chief.

He read it over slowly twice.

"Well, what is it?" asked his master.

"What Moro Trimmul wrote from Tooljapoor—what they asked you, my lord, to join in; and here is your name with five thousand men in figures after it, and the Wuzeer's with a lakh."

"Is it genuine, think you? that is what we want to know," said Gopal Singh.

"Certainly," replied the Karkoon; "there is the private mark on the seal, and the signature 'Hé Venunti'—'this supplication'—is all the Maharaj can write. No one could forge that, it is too crooked. How did that man get it?"

"He stole it, Amrut Rao," said the chief; "and we are discussing whether he ought to live or to die. What dost thou think?"

"As a traitor to the salt he has eaten, he ought to die, master," said the Karkoon, looking at the Lalla, who felt that his fate was in the Brahmun's hands,—"but——"

"That is just what I said! he is not fit to live," interrupted the chief. "Let him die. Ho!"

"But"—continued the Karkoon in Canarese, persistently interrupting the chief, and waving back Lukshmun, Rama, and others, who were advancing—"if I may speak. He says he wants to take them to Beejapoor. Let him have his own way. A bargain may be made with Ali Adil Shah through his secretary the Meerza—not by him" (and he pointed to the Lalla), "but by us. The letters will not alter the matter one jot, and my lord can act as he pleases afterwards. We can send people with the Lalla."

"Excellently spoken, Amrut Rao; ye have all better brains than I have. Then the papers are valuable?" said Pahar Singh.

"Yes, my lord, if properly vouched for; and the man who stole them can give a better account of them than we can. The King might give any money—a lakh of rupees—for them. He already more than suspects the Wuzeer and Sivaji Bhóslay of being in league with the Emperor, and would rejoice to get such proofs of their treachery."

"Hark ye, Lalla," cried the chief, changing the language to Oordoo, which he spoke well, "what didst thou expect to get for these papers? What is the price of them?"

"My lord," he replied, simpering and putting up his joined hands, "they may be worth lakhs—so the Gosais at Kullianee told me—anything I liked to ask. They will negotiate the matter with the secretary and the King for me; and if my lord would only condescend to assist, I—I—would give—yes, he might be sure of a share."

"I of a share!—of a bribe! Art *thou* feeding me with a bribe? O base dog, and son of a dog! Pig! I a share? O Lalla, thou art surely mad, and fated to eat dirt. Enough of this! Ho, without! —Lukshmun!—hunchbacks!—away with him; give him the handkerchief in the outer court. Quick!" roared Pahar Singh, relapsing into fury.

"Uncle! father! not now," cried Gopal Singh, entreatingly, and touching his feet; then rising and stepping forward with joined hands, "calm thyself. Not to-day, when I am safe; not to-day, when I promised him life! Give his life to me for this day; after that, as thou wilt."

"It is valuable, my lord," added Amrut Rao. "These papers cannot tell their own story. Where could we say we got them? He must go with them to authenticate them. Gopal Singh and I can go to the city with him, and, after all, he deserves well of Ali Adil Shah, though he has been a traitor to his own King. Give him to us, my lord; we may get good out of him."

"No," said the chief, after a moment's pause, "no, Rao Sahib, I will go myself. I will see the end of this matter. Thou shalt come with me, Maun Singh; and we can work through thy brother, Amrut Rao. A lakh, saidst thou, O Lalla? Well, I will give thee a share if thou art true. And now I give thy life to thee—buksheesh! —a free gift—a new life, O Lalla. See that thou make good use of it, for what I give I can recall. Go: they will see to thy food and comfort, and thou wilt eat in a Rajpoot's house of the race of the Sun."

The Lalla would have said something about his gold and his horse; the words were in his mouth, and it was well, perhaps, he could not speak. The revulsion was too great for him, from life to apparently imminent death, and again from death to life. Weary with travel and faint with hunger, he had sunk down insensible, and they carried him away into the court.

"The King has been seeking my life, friends, for some time past," said the chief musingly. "Perhaps it would be well to use these papers—that is—— Yes," he continued, "I have eaten his salt—I and my father—and we eat it now. My heart revolts at this treachery, and we can be faithful with many another. Let us rouse the boy. There should be good stuff in Mahmood Adil Shah's son, and I will try it. As for the Wuzeer, I know what he would have me do, but I will not say it, else should we have been left quiet so long, and the army so near us? Stay ye here, Gopal and Amrut Rao. If he send for me, go to him at Nuldroog; 'tis but a ride. Go and take his money, then come to me at the city. I shall be in the old place; and bring the hunchbacks with you, there may be work for them."

The Lalla recovered as they carried him gently into the open air, and bathed his face with water.

"Ah!" said Lukshmun, who was the most active of his attendants, and was unbinding the shawl, "see what care I take of thee, O Lalla; better your fingers are sound than roasted; better your neck straight than twisted; better have to eat good food here—it is so good—than have thy mouth filled with mud and water in the river yonder——"

"My gold, my gold!" gasped the Lalla, interrupting him, "who has got it? at least get that for me."

"He has got it," replied the hunchback, pointing with his thumb backwards. "Better he, than I or my brother; we should only spend it—he won't. Thy star is bright to-night, Lallajee. When thou art set free do not forget us, that's all. Come."

They conducted him to a small chamber within, where two decently-clad women awaited them—slaves or servants—and informed the Lalla that a bath had been prepared for him, and food would be served to him in the eating-room.

We are assured, therefore, that the Lalla was left in good hands. There was perhaps a shade too much garlic in the cookery, he thought; but he was not particular, and appetite returned with absence of fear. When he had finished, he was summoned to the chief, and it was not without apprehension that he went; but he was now received kindly, though with a rough sort of civility, and motioned to sit near Gopal Singh. So assured, the Lalla's habitual confidence soon returned, and he took his part, with much ability, in the discussion that followed, in which his information in regard to the Emperor's designs was most valuable.

How the consultation ended will hereafter appear in another locality, to which we must now transport our readers.

CHAPTER XVII.

THE Azân, or evening call to prayers, had just ceased throughout Beejapoor. From mosque to mosque, and minaret to minaret, the sonorous and musical voices of the Muezzins had proclaimed the evening invitation to worship. It was still light, though the vivid hues of sunset were fading fast, and the warm red and orange tints, which had rested upon the minarets, domes, and gilded pinnacles of the palaces, mosques, and mausoleums of the superb city, were giving place to a sober grey. Here and there a star already twinkled in the heavens, and a few rosy clouds, on which the sun's rays rested lingeringly, floated away eastwards before a gentle breeze, that rustled among the tall palm trees. For a time the busy hum of the populous city seemed to be hushed, and the stillness and seclusion of the spot we have to describe, prompted those feelings of devotion which the time required.

It was one of those small yet elegant mosques, which are found scattered everywhere about the ruins that now exist, surrounded by enclosures that were once gardens, in which broken fountains and dry watercourses now only suggest visions of their former elegance and comfort, and where low brushwood and tangled grass have displaced the fragrant flowers and useful fruit trees of former days. Here and there a jessamine, now wild, trails over ruined walls and once trim garden terraces, or a long-lived hardy lime tree struggles for existence in the unwatered soil.

At the period of our tale, however, the building was in its full freshness and beauty. A single arch, of low Saracenic form, led into a square room vaulted by delicate groins, leading from the corners to the base of a cupola above. The floor was formed of chequers of black and white marble, highly polished; and the sides of the room, deeply indented by arched niches, were finished with stucco, which rivalled the marble in polish and purity of colour. Around the largest niche, at the end opposite to the entrance, and the arch in which the pulpit stood, were borders of delicate arabesque foliage, into which texts from the Koran, in coloured enamel letters, were skilfully and elegantly interwoven; while above the pulpit itself, in gold letters on a black ground, was the Arabic text, "La Alla, il Alla, Mahomed russool Alla;" "There is no God but one God, and Mahomed is the prophet of God." Two plain cotton carpets, striped red and white, had been placed before the pulpit, to be used by those who might come to the evening prayer.

Outside, the front of the mosque was composed of the dark-coloured basalt used in all the buildings of the city, beautifully finished as to the fitting of the stones, on which bold cornices and rosettes had been executed round the entrance arch, and about the projecting portion which supported the small minarets. Immediately above the archway, broad stone eaves crossed the face of the building, resting upon deep and richly carved brackets of black basalt, surmounted by a bold cornice, over which were fleurs-de-lis, forming the upper ornament. Under the projecting eaves, and on the crest of the entrance arch, were bright flowers in coloured enamel, bordered by frames of delicate white stucco work, which relieved the rich but monotonous tint of the stone, without disturbing the chaste effect of the whole. In the centre of the terrace, before the mosque, was a small fountain, for the purpose of ablution, which threw up a tiny thread of water to some height in the air, descending in a shower of light spray, and producing a faint, plashing sound, very grateful to the ear.

Above the mosque, and mingling with its slender minarets and thin gilded spires, a few cocoa-nut trees waved their graceful pendant leaves; and with them the heavy foliage of the fragrant moulserry, and the broad leaf of the plantain, with its tender yet vivid green, formed an harmonious contrast. Nearer the terrace was a group of orange trees, some weighed down by clusters of golden fruit, others covered with blossom, which, with the tuberoses around the fountain, and the evening jessamine now opening, gave forth to the cool evening air a fragrance almost overpowering. By day, the sun hardly ever reached the mosque, and it always appeared invitingly cool and quiet; but at this evening hour, shadow was rapidly deepening into gloom, adding a solemn effect which enhanced the beauty of this secluded spot.

Two persons stood by the fountain. They had just performed their ablutions, as the last quivering chant of the Muezzin, "La illa, il Ulla," issuing from the tall minaret of one of the neighbouring mosques, floated to them on the soft breeze: yet they appeared to hesitate ere they entered the mosque for the evening prayer. One of them was an elderly woman, clad as befitted the position of the favourite nurse and confidential female servant of a wealthy house, in a blue cotton petticoat of thick but fine texture, over which, and around her body and head, was a white muslin scarf. Her features were homely, yet good-natured, and she evidently regarded her companion,—who merits a fuller description,—with pride mingled with deep affection.

And, in truth, there were few fairer maidens in Beejapoor, even among the wealthy and high-born nobles, than Zyna, the only daughter of Afzool Khan. Her features might be called irregular, according to any European standard, but they were soft and inexpressibly charming; and in her large lustrous eyes, of the deepest brown, there lurked a world of deep feeling which the excitement of life would call into action. About her rounded chin and small mouth, whose full and bow-shaped lips had somewhat of a voluptuous expression, there played a thousand charms, which, though they might not disclose themselves or be observed while her features were at rest, yet, as her first timid reserve gave place to the excitement of conversation or passing incident, exercised a strange but irresistible fascination over those about her.

She was very fair for her country. Her mother's bright Georgian complexion was but little deepened in her daughter's richer and browner cast of colour; the skin appeared to possess that transparent softness which gave a bewitching charm to the delicate yet decided features; and her cheeks and neck flushed, under any excitement, with a warmth which told of her southern and more excitable temperament. Whenever she spoke, the upper lip was raised higher than usual, disclosing a rosy mouth, with teeth which glistened like pearls, even and small; and from the absence of any ornament in the nostril, it was evident that, as yet, no marriage rite had been performed. Her age might be fourteen, or even less; but her figure, from its rounded proportions and grace, would have induced a presumption that she was older.

Yet it would have been only a passing thought. One look at that innocent, almost childish face—where, though full of bright intelligence, the world had as yet fixed no stamp of care to check the natural joyousness of her spirit—would have dispelled it instantly; and if the habitual brightness was sometimes dimmed, it was but as the breath upon a mirror—the passing shadow of some gentle disappointment, which enhanced the beauty as it passed away.

There was no mark of rank or wealth about her, except in the solid gold anklets of heavy chainwork she wore, which fitted closely over her high bare instep: a ring of gold hanging loosely about her neck, and a rosary of large pearls usually worn there, but which were now passing rapidly, and apparently mechanically, through her fingers, as if the thoughts that urged them were somewhat agitated. There was, too, a slight knitting of the brow while she idly, and perhaps somewhat impatiently, dabbled with one naked foot in the water which was welling over the rim of the fountain, sending circles of small wavelets over its otherwise unruffled surface, as she looked eagerly to the entrance-door of the garden as if in expectation of some one. As she stood thus upon a step, her foot resting upon the raised rim of the fountain—the vivid scarlet of her satin petticoat, and the white of the fine muslin scarf which, wound about her person, and passed over her head—were reflected in its trembling waters; and, with the mosque and dark trees behind her, and the figure of the old nurse sitting on the step at her feet, a picture was formed such as no man could have looked on without emotion, and admiration of a being so eminently lovely.

"You are my witness, Goolab," she said at length, looking down on the nurse, "that he said he would come to evening prayer, and that I have waited thus long. The time is passing fast, and you know this is the second night he has disappointed me. O, that he may not be careless to God's service! He used not to be so. But I am not angry with him, nurse," she continued, looking down to the attendant; and as she spoke, every trace of displeasure, if it had ever existed, disappeared at once before her habitual good humour and sweet smile; "he never disappointed me, that he had not some very good reason for staying away—and yet——"

"Nay, my soul," returned the woman, "the Azân is but just said, and there is yet ample time for prayer; the carpets have not been half spread in the Jumma Mosque yet. Why should you be impatient? But listen, was I not right? My young lord comes, so think him faithless no longer."

As she spoke the door of the garden court opened, and with a cry of joy Zyna sprang to meet her brother, as with rapid steps he traversed the garden, and ascended the low terrace before the mosque.

Still of tender age, Fazil Khan was already a remarkable figure. The down of youth had not yet hardened upon his lip and chin; but his tall athletic frame, and erect and confident carriage, proved him to have been engaged in the actions, if not the strife, of the world. His animated features strongly resembled his sister's, but with a sterner and bolder cast of expression, while his colour was much darker. A large grey eye, with remarkably long lashes, which he had from his mother, increased their grave, thoughtful, yet tender, and perhaps almost mournful, expression; the same sweet smile as Zyna's played about his mouth as he returned her joyous welcome, while his glistening eye and excited manner proved that something unusual had occurred, not only to delay him, but to cause an emotion he could not well repress.

"Ah, thou art a sad truant, Fazil," said Zyna, as, after their first greeting, he laid aside his sword and shield, loosened his waist-band, and prepared to perform his ablutions; "armed, too, more heavily than usual, while thy face tells me thou hast met with some recent adventure. Thou hast not been in danger . . . . Fazil, my brother!"

"Danger!" echoed the youth; "if to walk the streets of Beejapoor amidst contending factions, where one can hardly tell a friend from an enemy, be danger, why then, dear sister, I have had my share even now. But, trust me, there is no real danger to me. Come then to prayer, for the Azân is said, and the light already fails us."

So saying, they ascended the mosque steps together. Their carpets were already spread, and they at once engaged in the service of the evening,. well known to the youth, but in the performance of which, his sister was as yet only his gentle and docile pupil.

It would seem that their appearance, as they descended the steps of the mosque together after the prayer was finished, and came out again upon the terrace by the fountain, had more than ordinarily attracted the nurse's attention, for she advanced, and passing her hands rapidly over them from head to foot, pressed her knuckles against her temples; and as they cracked loudly, ejaculated a fervent wish for a thousand years' life and prosperity to each. Such acts are common to the privileged native servants of India, and old Goolab had been their faithful attendant since they were born, and had carefully watched their growth. Both loved her warmly, and there was nothing either would have grudged, to soothe the declining years of their old favourite.

"Enough, enough, Goolab," cried Fazil, as, after several repetitions of the ceremony we have just mentioned, she stroked his chin with her fingers, and kissed their tips; "what evil do you think has come to me that you take it on yourself?"

"Alas, I know not!" said the nurse, sighing; and as she spoke her eyes filled with tears; "but my lord said there had been danger, and I would not have it so. And what evil glances may not have been cast on my beautiful child all through the streets to-day?"

The youth made a slight gesture of impatience, but it was lost on the fond old woman. Checking the feeling which had prompted it, he cried cheerfully, "No, no, Goolab, believe me, I meant no more than ordinary danger; are we not always in it? And who can tell the hour of his death?" he added after a pause, and looking reverently upwards; "or whether it is to come by a bullet or a sword-cut, long wasting fever or sudden sickness; nay, here as we stand! When the message comes we cannot stay."

"Hush, say not so, brother," said Zyna, gently laying her hand upon his mouth; "talk not so of death."

"Nay, my rose, he says but the truth," added Goolab; "and who knew it better, than the pure saint your mother, who sleeps yonder? Well, it was God's will, and who shall gainsay it? Meah is right, my pet, but death should not be sent to the like of you; only to the old servant who is ripe for the harvest——"

"We linger," said Fazil to his sister, interrupting her; "and the darkness is fast spreading. I have much to do ere midnight, and I must go to prepare for it. I will meet thee at the evening meal before I start—— Yet once more to take leave of thee, O mother!" he said to himself; "there may be danger to-night, and if it should be—— Come, Zyna," he resumed, "a few flowers for the tomb, and I must go. Get a light, Goolab—the lamp may as well be lighted now."

"I had placed them before you came, Fazil; but come; again may she look down on her children together," said his sister.

So saying, she gathered a few jessamine and moulserry flowers and, with her brother following, passed to the end of the garden court, where, among some others, stood a high tomb of polished black stone, with a pillar at the back in which was a niche for lamps that were lighted every evening.

Reverently and tenderly were the fresh flowers laid at the head and feet of the tomb by both. One could see no morbid motive in the act, and there were no tears or vain regret. Their creed, imbued as it is with fatalism, had taught them submission, and the offering up of flowers every evening after the Azân, as the lamps were lighted, had become a simple duty, never committed to others. If those two loving and simple hearts believed that their mother's spirit was thus rejoiced, it will account to us for that constant remembrance of the dead which is so affecting, and generally so sincere, among the Mahomedan families of India.

"Come," said Fazil, "we must not delay; though indeed, O sweet mother! I could stay long with thee to-night," he added, touching the foot of the grave gently, and raising his hand to his head. "I kiss thy feet, O mother! may thy blessing rest upon me. Be not far from us, O beloved! Come, Goolab, give me the lamp, and I will place it myself to-night."

"What ails the boy?" said the nurse to herself, as Fazil advanced with the lamp, lighted the others, and placed it in the niche with the customary prayer. "What ails him to-night? Truly there is danger, and he has done all those things himself that he may meet her—— If it be the will of Alla, who can gainsay it? but not so, O Protector!" she muttered; "not so. I vow Fatehas at the mosque next Friday if he is spared," she said inwardly, weeping.

Fazil's errand was done, and as he turned he saw the old nurse wiping her eyes. "Ah, weeping, Goolab?" he said. "No, no, that is of no use now."

"No, Meah, truly of no use," she replied; "but memory is often too much for me when I think upon her. Yet I will not weep—of what use would it be?"

"None, old nurse, none; come, get me my dinner, for I have much to do ere midnight."

"Will our father join us?" asked Zyna.

"I think not; I left him engaged with affairs of importance with the King's secretary in the Durbar, and he did not speak of return. I will wait a little for him, but should I not see him, thou must tell him, Zyna, that I am gone on the King's business. But hurry the dinner; I go only to give a few orders, and I will be with thee presently."

So saying he left them, and quitted the garden by another door which led to the outer court, where the guard-houses allotted to the retainers of his father's house were situated. Goolab followed to bar the door after him, which was kept closed on the inside, and, returning to Zyna, said, "Did he tell thee what he was going to do, my life?"

"No," said Zyna sadly; "he would not tell me, nurse, and I dared not ask him. He said he would explain all by-and-by, and he will. I know he will," she added, clapping her hands; "he always trusts me."

"I only hope he is in none of these plots that they say are going on," returned the nurse.

"What plots, Goolab?" asked Zyna with apprehension.

"O, I know not," replied the old woman, with a puzzled air, and passing her hand across her eyes; "only people in the bazar say so; and the Bangle woman, after she had put on your new set the other day, said something about the Mahrattas and Sivaji Bhóslay."

"O, the Kafirs!" cried Zyna, laughing; "I have no fear for them, if that is all. I was afraid of worse. But come, or we shall keep him waiting."

CHAPTER XVIII.

ENTERING another small court, in which there was a stone porch formed of pillars connected by arches, supporting a dome in the shape of half an octagon, projecting from a side-wall, which served as a private place of audience—Fazil passed through a farther door into one of the large exterior courts of the mansion, which contained an open hall composed of a triple row of pointed arches covering a large space. Generally, it was filled with the better classes of horse-soldiers; Silladars, or cavaliers who rode their own horses and sat there when not on duty; also by the officers and men of the young Khan's own guard: and occasionally was used by his father when were held great ceremonies, festivals, or rejoicings in the house.

On the three other sides of the court were arches or cloisters, slightly raised from the ground, in which lounged or slept soldiers of all classes, on duty or otherwise, generally collected into groups, playing at chess, or pacheese, or cards, singing, or telling stories. Just then, however, most were idle; for the lamps, which stood in niches in the centre of each arch, had not been lighted. The large hall was nearly empty; but in one corner a group of Karkoons, or clerks, sat with a large brass lamp in the midst of them, occupied with accounts, and making fair copies of letters to be despatched by that night's post.

All the men assembled here were strictly the retainers of the house;

for the guard of troops belonging to the King had another post in a different court, and were comparatively few in number. Afzool Khan's household force, or Päegah, as it was called, was supported out of royal estates, granted or assigned for the purpose. It belonged strictly to the royal service, but the men looked to their own lord for employment and maintenance, followed him to the field, and were for the most part hereditary retainers, with no claim upon, or expectation from, royal favour. Such was the condition and constitution of the greater portion of native armies at the period of our tale, and such it continues to be in native states where troops are maintained.

Fazil Khan was the idol of his men, both Moslems and Hindus. His martial exercises had begun early, and he had proved an apt scholar. Any of the men who particularly excelled in the use of a particular weapon had, in turn, the young noble for his pupil; and in all field accomplishments necessary to the soldier and gentleman of those days, the young Khan was well skilled. No doubt these, and his daily systematic exercises, had developed a frame always strongly knit; and his broad deep chest, round muscular arms, and thin flanks, amply testified strength and activity.

On horseback with the Mahratta spear or matchlock, it was no hyperbole to say that, at full gallop, he could pick up a tent-peg driven into the ground with the former, or shatter one at a fair distance with a bullet from the other. Such martial accomplishments never fail to gain the respect and attachment of an inferior soldiery; and when to these were added a disposition open and cheerful, somewhat hasty perhaps at times, but in reality generous and affectionate,—a hearty frank manner, which few could resist, and a countenance, not strictly handsome, but which expressed all this and even more,—it will not be thought strange, that the young Khan should have become a universal favourite with his retainers, and the especial darling and idol of a few.

Chief, perhaps, among the latter, was Bulwunt Rao Bhóslay, who held rank in the Päegah as Duffadar, or leader of a small "duffa," or subdivision of men. He was a Mahratta of good, nay, originally noble family—a Silladar, or cavalier who maintained not only his own horse but five others, with which, mounted by dependants of his own, he had originally visited the capital and joined the service of Afzool Khan.

Him, had the young Khan selected as his especial instructor in the use of the sword; for at the annual festivals and games before the King's palace, Bulwunt Rao's feats of slicing betel-nut on the ground, cutting a lime in two on the palm of a man's hand, or a ripe guava on his head, were unrivalled; and their yearly repetition was looked for by the people with great interest, and always rewarded by hearty acclamations.

Bulwunt Rao was worthy of his young lord's confidence. Daring and resolute, he had already led Fazil Khan into the midst of some sharp cavalry affairs with the Moghuls, and brought him forth safe, while he himself had been wounded several times in protecting him from sword-cuts. Wily, yet full of energy, if there were any necessity for action, open and frank in his manner, he had early won his young lord's affectionate regard, which he very heartily returned, while he rejoiced, with all a soldier's pride, to see him growing up as manly and true of heart as his boyhood had promised.

Fazil's arrival among those assembled—so suddenly, and at an hour when he usually withdrew to the zenana and his studies—caused no little excitement among the men, and they eagerly crowded round him for the news which he might have to tell them.

"What tidings hast thou for us, Meah Sahib?" cried a fine bearded fellow of his own tribe of Pathans, also a favourite. "May thy prestige increase! but there should be something by thy look,—a march against those zenana dogs of Moghuls, or a fray over the border against Golconda."

"A hunt of Moghuls!" echoed several. "What better sport, Meah? There are some pickings of Delhi gold to be got in their waist-bands and pockets."

"And what has my lord for his servants to perform?" asked Bulwunt Rao, now advancing with his usual easy yet deferential manner. "Speak but the word, and we are in our saddles directly. Shall I order the Nagara to be beaten, and cry to horse!"

"Not so, Bulwunt," said the young man, taking him aside; "what I have to say is for your ear alone. Come into the private court and listen."

"For me alone, Meah?" returned Bulwunt Rao, laughing. "What brawl have you fallen into? whom have you slain to-day, sir?"

"Let us all follow if ye are going out," cried several others; "don't leave us behind."

"We have had nothing to do for a month," added one.

"And our swords have lost their edges, Meah," shouted several.

"Peace, all of ye," exclaimed the young Khan; "let no one follow us. This is no fighting matter. Am I wont to plunge into street brawls, Bulwunt Rao?"

"We were none of us with you, my lord, to-day," cried several, "and it is not safe for you to be alone in the streets in these times."

"I had others of the King's, and was quite safe," returned Fazil; "but come, Bulwunt, if you are fit to listen to me; I only fear that ganja pipe of yours is at fault, and your brain is hardly clear. If not, I had as well hold my tongue; yet I had rather trust you, old friend," he continued seriously, "than any other."

Fazil's altered tone and manner had their effect upon his companion. "Wait for a moment, Meah," he said, "I will join you instantly;" and so saying, he ran quickly back to the spot where he had left his carpet, seized a brass vessel of cool water, poured some into his hand and dashed it upon his face, then swallowed several rapid and deep gulps, and returned. "Now, I am fit to listen to the words of the holy Krishna himself if he were on earth; therefore speak on, Meah Sahib, and behold your servant ready to think for you, or to fight for you, as you please!"

"Ay, there is some soberness about you now, Bulwunt," said the young man; "less redness about the eyes, and they are looking straight out of your head, instead of rolling about in it. Now, can I trust you not to prate of this matter before the people yonder, or over the ganja pipe——"

"Nay, Meah, be merciful, and pardon me for once," said Bulwunt, closing his hands and putting them up to his forehead; "the ganja has grown on me, but not to the discredit of my faithfulness, Meah; and when I smoke I never talk. Now, say on, I will be silent as death."

Fazil proceeded some paces through the court without replying to his retainer, and tried the garden door, but it was fastened inside. "We must be content here," he said. "Go, shut the door, we shall at least be safe from interruption."

"In the name of all the gods, Meah," said Bulwunt Rao, as he returned and sat down on the step of the porch beside Fazil, "what hast thou to say to me? Why all this need of caution? Has the Wuzeer revolted, or what?"

"Silence," returned Fazil, "hear me. In one word, you are a Mahratta—is Tannajee Maloosray known to you?"

The question seemed for an instant to stun the faculties of the hearer. He passed his hand dreamily across his forehead and eyes, and, pausing, seemed to gasp. Fazil thought it might be a sudden dizziness—the consequence of the strong narcotic he had been smoking—and was about to ask him, when Bulwunt Rao spoke.

"Tannajee Maloosray! Meah? Do I know Maloosray? Ay, truly, Khan; as the wild dog and the wolf, as the wild boar and the tiger know each other, so do I know Tannajee Maloosray. The destroyer of my house, the usurper of my possessions, the plunderer of my ancestral wealth. Yes, there is a feud between us which can be washed out only by blood. Listen, Meah," continued Bulwunt Rao, and he got up and walked rapidly to and fro: "hast thou time to hear a short story about Tannajee?"

"Yes, speak on. I am listening."

"I was a youth," continued Bulwunt, "younger than you are by several years, when Maloosray aimed his blow at my family. My father was dead; had he lived, Tannajee dared not have done it. My uncle, Govind Rao, was a timid man, looking only to the farms and to money-making while he lived. At last he died also. But he left another brother, Ramdeo, whom we loved much, and he took care of us all. My younger brother, Seeta Ram—why speak of him, Meah? he would have been as beautiful as thou art—and some of the women and myself, all lived together in the old house. They came at midnight, Tannajee and a band of his Mawullees. I do not remember much, Meah; but look here;" and he took off his turban and showed a deep scar on his shaved head. "That is what I fell from, under a blow of his sword. I don't think," he continued dreamily, "that I have been quite right in my brain since, but it does not matter.

"Next morning there were seven stark corpses in the house, and great pools of blood. My uncle, my grandmother, two servants—how can I say it?—yes, my mother and my little brother, and my mother's sister, who was a widow. One blow of a sword had killed my brother and my mother. He was in her arms, and had clung to her. Enough; who could have done this but Maloosray? There is not a sword in all Maharastra which could have struck such a blow as that was—but Maloosray's.

"When I recovered consciousness in the morning, the women that remained, and some servants, were wailing over the dead, but they were barely alive from terror. Neighbours however came in, and some of our tenants and servants, and the place was cleaned up. In the evening there were seven piles made near the river for the seven corpses, and they were burned. My wound had been sewn up by the barber, and I was carried to perform the last ceremonies, and I then swore upon their ashes to revenge them, and I will yet do it. Now, by thy father's salt, tell me what thou knowest of that villain Maloosray, and how his name comes into thy mouth?"

"And was nothing done for justice, Bulwunt? Was justice dead in that country?" asked Fazil, deeply interested.

"Justice!" echoed Bulwunt Rao, "justice! Ah, Meah, what can the poor do for justice? All the wealth of the house had been plundered. Maloosray had brought a hundred of his brethren in that Duróra, and he had promised them the plunder. His object was my life, but the gods spared it, and I came here to serve the King, till—till Tannajee is dead, or till I kill him, Meah! That is the only justice I want: that, and the land he took from me. I thought to tell thee all some day, and now I have said it; but, by thy soul, tell me how Maloosray's name is known to thee, and why?"

"Should you know him again, Bulwunt, if you saw him?" asked Fazil.

"Know him, Meah—among a thousand—among a thousand. It is years since we met; but, before that quarrel with my father about the land, he came to us often, for he was my mother's relative. He hunted large game on our hills, when I went with him, and I was a great favourite of his. Most of the sword-play I know, he taught me. Know him? Yes. That night I, a stripling, crossed swords with him. I had wounded one of his men, and he heard the cry. He had been seeking for me. What could I do, Meah, a weak boy, among a crowd of screaming women? Yet I crossed swords with him; and there are few alive who would dare to do so. Forget him? No, I should know him among a thousand. His eyes, Meah, his eyes! Hast thou seen them?"

"Nay, I have not seen them yet, Bulwunt; but I think I know where he is to be found," returned Fazil.

"Here, Meah? in Beejapoor? Tannajee Maloosray in the city?"

"Yes, here. You are always rambling about the city at night, and know all the mudud khanas; canst thou guide me to one Rama's shop—Rama of Ashtee? It is in the great kullal's bazar, and near a Hindu temple."

"I know it, Meah; I know it well. Rama sells the best ganja in Beejapoor. Yes, I can take you there, but not in those clothes."

"Not now. Let the night wear on a little; they will not be there till just before midnight," replied Fazil; "and we have to watch the temple, too. Is there one near Rama's, with trees about it? Some people meet there first, and then go to Rama's."

"Yes, Meah, there is the temple of Dévi, in the plain beyond, among the tamarind trees; a lonely place it is, and Byragees put up there. Yes, I know it."

"Then I am right," continued Fazil, "for I saw it myself to-day. Now, as Maloosray is desperate, should we not take some picked men with us? There is Raheem Khan, and——"

"Men?—to take Maloosray?" cried Bulwunt. "O Meah, you are simple to think it. Maloosray will have twenty, aye fifty, spies out, and old Rama is chief of them. One soldier a coss off, and Tannajee would be warned. But why go, Meah?" he continued, after a pause. "I will take my own men and bring him. "O," cried Bulwunt, speaking through his teeth and to himself, "for one good chance and a fair field with him now!"

"No, Bulwunt, I must go; it is the King's business," returned Fazil; "besides Persian may be spoken, and you do not understand it."

"Persian, my lord? then this is a Moghul affair?"

"I cannot say, friend," returned Fazil; "all I have discovered is, that Maloosray will be in the temple, or in the mudud khana, and a 'Lalla.' There is no good, I am sure, at the bottom of it, and we must find out what it is. We know the Moghul emissaries are busy, and it is important to check their plots."

"And Sivaji Bhóslay's also, Meah, they bode no good; for my

people write to me that he and Tannajee have leagued together, and——; in short, they write foolish things, sir."

"Bhóslay? that is your family name, Bulwunt," said Fazil, musing.

"Yes," he replied, "and we are of the same house; but he is rich and I am poor. And now people tell wonderful things of him; how the Mother—that is, Bhowani, speaks in him sometimes, and he prophesies great events. One thing is certain, Meah, Sivaji Bhóslay is no friend to Beejapoor, nor to any Mussulman; and if Maloosray has come here for him, it is with some object which is worth the risk to discover."

"Then they are friends?" asked Fazil.

"Ay, Meah, as thou and I, and nearer still. Maloosray believes Sivaji to be an incarnation of the gods, and would give his life for him. So, too, many another; and the people have begun to write ballads about him, which are sung in Beejapoor even sometimes, and they set one's blood dancing. No wonder the people of the wild valleys love them; wild places, Meah, which ye know little of as yet."

"Yes, it is worth the risk to find out what is doing. One thread of those dark intrigues in my hand and I am not my father's son if I do not discover more," replied Fazil; "but you said we should be disguised."

The Mahratta thought for a moment. "What sayest thou, Meah, to becoming a Hindu for the time? I could paint the marks on thy forehead. Nay," he continued, as he saw the young man shrink from the idea, "they will only be very temporary 'abominations,' as the old Khan calls them, and water will remove them when we return."

"Good," returned Fazil. "I will suffer 'the abominations' in the cause of the Shah and the faith. And, now, begone. I will come to thee here, after the evening meal, and we can dress unobserved. But swear on my neck, Bulwunt, no more ganja to-night."

"No, no, Meah," returned the man, laughing, and touching his young lord's neck and feet; "I swear I will not touch it. We both need cool heads for this work, and I will not fail you."

"Then go," added Fazil. "I will send Goolab to you when I am ready."

CHAPTER XIX.

Fazil was as good as his word to his fair sister, and having seen Bulwunt depart, gained the door which led to the private apartments, and proceeded to that in which he knew he should find her.

The room was upon the first story, which, by means of deep stone brackets, had been constructed so as to project somewhat over the rooms beneath. It contained, indeed for the most part consisted of, three large oriel windows, overhanging the line of the walls, so that they commanded a view up and down the main street, which led to Toorweh and the royal palaces. These windows were large enough for several persons to sit in and enjoy the air; and the floor of the centre one, which was the largest, was raised a step above that of the room, so as to form a dais, on which a thickly-quilted cotton mattress, covered with clean white muslin, was laid every day, and furnished with large pillows, so that those sitting there could recline luxuriously, if they pleased. Between the stone mullions of the windows, carved screens or shutters of wood had been inserted, which were fixtures, except a portion in the centre which opened on hinges. Without them were heavy wooden shutters, lined with iron, with openings to fire from should it be needed.

The other windows did not project so far, and were in fact single arches, filled deep with carved lattice-work, closed during the day, but open in the evening to admit the fresh air. Beside each was a large Persian carpet and a pillow. The floor of the apartment had also a thin carpet of quilted cotton cloth, covered with white muslin; and the perfect neatness of the whole, the walls being pure white without ornament, gave evidence of very vigilant superintendence by the Khan's present wife, perhaps by Zyna herself. One lamp burned in a corner, and, being agitated by the wind, which blew freely through the apartment, gave a flickering light, which left much of the space in actual gloom.

Zyna had been there some time, and the sweet freshness of the evening air had tempted her to throw open the lattice window to admit it more freely, as she sat in the balcony or oriel window already mentioned. Looking out upon what was passing below her, she did not observe her brother's entrance, and almost started as he spoke.

"I did not hear thee, brother," she said, rising and making way for him. "Come and sit here, it is so fresh after the rain. What kept thee so late? We hear the Durbar was very full to-day, and that there are more rumours of war. O, I pray not, brother?"

"True, sister, there are such rumours," he replied; "but nothing new. The Wuzeer is at Nuldroog with the army. The Emperor's forces lie about Dowlutabad, so there is no change. But I was not in Durbar. I was looking after some other matters. Come and sit here, Zyna, and I will tell thee. See," he continued, as she seated herself by him, "the city looks calm and beautiful, does it not? Yet, who can tell the wild acts now in progress there, and the wild plots which disgrace it?"

In truth it was a fair scene. The house or palace of Afzool Khan stood somewhat apart from other buildings, upon a slight eminence, and the room they were in overlooked a large portion of the city to the south, west, and north. Between the combined twilight and light of a moon about half-full, the outlines of the city generally, and of some of the most remarkable buildings, could be seen distinctly, and formed a picture of great beauty. To the north, the large dome of the mausoleum of Mahmood Adil Shah stood out boldly against the clear grey sky, as well as the high dark masses of the King's palaces in the citadel, and of that of the "Seven Stories" in particular, in the windows of which lights already twinkled here and there, and disappeared.

A little on the left of the palace was the massive cavalier of the "Oopree Boorje," with the King's flagstaff on its summit; below, the dark lines of the fortifications, with lights gleaming from each guard-room upon the bastions. Thence the eye travelled round the city, resting here and there upon massive domes and slender minarets, shining tenderly in the moon's rays, which also fell softly upon the outlines of terraced houses and palaces, and upon the dark masses of foliage of their gardens. Over the most populous parts of the city also nearer to them, the evening smoke hovered like a thin mist, catching reflection of the thousand lights and fires beneath: and a hum of voices arose from thence:—otherwise, all was still around them, and the broad street leading to Toorweh nearly deserted. Night was fast falling, and a bright star here and there already sparkled in the sky.

"Yes, it is a fair scene, sister," he continued, as she drew closer to him. "Yet, even now, men are plotting villany and treachery. There is no peace in it."

"No peace, brother!" she said, echoing his words; "cannot others be as we are—enjoying what Alla sends them without strife? Why should it not be so?"

"Why, Zyna? because of ambition, which, with the hot thirst it begets, dries up men's hearts; because of avarice, driving them to barter kingdoms and honour for gold; because of fraud, and deceit, and lies, and profligacy. Alas, girl, where ends the catalogue? Even now I fear the evil thoughts and treacherous plots of our fair city."

Zyna shuddered, and nestled closer to her brother. "Why is thy speech so sad to-night, Fazil?" she said timidly; "does aught threaten us or our friends?"

"Listen, sister, and judge," he returned. "I cannot help these fancies. Ah, Zyna! if I had one like thee to be with me always—to be more to me even than thou art—perhaps the world, fair as it lies there, would have few charms for me."

"She would be forgotten before a bright sword or a gallant horse, brother," replied Zyna, in a tone of raillery.

"Not so, by the Prophet!—by your head and eyes; no, Zyna," cried her brother earnestly. "Let such an one come, and thou wilt see what she would be to me."

"Would it were so, brother! and yet I know of no one—not one as yet—whom thou couldst love like me. None of the maidens of this city are worthy of thee; no, not one, Fazil."

"Ah! nothing less than one of the blessed houris of Paradise would content thee for me," returned the young man, laughing; "but one like thyself would quite content me, sister. Perhaps even now thou hast been thinking I have some love-secret to tell thee, for I have not accounted for my delay these two evenings, but love there is none, dearest. No—none at all," as she shook her head and laughed incredulously,—"none. A graver matter, truly, if I am right. Listen, Zyna, I have told thee of Kowas Khan before—my friend, the Wuzeer's son——"

"What of him?" she returned, so abruptly that her tone of alarm startled her brother. "Yes," she continued, correcting herself, "surely—often—dear brother, hast thou not told me of his bravery when the Moghuls besieged the city? but do not mention him, else I will go away."

"Nay, go not, Zyna. I will not tease thee," he replied, "yet why should I not speak of him? Is he not a hero—a very Roostum? Is he not beautiful?—a youth for a maiden to love, or a man to make his friend! But enough of this," for he perceived the confusion his last words had occasioned: "to say the truth, I am anxious for the whole family, and there is much cause to fear; the Wuzeer is not keeping his faith with the King. But for that, indeed——"

"Hush, brother!" said Zyna, again blushing, for she knew that she had been sought in marriage by the Wuzeer for his son; "may God forbid evil to him or any of them; and men have as yet spoken well of him. Why should he be suspected?"

"Alas, who can say?" replied her brother sadly. "Who can tell to what crimes pride and ambition may not urge a man? Truly, sister, it will not be marvellous if the Wuzeer, seeing the danger of the Moghuls on the one hand, of Sivaji Bhóslay on the other, and knowing better than we do the divisions among our own nobles, should forget his faith, and try to strike in for himself. 'Twas thus, so writes the historian of honoured memory, Mahomed Kasim Ferishta, that our own kingly house rose into existence, and the Nizam Shahy and Kootub Shahy dynasties also; what wonder, then, that Khan Mahomed—the rich, the honoured, the powerful—should be tempted to follow examples so successful and so prosperous?"

"What! and forget his King, who has raised him from—from——" she could not add slavery; "forget honours, titles, lands, wealth? O brother!"

"Ah, Zyna," returned Fazil, sighing, "believe me, there are few minds so noble, and so humble too, as to despise power in little things; how much less a position so exalted as that of monarch of these noble realms. Men have already forgotten 'Rehan' the slave, in 'Khan Mahomed,' the Wuzeer of Beejapoor. We know what he was, we see what he is, and we can think what he might be. If he is playing for the highest stake, it is a game in which his life is of no account."

"I would I had not known of this, brother, from thy lips," said Zyna sadly. "True, it seems to have a terrible distinctness: and his son?"

"Nay, by your head and eyes, he is pure, Zyna. My own dear friend," he exclaimed, "I would answer for him with my life. As for the rest, 'tis but suspicion as yet. Whatever the matter I know of may lead to, I am resolved to see the last of it. Listen.

"Last evening I was coming from the Durbar, and, dismissing the men who were with me, I rode to some open ground to exercise my horse. It is not far from the King's palace at Toorweh: and to get there I proceeded through the outskirts of the city, which lead to the quarter of the lower orders of the people. I had not ridden far when I met the palankeen of the King's secretary, attended by some horsemen. It seemed strange to meet him there, because, when I left the audience hall, he seemed immersed in business. So I rode up towards it with the intention of saluting him again, when he shut the door as it were carelessly, but, as I thought, with an evident desire not to be seen: this stimulated my curiosity. I had no pretence for following him, only there happened to be an acquaintance, who was in command of his escort, and who called me. I joined him, unobserved by the Meerza, and accompanied him under pretence of friendly chat. By-and-by, as the better part of the town grew more distant, I asked him banteringly what had brought so great a person as the King's Meerza into so mean a quarter, and whether I might see the end of the adventure; and looking about him—to be sure the rest of the escort were out of hearing—he told me that, after leaving the court, the Meerza had first gone to a respectable Hindu house in another quarter and remained there some time; and when he came out he was attended to the door by a Hindu soldier, who bade him depart, and told him not to forget the shop of Rama of Ashtee, in the 'kullal's' quarter, and Tannajee Maloosray. Thence a man was sent as guide to another house, and he showed him to me then running with the bearers before the palankeen. 'So I can only suppose it is some work of the King's,' added my friend, 'with which we cavaliers have nothing to do.' I thought otherwise, for Tannajee's name is famous; and we rode on.

"After some time the guide stopped at the door of a decent house, which I think was a Jungum's Mutt. The Meerza did not get out of his palankeen, and a man came to the doorway and began to speak in Persian, after having looked round suspiciously at all of us. I shall not forget the man, Zyna, for he had piercing grey eyes and a hooked nose. I suppose he thought no one could understand him, for he did not speak low. Still, as his head was partly inside the door of the secretary's palankeen, I could not hear all, and could only approach, indeed, on pretence of my horse being restless. I heard, however, the man's direction to the secretary, a Hindu temple of Bhowani, in the plain on the east of the fort, where papers were to be shown at midnight, and the Wuzeer's name was mentioned. Thither I will go, 'Inshalla!' to-night. I can disguise myself, and my speech is Mahratta or Canarese, as I please, and Bulwunt Rao goes with me."

"Go not, my precious brother," said Zyna, interrupting him; "there must be danger among these plotters. Remember what thou art to us all, Fazil."

"If my love were not what it is for Khan Mahomed's son," he replied, "I would not hazard this matter; but we, thy father and myself, owe the Wuzeer many favours, and I should hold myself false did I hesitate to peril something in their cause. Even thou, Zyna, hast not forgotten how Kowas Khan and our brave Bulwunt Rao fought over me when I had been stricken down in the Friday's fight with the Moghuls, and but for them I had perished. Yes, sister, I must go."

"Go? whither, son?" said Afzool Khan, whose entrance had not been observed by either; "whither wouldst thou go, and for what?"

"Father!" uttered both at the same moment, and, rising, saluted him reverently.

"Be seated, my children," he said; "I too will join you. Your mother hath not been here?"

The allusion made was to their father's second wife, whom he had married after the mother of his children died, and who received from them all the honour and respect, if not the tender love, of their real mother. Her name was Lurlee, to which her title of Khánum being added, she was known among her friends and dependants as Lurlee Khánum; and she will appear presently in her proper person.

"No, father," replied Zyna, "she was going to cook something for you, and had something to do with her tables; and said that there was something going to happen, for that Mars and the moon, or stay—really I don't know, father, how it was—I forget."

"Ah," returned her father, smiling, "bicharee—poor thing!—those stars are a sad trouble to her. But what art thou going to do, son?"

"Tell him all you have told me, brother," said Zyna.

Fazil recapitulated what he had told his sister, and finding his father interested, again stated his intention of following up the secret, whatever it might be.

"Go, my son," said the old Khan, "I cannot gainsay thee in this matter. If we can protect Khan Mahomed or keep evil from his house, or if any of these vile plots can be traced to those concerned in them, a few sharp examples may deter others. But why not take some of the Päègah? those are dangerous quarters by night."

"Impossible, father, they are too wary; and Bulwunt Rao says there will be spies and scouts watching everywhere. So we are better alone, and with your leave, father, I go to prepare myself."

Afzool Khan opened the casement, and looked out. He partly leaned out of the window, and appeared to be gazing abstractedly over the city. The young moon was now low in the sky, and the stars shone out more brilliantly than before; but clouds were gathering fast in the south-west, which, from the lightning flashing about their tops, boded a storm. As yet, however, the gentle light of the moon pervaded all, glinting from the bright gilded pinnacles of domes and minarets, and resting tenderly upon the white terraces, walls, and projecting oriels of houses near him—upon the tapering minarets of his own private mosque, and the heavy but graceful foliage that hung about them.

"It is a type of what is coming," thought the Khan—"here the moonlight only partially dispelling the gloom, which will increase; there heavy night-clouds already threatening. Even so with our fair kingdom: the tempest of sorrow may break over us. We cannot stop it, but we may at least endure the trial, and be true to our salt."

He was long silent, and the beads which he had removed from his wrist were passing rapidly through his fingers, while his lips moved as though in prayer. Zyna dared not speak, yet he looked at her lovingly as his lips still moved, and passing his arm round her, drew her to him. Perhaps with that embrace more tender thoughts came into his heart, some memories that were sad yet grateful.

"There will be no danger, Zyna," he said assuringly, as he felt her trembling, and guessed her thoughts; "Fazil and Bulwunt Rao are both wary. The moon, too, is setting, and it will be dark, perhaps raining. He comes, daughter," continued the Khan, as Fazil's foot was heard on the stairs; "let us look at him."

As he spoke, Fazil entered the room and made the Hindu salutation of reverence to his father. "Should I be known as your son, father?" he asked.

"Nemmo Narrayen Baba," cried Afzool Khan, laughing, and returning the salutation in the same style. "If thou knowest thyself, it is more than I can say of thee."

The disguise was indeed perfect. Fazil was naked to the waist, and a coarse cloth of some length, which might serve as a sheet if unwound, was crossed upon his shoulders and chest in thick folds. A long scarf of thick soft muslin was tied about his loins, leaving his muscular arms bare and free. On his chest and about his neck was a necklace, consisting of several heavy rows of large wooden beads, which, with the cloth, might turn a sword-cut, while both served to protect him from the damp night wind. About his head was a turban of coarse cloth, and a strip of finer material, passing under his chin, covered his mouth and eyes, and was tied in a knot above his turban, leaving two hood ends hanging down on each side. His face was smeared with white earth, and above his nose the broad trident of Krishna was painted in white and red, covering nearly the whole of his eyebrows and forehead. The loose Mahomedan drawers had been changed for a Hindu waistcloth, or "punja," tied tightly about him, and reaching barely to his knee; while the ends were rolled up, leaving his legs and most part of his thighs bare, which, with his arms, were covered with brown earth to subdue the fairness of the skin. The whole of his clothes were of one colour, a deep reddish brown, which is called "bhugwa," and is the sacred and distinctive colour of all religious devotees. At his back hung a broad black shield with steel bosses upon it, and he held in his hand a sabre with a plain steel hilt and black scabbard, which his father recognized as a favourite weapon. Nothing could have been better suited for his guise than the whole equipment, nor was there anything left to desire in its perfect adaptation to resistance or flight, should either be necessary.

"Bulwunt waits for me in the garden, and I go. Thy blessing, my father," said Fazil, stooping forward.

"Go. May Alla, and the saints, and the holy Emaon Zamin protect thee!" said the Khan, rising, and placing his hands tenderly on his son's head. "Go, and return victorious!"

"Ameen! ameen!" (amen!) sighed Zyna, for her heart was with her brother, as he turned to depart upon his perhaps perilous mission.

CHAPTER XX.

"You have not stayed long, Meah, after all," cried the cheery voice of Bulwunt Rao, as he saw his young master approaching the place of meeting, a large peepul tree, which stood at a back entrance to the garden. "And you are as good as your word. I thought there might be some lecture from 'the Mastu,' and some remonstrances from the Khánum, and possibly that the stars were not to be overcome; but all seems to have gone well. Did they know you?"

"My sister seemed rather frightened as she saw me, and shrank back, but my father declared me perfect, and bade me God-speed," replied Fazil; "but look over me once more: dark as it is, it might be a matter of life or death if we were discovered."

"Discovered, Meah! No, trust me for that!" replied Bulwunt. "Only keep that courtly tongue of yours quiet, or if you speak at all, let it be in Canara, which somehow suits you better than our soft Mahratta, and let it be as broad as you can make it. Leave the rest to me. 'Mahrattas know Mahrattas,' is one of our common proverbs, not untrue either. No salaams, Meah! If there be occasion to salute any one, you know the mode. So—join your hands and thumbs together, carry them up to your nose. There, your thumbs along the nose—good. Now a gentle inclination of the head, very little—— Shabash! that was excellent. Take care that no Bundagee or Salaam Alyèk—or other Moslem salutation escape you: if you have need, a soft 'Numuscar Maharaj,' or if we meet a Gosai, 'Nemmo Narrayen Bawa!' Or, better than all—why risk anything? keep a silent tongue, and leave me to talk."

"Nay, not so fast, friend," cried the young Khan, smiling at his follower's earnestness, "fear not for me; I know enough of the customs of the dress I wear to bear me out if need be, and I would fain have my tongue as my hands are—at liberty. No ganja, I hope, since your brain is clear."

"By your head and eyes, no, Meah, I have only drunk water since you first called me," he replied earnestly; "look here," and he executed one of the most difficult of the movements which accompanied his sword exercise,—"will that do?"

"Let us on then, friend, in the name of all the saints, for we have enough to do ere morning, and it is some distance to the temple."

"Nearly a coss, Meah, and we have to pass some bad places beyond the deer park. Come, let nothing induce you to enter into a brawl, or notice insult, or we shall fail. If we are attacked, we can strike in return. Come!"

So saying, they moved on rapidly and silently to the Hindu temple which Bulwunt Rao knew of. Their appearance—for both were attired as nearly as possible alike, except that Bulwunt had concealed more of his face than his companion—was too common and unobtrusive to attract attention, and they passed unnoticed through the respectable portions of the city, meeting, however, few passers in the now dark and deserted streets.

Passing the wall of the deer park, and skirting the walls and glacis of the citadel, patches of open rocky ground succeeded, where a few sleepless asses picked up a scanty night meal, and the houseless dogs of the city snarled and fought over the carrion carcases of cattle, or the offal which had been thrown out there, or disputed their half-picked bones with troops of jackals. Now they met men at intervals, who, with muffled faces and scarcely concealed weapons, watched for unwary single passengers, from whom by threat or violence they might be able to extort the means of temporary debauchery. Some such looked scowlingly upon the friends, and sometimes even advanced upon them; but seeing at a nearer glance no hope of anything but hard blows, passed them by unheeded.

"Many a good fellow has had an end of him made hereabouts," said Bulwunt in a low voice, as they passed a more conspicuous group than usual, who seemed inclined to dispute the way with them. "How much would there be found of a man by morning, to ascertain what he had been in life, if his body were thrown upon one of those heaps of carrion, which the hyenas, dogs, and jackals are fighting over? Do you not hear them yelling?—Bah! that would be an ugly fate, and that is why I seldom venture into this quarter by night."

"Then you come sometimes?"

"Why not, Meah? Are there not adventures enough for those who seek them? I tell thee, many a young noble, ay, and old one too, that I could name, come here after dark and amuse themselves gaily for an hour or two; but thou art not of that sort, Meah; else I had brought thee long ago."

"And that is the quarter yonder, I suppose," said the young man, "above which the light gleams brightly."

"You are right, Meah; a few minutes more and we enter it."

A scene it was of coarse open profligacy. Shops of a low character for the sale of spirits were everywhere open, filled with flaming lamps, or before which stood large iron cressets filled with cotton seed soaked in oil, that burned brightly, sending forth a thick ropy smoke, and showing groups of men, women, and children too, sitting on the ground, drinking the hot new liquor, or the more rapidly intoxicating juice of the date palm-tree; which, contained in large earthen jars, was being dispensed by ladlesful to people clustered around them. All this part resounded with obscene abuse, and songs, and violent wrangling. In one group two men had drawn their daggers, and were with difficulty held back by women hanging about them. In another place, two women had hold of each other's hair, and were beating and scratching each other with their disengaged hands.

They passed through all; many a gibe and coarse invitation familiar to Bulwunt Rao, who, had he been alone, could not have resisted them, followed them from men and women. But he was for the time steady, checked by the presence of his young chief, and with the fierce desire of meeting his hereditary enemy burning at his heart. They were now near the place in regard to which

Bulwunt thought he could not be mistaken. A little further there was a Hindu temple gaily decked out with white and orange-coloured banners; people were singing evening hymns within it, and their voices rose even above the hoarse murmur of the crowd, and there was a clash of cymbals accompanying them. Bulwunt stopped, and laid his hand on his companion's arm.

"That is the temple," he said, "by which I know the kullal's, and that is where we shall meet Tannajee, if at all. That is Rama of Ashtee's shop across the street."

"And is the other temple far off?" asked Fazil.

"Not now; a few more turns down the back lanes yonder, and we shall find it among the tamarind trees in the plain. We will go there at once."

Bulwunt knew the place perfectly. A quiet secluded spot, where often, stupid from the effects of ganja, or drink, he had gone to sleep off the effects before he went home. A place where one or two Jogis, or Gosais, or Sunniasis of ascetic orders, usually put up, or travellers sometimes going eastwards, who had to be clear of the city before dawn. The grove, too, was a favourite place for encampment, and droves of Brinjarries, or other public carriers, halted there in fair weather. Now, however, it was quite vacant, and the natural gloom of the place was deepened by the darkness of the night, while the glare to which their eyes had been exposed, caused it to seem more gloomy still.

"An evil-looking place, friend, at this hour," said Fazil.

"Ay, Meah, dark enough; yet better than the light we have left yonder," he replied, pausing and looking back to where the glare of the kullal's quarter rose into the dark night air above the houses;—"better than that. Yet it is a strange place to come to at night, unless there be any one here. Be cautious, Meah, I will look in."

The temple was a small one, upon a low basement; the high conical roof or steeple could hardly be traced among the heavy foliage that enveloped it. There was a court around it, the wall of which was not so high on one side but that a man standing on tip-toe might look over it; and as Fazil was about to do so, Bulwunt Rao pulled him back.

"For your life, no," he whispered, "some one is there. I saw the flicker of a fire yonder; come round to the back of the verandah. I know of a hole in the wall which is not filled up."

Fazil followed. His companion was right. A hole had been left in the wall for light or air, and some loose stones and bricks stuffed into it. Just enough aperture remained for both to see plainly what was therein. On two sides of the small court, opposite to the temple, was a terraced building roughly built, the pillars supporting the clay roof being of rudely-hewn timber. The basement was level with that of the temple, and ascended by three low steps in the centre. Three persons were sitting on the floor near the embers of a fire; two enveloped in white sheets, which were drawn over their heads, and partly over their faces; they might be Brahmuns, who had been worshipping at the temple. The other was a "Jogi," or ascetic, who, in all his majesty of dirt and ashes—his hair matted and twisted about his head like a turban, the ends of a long grizzly beard tucked over his ears, and naked to the waist—sat cross-legged upon a deer's skin before the embers, which cast a dull and flickering light upon his naked body.

Occasionally, with his right hand, he took ashes from the fire and rubbed them over his broad hairy chest and sinewy arms, and occasionally over his face, telling his beads the while with his left. None of the men spoke. Could they be the persons of whom they were in search?

"I fear we are wrong, Bulwunt," whispered Fazil, "these must be Brahmuns with that Jogi."

"I know of no other temple, Meah," returned Bulwunt; "but wait here, I will go round to the door and question them."

"Be careful, friend; I like not the look of the old Jogi; be careful," interrupted Fazil."

"Nay, I am not going to quarrel with him," continued Bulwunt Rao; "but watch what they do. You will see all their faces if they turn to me." And with cautious steps he moved in.

The door of the temple was in front. Bulwunt had seen it was partially opened when they arrived. Fazil heard it creak on its hinges as Bulwunt opened it, and saw him emerge from behind the basement of the temple; and amidst a rough cry of "who comes?" "who art thou?" from the three persons, walk slowly and firmly up to the basement of the verandah, and make the customary reverential salutation.

"Thou art a bold fellow," exclaimed one of the men covered with a sheet, who stood up, looking at Bulwunt from head to foot, "to intrude upon respectable people unbidden. A Gosai, too, whence art thou?"

"I am a poor disciple of Amrut Geer, of Kullianee, if ye know the town," answered Bulwunt, deferentially; "and they call me Poorungeer. I have come to the city on business, and have travelled far to-day. I often put up here, and, as I saw lights, I entered, in the hope of shelter for the night. It will rain presently, and, with your permission, I will take a drink of water and rest here."

"There is plenty of water in the well without," returned the man sulkily; "and there are the iron bucket and cord—take them and begone. There are a thousand Gosain's Mutts in Beejapoor, why shouldst thou stay here?—begone!"

"Nay, be not inhospitable, O Bawa!" returned Bulwunt. "I am weary and footsore; it is a long way to the only Mutt, I know, and it is not safe for a man alone to pass the plain at night."

"I tell thee begone," said the Jogi; "there is no room for thee here; begone, else we will turn thee out."

"Direct me, then, to a resting-place, good sirs," replied Bulwunt. "I would give no offence; I pray ye be not angry. "Nay," he continued, observing a gesture of impatience; "behold, I am gone. I would not be unwelcome. Only say, O Jogi, what this temple is called?"

"This is the temple of Toolja Dévi, and dedicated to the Holy Mother at Tooljapoor," replied the man. "If thou hast need to visit it, come to-morrow, and thou wilt see the image. Depart now, or these worthy men may be angry. Thou hast interrupted already a discourse on the mysteries——"

"Which would have benefited me, Bawa, also. I shall not forget their inhospitality. Now I depart." And saluting the Jogi, who lifted his hand to his head, and staring fixedly at the others, whose faces were plainly visible by the light of the fire, which had blazed up, Bulwunt Rao left them.

"Listen, Meah," whispered Bulwunt to Fazil, as he rejoined him. "These are the people, no doubt; there are some holes in the wall behind them, which I saw when within; come round to them, we shall see and hear better, and can listen to the old Jogi's discourse on the mysteries; no doubt it will be edifying. The old Jogi is some one, I think, in disguise, but it is well done. Come, and tread softly."

The light tread of their naked feet was not heard amidst the rustling of the trees above; and, as Bulwunt had said, there were several holes in the wall which enabled them to see and hear perfectly, except when the conversation was carried on in the lowest whispers. They were, however, on the highest side of the court wall.

"We are right now," whispered Fazil; "but have the weapons ready in case of need. I like not the Jogi nor his friends."

The inmates of the little building were silent for some time, and one of them, who had kept his face concealed, at length lay down, and drew his sheet over him. The other two smoked at intervals. Now one, now the other, lighting the rude cocoa-nut hooka with embers from the fire before them.

"Didst thou know that lad, Pahar Singh—that Gosai?" asked his companion. "Methinks he was more than he seemed. I know most of that old robber Amrut Geer's cheylas, too, but not him; he may be a new one perhaps. Only I wish I had not seen him; there was an evil eye in his head;" and the speaker's shoulders twitched as though a slight shudder had passed through him.

"What dost thou care about evil eyes, Maun Singh?" replied the Jogi, laughing. "I know not the man, and why should he trouble thee, brother? Depend upon it he was no more than he seemed, else why should he have named Amrut Geer of Tooljapoor? Why art thou thus suspicious?" And he again applied himself to the hooka, whose bubbling rattle rang through the building.

"Nay, it does not signify, only one does not like to be intruded upon, that's all. I had as well shut the door of the temple, brother."

"Do not bolt it," cried the Jogi; "they will be here soon," as the man went and closed it; then returned, and with another shrug or shiver, lay down, when both relapsed into silence.

"Pahar Singh!" whispered Bulwunt to the young Khan; "the robber, murderer, rebel, what you please. The man after whom we wandered so long last year. Ah, 'tis a rare plot, Meah, if such be the instruments."

"Hush!" said Fazil; "they are speaking again. Listen!"

"Where did you get those papers, O Toolsee Das?" asked Pahar Singh of the man who had been lying down. "What, hast thou been asleep? Tell me again, lest I make a mistake."

"Not I, please your Highness," replied the person addressed, raising himself upon his arm; "but if you talk in that gibberish language of your country, what am I to do? It is dull work waiting when one's eyes are heavy with sleep, and I am not rested from that fearful ride."

"Ha, ha, ha!" laughed Pahar Singh; "that ride, Lalla! O man! it was but a child's ride after all, only forty coss. You will be lively enough by-and-by. Now, if you can speak without lying, tell me truly, are those papers genuine or not?"

"My lord," replied the Lalla, sitting up; "they who come will best know that. If they had not been genuine they would not have been worth the stealing, nor these long journeys, to which your servant is not accustomed, nor the risk of being compared with original documents. I told my lord this before, and——"

"True, Lalla," said Pahar Singh, interrupting him; "but one likes to hear a thing over again when it is pleasant. Ha, ha! when it is pleasant, you know——"

"When the honour of great houses is at stake we Mutsuddees have to be proportionably careful," returned the Lalla pompously; "and when your poor servant saw what these were, you see—my consideration for the king—for this state—may it flourish a thousand years—was great, and I—I, ahem—brought them away——"

"You mean you stole them, Lalla? Out with the truth, good fellow."

"Well, sir, if you don't like my words. Yes, I stole them, and it was a blessed chance which has enabled me to turn them to such good account," said the Lalla, smiling blandly. "Excellent indeed, my lord; and I," continued the Lalla, rubbing his hands, "ha! ha! my lord, and I——"

"Ha! ha! ha!" responded Pahar Singh, interrupting him with a coarse laugh. "We shall see. No blood in that robbery, Maun Singh. Ours are seldom so neatly done, I think; but the Lalla is a master of his craft. Well, and if they are genuine, you will have a rich reward. O, much money; gold perhaps, who knows? and half is mine for not cutting that lying coward throat of yours, or hanging you like a dog, Lallajee."

"Noble prince, I have not forgotten the agreement, nor my lord's hospitality," returned the Lalla, joining his hands.

"Ah, that is well," returned Pahar Singh grimly. "One should not forget obligations, and they are only five days old. By your child's head, Maun Singh, he had a narrow escape, only for the boy and thee. Ah, it was rare fun. A coward—a peculiar coward! He did not think he should live, and he told us of the papers; only for that, they would have gone into the river with his carcase. Ah, yes; it was well done. What if they are false, O Lalla, and we have been brought so far in vain! O man, think of that."

"Yes, think of that, Lallajee," returned Maun Singh, turning himself lazily round to speak. "There are few like thee who are made guests of, and fed instead of becoming food. Ha, ha, ha! art thou not afraid?"

"My lords, I can say no more. I have told you all I can, and the rest is in their hands who come," said the Lalla, humbly putting up his hands to his nose. In his heart, however, the man was chuckling secretly. He thought those who were to come would be attended by a retinue, and he purposed to watch his opportunity and denounce the robber, who would be seized on the bare mention of his name; and when he, Toolsee Das, should not only get the price of the papers, but, he felt sure, be rewarded for having enticed so wary a robber into a trap. The Lalla, therefore, endured the raillery and coarse abuse expended upon him with a peculiarly grim satisfaction.

"Yes, a cowardly knave, by your eyes, Maun Singh," continued Pahar Singh, while both were laughing heartily. "Ah, how he begged for life! And we have fed him well since too, though I am not sure that I did right in bringing him here, after all. I think I ought to have sent thee after thine ancestors, Lalla!"

"I doubt not, valiant sir, that your worship hath slain many of the King's enemies," said the Lalla, trembling in spite of himself, but inwardly determining to show no mercy, "and you are pleased to be merry."

"Dog, if thou hast deceived me, and brought me fifty coss for nothing, to save thy miserable life," said Pahar Singh, fiercely, "thou shalt not escape me twice. Hark! what is that at the door?" for it was now shaken violently; "they are come, Maun Singh. Remember, Lalla, I am no Pahar Singh now, or thou diest on the spot. See what I have for thee here," and he showed the shining naked blade of a sword concealed under the ashes. "Enough, don't be frightened, only be discreet. Go, Maun Singh, brother, open the wicket quickly," for those without again shook it impatiently. "Two are to come, only the two; there might be treachery with more. But ho, ho, ho! Pahar Singh is a match for ten, is he not? Now, see thou speakest the truth, O Lalla," he continued; "and my vows for the temple, and the well, they are not to be forgotten—nor—the feeding—five thousand Brahmuns. Forget not this on thy life. I am thy Gooroo, teaching thee 'the mysteries.'"

These words came from him, jerked out, as it were, by morsels, during the brief interval that elapsed before those he expected arrived; and which he employed in rubbing additional handfuls of ashes from the edges of the fire upon his face, body, and limbs, so as to render his disguise more complete, and in heaping up ashes on his sword, the hilt of which lay towards him, ready for action. As he finished, he took a string of wooden beads from his hair, and settled himself on his heels, in an attitude of austere devotion; for, after a brief parley at the gate, steps were heard advancing, and the Lalla, though his heart sank within him at seeing only two persons accompanying Maun Singh, rose as they ascended the steps of the basement, and were clearly visible by the light of the fire, which Pahar Singh had caused to burn brightly.

Fazil Khan's heart beat fast as he saw that one of the persons who ascended first was the King's secretary, his most trustworthy and confidential servant. His handsome, grave, Persian face, and long grey beard, with the lameness he was known by, which resulted from a wound, were unmistakable. The other, who had his face partly concealed, and who might be taken for an ordinary attendant to the Secretary, seemed nowise remarkable; but, as the pair sat down before him, and this person removed one fold of the scarf about his face—though he kept his mouth and nose still covered, as if to exclude the night air—the large sad eyes of the young King were plainly visible.

Fazil beheld him with an intensity of wondering interest, which it is impossible to describe, and fairly panted with excitement. "If he had known whom he was to meet here," he thought, "he would not have exposed himself to this risk: Alla and the Prophet have sent us." And as this escaped him, partly interjectionally and partly in devout prayer, the young Khan seemed to swell with the consciousness that his King might owe his safety, nay, even life, to them.

The Secretary was a veteran soldier, but he was unarmed, except a small knife-dagger in his girdle. Fazil, therefore, loosened his sword in its sheath. "Be ready," he whispered to his companion, who pressed his hand silently, in acknowledgment of the caution. Bulwunt had evidently not recognized the King; indeed, it was well perhaps that he could not see the face, or have his suspicions awakened: he might not have preserved the same composure as his young master.

CHAPTER XXI.

THE silence was becoming oppressive, though only of a few moments' duration, when Fazil observed the Jogi twitch the sleeve of the Lalla's garment as a sign to begin. Though it had cost him a pang to think he had no present hope of securing the robber, Toolsee Das, in truth, was pretty much at his ease. The position and rank of the King's secretary were unequivocal; who the other person might be, he could not conjecture—perhaps an assistant, perhaps a son—he might be either. There was something, certainly, in the look of those great black eyes, which was uncommon; but they gave no response to the Lalla's rapid but curious investigation of them: they could not be fathomed at a glance.

There was nothing in the demeanour of either of the persons before him to excite personal apprehension; and the Lalla was quite sure that Pahar Singh would not give him up, or the papers either, without an equivalent in money; and as he could not have Pahar Singh taken, it was assuring to think that he need not be apprehended himself, for it was quite certain that the robber would get more for the secret here than if he and the papers had been conveyed to the Imperial camp. There, a short questioning, and the executioner would be sure; and the Lalla shuddered for an instant at the thought of what would have followed. Here, as one who could give information of the enemy, and who could disclose state counsels, to what might he not aspire? If the people and their language were barbarous in northern estimation, yet he had seen enough of the city to be satisfied of its beauty; and were not many of the northern people already settling among the Dekhanies?

Such thoughts were flashing rapidly through the Lalla's mind—far more rapidly than we can write them—when he felt the sudden twitch we have already mentioned: he joined his hands together, and began, in a mincing accent, some of those courtly Persian phrases of complimentary welcome, common to the Mahomedans of the north, and which we need not repeat. The Secretary, however, was not in a mood to endure them.

"Peace, Lallajee!" he said; "we are rougher people here than those from whom you have brought these idle compliments, and you can keep them till you get back. Now to business—do not detain us."

"Ah, yes. My lord desired to see some letters of which I spoke to him," he replied; "some that I mentioned yesterday."

"It is therefore that I have come, and it will be well if they can be produced. You have higgled for them overmuch, good fellow," replied the Secretary, curtly.

"Nay, if my lord regrets," said the Lalla, "there is no need to press the matter further. Baba!" he continued to the pretended Jogi, "thou canst burn them in the fire there, only perhaps the King——"

"Not so fast, good sir," said the Meerza, speaking more blandly. "I remember all that has passed between us and that valiant gentleman yonder," and he pointed to Maun Singh, "and I am willing to perform my part of the bargain. And is this the Gooroo of whom ye spoke?"

"Sir, it is," replied the Lalla. "A holy man—one unused to the ways of the world, and who travels from shrine to shrine in the performance of sacred vows. Such were the Rishis; such are those from whom holy actions emanate; and such are the virtuous Jogis of the present day, of whom my Gooroo is a noble example. He, desiring the welfare of the Shah—may his splendour increase, and live for ever!—sent me to inform you, O fountain of eloquence and discretion! that they were in existence——" Here the Jogi gave another twitch of interruption, and a look, with a low growl, which the Lalla well understood, and continued—

"You see, noble sirs, he hath already suffered the interruption of his devotional abstraction, and is uneasy; for he never speaks unless to bless his disciples, or removes his eyes from the end of his nose: in continuing which, and repeating to himself holy texts and spells of wonderful power, he is pre-eminent in absorption of his faculties. So my lord will excuse him, and will remember the condition attached to the perusal of the papers."

"The gold, the gold—the money first!" growled the Jogi. "My son, my vow, my vow!"

"Noble sirs," continued the Lalla in a deprecatory whine to both, which appeared perfectly natural, as he looked from one to the other, with his hands joined, "you must pardon him; he is not a man of courts or of the world, but of temples, and holy shrines, and ascetic exercises; and some time ago he made a vow to build a temple on a spot where he had an ecstatic vision of heaven, and to dig a well, and feed five thousand Brahmuns, and to pass the remainder of his days in assisting poor travellers and in holy contemplation. A holy man, therefore, noble gentlemen, and he is anxious about the gold, not as filthy lucre, but for the sake of the temple and the well."

"Peace!" interrupted the Meerza. "What, in the name of the Shytan, are the well and the temple to us? Let us get up and depart, Sahib," he said to his companion, "they have no papers; this is but a scheme to raise money. I like them not, my lord," he added in a whisper, "and bitterly do I regret having brought you here unarmed and unattended. May God and the Prophet take us safe hence!"

The Lalla was not watching their faces in vain; he felt that he had gone far enough; and a fresh scowl from Pahar Singh, which was not to be mistaken: and his action, as he turned up a corner of the deerskin on which he sat, exhibiting a small red satin bag which might contain papers, assured the Lalla that he need not delay longer.

"Nay, my lords, be not impatient," he said blandly. "When was —he, he!—business of importance ever well done in a hurry? Behold!" added the Lalla, taking up the bag, "here are the papers which the holy father has kept safely for me beneath his deer's hide. Have I your permission to open them, Baba?"

"Open, and be quick," was the short answer of the Jogi.

"Simply then, noble sirs," continued the obsequious Lalla, taking some Persian letters out of the bag, "here they are; and if either of ye know the handwriting, the signature, or the seals of Khan Mahomed, Wuzeer of Beejapoor, he will, Inshalla! be able to recognize them. I do not know them myself, but that makes no difference; they are no forgeries. If you, my lord," he added to the Meerza, "know them, you will find that your poor servant has spoken the truth. Look at them carefully."

The Meerza received the packet with trembling hands, but he said firmly, "Thou knowest the penalty thou hast incurred if these be forged; and if a slave like thee shouldst have dared to question falsely the honour of one so exalted as the Wuzeer, beware!"

"I know—I know, O most exalted and worthy sir!" replied the Lalla, humbly but confidently shutting his eyes, folding his hands upon his breast, and bowing his head over them; "your worship told me before it would be death. But it will not be so. O no! In your poor slave's destiny is written favour and advancement at your hands, and his planets are in a fortunate conjunction."

"I would hang him to the highest tree in Beejapoor, to the topmost branch of the Goruk Imlee, to feed the crows and kites for a week. What a rascal he is, Meah!" whispered Bulwunt.

"Hush, and be ready! there is a life on every word," returned Fazil, hearing the King speak in Persian in an under-tone to the Meerza.

"There is no escape from death," he said in a sad tone, "if these papers be not false."

"True!" exclaimed the Jogi, abruptly, but whether it had reference to the Lalla's speech or the King's, could not be certain. The King looked at him suspiciously, but the man appeared once more to have relapsed into abstraction.

"O, that I know, worthy sir," returned the Lalla carelessly, "we must all die in the end: we are all mortal: what saith Saadi?" and he quoted a verse from the Bôstan. "I have no fear of them, noble gentlemen! May it please you to look at them first, and then determine about killing me afterwards. He, he, he!"

"He does not tremble under those eyes," whispered Fazil to his companion. "This must be true. God help them all!"

"If there be faith in handwriting and seals," resumed the Lalla after a pause, "I fear not. If these documents had not been so precious, why should the asylum of the world, my master, have kept them so carefully in his own writing-case? The time is not come, O Meerza! but you will yet hear of a reward having been set upon your poor slave's head. Be it so; I claim the protection of Ali Adil Shah for the service I now do him, Bismilla! Open the packet there, and say whether I have death and infamy before me, or life and honour in the King's service, for there is more at stake in this matter than my lord knows of. Bismilla! open it."

The Meerza held the packet irresolutely, as one who almost feared a knowledge of its contents, and looked for a moment to his companion——

"Bismilla!" said the King, eagerly speaking in Persian, "open it; this suspense is intolerable. Dost thou fear for Khan Mahomed? art thou his friend?"

"By your head and eyes, by the King's salt, no," answered the other. "For good or for evil, Bismilla! I open it,"—and he tore the cover hastily.

The heart of Fazil Khan beat so hard in his bosom that its throbbings seemed painfully audible to himself, and he almost fancied they must be heard by all inside; but he was still, as was also his companion.

As the wax-cloth covers were withdrawn, there appeared several letters in the bundle,—large, and the paper covered with gilding, such as are sent to persons of the most exalted rank only. Eagerly, most eagerly, did the practised eye of the Secretary run over each superscription, and each was narrowly scrutinized. One by one he passed them to the King, and Fazil could see that, whatever they were, they caused the deepest expression of interest in both their countenances. Suddenly the Meerza came to one which, having examined even more narrowly than the others, he passed on, with a deep sigh, to the King.

It was taken eagerly, and at once opened and read, while the Lalla turned from one to the other with an intense expression of curiosity, fear, and hope blended together, marked on his features.

"Does that Jogi understand Persian, thinkest thou?" asked the King of the Lalla.

"Not a word, I will answer for it with my head," returned the man confidently. "How should he?"

"And thyself?"

"Surely, excellent sir; I have long served in the royal Dufter, else how should I have known what to take and what to leave?" He spoke now in Persian, and the conversation continued in that language.

"If there were more, why didst thou not take all, Lalla?" asked the Meerza.

"All, Meerza Sahib? that the theft might be discovered before I had time to get away? Ah, no, good sir! A Mutsuddee may be a rogue, but he should have discretion," and he quoted the Persian proverb to that effect; "and to all appearance the royal desk still holds the same packet which I made up with other papers, and sealed with the private signet as it was before. No; the theft is not suspected yet, unless that packet have been opened by the Emperor when I was missed——"

"And thou knowest the contents of this letter, Lalla?" inquired the King.

"I could say them to you, for I have them by heart, noble sir; perhaps they are somewhat remarkable, for when I read them, I thought Ali Adil Shah would like to hear them, so I committed them to memory. I will even repeat the letter to you if this worthy Meerza have no objection. I presume," he continued to the Secretary, "that your friend is in the King's confidence as much as yourself."

"Surely," was the reply. "I may say that he is more in it than I am myself, else I had not brought him."

"Enough," said the Lalla; "I am satisfied. Now, open the letter and compare it with what I repeat. There is no Alkab."

"True," said the King, "he has drawn a Mudd at the top."

"Proceed after the Mudd, then," continued the Lalla, "the letter runs thus:—

"It has been the will of the all-powerful that the forces of my lord, the ruler of both worlds, should retire. Let not that trouble his heart. By the favour of the most merciful, matters will yet take a prosperous course for my lord's true interests. All here, with this poor suppliant for his bounty, are day and night labouring in his behalf: and already many, as by the endorsed list, with their adherents, have been gained

to the true cause. Others demur, but will repent; again, others are obstinate, and cannot be moved, but they are not many. A few months more, and when the season opens, the harvest will be ripe for the gathering. Then, there will be no turning back for my lord from this city; for its people, with this poor servant, rejoicing to escape tyranny, will at once turn to the asylum of the two worlds, and give my lord's fortunate footsteps a happy welcome. We are tired of the false religion; and as to the King, he is but yet a boy, and has neither power, knowledge, nor any friends: and are men of venerable age to submit tamely to his idle fancies? Surely not. He can be ultimately provided for. For the rest, my lord's promises are undeserved by the least of his servants, who is not fit to kiss his feet; but my lord can at least rely that his administration will be carried on entirely in his interest, and to his honour and glory. What need to write more? it would be beyond the bounds of respect. May the splendour of dominion and honour increase! The signature of Khan Mahomed, Wuzeer of Beejapoor."

"Ay, what need of more?" sighed the young King. "Enough here—enough to prove the man's treachery, the least deserved that ever the false world saw. Yet, Meerza, there are still many true to the King: there are some suspected ones in the list that we know of," he continued, his eye running rapidly over it, "but Afzool Khan, and many of note, are not here, and yet rumour has assailed them also."

"Yes, they are intimates," said the Secretary, "but no more, I think."

"Then I have won my reward and my life!" exclaimed the Lalla anxiously, in his own tongue.

"Your life, surely," replied the Meerza; "but for the reward, we need to make some further scrutiny into those papers ere that can be disbursed: they must be compared with others in the King's possession. Therefore I will take them with me to-night, and if you will come to me—you know my house—early to-morrow, all will be arranged to your satisfaction."

"But, my lord—noble sirs," cried the Lalla, in evident dread, "that was no part of the bargain. Did we not settle——" He could not, however, finish the sentence on account of a rude and decisive interruption.

"I forbid it. I forbid one paper or one of you passing hence this night till the money is paid," said the Jogi, severely.

"And who art thou?" demanded the Meerza, haughtily. "Peace! withdraw; this is no place for thee, or the like of thee."

"Who am I?" retorted the ruffian. "Who am I? One who has the right, as he has the power, to demand what he seeks." And as he spoke he snatched from beneath the heap of ashes before him the heavy sword he had kept concealed there, which flashed brightly in the firelight, and started to his feet, as did also his follower. "Stir not!" he exclaimed to the King and Secretary, who had been too much startled by the sudden action to rise with the Jogi; "stir not, or ye die on the spot!" Drawing himself up to his majestic height, Pahar Singh laughed scornfully. "Ha, ha, ha! a boy and a penman against me! Ha, ha, ha! put up thy weapon, Maun Singh, there is no need of it."

"Who art thou?" demanded the King, rising notwithstanding the threat, and returning the glance as steadily as it was given.

"It concerns thee not," answered Pahar Singh. "Pay me the money promised on those papers—ten thousand good rupees—on this spot, or you pass not hence alive. Brother," he added to Maun Singh, "be ready. They have brought the money, and we must get it."

It was a moment of intense anxiety to Fazil Khan and his companion. A word—a sound from them, and the life of the young King was gone. Fazil could see that, except a small dagger in each of their girdles, the King and his Secretary were unarmed. To rush to them soon enough to be of use, was a thing impossible; they would be dead ere he could strike a blow. There was no absolute peril, however, as yet, and too much at stake to risk anything. Pahar Singh appeared to have no evil intention; but, if provoked, it was plain he might do violence, and would not hesitate to use his weapon if rescue were attempted.

The King saw his danger. There was little avail in temporizing, and his thought and action were alike prompt. His own life and his friend's were both at stake; and what did the money signify? Not a feather in the balance. Could his attendants, whom he had left at a distance, even hear of his danger, he must perish ere they could approach him.

"Hold!" he cried, "whoever thou art, Jogi. If the Lalla says thou art to have the money, it will be given. Our bargain was with him."

"And his with me," returned the man. "Give it me;" and as he spoke he advanced close to the King.

"Pay it to him—let him have it," cried the Lalla to the King, "and keep back your men if you have any with you, else there will be bloodshed. He is desperate, noble sirs; do not provoke him."

"I would do him no harm," said Pahar Singh to the Secretary, "but it is as well to be certain in case of treachery;" and he drew a small dagger from his girdle with his left hand, and held it in an attitude to strike into the King. "Go, if the money is here; bring it quickly; but beware of any attempt to rescue him, or you will cause his death. You could not reach me ere I had struck him down.

Go then, Meerza Sahib, my friend Maun Singh will bring the bags: he is strong enough."

"Go, friend," said the King, "do as he says. If the people ask questions, say I am safe, and will be with them presently."

"And leave thee with him!" said the Meerza, anxiously. "I will not stir; there is peril, and my place is beside thee."

"There is no peril if ye are true," said Pahar Singh; "much, if ye are false. Go!"

"Go, friend, I will trust him; his object is money, not my poor life. Go! I am not afraid of him, nor he of me," said the King.

"How noble he is!" whispered Fazil to his companion.

Both would have given all they possessed to have been by the King's side to have struck down the ruffian.

"Ay, Meah, I would we were by his side," returned Bulwunt. "Who can he be? Whoever he may be, he is indeed fearless; but he will not be harmed if they bring the money. Hush! they may speak again."

The Meerza turned silently to go, and descended the step, accompanied by Maun Singh.

"Come," said the latter to the Lalla; "help to carry the bags, good man; it will save me another journey. Come!"

The Lalla followed, and the two remained standing face to face, the young King and the outlaw looking steadily at each other.

"Afraid of thee?" said Pahar Singh in a low voice, and dropping the arm which had held the dagger uplifted. "Afraid of thee? No, proud boy: he who defied thy father's power at its greatest, hath little to fear from thine. Ali Adil Shah, thinkest thou that this poor disguise could conceal thee? Yet thou art bold and true, and I rejoice that I have had proof of it, for men told me thou wert a coward—a boy of the zenana—only fit to herd with women. Now thou hast met the 'Lion of the Hill' bravely," he continued, using the play on his own name, "and he will turn from thee peacefully. Thy life hath been in my hand—nay, is now in it were I to strike—but I give it to thee freely; promise me mine in return, and swear by thy father's spirit that, once gone from this, thou wilt not turn back, nor suffer any one of thy retinue to do so."

The King started as the man covertly declared his name, and the covering fell from his face.

"Thou Pahar Singh, the Lion of Allund?" he said.

"Even so, monarch," returned the chief. "Ha! ha! The man whom thy slaves—cowards—tell thee they pursue. Aha! they dare not. Pahar Singh is monarch of his own wilds; no royal troops dare to come near them. But keep thine own counsel, and now listen. Thou mayst need me yet, and I may do thee good service. Two thousand good hearts and stout arms, such as thy money cannot hire, serve Pahar Singh. Swear to keep faith with me, and I will be true. Hadst thou been a coward, and quailed at the sight of this weapon, I should have been tempted to slay thee, Adil Khan, like a dog, for never yet did coward sit on the throne of Beejapoor. For what has happened, thou hast my respect. Enough! remember Pahar Singh, and in two days or less I will send thee more tidings, or come myself. Thou mayst kill the messenger, but he will not tell of my hiding-place; and if harm come to him, I swear to thee, by the Lady of Tooljapoor, my Holy Mother, that I will take a life for every hair of his head, and burn a hundred villages. Now, silence! I have spoken. Am I free to go, scathless as thou art? Thy hand upon it, monarch!"

It was frankly given, and the rebel and outlaw, instead of taking it rudely, and as if prompted suddenly by a kindly feeling of reverence for his King, bent his head gently, touched it with his forehead, and kissed it.

"Thy hand has touched my lips—put it upon my head, and swear by thy father not to harm me," he said, quickly.

"I swear by my father not to harm thee, Pahar Singh: only be thou henceforth faithful to thy King's salt," he replied, as he placed both his hands upon the outlaw's head.

"Enough," returned Pahar Singh, removing them, pressing them again to his forehead, and kissing them reverently; "I will be true to thy salt, O King; but speak to no one of me, and wait patiently till I come—I may have news for thee. A fakeer's rags and a beggar's cry admit me everywhere—'Ulla dilâyâ to léonga'*—by night or by day, wherever thou art, in durbar or zenana, whenever you hear it—admit me, or order me to be confined, and send for me—I shall bawl loudly enough. If I come not in two days, do not doubt me; but stir not in this matter till I arrive—it may be very soon, I cannot say. Now cover thy face; they come," and he resumed his former threatening attitude.

The Meerza, with the two others, emerged from behind the temple almost as he spoke, and in a few moments had ascended the steps of the apartment. Maun Singh drew a heavy bag from beneath the scarf which was round his shoulders; but the eye of the robber at once detected its small size.

"Those are not rupees, Meerza; beware of treachery with me. I have not harmed him," he exclaimed.

"No, it is gold, holy Baba. Behold!" and he opened the bag, and poured the contents carefully into a little heap on the floor near the fire. "There is more than *he* bargained for," he continued, pointing to the Lalla, "but it does not matter; you are welcome to it, for the temple and the well."

* "If God give I will take."

"Enough," returned Pahar Singh; "I am satisfied. Go, take your papers, and begone; molest me no more." And, sitting down on his deer's hide, he heaped up the gold coins carefully with his left hand, while his right still held the sword.

"And my reward, O Meerza Sahib!" cried the Lalla eagerly, as he and the King turned to depart; "thou wilt not abandon me to him."

"It is there with the rest," answered the Secretary; "Lallajee, help yourself, we must begone."

"Nay, but I want it not; only take me away—take me away. I fear him," cried the man, in a piteous voice, and trembling violently.

"Peace, fool," exclaimed Pahar Singh, rising and holding him back powerfully. "Peace, I will settle with thee!"

CHAPTER XXII.

For a moment the natural presence of mind which Fazil possessed deserted him, and his brain seemed to reel under conflicting thoughts, and the weight and importance of the secret of which he had become possessed. Should he disclose himself to the King as he passed out, and urge him to allow Pahar Singh to be taken? The retinue which awaited the monarch would be enough to surround the temple, and the robber's capture or death was certain. It was a deed to do to prove his devotion, and the country would be free of a bold and mischievous marauder, who plundered it up to the gates of the city. But the King's promise to the outlaw was for the time sacred, and there was, perhaps, further service to be done by the man, which could not be delayed. As regards the Wuzeer and his family, also, he must avow his knowledge of the secret to the King, when he might be charged as his spy, and so share the Wuzeer's fate. These thoughts checked the impulse which had so nearly carried him on,—it might have been to destruction.

"Shall we follow him? shall we speak to the King?" asked Bulwunt hurriedly, observing Fazil's irresolution. "Say quickly, Meah,—we have not a moment to lose."

"No, no! we are better here," replied Fazil. "The avowed knowledge of that secret might chance to be our death-warrant; and has not the King given him kowl? Let us watch still—we may gather further particulars; but to follow the King is madness. Listen! they are speaking." Again, therefore, they resumed their respective positions.

A few sticks had been thrown on the embers, and Maun Singh was kneeling down and blowing them into a flame, which, bursting through them in small flashes with every breath, partially illumined the figures around it and the blackened walls of the apartment. Pahar Singh sat with the gold coins before him, counting them one by one. A large portion were already laid on one side, which he proceeded to drop into the bag. The expression of his coarse and savage features could now be distinctly seen; for not only was the light from the fire becoming steady, but he had removed from his original position, so that he sat with his face nearly full towards Fazil, though from Bulwunt Rao he was more concealed than before. It was a face which, once seen, could never be forgotten. Men saw it and quailed before it: women saw it and shuddered: and Fazil remembered how often old Goolab, when he was yet a child, had frightened him by the mention of Pahar Singh: while tales of his occasional frays and bloody deeds were of everyday report in the bazar.

There, then, he sat. Turban he had none: his matted hair, twisted into a rough rope, was tied in a knot on the crown of his head, and covered with ashes, showing the high narrow forehead—on which, though crossed by deep wrinkles, the forked veins, swelled by his excitement, stood out like ridges, betokening passions wild, fierce, and uncontrollable. The eyes, always bright, glittered restlessly and suspiciously from beneath the heavy brows, to which, and to the lids, the white ashes, smeared on his face from time to time as he sat, had adhered; and his hard grin disclosed the prominent eye-teeth, which he chose to call tusks, in allusion to his name.

When we last saw this face at Itga, it was excited, but there was a softening influence exercised by the presence of his adopted son, and Pahar Singh was under some restraint. Now there was none, and it was difficult to recognize the features at all under his disguise, which served to increase the natural ferocity of the expression.

His rough moustaches, of a sandy-brown colour at the ends, mingled with a straggling scanty beard, were usually parted in the middle, and turned over his ears; but now, being loosened, they were tied together in a knot under his chin, in the most approved Jogi fashion. His broad chest was covered with grizzled hair of the same peculiar colour as his beard; and his chin, originally fair, had become of a deep brown, except where it retained some of its original colour. His arms, which had appeared so muscular when he suddenly started up to threaten the king, seemed even longer and more powerful, as he sat stretching out one over the blaze, while the fingers of the other hand played among the gold pieces before him. Pahar Singh's countenance was now very repellant. It seemed to Fazil that mercy could never issue from those pitiless lips which, with the full nostrils distending and contracting rapidly under the action of feelings not yet expressed, produced an effect which fascinated, while it shocked one unused to it.

"Lallajee," he said, every now and then looking up: "O friend, dost thou love gold? See, this is red and pure—ah, yes, lovely—and so it need be, coming out of the King's mint direct. More than ten thousand rupees, too, they said. Well, there are just five hundred and fifty ashruffees. That is—how much, Maun Singh? thou art a better accountant than I am."

"Somewhere about eleven thousand rupees, I believe, Maharaj," said his follower.

"Well, that will do, Lallajee," continued Pahar Singh. "That is my share for taking care of thee, thou knowest, and getting thee a good market for thy papers. The gods be praised! I vow ten of these to the Holy Mother's necklace at Tooljapoor," and he took up ten pieces of the number that remained.

"Nay, valiant sir," interposed the Lalla: "that is your Excellency's share in the bag yonder. These are mine, not half, as we agreed, but enough perhaps for the poor Lalla. It would be no merit for my lord if he were to give to the goddess——"

He could not finish the sentence, whatever it might have been intended to mean, for the rude interruption—"Ill-begotten!" cried the robber, snatching a brand from the fire and striking the Lalla's hand, which had advanced towards the heap,—"dare to touch the gold, and thou diest! That for the like of thee!"

"I am your slave," whimpered the man, wringing his hand; "but why did my lord strike so hard?"

"Listen to the coward, brother," said Pahar Singh with a sneer; "a woman would not whine like that. Now, thy share, Maun Singh."

"Of course," said that worthy, "after being dallal in the matter, and putting my head into jeopardy, running after that mad Secretary into the very palace—where, had any one chanced to recognize me, I should have been cut down or speared like a mad dog—truly, considering the risk, and that day and night's ride to boot, mine comes next. Ah! thou art a just man, O Jemadar."

"Well, then, hold out thine hand, brother," returned Pahar Singh, taking up a few coins and dropping them into his hand. "One, two, three, four, five, six, seven, eight. Good gold, good gold, Lallajee!" he said, looking up: "but it is of no use giving it to him: he will only spend it on women and liquor. Better I should have the rest, who can take care of it, Lalla, and give it him as he needs it—dost thou not think so? Yet, stay, I may as well —nine, ten, that's two hundred rupees, brother—enough for thee.

Who would have thought of a bundle of old papers bringing so many bright ashruffees. And after all, O Lalla—by your head—were they true or false, O mean thief?"

"True; I swear by your head and eyes, by the holy Krishna and his temple at Muttra. Canst thou doubt, after what has passed, O Jemadar?" cried the Lalla earnestly.

"Nay, how could I understand thy jabbering of Persian? That was no honest talk, Maun Singh; they meant to cheat us by it, and this slave joined in it. Twenty-one, twenty-two,"—he was counting the remainder of the gold, and dropping the coins into his own bag as he spoke, "twenty-three. Dost thou think, O Lalla, that I am a cheating Mutsuddee, like thyself?—twenty-four, twenty-five.—Ill-begotten clerk, say—am I—Pahar Singh—a liar and a thief like thyself?"——

"May I be your sacrifice, Maharaj, no," cried the Lalla, terrified at his manner, and watching, with evident and ill-concealed uneasiness, coin after coin disappearing into the bag. "Why should my lord be angry if I spoke in Persian?"

"Ho, ho, thou art frightened again—art thou? Well, perhaps thou couldst not help the Persian, as the letter had to be read; but I understood it all the time, O Lalla. Thou couldst not have cheated me—listen!" he continued in that language, speaking it with a broad Mahratta accent; "what part of this sum dost thou expect for thy share—twenty-six, twenty-seven. There is yet much, Lalla. What sayeth the poet Saadi? Expectation—— No matter, I forget the verses we used to learn at school. How much?"

"Nay, Maharaj, I know not," returned the man in a bewildered manner. "My lord said half would be mine, and the Meerza told us there were more than ten thousand rupees."

"Good, O Lalla, thou patron of valiant men like me: but dost thou expect it? Five thousand rupees! dost thou think that such a sum will come to thee?" and his hand passed to the hilt of his sword.

"My lord! noble prince! I—I—I," stammered the now trembling wretch. "I—I—mean the promise to me. Nay, look not so, Maharaj," as he observed the robber's face distorted with suppressed rage, the veins of his forehead swelled, and white foam gathering about the corners of the mouth. "Nay, look not so angry! Behold, I kiss your feet: I am a very poor man, and a stranger;" and he joined his hands in supplication as he rose from his heels partly to a kneeling posture. "Would my lord ever have known of the value of those papers had I not told it? Would they not have been thrown away, scattered to the winds, if my poor life had been taken at Itga?"

"My promise!—my promise to thee, O son of a base mother! Didst thou not swear to me they would be worth thousands?—

lakhs!" cried the robber, raising his voice and gesticulating violently, as he now took up the gold pieces by handfuls, and thrust them into the bag. "A lakh of rupees! and here are only a few paltry coins, for which thou hast brought me fifty coss! What will Anunt Geer of Kullianee say to this poor instalment on his debt? Thief! get me the rest—the rest of the gold they have put aside for thee. Didst thou not promise a lakh?"

He had now lashed himself into a fury, which had been his object evidently from the first; and he struck the Lalla with his clenched hand violently upon the head, so that he fell backwards, and lay apparently stunned; but it was only fear.

"He will kill him—not that he does not deserve death, the mean hound!" said Fazil Khan, hurriedly to his companion. "When was Pahar Singh ever known to spare a victim? What is to be done, Bulwunt? shall we attack them?"

"Alas, Meah!" returned the other, "what can be done?—a sound, a word, and the man is dead. We cannot reach them; and the door was closed and barred when the others went. Ai Bhowani! ai Khundôba! ai Bhugwan! save him! O, that I had brought my gun with me, or even a pistol, Meah; but he dare not kill him; he is only frightening him out of the money. Hush, and listen!"

"Raise him, brother," continued Pahar Singh to his companion, laughing; "we will soon see whether this fear is true or feigned; or is the coward soul really gone out of his body?"

"Nay, Jemadar, but he breathes," said Maun Singh, raising the Lalla. "Speak, O Toolsee Das! art thou alive?"

"My lords! O my lords!" gasped the terrified wretch; "what have I done? what have I done? why am I beaten?"

"My thousands, I tell thee!" cried the robber hoarsely. "Where are the papers that were to bring me thousands? Thou hast concealed them to sell to others. Liar! liar, and base-born coward, as thou art!—— Enough, Maun Singh," he continued, in another language, which was not understood either by Fazil Khan or his companion, and which both often thought of afterwards; "he must die; the goddess has sent him; he must die for her, lest he lead other men astray."

"Ay, he is good Bunij, Jemandar," returned the man coolly. "Methinks this would have saved trouble long ago, and your worship's getting into a passion. We ate the goor this morning——"

"Surely, brother, but no blood. I would not soil my sword with carrion like him; and yours is a certain hand with the handkerchief."

What words can describe the terror of the devoted wretch? He could not speak or cry out. Of what use if he had? He knew the temple was far from men's abodes, and the wind moaned hoarsely in the trees above, as the branches swayed to and fro before a brisk gale now rising with the clouds. He tried to swallow, but in vain. He sat paralysed, as it were, his eyes wandering vacantly from one to the other, while his lips were tightened into a ghastly simper of fear. Neither of the men spoke; but Maun Singh was carelessly twisting a handkerchief into a peculiar form, and tying a knot at the end of it. "Thou wilt not feel it, Lallajee," he said jocularly, but in the strange tongue; "my hand is sure, and I am the best Bhuttote in Allund."

What the Lalla understood or guessed it was impossible to conceive; but Fazil felt assured that murder was to be done. "By Alla and his Prophet!" he said to Bulwunt, "come what may of it, are we men to stand by tamely and see foul murder committed before our eyes? Were the wretch a hundred times more liar and coward, one good blow should be struck against that ruffian. Ho, Pahar Singh! Maun Singh!" shouted the young Khan before he could be prevented by his companion. "Hold! would ye do murder?"

"Hur, Hur, Mahadeo!" cried his companion at the same moment, and both rushed to the place where, on the side they had been standing, the wall seemed the lowest; but it was still too high to be reached without a scramble over rough stones, which delayed them longer than they had thought. The top once gained, they leaped into the enclosure with drawn weapons; but as they did so, Fazil saw one man on the top beyond, another climbing up, aided by his companion. For him and Bulwunt Rao to rush across the court was the act but of an instant; yet they were too late: the Jogi—Pahar Singh—had escaped, and his companion was in the act of dropping down, when, aided by a bound, the well-aimed weapon of the young Khan reached him. Where or how Fazil Khan had wounded the robber he knew not; but when he examined his bright blade, there was a broad stain upon it which could not be mistaken. As he looked, hesitating whether he should leap down and follow, he could just distinguish two figures dimly, running at desperate speed through the trees across the plain, which were quickly lost in the gloom.

Bulwunt Rao was at his side. "Another moment and we should have had both: the gods have protected them; and it is of no use following, Meah," he said.

"No, no, they are gone," returned Fazil; "it is useless to follow: better for us to see after that poor wretch yonder—the villains may have murdered him, after all;" and they hastened to him.

The flickering blaze was still playing about the little fire, and served them with enough light to distinguish the objects by it, disclosing, too, more of the apartment or verandah than they had yet seen; and as both entered the place at the same moment, a cry of execration burst simultaneously from them.

"The villains have been too sure! While we scrambled among those stones they killed him. See, here is an ugly gash, Meah!" said Bulwunt Rao.

"That would not kill him," said Fazil, stooping to raise up the body—"and he is quite warm. I most fear this cloth about his neck; but look for some water. I would not have him die. So now—dash some in his face—his heart beats, too—he lives, Bulwunt Rao!"

"Praise to Narayun! there is at least a chance for him," cried Bulwunt. "Awake—arise, O Lalla! and fear not," he continued to the wounded man; "your enemies are gone, and you are with friends who can protect you. Here, drink some water. I am a Hindu who give it; and speak, O man with a small liver!"

These cheering words, accompanied by a few gentle blows on his back, and a little water forced into his mouth, restored something like consciousness to the wretch. He opened his eyes and stared wildly about, and into the faces of those who stood over him: then he put his hand to his throat as if it hurt him.

"Ay, I dare say," continued Bulwunt—"I dare say they hurt thee badly; but fear not, Sree Swami has sent you friends; drink, and it will do you good. Tut, man, you need not be particular about caste; here is my junwha, and there is no need to ask further. That's well—can you speak?"

"Ye are not they," said the Lalla huskily, and in a low tone. "Friends, how came ye here? Hai, Hai!—alas, where is my gold? and where are the robbers who would have killed me? May their mothers be defiled!"

"Perish the gold, meanhearted," cried Fazil; "with thy soul hovering betwixt life and death, is thy first thought for thy gold?"

"I worship thy feet, brave Gosai," returned the Lalla; "but it was all I had, for which I had risked much. Hai, Hai! it is all gone now, and I am in a strange place without a copper or a friend;" and he turned to the wall and sobbed bitterly.

"It was a round sum to lose, certainly," said Bulwunt; "but thy life is safe, and thou hast only to steal again, Lallajee!"

"Better to have died—better to have died, sirs!" cried the man distractedly. "When shall I see so much gold again? Look, noble sirs, is all gone? has he taken all?"

"It was here they counted it," said Fazil; "look about—a piece or two may be found; or they may have dropped some in their flight."

Bulwunt blew a dry stick into a blaze, and looked around. He was fortunate—a few coins had escaped Pahar Singh, which he gave to the Lalla, who tied them up in his waistcloth.

"Look for more—look yonder, kind sir; and the blessings of a poor Khayet be on you both," returned the Lalla. "My eyes are dim:

alas!" he exclaimed, as he put his hand to the back of his neck and felt blood,—"I am killed—I am dying!"

"Peace, fool!" cried Fazil impatiently, "a child would have cut deeper: it has been a strange escape. Give me your scarf—I will tie up the wound."

"And here is some more money for you, too, Lallajee," said Bulwunt, who had now returned, having picked up several gold pieces in the line which Pahar Singh had taken across the court. "There may be more, and if you come to-morrow early, you may find them."

"But now we cannot wait, Lalla," added Fazil; "there is no further fear of your life. The clouds are gathering fast, and there will be rain; we will see you safe to a guard-room, and I will have you cared for in the morning; or you can sleep here if you like."

"Ah, leave me not, gentlemen! I am poor and in great pain," replied the man. "My clothes and horse are a long way from hence: how shall I get to them? Take me with you and I shall live, else he will find me out and kill me—that Pahar Singh."

Supporting the wounded man between them, the two friends unfastened the door of the courtyard and passed out. The glare and noise of the bazar seemed only at a short distance, and knowing that a strong guard was placed at night near the end nearest the city, they went to it as directly as they could. A few questions were carelessly asked as to the cause of the wound, and as vaguely answered. A traveller found wounded, who had been robbed, was probably cause enough to acount for his condition.

"We cannot delay, Lalla," said Bulwunt, in answer to his cries that one at least would stay with him. "We have far to go, and the night is passing fast. The clouds, too, are gathering, and the thunder is growling in the distance. Hark! there will be a storm. Come, Meah," he whispered, "we may miss him whom we seek. See that the man's wounds are dressed, Duffadar," he continued aloud to the officer of the guard, "and let him sleep here."

CHAPTER XXIII.

As Fazil parted from the wounded man, the scenes of the night, the horrid truth regarding the treachery of his friend's father, the danger which threatened both, and indeed the whole family, caused him many an anxious thought. His worst suspicions had only been too deeply verified, and even now there arose some struggle between duty and allegiance to his King, and affection for the Wuzeer's family, for the sake of his son. Bulwunt had again avoided the principal street, and they were once more in the open ground beyond the houses.

Fazil walked on rapidly and silently; but at length the oppression of his thoughts found vent in words. "Let him decide," he said aloud, in allusion to his father; "wisdom abides with him; and in a matter like this his advice is precious."

"And what think you of all this, Meah?" asked his companion, for an instant slackening his pace; "what will the noble Khan Sahib say to it?—not indeed that he and the Wuzeer are very intimate friends either. I tell thee, were not my heart turning to that devil Tannajee Maloosray, I should be lost in wonder at the Wuzeer's folly."

"Even so," said Fazil, sighing; "a man in whom I would have placed confidence as in my own father—one who ought to be honoured and loved for his faith—is but a poor knave, after all, Bulwunt—not better than that miserable Lalla whom we have just left—a thing for men to spit upon. Alas for the world's honesty, brother! A heap of gold, a few empty titles, the smile of a woman,—and power—which does but make its possessor miserable when he has gained it—turns right to wrong, justice to oppression, virtue to vice, honesty to knavery, faith to treachery. We look for it in the highest, but it flies from us; we seek it in the lowest, and turn from them but too often in despair. Should not one sigh at depravity like this, which finds no echo in one's own heart?"

"True, Meah, and may it long be so with you," returned his companion; "but your experience of life is as yet small, and as it increases I fear you will search in vain for the purity which your own heart now pictures. Perhaps it may exist among women. Sree Swami knows, and you may find it there. I have not, Meah; but in the world abroad, when you have more to do with it, your sensitive spirit will become blunted by degrees, and, though a serious matter like this will trouble it, you will gradually learn to pass many a broad lie or rogue's trick which now vexes you, without notice beyond a passing curse or a hasty blow. Patience, Meah Sahib! thou hast much to learn yet; would it were good, and not evil!"

"Ah, would it were, Bulwunt Rao! Your experience is from the crooked ways and thoughts of your own people, of which men make proverbs; but for a noble of the state to betray his salt in this base manner, makes me sick at heart. But this is no time, friend, to think of aught but the work we have to do; and what more has to come of the night we know not. Hark! the thunder growls again, and the storm is coming up fast—we had as well run on to shelter; and what more may follow, Alla knows!"

So saying, they hastened as rapidly as the rough ground and increased darkness would admit, Bulwunt Rao guiding his young master through narrow lanes and over deserted spaces, till they again emerged into the now nearly deserted bazar. It was just past midnight, for the trumpter at the guard-house, taking up the signal from the fort gate, had blown a flourish, which was understood by the keepers of liquor-shops in the quarter. The booths were still open, as well as those of confectioners and bhung or opium sellers; but the lights were being extinguished, and the groups which had been concealed within turned into the street.

A wild company truly! Some staggering in the last stage of idiotic drunkenness from opium, others tossing their arms wildly in the air, while their obscene and fearful curses and imprecations mingled with the low muttering of the thunder, which hardly ceased, and seemed to grow nearer every moment. Many forms lay prostrate in the street—some sleeping off the fumes of drink, or groaning in helpless intoxication; and they were often beset by women, whose loosened hair and disordered garments, and the wild leer of their glistening eyes, bespoke their depraved condition. But, casting those who were most importunate violently aside, they at length gained the temple, which was close to the drinking-shop we have before mentioned, and paused for a moment near the gate, which was now shut, while all was silent within.

"Let me look over thee, Meah," said his companion, "as we have a little light, and are free from those drunken wretches. Dost thou know, Meah, I have been like them sometimes, I fear; but this sight sickens and sobers me."

"God grant it, friend, it is the only thing I have ever feared in you," he replied warmly.

"Yes, it will do," continued Bulwunt; "the disguise is complete. So—the chin scarf a little more over the end of the nose: there—no one would ever suspect you. Now, I have a plan in my head, which thou wilt say could only come of a Mahratta's brain—crooked and wilful. It is this: I think, from bazar gossip, that Tannajee and Pahar Singh are one, and that they have met at Tooljapoor at the temple, or at that old villain Bussunt Geer's, at whose Mutt Tannajee's people put up, or that they have corresponded with each other through him. It is not very long since I was there—about two months ago, Meah. They were very busy—so much so that the old fox would hardly let me stay; but I was certain there was something going on; and now I have seen Pahar Singh, I am sure he came one day and held counsel with the old Gosai. Now, if Tannajee has not been there—as I will find out, if possible—I can personate Poorun Geer, the disciple of Bussunt Geer, and we may find out more of this plot. But be thou silent—a vow of silence for a year. I dread thy courtly speech breaking out even of our rough Mahratta tongue or a Mussulmani oath. Trust to me, Meah: I will not fail thee if we meet this fellow!"

"I would we had brought the guard with us, Bulwunt," said Fazil.

"Guard!" said his companion, laughing. "Look, there are his

sentinels. That fellow," pointing to a figure seated at a little distance on the ground, muffled in a black blanket, and hardly to be distinguished from an animal or a stone, "is one. I saw him shift his position so as to watch us; and I see three others in different directions, Meah; one will cough, or sneeze, or make some signal when we move—and there is old Rama in the doorway, listening. Guard, Meah! no, no; we may kill Tannajee if we are lucky, but were a guard to approach, he would be off into the deserted ground at the back, and who could find him? Now, come; and may the gods protect us!"

It was but a few steps. As they moved past, a low cough proceeded from the sitting figure on the watch, and a light streamed from the doorway as the publican, Rama, moved in.

"Did you see that?" whispered Bulwunt—"is it not as I told you? Keep your sword ready, Meah; but be not hasty, whatever you may see or hear."

So saying, they stepped into the vestibule of the shop—an open space, around which were benches of raised earth or brick, neatly plastered over. A counter with some brass measures and a large copper vase, brightly polished, containing spirit, stood at one side, and a lamp burned in a niche.

Bulwunt took one of the brass drinking-cups and rattled it against another as a signal; for, as he supposed, the owner of the place had gone to an inside apartment. As he came forth, Bulwunt accosted him, and requested two hookas to be filled—one with tobacco, the other with ganja, and was advancing to the inner apartment when the man stopped him.

"There are no hookas to be had here to-night; it is past the hour, Babajee," he said, "and I am out of ganja till to-morrow. Nor can you go in there, for the place is engaged; and they who are within will not brook being disturbed."

"Ha! then there is play going on, Rama; and that is what we came for—a new hand is always welcome. Go and tell them there are two *gentlemen* without who would join."

"Play? No, truly," cried the man—"they have other work to do. But go your way, both of ye, for I cannot admit either of you at this time of night, and have no hookas for you to smoke. Begone; there are plenty of mudud khanas in the street besides mine, where you can get all you want. Begone, ere the rain increases."

"Nay, be not inhospitable, good fellow," returned Bulwunt, soothingly; "and here is a trifle for thee—even for shelter. Hark to the thunder!" And as he spoke, another blinding flash of lightning illumined the interior of the shop, while a crashing peal of thunder followed hard upon it. "We shall have more of that, Rama; and as to stirring out in the rain,"—for it had come plashing down with the thunder—"whose dog am I that I should go out in it—I or my brother either? Is this a night to turn two votaries of Sree Mahadeo into the streets—strangers, too, who know no other place of shelter? And were we not told to come to Rama's shop near the temple?" he added to Fazil; who, sitting down, nodded assent, and followed his example.

"There is a Gosai's Mutt hard by, round the corner," returned the man doggedly, "and a temple of Bhowani away yonder, in the plain at the back, among the tamarind trees. You will find your brethren in one, and shelter and water in the other, if ye need them. Begone, and trouble me no more. Get up; why sit ye there unbidden? Get up!"

"Get up and go to a Mutt, indeed!" retorted Bulwunt, who did not move, but, on the contrary, settled himself more determinedly and doggedly upon a seat. "Not I—in this rain! How, brother?" he added to Fazil, "shall we attempt to enter the Mutt at night through barred doors?—be taken for thieves, and be fired upon for our pains, perhaps?" Fazil shook his head. "No: we were told to come here to Rama's—is thy name Rama, friend?—and here we are."

"Who told ye to come here?" asked the kullal.

"It concerns thee not, good man," replied Bulwunt, "unless they call you Rama."

"That is my name; and what is your business with me?" he returned sulkily.

"That you will know by-and-by," replied Bulwunt. "Meanwhile, as to the Mutt and the temple, who knows whether there is either the one or the other; and who can go to look in this storm? Wherefore, worthy sir," he continued to the keeper of the place, "we are very comfortable, and intend to remain. We are not beasts to be turned out in rain like this. So, kindly bring the hookas, and when we have smoked we will rest after our long travel to-day. As to those here before us, we are not likely to molest them; and if they do not let us alone, we have weapons, and can defend ourselves. Therefore, be reasonable." Bulwunt spoke loudly, that he might be heard by the men within.

"What noise is that?" suddenly asked a strange voice from behind a partition close to which they were sitting. "Did I not tell thee, Rama, to admit no one?"

"May I be your sacrifice, Rao Sahib," returned the kullal, joining his hands together, and advancing to the door of the room, "your slave desired these two Gosais to depart civilly, but they will not move; they say they were told to come here, and ask for hookas. When I told them to be gone, one fellow talked about his weapons, and I believe they are drunk."

"About weapons, did he, Rama? and who art thou, mad youth,

who venturest here into the privacy of gentlemen?" said a tall man, who now advanced from behind the partition with a sword in his left hand, while, observing that Bulwunt Rao and Fazil were armed, his right hand passed to his sword-hilt, and rested there, with a determined action.

How the stern tones of his voice thrilled to the heart of Bulwunt Rao, as he listened to them after an interval of many years. When he last heard them he was a mere youth. Shrieks of women were ringing in his ears, and his enemy's fierce commands to kill and spare none—hurried shouts, and the clash of steel. As he stood, the past recurred to Bulwunt Rao so vividly that, though years had intervened, it seemed only as if that night had gone, and morning had succeeded. There could be no doubt he was in Maloosray's presence. The same grave, determined manner—the same large black eye—as the proverb about him said, "Gentle as a fawn's, or fierce as a tiger's—the same deep-toned voice. Time had hardly tinged his whiskers and moustaches with grey, but his face was weather-beaten and seared, as it were, by the sun, and his large bony frame more developed, than when they had last met—the boy and the cruel fiery youth. The light from a rude lamp in a niche of the wall threw a strong glare upon his face, which he did not seek to evade; while the features of Bulwunt Rao and his companion were in a great measure concealed by the shadow thrown upon them in the corner where they sat.

"A poor Gosai," answered Bulwunt in the Mahratta tongue, but in a tone as haughty as that in which he had been addressed, "who, with his brother, has sought shelter here and refreshment. Why shouldst thou interfere?"

"Ha! a proud speech, young sir; and your companion, why does he not answer?" returned Maloosray.

"He has a vow of silence for a year, made at the shrine of our Mother of Tooljapoor," returned Bulwunt, doggedly.

"Enough," cried Maloosray, "begone in her name! There is a temple of hers a gunshot from hence; begone to it."

"We must know who it is that has the power to send us hence ere we stir foot to depart," retorted Bulwunt, rising, and raising his really fine figure to its full height; and as Fazil Khan followed his example, both were ready to meet any sudden assault. "Who dares, I say, send us out in such rain? Are we men or dogs, to be put out with insult from a public place in such weather?"

Tannajee's sword was drawn in an instant, and flashed brightly in the flickering glare of the lamp. The others were as rapidly unsheathed; but both parties stood on the defensive,—neither struck.

"For the love of Mahadeo, for the love of Bhowani, by your fathers' heads! no blood-shedding here, good sirs!" cried the keeper of the house imploringly, passing between them, and stretching out his hands deprecatingly to each in turn. "I shall be ruined! fined!—they will hang me! Hold! there will be blood shed. Help! help!" he shrieked in a frantic manner, seeing Tannajee advance a step.

Hearing his cries and the altercation, two men rushed from the inner apartment with drawn weapons, and would have attacked the others at once, but Tannajee withheld them.

"Peace!" he cried; "put down your weapons, friends. Peace, bold youth!" he continued to Bulwunt Rao; "you have run a fearful risk unmoved, which you do not know of. Who are you?" he asked rapidly.

"A Gosai: I have said it already," replied the other.

"A disciple of what teacher?"

"How are you to know, even if I tell it truly, who my Gooroo is?" returned Bulwunt. "Is Bussunt Geer of Tooljapoor known to you?"

"Ha! Bussunt Geer of Tooljapoor? but his cheyla is Poorun Geer, not thou?"

"Maharaj, it is true; but I am the younger. Poorun Geer stays with the Gooroo."

"And your name?"

"As-Geer."

"When were you made a cheyla?"

"About a year ago; and I was at Bhaga Nugger and Golconda till lately; in the house there."

"And what has brought you here?"

"I do not answer questions except upon the Gooroo's business," replied Bulwunt haughtily.

"Good, thou art discreet, O Babajee! And thy companion?"

"He is a novitiate under a vow of silence for a year."

"Good. Let there be peace between us for a while, till I prove thee true or false."

Bulwunt was about to make a passionate reply, when the imploring look of Fasil met his eye. It seemed to say, Go on with this deception; and, after a moment's thought, Bulwunt Rao determined to do so, and to refrain from violence so long as it suited his purpose. Ready himself to strike if needful, he might be able to throw Tannajee off his guard.

"Listen," continued Tannajee; "by one question I shall know if thou art true or false. If true, well for thee, Baba; if false, by the holy 'Mata!' hadst thou ten men's lives, and ten others to back thee, thou shouldst die like a dog."

"That is easier to say than to do," returned Bulwunt in a contemptuous tone. "I have seen enough of bullies at Bhaga Nugger to fear big words. But speak; if I can answer your question, well; if not, what is in my hand may reply to anything further."

Maloosray laughed aloud—a short bitter laugh, very grating to hear. "How much ganja hast thou smoked, O Baba?" he asked with a sneer; "but stay, this is folly. If thou art Poorun Geer's cheyla, thou knowest Pahar Singh?"

"What Pahar Singh?—him of Itga?"

"The same: we call him of Allund."

"The Hazaree?"

"Ay—Hazaree, robber, Gosai, murderer, if thou wilt. If he is known to thee, why ask? By Khundoba! I distrust this fellow," he added to the two others, who closed up to him; "why did he ask?"

"I know him," said Bulwunt doggedly, "he is here."

"Where?"

"He was in the temple of Bhowani behind there less than half an hour ago, for I spoke to him."

"Thou? why?"

"I had a message from the Gooroo for him."

"And where is he now?"

"Nay, how should I know? I saw him there with one Maun Singh, and another, whom I knew not."

"Strange that he should not have come," continued Maloosray, after a pause. "Art thou sure of the man?"

"As sure as that——" Bulwunt had nearly spoken his adversary's name, but a twitch from Fazil checked him. "As sure as that I see thee, O Maharaj."

"And who am I?"

"Nay, I know not, nor care. My message was to Pahar Singh, and it was delivered. I was told to come here to meet some others; ye may be they. Pahar Singh may be yet at the temple," observed Bulwunt, who trusted to his ingenuity to get rid of one of the men. "Why not send for him?"

"A good thought," said Maloosray; "go at once, Abajee," he observed to the smaller of the two men. "Here is my blanket—the rain will not signify, and take one of the men with you."

"And bring Pahar Singh here, Maharaj?" asked the man, sheathing his sword, and turning to look for his shoes, which were near a door they had not observed.

"Yes. Tell him I am here with Bussunt Geer's cheyla, and that there is no fear. If he be gone, come away; we will await you."

As Maloosray turned slightly to speak the last words, a look of intelligence passed between Fazil and Bulwunt; but though the odds against them had been withdrawn, Maloosray's suspicions had apparently not relaxed in the least, for he stood, his weapon ready for action, and his shield advanced before his body, so that Bulwunt had as yet no opportunity to strike as he desired. His account of himself was plausible enough, but it did not apparently satisfy the wily Mahratta.

"And Pahar Singh was there, Baba?" he asked; "know you for certain? What message had you to him?"

"Nay, it was easy enough, Maharaj," returned Bulwunt; "all he told me was, to meet Pahar Singh at the temple of Bhowani, near the kullal's quarter, this night, and afterwards to come to Rama's shop near the temple, where I should find some Mahrattas who would give me a message. I have reached Beejapoor in four days, and must return to-morrow. If you are the person I was to meet here, tell me what I am to say, and I will go; for we need a lodging for the night, and our horses are in the city."

"Where?" asked Maloosray.

"At the Taj Bowree;* but I shall be away by early dawn."

"But the fort gate will be shut, Baba."

"I have a friend at the wicket who will let us in. Do not fear for that, Maharaj!" replied Bulwunt confidently.

Maloosray thought for a moment. "It must be true," he added. "Now, Baba, listen; if I trust thee, couldst thou help the cause Bussunt Geer has at heart?"

"I will be faithful to him; is he not my Gooroo?"

"And thy companion?"

"Surely, as myself. We are one."

"Then listen," said Maloosray, for once thrown off his guard, and now leaning upon his sword. "I believe this tale could not have been invented, for no one knows, but the Gooroo, why Pahar Singh would venture to Beejapoor, and what need he had to bring me here. I do not care to see Pahar Singh, who is a stupid ruffian; but if thou wilt deliver my message to Bussunt Geer in four days, it may save trouble to many people, and help what we have in hand. Tell him if he can get the Lalla's papers, to keep them; if Pahar Singh has them, to make him keep them till Khan Mahomed can redeem them. They will be worth thousands—lakhs, perhaps, if they are what I think. Tell the Gooroo that Sivaji Bhóslay will not be unmindful of his care in this matter; say also that Pahar Singh has disappointed me, and it is better the message went through thee; for who can trust one who has a double face, and who is with the King to-day, Sivaji the next, Alumgeer the day after—fickle and covetous, looking only after gold. Yet, if he please to meet me, he knows the place and the time. Hast thou comprehended all this?"

* The Royal well, which is surrounded by cloisters and rooms, where travellers still put up.

"Fully; but thy name? Thou mayst be an impostor. Whom shall I tell him I met at this place, and whose message am I to believe?"

"He did not tell thee? He was afraid, perhaps, my name should be heard in Beejapoor; but I laugh at such precautions. Say that the servant of Sivaji Bhóslay—one Tannajee Maloosray—bids thee say what I have told thee."

"Tannajee——"

"Ay! Tannajee Maloosray. If thou art from Poona thou mayst chance to have heard of it."

"Maloosray of Rohéla?"

"The same; there is no other Tannajee Maloosray living——"

"And I, villain and murderer! am Bulwunt Rao of Sewnee," he shouted, no longer able to control himself, and assaulting his hereditary enemy with all his force. "Upon them, Meah, in the name of the King! Hur, hur! Mahadeo!"

It was well for Maloosray that the point of Bulwunt's sword caught a projecting rafter of the low roof as it descended, else he had never spoken more. Nevertheless it reached him; and though a steel chain had been woven into his turban, which prevented a severe wound, the force of the blow somewhat stunned him; and so fierce and unexpected was the assault, that for an instant his habitual presence of mind failed him. But for an instant only. Ere Bulwunt could repeat the blow, Maloosray had leaped aside, and began to press his impetuous adversary very closely. Fazil, in his turn, had attacked the companion of Maloosray, and found him a wary swordsman; and the place, confined as it was, afforded no room for rapid movement; while the light was dim and treacherous. Blows were, however, rapidly exchanged. The quarrel could not continue long: for the shouts and cries of the keeper of the house, and of several of Maloosray's scouts, who were unarmed, aroused the guard, who rushed to the spot with loud exclamations and drawn weapons.

Tannajee felt in an instant that he had no chance if they entered, and he knew that if taken his execution would be immediate and certain. Just, therefore, as the dark figure of the foremost of the guard was entering the shop behind Bulwunt, and by whose rapid tread and shouts he was somewhat thrown off his guard, Tannajee gathered himself up for a desperate blow, and delivered it with an abusive imprecation. "Once I failed," he said—"not now!" As he spoke, the heavy weapon descended with all his great strength; Bulwunt tried to stop it, but it caught the edge, not the face of the shield, and, though he partially succeeded, or he had never breathed more, glancing from the hard and polished edge of the shield, it lighted upon Bulwunt's bare neck and shoulder, cutting down to the bone in a ghastly manner.

Maloosray saw with exultation that the blood poured forth in a torrent, and, as Bulwunt staggered and fell back, he called to his companion to follow him, and both darted through the back apartments into a court leading into a narrow street beyond, and as they passed they closed both the doors behind them.

"Follow me!—a thousand rupees for Tannajee Maloosray's head!" cried Fazil to the guard; and though they pursued him for a short distance, all chance of capturing him was hopeless in that murky darkness and heavy rain.

CHAPTER XXIV.

It was no fear of Maloosray or lack of enterprise that caused the young Khan to desist from his pursuit; but finding that his retainer had not followed him, nor, indeed, any of the guard—the fear that Bulwunt might have been wounded occurred to him, or that he had been apprehended and detained. It was hopeless also to trace Maloosray, or to ascertain which way he and his companion had proceeded, as they issued from the door of the courtyard into the lane behind. Turning back then, after he had run a few paces, by the way he had come, and directed by the clamour inside the house, he passed rapidly through the yard, and entered the room where the quarrel had taken place; this he found filled with armed men, with several torch-bearers standing around what appeared to be the dead body of his friend.

Fazil had observed Maloosray's violent attack upon him, and that Bulwunt retreated a step or two to avoid it; while at the same time he had advanced towards his own antagonist. The consequences of that blow, therefore, were not immediately seen by him. Now inexpressibly shocked and grieved by the result, Fazil heeded no one; but pressing his way through those assembled, somewhat roughly, he threw himself on his knees beside Bulwunt, who was quite insensible, and, laying aside his sword, strove to raise him up. He saw indeed with great grief that Bulwunt had received a very severe wound; and the pool of blood flowing from the cut, which had not been stanched, and his apparently lifeless condition, caused the most lively alarm.

"Will no one help me?" cried Fazil, looking round, while vainly endeavouring to stanch the blood which occasionally welled from the gaping wound, as Bulwunt breathed heavily. "For the love of God and the Apostle lend me thy waist-band, good sir!" he continued, addressing a respectable-looking man who had accompanied the soldiers, and who was, in fact, the petty officer over them; "or bid some one loose my waistcloth, else he will perish. Alas, my true friend and brother!"

"And who are you," returned the man contemptuously, "who, in the dress of a Kafir Gosai, dares to take the name of the holy Apostle? —on whom be peace!—a thief or murderer, I warrant. How say you, brother! He may have done this himself, and now mingles with us to pretend grief and avoid suspicion. Here is some evil, depend upon it; seize him and bind him fast."

"Yes, my lords," cried the keeper of the house, who now ventured forward, "bind him fast. That is the fellow who did the murder. They quarrelled over their ganja; and though I did all I could to prevent them——"

"Peace!" cried Fazil, accustomed only to command, and who could ill brook the measures threatened; for several men had closed about him at their officer's order, while another had kicked away his sword, which one of the men was picking up. "Peace, I say; raise him up! See, he is badly wounded; have you no compassion? He will die!"

"Whether he dies or whether he lives, one would think it was little concern of thine, boy," replied the man; "and there is blood on his sword, too," he added, as the man who had possessed himself of it held it up to the light. "Seize him, brother, and bind him fast; he will have to answer for this in the morning. Who art thou, ill-born?"

As the leader of the party spoke, several of the soldiers had thrown themselves upon Fazil, who still kneeled beside Bulwunt, and, holding him down, pulled the turban rudely from his head, and in an instant bound his arms with it so tightly behind his back that the act caused him immediate and exquisite pain.

"Who art thou, knave?" asked the man again peremptorily.

"Speak," cried several of the men, shaking him rudely; "don't you hear what his worship says to you? Speak!"

"It is useless for me now to say who I am," replied Fazil looking round. "Enough that I am one of your own faith, as ye will know when the morning breaks;—one who may be able to punish you for rough uncivil usage, or reward you if that poor fellow is speedily aided. I care little what happens to myself; but if ye know of a physician near, or a skilful barber, I pray, good sir," he continued, addressing himself to the officer, "send for him, that a valuable life may be saved."

This speech was received with a shout of derision by most of the party; but their leader was not unobservant, and he saw at once, by the manner and speech of Fazil, that he was no common person; certainly not, what his attire proclaimed him to be, a Gosai. There was a chance that he might be some one of rank in disguise. The keeper of the house had declared him to be the man who had struck down the unfortunate Bulwunt; but, again, the consideration of his return to the spot, and his sincere grief at the poor fellow's wound, went far to assure the officer that his prisoner had not done the deed, and that whoever did it had escaped. These thoughts rapidly occurring, caused the Duffadar to doubt whether rigour was needful. "Art thou a Gosai?" he asked again. "Answer truly!"

"There is no God but God, and Mahomed is the Prophet of God," exclaimed Fazil, repeating the creed, and, as rapidly as possible, in Arabic, the first part of the midnight prayer. "No, good sir, I am no Gosai, but a humble disciple of the Prophet, on whom be peace!"

"Toba, Toba! now shame on me that I should have put a Mussulman to disgrace," exclaimed the Duffadar. "Loose him, friends—we will see to this; and run one of ye to the respectable Meer Hoosein, who lives in the alley yonder, and is a skilful doctor; and, if I mistake not, there is a clever barber, one Nunda, who lives near him, and who is accustomed to matters of this kind. Bid him bring his needles to sew up the wound. And, hark ye, no excuses from either about the rain and lateness of the night; this is the King's business, and a matter of life and death."

Then turning to Bulwunt, who had been raised up while Fazil's arms were being unbound, and who appeared sensible, he spoke cheerfully to him, biding him not to be afraid, for he would be well treated.

"Water!" gasped the poor fellow, looking dreamily about him and pointing to his mouth—"Water!"

"Here is a vessel full," cried a bearded soldier, advancing; "drink, friend."

"Hold," said Fazil, "he is a Hindu; he will not take it from you. Where is the kullal? Let him get some."

"Here, great sir," said the man, advancing with a brass vessel full. "Who is he? May he take water from me?"

"He is a Mahratta," replied Fazil.

"Then there is no fear," added the kullal, and he knelt down and poured a little into Bulwunt's mouth, who drank it eagerly, and, laying hold of the vessel itself, took a long draught, which seemed to revive him; while the kullal, untying the scarf about his chin, wetted it with water and applied it to the wound; and, removing his turban, also wetted his head.

This treatment soon revived Bulwunt, who now sat up and passed his hand dreamily over his eyes, but did not speak.

"He seems recovering," said the Duffadar to Fazil, who had been pulled to one side and was held by two men, though his arms were untied. "So far thou art fortunate, young sir; but, in the name of the saints, why didst thou strike him down? Was this well?

'Twas but yesterday that the Kótwal swore on the Koran that he would have the right arm of the first brawler who should do murder: pity such fate should befall thee, young as thou art! Are there not enough of the Shah's enemies abroad to try thy weapons upon, without mixing in midnight brawls? But speak to thy friend, if friend he is. It may have been a hasty blow, deeply regretted."

"Sir, you are under some extraordinary mistake," said Fazil, who had several times tried to interrupt the speaker. "I am not the man who did this. Ho! Bulwunt, Bulwunt!" he continued, "speak if you can, and fear not. I am here, and these are friends."

"Meah," said the poor fellow very faintly, "I am badly hurt. I may die, Ai Narayun! Ai Bhugwân!—Water, Meah! I am faint and sick,"—and he fell back almost insensible.

"Loose my arms, good sir," cried Fazil impatiently; "I am no thief to run away. If there be a Hindu among you, give him some water. I may not do so."

"Let him go," said the Duffadar to the men, "there is some mistake here, I think, and no enmity between them; and do thou, Jewun Singh, fetch a vessel of water—he will drink from thy hand freely."

Fazil's first act on being released was to examine the wound, which was severe, and required care. The sabre of Maloosray had cut deep into the neck, close to the shoulder, and the loss of blood had been very great. A little higher up and the wound must have been instantly fatal. To wring out the scarf which the kullal had placed upon it, and replace it wetted, was Fazil's first care, and in this the Duffadar and some of the men now lent a willing hand. Fresh cool water was also brought by the man who had been sent for it, and Bulwunt Rao, having again drunk freely, sat up supported by his young lord.

"Ask him now, Duffadar Sahib," said Fazil, "whether it was I who wounded him, and, on his reply, give me liberty or not as seems good to you. Speak, Bulwunt Rao, did I hurt you?"

"Now may his tongue rot who says so," replied the wounded man, looking wildly about him. "But thou art safe, Meah!—and did they escape?"

"Who?" asked the Duffadar sharply.

"Tannajee Maloosray, the friend of Sivaji Bhóslay," returned Bulwunt. "People know of him, perhaps!"

"Tannajee Maloosray? Thou art dreaming, friend," said the Duffadar, with an incredulous smile. "Tannajee dared no more enter Beejapoor than—than——"

"Than you, good sir, dare go to him, I suppose," said Fazil, ending the sentence. "Nevertheless, he was here, and but for a mischance would have been lying dead there."

"Tannajee here!" mused the Duffadar; "this must, then, be some deep plot, and the city is full of plots. Sir," he said to the young Khan, "the mention of that name, and all the events we have seen, cause many suspicions in my mind which I am not competent to dispose of; therefore, whoever thou art, release is impossible till the morning, when I must give an account of all matters to the Kótwal, who has cautioned the guards to be watchful against Mahratta parties and Moghul emissaries."

"Willingly," replied Fazil. "I could not leave him now, nor till his wound is dressed. As for myself, I am Fazil, the son of Afzool Khan, though I may not tell why I am disguised as an infidel, and why found in this place; suffice it to say it was in the King's service."

"Now may I receive my lord's pardon," cried the old man, presenting humbly the hilt of his sword as an offering. "Why did he not tell me sooner, and this offence and presumption would have been spared? Who among us does not know the valiant Afzool Khan, and have not all heard of his son Fazil Khan, the pillar of the state?" he added to the men, who fell back, saluting the young man with mingled curiosity and respect.

"Give me some water," said Fazil. "This dress and appearance are against me, Duffadar," he continued, laughing; "and if I had told who I was when ye seized me first, my arms might even have been bound a screw tighter perhaps. It does not signify now, for you only did your duty, as I can bear witness. Ah, the water is come—pour it over my hands, good fellow, and after the paint has disappeared, some of ye may know me."

"I know you, my lord," said a youth who pressed forward, as Fazil turned again to the light from the door where he had been washing his face. Yes, father," he continued to the Duffadar, "this is truly the brave young Khan—no doubt of that;" and he stepped forward and touched Fazil's feet.

"Too dangerous, too dangerous," said the Duffadar, "for one like him. Yes, thou art right, Ashruf—now I know the face too; but the disguise was perfect; who could have guessed it? Too dangerous: and thou the only son of the noble Khan! Ah, sir, had any evil befallen thee——"

"No matter if I had died," cried Fazil, "it would have been in the Shah's service; but here are the physician and barber, and my friend's wound must be dressed; and do one of ye see for that kullal, who knows more of Tannajee than any one else. Where is he?"

While some of the men went to search for the kullal, the barber, having trimmed the lamp and increased the light by several wicks, unfastened a leathern case containing razors and other instruments, and selecting two cróoked needles fitted with waxed silk thread, put them aside, while he washed the wound clean in a careful and confident manner. A few stitches brought the lips of the cut together, after which it was bound up with fresh leaves of the neem tree, which cooled the wound and refreshed the patient.

All this having been effected, Bulwunt Rao was carefully raised up and borne by several of the men to the chowree, or guard-room, which was hard by, but at the opposite side of the quarter to that in which the Lalla had been lodged.

CHAPTER XXV.

WHILE search was being made for the kullal, Fazil's thoughts reverted painfully to his father and sister. He could not leave Bulwunt without exposing himself to further suspicion; but he might at least send news of his safety, and his application to the Duffadar for a messenger was promptly acceded to.

"Surely, Khan," was the prompt reply, "I could hardly refuse your going yourself, if you asked; but it is better you stayed. Men's tongues are bad, and I am only a humble man. Verily I will send my own son Ashruf, and he will do the errand carefully. He is gone—that is, my son Ashruf—my lord, to see the barber home, and will be here directly. A brave youth, O Khan, and with a large heart. Does my lord remember the Friday's fight with the Moghuls in the plain by Allapoor? Well, in that my boy did good service, and in killing one of the enemy got a sharp cut himself over the arm, but he did not care for it; and was he not fighting on the strength of the King's salt?"

"Indeed, I remember it well, Duffadar," returned Fazil, "for I was beaten down, and wellnigh killed myself, when this poor friend of mine here rescued me. How, Bulwunt! was it not that day?"

"Ay, Meah, that very day," he said faintly; "the last battle Bulwunt Rao will ever see in thy service. I am very faint, Meah. These films before my eyes seem to precede death. I pray thee leave me not here."

"Nay, fear not," replied Fazil; "the barber said there was no danger of life. Be of good heart, Bulwunt—no bones are cut; and though there is much weakness from loss of blood, you will soon be well. Get to sleep, we shall not leave before daylight."

"I do not fear, Meah. Death has no pain or regret for me. My only wish was to die in the service of your house. I am the last of my race, and have no one to mourn for me like thee, Meah! I would live for thee if it be the will of God; and but for this, death would be welcome."

"Peace! do not speak, friend," returned Fazil; "go to sleep, and thou wilt be strong ere morning. Does not the barber, I tell thee, say there is no danger? so be comforted."

"None perhaps of life, Meah; but this arm, which was all I had to live for, it will never hold sword more, Meah—never, never!" and he sobbed like a child.

"Fear not," cried the Duffadar cheerily; "I have worse wounds on me than that, Rao Sahib, and yet my arm can strike a blow for the Shah; so be comforted, and get to sleep."

Bulwunt sighed. "If I had only slain him," he said, "and revenged the dead, then I could have died; or if this arm had gone for that, its best service in life would have been done. I shall never have such a chance again, Meah. But the gods have need of him, and he has the protection of Dévi. He and Sivaji Bhóslay both have it, as ye will see hereafter, Meah. Who can resist them?"

"This is the youth of whom I spake, Khan Sahib," said the Duffadar; "a brave boy—a brave boy he always was."

And truly there was much in the appearance of the youth to corroborate this. An open, dare-devil, good-humoured countenance, with bright merry eyes, which, as he spoke, seemed to close up till two bright sparks only were visible; and a wide bow-shaped mouth, about which fun, and perhaps some mischief, played in perpetual smiles, conveyed an impression of recklessness of danger, as a lithe rapidity of movement did of extreme activity of body, and perhaps endurance.

"A brave youth, doubtless, Duffadar Sahib," said Fazil; "his eye speaks for him; a boy to be proud of. How sayst thou, lad? Wilt thou do an errand for the son of Afzool Khan?"

"Ay will I," replied the boy promptly, while he presented his sword-hilt to the young Khan, as his father had done; "and gladly too; and if my lord will pardon me for saying it, I have long known him. Who does not know the brave son of a brave father? Ah, Meah Sahib! if I had only been on a horse when Afzool Khan's Paigah dashed into the Moghul's that Friday, I would have struck a blow with you. I watched you as you rode by close to the standard-bearer. Then there was a fierce fight, and men said you were cut down. Ah! I was only on foot, for we are too poor to ride; and I was—a little wounded," he added, dropping his eyes modestly, "and father led me away. But for that, Meah Sahib, I would have been with you, even on foot."

"Boldly spoken, and with a true heart, Ashruf!" exclaimed Fazil; "and if you do this errand carefully and quickly for me, you shall ride ever after with me in my troop—that is, if your father will permit it. Afzool Khan's stables have enough horses to find one for you. Of that, however, more hereafter. Go now to the house, ask for Goolab the nurse; tell her I am safe, but that Bulwunt Rao is wounded badly, and a palankeen must be sent for him with all speed, and my clothes and shawls put into it. If my father be asleep, he is not to be awakened, but my sister must know that I am safe. Now begone; here is my ring, which will pass you through the fort. Let us see how soon you will return."

"Come, Shékh Hoosein," said the lad, addressing a young man standing near; "we had better be two. Tie up thy waist-band tight, for we shall not draw breath till we reach the city gate. Come!"

Both loosened their waist-scarfs, and retied them tighter, and after a few words of caution from the Duffadar, they dashed down the street at full speed.

As they left, several of the men came in, leading the kullal by the end of his turban, with which his arms were tightly tied down. Bareheaded, covered with mud, and bleeding slightly from his nose, his face wearing an expression of fright and pain combined, Rama was a very different-looking person to what he had appeared when Fazil Khan and Bulwunt entered his shop. His first impulse was to cast himself on the ground before Fazil, and lie at full length moaning. The men who were with him did not interfere. The act was a deprecation of anger which it would have been unmannerly to deny.

"Get up," cried Fazil; "get up, knave and liar! Say, was it I who wounded that poor fellow yonder?"

"Pardon! pardon! Noble Meah, pardon! Your slave will not rise till he has pardon," cried the man abjectly. "It was all a mistake; and how could I know the son of Afzool Khan? Pardon! and I will tell all I know."

"If thou dost not, hound! thou wilt hang upon the highest branch of the Goruk Imlee to feed the crows before morn," replied Fazil. "Get up! If thou tellest the truth, I give thee kowl; if not—if I detect one word of lie, nothing can save thee. Dost thou hear? Rise!"

"Get up, Kafir!" cried the man who held the turban, giving it a jerk, which caused a corresponding exclamation of pain. "Don't you hear what my lord says to you? He will give you pardon if you speak the truth. Get up, and tell him all. My lord," he continued to Fazil, "he knows much, and he has some papers which one of the fellows—Maloosray, he says—dropped as he left the house. We wanted them, but he said you would pardon him if he gave them himself. We found him hiding in the wood stack near his still, and the fool must needs struggle and try to wrestle with one of our men, and so got a fall; but he is not hurt."

"Loose my arms, noble Meah—tell them to loose my arms. They are swelling already, and I am sick with pain," said the kullal, rising.

"If my lord allows me, I will loose him. There!" continued the soldier, on receiving Fazil's sign in the affirmative; "see thou speak the truth, else I will tie them tighter than ever, and they will not be loosened again while thou art alive."

"My lord, don't threaten me, or I shall lose my senses," said the kullal, the horrible vision of hanging, as he had seen many hang to the branches of that famous tree, coming vividly to his mind. "If there be a good Hindu among you, give me a drink of water. Ah, my arms! my arms!" he cried, sitting down again, and sobbing as the rope was loosened.

"Here is water," said one of the men, advancing with a brass vessel full. "I am a Rajpoot—drink."

The draught refreshed him, and he began his tale. It was in the main correct, and as we have already related it. "Tannajee and his companions had been at his shop only a few minutes before Fazil and Bulwunt came in. They had been very careful, and before they entered the house placed scouts to watch all the approaches. They spoke in low tones, and, beyond a few words now and then, he had caught nothing of their conversation. All that he could gather was, that Pahar Singh and a Gosai from Tooljapoor were expected, and they were so impatient for their arrival, that two of the men had by turns gone to see after them."

"Had they ever been at your shop before?" asked Fazil.

"Yesterday one of the men was there twice to say the place would be wanted in the evening," replied the kullal; "and he gave me ten rupees to say I had neither spirits nor ganja; so I told every one I had none, and no one stayed but you."

"You might have suspected they were after no good," said the Duffadar. "Why did you not give warning here?"

"Ah, sir, I am a poor fellow," returned the man, "with a large family; and if gentlemen sometimes like a private room to smoke, to play, or to talk in, am I to forbid them? Would they not get it elsewhere?"

"True enough—thou art not to blame," said Fazil; "but the papers—what of them?"

"After you were taken away, my lord," replied the kullal, "I took the lamp inside towards the door, for I thought I saw blood on the ground, which indeed there was; and one of the two men who escaped must have been wounded. I followed the trace of blood to the door of the yard, and there I found this little bag, noble sir; here it is."

As he spoke he produced a small silken bag, apparently filled with papers, from under his waistcloth, and handed it to Fazil. In it were several letters, and bundles of accounts written in the Mahratta character.

"I cannot read these, and they may be of importance; so we must wait, for this poor fellow of mine is asleep," said Fazil.

"No, Meah, I was dozing while you spoke, and am easier now, for the bandage has cooled my wound. Papers? What papers?" said Bulwunt, rising slightly, and supporting himself on his left arm. "Give them to me."

"There are some in Mahratta, which Tannajee, or one of his companions, dropped in their flight. Can you make out what they are, Bulwunt?" asked Fazil.

"I will try, Meah; put the light here. Stay; open them separately. I forget that I have but one arm now."

The papers were given to him one by one, and his eye glanced over several in succession as of no importance; but one appeared to interest him greatly, and Fazil observed his eyes return to the commencement after having looked over it hastily, and his lips to move as if reading it word by word, while the expression of his face changed to one of intense concern.

"Yes, Meah, this is indeed important," he said; "but no one must hear it but thyself or thy father. Listen," he continued, whispering; "that is from the old Gosai at Tooljapoor, about those letters the King has obtained. Those whom they concern are mentioned in feigned names, and it will puzzle me not a little to understand their meaning fully; but we have a clue in what occurred at the temple, and I will unravel it when we get home. Now my eyes are too weary. Stay, there may be something from Sivaji. . . . No," he continued, after he had looked at them one by one, "there are none from him, but several from Yessjee, who is his friend. No, they are too wary to write letters; but no doubt there is much intrigue afoot, Meah—much."

"Enough," replied Fazil; "now go to sleep, Bulwunt, till daylight brings people from the house. I too will rest, if I can, after all this excitement, with your permission, Duffadar Sahib——"

But the old man had lain down on the floor while the papers were being examined, and was fast asleep; so also were the men of the guard, except one sitting at the doorway as sentinel, the gurgle of whose hooka mingled with an occasional snore from a sleeper on the floor. Those about the kullal, who had been removed to a little distance, asked how he was to be disposed of.

"Take him to his house," said Fazil, "and keep him there till he is wanted. Go with them, Rama," he continued to the man, "and be ready when I send for thee. I will answer to the Kótwal for the night's events."

"That is all I wanted," he replied. "My lord is very kind and merciful."

"Not yet. I have much to ask and much to hear. If thou canst speak the truth, well for thee; if not, beware!"

CHAPTER XXVI.

How slowly and wearily night passes when a sense of impending evil overpowers sleep, and renders every faculty sharply sensible to sounds and impressions otherwise of ordinary occurrence,—when a thousand vague phantasies flit before the imagination hardly more definite than the keenly-painful thoughts they awaken! How difficult thus to endure delay or uncertainty, and to account for causes of either, so as to gain consolation or assurance to one's self, far less to impart comfort to others whose fears and apprehensions are perhaps greater than our own.

Thus heavily was hour after hour counted by Afzool Khan and his fair daughter in the apartment we have already described. The Khan busied himself, or seemed to do so, with a pile of Persian papers, on some of which, from time to time, he made notes: but it was easy for his daughter to see that his eye often followed vacantly the lines of the writing, and that his thoughts wandered far from the subjects before him.

The Khan's wife, Lurlee, had come, and been dismissed with an injunction not to interrupt him, and that he should be late. Zyna did not disturb her father, and found a partial occupation in some embroidery, which helped to dispel for a time her fears for her brother; gradually, however, as the night wore on, it was easy for her to see that her father's anxiety increased. It was true that Fazil's return was not expected till after midnight; but that, under the thought of his perilous errand, brought no consolation with it, and she sat watching the expression of her father's countenance, yet not so as to be observed, and withdrawing her eyes when he looked up. A few careless words fell from time to time from both, and a few entreaties by the Khan to his daughter that she would take rest, were met by requests that she might be allowed to share his watch, for that she had promised her brother to await his return.

Thus midnight came, and with it sleep to the young girl, that would not be denied. She had folded her scarf about her person, and lay down where she was; and her father now watched his sleeping child, almost wondering at her beauty, as the light fell upon her, and projected a shadow from the long eyelashes upon her soft downy cheek. So, with the image of the dead before him—for he remembered her mother even such an one as her child—Afzool Khan's thoughts wandered far back into the past,—far back to the time when, with life before him and easy competence, the servant of a noble and united kingdom, the future had not concerned him, save only to wish that the happiness he possessed might endure.

But that bright future was long past. The present was dark, uncertain, menacing. Had there been any one to listen, the bitter sob of the old Khan—a sob of exquisite pain as his thoughts alternated between the happy past and a gloomy future—might have been heard,—such pain as those alone can know whose affections and memories of the past arise most vividly to augment any new suffering that may be present. The years of happiness in his home, which might have been his lot had his wife been spared to him, rose to the mind of Afzool Khan as a sad mockery; for though the grave had long held her whose fair form seemed renewed before him, it appeared almost as if she were again present to him in all her beauty.

"Thou art a fair blossom. May God love thee! May the holy saints keep thee! May thy mother watch thee, my child!" murmured the Khan, as he bent over his sleeping daughter. "Even such was thy mother in those first days, as guileless and as beautiful. Nay, thou art but the copy, Zyna. And had she but lived to see thee and thy brother as ye are it would have been well. Yet why not well as it is?" he resumed after a pause; "surely Fate is good whatever it be. If my heart warns me of coming ill—nay, if he too be gone from me, well; he is with her, and the old man will soon follow, and there will be peace, peace, peace! Yet I would live still a little for thee, my child—only for thee! else the first shot or keen sword-cut were welcome to Afzool Khan."

So he thought and watched, and at times gently fanned his child with the papers in his hand that her sleep might be the lighter, and again resumed his occupation of reading. All was silent, but the night wind sighed mournfully through the open trelliswork of the window, and seemed rising; and as he listened, there were mutterings of a coming storm.

Opening one of the small casements, he looked out. The city was dark beneath him, and still; even the dogs seemed to have gone to sleep. Far distant, the wailing howls of a pack of jackals came upon his ear fitfully, and again ceased as the sound was blown away by the wind. Over the face of the sky the wild dark clouds were now hurrying ragidly along, disclosing here and there a star, which was again as instantly hidden. In the west, the horizon was black and threatening, and the edges of a heavy bank of cloud, now fast rising pile over pile, were illumined like burnished silver, as lightning flashed rapidly through them, lighting up the city, and the bold domes and tall minarets of the mosques and mausoleums, with a sickly glare for an instant, to disappear as rapidly as a thought. One of the night-storms of the season was evidently approaching, and the cool fresh wind was grateful to the Khan, as he leaned forth and looked into the void of darkness abstractedly.

The papers he had been perusing had been the subject of consultation that day at the court between the King, his Secretary, and himself. They were reports from the governors of the west and north-west provinces—a country which Afzool Khan had governed some years before, and knew perfectly—and related to a growing disaffection and a rising spirit among the people of the mountain valleys, which could not be accounted for save by the intrigues and machinations of Sivaji Bhóslay and his adherents. Sivaji, as a restless youth, had before risen in petty insurrection, and had resisted small forces sent against him, but had renewed his fidelity to the State, and had been pardoned. Notwithstanding, however, he was believed to be active in evil designs; and report assigned to him constant communication and intrigue with the Moghul emperor Aurungzeeb, as well as endeavours, on his own account, to excite the people.

Afzool Khan was no indifferent spectator of these events. He was one of those who, with others of his rank, had received profuse promises from the Emperor during his first invasion of the kingdom; and though Aurungzeeb's intentions had not been finally declared, yet Afzool Khan knew that if he favoured his cause, even secretly, for the present, he was certain hereafter, should the Emperor prevail, of high rank and rewards far beyond those which he now possessed, and also that the weight and influence of a few men like himself would at once turn the scale against Beejapoor, which already trembled in the balance.

The Moghul party, he well knew, was strong in the city. Many who had been disappointed of court influence almost openly professed it: they had nothing to lose and everything to hope for. But there were others—like the prime-minister, Khan Mahomed, for instance—who, in the enjoyment of large estates, high commands, and immense wealth, still desired more; nay, even the partition of the kingdom, that they might hold what they possessed as independent princes.

Again, Aurungzeeb's zeal for the cause of his faith was a well-known element of his character. He was a strict Soonnee, who held the heretical belief of the Sheeas in hereditary hatred; and the sight of the noble domes of the mosques at Beejapoor filled him with a fervour of bigotry even stronger than the lust of territorial dominion, to subvert the royal house which held those detested tenets.

Afzool Khan was also an orthodox Soonnee. He looked with abomination upon the Sheea ceremonies at the great mosque. He could not join in prayer there, nor could he enter save with the certainty of being offended and insulted by the religious ceremonies of his King. It was equally certain that the doctrines he professed belonged to a strong party in the city, who on all possible occasions urged amalgamation of the country with the empire of Delhi, in order to insure the supremacy of their own creed. Yet he was true.

Like him, the minister Khan Mahomed had been faithful through many temptations; but of late, though he still preserved a fair and honest appearance with the young King, rumour had become busy with his name, and, intimate as was their friendship, the old Khan's trust in him was much shaken under an accumulated mass of suspicion, though, as yet, nothing definite had transpired. Hitherto also the minister's apparently unflinching adherence to what was feared to be a falling dynasty, and to a government which, under foreign invasion, and internal disunion and distraction, had become weakened, had retained Afzool Khan's respect and affection; for this, combined with Khan Mahomed's professed devotion to the young King, who, with excellent dispositions and a fair promise of ability, was yet without experience, formed a strong bond of union between them.

Private friendship, and the free intercourse of camps and battle-fields, had existed for many years; and as their children grew up together, and the beauty of Zyna became notorious, the minister's son, whom we have already mentioned, pressed upon his father, very importunately, the necessity of formally asking her in marriage. But under his own secret hopes of the eventual ascendancy of the Moghuls, and his convictions that the obstinate fidelity of Afzool Khan would sooner or later lead to a serious breach between them, the minister had as yet refrained from taking any steps in the matter; and on his own part Afzool Khan had been equally guarded.

The events of the night, however, would disclose the real tendency of the Wuzeer's conduct; and the thought that there were grounds of more than ordinary suspicion, could not fail to increase the feeling that he was actually guilty, which for some time past had lain at Afzool Khan's heart. He had fancied, too, a growing coldness on the part of the Wuzeer towards him, unlike the spirit of their former free and unrestrained intercourse; and he could not fail to observe, in his visits to his court, that men to whom rumour attached the same suspicions as to the Wuzeer, were preferred as counsellors to himself.

All this, however, had as yet produced no personal disagreement: it was only mistrust, arising from suspicion on both sides; but the Wuzeer well knew that, if his designs were discovered for certain in any degree, he should find in Afzool Khan a powerful and bitter enemy, whose fiery temper and habit of prompt action would make him a far more dangerous enemy than the young King himself. No one, also, knew better than the Wuzeer the temptations to which Afzool Khan had been exposed, and through which he had come as yet unsullied. He knew that in the Moghul army many ties of clanship and acquaintance existed for the Afghan, which the service of Beejapoor did not afford, and that the Emperor, desiring to gain one so faithful, brave, and skilled in the field, who was also a Soonnee, had offered rank, titles, and estates, with his personal friendship and confidence, as yet in vain.

There had been times when Afzool Khan, wearied by petty slights, uncertain as to the future existence of Beejapoor as a kingdom, and comparing the wide field of honour in the imperial service with the narrow circle of Beejapoor, had felt tempted to accept these offers. But the thought had been as often repelled, and had led to a more steadfast and more healthy attachment to the young King; and when Ali Adil Shah, who had but recently succeeded his father Mahmood, displayed the possession of vigour and manly thought, and his disposition and talent appeared really equal to the maintenance of his dignity,—Afzool Khan's fidelity was no longer doubtful, and his openly-evinced confidence in his King had rallied the wavering attachment of many.

A more than ordinary proof of this had been that day given by the King in public Durbar. The Wuzeer was then absent from Beejapoor on service, watching the frontier, with a force to oppose Moghul incursions; and the King had, as an unusual act, invited Afzool Khan into his private chamber, to discuss the contents of the letters of which we have already seen the Khan in possession. They were many, and on many subjects; and the King's trust in the old noble could not have been more heartily evinced than by permitting him to take them home for perusal alone.

They were a tangled skein of intrigue, alarm, and disaffection, of exaggerated rumour and detail of actual occurrences, which were not without signification in the aggregate. If, in reliance on the gradually increasing ability of the King, Afzool Khan had no longer hesitated, but, with the sincerity of an open and faithful heart, showed that he for one no longer doubted, and that his allegiance would be true—others as high in rank, and holding equal or greater territorial possessions, were not so; and, as we have already stated, there was much disaffection, not only in the city, but in the army, and also in the provinces.

So long as the Moghuls had beleagured Beejapoor, men of all parties, and, we may add, creeds also, had united in the common bond of self-preservation; well knowing the plunder and devastation which would ensue if the city were taken by storm or in the course of actual war. This also had been foreseen by the Emperor; and his advices from the traitors within, at the head of whom was the Wuzeer, led him to the conclusion that nothing was to be gained by open force at present. Enough that the seed of disaffection had been sown, which he trusted would, in a comparatively short period, bear the fruit he desired. On these considerations, Aurungzeeb had raised the siege, and lay at a distance in seeming inaction; nevertheless watching the course of events not only with eagerness, but with astute foresight and untiring intrigue. Emissaries were busy in the city, and among the wavering and discontented gained many converts. Money, promises and assurances of protection were freely lavished, not only among the courtiers, but among the frontier chieftains, powerful tributaries, feudatories, and zemindars, who possessed influence over the people, and wherever else it was possible. Village authorities were also canvassed; hereditary rights and immunities guaranteed, with confirmation of former grants from the Beejapoor princes.

All such were openly encouraged to revolt, to withhold payment of revenue, and to harass the government of the State by every means in their power. During the confusion attendant upon the Moghul invasion, many districts had been wrested from the State which could not be regained except at great cost and by the employment of separate forces, which weakened the general efficiency of the army. In some instances, those who had recovered and held such districts, had themselves retained possession of them, fortifying the village ghurrees or castles, occupying and repairing hill-forts, under pretence of assisting the King's cause, but in reality to strengthen their own positions. Of such, was the Mahratta prince, Sivaji Bhôslay.

The letters which Afzool Khan was perusing were of the tenor consequent upon such events. They were chiefly from governors of provinces, forwarding reports from their subordinates to make their own views more intelligible. Most applied for the assistance of fresh troops, permission to raise local levies, and funds to pay them; while they gave accounts of opposition and imperial intrigue, which were only too certain and progressive. Others detailed plots and rumours, or preparations for revolt which should be checked.

Around Beejapoor itself there was perhaps no apprehension; but everywhere at a distance the same confusion existed, and it seemed to Afzool Khan as though it were impossible to provide against the spread of growing disaffection which, if he had before only partially guessed, was here developed in all its hideous and most perplexing detail. Letter after letter was thus read and thrown aside, till, weary of the subject, and sick at heart with apprehension, unable also to determine upon any definite course of state policy, he had put aside the correspondence, and was reviewing the detail in his own mind as he looked out on the city from the window.

The question to be determined in particular was as regarded the condition of the country to the west and north-west, which heretofore had given no cause for alarm. When Afzool Khan himself had governed it, he found the people, if ruder in manner than those nearer the capital, yet peaceable and industrious farmers; and beyond checking local feuds, there was little need for exertion or apprehension of any kind. Now the governor wrote of large assemblages of armed men, of habitual indifference to the authority of the officers of the State, and of the growing influence of Sivaji Bhóslay, before which he felt it next to impossible to maintain his own position or collect the revenue, much less to bring him to subjection.

The latest letters, too, described emissaries from the imperial camp having been traced in disguise to Sivaji's strongholds among the mountains, and an increasing belief among the people that he was destined to become a great prince for the subversion of all Mahomedans; while it was very evident that, by some secret means, they were being organized either to revolt for Sivaji himself, or in the cause of the Emperor.

The writer was a personal friend of Afzool Khan's—one whom he had no reason to believe would write either from fear or from an incorrect view of existing circumstances; and on this account his recent letters had not only become more important, but in a higher degree more interesting. He had forces at his disposal sufficient to repress any outbreak, but his knowledge of the people and the country, and the use they might be put to by the Emperor against the State at any critical moment, had confirmed apprehensions under which he had written, temperately but firmly, to the King, not to neglect or underrate those signs of the times; and to seek among the counsellors and nobles at Beejapoor such advice in respect to the prevention of local disaffection as might be practicable.

"If Fazil is right," murmured the Khan to himself, as he revolved these questions in his mind, "we may obtain confirmation of the designs of the Mahrattas and the Emperor, which will assist the comprehension of these letters. But it is strange that they have any common cause, or that such discordant elements should unite, even with the hope of mutual assistance."

A low cry from his daughter aroused him from his reverie. As he drew himself within the lattice, Zyna had raised herself, and was looking about scared and half awake. "Fazil!" she said. "O father, I dreamed I saw him laying before me, looking as though he were dead, and then he seemed to change to you; and I was terrified and screamed out."

"Be calm, Zyna," he replied, supporting her tenderly; "thou hast been much excited, and needest rest, and no wonder that an evil dream came to thee. Fear not; he is safe, and I am beside thee."

"Safe, father? then he is returned, and I have been sleeping carelessly."

"No, daughter, he is not come yet. He has most likely taken refuge from the storm, which was severe."

"In my dream I heard the thunder, father, but it seemed as though it were cannon. I marvel that I slept through all."

"And soundly too, Zyna; but look, the morning will be fair for their return," and he opened the casement.

The black pall of clouds which had hung over the city had passed away, and the wind had fallen, except a cool gentle breeze which blew freshly in at the window, and rustled among the foliage of the garden. Here and there the silence was broken by a gentle and distant murmur in the city, for, early as it was, some were already astir.

"I will watch now, father," said Zyna; "surely you have not slept at all. I am quite rested, and will wait for Fazil."

"It is near the third watch of the night, Zyna; thou art not afraid to be alone if I sleep? If Fazil come not before dawn, I will mount the Paigah, and we will soon bring him to thee; but I have no fear now, and say this only to content thee. I will try and rest my head for a while, daughter; for it is weary, and these papers have caused me much thought." So saying, he lay down on the divan where he had been sitting, covered his face with a shawl which Zyna gently cast over him, and at once fell into a deep slumber.

CHAPTER XXVII.

ZYNA sat beside her father, trimming the lamp as it needed, wondering much at Fazil's strange absence, and occasionally taking up one of the papers with which her father had been occupied, and reading it vacantly. Zyna could read, which was unusual in girls of her age and class: and, originally of a studious character, she had learned enough Persian with her brother from their old teacher, a superannuated secretary, to be of use both to her father and brother; more especially to her father in his confidential correspondence. Apparently she found nothing to interest her very much, for she laid down letter after letter after reading the superscription, and looked out through the lattice impatiently, as it were, for the coming dawn. The bright morning star now appeared above the tops of the trees, and a glow overspread the whole east—the false dawn; which, while it as yet gave no definite form to the surrounding objects, yet relieved the extreme darkness of the night. As Zyna sat, she fancied she heard a sound of voices at the gate, but it died away. It could not be her brother; he would have been admitted at once. Again, as she listened, and the silence seemed painful, the murmur was renewed, and she started up.

"It is he—Fazil is come!" she cried eagerly to her father, awaking him. "O, father, go to meet him; would I could go myself!"

Afzool Khan listened from the window, and Zyna could see that the expression of his face increased in gladness, and the revulsion in her own heart caused agitation which she could not restrain.

"He is not come," said her father; "it may be some messenger. God grant there may be no evil tidings! Be calm, my child; I will go below and ascertain, and will return or send word about him!"

Hurrying down to the gate, he found the sentinel in altercation with the lad we have before mentioned. It was evident that the boy had been there some time, and the sentinel, being informed that his young lord was safe, had no idea of wakening any one before the usual hour of morning prayer. As Afzool Khan approached the gate alone, he heard the lad's earnest prayer for aid answered by a dogged refusal.

"Begone!" said the man through the wicket; "thy tale may be true enough, and the Sahib Zadah* may be where he is; but, look you, the great Khan Sahib is fast asleep, and cannot be awakened. Everybody is asleep; there is no woman here to send to him in the zenana. Begone therefore, or lay down at the gate. When morning prayer is over, thou shalt have speech of the Khan. Till it is broad daylight, I draw no bolt. If thou wilt not go, at least sit quiet, for there are gentleman in the guard-room here who might treat thee roughly if disturbed in their sleep."

The boy was turning away sadly, when the voice of Afzool Khan was heard calling from the inner court, as he unfastened the door leading to the larger one.

"Whose is that voice?—who speaks without?—why is he not admitted?" he asked.

"My lord," replied the man on duty, "the Sahib Zadah is not here, but there is a boy who says he knows of him."

"Was it well, Yousuf, to turn him away?" asked Afzool Khan. "Suppose my son had had need of us."

"Nay; but my lord slept, and the Sahib Zadah was safe. Bulwunt Rao only is wounded—and there were no women to send—and I did but tell him to wait," stammered the man.

* The respectful title of a son—literally, "lord's son."

"No matter—where is the boy? Open the wicket," said Afzool Khan impatiently.

"He does not consider who may be behind it," said the soldier, as he unfastened the ponderous iron bars and unlocked the padlock of the wickets, "and that this may be but a device to attack the gate. But he will always be headstrong."

"I am here, Khodawund," said the lad, from without, and squeezing himself through the opening between the wicket-door and the chain which fastened it. "Behold I am now before you, valiant sir," he said to the sentinel, "whom you took to be a thief; but I would have speech of the noble Afzool Khan himself, if it be possible to have him aroused."

"I am he," returned the old Khan, stepping forward. "Speak on, if what there is to be told may be said before these men;" for several had now arisen, saluted their master, and were standing by him.

The boy touched the old Khan's feet reverently. "Fear not, noble sir," he said hastily, "for the Sahib Zadah is safe. He met with no hurt, though he was in danger."

"Ul-humd-ul-illa!—Praise be to God," broke from the old man fervently, and was heartily re-echoed by all around; for men were arriving every moment from the different portions of the court, and crowding round to hear the news. "Ul-humd-ul-illa! O holy Geesoo Duraz!" * he continued, looking up, "I vow fatehas to thy tomb, and a new covering shall it have of the costliest cloth-of-gold. But go on, boy, and fear not. Is there aught for my private ear?"

"Nothing, my lord—nothing. There was a fray, and Meah Sahib's attendant or friend was badly wounded. I want a palankeen for him; that is all."

"And my son—why did he not come with thee? And who art thou?" asked the Khan.

"They call me Ashruf, and I am the son of Peer Mahomed Duffadar, and Meah Sahib could not come, because," added the lad, dropping his head, "he was my father's prisoner—and——"

"By the Prophet, but this is too much!" exclaimed the fiery old Khan. "Who art thou, knave, that dares to say the son of Afzool Khan is a prisoner to any one?"

"May I be your sacrifice, O Khan," returned the boy, nothing daunted, though the Khan's angry speech was re-echoed by all gathered around him. "May I be your sacrifice, there is no harm meant to your noble son, whom we all know and honour. He it was who in my hearing declared that, in order to save my father,

* *Huzrut Syud Geesoo Duraz*—"Prince of the Long Locks"—the name of a celebrated Mahomedan saint, whose tomb at Gulburgah is esteemed the most holy, as the saint is the greatest favourite of all, perhaps, in the Dekhan.

he would attend the Kótwal's court; for it was but yesterday that the Kótwal swore he would have the right hand of the first brawler taken, cut off, and hung up in the chowke,* and that he would degrade the first officer who failed to apprehend those concerned in any riot. Be not angry, therefore, noble sir, for my father explained all this, and your son goes of his own freewill. My father could not help it, you know, my lord," added the boy, apologetically, "for a man had been wounded, and there was blood on your son's sword."

"Ay! Jehándar Beg is likely to be a man of his word, too," said the Khan to those about him, "and force will do no good. But it were as well that my son should be attended, I think. What say you, gentlemen? So be ready some twenty of you, and call up the spearmen; the palankeen and bearers, too, for Bulwunt Rao. We could ill spare him, poor fellow, from among us."

"Nothing could have happened if Meah had taken some of us with him," cried several of the men at once. "We all wanted to go," added Raheem Khan, "but he bade us mind our own business, and took Bulwunt Rao with him; and see what has come of ganja smoking."

"And Meah might have been wounded or killed," added several.

"My friends, there was need to do it," answered Afzool Khan; "a secret service for the King cannot have too few witnesses. As to his life, or mine, or that of any of you, do we not eat the salt of the King, and should our lives be grudged? Peace, then, and hasten to get ready: the morn is fast breaking, and by daylight we should be in the saddle. Keep the boy; he must accompany us." So saying, he turned back into the private court in order to seek his daughter, who had followed him. Goolab had been beforehand with her, and had communicated the news in her own way, with many marvellous additions, while the Khan was giving his orders to the men. Now, therefore, on hearing her father's brief confirmation of Fazil's safety, all past anxiety was at once forgotten, and, with glistening eyes and a thankful heart, she clung to him as they entered the small court of the zenana apartments together.

By this time, too, Zyna's second mother, who as yet has been barely mentioned, had been aroused from her sleep by the prevailing bustle; and as she habitually indulged in long rests, and disliked early hours most particularly, she met the Khan and Zyna in a mood of very querulous character, which arose partly from having been robbed of a large portion of sleep, and partly from having heard Goolab's exaggerated report of Fazil's danger. Now, the good lady had not even known of his going out, nor, as her lord had requested not to be disturbed, of the manner in which the weary night had passed.

* Market-place.

"Blessed be the holy saints that he is safe!" was the exclamation of Zyna, as she threw herself upon the lady's neck; "there will be no delay now, and my father will bring him to us. O mother, are you not thankful?"

"It was well done of thee, Khan," cried the lady ironically, disengaging herself from Zyna, and not heeding her words, "to send that poor boy out in such a night as the last has been. Such thunder and lightning! Naked, too, I hear—to run the chance of cold and wounds. Ugh! and thou sayest thou hast a father's love for him? Toba! toba! I swear to thee, had he been my son, he should never stir out without my permission. I would take care of that. He should not go hence, Khan Sahib, until I knew that the planets were propitious—a thing—Alla defend us!—that some people care as little about as—as . . . and then to think what a tempting of destiny it was to send the boy from home without asking or caring for the positions of the stars, or finding out whether there was not an adverse planet in a threatening house. As it is, we hear that Fazil is wounded—that is, he might have been; and that Bulwunt Rao has had his head cut off—that is, nearly, for he has a horrible cut in his neck, and his head is hanging all on one side; and," she continued, wiping her eyes with the end of her scarf, and in a whimpering tone, "all this comes of not asking me. What am I in the house but less than a dog? O Khan——"

"Peace, Lurlee!" returned Afzool Khan tartly. "What cross words are these so early in the morning? Enough for thee that the boy is safe, and that we have subject for thankfulness in his escape from danger, and not of sorrow. Peace! is it thus Alla should see thee after His mercy? Fazil will be here presently, and will tell thee perhaps as much as I know."

"Ay, perhaps!" retorted Lurlee. "I, who am less than a cat in the house, and as gentle as a sheep, am thus treated! O Khan! shame upon thee that I know everything only when it is stale, and comes to me through the bazar! Are not all your goings and comings hidden from me? and now I hear you and Zyna sat up all night together; and I was told you were not to be interrupted, and had to eat my dinner by myself, and to get to sleep as best I might. O Khan! am I less than nobody? I who am of the family of——"

"Thou wouldst only have been anxious and fretful, Lurlee," returned the Khan soothingly. "The planets would have troubled thee. We meant only well in not telling thee. It was an urgent matter, and we could not wait for the astrologer to read the tables for us, or tell us what star was in the ascendant. Go, see after some breakfast, or whatever can be got for Fazil; we may be detained, and I'll warrant he is hungry enough already. We cannot wait for lucky hours sometimes, but must take what Alla sends us."

"I will not go, Khan. I will not be put off with empty words," she cried, angrily; "and if you do not choose to read the stars, what does it signify? are not the consequences of your error on your own head? When was it that the stars were aught in your eyes? Have I not read you many a warning, which, had it been heeded, would have saved much trouble—much! When Fazil went forth to battle, did I not warn you not to let him depart? and did he not come home wounded and senseless? And when I told you one day, when one of the horses died, that something bad must befall us because of the evil aspect of the stars, I was only laughed at. Is this true or false? And yesterday, if I had but been asked beforehand, could I not have told all that was going to happen? Behold!" and the lady drew from her bodice a table regularly constructed to aid her astrological predictions and researches—"behold! were not Saturn and the Moon in conjunction? Is not that bad enough? and cannot you see that is the reason why Bulwunt Rao, poor fellow, has had his head cut off?"

"Peace, Lurlee!" again cried the Khan, to whom his wife's astrological wisdom had long proved a serious annoyance. "If all the planets in the sky had come together for good or evil, Fazil must have gone last night, for it was an errand of life or death. Now all is safely over, go and prepare some sheernee for distribution, and be thankful for what is, rather than anxious about the stars——"

"Toba, toba!" exclaimed the lady, interrupting him; "for shame, for shame! O Khan, to blaspheme the stars! May your sin be forgiven!"

"Nay, mother, but he did not blaspheme," urged the gentle voice of Zyna. "He did but mean that Fazil was safe everywhere; for thou knowest, dear mother, that he is in the hands of Alla, and that the blessed Alla is above all."

"He is not above the stars," retorted the lady angrily, and over-anxious to establish the truth of her favourite superstition—"that is, He—I mean—He is above them; but then——"

"Ah, Lurlee; better leave them alone," cried the Khan, laughing. "Art thou not sinking deep into the mire of thine own conceit, lady? Well, thou art welcome to them if they will teach thee not to be wilful, and not to do thine own desire, which is ever ill controlled and variable; and as to their being higher than Him who made them—why, I have no more to say."

"I said no such thing," retorted the lady doggedly; "but it is ever thus. Take care, Khan, of wilful disregard of warnings."

"Another time, perhaps, wife. Now we cannot delay, for the Kôtwal has got hold of Fazil, and that is worse than an adverse conjunction of planets. But fear not," he added, seeing that the countenance of Zyna betrayed alarm; "a word from me, and he will be released."

"If he is not, I will go to my cousin the Wuzeer's wife, and beg for him," replied Lurlee.

"Ay, in spite of the stars? Well, well, beebee, I hope it will not be needed," said the Khan cheerily. "We are not yet come down to asking favours of our cousins' wives. No, Lurlee; keep thine interest for another time, and see to it that thy cousin doth not require thine aid ere thou hast to ask hers."

"Impossible, Khan!" cried the lady sharply. "Thou art pleased this morning to underrate my poor self and my relations. It is well, O Afzool Khan!" (she meant to be very impressive when she called him by name)—"it is well—I say it is very well, that you speak thus. See to it that thou, too, want no aid from them."

"I do not need them, Lurlee," replied the Khan. "As to their aid to me—nay, be not angry—I have not much hope of it; and for the rest, if I am right in what I think, there is evil impending over the Wuzeer's house, which all the stars will not tell thee of, nor him either. May the saints avert it! If it be true, thou shalt know of it ere many hours be past, and we will try to aid him; but at present let there be peace between us. By-and-by thou wilt say to Fazil, It was well done, though our news may not please thee. Go, girl, bring me my sword," he continued to Zyna. "Bring a shawl too, for the morning air is chilly."

Zyna was glad to escape, for, in truth, bickerings such as we have noted were too frequent in the house to be very tolerable, and sometimes one side, sometimes the other, was in fault; most frequently, perhaps, the lady, who, having had no children of her own to care for, and having in her youth been instructed in Persian, had turned to divinity and astrology with great zeal. In the latter she had indeed great faith, and professed herself able, as no doubt she was willing, to direct all affairs of the house, as also of the state, by planetary influences. Thus, no event could happen without its being, to her perception, plainly written in the book of destiny, which the light of the planets rendered easy reading; and if a dish happened to break, or a cow or bullock died, or a horse had to be purchased or exchanged, or any household rejoicing made, or trouble endured, all were found to have connection with the planets, or to be the consequences of the lucky or unlucky days and hours of which her life was composed.

Lurlee Khánum being a scholar, was also an object of envy to many of her female friends, and was consulted by them upon various turns of their fortunes; and in regard to lucky colours for dress, lucky moments for putting on new clothes, settling matches and marriage days, the weaning of children, putting them into new beds, cutting their hair or nails, and the like domestic matters, she was an unquestionable authority. She, according to the rules laid down in her book, had written several charms, and given them to her friends, which, together with the virtues of certain herbs and medecines, had been the cause of relief to babies when cutting their teeth, and when they cried at night, or had bad dreams, or infantine ailments; and had been efficacious also in averting evil spirits, evil eyes, and the envious wishes of others.

For these accomplishments—especially her skill in astrology, which was believed to be very wonderful, indeed almost a special revelation—Lurlee Khánum was held in vast respect by all classes in her quarter of the city; and her opinions and interpretations of the stars were decidedly preferred to those of Meer Anwur Ali, the old Moolla of the public mosque nigh at hand; and a considerable feud existed between them in consequence. For the Moolla considered her as an interloper, and as one by no means instructed or qualified to have converse with what she professed, whether astrology or medicine; and had been known to say, irreverently no doubt, that more people died of Lurlee Khánum's medicines than the angel of death knew what to do with. In short, Lurlee Khánum, the second wife of Afzool Khan, was a much more popular person than the first had been; who, being a foreigner, and absorbed in her husband and children, cared little about her neighbours; whereas her successor was in most respects the exact reverse.

Lurlee Beebee had once been handsome. She was of somewhat dark complexion, but had very large lustrous eyes, with a prominent nose, and had not escaped marks by smallpox, though they were not disfiguring. When the Khan married her, her figure was perfect; but she had lately, much to her mortification, increased in size; and though she took many infallible receipts to prevent fat, it would accumulate. For many years she had had hope of children, and had made vows to all the shrines in Beejapoor, had sent gifts to those at Allund, Gulburgah, and Gôgi, and had vowed to make vast distributions of money, and to do other charitable acts, if her prayers were granted. Now she began to fear she had no chance, which had vexed her not a little, and had combined, with other troubles, to give a sour, grim expression to her countenance, which rarely left it.

There were times, however, when she was bright and pleasant; for, really kind at heart, few had greater powers of pleasing than Lurlee Khánum; but as her husband became more and more occupied with public affairs, estrangement had begun, and was progressing. There was one fear which had beset Lurlee for many years—that her lord, seeing she had no children, would marry again; and the idea of a sister-wife was very intolerable: this, however, had passed away. The Khan was advancing in years, his children were growing up, and she had no fear of another usurping what affection remained, or interfering with her household management.

To the Khan's children Lurlee was fondly attached; indeed, they were now the principal links between her lord and herself. Their mother had died when they were of tender age; and, after Lurlee's hopes of children ceased, she took more kindly to them than before, and had done her duty by them. Nor did their father interfere with that deference to her judgment in matters concerning them, of which she had better knowledge; but her increasing faith in her own infallibility had begun to distress both, as they could not help estimating at its proper value the superstition upon which the majority of her acts and opinions were founded once for all.

Such was Lurlee Khánum, the only lady in the harem of Afzool Khan. Other nobles of his rank would have married as often as the law allowed, without reproach; but the old Khan's affections had seemingly died with Zyna's mother; and the excitement of war, of political events, and provincial government, together with the management of his fine estate of Afzoolpoor, had apparently filled his mind to the exclusion of other subjects.

In a few moments Zyna had returned, bearing the weapon, which her father took from her; and having entered the garden with her, they performed their ablutions in the mosque before mentioned, and went through the usual forms of the early prayer. The Khan then returned to the zenana, where Lurlee Khánum met him.

"I have put up some food in the palankeen," she said; "see that Fazil eats it. I would all this were safely over," she added, after a pause. "Thou art not angry with me, Khan—with your Lurlee? do not go forth angry with me, my lord."

"No, no! not angry, dear one," returned the Khan, much moved and softened. "I am not angry, but impatient; forgive me, Lurlee. Alla keep you till I return: and you too, my child! Fear not; I will bring him safely to both of you."

The Khan's horse awaited him in the outer court, and with it a strong troop of his best horsemen, with a company of spearmen, whose combined force seemed enough to have rescued Fazil, had there been need. Afzool Khan was greeted heartily by all, and as he cast his eye over the group of steady and oft-tried retainers, he felt that confidence which results from habitual companionship with others, and that no danger could reach Fazil which they could not share or overcome. The greeting was as heartily returned as given; and the gates being thrown open after a few questions to his son's messenger, and preceded by him and the band of spearmen who ran before his horse, Afzool Khan and his retainers pushed forward at a rapid pace.

It was now broad daylight, and the freshness of the morning, and its clear bright atmosphere, rendered every object more beautiful than it had been before the rain. Every stately mosque and minaret, palace and mausoleum, with their bright gilded spires, caught the fast-increasing light, and stood out boldly against the clear eastern sky; while the rich foliage of the trees, unmoved by any wind as yet, hung in heavy masses, and seemed refreshed by the moisture they still retained. As they passed the various gardens, the rich fragrance of tuberose, lime, and orange flowers loaded the air almost to excess; while the very ground gave forth that refreshing earthy scent which, in India, after rain, mingles so peculiarly and yet so gratefully with every other perfume. Few persons were yet abroad; and with the exception of an occasional devout Mahomedan proceeding to early morning prayer at the mosque—a young rake, with a small band of sword-and-bucklermen, returning from the night's questionable companionship—a few humble carriers of fruit and vegetables coming from villages without the walls to the morning market, with here and there small companies of travellers starting on their daily journey,—all was silent and deserted; and the heavy tramp of the horsemen, as they proceeded at a rapid pace, sounded strange and suspicious at that unusual hour.

CHAPTER XXVIII.

THE young Ashruf ran lightly along before the party, leading them, by narrow lanes and streets familiar to him, direct to the spot where the occurrences of the night had taken place; and under such guidance—for the boy's speed never flagged for a moment—Afzool Khan and his men arrived at the building where Fazil was waiting, almost ere the sun's rays were sparkling upon the tall minarets and domes of the city.

He had looked anxiously for their coming long ere dawn broke; for he had awakened as usual for the morning prayer, in which he was joined by the Duffadar and several other devout members of the guard: and since its conclusion he had been sitting on the step of the guard-room, or watching Bulwunt, who slept heavily but restlessly, and speculating on the reason of his young messenger's delay. Truly cheering was it, therefore, after hearing from a great distance the rapid advance of a body of horsemen borne on the still morning air, to see the well-known band of spearmen, led by the young Ashruf, turn the corner of the street, and immediately following them the tall figure of his father, and with him perhaps fifty of the Paigah.

A few moments served to bring the party to the spot. As his father strove to alight rapidly, Fazil sprang to aid him with a joyful cry; and when the old Khan could disengage himself from his stirrup, a hearty embrace followed, to the no small wonder of a crowd of neighbours, whom the unexpected appearance of a well-known nobleman and his dashing escort had collected: and who could not understand the warm greeting and embrace between what appeared to be a Hindu beggar, still much besmeared with wood-ashes and paint, and so gallant a cavalier as Afzool Khan.

Led by Fazil into the apartment we have already mentioned, the Khan submitted to be seated upon a carpet; and the room being partially cleared, he proceeded to inquire into the circumstances of his son's detention, and of the fray of which Ashruf had informed him. Upon Bulwunt, the sound of the old Khan's voice acted like a charm. Weakened by loss of blood, he had fallen into a dreamy kind of doze rather than sleep, which the trampling of the horses, and exclamations from their riders as they arrived, had converted into an imaginary battle-field, on which he lay wounded and helpless; but when the well-known voice of his lord was no longer doubtful, he was aroused, and, raising himself feebly, earnestly requested his master to come to him to hear, as he thought them, his last words.

"He is not in fault, my lord," he said faintly, and pointing to Fazil. "They would have made out that he wounded me—may their tongues rot! He will tell you all that happened, and how the enemy of my house, Tannajee Maloosray, has given me my death-blow."

"Not so, brave Bulwunt," said the Khan, cheerfully; "there is no fear of thee, methinks. Thou art weak, and thy sight fails thee; but keep a good heart, friend, thou will strike many a blow yet for Afzool Khan; a few days' rest, and this trouble will be forgotten."

"Has he told you all?" asked Bulwunt.

"Not yet, not yet, friend; but I shall hear it ere long."

"Track him, track him, my lord," continued Bulwunt; "Maloosray cannot be gone far. He is even now in the city, at one of the Mutts or Serais. He could not escape if the gates were watched. He might even be found at——"

But speech suddenly failed the poor fellow, and, exhausted with his effort, he sank back, fainting, on the pillow.

"What did he say, son?" asked the Khan, quickly; "what of Tannajee Maloosray? Him of Pertábgurh—the friend of Sivaji Bhóslay?"

"Even so, father," replied Fazil. "I did not mention him, as there were so many listeners, and the matter was for your private ear; but, as Bulwunt has said it, no matter now. Would that we knew his haunts! Perhaps he knows, but he is too exhausted to speak."

"Tannajee Maloosray here!—in Beejapoor!" exclaimed the Khan, "and hath done this deed! O that we knew where the villain were hiding! Nevertheless, the gates shall be well guarded; that was a good thought of thine, Bulwunt. Ho, without there! One of ye ride to each gate of the city—tell those on guard there, that Maloosray hath been seen within the city last night, and all that pass out are to be well looked to. Do ye hear?"

"Jo Hookum," cried a number of the men who heard the order; and after a brief consultation together, single horsemen dashed away to the several places to which their errands tended.

"And now change thy dress, son," continued his father; "this disguise is hardly seemly to thee. Here is a suit, and there will be water outside."

"If the Duffadar here have no objection," returned the young man. "You forget, father; I am his prisoner of my own free will."

"Chut, chut, boy! thou art no prisoner—be quick," cried the Khan.

"The saints forbid," interposed the Duffadar, "that any one of such exalted faith as the son of Afzool Khan should be ever suspected of being an infidel. When——"

"There, there, Fazil! go!" interrupted the Khan, laughing; "I have no eyes for thee in that abomination; let us see thee in thy proper shape."

"Then follow me, father, into this apartment," replied Fazil; "I have that to say which will not bear witnesses—much that is marvellous."

"That I doubt not, son. I will follow when Bulwunt is cared for; I see they have brought up the palankeen."

So saying, the Khan tried to raise the wounded man, while he spoke cheerily to him. Again, at the sound of his lord's voice, the spirit of the retainer rallied, but it apparently hovered between life and death; for, after another faint attempt to speak, he fell back exhausted.

"It is of no use," muttered the Khan; "he will die, I fear, and we can ill spare him. Ho, without! bearers or spearmen! Come in some of ye. And look ye," he added, as several entered, "take up Bulwunt Rao, carefully, as he lies, by the corners of the blanket; put him into the palankeen, and take him home at your easiest pace. He is to be lodged in the private apartment of the Khilwut. Get a bed from the house, and send for our physician directly, and the surgeon of the palace. . . . Now, begone."

Carefully and gently the men raised him up, and bore him out. He groaned heavily as he reached the open air, yet it seemed to revive him, for he looked around. Some of his comrades who crowded round spoke cheerily to him, and he recognized them and smiled. He was at once placed in the litter, and the bearers, at a rapid but easy pace, proceeded homewards.

"I dare not have spoken to thee, my son," said the old Khan, when he had joined Fazil, who was busily engaged washing the ashes from his face, neck, and arms, "before those people, though I was burning to do so. So thou hast really discovered something by the night's adventure. This Tannajee,—what of him? Tell me quickly?"

"Alas! father," returned the young man, sadly, "I know so much, and of such weighty matters, that my soul trembles under them. I would almost that I had not gone out last night, or that other lips than mine had to tell thee a tale of treachery and wrong-doing."

"Son! I see it in thy face. The Wuzeer!" exclaimed the Khan, starting.

"He is false, father—false," continued Fazil.

"Ah, I feared so; but speak, boy, how is it? Who told thee?" cried Afzool Khan, impatiently.

"I need not say more to confirm it than that the King knows it," returned Fazil; "and that he has papers now in his possession which leave no doubt of Khan Mahomed's treachery; Mirza Anwur Ali and the Shah took them last night, and paid for them."

"Ya Alla kureem! and where was this? By the Prophet, tell me, Fazil! My soul eats your words! speak, boy, quickly."

Then Fazil rapidly sketched the scene of which the reader already knows the detail, while the old Khan listened in silent amazement, his forefinger between his teeth.

"Ya Khubeer-o! and hath all this been so easily found out?" he exclaimed. "Ah, Khan Mahomed! often has your poor friend warned you; but in vain. Now you are lost, alas, alas! and for that insane ambition which would not be repressed."

"We must save him, father!" cried Fazil; "he must not perish. At the risk of my own life would I do aught possible to avert the danger which threatens him. What can we do? Implore the King to spare the ancient friend of his house? or write and warn him? Ah, father, you are his most valued friend, and his son is as a brother to me! Speak; what can be done?"

"Alas, I know not yet, son," he replied, sadly; "but tell it again; all, Fazil—all that the King said. I will think it over. Wishing to save, we must not destroy."

Fazil again narrated what he had seen, and, as well as he could remember them, the contents of the letter which the Lalla had repeated. But the Khan thought long and deeply on the whole matter ere he could see his way to action. At last he said to his son—

"What I have determined upon ought to suit both parties. I will go instantly to the King, and try if his purpose as to the Wuzeer can be discovered. I must take the papers he gave me in any case. Do thou, Fazil, go to thy friend—it may be that he knows all; but, if not, he can be warned of the danger. Timely submission may alone avert it; but the peril is fearful."

"Alla is just, and it will be as He wills," returned his son, devoutly; "but we must not forget that Lalla; his presence may be of moment, and it were well he were cared for; his wound was a mere scratch, and he may be able to ride; let us send for him."

So a messenger was despatched to bring him, or to ascertain, at least, whether he could ride; as, if not, a litter would be provided. To the vexation of Fazil, however, and his father, the messenger returned, saying that a litter had already been sent by the Kótwal's orders, about the time of morning prayer, and he had been taken away to that officer.

"Jehándar Beg is faithful," said the old Khan. "He is as true to the King's salt as I am myself, else I should have feared the result; but who can hold the Lalla's tongue?—that is what I dread, Fazil."

"And he did not appear over-discreet either, father," replied Fazil; "however, the best thing we can do is to follow up the information, and go to the Kótwallee; it is my duty, too, to see the worthy old Duffadar safe through the matter, for truly he did what he could."

"True, son," returned Afzool Khan; "and I will accompany thee. Jehándar Beg may not have forgotten some matters in which I have been able to befriend him now and then. No; that Lalla must not slip through our hands, Fazil."

By this time Ashruf had saddled his father's ambling pony, and stood waiting without, so the cavalcade was soon ready. The Khan's men were all mounted, and a few of the Duffadar's guard attended as escort to the kullal, for whom his own pony had been provided, so that there was no delay; and as Fazil and his father stepped from the guard-room, the young man's appearance was the signal for a shout of congratulation from all, which being duly acknowledged, Fazil turned with a smile to the old Duffadar, and told him "his prisoners" were ready.

"If I can but assist ye, noble gentlemen," said the old man, respectfully, "in this matter, it will be a happy thing; and if my son——"

"Bismilla!" exclaimed Afzool Khan, mounting his horse, and interrupting him; "we are no evil-doers, to fear justice. Move forward!"

The building where the Kótwal's morning court was held, was at no very great distance, in the city itself; the other court was within the fort, not far from the King's palace; and they proceeded to the former at a rapid pace. By-and-by, as they drew nearer the place of their destination, a horseman dashed on to give notice of the near approach of the Khan, in order that he might be met, and greeted in a manner due to his rank.

"What can bring Afzool Khan, the pious and true, here?" asked one of the under-officers on duty at the entrance guard-room of the outer court. "He is no brawler or intriguer."

"Who knows, Meer Sahib," replied the person addressed. "In these days the world is turning topsy-turvy, and one has to see and believe strange things. There is already a report that the young Khan is in fault, and has wounded the man who was brought in a little while ago upon a bed, and killed another; for a body was found this morning near a temple beyond the fort. I was at the Bazar mosque at early prayer, and they said there it would be a bad business. What matter? Afzool Khan has plenty of cash, and a sharp fine will set all straight."

"I pray it may be no worse, friend," returned the first speaker; "but I have heard Jehándar Beg swear upon the holy book to spare no one if blood hath been shed; and here is one man dead and one wounded to be accounted for. A bad business, friend—a bad business; but we shall see. God grant it may not lead to that!" and he pointed to the corner of the court, where lay a hand in a pool of blood—a ghastly evidence of summary justice on a criminal but just performed. "But we shall see; the Khan is heavily attended, and methinks it would be as well to let him alone."

"Ay, friend, he is one of the old stock, well tried and trusted; the peace of God and the Prophet be upon him and his; and that is a brave boy, 'tis a pity he should be in any trouble. Would we had more of them about the King! Truth is lie, and lie is truth, friend, in these days; and men whisper that Jehándar Beg is no friend to Azfool Khan, nor the Wuzeer either, and they are of the same party; but we shall see. What will be, will be."

CHAPTER XXIX.

ALMOST as they spoke, the Khan's retinue approached, and, preceded by its band of spearmen, some horsemen, and the party of the old Duffadar, swept round the corner of the adjoining street. Very conspicuous among the cavalcade were the figures of the father and son riding together; the Khan in his morning suit of heavy cloth-of-gold, which glittered richly in the sun; his son, plainly dressed in white muslin.

Fazil rode a led horse of his father's, which he sat with perfect confidence and control of the fiery animal; but his countenance expressed anxiety which he could not restrain. In truth, he felt, notwithstanding his assurance to his father, that if he were subjected to a strict examination, he should be ill able to account satisfactorily for the various events of the night without compromising others. In regard to Maloosray, he had one witness in the kullal; and there was nothing to implicate him in the occurrence at the temple, in case it should form subject of inquiry. No, he could not now recede.

As to the old Khan himself, no thought of fear disquieted him. He considered that he was only humouring a whim of his son's in accompanying him, that he might insure the Duffadar's being freed from blame. Suspicion of aught affecting the safety or honour of his house had never entered his mind; and he had ridden along gaily, causing his fine war-horse to caracole and bound, free from all thought of uneasiness, except what might result from the delay.

As the party entered the gate, they were met by several persons deputed to receive them, and returned the respectful and hearty greetings of the soldiery on duty, to whom they were well known. Dismounting at the end of the court, they passed through to the next, where already many suitors and complainants were assembled. There, too, on a bed which had been placed in a side-room, lay the Lalla, with a sheet drawn over him, which Fazil saw was stained with blood. The Lalla had covered his face; but the pink colour of his turban, and its peculiar tie, were not to be mistaken. So, passing all, and receiving and returning salutations, they entered the room of audience, where, surrounded by a few Mutsuddees, or scribes, sat the Kôtwal himself.

Jehándar Beg was a Persian by birth, a man of some learning and much cunning, but really intelligent. Those were times when the service of Indian princes was eagerly sought for by Persians, Turks, Affghans, and even Abyssinians; and adventurers often rose to princely rank and honour in their service. Jehándar Beg was one of these. When young he had accompanied a relative to the Dekhan court, the prince of which was a Sheea—his own faith—and where, among others of his countrymen, the historian Mahomed Kasim Ferishta had been distinguished. He had risen steadily in the King's service, and proved himself brave in the field, as well as sagacious and trustworthy. Having attained to his present office, he was, in the main, respected, and was the dread of all night brawlers, sharpers, and thieves, whom he punished heavily; but he was fond of money, and it was whispered that, in grave offences, he had his private price. After all, what mattered that? Occasionally a great person was fined, or otherwise punished, and so men's mouths were stopped, and the Kótwal believed to be a great man.

Jehándar Beg's appearance was magnificent. He always wore the peaked lamb's-wool cap of Khorassan, and the Persian robe; and his rich brown complexion, and dark-brown curly beard, grave features, and large soft black eyes, combined to render his face a remarkable one, not easily forgotten. The expression seldom varied; nothing ever caused him to laugh in his court—rarely to smile—nor did he ever express anger. Happen what might, his habitual gravity never relaxed for a moment, and there was no man who could tell a lie, conceal a fact, or change an opinion—or, in the course of duty, order the torture, and look upon it, with such perfect imperturbability as he did.

His office was at once arduous and difficult, but he was not restricted in power. In cases of life and death, perhaps, and if the criminal were of importance, reference might be made to the chief legal authority or to the King; but, as far as minor punishments were needed, the lopping off of an arm, a hand, or a foot,—torture and imprisonment, or the like,—no one questioned the Kótwal's acts. As chief magistrate of a city which contained a large proportion of lawless population, he often found it necessary to make sudden and severe examples in order to check disorder and crime: and, recently, the city had been agitated by conspirators: parties ran high; and duels and brawls, generally attended by fatal consequences, were frequent.

The old Duffadar was right when he told Fazil of the Kótwal's oath to punish severely the first brawler who should be apprehended, and he trembled for the consequences of the inquiry into the night's disturbances. Here were two men wounded, and, as far as he knew, another who had been taken off, or who had got away; and one dead body, found near the temple of Bhowani among the tamarind trees, was fresh, though torn by wild animals, and the blood had been traced back to the temple wall, on the top of which some stones had been displaced.

Altogether, matters had an ugly appearance; and the old man could not help thinking that Fazil was concerned in both affairs. "May God be merciful to him," he said to himself, "for he is a brave youth, son of a gallant father; better a hundred battle-fields, and a fair chance man to man, than the crooked ways of this court, and the merciless character of Jehándar Beg. Be wary, my lord," he whispered to Fazil, as, having made his obeisance and report, he was falling back to get free of the advancing parties; "Jehándar Beg's looks are not pleasant this morning, and you need to be careful. I should not warn you without there were need; be careful in what you say, and I will guide you by my looks from time to time."

But Fazil had no fear. Unused to such scenes, he could only feel that his word would pass him free from all suspicion, and that his father's rank and good faith were above question.

To the old Khan, the Kôtwal's greeting was one of respectful deference; and the seat of honour was assigned to him. To Fazil, however, he maintained a stiff reserve—so pointed, that the Khan could not but notice and remark upon it.

"That is my son," he said, after an awkward pause which no one apparently dared to break, "and I would have you acquainted with him, Meerza Sahib. Shookr Ulla! he is not utterly unknown among the ranks of those who are true to the King in Beejapoor, though he is but a youth."

There was no reply, however, given to this speech, and the embarrassment of all grew more painful. The clerks and guards looked from one to another, and the old Khan to them in succession, with increasing indignation at their demeanour.

"By the Prophet!" he exclaimed at length, ironically, "ye seem marvellously engaged, gentlemen," as, on hearing him speak, every one looked away, or into the papers before them, "that a civil greeting does not obtain a civil answer. Your politeness, Meerza Sahib, is proverbial in the city; but it seems to have deserted you on this occasion, or is reserved for thieves and loose women. Come, my son—come; we intrude here. Jehándar Beg has his own private work to do, no doubt, and does not need our company."

"Hold!" cried the Kótwal; and, as he spoke, several of the armed attendants closed up the doorway with their long broad spears, while others without blew the matches of their guns. "Hold! Thou mayst go, Afzool Khan, for what may follow may grieve thy brave heart; but there is blood on thy son's sword, and it must be inquired into. Young man, what is this they say against thee? A man killed in a drunken brawl in the worst quarter of the city? Was this to be expected from the son of Afzool Khan? Speak, and speak truly, before God and his Prophet." The Meerza's eyes flashed and dilated as he spoke; and as they rested upon the young man, who had not seated himself, they were met by a gaze as bold and fearless as his own.

"I am no brawler, Meerza Sahib," he exclaimed, in reply. "Astagh-fur-oolla!—nor drunkard either. Peace, father! sit quiet; let me answer for myself—I am not afraid," he added, as the Khan attempted to rise, and was evidently provoked beyond endurance. "Ask the Duffadar who accompanied me, and the man in whose house it happened, whether I am to blame. Their statements will suffice."

"There are two matters to answer for, Meah Sahib," said the Kôtwal. "Were you not in the dress of a Gosai last night, and another with you? Nay; no denial!"

"I have nothing to deny, Meerza Sahib," returned Fazil. "My father knew of it, and I went by his permission."

"Good. Now, Peer Sahib, what happened to you?" asked the Kótwal of another officer present.

"My lord, it was just before midnight," he replied, "when two men, Gosais, brought a third person, who was slightly wounded, but complained much of his neck. He is a foreigner, for he speaks the Delhi language. They said he had been robbed, and told us to keep him safe till the morning, when they would come for him; and as the man was very helpless, we put him on a bed in the guard-room, and have brought him here. Again at dawn, some of the men were going towards the temple of Toolja Bhowani, when they saw the dead body of a man, with a deep wound in his back and a stab in his breast—a Hindu, for he had on a Brahmun's thread, so he may be a Rajpoot; but no one knew him. Several mohurs were picked up by him and others between this place and the temple:—the Mutsuddee has them—eleven, I think,—and there was blood all the way along. It was a desperate cut; and how the man could have run at all with those wounds, it is hard to say."

"He was murdered, then," thought Fazil; "would I had not struck him! yet there is one traitor and robber the less."

"And the man who was brought in, what of him?" asked the Kótwal.

"He moaned and groaned, my lord, worse than a woman; said he had been robbed at the temple; spoke of Pahar Singh who had wounded him, Maun Singh who had throttled him, then of the Shah's secretary—may his name be honoured!—and some ten thousand rupees. In short, noble sir, we could make nothing of the matter, for he began to weep if we spoke to him, and told us to take him to the King without delay. So we brought him here, and must speak for himself. It appeared to me like the dream of some opium-smoker," continued the speaker to those about him; "we could not understand it at all."

"Shouldst thou know the men who brought him?"

"Well, my lord, I can't say for certain," replied the officer, "but one of our people said they were not what they seemed; and he thought one was Bulwunt Rao, who is a Silladar of the noble Khan yonder, and who goes about bazars at night, sometimes; the other's face was tied up, and he did not speak."

"I was the other, Meerza Sahib," interposed Fazil, quietly.

"I thought as much," said the Kótwal, drily. "Were they armed, Peer Sahib?"

"Yes, to be sure, my lord," he replied; "would any one go about in those quarters at night without being armed? Yes, they had sword and shield."

"Where are the weapons?"

"Here, my lord," replied the other Duffadar, who now interposed, "in my keeping; the young Khan gave them up to me. He has another sword now."

"Yes, there is blood on the blade, and here are cuts, fresh ones, on the shield," said Jehándar Beg, examining Fazil's weapons. "How, young sir, do you account for these?"

"I will reserve what I have to say; it is no use speaking now," returned Fazil, who had observed his old friend shake his head, and who again nodded approvingly.

"Bring in the wounded man," cried the Kótwal; and the bed on which our poor friend the Lalla lay, was carried in and set down; "we must confront the parties."

"Get up, good man," said an attendant Mutsuddee; "this is the Kótwal; make your reverence, and tell what happened to you."

"Ah, protect me, befriend me. I have been robbed and murdered . . . . I cannot get up . . . . I am a poor man and a stranger. Look at my blood," gasped the Lalla by turns to all about him.

"Who did it? and who art thou?" cried the Kótwal. "Where hast thou come from?"

Now, it might be awkward for the Lalla to answer these questions. He knew he had a few gold coins left, enough to keep him for some time—for he had been used to poverty, and could endure it—if he could only get free. Any man with quick wits, could do something for himself in the city; and had he not done good service? These thoughts passed rapidly through his mind ere he spoke.

"Asylum of justice!" he said, in his most humble tones, "I don't know who did it, but I was robbed in the temple."

"Of ten thousand rupees? Speak truly."

"Ah no, sirs. What would a poor Khayet like me do with ten thousand rupees? No, but of what I had in my humeana."

"And Pahar Singh? they tell me he was mentioned by thee."

"Ah, noble sir, I am a stranger and a foreigner; what do I know about Pahar Singh, or anybody? I am very weak," added the Lalla, in a feeble voice; "will no one help me?" and he lay down, as well to escape further questioning, as to excite pity for his misfortunes.

"This will not serve thee, whoever thou art," returned the Kótwal; "answer truly, where art thou come from, and what took thee to that lonely temple at night?"

"My lord, I am a poor Khayet from the north, seeking service; and I fell among thieves who decoyed me thither and robbed me. See, they wounded me also, and tried to strangle me. What more can I say?"

"That is not enough, friend," resumed the Kótwal; "we must know how it happened, for others here appear concerned in the matter, and murder hath been done."

"Murder, my lord!" cried the Lalla, again raising himself;

"there was no murder, though perhaps they thought they had killed me when they took what I had."

"Who, Lalla? be not afraid," said Jehándar Beg, soothingly.

"A seeming Jogi and another. They ran away, and left me senseless. Then two Gosais came and raised me up, and gave me water, and took me to the guard-room. May the gods recompense them, for they bound up my wound!"

"Two Gosais—ah, this may be some clue!" said the Kótwal; "this agrees with the other statement. Then thou art one of them, Meah Sahib?"

"I have already said so," replied Fazil; "and my retainer, Bulwunt Rao, was the other."

"What took you there?"

Fazil considered for a moment. What he had been witness of could not now be related, and he replied, "It was a matter, Meerza Sahib, in which I am not bound to answer you. If those it concerns are to hear of it, they shall know otherwise."

"Beware, young sir!" said the Kótwal, gravely; "there can be no secrets here."

"Nevertheless, I cannot answer. It is enough that I have told my father of it," returned Fazil.

"Yes, Jehándar Beg," said Afzool Khan, "he has said enough to prove he was no robber, and that ought to content you."

"Yet there was murder done, my friend," replied the official, quickly; "blood was on the wall of the court, and a corpse not far from it, and there is blood on this sword of your son's. He should clear himself of this horrible suspicion. But stay; there is the other affray to be accounted for,—that in the wine-shop—a drunken brawl, I fear."

"I am no brawler, Meerza Sahib, nor drunkard," exclaimed Fazil, indignantly. "The man is present in whose house it occurred; let him say what happened."

"Let him be brought forward, and let Fureed Duffadar state what happened," said the Kótwal, authoritatively. "Till then be silent, Meah."

CHAPTER XXX.

The old Duffadar's account was clear and circumstantial, and the Kótwal listened attentively. When it was finished, the Kullal was called, and, prostrating himself, began by imploring protection, which was granted.

"It is a weighty matter, my lords," he said, "and needs much inquiry. May it please you to listen," he continued, after a pause, as if to collect his thoughts. "Your slave would represent that he heard a conversation between the young Khan there and a man whose name may hardly be mentioned in Beejapoor, Tannajee Maloosray."

"Maloosray!" echoed the Kótwal. "Protection of God! thou art not mad to say this? or drunk?"

"May I be your sacrifice!" continued the man, evidently observing that his words had made an impression, "I am not mad, and I have an oath against wine. I swear by the King's salt, that he spoke with Maloosray."

"And he was disguised like a Gosai, Fureed?" asked the Kótwal of the old Duffadar.

"Khodawund! what did he tell you himself he was?" replied the man. "He changed his dress when his father came. Even now the ashes may be on his body."

"What said the young Khan to Maloosray?" asked the Kótwal of the Kullal. "Speak truly, or I will have thee flogged through the bazar, and all thy property confiscated for irregular hours in thy shop."

This was what the man feared from the first. Had Fazil appeared in favour he would have appealed to him for explanations in regard to the affray, for which he dreaded he should be punished; but Fazil seemed already unable to help himself, so he had determined to take his own course in the opposite direction.

"Why should I tell a lie?" he replied, holding up his hands humbly and with a gesture of supplication. "I swear by your feet it is true." Pointing to Fazil, he continued—"He said he knew Pahar Singh was at the temple, and they sent a man for him; and if he did not come, that they should meet again. Then Maloosray said something about Sivaji Bhóslay, and the Moghuls, and the Shah Aurungzeeb, and armies, and there was another message to Pahar Singh. Then another man struck a blow at the Maloosray, and they fought, and I screamed out for the guard, and Maloosray ran off; but I secured him," and he pointed to Fazil.

"O base-born!" exclaimed Fazil, "thy mouth is full of lies——"

"Hear him," interrupted the man; "he had me tied up till the blood nearly burst from my fingers, and made me promise not to reveal this. Behold, my lord, the marks of the cords, and how my arms are swelled. By my child's head, it is true, noble sir, it is all true. How could I, a poor seller of ganja and bhung, have dreamed such things of Tannajee and Sivaji? Do not men tremble at their names? Search the young Khan, he has papers which Maloosray gave him. I saw them myself——"

"Alas, it is but too clear to me," said the Kótwal, interrupting Afzool Khan, who was about to speak, "that there is deep treachery here. Deep plots are being laid, but this poor servant of God has a clue to one at least. Inshalla! it will be sifted to the bottom. Enough of suspicion was there against you, young sir, on the other matter, but this is graver still. Yield, therefore, Afzool Khan, and you, Meah; resistance is vain, and I would fain spare blood."

As he spoke, the soldiers and attendants, who had gradually gathered round them, closed in so near that they could have been seized or overpowered at once, if the old Khan's sword had not been drawn by him the instant their movement was made. Now, as he stood prepared to meet any attack, his eyes flashing and his tall figure drawn up to its full height, no one ventured a step towards them, nor offered to seize his son, who, on his part, made no attempt at resistance.

"Draw, Fazil, draw!" cried the Khan; "let us see which of these sons of vile mothers will first die. O that we had a score of our fellows with us, this insult would not have happened. Draw, boy! a few good strokes will see us clear of this gang of executioners, and there are enough men without to carry us through the city. Come on, in the name of God! Bismilla!"

Saying this, the old man advanced a step, while those before him, so sudden and determined was his movement, fell back as though they would have allowed him egress. Fazil, however, saw his father's danger, not only from the chance of a sword-thrust or blow in the struggle which must ensue, and the certainty of an attempt at rescue by the men without if they heard of it, but in the disgrace and suspicion which would fall upon them if the inquiry were forcibly interrupted.

"Father, father!" he cried, passionately, "do not stir. I implore you, move not. You know how false this base charge is, and I beseech you not to let it be said that we feared to meet it, and evaded justice. Yes, let it be first done on this lying dog, who has misled Jehándar Beg. See, for one, I surrender myself and my weapons;" and, as he spoke, he threw his sword and dagger on the floor, which were eagerly secured by an attendant.

"Degenerate!" cried his father. "Dost thou fear death, boy? When did an Affghan ever surrender his weapons but with his life? Fie on thee for a coward, to hesitate to strike a blow for me!"

"Coward!" exclaimed the young man, sadly. "Father, you know not what you say. Why such bitter words? is this a time for contention?"

"Khan Sahib," said Jehándar Beg, who had risen with the others, and now advanced, "listen to your son's words of peace and reason. You are alone, and, though one or two might fall, there would be no escape. The blood of Afzool Khan, or his son, should not flow in a court of justice, but against the King's enemies. Put up your weapon, and wear it, Khan; and you, noble youth, yours.

Appearances are against you both; and these plots have been so long hidden from us, that your poor servant, the slave of the King —may his splendour increase!—has no alternative but to detain you till the pleasure of the Wuzeer is known."

"Father, I beseech you to listen to reason—to advice kindly given and well meant," cried Fazil; "consider what is at stake, and that the moment we have speech of the King there will be no fear."

Afzool Khan looked from one to the other and around him irresolutely, and the tears rose to his eyes, and fell over in large drops. Any advance would have decided him to an act of desperation; but his son saw the struggle in his mind, and, throwing himself before him, grasped his feet.

"Father, save your honour," he cried, earnestly; "save your life by my example. Shall it be said that Afzool Khan died a traitor, or that a breath of suspicion rested upon the truest, most loyal name in Beejapoor?"

A moment the old Khan hesitated, but his sword-point dropped, and he dashed his hand across his eyes impatiently. "My spirit chafes at the thought of restraint, Fazil," he said; "yet for thy sake, boy, I submit. But I pray thee, Jehándar Beg, let thine errand to the Wuzeer be done swiftly, or, by the Prophet, there be those in my service who would reck little of a rescue. Stay, I had better write; that will assure them more."

A few lines were hastily written by Fazil, and sealed with the Khan's private signet. One of the escort was called up, and the note given to him by Fazil himself, with an order to take the men home, and a caution to be discreet. The soldier looked about him incredulously.

"Do you remain of your own pleasure, my lord?" he asked.

"Yes," replied the Khan; "we have business here for to-day which cannot be deferred. Keep quiet, all of ye; but be ready," he added, in an under-tone; "when I need ye I will send word."

"Very good," cried the man in a loud voice, in order to cover the Khan's whisper, "very good; I understand; it shall be done."

"You had better withdraw to the private apartments, Khan," said the Kótwal, respectfully. "I know too well the honour of a Puttán to question you. Stay there till I return. Refreshment, too, shall be provided; and I pray you to consider this poor house as your own while you stay in it. The Wuzeer was at Almella yesterday, and is expected this evening."

Afzool Khan hesitated, but his son whispered, "We shall be better there, father, than amidst these curious gazers," and drew him along gently. He did not resist, but followed passively. "Stay, however," added Fazil to the Kótwal; "where is Fureed Duffadar? I would speak with him."

The man advanced a few steps. "I am here, my lord; what are your orders?"

"None from me," returned Fazil; "but look you, Meerza Sahib—for the sake of justice ask of this good man what that Kullal told us; for it is in the law that the word of a true believer is better than the oath of a Kafir. And, pardon me, Meerza, but my father and myself, in the name of the King, hold you responsible for the custody of that man. How came Maloosray into his shop, or to remain there while a King's guard was within ear-shot? Ah, liar," added the young man, as the Kullal was advancing, with joined hands, and about to speak, "no more; thou hast told enough lies for the present; by-and-by there will be other questions. Beware of them."

So saying, he passed with his father into the door which the Kótwal himself held open. It was a quiet, secluded place—a small apartment supported upon wooden pillars and arches, which opened into a court shaded with trees. Carpets and pillows were there in abundance, and the place was cool and neatly furnished.

"The papers, whatever they are, Meah, remain with you," said the Meerza. "Shall we examine them here privately?"

"They will be shown to the King only," said Fazil, dryly, "for they concern no one else; meanwhile I am responsible for them."

"Then I will leave ye, noble sirs," returned the other; "be pleased to rest yourselves."

"O for a moment's speech of the King!" cried the Khan, as they were alone. "Now it is too late, and Khan Mahomed is lost. Nay, son, 'tis a pretty court, and not unlike our own Khilwut; but I cannot breathe freely. Canst thou, Fazil? it chokes me."

"Fear not, father; all will be well, I trust," replied his son. "Unobserved, I gave a message to the lad Ashruf, who seems faithful, to be delivered to Kowas Khan. If he comes, all will be well, for he can warn his father. No harm can happen to us except from the Wuzeer, and he may——"

"He dare not," cried Afzool Khan—"he dare not think of us; he will have enough to do to save himself. If the Shah acts—acts firmly—as—as—I would, son, were I in his place and were it my dearest friend—he should die. O Khan Mahomed! O friend!" exclaimed the old man bitterly, "how often have I remonstrated and implored, but you have not listened! He spoke me fair, Fazil, always,—see what is in his heart. But what is written, is written. Let it be; we cannot prevent it."

"Ameen, father! we can only do what is possible to save——"

"I tell thee, boy," resumed the Khan, interrupting him, "I doubt whether it would be meet in us to interfere with God's designs, and to help treachery to escape its deserts. The danger is too great to the King, and, next to God and the Prophet, he is to us dear and honoured. I tell thee, son, we had better not interfere; it may not be good for us."

"Nay, father," said Fazil, "so long as we speak friendly truth and warning, there can be no fear; and what is written in the Wuzeer's destiny will be fulfilled."

'Thou wilt see to that door with thy life, Nasir," whispered the Kótwal to one of his chief attendants, a burly Abyssinian slave. "See that no one passes out or in without my orders. If violence is attempted, strike,—dost thou hear?—to the death! Proud as Afzool Khan is, he may yet lower his head, perhaps with his life. And they have papers, which we must take, Nasir—forcibly, if we cannot otherwise get them:—ere the sun sets, too, or he passes hence."

"Are we strong enough to keep the Khan, my lord?" asked the man doubtingly.

"Ay, true; we need be stronger; send this ring," and he took off his signet, "to the Wuzeer's son. Say we need five hundred men to reinforce the guard. Yes, we should otherwise be too weak, if those mad Affghans were to attempt a rescue. Return here when the messenger goes."

"On my head and eyes be it," replied the slave; "no one shall pass hence save over my dead body."

CHAPTER XXXI.

MALOOSRAY had too much at stake to risk aught by delay, and he and his companions fled from the back door of the house already described, screened by the rain and thick darkness, leaving, however, one of the scouts to inform their companion of what had happened, and with directions for both to join him at their place of concealment as quickly as possible. They proceeded at a rapid pace, leaving the suburb, and striking across the open plain, eastwards, in the direction of the small hamlet of Allapoor, bearing the wounded man with them. Heretofore, in his stealthy visits to the city, Maloosray had found shelter and concealment in a Mutt or monastery of Jogis, who, in their annual pilgrimages, had become known to him, and assuming their garb, and even joining them in their morning perambulations in search of alms, he had been enabled to visit those persons in the city with whom his intrigues were being carried on. Now, however, the Jogis had warned him that their Mutt was no longer safe. Jehándar Beg had received information which led to several visits by his men at night; and though not interfered with, or even aware of the reason of suspicion, the Jogis knew they were watched.

But they were true to his interests, and had prepared a place more secure, because without the walls, and more secluded, than their own Mutt, which was the resort of travellers and devotees from all parts of the country. This was the cloister of an old Hindu temple which stood by itself in an unfrequented part of the plain, and which, either by some act of desecration, or because of its inconvenient situation, had been long neglected. The cloister round it was, however, in good repair, and a little plastering with clay, and cleansing of the chamber from the accumulated dust of years, made the place comfortable enough; and one of the Jogis attended in turn, brought provisions, and acted as cook to the party.

It was easy from thence to reach the city unobserved. Not far distant was the small hamlet of Allapoor, yet sufficiently far to deter prying persons from coming to see who lived in the deserted temple; and if any one were observed, it was, to all appearance, only a Jogi. When, therefore, the Patel, or chief elder of the village of Allapoor, was told by the shepherd boys that some mendicants were repairing the cloister of the old temple and staying there, he bade no one interfere with them; and his good-will was by-and-by secured by an occasional present from time to time. No one suspected the place or its inhabitants; and few frequented the plain about it, which, being hard and stony, was uncultivated, as it still remains, and was used here and there for cemeteries; but the greater part was left to nature, and to flocks of hardy sheep and goats, which picked up a scanty subsistence.

It was not without some apprehension that Maloosray had first trusted himself to the new shelter; but in the course of several visits he had become accustomed to it, and found that he was at once freer and safer there, than in his old quarters inside the walls. The horses, too, were excellently provided for in the crypt of an adjoining Mahomedan tomb, which had never been finished, nor had any use been made of it. Below the foundation terrace was a spacious arched vault, above which the walls of the mausoleum had been partly carried; and the entrance was so overgrown with matted creepers and bushes, that it could not be seen unless examined very closely. Within, three horses, and as many stout ponies, found excellent shelter and concealment; and Maloosray's scouts—who were, in fact, his retainers and escort—lived with them and tended them.

To this place Maloosray proceeded as fast as the wet ground and the rough by-paths would permit—supporting his companion when needful, and helping him over stony places. The wound was not dangerous, yet it had caused considerable loss of blood, and the hardy mountaineer was more weakened than he liked to admit. Once they emerged upon the plain, the temple was soon reached; and, after having the sword-cut dressed and bound up, the wounded man was left to his repose.

Maloosray's next care was for his horses, and he proceeded to the crypt. Safe now from observation, for it was long past midnight, the men there were busy with preparations for the morning meal—for they could cook only at night. Two were grinding millet-flour in the hand-mill, which they always carried with them; another was kneading dough in a wooden trough; a fourth shaping portions of it into cakes, which he patted between his hands into the desired form, and a fifth was baking them upon a large flat iron pan or girdle—which held several at the same time—and removing them to the side of the fire to harden, as fast as baked.

A goodly pile of bread had already accumulated; and in two earthen pots simmered messes of vegetables and split-peas, from which a strong, and not unsavoury, smell of onions and garlic proceeded. The fire, fed by dry sticks from time to time, lighted up the space around, resting upon the rough stone arches and heavy massive groins of the crypt; and upon the forms of several men lying asleep, wrapped in their strong cotton sheets or rough blankets, while others reclined lazily, talking occasionally to those employed. There were three horses—two lay asleep among the men, the other, a powerful silver-grey mare, was feeding, and looking round occasionally to the man baking bread, expecting, with a low whinny, her allowance of buttered cakes.

The scene was peculiar and striking: for the gloom of the vault was so deep, except around the fire itself, that every object seemed to stand out in sharp relief as the light caught it. Just then, too, a brighter blaze than before rested upon the coat of the mare, and, shining on the soft glossy skin, caused the graceful outline of her form to project from the deep gloom behind it in a remarkable manner.

"What! awake, and no one guarding the door? Ah! would ye have the Kótwal's men upon ye, my sons?" cried Maloosray, entering unobserved. "Beware, all of ye, the risk is great."

"Master, we had the watch set," answered a man, standing up and making a clumsy salutation, while others started to their feet. "I only came in for a moment to see to the mare, for the rest were busy."

"Has she not slept?"

"O yes! She just now woke, got up, shook herself, and neighed. That was what brought me in; I thought she had no fodder, and that the others might be asleep."

"Then she is fresh for a journey, in case we have a rapid one, Ramjee?"

"Ay, master; you may be at Poona in three days if you will, or at Pertâbgurh either. She will do it."

Maloosray approached the animal: she stretched her head towards him with a low whinny, and rubbed her nose and eyes against him. "Yes, Rookminee," he said, caressing her, "thou wilt have sharp work, perhaps. Art ready, lass?"

There was another low whinny in reply, as she licked the hand held out to her. She at least understood the caress, and responded to it. He passed his hand over her sleek coat, which glistened like silver in the firelight, and down each leg, and taking up each hoof, narrowly examined every shoe and nail in it in succession.

"Ah! if you can find any fault there, master, you may do as you please with me," said Ramjee. "No; Balla at Jutt knows his trade too well to allow a nail to slack, and he knows, too, whose mare he is shoeing! What does he say? When Sivaji Bhóslay comes with a hundred thousand horse, then I will ride with him on his raid to the south, and not a horse shall drop a shoe, be the journey ever so long."

"And he shall, Ramjee," cried Maloosray, laughing. "The fellow is a braggart, but he is useful."

"Ah! master, that was a rare meeting. Was it not curious that so many horses wanted shoeing that day? Well, so thought the royal horsemen stationed there; and they went about twisting up their moustaches, and swelling themselves out as you never saw, my lord. Many good fellows there were, who would not have cared for a chance with some of those gallants in the open plain. When are we to begin, master?"

"Ay, when?" echoed a number of the men, who ceased their occupation for a moment, or raised themselves on their elbows while the answer was given.

"Not yet, my sons, not yet; we bide our time. And now for work," answered Maloosray. "Go thou, Ramjee, to the Paigah of Afzool Khan early, and see if that dog Bulwunt Rao is dead. Well was it that I tied chains in my turban folds last night, else he had cloven me to the teeth. I have vowed a silver horse to the shrine of Khundôba at Jejoori, for the deliverance."

"And was he slain, master, at last?"

"Nay, that is what I want to know," he replied. "But I had a fair blow at him, and I rarely miss. Go, and bring news quickly."

"Master," said Ramjee in a tone of entreaty, and reverentially touching Maloosray's feet, "I will go. Let there be no risks like this again. What would the Maharaja do without you, and what is there to be gained here that is worth such peril?"

"Ah, yes!" added another, "what if ten thousand such as we are were expended, it would be nothing were Tannajee safe. Only that two of us in the lane behind Rama's, misdirected a party of the King's men, ye had been beset, before and behind; and if the King had got hold of any of ye, the kites and crows of the 'Goruk Imlee' would have had full bellies by this evening."

"Well, it was not of my seeking," returned Maloosray; "for Bulwunt Rao was reported dead—killed in battle two years ago; so, at least, we heard. It was like fighting a spirit, my sons; and I missed my blows. . . . Hark! who is that without? Netta? What news, brother?" he continued, as a slight, active-looking man entered hastily. "Didst thou find Pahar Singh, the old robber?"

"Maharaj!" returned the man, "there was no Pahar Singh. We found a fire burning in the verandah of the temple, and I took a lighted brand and looked about. All we could discover was a little fresh blood on the floor and three gold pieces among the ashes. But there was blood on the wall too, and we tracked it for a few paces, when the torch went out in the rain, so we went on and heard a man moaning in a nullah, and some jackals were standing by him as we went up. Dost thou remember Maun Singh, who is with Pahar Singh always? Well, we could hardly see, so Limba went back for another brand, and brought it under his blanket, and then we saw the man's face. He was terribly wounded, and could not speak sensibly, but one or two names escaped him, one of which was Pahar Singh, and Limba knew his face."

"Ye did not let him live, the foul traitor and liar?" cried Maloosray, excitedly. "O that it had been 'the Lion' himself! Ye did not let him live?"

"Master, he will speak no more, nor yet tell lies. I have made that sure enough," said Limba, approaching and touching the feet of Maloosray. "I knew him after what happened in the old Gosai's Mutt at Tooljapoor, and Moro Punt would have had me kill him then and the other too, only I could find no opportunity. They had some fifty horse with him, and were as shy as deer. Now I have settled that account."

"Good, my son," replied Maloosray; "but what had happened, Netta? Was there no further trace of them?"

"None, Maharaj; we were fairly puzzled. We returned, and stayed in the temple by the fire, in hopes that Pahar Singh might come back; but it was no use. Then we went and listened behind the guard-house, and heard there was a man wounded in an affray—a 'Gosai'—and there was a barber dressing his wound."

"Then he did not die? I had hoped he did."

"Holy Mother! was this thy work, master, and all of us away?" cried several of the men.

"No; Ranoo remained with me," replied Maloosray, "and has got a scratch; but what of the man wounded? What think ye of Bulwunt Rao, my cousin, dead long since, as we thought, but come to life, Netta?"

"My curse on him! And he escaped you, Tannajee?"

"I am going to see if he be dead, brother," interposed Ramjee; "the master's blows are not little ones."

"You see, friends, they—those two Gosais—as they appeared, must have met Pahar Singh, who directed them. I see it all now—the villain's attempt to decoy us into that trap by the temptation of news of the Wuzeer. Depend upon it, he has been bought over, and is not to be trusted; and he set them on our track."

"He never was," cried both the men; "he has only one king and one god—that is money," added Neeta; "and he has gone where he could get it."

"Yes, friends, those men knew us," continued Maloosray; "and to my mind the place is no longer safe: so we had as well be ready. If they have given the alarm—and Bulwunt would do so if he had any sense—we shall have horsemen scouring the plains to-morrow, and that fine lad, Fazil Khan, at the head of them. So away, some of you: watch the gates; let the horses be kept saddled all day; and let them have bread as fast as they can eat it. I would go at once, Nettajee," he added to that person, taking him aside; "but the Wuzeer must be seen and spoken with first. He was at Almella yesterday, and will be in the city by the afternoon. Without having speech of him, I dare not show myself before the master; and the object of our journey would be incomplete. I think we may trust him."

"Alas! I fear not," replied Nettajee; "ye are too sanguine, you and the Maharaja. Khan Mahomed will not league with us; he leans to the Moghuls, and calls us 'Kafirs of Hindus,' and kills cows wherever he can. I know it. Why do ye trust him, when he is faithless to his own salt? Suppose he chose to turn round and hang up Tannajee Maloosray to the 'Goruk Imlee tree,' would not that keep him fair in his master's eyes, and blind them to his intrigues with the Padshah? Ah, brother, trust him not: one who will deceive the master who has raised him to what he is, will deceive you. A slave born, he will be one to the last; and he is not fit to strike in with free men like us! Leave him to the Moghuls, to whom he will be a slave, as he was to Beejapoor: we have our own road between both. But come now to Ranoo: is he fit to travel?"

"He will be better after he has slept. We were owls, Nettajee, not to see through those flimsy disguises," returned Maloosray.

"Bulwunt Rao is better living than dead, brother; and we may yet bring him round," said Nettajee.

"I tell thee, O Netta," interrupted Tannajee, fiercely, and grinding his teeth as he spoke, "I would cut him down with my own hand at the feet of the Maharaja, rather than he should have speech of him. Never name him to me, else we may differ."

"Ah, that blow of his still rings in your head, Tannajee," replied the other, laughing. "But come; if you don't need sleep, I do. He sleeps," he continued, as they entered the cloister where the wounded man lay; "that is well; and I will do the same, Tannajee;" and so saying, he took down a sheet from a cord on which it was hanging, and, wrapping himself in it, lay down, and was soon snoring loudly.

But Maloosray could not sleep, and after a while, got up, and ascending the steps to the roof of the terrace, looked over the plain suspiciously. All, however, was still. To the east, lightning was playing about the tops of the clouds in dim flickering flashes. Everywhere else the sky was clear, and the stars shone with great lustre. A few jackals howled in the distance, and their cry was answered successively in many directions. Then the drums and horns of the several guards at the gates and on the outer walls and bastions of the city, sounded deep and shrill one by one, and were taken up by those in the "Ark" or citadel of the palace, and so died away in the distance.

His eye followed the line of towers and battlements, and narrowly watched every light which might betoken a stir among the troops within; but there was none. The huge dome of the mausoleum of Mahmood Adil Shah, not long completed, stood out in a dark heavy mass against the clear sky: and beyond it the outlines of the Palace of the Seven Stories—the great Cavalier—and a confused mass of trees and buildings intermingled; nearer, too, the massive walls and arches of the tomb of the mother of the late King, then, as now, unfinished.

All was still. High up in the palace a light twinkled now and then faintly, on which Tannajee speculated dreamily. Was the King awake? the light was in his private apartments. What could he be doing so late in the night? for the drums and trumpets had sounded the third watch. O that he would join heartily with his master, and defy the Moghuls! Would no one tell him this was his best policy? Better a thousand times to secure the fidelity of a large portion of his own subjects by timely concession, than to defy and coerce their chieftain. Now, too, though the Moghuls had been once beaten off, it would not be so again. They were resting and gathering strength, and one by one the independent kingdoms to the north had fallen before them.

How long would this remain?—this, the most extensive, most valuable, and most heretical. Better far, then, to secure the Mahrătta people, than to lose all by a double war with them, and with the Moghuls. "Will no one tell the boy this?" thought Maloosray. "We do not wish him evil; but the master must be free, and will be free. The people will assemble at the Dusséra, and the King can then have his choice between a lakh of Mahrattas and a lakh of Moghuls, or both combined; and yet this old family should not pass away—it should not pass away at our hands."

But we need not follow his thoughts further: better to transport ourselves to that twinkling light high up in the Seven-storied Palace, and see who sit beside it, and hear what they say.

CHAPTER XXXII.

The Palace of the Seven Stories still exists as one of the most noble and picturesque ruins of the Fort of Beejapoor. Of the Seven Stories, only five are now traceable; the two upper have been destroyed, perhaps by lightning, or have fallen from decay and disrepair; and it is only in the third that the remains of the beautiful chamber still existent there convey an idea of the effect of the whole structure when it was perfect. Even this has been much damaged. The gilding of the walls, of the groins of the arches and fretted roof, and of its delicate arabesque borders, has all been scraped off, and the fresco paintings are so destroyed by exposure, that but little exists to tell the history of the beautiful Bhagiruttee, the mistress of the monarch who built the palace for her.

Enough, however, remains to show what the general design and execution of the work were; enough to prove the exquisite taste which had directed its completion, and the skill and boldness of the architect who had raised the dizzy tower so high. Then, the spacious arches and oriel windows were filled by richly carved panels and shutters of teak wood, which admitted sufficient light and air: now, these are all gone, the windows are open, and the rain and sun and wind are rapidly causing decay and destruction of what remains. The upper stories are so broken that they cannot be ascended; but in the one of which we speak, the traveller will be tempted to sit a while looking over the masses of ruins beneath him: and over the still perfect walls of the citadel. Beyond, the undulating plain studded with mounds, shows lines of streets, with broken arches, minarets, and some still perfect mosques, mausoleums, and palaces, which have withstood the effects of time and the spoiler, and remain as proofs of the splendour which once prevailed.

At the period of our tale all these were perfect. The city spread away to the south and west, covering many miles of plain with those streets and houses of which the lines of mounds alone remain. They are interspersed with villages, which are probably portions of the old city, never entirely deserted, and to which the descendants of the population of those days have clung through all vicissitudes. To the east and north, after looking over the greater part of the citadel, the eye followed the plain beyond—the proper esplanade of the fort—and the undulating rising ground to the north-east, from which the Moghul batteries had so recently poured a storm of shot upon the defences, yet happily with no effect.

The King's apartment opened to the west; and, like Afzool Khan about the same time, he sat courting the breeze, which played gently round the rich clustered mullions of the oriel window, and refreshed and soothed him. The storm had died away, and the night was clear and fresh; while, from the garden below, ascended the mingled perfume of champas, limes, tuberoses, jessamine of various kinds, and other sweet-scented flowers, which loaded the air almost to excess.

A silver lamp, on a tall silver stand, stood in a recess sheltered from the open casement, and its seven wicks burned brightly, illuminating the chamber, and by their strong light causing the gilded roof, arches, and groins, with all their delicate colouring of rose-colour, yellow, light-green, and blue enamel, to assume a soft harmony of effect—different from the light of day, yet perhaps more beautiful.

Furniture there was none; but in the space enclosed by the oriel window, there was spread a rich, soft, Persian carpet, which filled its area, on which, in the corner near were the young King was sitting, lay a thick quilted mattress of green satin brocaded with gold, and a large pillow of the same material, both covered with fine muslin. This had been the King's seat, and it was thickly strewn with papers—some Persian, some Mahratta—which, to all appearance, had been under examination, and he had evidently just left it and placed himself by the casement which he had opened. He was alone, but, by the frequent glances towards the doorway, which was covered by a heavy curtain, some one seemed impatiently expected.

The events of the night had aroused unusual energy in the young King; nor, since his accession to the throne, had any occurrence excited him like the discovery of treason in the man he had, perhaps, most trusted—his prime minister, Khan Mahomed. It was so unprovoked, so undeserved. Early in life great ability and aptitude for business had been remarked in the Abyssinian slave, Rehân, by the late King; and he had risen, as favourites among Asiatic princes often do, rapidly to rank and wealth, with every honour which an attached and grateful prince could bestow upon him. Finally he had reached the rank of prime minister or Wuzeer, as we have already mentioned, and, amidst all the distractions and intrigues of faction, had succeeded in preserving his monarch's attachment.

In this position he was maintained by the young King on his accession to the throne, notwithstanding the insinuations of many that the Wuzeer was unfaithful. The King had not heeded these suspicions, nor, indeed, beyond mere rumour, was there anything which could lead to confirmation of them; and as the Wuzeer desired it as a proof of his fidelity, the Abyssinians under his command had been pushed on to the north to watch the Moghul armies; for it was better to submit to the turbulence of the Dekhan chieftains at the capital, who could be controlled by neutral forces like those of Afzool Khan, than to risk the possible misconduct of the others. Again, the Dekhanies could not be trusted with the frontier; and the King, impressed with the fidelity of Khan Mahomed, had left him at his post.

At this period the Dekhanies and Abyssinians were rival factions in the state. The latter were more amenable to discipline than the former, who were descendants of those Mahomedan warriors—Toorks, Tartars, and Affghans—who, at the close of the thirteenth century, under Alla-oo-Deen, had invaded the south of India, and wrested the territory in which they had settled from the Mahrattas of Deogurh and the Canarese dynasty of Beejanuggur. They had founded, and maintained the dynasty of Gulburgah, against the attacks of powerful Hindu states, and, when they separated from it, had attached themselves to the founders of other dynasties, which rivalled, and, indeed, exceeded in splendour, the parent one.

Those who were in Beejapoor had joined Ibrahim Adil Shah, when he declared and established his independence of the Bahmani dynasty of Gulburgah, and they had risen to rank and wealth with the state. They had been led to victory by that monarch and his successors; they had conquered province after province from the infidels of the southern Hindu states, and they had at last finally subdued and overturned the ancient Hindu monarchy of Beejanuggur, which, for several generations, was their bitter enemy and rival. Was it wonderful that they at length became arrogant, and that, to maintain an equipoise against them, another element, the Abyssinian, was admitted into this state? It is the old story in the history of the world of exclusive military power; the old play which has always been played out when the characters are brought together.

There were proud names among these old Dekhan families, which still exist, Tartars and Toorks, who ill brooked the control of slaves like Abyssinians. They were free, and held themselves equal in rank to their own king—proud barons in fact, who seldom accepted administrative service, and were rarely fit for it; men "who could fight, but could not write," as they boasted; turbulent, arrogant, quarrelsome among themselves, split into as many factions as they were families and tribes. The "Dagtorays," "Alla-ool-Moolks," "Bhylmees," "Kalla Chuttrees," "Saféd Poshs," and a host of others, were faithful to their own state, while they were an unceasing source of anxiety, and often distress, to its administrators.

So long as the Moghul armies had threatened the capital, or there was employment daily in the field to meet a common danger, these tribes and their chiefs had found occupation against the common enemy, and had fought valiantly and successfully. The best cavalry of the Moghul army was no match for these fiery Dekhan cavaliers. Reckless of life, well mounted, each tribe and appellation vying with each other, whenever there was a chance in their broad plains, they had not neglected it, and were ever in advance of the more disciplined though slower moving bodies of Abyssinian horse and foot, whom they despised as slaves.

Between the extremes of party were those who, like Afzool Khan, belonged to neither, who held a common interest and faith in the dynasty they served, and whose arms had often been turned against Abyssinians, and against Dekhanies, whenever revolts or mutinies of either rendered it necessary.

Among these contending factions, and ever present rivalries, the course of the young King had been difficult and devious since his accession; but respect to his father's memory and experience, for he had been a wise prince, a successful administrator, and a valiant warrior in the field, had, in the end, induced him to continue the predominance of the Abyssinian element in council; and to allow the Dekhanies scope for their ambition in military commands and active service in distant provinces of the kingdom, retaining those only at the capital who would prove a counterpoise to the Abyssinians, in case of need. Influenced by personal esteem, and even affection, for the man who had been his father's most trusted counsellor and friend, he had retained Khan Mahomed in office, notwithstanding the evil reports of his Dekhan officers; and under these circumstances the distress, and even dismay, of the young King at the discovery of the treachery, which had long existed, was hard to endure. It was his first bitter lesson in life, and there were few to fall back upon for advice or consolation.

In his extremity his thoughts had turned to Afzool Khan first, perhaps, of all: but again, his known intimacy with the Wuzeer; the report that the families would soon be united by the marriage of Khan Mahomed's son to the old Khan's daughter; the notorious friendship of the young men; and, above all, a certain reticence in Afzool Khan's expressions whenever the Wuzeer's character or actions were discussed—recurred to the King, and his thoughts turned from Afzool Khan to others in succession, yet finding rest nowhere.

Of all his officers, on whom could he depend? Jehândar Beg, who should have been his executive in any arrest of the Wuzeer, was known to be his dependent: and thus speculating on each, he estimated bitterly how really weak he was in personal adherents.

At first all appeared to be decided in his favour, but gradually requests were made under one pretext or other, which disclosed the true objects of his courtiers, and the young King had sufficient discernment to estimate their professions at their full value. It was these experiences which threw him back upon himself, and upon the Wuzeer, who was, at least as he thought, moderate and unselfish. Moderate, certainly, to him; yet, at heart, more grasping and more treacherous than any.

There was no doubt of that now. Again and again had the King taken up the letter we have before read, and examined it closely, and had each time laid it down with increased conviction that it was genuine. There could be no doubt either as to the seal or the writing. Khan Mahomed's own hand was too peculiar to be imitated; yet he had doubted—still doubted. It is hard to admit conviction of guilt when one's affections are pleading innocence, but here it was not to be resisted; and, as most generally follows such conviction, those very affections were fast becoming the most unrelenting judges.

"Let them but confirm this," said the King, aloud, as he looked out, and again turned to the papers, selected the letter, looked over it, and hastily put it down with a shiver. "Let them but confirm it, and then—— O, my father! wert thou here it would be the same, and your son will not flinch from the necessity, be it what it may."

CHAPTER XXXIII.

As yet the King's thoughts had admitted nothing definitely; the blow had been too sudden, the provocation too great, for aught but a numbness of perception which checked conclusive determination; but this was passing away fast, and it was becoming still more apparent that, if Khan Mahomed's plan had succeeded, he must, if he survived it, be the dependent of his own slave and his father's. Were the other letters, which they had looked over hastily, true also? Men's tongues had before been busy with the Wuzeer's reputation, and now were so again—the same subject and the same man; and it was—"true, true!"

Unconsciously he had spoken aloud in his reverie, and the word seemed to come as if an echo of his own thought.

"Who spoke?" he cried, looking round—"Who spoke?" His very question seemed to make the silence more impressive; and, as he strained his eyes into the gloom of the chamber, there was no sound but the gentle sough of the night wind, laden with moisture, among the trees below and the open latticework of the windows. "The spirits of the dead are around me to-night," he continued to himself, shuddering. "Listen, O father! Listen, sweet mother! O Prophet of God, on whom be peace, assist and hear me! O thou fountain and dispenser of justice, make me true and bold; make me, as I should be, thy agent among thy people. If I have been a child till now, forgive me—that is past. . . . He writes to the Emperor, that I am a boy!—that I am a boy! Inshalla! No! that is past!" As he spoke, the sound of voices below, and of footsteps ascending the narrow stair were distinctly audible, and he paused to listen. "It is they at last, and the Meerza has not delayed. Enter," he cried, as the steps appeared to reach the landing-place and doorway —"enter, I am here."

The heavy quilted curtain was pushed aside, and three persons advanced—one the Meerza or secretary we have before mentioned; the other two we have not yet seen; but they had been often employed as confidential advisers by the King, and he had now sent for them. When they returned from the temple, the King and his secretary had examined the papers they had obtained, with great care and anxiety, and they proved to be far more voluminous and important than even our friend the Lalla had imagined.

The dates of the letters extended over several years. Some, of later date, within the year, had evidently been sent secretly, for they were rolled up into the smallest possible compass, in lead, and so that they could be put into the mouth, or otherwise hidden; the handwriting was disguised, and several were written in cypher; but the most recent were not disguised at all, and the seals were perfect. The whole formed a series, and they had hastily put them together. Each letter confirmed the other, or seemed to do so, and yet, considering the issue at stake, neither cared to trust their own judgment: and the papers needed confirmation, as well of their authenticity as of their reference to former occurrences and dates.

Of the Mahratta documents, however, they could form no opinion, as neither could read the character; but the secretary was familiar with the seal, and even the rude signature, of Sivaji Bhóslay; and these letters might throw some light on the subject of reputed intrigues with the Emperor, and prove a guide to future proceedings.

The two persons who had been summoned so hastily to the night council were, in the first place, Peer Dustageer Khaderi, a holy Syud, or descendant of the Prophet, of the purest lineage, and the head of a religious house or establishment of Durwaysh, or, as we familiarly call them, "Dervishes," which had been largely endowed by the State, and for whose ancestors, buried in the precincts of the shrine, miracles were now becoming ostensibly claimed. As a consequence, the holy influence of the "Peer" was decidedly on the increase; and as he had been chosen as religious instructor to the King, he was at that time his "Moorshid," or spiritual guide; and being a shrewd, well-educated person, possessed of deep local experience, and, from his position, able to obtain information of a trustworthy nature, he was frequently consulted. To give him due credit, the Peer had proved, on more than one occasion, to have rendered valuable service. Him, therefore, had the King named as the person best fitted to be intrusted with the secret they had obtained.

The other was an old Brahmun, who entered leaning upon a long stick with a gold head, yet not so as to evince weakness, and was as remarkable in his degree as the person whom he accompanied. Neelkunt Rai Pansay, in the outset of his life a humble Karkoon, or clerk, in the revenue department of the State, had served, in succession, three generations of its kings, and, at upwards of eighty years old, was still clear-headed, astute, and faithful. He had risen to the rank of "Peshcar," or finance minister, by his valuable services in that department; and though an "infidel," as he was termed by the Peer, was beloved and respected, and consulted on occasions of more than ordinary solemnity or embarrassment, more particularly in regard to the affairs of his own people, the Hindus of the kingdom.

While the secretary advanced to the King, the others stood at the further end of the apartment. Neither knew why they had been summoned, and the hour of the night, the, to them, strange fact of being together in the most private apartment of the palace, and in the King's presence, caused them to look at each other wonderingly.

These were not persons who could ever unite in private friendship; for the Peer, a bigoted follower of Mahomed, and a holy saint to boot, was one of those who, as warriors of the faith, would have led armies against the infidels, and utterly exterminated them. That king of Gulburgah, Feroze Shah, was in his eyes a true Moslem, and now surely enjoying Paradise, who, in pursuance of his vow, had slain a hundred thousand of the infidels of Beejanuggur, and made pyramids of their heads at the gate of his city. If the kings of Beejapoor had been such it would have been well; but, alas! in his eyes they were degenerate. Here was a proof: the infidel minister sent for to confer with him! the Syud! "Astagh-fur-Ulla!" (God forbid it!) gurgled in his throat, and he edged away and gathered up his garments with a gesture decidedly contemptuous.

This did not escape the old Brahmin's notice, but it was no time to resent it, for they were called forward. A word from the secretary had decided the King to have the Mahratta letters first examined. Aroused from his sleep, and in the presence of a Brahmun, the Syud was not likely to discuss any matter temperately with one; nor, indeed, in a subject in which Mahomedan honour was involved, was it politic, perhaps, to reveal particulars to a Hindu; but the fact or otherwise of Sivaji Bhóslay's attachment or treachery so affected the Wuzeer's position, that it could not be concealed from one who, whatever his faults of religious arrogance might be, was at least a firm friend of the young King and of his government.

"Salaam-o-alykoom! Khoosh amudeed! (you are welcome)," said the King, using the Persian salutation to the Syud, and rising as he advanced.

"Salaam-o-alyk!" returned the holy man, advancing, as was his wont, in a peculiar but characteristic manner; that is, he bent his head forward, so as to assume a stoop which might be supposed reverential, but which was, in fact, patronising in the extreme; stretching forth his arms in an attitude of benediction, and, having set his feet nearly at right angles, he shuffled with short steps towards the edge of the carpet on which was the King's seat. "My lord's health is sound, and his brain is clear?"

"I am well," returned the King; "be seated."

The Peer looked for a place as near the King as possible, and, with another wave of his hands, settled himself upon his heels with two motions—first, to drop on his knees, and second, to subside upon his heels, very much after the fashion of a camel when it is to be loaded. This done, he joined his hands together, and smiling blandly, again ventured to ask whether "My lord and prince were well."

"By your favour and the mercy of God," replied the King, "I am well."

"Ul-humd-ul-illa! (Praise be to God!) Shookr! shookr! (thanks, thanks!)" ejaculated the Peer devoutly, as he settled himself more comfortably; then, taking his rosary from his waist, began to tell his beads with great rapidity, as the old Brahmun, following to the edge of the carpet, and making a humble and reverential salutation, stood awaiting the King's pleasure.

"Be seated, Neelkunt Rai," said the King kindly; and as the old man stooped to the ground, supporting himself by his stick, the secretary compassionately put his hand under his arm, and let him down gently. The scowl from the Peer at this unwonted act of courtesy was lost upon the secretary, but not upon the old man himself; nor was his look of thanks to the person who had assisted him unremarked by the Syud. "I will watch them," he said inwardly: "these two seem to understand each other."

CHAPTER XXXIV.

The King spoke first, breaking a silence which, though only lasting for a few moments, seemed interminably oppressive.

"I have called you, Neelkunt Rai," he said, "to examine and read to me some papers which have come into my possession. There is no one about me from whom I can expect more true fidelity than from you in a delicate matter. Give him the papers, Meerza; they are before you."

"May my lord's favour and condescension increase," returned the old man, bowing humbly. "I have never deceived the State, and am too old to begin; and as the grandson is now, so were the father and grandfather always towards me; true confidence is rarely disappointed."

The King sighed. "Alas," he said, "would it were so! Read and judge for yourself."

Neelkunt Rai took the papers, cast his eyes over a few lines, put them down, fumbled in his pockets for his spectacles, which finally were found in a fold of his turban, put them on, and looked first at the end of the paper.

"The letters are from Sivaji Bhóslay, my lord. Doubtless some renewal of his former excesses, and his usual apologies for them. Shall I read them."

"If that were all, Neelkunt Rai, we could forgive them," replied the King; "but read; we may perhaps be in error about them, though truly our vassal grows in power, and heeds not warnings or advice."

"It is only a few months since he took the four forts," interposed the Meerza, "and the letters given to Afzool Khan mention that he is repairing and putting grain into them, and that Pertâbgurh, where he lives, is now impregnable, and that——"

"Let him read, Meerza Sahib," said the Peer ironically: "one so high in the favour of the King should not be interrupted;" and he stroked his beard gently with one hand, while the beads of his rosary passed rapidly through the fingers of the other, and his lips repeated the particular invocation of the divinity which suited every bead. "Let him read; my lord is already listening."

Neelkunt Rai proceeded. He had been deceived by the address, which was that usually written to his own sovereign, and had read the letter through unsuspiciously; but as its purport became evident, it was clear, by his change of countenance, that this was no ordinary communication, and after a while he stopped suddenly.

"It is not fit for my lord to hear," he said excitedly. "This is treason!"

"Be not afraid, Neelkunt Rai, we would know the worst," replied the King.

"Yes, my lord should know who are true and who are false," added the Peer, pompously. "It is true wisdom!"

"As you will," returned the old man, bowing to the King, and not noticing the Peer; "your servant is not responsible for what is written, and you must be patient with it;" and he read and translated as he went on.

There could be no doubt that the treason was unmasked and unconcealed. The wrongs of his father, wrote Sivaji, who for four years had been imprisoned in the dungeon of the citadel of Beejapoor, near the gate, called for revenge; the wrongs of the people, suffering under endless local oppression and exaction, called for redress, which it was hopeless to expect at the hands of a boy, priest-ridden and under the domination of bigoted and ignorant ministers. The conclusion was characteristic of the writer. All he desired was confirmation of his ancestral rights, and permission to serve, with his forces, in the imperial interest.

Letter after letter was read, all much to the same purpose; those of the latter dates being more particular, perhaps, than the former.

"Enough," cried the King at last, "we are weary of these details. What dost thou think, Neelkunt Rai?"

"My lord," said the old man, joining his hands, "mine are not the words of flattery; nor is my advice given without reason. I cannot control men's tongues, nor can I hinder the actions of such as Sivaji Bhóslay; nor yet am I a soldier, to estimate whether his means are proportionate to the end he proposes to attain. If I may speak, I will do so truly, and as one who is near death now; but my lord must not be offended, else I am silent."

"Be careful, and do not transgress the bounds of propriety and respect," said the priest.

"Let him speak as he will, Synd," cried the King, hastily; "do not interrupt him. Fear not, Neelkunt Rai."

"I fear no one, because I have no reason to do so," returned the old man simply, and looking steadily at the priest. "What I have to say is this: the disaffection of Sivaji Bhóslay may spread, but it has not yet become dangerous. That it will be so, if not checked, there is no doubt, for the whole Mahratta people are with him; and there are many signs among them that he will be great——"

"That he will be great?" echoed the King.

"My lord," interrupted the Synd, "I know all about that. Some of my disciples who live at a distance, have come to me from time to time lately, and told me of the damnable doings of the infidels; and how this Sivaji is supposed to have revelations from their gods; but they are but stones—they are but stones, and gold and silver. Now, what saith the blessed Prophet, on whom be peace, about such infidels?"

"Spare us, good Synd," returned the King, interrupting him gently, "we know the passages; but God hath seen fit to give our house subjects of this faith; and they are all our children—they—as well as the true believers. We can see no difference."

"Astagh-fur-oolla! No difference!" cried the Synd. "Is it not written in the holy book, how they shall be burned in the fires of hell, and thou sayest there is no difference! Some one hath surely bewitched thee with sorcery, my son, and I will say exorcisms for thee—and——"

"Enough," returned the King, coldly; "we have not time to waste in discussion on such matters now. Proceed, Neelkunt Rai."

"The Syud is a holy man," said the old minister, "and he and his house are venerated, and he should be merciful and considerate to all; but as he, too, hath heard the rumours in regard to Sivaji, my lord will believe them. And it would be well not to disregard them entirely. A people's enthusiasm is not to be trifled with."

"There is but one cure for it, if they are infidels, and that is the sword," murmured the Syud. "What saith——"

"We cannot suffer these interruptions," interposed the King, haughtily.

"Peace, Meer Sahib," whispered the Meerza, laying his hand on the other's arm, as he was about to rise. "Peace, and be still. In what will come afterwards we have need of thee—much need; be still."

"My prince," said Neelkunt Rai, endeavouring to rise, "I have done what was needed, and beg leave to depart in peace. My King knows the worst. What his servant would advise will not now be listened to, were he even to speak."

"Say on," cried the King, interrupting him; "thou hast a right to speak. Say on; we will not prevent thee."

"But he will," returned the Karkoon, pointing to the Syud.

"If he speaks no irreverence against the people of the true faith, he may talk till morning," said the Syud, with a wave of the hand. "I shall be dumb and deaf."

"I have little to represent, my lord," replied the old man. "It is hard to say whether rebellion such as this, should be crushed or forgiven. If I should advise the former, can it be done? If the latter, I may be suspected of partiality. Ah, my prince, if you gird up your loins to fight Sivaji, it will but be trying to grasp the wind; and your best troops will be taken into his mountains, leaving their places empty for the Moghuls to occupy, and that were a dangerous risk. No! send your royal 'kowl' to the Bhóslay—invite him here—ennoble him—treat him as your ancestors treated the Beyder chief of Suggur, and you will secure him. If a time of trial should ever come, which may the gods avert, the old Brahmun's words and cautions for the adoption of a merciful policy will not be forgotten. May I depart?"

"Yes, you have permission to depart, Neelkunt Rai," said the King, interrupting the Syud, who was about to speak angrily. "It is even as we suspected in regard to those letters, and the Bhóslay's treachery to the State. We would ask one thing more:—what force hath Sivaji in reality?"

"My prince," returned the Brahmun, rising and leaning on his staff, "what shall I say? Have you no reports? Were not letters given to Afzool Khan to read? Ask him; he knows that country better than I do—far better. Ask the Syud what his disciples tell him."

"No, no; I will have your opinion," interrupted the King. "Speak! what do your people, the Brahmuns, say about it?"

"May I be forgiven, my lord, if it prove untrue. Yet I will speak as I hear," replied the old man. "My prince knows that I am not of this country, nor of this people; I have no interest in them except as Hindus; but you may be assured there is not a Mahratta breathing who will not follow Sivaji, and the divine call he is believed to have received. No man who can wield a sword or carry a gun, or who has a horse to ride, that will not go to the places of meeting when—'the fire is on the hills.' How many there may be, the gods only know! Lakhs! lakhs! who can count them? Beware of them, my prince, and secure their chief ere it be too late."

"What has passed here is secret, Neelkunt Rai," said the King. "Thou mayst go; we will send for thee again in this matter ere it be concluded," and with a deep reverence to the King, and salutations to the others, the old man retreated a few paces backwards, then turned, and passed out of the chamber.

"Blessed be God and the Prophet!" exclaimed the Syud when he was gone. "The air was defiled by his breath! Ul-humd-ul-illa! a Kafir and a traitor, may he——"

"Peace, Meer Sahib, we have dismissed him, and that is enough," said the King. "Our father, on whose memory be peace, trusted him, and so did his father,—so also do we."

"As my prince pleases," returned the holy man, with a humble gesture, and checking the volley of curses he had prepared to hurl after the old Brahmun. "In this matter it seemed to me that his counsel was cowardly and dangerous. How say you, Meerza? Was Feroze Shah afraid of infidels when he and his true believers slew them by lakhs, and the pyramids of heads stood by the gates of Gulburgah? And is our prince less than he was, or are these Mahratta Kafirs more powerful than those of Beejanugger? Speak, man!"

"My opinion would be little worth," said the secretary, "even did my lord desire it, and there are others more capable of judging of the power of this Mahratta robber than I am. What you have to advise our master upon is another matter, Syud."

"Explain it to him, Meerza," said the King, sadly: "I am sick of treachery, which seems to be closing round me like a net on all sides."

"God and the Prophet forbid!" exclaimed both in a breath. "Treachery known, is soon disposed of. That which sits crouching in hidden places is alone to be dreaded," continued the Syud. "Ere I hear the detail, I have my fears."

"Nay, read thyself and judge," said the King. "Give him the letters, Meerza."

"I have compared the seals," said the secretary, "with those letters recently received by the King, and the writing also. Judge for yourself before you read."

The Syud obeyed. He examined and compared the seals, the superscription, and the paper of all, with much care and evident interest, as expressed in various ejaculations of wonder, and appeals to the divinity under various appellations suited to the circumstances, which may be spared. "No doubt, no doubt," he said, after the scrutiny had been concluded, "no doubt of these, nor of the superscription. They only confirm what hath long been in men's mouths, yet was undetected."

"Read," said the King. "Satisfy yourself."

CHAPTER XXXV.

"It is finished, my lord," said the Syud, looking up, after an examination of the papers which had appeared interminable, and as he spoke, the cry of the Muezzin of the Royal Mosque arose in the invitation to morning prayer, sonorous and musical, "Alla hu Akbur! Alla hu Akbur!" "It is finished," he continued, "and it is the will of Alla that morning prayer should come with the last words. Come, my lord, let us do this service, and ask a blessing on our deliberation. Come to the terrace in the fresh morning air."

We need not follow them. As they returned and seated themselves again by the oriel window, the first blush of dawn was stealing over the sky, paling the stars, and the gentle breeze of morning rustled softly among the leaves of the gardens below. The ceremony he had performed, the ablution, and the air of the terrace outside to which they had adjourned, had refreshed the King after this weary night.

"Speak, Syud," he said, as they resumed their seats. "What is it to be?"

"I need not, my lord," replied the Syud. "What Alla hath put into thy heart I now see in thine eyes, and so be it! Ameen! ameen! ameen! It is his destiny. He is not fit to live; let him die, perjured and faithless as he is. My lord, he had sworn on the holy book to me to be true. He had touched my feet and my neck as witness to his oath. Yet see, since then, nay, within a few weeks, this letter—worst of all—was written. But O, my prince! there must be no mistake. Even at the last, let not the blood of a guiltless man be on our heads."

The Synd's resolution had wavered for a moment, but was rallied by the secretary as the King shook his head, but did not reply.

"Meer Sahib," he said, "we have had the same doubts, my lord and I. Considering how we obtained the letters, can there be uncertainty?"

"God forbid!" replied the Synd—"God forbid! it is enough. I see in this revelation the hand of the All-wise, and we, his creatures, should not resist His destinies and His justice. We cannot do so even if we wished," and he bowed his head reverently over his beads. "Hark! what is that?"

"Ulla dilâyâ to léonga! Ulla dilâyâ to léonga! (If God give I will take! If God give I will take)" was suddenly shouted in an outer court of the palace by a powerful voice, and interrupted the priest for a moment.

"Listen!" he continued, grasping the Meerza's arm. "What is that cry, so strange, and so early?"

"It is but one of the city beggars," said the King, looking across to his secretary with a peculiar glance of intelligence, "who perhaps has not slept off his night's potions. One of thine own disciples, perhaps, Huzrut."

"I will go and listen," said the secretary, rising; and he proceeded to the terrace where the morning prayer had been performed.

"Ulla dilâyâ to léonga!" arose in clear deep tones, now unchecked by the heavy quilted curtain of the royal chamber. It was a common form of cry of fakeers or other beggars; but there was something in the rough tone of the voice which seemed to strike familiarly upon the Meerza's ear.

"Ulla dilâyâ to léonga!"

The last cry was followed by a remonstrance from the soldiers below, who, belonging to the guard of the private apartments, had evidently stopped the intruder.

"Gently, O Syn," cried one; "what dost thou here so early? Do not bawl so loud, friend, else they will be awakened up yonder, and thou wilt be whipped and put in the stocks. Come and sit here, and rest thyself if thou wilt."

"Ulla dilâyâ to léonga!" was the only reply.

"Nay, but thou canst not enter here, Syn. This is the private court of the Hareem, and thou must be silent," continued the soldier.

"Ulla dilâyâ to léonga!"

"The fellow is mad or drunk. Here, Jemadar," cried another voice; "what is to be done with this Fakeer?"

"Who can this be?" thought the Meerza. "This is no common cry. I must see the worthy Synd out, and get speech of the crier."

"Ulla dilâyâ——"

The Fakeer's cry was broken off abruptly, and there was a noise as if of a scuffle below. Could it be any one in the Wuzeer's interest, seeking for information, or perhaps with deadly intent. "Ho there!" cried the secretary; "what noise is that so early, disturbing the King?"

"Some drunken Fakeer, my lord," returned one of the guards, looking up, "who has intruded, God knows how."

"Keep him, and I will come down presently," answered the Meerza, not waiting for the reply, but re-entering the chamber.

"Some Fakeer, my lord," he continued to the King, but answering his look of intelligence, "whom I have ordered to be confined till the Darogah of the palace can deal with him for his insolence."

"If he be one of my men come after me," said the Syud, "he shall be punished. And now, my lord, have I permission to depart? Delay not in this matter; and may God givo you a safe deliverance from a traitor!"

"You may go, Meer Sahib," said the King; "and we thank you for this visit; but shall need you at noon."

"Your servant will be present without fail," returned the Syud, humbly. "Would that his power were equal to his devotion in the King's service!"

"Return directly," said the King, in a whisper, to his secretary, as the holy man waddled slowly to the door. "I know who it is; bring him hither at once. Hast thou forgotten the Jogi of the temple?"

"Hither? that fearful man!"

"Yes, and at once—any excuse—say he does exorcism—anything." The secretary hesitated.

"At once," continued the King, positively, "and without fail. I feared him not then, when I was in his power and helpless, neither do I now. Go, take this with thee," and he slipped his signet ring into the Meerza's hand.

"I will have him searched at any rate," thought the Meerza, as he descended the narrow stair. "Take care, Meer Sahib, the light is uncertain. Ah, here we are. Who is that, Abdulla, that was crying out?" he said to a eunuch, who, with others, kept guard at the foot of the stairs.

"I know not, my lord. He is some drunken Fakeer, no doubt; and they have tied him up, I hear."

"He may be wanted above," whispered the Meerza. "Let him follow me, and without notice or hindrance. Some exorcism is needed—you understand—within——"

The man stared, and only bowed assent over his crossed arms. "Who dared question royal secrets?"

"Coming, Meer Sahib; I only looked for my shoes," cried the Meerza to his companion, who had advanced a few paces.

Hearing the secretary's voice, several persons emerged from the guard-room, holding the Fakeer tightly. His face was distinctly seen in the morning light, and there could be no mistake.

"He is not one of my children," said the Syud, blandly, looking at the man, and seating himself in his palankeen, which had been brought up; "some drunken brawler, no doubt, who deserves a whipping. Send him to the Kótwal, my sons. I am departing, Meerza Sahib."

"Khoda Hafiz! (God be with you!)" returned the secretary. "At noon, you remember!"

"Of course, Meerza Sahib, the royal commands are on my head and eyes. Go on, my sons," and the bearers shuffled along at their usual pace.

"Shookr Oolla! (thank God!)" ejaculated the secretary, who had doubts of the priest, as he had of most others. "Who art thou, fellow?" he added to the prisoner.

"Bid them loose me," said Pahar Singh, for it was he, "and I will tell thee. Hast thou forgotten so quickly?"

"My lord," said one of the soldiers, "let us turn him out into the town."

"How he got in here," added another, "no one knows; yet he is not drunk, and he has done no harm beyond bawling and struggling. He has the strength of a fiend."

"Loose him, my friends; he is an exorcist, and there has been some trouble within," replied the secretary. "I must take him into the presence. He has no arms? Behold the royal seal."

"I have the amulet which shall restore health to the sick," growled the pretended Fakeer; "it is sorely needed, and time presses. The planetary conjunction is passing."

"Come, Syn; I will lead thee in," said the secretary, taking his hand.

"He has no weapons—we searched him well; but he will answer no questions," said several men, speaking together.

"Ah, my friends," replied the secretary, gravely, "those who cast out evil spirits are not to be questioned. Come, Syn, follow me."

The men shrugged their shoulders incredulously. What could it mean? To all except the Meerza the entry of such a character to the private apartments at any hour would have been impossible—but now, and under the King's seal? How had he entered the citadel? The guard at the gate had not seen him pass; and this mystery, with the fact of his having been expected, furnished plentiful cause of speculation to those who had seized him.

CHAPTER XXXVI.

"WHAT is it?" asked the Meerza anxiously, as they passed into the inner court. "Why hast thou come, Pahar Singh, thus early?"

"Is he above—Ali Adil Shah?" asked the robber; "what I have to say is for him alone. And thou hast recognized me, O Meerza?"

"He is," replied the Meerza; "follow me and be silent. I will tell him. Yes, I knew thee, and he trusts thee."

The eunuchs of the lower guard bowed their heads on their folded arms as the two men passed and ascended the stair together. When they reached the terrace, the Meerza stepped on and drew aside the curtain.

"He is come, my lord," he said in a low tone—"he—the robber."

"I thought so," replied the King; "bring him in."

As Pahar Singh entered, the light of the lamp shone full on him, and revealed a haggard anxious face; his large eyes were gleaming wildly from among the heavy masses of his matted hair, now hanging about his shoulders; but the disguise as a Mahomedan mendicant was as complete as that of the Hindu Jogi had been. He made no lowly reverence, but advanced boldly—defiantly, as it were—to the edge of the carpet, and the King involuntarily grasped the hilt of the short sword lying beside him.

"The King might kill me," said the man, observing the action; "a word, and the head of Pahar Singh is struck from his body by those eunuchs yonder. There is no escape hence—is it not so? Yet I have trusted thee, O King, and do not fear thee, even as thou didst not fear me. I am here, true to thy salt; and what I have to tell thee is as true as I am."

"Fear not," said the King, "and speak freely; thou art safe here."

"Does he know all?" asked the robber, pointing to the Meerza.

"All, friend. Was he not with me, and are not these the letters?" returned the King. "Else——"

"I believe thee, Adil Khan," said Pahar Singh. "Now, listen: time is short, and much has to be done ere thou art safe."

The King started. "Safe?" he cried.

"Ay, safe, my lord. Khan Mahomed was at Almella yesterday, and is on his way hither now. He will be here about the third watch of the day, or sooner. What brings him, think you?" said Pahar Singh, rapidly.

"I sent him a letter of assurance, and he believes it," said the King.

"Believes it, King? He?" exclaimed the man derisively. "He? Thou art but a simple boy to think so. No, he has understood it rightly, and in reply has brought some hundreds of my men with him. What for?—it is in thine eyes to ask—what for? I will tell thee. Ah! thy heart tells thee now: there is no need for me to speak."

"Then his designs are evil, friend," said the King, with a slight shudder.

"King! without that letter he was not to be trusted. After he received it he knew his fate," returned Pahar Singh. "We—I—have an evil reputation, they say: and he believed I would do anything for money. He sent an express messenger for me from Nuldroog. I had come here with those letters, but my son went. Money was offered to him: rank—an estate—whatever he pleased. Money? yea, much money. A lakh of rupees—more. Why? thou already knowest. Yes—to kill thee, O Adil Khan, thou wert not to live over to-day. My son pleaded fatigue and my absence—time also to collect the men. That is why Khan Mahomed did not arrive yesterday. That is why he is at Almella now. My son is shrewd and wise—he secured all he could of the Wuzeer's money; and then—ah, blessed boy!—he rode on to meet me last night. Ha, ha! they thought he had gone to Itga to hurry on the men; but he is a good youth—he knew what to do. A gallant horse is that which that Lalla left with us; thy life was on its feet, O Prince! and my boy was in sore temptation. So he reached me last night, just as I had gained my hiding-place, of which he knew. Ah, I was sick at heart, for my brother was dead——"

"Dead!" cried the secretary; "God forbid! he was with thee, and well."

"Ay, dead, Meerza," continued Pahar Singh. "Yes, murdered—perish the cowardly hand that struck the blow in the dark. We were attacked by robbers, who had watched us, and he was struck down in the fight. I went for assistance to carry him, and when I returned he was dead, and a knife-wound in his heart. Enough, master," continued Pahar Singh, dashing his hand roughly across his eyes. "He died in thy service. Enough for him."

"And then?" asked the King.

"My son had consented to do the work; and that slave, the Wuzeer, believed him. The boy told me he pretended to hate the King, and that there was a death feud between our house and thine, Adil Khan—was it not good? O, he is a clever youth that. It was he who got those letters, too: and now he has received money from the slave. Enough! Speak, O King. Is the slave to be delivered into thy hand alive, or wilt thou give him to me—to me, Pahar Singh? Dost thou doubt me? I ask no money—no reward from thee. Thy house—thy very life—is in peril: Pahar Singh can save both, and ask nothing but to be held true to his master's salt. Nay, do not interrupt me," he continued, waving his hand, while he wiped away the foam which, in his excitement, had gathered on his lips. "Think, Adil Khan, was thy royal house ever so threatened before? Hath not the Wuzeer prepared the enemy to make his last swoop upon thee, even as a falcon on a hare; and wert thou dead, with no son to rally men around him, and Khan Mahomed holding the power,—could thy kingdom be preserved? Are the Moghuls idle? Is Sivaji Bhóslay indifferent? Above all, could thy royal armies have saved thee had I been a traitor?"

"Come hither," cried Adil Shah, from whose eyes the tears were welling fast as he thought upon his defenceless state, the deep treachery which had been meditated, and the rough earnest devotion of this strange man. "Come hither: let me put my hand on thy head."

Pahar Singh advanced. The squalid mendicant covered with rags—to all appearance what he seemed, so complete was the disguise—trod boldly upon the royal bed of satin and velvet; but he bowed his head to meet the hand which the King extended and laid upon it gently.

"As thou wilt, true servant," said the King, "for there is a stern and fearful necessity to be encountered. Whatever reward thou mayst claim hereafter is freely bestowed upon thee—all thou hast ever done against me or my people is forgiven. Take that slave for thine own if thou wilt, to deal with as it seemeth good to thee."

"Remember," cried Pahar Singh, seizing the King's hand and detaining it upon his head, "these words cannot be revoked. Whatever happens, I do but thy bidding, O King; and, only for the need for thee to know it, I had done the same even though I had not seen thee. Now I go, whither ye cannot trace me, but ye will hear of me ere the day is past."

"Go," replied the King. "I have no fear of thee or of thine acts. Alla and the Prophet direct and keep thee, O true friend, whom he hath sent me in my need. Go!"

"Only be careful," continued the man, withdrawing the King's hand from his head, kissing it reverently, and then releasing it—"only be careful! Stir not beyond the fort till the news comes to thee. The guards on the gates and within are of the true party, and thou art safe with them. Care not for revolt; the Wuzeer brings no men with him but my own. My son prevented those he brought from coming on, and they returned to Nuldroog from Almella. None of his party here dare stir. Yet, if there be any movement, send for Afzool Khan and his son Fazil; they are my bitter enemies, but they are true to thee. Nay more, the Wuzeer's son is not with his father in this matter, and is true to thee,

O King, because of the young Fazil. And now I go. Send me beyond the gate, for I must not depart as I came."

"I am ready to go," said the secretary. "They were marvelling at thy sudden appearance. How was it?"

"I may tell thee some time or other," returned Pahar Singh, smiling; "but come, it is almost day. Yet, ere I depart, my lord, I would kiss thy feet. The reverence I once paid thy father, the noble Sultan Mahmood, I would pay to thee." And so saying, he prostrated himself, embracing the King's feet, and kissing them respectfully.

"Would thou wert a true believer, and thou wouldst be as a brother. O, that I could reward thee adequately," said the King, with much emotion.

"I am better as I am—free," returned Pahar Singh. "When I have earned reward, Adil Khan, I may ask it if I live; and if I die, remember there was one true heart among thy people, and protect my Gopal—my son. Let us not speak of reward; there is nothing now between us but true faith, as thou art witness, O Meerza, and that faith was never yet given for gold."

So saying, he turned and passed rapidly through the curtain, followed by the secretary.

Was there any doubt in the young King's mind now? None; all was clear. There was no thought of mercy—none of receding from determination. There could be no question of Pahar Singh's story, else why had he, outlaw and robber as he was, trusted himself in the very palace? There was no appearance about that strange man which could lead to a suspicion of deceit, and his grim devotion in this emergency affected the King deeply. Even if Pahar Singh failed, the course was clear. The Wuzeer must be confronted with the silent witnesses of his treachery; and in Afzool Khan and a score of other trusty adherents, the King felt he had ample protection.

No; it was no deception. After a short interval of silence, the Fakeer's cry, "Ulla dilâyâ to léonga!" again arose more sonorously, more confidently than before, and the King, stepping out on the terrace, listened, speculating how far the man might be gone on his deadly errand, and what would come of it, so absorbedly, that the secretary's footsteps, as he ascended the stair, were not heard, and the King started as he spoke once more.

"He is gone, my lord, on his work. I saw him pass beyond the gate."

"Did he say aught?"

"Nothing—he did not speak again. As he passed out of the court he shouted his cry, and continued it, walking rapidly till he was beyond the bridge of the ditch. Many of the men saluted him, and some offered alms, but he answered no one, and, still shouting, pressed on so quickly that I could hardly follow. When I last saw him, he had turned by the 'Goruk Imlee' tree, and was running fast; and so God speed him!"

"Ameen!" sighed the King. "Thou must not leave me to-day, Anwur Ali. Order a Durbar at noon, and there will we await the end. He or I, Meerza, whichever God wills; but it shall not be said of Adil Khan that he shrank from his fate into his zenana. Go; sleep there on my cushions for a while; we both need rest," and by another doorway, the King passed to the inner apartments.

CHAPTER XXXVII.

THE day wore on; and it may be imagined that the anxieties of the lady Lurlee and the fair Zyna were not diminished by the continued absence of the Khan and his son. As the former had left his wife, he had requested her to have a "kichéri" of a particular kind, with kabobs, prepared for him when he arrived. "He should be hungry," he said, "after his ride so early, and Fazil too. It was a soldier's dish, and would put him in mind of old days in the field, and—Lurlee could dress it so capitally." We may remember a slight bandying of words between the Khan and his lady before he went out; and he had ordered this dish as a propitiatory meal at her hands, for he knew by experience that the result would be satisfactory: the little acerbity would disappear, and the planets, perhaps, would be forgotten.

Nothing could have been devised more soothing to the lady Lurlee's temper—nothing more certain of dispelling any clouds of dissatisfaction or disappointment—than this appeal to her affections through her kitchen. Even in these intellectual days, a similar result is not unfrequently attainable; proving that the motives and springs of poor human nature, and its tempers, show but little difference at the time of our history and among ourselves; and did we permit ourselves to moralize after the fashion of the day, we might possibly deliver a pretty lecture upon the subject.

But—and we may as well avow it once for all—we feel ourselves bound to relate our story without any moralizing digressions whatever, further than what may form part of its action; and therefore we will not follow the changes of the lady's mind, from its first expectant and interested condition after the mixing of the materials by her own fair hands (for on such occasions she suffered no one to interfere), to the setting them on the fire to be done exactly as her lord wished. With the Khan's loving order, had come a flood of pleasant memories to her—of old camp days, hard fights too, in which her lord—safe, generally victorious, and restored to her prayers—found his wife busy with some favourite dish; and they loved each other, in a homely fashion, better for the cooking and the eating of it.

Now, as the lady sat over her private brazier, on which were her own silver cooking-vessels, the Khan's special gift, she told Zyna of many an old time and scene—of many a narrow escape—many a rough march which she had shared with the old soldier, and done her part in binding up his wounds if he were hurt, or cooking for him if he were hungry.

"Your mother was not of our rough Dekhani sort, daughter," she said; "people tell me she never went out with the army: she was a weak, fragile thing, I have heard, but very beautiful. Peace be with her, for thy father loved her much, and hath never loved me as her. But no children have come, Zyna—no children, that is it,"—and the lady sighed, and perhaps tears gathered in her eyes, for she wiped them hastily with the corner of her muslin scarf. "Well, it is God's will, daughter; and though I could never understand it properly, there was something wrong in the horoscope which they cast when I was betrothed. You see, Zyna, my planet was then Mars, which represented water—no, it was fire;—no, that's a male planet, and so it must have been Earth. Yes, I think it was—Earth; and then he was Venus—no, that could not be either; it must have been Saturn, and that's for air. So you see, fire and air—no, let me see—air and water? no. What did I tell thee, Zyna? Was it Earth?"

"I do not understand it, mother; how can I tell?" said Zyna demurely.

"But you are not listening, girl; ah, wait till your own time comes. I'll warrant you anxious and curious enough to know whether you are fire or earth, or air or water; and whether he is air, or water, or whatever he may be. Now about myself. You see I was fire; no I am wrong. 'Humul,' 'Sowr,' 'Jowza' (Aries, Taurus, Gemini)," continued the lady Lurlee, telling off all the signs of the zodiac, in, Arabic, upon the ends of her fingers, and then the planets in succession, "'Mars,' 'Venus,' 'Mercury;' and now look, Zyna, if the house of the Lion is on this middle finger, and the planet Mercury comes to it, you see Mercury is in conjunction with—with the Crab. Did not I say the Crab, child? Now attend, else I shall lose all my reckoning. 'Humul,' 'Sowr'——"

"Alas, mother, but I do not understand it, and I can never remember the names of the planets or their houses,—indeed I cannot," said Zyna, piteously. "But ah, mother, look, it is burning!"

And so it was. In her astrological involvement, Lurlee Khánum had forgotten the kichéri, which, as the bottom of the pan became too hot, sent up a most unsavoury odour, and brown smoke issued from under the lid.

"God forgive me my neglect, daughter," exclaimed the lady, sorrowfully, as she examined the pan: "it is surely quite spoiled, and thy father is so particular. The least idea of burnt kichéri is enough to set him mad, and I could not look at him for a day or more. And he will be expecting this to be all ready. "Protection of the Prophet!" exclaimed the lady suddenly, "there he is. What shall I do?—what shall I do?"

That which had startled Lurlee was the arrival of the Khan's escort, and the beating of their kettle-drums in the outer court; and as she listened, and stood up, ladle in hand, expecting her lord's entrance, she was perhaps relieved by the appearance of Goolab who, as the general outdoor scout, brought tidings from the courtyard of occurrences of all kinds.

"They are not coming, lady," said the nurse. "They are gone to the Kótwal's, and will stay there. That's the news brought by Peer Khan, and a host of them. And there's Bulwunt Rao as good as dead; and he's to be put into the private apartments, and the King's doctor is to be sent for; and I must go and see to a bed for him, and a soft mattress, and pillows and sheets; and then they'll all be spoilt with his blood. His blood, indeed!"

"A blister on thy tongue, O prating woman!" cried Lurlee. "My lord taken to the Kótwal's? *My* lord! O Zyna! O girl, what is the world come to? Thy father taken to that man of blood, Jehándar Beg; and those cowards, the Paigah, have come here without him? O girl—what is it? speak, hast thou no sense?"

Indeed, Zyna had very little; the mention of that dreaded name, the certainty that if her father could have returned he would, and the fact of Bulwunt Rao being dangerously wounded, all combined to terrify, and Lurlee herself was no calmer.

"Was there no message, Goolab?" asked Zyna.

"O yes; that the Khan remains at the Kótwal's, and will eat his breakfast there. He has business, and will stay. That is all, and that Meah Sahib is well."

"That is all!" exclaimed Lurlee. "That is all! To have my lord in the Kótwallee, and that dish of kichéri dressed in vain! O woman of little grace that I am! why did I deserve this? what have I done? what have I done?"

"But it was spoiled, mother," said Zyna innocently; "do not care about it. Only thank God they are safe. O, I vow a Fateha——"

"Not care, child? and would it not have been the same had it been, as it was, dressed like food for the Peris? would it not have been the same? Would he have come to eat it? he, thy father? Why order it? why affront me by leaving it here to be spoiled? why did he not come long ago? This is not as it used to be of old. O, Afzool Khan! am I less than dirt in thine eyes? am I—I—I——"

Now, the lady Lurlee, like all other Mahomedan ladies, only mentioned her husband's name on very solemn occasions, or when excitement got the better of discretion; and here was an instance of it. She sat down upon the stool before her brazier, and, after rocking herself to and fro for a while, burst into an uncontrollable fit of sobbing. It was difficult to say, perhaps, what had most particularly affected her; but undoubtedly the burning of the kichéri was at the bottom of all. It had been so good. Then she knew how his face would have expanded under its influence as he ate; it would have reminded him of some old scene, whose history would have come out between the mouthfuls—he might even have caressed her. Ah, all was now gone—her trouble, her expectation of a loving greeting, all gone: and the sense of neglect and indifference under which she habitually existed, had for the time taken its place. But gradually the sobbing was soothed, and Lurlee, laying her head against Zyna's bosom, seemed lost in thought.

"There must be unfavourable conjunctions among the planets today, depend upon it, daughter," she said at length, rousing herself, and drying her eyes, "else all this would not have happened. Now, let me look steadily into it: perhaps we may learn something for our guidance."

"Look!" continued the lady after a pause, and a brief examination of an astrological table, which she usually carried about her, "look here. Ah, graceless and unfortunate that I am, I should have foreseen all that has happened, and he should never have gone out at all. Why, here is Saturn in the ascendant till the first watch of the day, and then follows the Sun, and that's what spoilt my cooking. Let me see—Aries, Taurus, Gemini, Cancer," she continued, counting the signs of the zodiac, as before, on her fingers, "Aries, Taurus—why, God be merciful! here follows Mars, and he's an executioner—and they are in the Kótwallee—the Prophet's mercy be on them! Yet, stay, Mars will last for only three hours; then comes, let me see—Mars, Jupiter, Mercury, Moon—no, Venus, Jupiter, Moon. Yes, I am right now, girl. That means messenger, and Venus is propitious. Ah, yes, don't you see it all, Zyna? Don't you understand? Look, first the Moon, that's we ourselves, as messengers; and then Venus will save them, if we can get past Mars. Of course it is quite plain. Don't you see?"

"Alas, no, mother! I do not," said Zyna, innocently. "I see figures and numbers, and angles and signs, but it is hopeless to ask me about them. You are a wise woman, and this is a marvellous science. Surely, and please God, you are right."

"O, I see exactly what to do; and it is well I can pick out a path among these mysteries," cried Lurlee, brightening, "or we had all been lost long ago. But we will eat first; I am sure some of the kichéri is good, and at any rate there are the kabobs, and Jameela will have bread. Come and eat, daughter, it will support thee; come, we have much to do ere noon. I see now, and when thou hast eaten I will tell thee. Jameela! O Jameela!" she cried to the cook, who, when her mistress came to usurp her functions, discreetly kept out of the way. "Jameela, bring some bread and some pickle; we must eat now."

"But you have the kichéri," said the dame. "Surely it is not burnt," she continued, sniffing into the pan with a cook's experienced nose.

"Begone, graceless!" cried Lurlee, who well knew the old woman was rejoicing in her heart over her discomfiture; "begone and get the bread."

"There is none but the men's bread, and it is coarse enough, for the meal was not sifted," returned Jameela. "When *you* take to cooking, of course I am not expected to be mindful of other light bread, and such things; but——"

"Begone, and do as you are bid," cried her mistress, sharply. A look from Zyna also, deprecating further discussion, was understood at once by the old dame.

"I will bring the best of it, Khánum," she said, "and there is some quite hot; but I can bake a few of your own 'phoolkas,' if you like; they will be good with the kabobs . . . . which seem savoury," she continued, craning over to look into the pot on the fire, and sniffing into it.

"Where is Goolab? Ah yes, do so, Jameela, and bring them quickly," replied her mistress; "thou art a jewel."

"I will send her, lady," said the cook, departing; "and I would bring the men's bread, only it is not fit for the likes of ye."

"Now, what is to be done?" asked Zyna. "O mother, thou seemest to understand everything, and art confident, and I am distracted with apprehension. O my father! O my brother! God keep you safe. I vow lights at Peer Sahib's tomb, and to feed a hundred Fakeers there to-morrow, if they be safe!"

"We must go to the palace, and inquire why thy father is detained," replied Lurlee decisively. "Ah, Goolab, where wert thou? But never mind," she continued, as the dame entered. "Lay out clothes for us; we must go to the palace; and bid some one go and say we pray to see the Bégum Sahiba, and order the palankeens and an escort to be ready. Inshalla! daughter, we will see what this evil-minded and base-born Kôtwal can do."

"And the jewels, Khánum?" asked Goolab.

"Ah! I had forgotten. Well, a few."

"No, mother, no!" cried Zyna, "not so. With our hearts heavy and sad, it surely is no time to put on jewels. Let us rather go with sober garments, and prostrate ourselves before the Peer's shrine on our way."

"I tell thee the Peer cannot help us," returned the dame tartly; "it is the stars and the Bégum. When they are safe, then do thy Fateha if thou wilt. Come here, eat, for we have much to do. Ah! Jameela-bee;" for Lurlee always added the respectful addition of *bee*, for lady, when she was in good humour, to her cook, who now entered with a tray of hot bread and delicate phoolkas, and a white cloth over her arm: "thou hast been quick, friend."

It must be confessed that the lady Lurlee's appetite, sharpened perhaps by her unusual fast and the process of her own cookery, did ample justice to the meal. Her confidence in the stars sustained her far better than Zyna's faith in her saint—that is, if one might judge by the resolute and satisfied features of the elder face as it bent over its plate, eating heartily, and the distressed, anxious, and tearful expression of the younger, endeavouring almost vainly to eat at all. It was of no avail that Lurlee encouraged her daughter, and even picked out tempting morsels from the kabobs, and set them before her, with the hottest of the phoolkas, as they were sent in short relays from the kitchen.

"Ah, daughter! he would have enjoyed this," said Lurlee, as she washed her hands over the ewer brought her at the conclusion of the meal, and sighed in a manner which plainly signified her regret not to be able to eat more. "Yes, the kabob was good, but thou hast scarcely tasted it; a trifle more pepper would have been better, perhaps; yet it was good. And now, girl, I am ready to face the Kótwal or the Bégum, or—the peace of God be on him—Adil Shah himself. Inshalla! we will see who dares to detain my lord when I, Lurlee Khánum, have cooked his breakfast."

CHAPTER XXXVIII.

Enough had transpired in the examination of Afzool Khan and his son, to satisfy Jehándar Beg that the young man and his father had attained knowledge of some secret relating to the conspiracies in progress, which they were reserving to tell the King; and we should be doing that very astute officer injustice, if we did not at once admit that he believed the secret known to them, or at least to Fazil, concerned the Wuzeer very deeply. Why the King's secretary had been mentioned he could not imagine. Did he know it also? Certainly it was important to find out everything that could be discovered, previous to the Wuzeer's arrival; and he purposed himself to go to his house, and have speech of him, before he should attend the Durbar, and appear before the King to inform him of the detention of Afzool Khan and his son, and of the events connected with them.

But Jehándar Beg, as police minister of that large city, had other sources of information; and whatever occurred at night was reported to him by his spies before the true business of the day commenced. Had not Afzool Khan come direct to the court, it is most probable that Jehándar Beg would have heard some account of Fazil Khan's night adventure before he appeared at all. As it was, there had been a reversion of events: and we must now follow the magistrate briefly, in his reception of the spies whom he summoned, directly the door of the court had closed upon the Khan and his son.

The room in which these persons were received, was one which could be entered from the large hall of audience: but there was a door also by the back passage which led from a street behind, and persons could come and go unobserved. There was nothing in this chamber—which indeed was very small—but a large pillow and a carpet, on which the Kótwal's sword-dagger, a heavy-bladed Persian or Affghan knife, and writing materials, were placed. As he sat down and clapped his hands, a door opposite was opened by a slave without, and a Brahmun, as was evident by his dress and the caste marks on his forehead, was admitted.

"Be seated," said Jehándar Beg. "Have you anything for me to-day, Pundit?"

"Yes," answered the Brahmun, taking a pair of spectacles from a fold in his turban, and placing them across his nose, and then producing some papers from a pocket within his dress; "these have just arrived by a special messenger from Moro Trimmul at Tooljapoor;" and he handed to the Kótwal several letters sealed with the private Mahratta seal of Sivaji Bhóslay, which Jehándar Beg examined closely; then, apparently satisfied, he made a Persian memorandum on the corner of each, with the date of receipt, very methodically, and put them into the side-pocket of his robe.

"And," continued the Brahmun, looking over his letter as the Kótwal had finished, "Moro Trimmul writes that his sister has been married to a Shastree at Tooljapoor, and that he has not been idle; but he cannot induce Pahar Singh to visit him or accept terms, and he is afraid to go to Itga himself; so it were better your worship advised our master to treat with him."

"Very good; I will mention it," returned the Kótwal; "but has Moro Trimmul been to Nuldroog to see the Wuzeer? It is not far."

"No, my lord; he was afraid to go unless a 'Kowl' were sent to him."

"Curious that, O Pundit!" added Jehándar Beg, with a sneer; "he is not scrupulous in general, I think."

"No, not in general, perhaps," replied the man; "but in this case he is—he is—not sure."

"Not sure? Well, I suppose he is certain of my being able to apprehend him, and make him so, on the Goruk Imlee tree."

"My lord is all-powerful; but Moro is careful—as much so as Sivaji Bhóslay or Tannajee Maloosray," returned the Pundit, dryly.

"Ah yes; no doubt, friend; he thinks himself so," replied Jehándar Beg, with a sneer; "but what of Tannajee himself? I heard just now that he is here, and was seen last night."

"Tannajee is everywhere," returned the man, smiling, "or some one else for him. If my lord requires him, he may be found at Wye: he would not trust himself in Beejapoor, I think; yet——"

"Why not, Pundit?"

"My lord can best answer that. Like Moro Trimmul, he is better at a distance till the time comes. He does not like 'those trees' of my lord's."

For once the Kótwal was at fault. It wss necessary to gain over the Mahratta interest, else the intrigue with the Emperor were abortive; but it was clear none of the Mahratta agents would trust the Wuzeer's party, without more assurance of its success than at present appeared likely; and the Kótwal felt this keenly. He might threaten, imprison, or even torture, but he could not penetrate beyond the surface.

"Tannajee was in the kullal's bazar last night," said Jehándar Beg, after a pause, "and had a narrow escape. He ought not to place himself in such peril."

"Indeed! I have said before there are Maloosrays everywhere," returned the Brahmun dryly; "I know what has been told you, my lord; but," he added, smiling, "I suppose you don't believe it."

"That is as may be proved hereafter. We shall know more by-and-by—to-day, perhaps," replied Jehándar Beg.

The man shrugged his shoulders. "Does my lord wish me to stay?" he asked.

"Not particularly. The master comes this afternoon, and may wish to see you."

"Certainly, I will attend; but about Maloosray? If he comes I will tell you," continued the Pundit, laughing; "but do not listen, my lord, to idle stories; Maloosray is everywhere, and in that is his safety. May I go?"

"Yes, go;" and the man, making a respectful salute, departed.

The Pundit was a clever agent, deeply devoted, like all his countrymen, to the Mahratta interest, apparently serving the Wuzeer's party through Jehándar Beg, yet at the same time revealing only what was advisable to be known, and gaining all the information he could. He had already seen Maloosray, and went direct to Jehándar Beg, on purpose to mislead him, in which he perfectly succeeded.

The Kótwal sat and mused a while on what had been told him. He believed the Brahmun about Maloosray. "And Pahar Singh would not join them? That is all he knows," said Jehándar Beg to himself. "My lord writes that he is sure of the robber, and brings some of his men with him. What can that be for?" He felt as though he had not been quite trusted; still the Wuzeer was coming that day, and would tell all. He could not perhaps write.

So another spy was admitted, evidently one of the royal eunuchs. He sat down where the Brahmun had been seated, and for a time was silent.

"Well," said Jehándar Beg, "is thy brain heavy with drink, Mahmood, or with secrets? Or is there bad news? Why art thou silent?"

"Good or bad, I know not, my lord," replied the man; "but it is at least curious, and you may understand it. I do not."

"Indeed!—say on, friend," returned the Kótwal, settling himself into an attitude of attention.

"My lord the secretary," said the man calmly, "was out late last night. He went to a temple somewhere, and there was another with him. He then returned to the palace, and the Peer Zadah and Neelkunt Rai were sent for and admitted. They sat till nearly dawn, when a Fakeer came, and was taken up to the Palace of the Seven Stories by the secretary."

Jehándar Beg took his beard in his hand, rubbed and stroked it, and mused for several minutes. "Anything more?" he asked.

"Some money was taken," added the man. "That is all I know, except that a Durbar is ordered after the mid-day prayer."

These tidings, strange as they seemed to be, troubled Jehándar Beg sorely. He had not been told of the Durbar. What could have happened? "Thou must go and find out who was with the secretary," he said.

"If I might speak," said the spy timidly, looking about him—"I think it was—" and he advanced and whispered in the Kótwal's ear—"the King himself."

"The King? Impossible; he never left the palace," returned the Kôtwal, aloud. "I know that he did not. The King?——"

"My lord cannot be mistaken," replied the spy, deferentially. "Nevertheless, I heard it——"

"Quite impossible! He could not have gone without my knowing of it, Mahmood; nor dare he venture out without being attended. Who were with the secretary?"

"Bundagee Sahib, and five others only; and the man who went with the secretary entered the private apartments with him when they returned. This I saw, for I was watching."

"Thou shouldst have gone into the court with them," said the Kôtwal. "What neglect is this?"

"I was going, but the guard stopped me," said the spy, as if ashamed. "They knew me, and turned me out of the fort-gate. What could I do? Since the last time I was drunk, they will not admit me."

"And the Fakeer?"

"I heard him calling inside, 'Ulla dilâyâ to léonga;' and when he got outside he ran, still shouting, towards the Goruk Imlee trees, and I lost sight of him."

"Then who told you he went into the palace?"

"O, the men on guard said one of the ladies had seen demons, and that the Syn had been sent for, to say incantations over her."

"Very likely," said the Kôtwal, calmly. "Now go and bring me the news I want. Was it the King who went with the Meerza, or his own son? Find this out for me, and return directly."

"Jo hookum!" returned the spy, "your slave will do his best," and he departed.

We need not follow Jehándar Beg in his other private audiences. He had many spies over many people.

If he had not been delayed by these communications and his own meditations upon them, and had gone to his prisoners at once, it is possible, perhaps, that the Khan and his son might have been taken by surprise; but they had been warned, and were prepared for him.

The lad Ashruf, who has been already mentioned, had been present during the first examination. No one noticed him; but he was shrewd and observant. He had asked his father whether he should run and bring down the whole force of Afzool Khan's Paigah to rescue the Khan; and perhaps the boy would have enjoyed a share in the mêlee which would undoubtedly have followed; but his father, while checking him angrily for the thought, bid him be on the watch, and should there be any danger, to give information of it. So the lad had remained in the Kuchéri, and was not noticed among the soldiers who lounged about there. As the Kótwal entered his private room, and was known to be generally occupied for some time, the various clerks and scribes took advantage of his absence, and had for the most part gone out; a few only remained, who seemed absorbed in their business. So, gradually, the lad edged himself close to the private door, which, as sometimes happens in Indian houses, did not close completely, on account of the hinges being outside the door-post. The lad could not see, but he could hear if he placed his ear, carelessly, to all appearance, against the place where the door joined the door-frame, and in this attitude he was not disturbed. Being questioned by a soldier, he answered lazily, that he was ordered to wait for his father's return; and apparently was settling quietly to sleep, leaning against the wall.

Ashruf had no idea at first of the results of the position in which he had placed himself; but a few words awakened his attention perfectly. To hear better also, he feigned to be sleepy, drew a part of his scarf over his face, and lay down; and by this means he could see under the door sufficiently to observe who came.

The Brahmun's communication did not interest him much; but as soon as the eunuch was seated, whom he knew to be in disgrace for habitual intemperance, he felt sure that his tidings would relate to the palace, and he listened more carefully than ever. Very little escaped him. He could not hear the eunuch's whisper, but the Kótwal had repeated the name of the King aloud—that was enough. It was necessary, at least, that the young Khan should know of it, and directly the eunuch had been dismissed, the lad got up and looked about.

It is frequently the case that, in houses of one floor only, like this, a staircase leads from the principal room to the roof; and in the corner, not far from the door we have mentioned, was one of this description. Ashruf watched his opportunity, and when no one was observing him, slipped gently behind the wall at the entrance of the steps, and ascended them quickly. He had remarked the direction of the court where Afzool Khan and his son were detained, and, creeping on his hands and knees to the edge of the terrace, looked into it.

At first he did not see them, because they were sitting upon the same side under one of the arches; but a soft cry of "Huzrut! Huzrut!" ("My prince! my prince!") in a voice very like a woman's, and a small piece of plaster thrown into the court, induced Fazil to get up and attend to the signal, whatever it might be. Looking up, he saw the lad's face peeping through an aperture in the open stucco-work of the parapet, and in a few moments had heard what he had to tell. It was important, because putting them on their guard against further questioning, which could only have one object, their continued detention; and thoughtful, because proving a faithful interest, which Fazil trusted to reward. It confirmed also, suspicions of the connection between the Wuzeer and the Kótwal.

"Can I do anything more, noble sir?" asked the boy, when his little story was done; "be quick, else I may be seen and flogged."

"Yes, two things," replied Fazil; "first, run to Kowas Khan, the Wuzeer's son; bid him come to me here well attended, but with no appearance of force; and then go to the Lurlee Khánum, at our house, with those papers"—and he threw what he had to him—"and tell her we shall not be at home early, as we have to attend the King's Durbar, and that we are well. She is to keep the papers till we come."

They saw the boy's face disappear, and heard him crawling back over the terrace. Fortunately he had not been observed, and he gained the bottom of the steps safely, and passed out among the soldiers, unchallenged, on his double mission.

But while he is running at a steady, unvarying trot, not staying even to take breath, we must follow what the Kótwal had to say to the old Khan and his son, which may be of importance in the elucidation of this history.

"Fear not, my father," said Fazil to him, as voices were heard at the door, "fear not, all will be well. The boy will do as he was told; and without alarm or force of any kind we shall be soon free. But speak not, let me talk; you are to know nothing, but that you went to fetch me when I sent for you last night."

CHAPTER XXXIX.

"LADY," said Goolab, again entering suddenly, "there is a boy in the court who says he must have instant speech of you. He will tell no one what he has to say, except that he has come from the master."

"A boy, Goolab? how old is he? can I see him? Quick, woman, my veil—anything to cover me," exclaimed Lurlee.

"Take this, mother," said Zyna, unfastening her scarf; "what need of concealment with a boy? I will go aside. Admit him, Goolab; he may have news of them."

The lad entered and prostrated himself before the Khánum. "Take these papers," he said. "My lord the Khan hath sent them; you are to keep them, and no one is to see them. He and his son are well and safe, and will go to the King in the afternoon."

"Prophet of God, what is this?" cried Lurlee. "Mahratta, too? Well, no one shall take them from me;" and, so saying, she stuffed them into that most convenient and unapproachable of all lady's hiding-places, her bodice.

"I am going, lady," said the lad, who had observed the action; "they are safe with thee now."

"Not before thou hast eaten, boy. There is some kichéri ready" —he will not mind its being burnt, she thought—"thou must be hungry."

Ashruf was, to say the truth, hungry enough; but he resisted temptation. "No, lady, let me go," he said; "I have another errand for my lord. May your house prosper."

"Thou art right," returned Lurlee, as he saluted her and departed. "Go; God speed thee; thou art a good lad. And now, Zyna, let us attire ourselves in fitting garments, and go to the palace, for time presses, and it is already past noon."

This, however, promised to be no easy task; and if Lurlee Khánum had had time to consult her tables in a fitting manner, the colour and particular kind of garment which would suit that period of the day, and in which the wearer would be lucky or unlucky, must have been decided. Goolab, too, and the other women, to whom the idea of the ladies going to the palace could be no other than an occasion for the display of the utmost magnificence, had laid out costly dresses of cloth-of-gold, brocade, muslin, satin; and a petticoat of gorgeous purple Italian velvet, trimmed with broad silver ribbon, with purple flowers upon it, a recent acquisition to the wardrobe, was especially tempting.

"Pardon me, Khánum," said Kurreem-bee, the "Moghulanee," or household dressmaker and mistress of the robes, "but on an occasion of this kind, and when a petition is to be made, we should know something of the mood her highness the Bégum is in, and the garments should agree with it. Yellow or red, with gold or silver, might excite bile—blue or purple would create phlegm; and when my lady Chand-bee, the wife of Jānee Sahib Dāgtoray, went to visit——"

"Now, in the Prophet's name, cease, Kurreem-bee!" cried Lurlee, interrupting her; "are we not in haste? and thou standest prating about Chand-bee, who never could dress herself except like a public dancing-girl. Peace, I say. Give me the green satin petticoat laced with silver, and the plain white scarf with gold flowers; these, with a shawl, will be enough."

Meanwhile Goolab and some other women-servants had made their preparations. The old dame was aware that her red satin petticoat, one of the Khánum's presents, would be much in her way, flapping about her legs as she ran by the litter; and as the ladies were settling themselves in their seats, she tucked it up, forming it, as it were, into a very efficient pair of baggy breeches, reaching to her knees, which could be shaken out when she arrived at the palace: and at the same time tied her clean muslin scarf about her waist and shoulders, in such a manner as to display a considerable amount of rotundity in directions otherwise perhaps not remarkable.

"Ah, you may laugh, impudence," she cried, aiming a blow at a fine sturdy lad, who, with others bearing spears, had just entered the court—"you may laugh, but that's the way to run;" and she kicked out first one leg, then the other, by way of proving whether the petticoat arrangements were firm. "I have run ten coss a-day when my lord was in the field, and carried my lady's hooka into the bargain. Peace, impudent knaves!" she continued to the men, as the laugh against her became more general when the bearers entered. "Take up the palankeen and let us go. Bismilla!"

There was no time for further colloquy, for the men, who had been turned out of the court while the ladies took their seats, now took up the palankeens: and the band of spearmen, arranging themselves in front, were joined in the outer court by a strong body of the Khan's horsemen, and the little procession quickly traversed the city, and arrived at its destination. There the litters, being carried into the women's court of the Palace of the Seven Stories, were set down at the foot of the stairs leading to the apartments in which the King had held his night council.

Goolab, having shaken out her petticoat, and put into her ears and about her neck, the gold ornaments she carried with her, appeared once more in her proper character: and received the salutations of the royal Mamas, who were to conduct the ladies to the chamber of audience.

We have before described this apartment; and the broad daylight, which poured through the now open casements, fully displayed its richness and beauty. Soft quilted cloths had been laid over the floor, and white muslin sheets tacked to them, covered the whole. Large pillows had been placed round the walls; and in the deep bays and oriel windows, numerous groups of ladies and their children were sitting conversing together merrily, and spread, as it were, upon every available space except the centre, which was kept clear.

Lurlee Khánum was not prepared for the display of rich dresses which had to be encountered, but assured by the kind tones in which she was welcomed by the Queen, sailed up to her with measured steps, causing her ample satin garment to swing in heavy folds from left to right, and back again, after the most impressive and courtly fashion.

Fyz-ool-Nissa, the King's wife, was as yet a girl, not, indeed, much older than Zyna herself. She could not be called beautiful, but there was a frank pleasant expression in her fair countenance which was irresistibly pleasing. The delicate hands and arms, sparkling with jewels, were all that could be seen of her person, buried as it was amidst the cloud of drapery which shrouded her as she sat on the King's seat in the oriel, and seemed an earnest of its grace; as also, indeed, her small graceful head and neck, which were loaded with costly pearl ornaments.

"The wife and daughter of the noble Afzool Khan are always welcome," said the Bégum, in her low sweet voice. "Come and sit here by me; 'tis a fair sight to see all the gallant people assembling, and they say it will be a great Durbar. And this is Zyna-bee? Ah, girl, they have often told me thou wert fair, but—— Well, I had better not say it. Come here, child, I am thy mother too; they tell me I have many children," she said, laughing. "O, so many!"

"May God fill your lap with them, may they climb about you, and may you live a hundred years to see them!" said Lurlee, earnestly.

"And here is one already," said the Bégum, seating Zyna beside her. "Ah, girl, we will have such a marriage for thee soon——"

As Zyna bowed down blushingly, Lurlee seized the opportunity of pressing her suit.

"Lady," she said, putting up her hands in a respectful attitude, "thine ear for a moment. I had a petition——"

"Ah, Khánum!" returned Fyz-ool-Nissa, with a look of disappointment; "I had marked this day for rejoicing; for the heavy cloud which has hung over my head so long is gone, and thou hast brought me a petition, and I hate them. I never get matters arranged as I like, and am vexed—— To-morrow, lady?"

"Only for my husband would I speak," replied Lurlee, firmly. "He and his son were decoyed to the Kótwallee early to-day, and they cannot get to the King. It must not be that Afzool Khan is counted a laggard. O lady——!" and here Lurlee, unable to contain herself longer, burst into tears.

Fyz-ool-Nissa looked to Zyna, and saw a confirmation of Lurlee's tale in the face—in those great eyes brimful of tears, and quivering lips.

"Hush!" said the Bégum, "this must not be known. O that there were any one to write!"

"I—I can write," said Zyna, timidly.

"Thou, girl? well done! Now," she continued, as an attendant brought a writing-case, "write what thou wilt, but be quick."

It was soon done. A few words, but enough for the purpose.

"Canst thou sign it, lady?" asked Zyna.

"Yes, child, 'tis all they could ever teach me," replied the Bégum, laughing; "and here is my seal, too. Ah! thou art a little clerk."

"Her father makes her write his letters," said Lurlee, apologetically, as the Bégum clapped her hands, and an old eunuch, who had been standing at the foot of the room, advanced.

"This must go to my lord instantly," said the Queen; "some one thou canst count on must take it, Daood, for me."

"Myself," he replied; "no other can do this errand. Fear not, lady," he continued earnestly to Lurlee, "thy noble lord hath friends he knows not of, and it is needful he should be in the Durbar to-day. Inshalla! thou wilt soon see him? Is any of the Paigah here to-day?"

"Yes," returned Lurlee, joyfully, "more than fifty men; they will be with the troops without."

"I will return presently," said the man, bowing over his crossed arms; "and if ye will watch your men ye will see whether the errand be done or not."

So the ladies sat and looked out. Bright flashed the sun's rays from spear and sword, morion and gauntlet, matchlock and shield, of the troops gathering before the hall where the King sat: while the gay turbans, vests of cloth-of-gold, satins and brocades, glowed in the bright sunlight like a bed of gorgeous flowers.

"There are ten thousand brave hearts throbbing for my lord!" cried the young Queen, clapping her hands. "Look, lady! O Alla, such an array of armed men is fearful, yet beautiful!"

"Ameen!" said Lurlee, earnestly. "A thousand times ten thousand are at his call, if he will only lead them! Why shouldst thou fear, lady? I have ridden with my lord in the battle and felt no fear. But look! a thousand thanks and blessings be upon thee! Yes, they go, Raheem Khan and all the spearmen. Dost thou not see them, Zyna?"

"Yes, to bring my father and Fazil," cried Zyna, in her turn clapping her hands exultingly. "Yes, they will repay thee, O my queen—my mother; they will repay thee with their lives."

"Nay, no tears now, girl," said Fyz-ool-Nissa gaily. "Look out over the cavaliers yonder, and wait patiently. Inshalla! your people will return speedily."

So they sat, silently now, praying inwardly for their safety, though the time seemed terribly long, as they looked over the gathering masses of men: over the gardens, mosques, and palaces of the nobility: and over the country beyond, where, in the quivering noonday light, and now fervid heat, the blue distance seemed melting into the sky.

CHAPTER XL.

Jehándar Beg felt that the communications he had heard might have somewhat disarranged his appearance, and he would not for the world be suspected by Afzool Khan of agitation of any kind; his ample beard must not be disordered, nor a hair of his eyebrows crooked. A glance in a small mirror, which hung in the anteroom, proved that the barber's skill was necessary, and he sent for his own servant. What other hand, indeed, could be allowed to meddle with that glorious beard, or to regulate the orthodox breadth of the moustache and eyebrows? Who understood the proper darkening of the spot in the centre of the forehead, as if it were always being rubbed against the ground in perpetual prayer, like Habeeb Méhtur, the chief of his craft? and finally, who so admirable a chronicler of all domestic scandal, in which Beejapoor was at least as prolific as other cities of similar size and peculiarity of social morals?

So Habeeb, having been summoned, found his master sitting alone where we last left him, reclining against his pillow in the small room before described, and saw, at a glance, that his spirit was troubled.

Having made his obeisance, which was not acknowledged, or barely so, the barber at once set to work, removing the conical lambskin cap which Jehándar Beg always wore, and subjecting the whole scalp to a series of manipulations which were inexpressibly soothing. How lightly moved the practised fingers along lines of muscles and nerves! how carefully was every stray hair put back into its proper place, or deftly eradicated with the sharp tweezers. Then, as the momentous matters of eyebrows, moustache, and beard were severally approached, and where the Kótwal's rough hand had rubbed his chin, pushed up the moustache, or disturbed the eyebrows—till every hair seemed battling with its neighbour or bristling in anger—all was soon reduced to order, and the cap replaced. Jehándar Beg felt a refreshing coolness pervade his head, the nervous excitement was removed, and a calmness supervened which he required for what he had to do.

Yes, a master in his art! Habeeb had made a masterly performance; and yet so quickly!—long enough, however, for those much-coveted papers to be taken far from his master's chance of possession to a place of safety.

"Shookr, Shookr, Habeeb!" (Thanks, thanks!), said the Kótwal at length. "Hast thou any news, friend?"

What was the barber to say? News? yes, plenty! There was no lack of that, such as his master relished; but would it be welcome?

"There was a grand entertainment at the Nawab Alla-ool-Moolk's last night, and some new singers from the Carnatic were there. My lord should hear one of them. She is very lovely," he replied cautiously.

"Except the blessed Mary, and Fáthma, and Ayésha—on whose names be peace!—I wish all women were in the burning pit," said Jehándar Beg savagely, and his hand approached his beard.

"Khóda na khasta bashud!" (God forbid!), exclaimed Habeeb, staying it. "God forbid my lord should touch what has been done! Even in that exclamation a hundred hairs have started up. May his slave ask what has discomposed the fountain of justice this morning?"

"There was some one ill in the palace last night, and a Fakeer was sent for, who shouted 'Ulla dilâyâ to léonga.' Who was that man? and who was ill?" asked Jehándar Beg, not heeding the question.

"My lord, no one was ill that I know of. About the Fakeer I will ascertain, if possible," replied the barber. "I can tell my lord one thing, however: the Shah—may his splendour increase—went out, even as the Khaleefa, of honoured memory, of whom we read—Haroun bin-al Rasheed—was in the habit of doing, to see after his subjects for himself, to hear with his own ears; and, if people say the truth, there is enough for him to hear, if he chose to inquire."

The men understood each other perfectly, and exchanged glances.

"People will talk, friend," said the Kótwal; "but where did he go? if thou'rt sure he went."

"Nay, that is more than your poor slave knows. They say he

took the young Fazil Khan with him, or else the Wuzeer's son. Sure he went? yes, my lord, quite sure," said the man, emphatically. "I was in the citadel, and saw him go out."

"Ay, indeed! Boy's tricks, boy's tricks, Habeeb; yet that Fazil Khan was accounted a steady youth: but he is in trouble about last night."

"Ah, master! we have all been like him once," said the barber, chuckling. "I suppose it was one of the new dancers——"

"Except that we did no murder, friend," returned the Kótwal, interrupting him.

"Is my lord *very* particular about a noble slaying a thief, or a night brawler?" asked the barber.

"O no! and it will be settled. And now you may go, Habeeb—find out who was visited last night; perhaps . . . no matter . . . and thou shalt have thy mouth filled, after our Persian fashion, with gold zecchins and sugar-candy. There are a couple in earnest of more."

"May the sun of your splendour increase in brightness, master!" returned the man, taking the money, and retreating backwards till he gained the door. "I will inquire——"

"And now for this boy and his rough father," said Jehándar Beg, speaking to himself, as the door closed on the barber; "if they could be gained? Well, I must see. If not—we cannot allow them to live; they are too powerful," and he rose and went into the outer hall.

"And no one has passed here, Jaffur?" said Jehándar Beg to the Nubian slave, who, with some others, watched the door of the court where Afzool Khan was confined.

"No one, my lord, except the servants with their meal."

"Did they speak to him?"

"Not a word, my lord; I listened carefully."

"Have the Khan and his son been speaking to each other?"

"Yes, frequently; but as they have moved to the other side of the court, which is now in shadow, I cannot hear them. My lord is going in? Should we not attend? They are armed."

"I am not afraid, Jaffur; put up thy weapon. Keep the door ajar, but do not enter, and, on your life, let no one listen. Do ye hear, all of ye?"

"Jo hookum!" (as you order), cried all together, dispersing as the Kótwal entered.

Afzool Khan and his son were sitting, as Jaffur had described, in the opposite corner of the court from the door; for the sun was now shining with a painful glare of heat into that side by which the Kótwal entered, while, opposite, the cool verandah was rendered more refreshing from the shadow of a large champa tree, which fell over the building and enclosure where they were. They rose courteously as the Kótwal advanced, and, saluting him gravely, yet without any expression of impatience at detention, requested him to be seated.

It was no part of Jehándar Beg's policy to attempt to bully. If he could find out what the affair of the night had really been, or obtain a clue to the truth of that which had been alleged of the King; in short, anything which might serve as a guide to action, or as means of warning to the Wuzeer, it would be enough.

"I trust my honoured guests have been fittingly attended to?" he asked, as he subsided on his heels at a respectful distance from the old Khan, joining his hands after the most deferential and most elegant of Persian customs. "I trust the repast was served hot. My lords must excuse my absence, and my being taken unawares. Had I expected the honour of their company, then, indeed, Zoolficar's skill should have been put forth."

"The kabobs and kichéri were excellent, Meerza Sahib," replied Afzool Khan, politely. "I was to have had the same at my own house; and there were other dishes, too. Verily, your cook must be a treasure; there is not such another in the city."

"My lord, a poor slave, who followed me from my own dear country, and has remained here with me. Yes, he has a pretty skill in the art, and . . . but you have yet to know what he can do. . . . If I might send him one day——"

"Shookr, shookr! (thanks), Meerza Sahib. Yes, we will see about it. Inshalla! inshalla!" replied the Khan, cheerily, "an excellent idea—and come yourself."

The Kótwal thought he had made a favourable impression. "After all, there was nothing in the murder matter that you need care about, Meah Sahib," he continued blandly, to Fazil Khan. "Pardon me if I was rude this morning, but when we are at business, you know, there can be no distinction of persons."

"None," said Fazil, gravely; "but who was the man found dead? You said one had been killed."

"O, only a Kafir Hindu; some son of a burnt father, who is gone to burn with him," laughed the Kótwal. "I don't know; the body is not yet claimed. By the way, Meah, it was strange enough that you should have been just in time to save that Lalla."

"Ah, yes; what has become of him?" asked Fazil innocently. "You promised he should be seen to."

"And I have done as I promised, Meah. Habeeb has dressed the wound, which is but a scratch, and the man has eaten heartily; perhaps he was not much hurt, after all."

"Perhaps not," said Fazil, significantly, "but it was well he fell into good hands."

"Yes," returned the Kótwal, musingly, "was it not strange what he told the Duffadar about Pahar Singh and the Shah's secretary? I have heard that my lord, the Meerza, was out last night late, and at a temple. Could it have been there?"

"To meet Pahar Singh? I should hardly say it was likely," returned Fazil.

"Nay, more, that the Asylum of the Faith—the King himself—was there also. At least—at least——"

Fazil saw Jehándar Beg was not sure. It was a mere guess, for which there was perhaps suspicion, but he laughed aloud and replied, "A good joke, Meerza Sahib; perhaps they say I was with him!"

"Well," returned the Kótwal, wagging his head, "the fact is, they do; and perhaps you were, my young friend. Let me see; his highness is about your own age. When I was as old I remember the Shah, with some others of us, used to have frolics now and then in the bazars of Isfahan. Ah, Meah, there were——"

Fazil made a gesture, as if his father, who was sitting bolt upright, with his eyes shut, might not like to hear the remainder.

"Yes," continued the Kótwal, "if ye did go, what matter?"

"I have before said that Bulwunt Rao was my companion, not the King; and the rest you know of," interrupted the young Khan.

"Not all, Meah; but we are out of court now, and I am quite sure of my young friend's good faith to let me know anything that concerns the state interests, the King, or the Wuzeer; and so, Meah Sahib, if we could examine those papers together——"

"Ah, yes! the papers, Meerza, you would not understand them—they were Mahratta."

"But we could find a Karkoon to read them, and you are known to speak that language, Meah?"

"True, Meerza Sahib, I do; but the papers are not here——"

"Not here, sir!" cried Jehándar Beg, with an ominous scowl passing over his face, at which Afzool Khan involuntarily allowed his hand to steal to his sword hilt, as it lay on the ground. "Not here?"

"Not here," echoed Fazil demurely, dropping his eyes.

"But they were here when you came this morning?"

"Certainly they were; and one of our people took them home for me."

"Yet you promised they should be forthcoming whenever I required them? Beware, Fazil Khan, how you entangle yourself in this matter," returned the Kótwal, sternly.

"I do not think I made any promise, Meerza Sahib," replied Fazil; "'tis you who must be mistaken, pardon me for saying so. I said they concerned the King, our lord and master, and would be shown to him only: and in Durbar to-day they will be presented to him. You will be there, of course?"

"By Alla!" exclaimed the Kótwal; "but if——"

At the oath the old Khan fairly took his sword in his left hand, and placed it across his knees, while he looked grimly at his host; and Fazil saw the upper portion of his father's moustache, where it touched his cheek, quivering with suppressed rage.

Jehándar Beg checked himself, and said, deferentially, "Forgive the oath, Khan Sahib, and you know enough of Persians to excuse it. It would have been pleasant, as fellow-servants of the King, to have shared your confidence. As it is denied, I yield the point; and you are welcome to all the credit of the service you will do my lord. But what say you, gentlemen, to assisting me to re-examine that Khayet who is detained without; you acknowledge, Meah Sahib, at least, that he was rescued by you—perhaps from death?"

"You have a strange memory, Kótwal Sahib, to-day," said Fazil, smiling. "I never said I rescued him, I think. Send for the man; no doubt you will hear all you wish from him, and will believe him. I do not appear to be very credible to you to-day."

CHAPTER XLI.

As the Kótwal rose to go to the door, the old Khan whispered to his son, "We can seize him, Fazil, if needs be, and put a dagger into him. The man is not fit to live. He is even now plotting something; I know it, trust him not, my son."

"If needs be, father, I am ready; but no violence yet," replied Fazil; "wait till the Wuzeer's son is announced."

"The man has been sent for," said Jehándar Beg, returning to his seat, "and will be here presently." He had given his own directions to the guard outside to stand by the door, yet no nearer than was needful for precaution.

The Lalla was not long detained. Almost as Jehándar Beg had seated himself—this time a little nearer to Fazil—he opened the door, which was closed after him, and advanced towards the party in a courtly but respectful manner. Fazil hardly recognized the man, so completely had rest and good clothes improved him. His face was clean shaved, his moustache and hair were trimmed and oiled. His small turban tied neatly in the Nustalik fashion of the imperial court, which was strange at Beejapoor. The clothes he wore, though somewhat too large, were yet clean white muslin; and a handsome Persian shawl over his shoulders, proved that his personal comfort had been well attended to under Jehándar Beg's orders.

"I trust you are better now," said Fazil to the Lalla, kindly, as, after his very courtly advance, in which he bowed his head very low, turned out his toes very wide, and put his elbows as far behind him as possible, he sat down much after the manner of Jehándar Beg, on the left hand of the Kótwal.

"My lord's house will prosper for his kindness to a poor stranger," said the Lalla. "What more delightful to exercise, what more grateful to God, than hospitality?" and he quoted a verse from the poet Saadi on the subject, which he followed by another and another.

"Enough, friend," said Jehándar Beg, laughing. "No need to prove your scholarly attainments; they are not needed at present. Now, we all bid you not to fear; but tell us, in plain terms, what happened before this brave young gentleman rescued you last night."

The Lalla was not very clear as to what course he was to take; he, too, was watching his game.

"My lord, noble sirs, they were Gosais who found me in the temple, and ye are Moslem gentlemen, or nobles."

"Very true," said Fazil. "Now, look at me carefully, and try if you cannot remember me as one who lifted you up after you had been robbed."

"Ah, yes, noble sir, now I do remember," cried the Lalla; "I owe my life to you, sir, my life. When I screamed, you must have heard me. I pray you, let me kiss your feet."

The action was an ordinary one of gratitude, yet enough to admit of Fazil's passing a well-known signal of silence to the man as he removed his hands, while the old Khan cried grimly—

"Make your reverence to your God, if you have one, not to my son. Is he an idol, that you bow down to him?"

"I mean no offence; pardon me, my lord," said the Lalla, humbly. "I was only——"

The opening of the door interrupted the Lalla's speech, which would have been very flowery and hyperbolic.

An attendant entered and spoke to the Kótwal. "My lord, Kowas Khan has arrived; is he to be admitted?"

"Tell him I kiss his hands; I am engaged with these worthy gentlemen," returned Jehándar Beg, looking round; "and pray ask him to excuse me for a short time. If he would like a hooka, or coffee, or sherbet, let him have all he desires."

"And his attendants?"

"Let any of proper rank sit with him, the rest can remain in the outer court."

"Very good, my lord," said the servant, and he shut the door.

During this interruption, a very pretty piece of pantomime had been executed between the eyes of Fazil and the Lalla. It would have been more complete, perhaps, could Fazil have used his hands also, but he dare not. As it was, however, the Lalla seemed to understand all that was required; and the delightfully comprehensive manner in which he half shut his eyes, bowed his head, and smiled blandly though almost imperceptibly, would have been fit example for any diplomatist. Nothing could be seen by the Kótwal, for, in order to speak to the servant, it had been requisite for him to lean behind the Lalla's back.

Jehándar Beg lost two points by his movement; one we have seen, the other was a more serious one. For as he moved, the letters which had been given to him by Moro Trimmul's agent, and which he had put into a side-pocket of his dress, protruded a little as he reached over, and, when he settled himself again, remained projecting half out of that receptacle. He was not aware of it, but they attracted Fazil's immediate attention. These he must have at any risk—for he had seen the seal of the rebel Rajah on them—and he again roused his father by the short cough they had agreed upon.

"Now, Lallajee, tell us all. You see you are among friends; but we are hungry for fruit—flowers do not satisfy us," said Jehándar Beg, jocosely rubbing his hands, and speaking in Persian, his own language.

"My lords, what can I say?" returned the Lalla, simply. "I am what you see, a poor scholar. Delhi is full of such, and we are starving. Every one said, 'Go to the King of the Dekhan; he is wise, he is generous, he is accomplished; he is a patron of literature.' So your poor servant prepared two copies of verses; one in Sanscrit, in which the third letter of every line is the same, T——"

"Mashalla!" said Jehándar Beg, laughing, "Te-tum—te te, te-ta-te to, Te ta-hah! Like that, Lallajee? O yes; our Brahmuns here make odes, in which all the words end in skri, pri, dri; or else msh, kshsh, rshsh-dshush. One would think all the mud in the Dekhan was squelching under their feet; but go on."

"My lord is pleased to be witty," returned the Lalla, with a bland smile, turning towards his host and joining hands. "Then I had a Persian ode. It was nothing—nothing—a poor thing altogether; only, if my lords wish, I could repeat it. Methinks there was some elegance about it, if nothing else."

"God forbid!" returned the Kôtwal, echoed by Fazil and the Khan. "Go on."

"Well, my lords, as you wish," continued the Lalla. "Some other day I may be more fortunate; and, with your permission, I will resume my history. I had saved a few gold pieces, and I had enough to keep my family for a year. I left them in my house, and I have gradually made my way hither by Ahmednugger and Sholapoor. That is all."

"Go on," said Fazil. "How didst thou get here from Sholapoor?"

"I came with some Gosais, as they appeared to be, who met me at a village, Al—, Al—. I forget—just after you cross the river Bheema."

"Almella," suggested the Khan, interrupting him.

"Yes, that was it. They said they knew of a comfortable lodging in a temple or a mutt; but if we arrived late we must be content with whatever shelter we could get. I do not know, sirs, whether they purposely delayed me by the way—for, indeed, the roads were very muddy; but we arrived after sunset, and they took me to a temple of Bhowani, in a grove. So long as it was light the place did not look amiss for temporary shelter; but when it grew dark, and the wind began to moan in the trees, I thought, sirs, that the men's looks changed, and—and I began to tremble, yet unable to help myself—as one lies bound sometimes in a dream.

"What could your slave do, sirs? At length they talked together in an unknown tongue, and all fell upon me, strangled me, and took what money I had, and my clothes, and I knew no more till this valiant gentleman and some one else roused me and took me to a guard-house, where I was well cared for."

"Why do you tell lies?" said the Kôtwal, who, though unable to make objection to the very probable story which the Lalla had invented, felt conscious there was no truth in it. "Ah, man with a burnt father, tell the truth; we are no enemies of thine! Do not eat dirt at our hands! Why did the Shah's secretary visit thee at the temple? Speak; it shall be well for thee. We are all friends of his Majesty's here."

A very slight compression of Fazil's under lip was sufficient guide for the Lalla. "The King's secretary? God defend us!" cried the Lalla, innocently; "what should I have to do with the secretary? Ah, sirs, why this oppression of a poor slave like me—a stranger without friends? Did you see the secretary when you came to rescue me, noble sir?"

"Not I, indeed; thou wast lying among the ashes, senseless enough. All we heard was a scream, which sounded like one in distress, and we entered the court," said Fazil, simply.

The Kôtwal looked from one to the other, but he could find out no sign of intelligence. He was fairly puzzled.

"Then why that respectable Duffadar's account of what you said to him in the guard-house?" cried Jehándar Beg, jerking himself suddenly round so as to confront the Lalla, while he seconded the movement by an emphatic blow on the floor. "What about Pahar Singh?"

As he did so, his sleeve caught one of the letters projecting from his pocket, which flew into the centre of the group. Fazil picked it up, and returned it with a polite bow, but not before he had distinctly seen the seal of the Rajah Sivaji Bhôslay upon it, and the memorandum in the corner, which Jehándar Beg had written for the Wuzeer, and marked private. Jehándar Beg's confusion on receiving the letter could not be concealed, and Fazil felt that, having seen what was not intended for him, he was in greater danger than before.

"What about Pahar Singh?" echoed the Lalla, who had observed the confused expression of Jehándar Beg's countenance, and seen also what he was quite familiar with, the rebel Rajah's seal. "My lord, your servant heard a great deal of him, as he came here through the country. Everybody, from Ahmednugger to Sholapoor, spoke of Pahar Singh, and warned me of Pahar Singh, but the Gosais did not appear to fear him, and said he never touched companies of travelling beggars. I remember now," continued the Lalla, dreamily, "I think some one asked me whether Pahar Singh had robbed me. Perhaps I said yes, I don't know; I might have said anything, good sirs, for I was like one in a hideous dream; and this robber everybody appeared to know:—in the bazars, in temples, mutts, serais—Pahar Singh, Pahar Singh—nothing but Pahar Singh all the way. I heard enough of him."

"Thou liest, Lalla. I have warned thee once, and again warn thee—beware of the torture!" cried Jehándar Beg savagely, and from between his closed teeth; "a word and——"

"Jehándar Beg," said Afzool Khan, interrupting, "you and I are old friends, and I am your guest, so also is this man. Good or evil of him I know not, neither do I care: but torture shall not be used; and so far as I know or have seen, he says nothing but the truth. We are helpless enough here, my son and I, but we will not allow him to be touched with any of your vile instruments. Question him otherwise as you please, it is your duty."

The tone of the old Khan's voice, habitually stern, seemed more so than usual to Jehándar Beg. Should he resent it and call in his men? It was the thought of a moment. He would have done this, but that he knew the Wuzeer's son sat without; he, at least, was faithful to Fazil, and might not object to prove his devotion to the old Khan, in the hope of its doing service in his suit for Zyna.

"Khan Sahib——" returned Jehándar Beg, putting up his joined hands.

He could not finish the sentence. Fazil, on pretence of arranging his shawl about his shoulders, threw it with a sudden gesture over the Kótwal's head, and closed it behind, throwing Jehándar Beg on his face, while, at the same instant, a dagger flashed from the old Khan's waistband, and was held by him close to the Kótwal's heart, and so that the point actually pricked the skin.

"Take out those letters, Lalla, from his pocket. In the name of the Prophet—if one sound escape him, father—strike deep and hard. Here is another traitor as bad as him we know of. There, hold his legs, Lalla. Wah, wah! thou art a noble fellow; fear not, friend—we are not like the Jogi. There, that will do; and well was it done," continued Fazil, as the Lalla rapidly passed an end of his own scarf round the Kótwal's arms, and tied it in a knot behind his back; "he is safe now. Where is his ring? give it to me, quick."

"Beware, Jehándar Beg," growled Afzool Khan, who leant over the prostrate man without altering his position, as the Lalla loosed the ring, "I do not want to kill thee, good fellow; but, by Alla, if thou strivest ever so little, this knife will go through thee. I am no friend to traitors, as thou well knowest; so keep quiet."

It was a bold stroke; but in such emergencies desperate efforts are generally the most successful. Fazil took the Kótwal's signet-ring, and went to the door. The slave Jaffur looked at it for an instant, bowed his head, and crossed his arms; while Fazil, looking round the hall, beckoned to his friend, who, attended by some twenty of his followers, sat upon the dais.

Kowas Khan arose instantly, and with him the men, who made their salutations, and advanced towards the door. The slaves believed that the Wuzeer's son had been sent for, and stood aside to let him pass: and as the young men embraced in the doorway, Fazil whispered to his friend to disarm them, and hold the door. A pressure of the hand was the sure reply.

"I will return with my shawl," said Kowas Khan aloud, going back towards his seat, "and I will follow you directly."

A moment afterwards Fazil and the Khan heard a few low cries, a struggle, and a slight clash of arms. The surprise had been complete. The slaves were disarmed, thrust into the Wuzeer's private room, and the doors closed.

"Fear not, noble friends," cried the cheery voice of the Wuzeer's son, as he stood in the doorway, "ye are safe, and no one is hurt. I have five hundred men of my own body-guard in the courts, on foot and horseback; and, Inshalla! we can hold the Kótwallee against an army. May I come?"

"Ul-humd-ul-illa!" cried the Khan and his son together, "hazar shookr, hazar shookr!—(A thousand thanks!) O holy 'Geesoo Duraz!' I vow to thee a thousand lights, and a chain of gold for the canopy of thy blessed sepulchre," continued the Khan, devoutly.

"Come, friend and brother," said Fazil; "come here and see what treachery doth in the most trusted places—nay, fear us not, Jehándar Beg," he continued; "we are not arbiters in your destiny—it rests in higher hands than ours. Father, take away the knife from his heart."

"I don't know that I ought," said the old Khan, grimly. "I shall keep it ready, and near thee, Jehándar Beg. I trust thee not, my friend."

"You are more lucky than I am," returned the Kótwal, sadly. "When a man's fate deserts him, he need not struggle—he is helpless," and he quoted a verse from the Gulistan to that effect.

"Shabash! a scholarly quotation," said the Lalla, gravely. "And now, gentlemen, if ye will trust a poor Mutsuddee, who has some experience, we will examine this worthy gentleman's pockets; and if he has any private writing-cases, something might be found in them also."

"Peace, Lalla!" cried Fazil, sternly; "what we do concerns thee not. But thou hast been faithful and intelligent, and we will see thee rewarded."

What was found in the search will presently appear; meanwhile, we need to see how those assembled with the King, in his royal court, were employed.

CHAPTER XLII.

THE great Hall of Audience in the Citadel was only used on state occasions of ceremony. It formed part of the oldest division of the royal residence, and was built, as report had it, after a model in Turkey or Persia, in both of which countries the founder of the dynasty, Ibrahim Adil Shah, had resided. But as no such model is known to exist, it is more probable that one of the Turkish architects whom he had invited to his camp, and to whose Europeanized skill and taste most of the noble Saracenic Gothic buildings of the city owed their origin, had designed and executed the whole under the direction of his munificent patron.

The "Ark," or Citadel of Beejapoor, is a fortress in itself, and the area is surrounded by a beautiful stone wall, having heavy bastions at intervals, and a fausse braye, also with bastions; both being protected by a broad wet ditch. The main entrance is by a causeway, defended by a gateway, flanked by bastions of great strength. The whole of the interior was laid out in palaces, under various denominations, and public buildings, such as the courts of civil and criminal justice, the treasury, the military and revenue record offices, and the like, and the great Hall of Audience, which now concerns us.

A broad road from the second gateway led nearly through the centre of the Citadel, as you entered, to the Màidân, or plain of exercise. The Palace of the Seven Stories, and the buildings connected with it, lay on the left hand, and the "Sunget Mahal," or Palace of Assembly, with other heavy blocks of building, public and private, to the right. All these palaces, at the time of which we write, were interspersed with courts and gardens; but the space before the great Hall, called the Màidân or Plain, was kept exclusively for the assembly, inspection, or exercise of royal troops on particular occasions, and also as the waiting-place of the "sowarees," or retinues, which attended those who visited the palace on ordinary business.

The hall itself was a very noble building. It stood upon a low basement, beneath which were crypts, probably used for archives, or as magazines; and was entered by flights of steps, which led into corridors at each side. The front was entirely open, consisting of one immense Gothic arch, ninety-two feet in span, and of proportionate height, and of two narrow lancet-shaped arches of corresponding height, one on each side, which opened on the side corridors.

The interior consisted of one immense room, unbroken to the roof; but upon its south side, and partially also east and west, there were projections built upon cloisters, which contained rooms and galleries; especially to the south, where there was a closed latticed balcony, where the ladies of the court might sit and look on at ceremonies of reception or rejoicing, and where the King might receive the petitions or salutations of the people without inconvenience. Above these galleries and balconies was another story, with open turrets at the corners, and suites of apartments above. As the building stands now, a mere shell, bereft of roof and floors, and with all, except its noble arches and cloisters, crumbling gradually to decay, it is a noble and impressive structure, and enough remains to estimate what it must have been when perfect.

A busy and interesting scene it was, even to those concerned. As each "sowaree" arrived at the entrance steps, it was met by a number of "chobdars," and mirdhas, or attendants, bearing massive gold and silver sticks, or clubs covered with chased silver or gold; dressed exclusively in white muslin, wearing small circular turbans, flattened out at the sides, muslin tunics, tight to the waist, and descending thence in thickly-gathered robes to the feet, which gave them the appearance of petticoats. These men attended officers of higher rank, who were, in fact, chamberlains, and whose duty it was to conduct the various visitors to the presence of the King, to proclaim aloud their titles, and to marshal them to their seats. Without, the royal Abyssinian and Dekhani guards prevented violence among their retainers.

Once the broad corridor at either side was reached by the visitors there was no further interruption; and though the war of struggle, gibe, and quarrel, peculiar to such an assembly, came hoarsely and with a stifled sound through the arches into the hall:—within, there was a decorous, if not, indeed, a solemn and impressive silence. Men spoke to each other hardly above their breath; and the soft murmur arising from thousands of such half whispers ascended and seemed to float tremblingly among the balconies, and up to the lofty roof of the building.

The King had early taken his seat. The musnud, or royal throne, was under the centre of the balcony before mentioned, upon a dais, raised a step above the general floor of the hall. There was no decoration visible upon it; and it consisted of a wide cushion and pillows, covered with white muslin, supported at the back and sides by a railing of wood, covered with plates of gold which, indeed, appeared as if of solid gold. On the right hand of the King, who was dressed in simple white muslin, with a single gold ornament in his turban, sat the Peer Bundagee Sahib, the religious instructor we have before mentioned; and at the back of the rail the Secretary, with two young nobles, whose hereditary office it was to wave over the King the jewelled Mórchas, or fans of peacock feathers.

Farther again behind, among the arches, closing up the entrance to the cloisters, and leaning against the pillars, were servants bearing the King's weapons, the Aftábgeeree, or sun-shades, the royal umbrellas, and the private guard of slaves, mostly Nubian eunuchs.

Like the monarch's seat, the whole of the floor was covered by quilted cotton carpets, over which white muslin was spread; so that, with the exception of here and there a coloured scarf or waistbelt, and an occasional turban ornament, the whole of the persons seated wore the same character of dress as the King, with little variation. In some respects the assembly had a monotonous appearance; but, on the other hand, the effect was chaste and solemn, and agreed with the plain undecorated character of the building.

The privileged attendants, however, who were allowed entrance with their masters, and who stood in files behind them against the wall, were dressed in the brightest and gayest colours which could be devised. Here were tunics of satin and cloth-of-gold, brocaded turbans and scarfs of the richest materials, mingled together in the greatest profusion; and this brilliant array, in which all hues seemed to blend with a strangely gorgeous harmony, formed a powerful background in relief of the white dresses, and white coverings of the floor.

Then beyond, the eye followed the graceful outline of the vast arch against a deep blue sky, flecked with light clouds. Below, it rested upon the plain, where, in the quivering heat, which gave a tremulous movement to the atmosphere, stood the serried masses of royal troops and sowarees, comparisoned elephants and led horses, litters and their bearers—all in the glowing colours which we have already seen from the Queen's balcony; and with bright arms and armour, which flashed and glinted in a thousand sparkles as the wearers moved.

The Secretary and the Peer had noted, carefully and jealously, the names of the several nobles and sirdars as they were announced by the mirdhas in attendance—presented their customary nuzzurs or offerings, according to their rank, and were conducted to their places;

and every now and then one or other whispered to the King, as neutral or suspected persons passed, or when the appearance of a well-known loyal friend gave assurance of support. Still Afzool Khan's place was vacant, and that of the Wuzeer. It was true the latter could not yet be expected, but his son might at least be present; and the double absence cast a gloom over the King's face, which he could barely conceal.

"I had counted upon Afzool Khan and his son Fazil," said the King, mournfully, to the Peer, "but you see they have not come. We might not expect Kowas Khan without his father; but I had thought Afzool Khan among the truest of my people—what think ye?"

The Peer could give but little consolation. He, too, had expected the Khan, and had had no doubts of his fidelity; so also the Secretary; but his unaccountable absence disturbed them both.

Just then the lady Lurlee's escort, entering the open space, wheeled up among other troops, and the leader, Raheem Khan, dashed at speed to the foot of the basement, made his reverence to the King, and followed his men to the position they had taken up.

"Ah," cried the Peer, joyfully, to the King, "those are Afzool Khan's 'sowaree'; the old Khan and his son are not far off now, Shookr-Oolla;" and he looked anxiously to the side entrance, in the hope of seeing him advance with his son from the archway in the corridor. Others came on, but neither appeared.

"What hinders Afzool Khan?" said the Secretary to the Peer, after a while; "who is detaining him?"

"Send and inquire," said the King.

"Go," said the Peer to a mirdha in attendance, "and see if Afzool Khan be in the corridor; if not, go to his officer and inquire where he is,—not as if our Prince had asked, but from me." The King, to whom the man looked for orders, nodded assent, and he departed and returned speedily.

"I examined both corridors, and he was not in either, Huzrut," he said to the holy man, "so I went to Raheem Khan, who tells me he has come with the Khânum;" and here his voice dropped almost to a whisper, "that Afzool Khan hath been at the Kótwal's, at Jehândar Beg's, since morning, and it is particular business, as both he and his son have been in private consultation with him since sunrise."

The King had leaned over the rail to hear the detail, but he had not noticed the first part of the message; and as the man receded among the attendants behind, looked from one to the other of his friends, but could gather no consolation from their faces.

"It is but too true, my lord," said the Secretary sadly; "we need not expect them; for the Wuzeer's son, with a heavy body of horse and foot, has just gone to the Kótwallee—he was seen with them not long ago passing the fort gate. Jehándar Beg is not come, and it is clear to me that they have garrisoned the Kôtwallee, and will defend it till the Wuzeer arrives, when they will declare revolt. Sending a party here is but a blind."

"And who are here to check it?" asked the King apprehensively.

"Many, my lord," replied the Peer earnestly; "all the Dekhanies are my disciples, and I will answer for them to a man. All the artillery are with them. Fear not."

The King looked inquiringly to his Secretary.

"Yes, my Prince," he said, "fear not: we cannot wait for them; nothing good ever came of vacillation or expediency. Bismilla! shall I order silence?"

"Bismilla-ir-rahman-ir-raheem!" exclaimed the King devoutly, looking up. "I am ready. Order silence," he said to one of the the mirdhas.

"Khámôsh! silence!" cried the man in a loud, deep voice, which rang through the hall, and sounded strangely, interrupting the loose murmuring chat which had prevailed before—"Khâmôsh!"

"Khámôsh!" was reiterated by all the mirdhas and chobdars stationed about the hall, and by the attendants behind, and was taken up by those in the corridors, spreading to the crowd without, and to the troops—"Khámôsh!"

The silence that ensued was almost oppressive. In the hall itself, after the men had once more settled themselves in their seats, there was not a sound or murmur. The struggles and gibes without ceased, and even the troops were still, save where a neigh, or the rattle of caparisons, as horses tossed their heads or champed their bits, broke the stillness; or an elephant, clashing his bells, and being admonished by his driver, lifted his trunk, and gave a short scream.

It was the Secretary's office to open the business of the day, and just as he was about to speak, the chief of the eunuchs entered, bearing the Queen's billet, and kneeling down behind the rail, while he spoke aside, covering his mouth, said to the King hastily—

"It is a matter of life or death. If Afzool Khan hath any favour in your eyes, O King, save him! there may be time."

"This is some trick on thee, Daood," said the King sneeringly; "we know where he is, and how employed. He is ours no longer, and hath left us of his own free will."

"His wife and daughter are with the Bégum Sahiba. Read that, and you will know why," answered the man firmly.

"Can it be true?" asked the King of the Peer, opening the note. "Ya Khubeer, O!" he continued, after a pause: "this is wonderful! wonderful! O friends! and yet we had suspected our noble friend. But he is true; see, here is our royal signet to this; no doubt, no doubt."

"What is it?" cried both the Peer and the Secretary in a breath, seeing the King much excited.

"Afzool Khan and his son are imprisoned at the Kótwallee, and prevented from attending. They must be brought instantly."

"Imprisoned?" cried both together.

"Yes, friends," continued the King, "there is treachery in this, for Jehándar Beg and the Wuzeer are one, it is clear now, and we must act at once. Ismail Khan," continued he firmly, to an officer who stood behind him clothed in a shirt of mail, "go thou with two hundred of the royal guard, and some of the mirdhas, bring Jehándar Beg to the presence, and with him Afzool Khan and his son."

"I beg to petition," said the eunuch, "that some of Afzool Khan's Paigah are here, who came with their mistress; they might as well go, if I might send them."

"Of course," replied the King, "why not send the whole Paigah?"

"Excellent," said the Peer; "take what are here with thee, Ismail Khan, at once, and send for the rest. Raheem Khan will not fail thee."

"I am gone, my lord, and will take him with me; he is my son-in-law."

"Ah, I had forgotten. Go; fear not; bring them safely and quickly, friend, for we have much need of their presence."

"Ya Ulla Kureem!" said the Peer devoutly, looking up, "this is thy doing. O, dear old friend! thou art not gone from among us as we had feared. Bismilla, let us proceed! first with these letters of Sivaji's, then with the rest. Afzool Khan will be here by that time, and the people will rise to his call as a man. Inshalla! your poor servant, too, will do his best. Let silence be called again."

It was necessary: for the entrance of the eunuch, the delivery of the note, followed as they were by the withdrawal of Afzool Khan's men, and some of the royal guard, had excited no little curiosity in the assembly. Afzool Khan's absence had been regretted by some, rejoiced in by others, but noticed by all; and now that his men were sent away, the speculations that ensued were various as to the cause; and while some feared disclosures, others already rejoiced in the prospect of his possible disgrace.

"Khámôsh!" again was cried by the same voice, which rung clearly above the buzz of conversation, and was taken up as before —"Khámôsh—silence!"

CHAPTER XLIII.

"O NOBLES, and well-wishers of the State!" cried the Secretary, in a strong, manly voice, "it is not mere ceremony for which ye have been called together this day; and it is not that the present urgent matters might not be disposed of by the Shah—may his splendour increase;—but in affairs of such moment, he would have the advice and assistance of older men, and of those who, for years past, have given their faith and their blood freely for the kingdom, and for his family; and surely nothing need be done in private, when ye, O Moslems! can be witnesses before God and the Prophet.

"Lo, friends in the faith! he hath called ye together because of those grievous rumours of treachery which prevail: and because of intrigues which have sown distrust between man and man in this city. Of these, two have been revealed to him by means little short of a miracle, and yet so true, that a child may understand them. Hear, then, what my lord the King will say to ye—listen!"

A low murmur arose through the assembly as men spoke in short, eager whispers to each other. Who was to be accused? To whom did these introductory remarks refer in particular? Many a secret traitor then sitting there, trembled upon his seat. Were he denounced, he felt there would be no alternative between detection and almost instant death, and there were not a few who repeated to themselves the dying confession of faith. If it was to be, it was to be; there was no escape now.

The King spoke from his seat, and though his voice was of a gentler character than his Secretary's, its silvery ringing tones were even more distinctly heard.

"O friends and subjects!" he said, "many words are hardly needful when the understanding is to have clear scope for action, and I desire all to consider what will be now put before ye. As God hath appointed me His deputy on earth to govern this kingdom, so I am answerable to Him for it, and for you, my people. This I clearly admit. If it be glorious, are ye not so? If it be tranquil, are ye not safe? If it be humbled, are ye not humbled likewise? Is any one weary of our service, let him leave it, but for the rest, let us be united: let it not be said by our enemies that we could be seduced and divided, or that our foolish quarrels are worse than the petty jealousies of the women of a divided house. O noble Dekhanies, put enmity and treachery from among ye: is it come to this, that they exist? Listen."

The King paused, and seemed to be searching under his cushions, while the sounds of his last words, rising to the vaulted roof, trembled in a sweet faint murmur, and died away among its fretted recesses; and as yet the rapt silence of the assembly was unbroken.

"A man," he continued, holding up a mass of papers to the view of all—"one whom we had venerated as a father—into whose hands we were given by our father on his deathbed—has been false. False to me, that is nothing,—false to the kingdom and to you, that is more,—false to his oath to an orphan as I am, and to God, that is most of all. Here is his writing, here are his seals,—look at them. These letters to the Padshah Alumgeer began ere that bad man were a king, and have been continued within a month; and by them we read now, that him we speak of would have given away our kingdom, but would have reserved his share. And yet, O Khan Mahomed! if we wrong thee in this, we will do thee justice before God and this assembly."

"Justice, justice!" echoed a thousand voices: "put out the treason!" while many rose excitedly to their feet and were pulled down again by their neighbours.

"Wait," continued the King. "Let him be heard in his own behalf when he arrives; do not prejudge him. If these are untrue, there is no honour we possess or can confer, that shall not be his. If true, let the just Alla judge him before ye all."

"Ameen, ameen!" cried the Peer devoutly. "Ameen, ameen!" was echoed by the assembly, in a hoarse roar, which filled the hall. Again there was silence.

"The next is a more simple matter," continued the King, with increased confidence. "Ye all know of Sivaji Bhóslay. How often his father rebelled, and was punished, and again forgiven by our father. How often the son hath been guilty of crimes. All these would have been forgiven. As a wise father corrects, while he bears with and forgives the errors of a wilful son,—so should we have forgiven also; but for treachery. Look, friends, here, in the same packet with those we have just mentioned, are these letters from Sivaji to the Padshah. We who have fed this wolf, are his enemies; those who have hunted him, are his friends. Here are lists of forts which will be taken and held for the Moghuls, of districts to pay for armies, of men who will join with their local levies. Between them they will share the Dekhan, and Sivaji will be the imperial Viceregent!

"Did ye hear, friends?" he continued, after a pause. "Do ye desire to serve under the infidel? I am young. I have no experience. I am a humble worm before God; but I am the son of one who led ye to victory. I am one who has been nursed in war, and will lead ye again! Choose, then, between them and the King of your ancient dynasty. If I have a place in your hearts, bid me stay; if not, a Durwaysh's robe and staff are mine, and at the blessed shrine of the Prophet I will abjure the world and die. I will trouble ye no more. No, no more—me, or mine."

For an instant the same sweet trembling murmur of the King's voice arose to the roof—but for an instant only. As if with one accord, a shout of "Deen! Deen! for the faith! for the faith! we will die for you!"—rang through the building, as men, no longer able to control their emotions, started to their feet and shouted the war-cry of Islam. Those who were without had observed the emotion in the hall, but had not been aware of its cause. Now, however, the familiar battle-shout fell on willing ears, and was returned, from the thousands gathered there, with an enthusiasm which knew no bounds. "Deen! Deen!" accompanied by the battle-cries of the various nobles and chiefs whose escorts were drawn up together.

Just then, and as the excitement from within and without had somewhat subsided, a strong body of horse, known to all as belonging to Afzool Khan, swept round the corner of the building with its standard unfurled, and its kettle-drums beating loudly. Among the serried mass of horsemen could be seen a palankeen closely muffled and jealously guarded, immediately behind which rode the brave old Khan and his son Fazil, with several of his officers. It was evident to all that the litter contained a person of consequence; and many from within the hall looked around anxiously, as Afzool Khan, his son, and several others with him, dismounted and placed themselves beside it. Could the Wuzeer have returned? If so, he was already a prisoner, and there was no hope. If not, whom could it be? The King had been about to address the assembly again, but he paused and turned to those behind him.

"Ah," he cried exultingly, "Alla hath heard our prayers, and here are our noble friends. I vow thank-offerings to thee, O Sofee Surmust! * O Geesoo Duraz! by thy hands, Peer Sahib, as thou wilt!"

"I said the planets assured me that my lord should destroy his enemies to-day," said the Peer, wiping his eyes, for his love for Afzool Khan was great, and he had feared seduction. "Shookr oolla! Shookr oolla! Hazarha-Shookr! thousands of thanks do we offer at thy throne, O merciful! and here he comes, Soobhán Ulla! Soobhán Ulla!"

Afzool Khan was well known, and a hearty shout had greeted him as he dismounted, looked proudly about him, and returned the salutations of his friends and the soldiery. The palankeen was, by his orders, taken up the steps into the corridor; and, room being cleared for it by the sticks and maces of the chobdars, it was carried on, the Khan and his son accompanying it, through the entrance hall and into the centre of the assembly before the throne, where, in spite of the remonstrances of the chamberlains, it was set down. Then the Khan, disengaging his sword from his belt, and bidding Fazil do the same, they advanced to the foot of the musnud, and enveloping the hilts

* A celebrated Mahomedan saint of the Dekhan, whose tomb is at Sugger.

in their scarfs, presented them as "nuzzurs" or offerings to the King, making, at the same time, their customary obeisances.

"Pardon for this boldness, my prince," said the Khan; "but as the merciful Alla delivered us strangely out of his hands who is there, we thought we had better bring him to 'the presence' at once."

"Who?" asked the king excitedly. "The Wuzeer? Khan Mahomed?"

"No, my lord," returned the Khan, "but Jehándar Beg."

"God be praised thou art safe, Khan," returned the King, putting out his hand and resting it upon the Khan's head, "and thou also, Fazil. Now, we have no fear."

"Ah, old friend!" cried the Peer, the tears fairly running down his cheeks while he pointed to the King; "he hath been so brave, so brave: my boy—so eloquent. Stones would have cried out at his words. Didst thou not hear the shouting?"

"Surely," returned the Khan; "but 'tis hardly a welcome sound in these days unless one knows the reason, so we hurried on. Eloquent! I knew he would be so. Brave! Ay, or he is no descendant of his royal race. May I open the litter, my lord?" he asked of the King.

"Bismilla! open it," he replied; and some of the attendants hastily untied the knots by which the cover had been fastened over the top. As the last fold was removed, the figure of Jehándar Beg sitting upright, his arms and hands swathed carefully in a shawl, and his eyes bound with a handkerchief, was displayed to all. The bandage was removed, and he looked wildly about him.

Jehándar Beg saw his position at once. He was no coward, and he perceived that all chance of life had passed away. The Wuzeer was not there, and Afzool Khan, stooping into the litter, took up the case containing Jehándar Beg's most secret papers, and presented them to the King. "May I be loosed?" said the Kótwal to the Khan. "My fate is in the King's hands."

"Surely," replied the King; "we fear him not, nor any enemy," he continued, looking round. "May God deliver them into our hands, even as he hath this traitor."

"Ameen! Ameen!" cried a tumult of voices, followed by the loud Khámôsh of the criers.

Afzool Khan spoke so as to be heard by all. We need not follow his recital, for the particulars have been already related; but the words were drunk in with avidity by the assembly. He disclosed no man's name; the papers would speak for themselves.

One by one they were read, Persian and Mahratta in turn, clearly and distinctly; while, by the King's command, several of them were taken round by mutsuddees to the principal nobles and sirdars, that the seals might be examined.

This necessarily occupied some time, during which, the litter having been removed to the door, Jehándar Beg stood in the centre, as yet boldly if not defiantly. Could the Wuzeer only arrive—and he was expected momentarily—all would be changed. Before him the King, bold as he seemed now, would quail; those friends in the assembly, who had already exchanged glances with him, would at once rise. There might be bloodshed, and of the result he had no doubt: it had been calculated beforehand, and was certain. Much depended on a mysterious arrangement of the Wuzeer's, which he suspected; but to the particulars of which he had not been admitted. Need he deny the papers? He dare not. They were facts which could neither be denied nor evaded.

"Unhappy, godless man," cried the King, when several had been read, and others were being examined, "are these true? Dost thou admit them? Hast thou eaten my salt and found it so bitter, that that of others seemed sweeter to thee? Speak, Jehándar Beg! are these true? are they thine own?"

Upon his reply hung many a life had he chosen to denounce those present; but with all his bad faith, there was no meanness in the man.

"The letters, my prince, are true; as they are addressed. I have no more to say. Whatever my fate is to be, let it come; I am ready to meet it," returned the Kótwal, firmly.

"And these for Khan Mahomed? The writing in the corner is yours, and the date of receipt is to-day."

"It is my writing; why should I tell a lie?" returned Jehándar Beg, sullenly; "but I know not the contents."

"Enough," replied the King; "my friends, we would do no injustice. Let us await the Wuzeer's arrival—it cannot be long now—and hear the result from his own lips."

CHAPTER XLIV.

"My lord, my prince," whispered the officer of the royal guard, stepping behind the rail in an agitated manner, "be careful of yourself; there is disturbance without; we will close round you; come away. The Wuzeer—the Wuzeer is—is—dead—killed, they say—at the outer gate as he entered. Withdraw with us—quick," said the man excitedly; "the news is spreading fast."

"Who hath done this?" cried the King, starting to his feet, and seizing his sword and shield, which, according to custom, lay before him. "The Wuzeer is dead, they say. Is there aught to fear? I move not, Afzool Khan, come what may. If I am to die, let it be here, on my father's judgment-seat. Will ye bear me company?"

"To death, to death!" exclaimed Afzool Khan. "Who dare

harm you? Ho! Alla-ool-Moolks, Bhylmees, Dâgtorays, all true men present,—rally round the King," shouted the Khan. "Deen, deen!" and his familiar battle-cry, "Futteh-i-Nubbee!" (Victory to the Prophet) rang high above the hoarse murmur which had arisen among the assembly. Now, however, those mentioned by the Khan sprang to their feet by scores, and their example was followed by hundreds. "Deen, Deen!" was shouted with increased enthusiasm.

"Here is one who brings particulars," said the Secretary, as an officer was led in, who prostrated himself before the King.

"My lord, the Wuzeer is dead," said the man, sobbing bitterly. "They murdered him at the gate. Those who did it went off across the plain, but they were men who had ridden with him. I was upon the bastion over the gate with a few others, and we saw them come rapidly along the road from Allapoor. I knew my lord's piebald horse, and his elephant was following at a little distance. We watched him till he was near the gate; there were only a few of us. There was no one present but a sentinel and one or two others, and a Kullunder Fakeer had spread his carpet just within the walls, and was crying, 'Ulla dilâyâ to léonga!' as passengers threw their cowrees to him. We were descending the steps to present our nuzzurs, when several of the men behind dragged the Wuzeer from his horse, and others on foot, who had been running with him, killed him with a hundred wounds ere he could cry out. What could we do, my lord? Ere we could mount the bastion again the whole had dispersed. We fired on them, but it was no use."

"And what became of the Fakeer?" asked the King, looking towards the Secretary.

"My prince, he stayed with the body, and shut the eyes," replied the man. "Then, as the Wuzeer's elephant arrived, he told the driver to take up the dead, and we saw him go towards the mosque, crying, as before, 'Ulla dilâyâ to léonga!' Hark!" he continued, "there he is."

"Ulla dilâyâ to léonga! Ulla dilâyâ to léonga!" The cry came nearer and nearer, never changing or faltering in its cadence or time —heard above all other noises and confusion within and without— "Ulla dilâyâ to léonga!"—up the steps, along the great corridor, into the hall, where every one made way before the brawny form and excited looks of the crier—who paused not, nor yet looked right or left, till he reached the dais. Afzool Khan and Fazil would have stopped him, but he strode on.

"Ulla dilâyâ to léonga!" he cried, looking at the King without saluting him. "Khan Mahomed is dead, from a hundred wounds. As I closed his eyes I saw this on the ground; it had fallen from him, so I have brought it;" and flinging a case, containing papers, to the King, he turned away without salutation; shouting the old, cry with his right arm bare, and stretched high above his head, he strode out of the hall, continuing it as he passed out of the building through the attendants and troops, and so away.

"Among these papers," said the Secretary, whispering to the King, "are many which, if now disclosed, might make men desperate; they are better kept secret."

"I am weary of them all," cried the King impatiently; "look at the judgment of God; we should own it reverently."

"Zoolm! Zoolm!" (injustice!) cried a knot of men who had collected at one side of the hall, and had risen from their seats. "Is murder to be done, and pass unchallenged?" Their tone was fierce and defiant, and boded no good.

"Peace, O friends!" cried Afzool Khan, stretching out his hands to them. "Is this a time for strife? who can say by whose hands he died? Yet better dead, than for this guilt to be proved before all, by these witnesses—his own hand and seals. O friends, brothers in the faith! there is the throne we have to defend, and we should count it holy martyrdom to die before it. We are ready; will ye be tardy?"

"Deen, Deen! listen to Afzool Khan! Futteh-i-Nubbee!" (Victory to the Prophet) the Khan's battle-cry, was shouted with deafening clamour. "Death to the unbelievers!"

"Silence, friends!" cried the Peer, as there was a short cessation of the shouting; "listen to me. One traitor is dead, but are we less than men that we permit Sivaji Bhóslay, his accomplice, to defile our beards? Deen, Deen! cry to God for victory. Deen, Deen!" he continued, rising and raising his voice to a shrill scream, as he stretched out his arms, "the Prophet hears us, and Ali, and the holy martyrs, and so will ye be martyrs and enjoy paradise if ye die."

Again, again his cry was raised, the fanatical cry of Islam, which no Moslem can hear without emotion; and grave men hitherto unmoved, roused with the rest to frantic enthusiasm by the holy man's words, threw themselves on each other's necks and wept aloud.

"And now, friends," continued the King, when he could be heard, "let him who would punish Sivaji Bhóslay for a thousand crimes and treacheries, take up the gage I place here. In the name of God and the Prophet, let who will take it, I accept him;" and so saying he motioned to an attendant, who, bringing foward a salver covered with a brocaded cloth, set it down on the edge of the dais before the King, and uncovered it.

On the salver lay a single birra of Pân, covered with gold leaf, one of those which, on the conclusion of the ceremony, would be distributed by thousands. Who would take it up?

"Are ye laggards, my friends, in pursuit of honour? I thought yonder gage would be a mark for men to strive for; are ye laggards, O faithful?" cried the Peer.

The mass—for every one had risen to his feet—swayed to and fro with emotion, but no one advanced; and out of it issued the hoarse ominous murmur that had several times arisen, and which, in the absence of any decisive action, caused involuntary apprehension.

At this moment Afzool Khan stepped boldly forward, and taking up the gage, pressed it to his forehead, eyes, and lips, then, saluting the King, held it high above his head for all to see.

"My prince, it is mine," he said, "if it be permitted, and if these my friends will join me."

"Ye have heard," said the King, turning to the assembly, "I accept him."

It was the crowning point of the ceremony, and the people, no longer withheld by court etiquette, swayed forward to the foot of the dais with tumultuous shouts of joy. Those without only knew that war had been proclaimed, and their cries mingled hoarsely with the rest.

"It is well this should cease, my lord," said the Secretary. "Men's hearts are hot, and enough hath been done to-day."

"Good," replied the King, "let the criers proclaim the Burkhast; and that there will be preaching in the Jumma Mosque daily, at noon, till the army advances."

"Be that my care," said the Peer, "and their hearts shall be kept hot, I promise you."

It was done. Attendants went round with trays of Pân, reserving Utr and other sweet essences for those privileged to receive them. The King sat to the last, and the great Hall was gradually emptied, save of the royal guards,—Afzool Khan and his son,—Alla ool Moolk, and other nobles, who had been desired to remain. The Kótwal's fate was yet in suspense.

"Bring forward Jehándar Beg," cried the King to the officer of the guard; and the prisoner was again conducted to the front of the dais, around which the nobles were now grouped. He saw no hope in those stern, pitiless faces.

"See what that case of papers contains, Meerza Sahib," said the King; "there should be no mistake in this matter."

"There is no need," said the Kôtwal, sullenly, to the King. "If you had died to-day, those who brought me here would ere now have been headless corpses. I will answer no more questions. Do with me as you will; except in prayer, my lips open no more."

"Take him away to death," said the King. "A kingdom that never punishes is too weak to exist."

Jehándar Beg was led away through the private cloisters. His head had fallen upon his bosom; but those who saw it never forgot the fire which seemed to flash from his large eyes, and the scowl of deadly hate which he cast upon all around him as he walked firmly on.

"We may now separate," said the King. "Forgive me, O friends, who have as yet known me only as a boy playing about your knees, if I have acted weakly in this first rough lesson of life. O noble Khan, there are those who await you with tears of joy. What can I say for this service you have done? This sword is known to you; wear it for the sake of Adil Khan. And do thou, Fazil Khan, take these, the first marks of honour thou hast won; but, Inshalla! not the last;" and removing the costly jewel from his turban, and a heavy necklace of pearls from his neck, he invested the young man with them with his own hands.

"I have but one boon to ask, my prince," said Fazil; "it is for my friend, the Wuzeer's son. I will answer for him with my life, that he was as true as I am. May I console him?"

"Take this to him," said the King, removing a gold ring from his wrist; "tell him that from Adil Shah he need fear nothing."

"Altogether," said our friend the Lalla, who had accompanied the Khan and Fazil, "these Dekhanies have some method in their rudeness; but, after all, they are mad,—quite mad. Such ebullitions of temper could not have been allowed in the Padshah's court. Mobaruk, mobaruk bâd, Khan Sahib," he cried, heartily yet respectfully, to Afzool Khan and Fazil, as they were passing out and receiving the warm greetings of their friends,—and of all, high and low, who could reach them,—"let your poor servant be honoured by his congratulation being accepted."

"Ah, friend, art thou there?" replied the Khan. "Well, thou must be seen to; come to my house and we will arrange something for thee."

"May it please my lord to make me news-writer to his army," cried the Lalla, joining his hands. "My style, Inshalla!—is——"

"Well," said Afzool Khan, interrupting him good-humouredly. "Son, wilt thou have him?"

"I agree, father," said Fazil, smiling, "if he will serve under one who may, after all, be only a Gosai."

"I am my lord's slave to death. I am but a poor Khayet, but I can be of use to a discerning patron," returned the Lalla.

"Come, son," said the Khan, "let us see whether Kowas Khan be returned. The King's message should be delivered ere we proceed home. Methinks he and all his people would be safer with us for a few days, until men's minds are calmer."

We will not follow the Khan on his benevolent errand; nor can we detail how much mustard and coriander seed were burned with frankincense before them to avert evil when they reached home: nor yet how often Goolab, and the other women-servants, and even the lady Lurlee herself, cracked their knuckles over them, till they would crack no more. One thing, however, was certain: the worthy lady was more than ever assured that she had read the planets aright, and, if she had not done so, a great evil would have befallen the family.

CHAPTER XLV.

SOMEWHAT later in the day, a few groups of men were assembled near those majestic Adansonian trees which still stand by the wayside between the Citadel and the outer gate of the fort of Beejapoor. The sun's rays fell slanting through their dense foliage, and cast broad shadows upon the bright green sward, which, with the trees themselves, glowed in the evening light. The wind had fallen, and not a leaf stirred in the oppressive sultry calm which prevailed.

On one side, upon a piece of faded carpet, torn and ragged, sat a Fakeer, to all appearance, with long matted hair streaming over his shoulders to his waist, and over his face also, so as partly to conceal it. Some coarse rags hung loosely about him, but he wore the tall felt cap of the Kullunders, and their quilted robe thrown over his shoulders. He sat upon his heels, leaning upon a bright steel rod with prongs at the end, which might serve either for support or defence, and spoke to no one; but now and again a low cry of "Ulla dilâyâ to léonga," was rather muttered than cried aloud. A few copper coins and cowries, which had been thrown to him by passers-by, lay on the carpet.

At a little distance from him were two parties of armed men—some Mussulmans, some Hindus—standing, lounging on the grass, and speaking carelessly together. One of these, from his dress and hair, seemed to be of more pretension than the rest, and might be the Jemadar, or sub-officer of the party, and was attended by two men armed with "Puttas," long, broad Toledo blades, set in steel gauntlets inlaid with silver, which hung at their backs, the hilts projecting over their shoulders. These men were both short, with round backs, and very powerful frames; and, from this brief description, our previous acquaintance with them under the banian tree will be remembered.

"Perhaps they have pardoned him, after all, and let him go," said Rama. "The King is young, and soft as a woman; and what will the uncle yonder say to that, I wonder?"

"Impossible," replied Lukshmun; "I was behind the guards all the time, and heard Jehándar Beg ordered for execution under the

Goruk Imlee. No, the King was as firm as our uncle when—— Look! what is that? Can it be they?"

As he spoke, a small procession was seen approaching, a litter tied up as though a lady were within; a few footmen ran beside it, and a few horsemen rode before and behind. Unobtrusive in character, its movements were nevertheless followed with the greatest interest by the men we have mentioned, and even the Fakeer looked aside to watch it.

At first it seemed to be proceeding by the road in the direction of the outer gate; but as it arrived opposite the trees, the leading horsemen turned suddenly across the sward and halted under them, followed by the bearers, who at once hastily put down the litter and retired apart. The leader of the party drew up his own men at a little distance, while the footmen were directed to remove the cover of the litter. As they did so, the person within, who was pinioned, put his feet out of it, and stood up.

"Where is Hoosein, the executioner?" cried the officer; "he was ordered to be here; and this is no time for delay. Have any of ye seen him?" he asked of the people around.

Some one answered, "He is not here;" and another cried carelessly, "Hoosein does not like doing service for his own master;" and a third called out sneeringly, "You will find him drunk in the bazar by this time; go and look there."

"God forbid," said the officer, impatiently; "go, some of you, and see if he be coming in any direction;" and several of the horsemen dashed off at full speed.

"Enough, sir," said Jehándar Beg, sadly; "a keen sword is all that is needed; and ye are soldiers. Loose my hands, I pray ye, that I may say my last prayer before I die. . . . Peace for a while, Syn," he continued to the Fakeer, whose chant had increased to a solemn wail; "here is something for thee. See thou to my grave, and to the Fatehas after death. This will be enough, perhaps," he continued, with a sad smile, throwing some gold coins to the man, which lighted upon his carpet, but were not noticed.

"Ulla dilâyâ to lconga!" was the only reply; but the tone, which had been raised as Jehándar Beg appeared, now subsided into a low murmur.

"Let it be here," said Jehándar Beg, stepping forward to a piece of smooth turf under one of the huge branches. "Will any one lend me a scarf? Stay, this will do," he continued, loosing his own shawl from his waist; "when I am dead, give it to the Durwaysh yonder." Then he spread it out on the ground, and knelt down upon it, with his face towards Mecca, settling the cap upon his head, smoothing his long curly beard, and the glossy brown curls which fell upon his neck. "There is no use asking for water for ablution," he muttered, "this will suffice;" and taking up a little dry earth, he rubbed his hands with it, allowing the dust to fall over his elbows.

Jehándar Beg looked once more around ere he began his prayer; above, to the stately trees, and their heavy foliage, among which a flock of noisy parroquets were fluttering from branch to branch, and screaming loudly; over the green sward, to the King's fort and palaces, on which, and upon the noble dome of the mausoleum of Mahmood Adil Shah, his first benefactor and patron, the mellow light of evening rested in a golden radiance, and away over trees, gardens, and minarets, all glowing in the same soft beauty; then upon the group around him, for a few chance passengers, seeing what was to happen, had gathered round the spot.

A shiver seemed to pass through him as he closed his eyes slowly. Not of fear, for the man, a Fatalist by creed and habit, was meeting his doom stoically as a brave Moslem can do; but a thought had crossed him which would not be put back—a vision of love and peace —of his girl wife in her rosy beauty, and of her fair boy, far away at his own village and home, in the blue mountains of Khorassan— and of a fond aged mother who lived with them. This season they were to have come to him. Who now would tell them of his fate?

"A word, Jemadar," he said to the officer. "Bid that Fakeer come hither."

"Thou wilt do it," he said, as the man rose and advanced, "for the sake of the gold. Give this ring to Afzool Khan—my worst enemy in life, and yet the truest man in Beejapoor—and these papers; he will know what to write to my—my—to my house. And now, friends, peace, and the peace of God and the love of the Prophet be with ye! When I have said the prayer, I would die."

It was finished, but as yet no executioner had arrived. Jehándar Beg sat resting upon his heels, his eyes closed, while his beads passed rapidly through his fingers as his lips moved in prayer.

"We cannot delay," cried the Jemadar to those around, "will none of ye strike a blow for the King? Here is the warrant, and here is a bag of money for any who will earn it."

"Go thou, Rama," said Lukshmun, nudging his brother, "thou art a surer hand with the 'Putta' than I am; but if thou wilt not, I will try mine on that rascal, who hath strung up many a better fellow than himself on these trees. Hast thou forgotten what he did to our people?"

"Yes," added Gopal Singh; "go, Rama, and end this play. See thou do it well, and they will give thee the money. Go!"

"If the uncle wills it," said Rama, hitching forward his long weapon, as he looked for a moment to the Fakeer, who bowed his head, imperceptibly to others, yet intelligibly to them, as he repeated his cry. "Yes, I will do it," and drawing the broad blade, on which the sun's rays flashed brightly, he felt its edge, then put his hand into the gauntlet which reached to his elbow, and fastened the straps over his wrist and arm carefully. He now advanced lightly, with circling steps, flourishing the heavy weapon, as though it had been a stick, round and round his head; yet, with every sweep, it was clear that he was measuring his distance more carefully. Another moment—a bright flash in the air—a whistling sound as the sword clove it—and the head of Jehándar Beg rolled to the ground, the lips still moving with the prayer which he had not finished, while the trunk fell forward quivering.

"The second to-day," said Rama, muttering to himself, as he wiped his sword on the sward. "Enough, enough!"

"Soobhan Ulla!" exclaimed the Jemadar. "A brave stroke. Thou shouldst be chief executioner thyself, friend."

"That is my brother, noble sir," said Lukshmun, interrupting the speaker, "and he does not like being spoken to after he has cut off a man's head. Give me the money, Jemadar Sahib, and let us begone; you see he is cleaning his sword; he might dirty it again if he were vexed."

"Take it, friend," returned the officer, "and away with ye, for yonder is Hoosein Jullâd coming, and ye may perchance quarrel over it. Begone!"

"Bid him and his party watch here till I bring men to bury the dead," said the seeming Fakeer, who had again risen and advanced, and who, having removed the bloody shawl, was rolling it up. "Watch with them, even though it should be night. This gold will suffice for all, and I will return." So saying, he stalked away rapidly in the direction of the fort, while his strange cry changed—"Ulla dilâyâ to leea, Ulla dilâyâ to leea!" (God gave and I took, God gave and I took!)

"Sir, here are the executioner's men, and they will watch; we need not stay," said one of the soldiers to their officer. "Let us go."

The litter was taken up, the soldiers moved rapidly away, and there remained only the watchers and two women, wrapped closely in heavy sheets, who had not been previously noticed, and who sat cowering behind one of the giant trunks, sobbing bitterly. Perhaps——; but no matter now.

The sun was sinking fast, and its rays fell upon a pool of blood, glistening, as it dried among the blades of the close sward,—upon a ghastly head, its face turned upwards to the sky,—and a headless trunk beside it, from which the crimson stream was still oozing. Above, on the high bare branches, sat foul birds and ravens, which had already scented the blood, and whose hoarse croaks mingled with the heavy rustle of the wings of vultures, assembling for a night feast;—no unusual matter, perhaps, in that place.

"A Fakeer says he must see you, my lord," said Goolab to Afzool Khan, as he sat quietly in his accustomed seat after the evening prayer. "He is in the court at the door, and will take no denial. He will not go away, but cursed frightfully when we said you were tired, and were resting in private."

"A Fakeer, Goolab! Do you know him?"

"All he says, master, is 'Ulla dilâyâ to leea,'" replied the woman, "and he declared he would cut himself with a knife and throw his blood upon us if we did not tell you. Hark! there is a shout."

"Ulla dilâyâ to leea!"

The Khan did not delay. "I know him, Goolab," he said. "Go, and say I come."

"Bid every one depart hence," said the man as Afzool Khan approached him, attended by several servants. "What I have to say to thee brooks no listeners. There," he continued, when all had gone; and flinging down the bloody scarf at the Khan's feet, "look, it is his blood who would have been true, but for him who went to hell before him. Here is his last request to thee, Afzool Khan, for he trusted thee only, of all this city. Take them, I have done his last bidding."

"His seal and these papers, Syn. More treason, perhaps. Did he say aught of them?" said the Khan.

"Only that they belonged to his house, and I should give them to you; and he died like a brave man as he was."

"Yes, as he was, Syn," echoed the Khan sadly—"as he was. And thou hast buried him? Else——"

"I have cared for that; it doth not concern thee, Khan."

"And who art thou, Syn? We have met before to-day."

"Ay, Khan, and before that often. Am I safe with thee? Put thy hand on my head; nay, fear not a poor servant of God, and I will tell thee who I am."

"Surely, friend," replied Afzool Khan, putting out his hand upon the high felt cap, "fear not."

"Not there, not there; on my head," cried the man, grasping the Khan's hand, and kissing it while he removed the cap; "on my head, on my head. Ask Ali Adil Shah of me, and remember—Pahar Singh."

"Pahar Singh!" exclaimed the Khan, starting back.

"Hush, fear not; I have been pardoned, and the Shah's hand hath been before thine on his head; fear not, I will be true to thee, for thou art faithful to him. Thy hand once more, Khan, freely and truly upon my head."

"Go, friend," said Afzool Khan, placing it as he desired. "Go, I doubt thee not, for I have heard what happened last night; go in peace. Whatever thou canst do for the Shah will not be forgotten."

"There is yet one more work to-day ere I sleep, Khan—one more, and I go to do it. God be with you."

As he departed, the men on guard would have stopped him, but again the old cry arose, and in his assumed character no one molested him, as the shout, rising and falling on the air, died away in the far distance.

Afzool Khan took up the bloody scarf and gave it to an attendant. "Let it be washed, and kept till I ask for it," he said. Not long afterwards some Persian merchants were returning to their country, and they bore the last requests of the unhappy Jehándar Beg, with such monies as could be saved out of his property, to his family.

That evening the crypt under the old tomb was again empty. Maloosray's scouts had brought him the news of Bulwunt Rao having survived his wound; and of the occurrences in the Durbar of the King, of which he had been advised by the Brahmun we have seen in communication with Jehándar Beg. Watching from the terrace of the temple, he had seen the Wuzeer's arrival at Allapoor; followed his course across the plain; and guessed, by the confusion and shots at the gate, and the dispersion of the horsemen with him, that something extraordinary had taken place, the particulars of which, and of the subsequent execution of Jehándar Beg, were related by his scouts. Under the presence of Pahar Singh, therefore, Beejapoor was no longer safe; and as night closed, the whole party, unobserved, left their hiding-place to its usual tenants, the jackals and hyenas of the plain.

CHAPTER XLVI.

As night fell, and as Maloosray knew all the Mahomedans would be engaged in their evening prayer, his little party emerged from the crypt, and took their way westward across the plain, avoiding the suburbs, and threading the narrow lanes among the fields, which on all sides skirted the city. One by one his followers and scouts had been despatched in advance to meet them at certain places; and a spot known to all, where the great northern and western roads diverged, was fixed upon as a final place of rendezvous. Thither, also, had been despatched the wounded man, Ranojee, who, unable to ride far at a time, was to proceed by easy stages with the scouts and other servants to Jutt, the chieftain of which town was a sincere adherent to their cause.

Maloosray himself, taking Nettajee, and the chief scout Ramjee with two others, to serve as grooms, had determined to visit Tooljapoor before he returned to his master. There were many active partisans of weight in the Bâlâ Ghaut; what had they determined upon, and what was his old friend Jeswunt Rao Bhóslay of Sindphul doing? It was impossible to write, and as long as personal communication can be insured, Mahrattas never write letters. It was above all things necessary that Moro Trimmul and Jeswunt Rao must have the first news of the Wuzeer's death; and except it were reported by royal express to the camp at Nuldroog, it could hardly be known at Tooljapoor next day. It was a long ride, certainly, but it was possible to reach Tooljapoor, and to secure Moro Trimmul's safety, in case it should be threatened.

The occurrences at Beejapoor had been very unexpected by Maloosray. At first sight they appeared to be a sore discouragement to the plans which had been almost matured; and for some time he rode in silence, brooding over the catastrophe we have recorded. He could not account for it. To all appearance the King and the Wuzeer had been on excellent terms, and Jehândar Beg their confidant; yet in one day both had been destroyed, and the party of Afzool Khan had suddenly become the leading one in the State. Was he ambitious, he might be prime minister. In his heart Maloosray acknowledged his fitness for the post. No other person would command the allegiance of the army, with whom Khan Mahomed had not been popular. "It will unite in the Khan, and we shall have enough to do to escape it," he thought, "but the young tree will bend to the storm when the old one will break, and we may find opportunity to strengthen ourselves, while we do not weaken the royal house."

Now the moon shone out brightly. There had been no rain since the storm of the previous night. The day had been hot and sultry; but as the night fell, a delicious breeze, soft and cool, had succeeded the calm of the evening, and the road was sufficiently dry to be travelled without inconvenience. Maloosray's noble mare seemed to feel, with her master, the invigorating effects of freedom of action,—and her light and springy movements, which conveyed to the rider an involuntary assurance of activity and endurance, excited within him a more hopeful spirit than that with which he had quitted the city. Now and again, as they passed some muddy rivulet, or stony portion of the road, a word of encouragement or caution from her rider would be answered by a low whinny, which was followed by a loving caress of her arched neck, and thus a perfect accordance seemed to be established between them.

"Shall we reach the river before daylight, Sidda," said Maloosray to his guide; "and can we get the boat? Will it be on this side?"

"The boatmen are all friends of mine, master," replied the man, "and will cross me at any village or at any time; fear not, I will say

I have dispatches, and they believe in this stick that I am on the royal service. No one will dare to stop one of the royal Hurkaras with this as his warrant;" and as he spoke he flourished the weapon —a short stout staff, gaily lacquered in rings of red, yellow, and black, with a heavy tuft of black cotton yarn at the end, from whence projected a formidable four-sided lance about a foot long, the point of which was carefully sharpened—lightly round his head.

They rode on, keeping the main track; now and again passing villages, where they were saluted by a chorus of barks and howls from the village dogs; again traversing long intervals between others, where the occasional piping of sleepless plovers, the wailing cries of ever-wakeful restless lapwings, and an occasional burst of howls and screams from packs of wandering jackals,—were the only sounds which fell on their ears in those solitudes.

They met no one at that hour, but they did not pass the villages, lying upon the road, unremarked. Here a shrill challenge was blown upon a horn as they passed a gate; there a drum was beaten, and other indications given of the village watch being on the alert, or a shot was fired from a bastion or watch-tower, the bullet of which sung harmlessly above their heads into the air. They were rough times those, when men ploughed with their fire-arms slung at their backs, and when the village cattle, while grazing, had to be guarded by parties of matchlock men against the raids of more powerful neighbours.

The moon set soon after midnight, and the wind again arose, sighing as it swept across the broad plains in fitful gusts, or rustling among the tall fields of grain which bordered the road. Light clouds, too, were rising from the westward, and hurrying across the face of the sky, partly obscured the stars, and caused additional gloom. Under other guidance Maloosray would have felt uncertain of the path; but the Hurkara never diverted from the track, or slackened his pace; and the party passed on unnoticed, at the greatest speed that the light and the road would admit of, without distressing their horses.

As they ascended one of the long undulating eminences, which are the characterizing features of the country, and which commanded a view for some miles around, Maloosray's attention was attracted by a light which, emerging from behind some grain fields from another direction, was advancing rapidly towards them, and apparently would cross the road a little in advance of them. It was evidently a torch, possibly that of some travellers; yet it moved too swiftly and regularly for men on foot; and to the keen practised ear of Maloosray himself, as well as of his followers, the tread of a body of horse was heard, while the slight occasional

T

sparkles from weapons, and the dull red glow of matches, were soon distinctly visible.

Could they have been followed? Had any one remarked their departure from the city? The little party halted at once, and drew up out of the track of the road to escape observation, and watched the movement of the light before them with beating hearts. Nor were they long in suspense. After disappearing for a moment in a hollow, the light appeared again upon the road itself, and the body of horse, which might be fifty or more, drew up across their way and halted.

Who could they be? Certain it was that the party was now posted there to waylay some one who was expected, and the information they were acting upon was apparently as sure as their movements were methodical. Not a neigh escaped their horses, nor was there any commotion apparently among the men. The place chosen was admirably adapted for a surprise. The road, as we have said, led up a slight ascent or spur of an undulation, the sides of which broke into small but rough ravines and watercourses intermixed with large loose boulders of basalt, difficult to be traversed on horseback even by day, and quite impassable by night. These features were the same on both sides; and the spur itself was a narrow neck, which widened, as the plain above stretched out, into one of the usual broad expanses of waste and cultivated lands.

"They have come by Hórtee," said the Hurkara in a whisper—"the village there in the hollow—and are waiting for some one. Master, dost thou fear them?—they will hardly molest travellers such as we are. Shall we go on?"

It was a difficult point to decide. There was certainly no way of avoiding them and yet keeping the road.

"Go, Ramjee," said Maloosray to his scout; "go and see who they are. Be careful! my mind misgives me about them."

"Master," replied the man, "this ground is higher than theirs, and if they put out the light they will see thee against the sky. Retire a little lower, and Enkôba and I will find it all out for you."

Maloosray saw the intelligence of the advice, and acted promptly upon it, while the two men, well accustomed to such proceedings, crept warily along under cover of bushes and inequalities of the ground, till they entered a tall field of grain, in which they could move without chance of observation up to the very party itself, and from which they looked with safety upon the horsemen.

As they had supposed, the body was drawn up across the road. One flank overlapped the cornfield, on the path by which they had come; the other rested upon a declivity where the same path descended to the westward. It was clear that the position could not be turned without great risk, and it was impossible to say whether the path to Hôrtee might not be guarded also.

In front of the party, and near a man who held a torch which he replenished with oil from time to time, were two persons mounted on powerful horses, whose wet coats and panting flanks showed that they had been ridden at a rapid rate; and it was also evident from the condition of the rest, splashed with mud and with similar evidences of fatigue, that, whatever might be the object, speed had not been spared in its pursuit.

"They cannot pass this unobserved," said the elder of the two, "and there can be no suspicion that we are on this road. Ah, there is no such trap, boy, in the country, not a rat could get by it. Well, we have not been idle; first Khan Mahomed, second the Kótwal, and now Maloosray and his friend Nettajee."

"You have not got them yet," thought Ramjee, "and Tannajee is not game for you, old fox. But for him, my dagger would have made acquaintance with you that day in the Gosai's Mutt at Tooljapoor. Ah! who could have told him of us?"

"I think, uncle, we had as well put out the torch," said a man, coming forward, riding a tall grey mare. "Tannajee is not a moth to fly into a candle."

"Good, Lukshmun," said the chief; "put it out."

"I think we were wrong, father," said the other leader; "a few men would have surrounded that den under the tomb, and no one could have escaped."

"True; but you would not have taken Tannajee alive, and here he will be helpless. No, it is better as it is; and he shall sit under the Goruk Imlees, and die like Jehándar Beg, before me."

"And Rama shall help him on his way to the gods, master, if you like," said Lukshmun. "He says he is quite ready, and he got the Putta sharpened again."

"Silence!" said the chief, as the light was extinguished, "not a word must be spoken now, nor a horse stir. Be careful, all of ye."

The scouts had seen and heard enough. The rustling of the high corn-stalks and their leaves, under the breeze, prevented their return through them being heard, and in a few moments they had rejoined Maloosray, who, with Nettajee, had descended the brow of the ascent for a few paces, and could not be seen from above.

"Master," whispered the scout, "'tis the Old Lion, Pahar Singh, and his cub, Gopal, and their men. I saw one of the hunchbacks, too, with them."

"Ha! the Old Lion thinks to have a feast to-day, Nettajee," said Maloosray, "but the man is yet to be born who will take Tannajee alive. And what did he say, Ramjee?"

"He said you should be taken alive, and that you should sit under the Goruk Imlees, and have your head cut off, like Jehándar Beg, by Rama the hunchback."

"Ah," said Tannajee, "he should not have brought a torch with him, Netta, else it was not ill-contrived. By the Holy Mother, there had been small chance for us had we got among them. And now, what is to be done?"

"We must go back. Beyond the rivulet and the date grove yonder is a path which leads to Boorga, and so to Churchan, if my lord does not care for a few coss more," said the Hurkara; "and, after all, it is as near as any other road to Mundroop."

"Good," said Tannajee; "let us be quick, they may advance."

So they moved carefully down the descent, beyond which was a small rivulet bordered by thin date trees and other brushwood. "See," said Netta, as they crossed the small stream, "we are but just in time: there they are!" and as Tannajee looked up, he saw several figures projected in outline against the sky, one of whom was pointing to the road leading to Beejapoor.

"I thought the Old Lion had been more wary," he said, "than to show himself in that manner; but he may cool his heart now; he had better have made for the ferry!"

It had, however, been a narrow escape, and one for which Tannajee vowed to feed a hundred Brahmuns at Tooljapoor; but the danger was past, and after a somewhat rough track for a short distance westward, the guide struck confidently into a broader road, which, like the preceding, led northwards, and, as the day dawned, the river-bank at the ferry beyond Churchan was safely reached. The guide's staff of office proved irresistible. In a few moments they were seated in one of the large circular coracle baskets of wicker-work, covered with hide, which serve as ferry-boats; and with the two mares swimming in front, and guided by the men who held them, and the skilful paddles of three lusty rowers, the party crossed the stream, and were beyond danger of pursuit.

CHAPTER XLVII.

In his last letter to Beejapoor, Moro Trimmul had directed his agent there to inform Maloosray that, at the day of which we write, there would be recitations in the temple, and, under cloak of this, that most of the heads of the Mahratta families were to assemble; it would, therefore, be advisable if he could meet them. It was partly on this account, but most particularly because of the murder of Khan Mahomed, that Tannajee had left the city so abruptly, and ridden through the night without a check.

Nor did Tannajee and his companion take rest anywhere during the day following, except for such refreshment as was absolutely necessary. They avoided all large towns and villages; and, as Tannajee knew the country perfectly by day, he guided his friend by cross paths, frequently through fields and waste lands, till, as the evening fell, they drew up before the gate of Sindphul, the village below the pass of Tooljapoor, which we have before had occasion to mention.

The owner, a distant relative of the Rajah Sivaji, by name Jeswunt Rao Bhóslay, was an intimate friend of Maloosray's, and a true and influential ally of the general cause in those districts. Maloosray's sudden arrival surprised him little, for in consequence of what Moro Trimmul had written, he had been expected; and, after a short conference, Maloosray urged that the news he had brought should be communicated to Moro Trimmul and those assembled with as little delay as possible, and in this Jeswunt Rao concurred.

So, after a slight rest and hearty meal, which both needed, the stout ponies, provided by their host, were announced to be ready in the courtyard of the house, and, accompanied by half-a-score of stout sword-and-buckler men, with matchlocks and lighted matches, they rode out of the village gate.

The active ponies, though well accustomed to the rough mountain-road, had paused for a moment to take breath on the level spot from whence the buildings could be seen below—the glare of light, spreading up both sides of the dell, revealing crag and rough wood, with the gilded pinnacles of the temple glittering brightly through the smoke of torches and of incense; but their impatient riders again urged them up the rocky ascent with all the speed they were capable of exciting. At the town gate there was no hindrance, for Jeswunt Rao was well known; so they were admitted without difficulty, and, leaving the animals at a house which belonged to him, adjoining the main street, the party proceeded at once in the direction of the temple.

It was no easy matter, however, to get there. As they approached the gate at the head of the steps descending into the ravine, and on the steps themselves, the crowds were almost impassable, but good-humour prevailed, and, after some struggles, the lower court and the great assembly were safely reached.

It was a remarkable sight. The court itself was crowded with spectators so closely packed that to move was impossible. They were sitting upon the paved floor in rows facing the centre, where an open space had been provided for the priests, and an avenue left for their communication with the shrine. Around this the most distinguished of the guests had been placed; and Maloosray observed with satisfaction, that many influential persons whom he desired to see, were present. So far, his visit could not have been better timed.

All round the court were huge cressets of iron, fixed into brackets in the walls and arches of the court. These were filled with cotton-seed which, fed with oil from time to time, threw a broad glare upon the people, and lighted up not only the temple and its quaint and fanciful ornaments, but the buildings around,—and above, the crags and precipices, with the houses hanging to them.

There was not a spot unoccupied; even the ledges and projections of the high pyramidal roof and spires of the temple were crowded, while the terraces of the vestibule and cloisters around, reserved for the ladies of the Hindu gentry of the neighbourhood, and of the chief visitors and priests, glowed with the gay colours of their garments, which stood out against the dark background of the mountain-side.

As the party advanced through the crowd, Moro Trimmul, who was among the Brahmun reciters, saw the tall figure of Maloosray behind that of Jeswunt Rao of Sindphul, who was struggling manfully with the crowd, and advanced hastily to greet him. He had hardly expected so prompt a compliance with his request, but was rejoiced that it had been made. He greeted Maloosray and Palkur heartily, and led them to the reserved space, where, recognized by many present, and speedily made known to others, they received a hearty welcome, and took their seats.

A few words whispered, sufficed to explain to Moro Trimmul the situation of affairs at Beejapoor, and the necessity for immediate action.

"We must dismiss the assembly earlier than usual," he said, in reply to Maloosray's anxious question as to how long the ceremonies would be continued, "and I will hasten what remains. Do not heed me; I have to take my part now, and as the assembly rises I will rejoin you."

Thus saying, Moro Trimmul passed into the dark vestibule of the temple, and was divesting himself of his upper garments and turban, when, from a pillar behind, the girl Gunga came towards him.

"I have been searching for thee," she said; "they wanted thee. Where hast thou been so long?"

"No matter where," he said gloomily. "Thou couldst have found me without, if needful. What hast thou done?"

"Nothing," she replied. "I cannot get speech of her, and the rest will not join me; they are afraid."

"So art thou, Gunga," he replied; "afraid, afraid of a girl? Ah, coward and liar!"

"Thou art afraid thyself, Moro Trimmul," she retorted. "Go! take her away. There she stands, no one will prevent thee; there, by the door—alone."

Moro Trimmul stepped from behind the pillar, still keeping within the gloom, and looked forward. Before the blaze of the shrine, and the lamps without it, stood Tara, in the act of bearing garlands of flowers to the altar. A number of them were hanging upon her left arm, while, with her right hand extended, she was delivering some to the priest.

As she stood at the door, in the full glare of the lamps within, the light fell upon her rich crimson silk drapery, its heavy borders and ends of flowered gold, and the massive gold zone which confined it round her waist; while the attitude she had involuntarily assumed, as she turned towards the shrine, showed the graceful outlines of her figure to peculiar advantage. She had wreathed a long garland of white flowers into her hair, which fell about her neck and bosom; and another was twisted round her brows, so as to form a coronet. It was a fanciful but simple and beautiful decoration, which suited the character of her small graceful head, and added to the charm of her attire.

Moro Trimmul watched her intently as she delivered the garlands to the old priest; then, as if a service had been done, she advanced to the centre of the doorway, and, making a low reverence, stepped aside and stood erect, looking into the vestibule in expectation, as it were, of further devotees. Moro Trimmul could see the sweet mouth parted in a smile, the pearly teeth glistening within the rosy lips, and the soft eyes flashing as the strong side light fell upon them. Beyond her the deep gloom of the recesses of the temple could not be penetrated. So her figure stood out against it in a power of effective relief which was almost startling.

It was a strange contrast. Within, the dreaded image, richly attired and covered with priceless jewels, the tiara on its head, and the weird ruby eyes, now sparkling brightly, now changing and glowing fitfully amidst the clouds of incense which was burning before it, and the black, stony, changeless features, seeming even to vary in expression with the passing effects of light and shadow. Without, Tara in her rich attire and glowing beauty, and that rapt expression in her countenance, which the excitement of the scene and the service of the "Holy Mother" had caused it to assume.

Moro Trimmul sighed. With all the fierce desire which burned within him, and which now gave him no rest night or day, there was mingled, curiously perhaps, a loving reverence for the girl, which, as yet, had restrained him both from violence and insult. It might be her character and position which had excited it, but rather, perhaps, her own innate purity and modesty of mind, and the charming simplicity of character, which he saw in daily exercise in her house, that controlled the fiery passions of his nature and his avowed unscrupulousness.

"If I were a man," sneered his companion, as she stood with him concealed behind the large pillar, "I should not be a coward when such a woman as that was burning at my heart. By the gods, she is no woman, but an incarnation of beauty. Look at her now!"

"Peace, devil," cried the Brahmun in a hoarse whisper; "hast thou forgotten the gold, and thy promise by the Pâp-nâs?"

"No, I have not forgotten," said Gunga, "I have part of it here;" and she shook her foot, on which the gold anklets tinkled slightly; "and I want to change this silver thing round my waist for a zone like hers yonder. Ah, how it glows among the rich silk! But thou art a coward, Moro Trimmul, else I had earned it long ago; and I could have helped thee."

"Go and speak to her, Gunga, and I will believe thee braver than I am," he replied tauntingly. "If she cannot be spoken with, how wilt thou earn the zone?"

The girl regarded him with a look of defiance, and, without reply, stepped forward into the light, advanced towards the shrine, making a slight reverence to the image, glided forwards, and stood opposite to Tara.

"Thou hast served many hours, sister," she said, in an assumed voice of kindness, "and must be weary; sit down within for a while, and I will do what is needed; 'tis my office," she continued, laughing, "as well as thine."

Moro Trimmul marked the involuntary shudder of aversion which spread over Tara's countenance, and the action of withdrawing the skirts of her garment between her ankles, which accompanied it. Then she spoke.

"I am not weary of the Mother's service; when I am I will come no more," she said gently. "Go away; I will not speak with thee or thy people, and that thou knowest full well; go."

"And why should I go?" cried Gunga, excitedly; "am I not a Moorlee like thyself, and have I not served the Mother longer than thee? To be sure, I am neither a Brahmun nor a widow to be nice as thou art; yet I bid thee go, and let me have my turn: thou hast had more than thy share of money already to-day."

"It is all in the shrine before the Mother," said Tara, shrinking from the bold glances and excited manner of the girl. "I have taken none of it: I need it not."

"That does not matter," said Gunga; "I will have my turn now. Go away; thou art not wanted. Those that will not dance before the Mother are not worthy to serve her. Go, else some of us will push thee out."

"Me!" cried Tara, drawing up her slight figure proudly, her eyes flashing, and her features quivering with indignation,—"me! you dare not; you are impure, and the Mother loathes you: touch me, and she will strike you dead!"

Gunga shrunk from the trial; and others of her sisterhood, who had stood apart ready to advance, slunk again into the gloom behind the pillars. Gunga looked round as if for countenance, but no one seemed disposed to join her, while the old priest at the altar, who had caught the sound of voices, came to the door, and, seeing Gunga, waved her off.

"Away with ye, and the like of ye!" he cried. "Outside do as ye please; here ye are an offence. Away! let her stay;" and he pointed to Tara. "Do not molest her."

"There is some spell about thee, Tara, which shuts my mouth; beware!" muttered Gunga, retreating; "it may not always be so."

"Bear me witness," said Tara to the old priest, "she is threatening me."

"Ah, daughter," he replied, smiling, "fear not such as she; the Mother is good to thee; and they cannot harm thee so long as thou art holy and pure."

"I did not tell thee to quarrel with her," said Moro Trimmul angrily, seizing Gunga's arm as she approached, and dragging her within the shadow of the pillar. "Art thou mad, or has any one given thee drink, Gunga?"

"I spoke to her kindly, which is more than thou darest to do," retorted the girl sharply. "What answer did I get? Pure? Why should she be pure? I tell thee there is a spell about her neck—I saw it glittering among the flowers—which put me back: I could not speak. Yes, Moro Trimmul, if it be only to put that spell under my foot, and crush it with her throat, I will do it; yes, I will earn the gold; let her see to herself."

"Good," he replied; "then I can trust thee. Come to me to-morrow, and fail not." And then, naked to the waist, with his soft glossy hair falling over his shoulders, and his fine figure displayed to the best advantage, Moro Trimmul passed out, and took his place among the reciters.

Gunga's eyes followed him. "Drink!" she muttered; "drink! he said that. Well, better drink than this madness, which is worse." And, sitting down, leaning against a pillar, she hid her face in her garment, and sobbed bitterly.

Just then, one of the ordinary processions round the temple formed opposite the shrine. Priests, bearing offerings of flowers and lighted lamps, holy water and incense, preceded by musicians, and chanting a hymn, passed out into the court. Several of the temple girls were dancing before it; and Tara, led on by an excitement she could not control, had seized a pair of cymbals, and began to clash them in the cadence of the hymn as the procession moved.

Three times round and round did the priests pass, and at the second Gunga joined it, dancing wildly and tossing her arms on high as she circled with the rest. Tara, however, remained among the priests, singing with them; yet, in the elastic grace of her step, as well as in the expression of her face, it was evident that she shared the fervour of the scene, and could not control herself, while her clear ringing voice mingled sweetly with the deeper-toned chant of the men.

Maloosray saw Tara, and watched the eyes of Moro Trimmul wandering from one girl to the other with an intense expression of passion. "Ah, my poor friend!" he said to himself, "that is the devil sitting at thy heart, and looking out of thine eyes! Alas! alas! who is she—that girl?" he asked of Jeswunt Rao, who sat by him.

"She is our new Moorlee," replied the man; "is she not beautiful?—But listen to Moro Trimmul."

CHAPTER XLVIII.

NEVER had the Brahmun's art been so effectively exercised by him before. In the recitation of passages from the Ramayun his voice, high and sonorous, pervading every portion of the court, delivered the appeals to war, the description of the demigod's forces, and portions of the battles, with a power which was listened to with breathless interest; while the pleadings of Seeta, the beloved wife, and her passionate confessions of love, were accompanied by tender actions, and tones as low and sweet as a woman's. Now rolled forth the majestic Sanscrit verse in its measured numbers, and again it was changed to the sweet Mahratta vernacular, that all could understand. At every interval the applause of the whole assembly arose in hoarse murmurs and loud clapping of hands, while many wept passionately.

No one would have moved till morning, but there was yet much to do; and, as Moro Trimmul sat down, Vyas Shastree ordered the distribution of wreaths of flowers to the chief guests, which announced the close of recitation for the night. Now, therefore, the main body of the people got up and began to separate, and in a short time only those were left who had been specially requested to stay. Now, too, the cressets, no longer fed with oil, went out one by one; and the deep gloom of night was fast spreading over the courts and buildings around.

"Will you not remain, Shastree," said Moro Trimmul, "to speak with these people?"

"No," he said; "no; there is no one to go home with the women. I thought you would accompany them."

"It will be late," he replied, gloomily; "no, I cannot come to-night."

"Your declamation was noble, Moro Trimmul," said the Shastree; "I had never heard the passages so spoken. Who taught you this style?"

"That is the way our master likos them said. No one taught me," he replied; "and if you could hear the whole in one of his assemblies in the deep forest, you would feel that you were a Mahratta."

"So I am—so I am," returned the Shastree quickly; "do you doubt it?"

"Not your faith, Vyas Shastree," replied Moro Trimmul, "only your energy. But go; I will come early to-morrow;" and, turning away, he entered the vestibule and joined Maloosray and others who awaited him. Guards of men, he saw, had been placed at each of the porches, so that no one could enter but those privileged.

A solitary lamp flickered on the altar where the image still rested, and cast a feeble and uncertain light into that portion of the vestibule which was immediately before it, and where Maloosray, Moro Trimmul, and the rest now seated themselves. Otherwise the spacious area was altogether in deep gloom, a portion only of its massive stone pillars catching rays of light, and seeming like giants standing around in solemn array.

We need hardly, perhaps, follow Maloosray in his narrative, which was listened to with breathless interest by his hearers. He had never as yet come among them, but his name and feats were well known through many a rough ballad both of love and war. There he sat, face to face with them; his large soft eyes flashing with excitement, and adding force to the few but burning words he spoke. Tannajee was no novice in the art of reading men's hearts; and among the mountains and valleys where he lived, there were already thousands of the best youth of the country at his command.

"Now," he said finally, "ye have heard all. We are before the Holy Mother, who comes to our Prince in his dreams, and tells him what to do; she who will scatter these impure cow-slaying Moslems like sheep before the wolf. O Holy Mother!" he continued, rising and bowing with joined hands in adoration to the image, "here are thy children; bless them, make them bold and true; they will swear not to hang back when 'the fire is on the hills,' and when they can strike for thy honour. Hear thou the oath, and accept it."

As he paused and looked round there was at first a low murmur of acquiescence. Then they who had been sitting started to their feet, and as many as could reach it rushed to the threshold of the sanctum and touched it reverently:—those who could not, stretched out their arms towards it over each other's heads, while wild cries of "Jey Kalee!" "Jey Toolja Mata!" "Bome, Bome!" (We swear, we swear!) rang through the vestibule, and were taken up by those without.

"Now, let us write the names," cried Maloosray, when the excitement had in some degree subsided; "sit down again, friends, and if there be a scribe among ye let him come forward."

The Putwari, or hereditary clerk of the temple, was there, with his writing materials tied up in a bundle, and he sat down and took them out.

"Light one of the large lamps," said Moro Trimmul to an inferior priest, "and set it in the midst; we are not afraid of our faces before the Mother."

As the wicks were lighted, one by one, the assembly seemed to dilate. Light after light flickered, but grew stronger. "A true omen," cried Maloosray, with fervour; "that is as we shall be, my friends. Light after light will appear to ye from afar; each may waver for a while, but when 'the fire is on the hills' ye will see all plainly. Be silent now, and let us write."

It was, indeed, a strange and impressive scene. In the midst sat Maloosray and Moro Trimmul, with the scribe; around, the heads of local families, Nimbalkurs, Bhôslays, Sindias, Ghoreparays, and a host of others, each anxious to be named in the record, and leaning forward to catch the eye of the scribe. Beyond them—some kneeling, others standing—was a crowd of eager faces, all bearing the same expression of excitement—one behind another on every side—while the light fell upon their bronzed features and glistening eyes, till those in the background were scarcely distinguishable.

One by one—chiefs, gentry, yeomen—gave in their names and complements of men, and page after page was filled by the record till no more remained.

"It is done, friends," said Maloosray, rising, as the Putwari had added up the totals, and signed his name as the scribe; "there are more than fifteen thousand men recorded. Enough for the time, and more hereafter. By-and-by, when 'the fire is on the hills,' ye will be welcome; till then, separate and be quiet, else Afzool Khan will come upon you, and we can give you no help. We will abide the storm and let it pass over us, and so must you all."

As he spoke the last words, those who had been sitting rose, and all in turn saluting Maloosray, the meeting broke up. The retainers of the respective leaders gathered round their masters, and the several parties followed each other out of the temple precincts.

"I shall depart before daylight, Moro Trimmul," said Maloosray, as they proceeded to the postern which led to the bottom of the ravine, below which their ponies and attendants awaited their coming; "wilt thou follow?"

"I have more to do here, Tannajee," he replied; "but after the Now Râtree I will come. I must watch Afzool Khan and Pahar Singh."

"Take care they do not watch thee," returned Maloosray. "Yet I fear not for thy enemies; of them thou art careful. I fear for thee, because of that girl who played the cymbals. She is the devil that I see sitting at thy heart, and looking out of thine eyes. I watched thee as they followed her. It were well for thee to come now, even now; come!"

"Impossible," returned the Brahmun, turning away. "Go!"

"As thou wilt, friend," returned Maloosray. "Words were always useless with thee; but be wary."

Moro Trimmul watched the party as they descended the steps to the tamarind trees below. He saw them mount and ride off, the torches with them throwing a ruddy glare upon the crags and brushwood above the path,—and his heart bade him follow; but as one of the temple watchers was about to close and bar the door, he turned aside. All in the building was dark and deserted now. The image had been taken from the altar, and put into its silken bed for the night, and a faint lamp occupied its place. A few attendants flitted hastily here and there across the dark courts and still darker vestibule, anxious to get away, and the watchers only were all that would soon remain.

"Maharaj!—Moro!" said a female voice in a low whisper, as he passed between the pillars of the temple, "stop!"

Moro Trimmul knew the voice. "Why art thou so late here, Gunga?" he said hastily. "Begone!"

"I feared you were angry with me," said the girl, putting her hand on his arm. "You would not look at me as I danced, only at her. I could not go till I had spoken with you. Ah, you are not angry with me? Lo! I will do your bidding, though my heart break and I die. Sit here, beloved, and speak to me; come," and she tried to draw him to her gently.

"Thou art one of the devils that are pulling me into hell!" cried the Brahmun fiercely; and, pushing her violently from him, he rushed wildly across the court.

Gunga fell back heavily against the pillar nearest to her, and as she recovered herself, the pain of the fall obliged her to sit down, involuntarily leaning against it. She drew her hand with a gesture of weariness across her face and brow, then looked to see if there were blood upon it. "Hath it come to this?" she said bitterly; "hath it come to this—and for her? Ah, me for her!"

The girl had listened unobserved, in a dark niche near the shrine, to what had transpired at the meeting, and her first thought now was revenge, sure and deadly. A word from her, and the Mahomedan officer in charge of the town would seize Moro Trimmul, and imprison him in Nuldroog. As the thought occurred to her she rose, and, hastily traversing the court, began to mount the steps which led up the ravine; but her heart failed, and ere she had ascended a few of them she wavered, sat down, and wept bitterly.

"They would kill him," she said, "and he must not die. No; I was wrong, and he will forgive me; and to-morrow I will go to him as he desired." Hers was a callous heart: but it had softened to her lover, and refused to do him harm.

Time or country, what matter? How often is the history of woman's love and man's passion like this! how often does such erring love frame excuse for bitter wrong, endured from him who, —of all the world,—should least inflict it!

CHAPTER XLIX.

A FEW days had elapsed, and it was a quiet afternoon in the Shastree's dwelling. The household work had long been done; the visit to the temple and the noonday worship were over. Vyas Shastree had remained there in discussion with other Brahmuns; Radha, complaining of a headache, had fallen asleep; Tara had read all that her father had appointed her to study during the day, and was waiting his return to have certain passages explained to her before she proceeded with her task.

The house was perfectly still, and from the town no sound reached them, for the heat without was great, and until evening there would be comparatively few persons astir. It was calm, and large white clouds were sailing slowly over an intensely blue sky, gathering into masses pile upon pile, of dazzling brightness, as the sun's rays fell upon them. The heat and peculiar state of the atmosphere caused the outlines of buildings and of the mountains to waver; and wherever the eye rested on any object, the air between seemed to quiver with a tremulous motion.

Hot as it was, Tara had not been deterred from her self-imposed duty. Throwing a heavy folded sheet over her shoulders and head, she had accompanied her father to the noonday service; nor, since the occasion when she took upon herself the office of the priesthood, and devoted herself to the duties of the shrine, had she on any pretence missed or evaded the necessary attendance.

At first, perhaps, it was a severe trial. The licence, accorded by general custom to the attendant priestesses, was to her abhorrent; and, on the other hand, Tara's unapproachable purity had given offence to them. While Gunga, therefore, and two or three others, proposed the prohibition of Tara's service, the rest, fearing the consequences, and having a real respect and love for the girl whom they had watched from her childhood, refused to interfere with her.

Tara did them no harm, they said, and her father could punish all, were any annoyance given to his daughter.

It is probable that matters might have continued in this state for some time longer, but for the scene we have already recorded, and the increasing jealousy of Gunga, expression of which could hardly be repressed by her; and on the day we now write of, the girl's behaviour had been studiously offensive to Tara until rebuked by the attendant Brahmuns, when she retired sulkily.

More insulting than that, however, was Moro Trimmul's manner to herself; and for the first time Tara had felt what she long dreaded,—the shame, as it were, of her vocation—the unavoidable exposure to any libertine glance which might fall on her; but she had rallied herself at the shrine, and, secure in the protection of the "Mother" she adored, had persevered in her duty without interruption.

There was, as we have said, perfect stillness in the house, only broken by the dull monotonous whirr of the spinning-wheels, as her own and her mother's flew swiftly round, with which the buzz of flies in the verandah and court seemed to harmonize. Her mother appeared particularly intent upon spinning some remarkably fine yarn; and as the thread had broken on several occasions, when Tara had spoken to her, and she had complained of it, both had fallen into a silence, which had not been interrupted. Gradually, then, the small troubles which had gathered about Tara returned to her recollection; and, as is generally the case on such occasions, began, in spite of herself, to increase in proportions.

Tara's was not, however, a suspicious nature, and she had soon struck out a course for herself in regard to the sisterhood. "It is the money they want, not me: "if I save it all, and give it to the Putwari to divide amongst them daily, it will surely be enough," she thought; and this she determined to do. In regard, however, to Moro Trimmul, it was very different. "Why did he look at her as he had done that day?"

Then her thoughts reverted to the time when she had first remarked him in the temple, a solitary stranger worshipper, to whom her father had spoken kindly. Her memory followed clearly his gradual steps to intimacy; but there was nothing she could charge him with, as an approach to familiarity in their intercourse. Through all the licence of the marriage time—through all her visits to his aunt and sister—there had been no violation of propriety; on the contrary, an habitual and respectful avoidance of her—or, at most, a distant and courteous salutation. Why should it have altered?

But since the night on which Gunga had spoken to her, and Moro Trimmul had made his famous declamation of the scene in the Ramayun, there had been a change. He either avoided her altogether, or his eyes dropped furtively as she passed, or met hers, as they had done that day, in a glance new to her, and inexpressibly offensive. Tara shuddered as she remembered it, and the action broke the thread she was spinning. She did not resume her work, and her hands fell listlessly on her lap as her foot ceased its motion. For a time her eyes wandered vacantly among her flowers, about which some gay butterflies were flitting and chasing each other in the bright sunlight; but suddenly a large dragonfly, which had been hovering over them, darted at one and carried it off; and as she started forward, gazing intently after it, a bird chased the insect, caught it, and flew away.

Perhaps the sudden cessation of the whirr of Tara's wheel had attracted her mother's attention; for after a while, as it was not resumed, she looked up. "What dost thou see?" she asked, anxiously; for ever since the day on which Tara said the goddess appeared to her, Anunda had been anxious, she hardly knew why: but she dreaded a return of that strange and violent excitement. "What dost thou see, beloved?"

Tara did not apparently hear the question, or did not notice it. Her hands, which had been involuntarily extended, fell upon her lap listlessly as before; but she turned towards her mother. "How long does he remain, mother?" she asked abruptly.

"He! who, daughter?" returned Anunda.

"Radha's brother," replied the girl, as a shiver seemed to pass through her; "Radha said he would go after the marriage, yet he delays. Why, mother—why does he not go?"

"Nay, and how should I know?" replied Anunda. "What is he to me? All I wanted was Radha, and we have got her; and he may go or come as he pleases. Thy father told me he had business here with the Nimbalkur and others till the Now Râtree was over, and he assists in the recitations. More I know not. Why dost thou ask? What is he to thee, Tara?"

"Nothing, mother; but so long?—will he stay so long?"

"Radha told me yesterday he must soon rejoin his people in the west, and leave her; and she was crying about it. Does that content thee, Tara?"

"I would he were gone, mother," said Tara, rising from her low stool, kneeling, and throwing her arms about Anunda as she sat on a similar one, while she hid her face in her dress. "Cannot he go sooner?—cannot Radha send him away?"

"Why, daughter? why?—Ah! he hath not spoken to thee, child; he dare not! Tell me," she continued, in a more agitated tone, as her daughter clung almost convulsively to her, "what is this? Why dost thou fear him? Thou—thou dost not? . . . thou canst not——"

"No, no, mother," cried the girl quickly, guessing her mother's thoughts, and looking up innocently; "fear not. I am not a Moorlee to love; . . . fear not! But ah, mother, I dread him! I will not go to the temple while he is there. I . . . I dare not—I dare not go. May the Holy Mother forgive me for neglect; but when he departs, I will serve her night and day."

"Thou art very beautiful, my child," said her mother, smoothing back the glossy hair and stroking the soft cheek which lay passively in her lap. "Ah, thou art very beautiful; and I fear such as he! Yes, if it be as thou sayest, it were better, indeed, to live secluded for a while. I will tell thy father, and he will understand it."

"Yes, he will surely understand," said Tara absently; "but ah, mother, was not that an omen? I thought it was, and I came to thee."

"What omen, Tara? I saw nothing, child."

"A thought came into my mind, mother," she said sadly, "that I was the butterfly sporting among the flowers, and he the fierce glistening insect that darted upon it and bore it away. But then, mother, the bird came and took both. Why was that?"

"Thou art not well, Tara," replied her mother, not understanding her, for she had not noticed the occurrence, and, seeing her shiver, thought her feverish. "Thou art not well; lie in my arms for a while, and the cold will pass away. O Holy Mother!" she cried aloud, as Tara, sobbing convulsively, hid her face in her bosom, "let not evil come to this child—thine and mine. O, be good to her, as thou hast taken her!"

"Would that it were so," said the girl, after a while, and still sobbing. "I would go, mother, if she would take me. What use am I in life? It would be bitter to leave the house and all of ye, but I should be with her. Did she not promise this when she touched my hair? Ah, yes; and she will not forget it."

"Hush, child; let this fancy pass from thee. Sleep, now, here. I will sing thee the old song. Nay, thou shalt not leave me! There is room at thy mother's heart, and strength still in her arms, to hold thee safely."

As Tara laid herself softly down in the old place, and her mother, rocking herself to and fro, sang the low sweet lullaby of childhood, —the girl's sobbing gradually stopped, and a gentle sleep fell upon her. Anunda watched the change anxiously. At first her brow was contracted, as if with pain, and a broken sob came now and again with her breathing; but gradually the head fell back on her arm, the sweet mouth opened slightly, and tears, which had had no vent before, welled gently from under the closed eyelids as the features relaxed into a smile.

"Yes," thought Anunda, as she bent over her child, while her own tears fell hot and fast, "the Mother is with her now, and she is again happy."

"What hath happened?" asked Radha soon afterwards, as, refreshed by her sleep, she rose, and came gently towards the low spinning-chair on which Anunda still sat. "Is she ill?"

"Hush!" returned Anunda, in a whisper. "If we can lay her down I will tell thee, but we must not wake her. I think . . . . I think the Mother hath been with her again; but I will tell thee."

Radha hastily spread out a soft mattress and pillow close to the stool, and, raising Tara together, they laid her down upon it, as they would a child. Her mother patted her gently as she lay, and gradually the same sweet smile as at first again stole over her face.

"Look, she sees the Mother!" said Anunda reverently. "It is always so, and nothing can wake her till the time is past. Ah, thou art happy now, my child, be it ever so with thee!"

"What did she say, sister?" asked Radha, as, having thrown a light sheet over the sleeping girl, they sat down to watch her apart, lest the noise of the wheels—for Radha had taken Tara's and joined the broken thread—should awaken her. "What did the goddess say?"

Anunda hesitated. As yet no difference had arisen between them, and Radha still looked up to her, more with the respect of a child for its mother than as a sister-wife would comport herself to her equal. Should she tell Radha all? It had occurred to her that he had imposed upon her some task which she hesitated to perform—that Radha had some impatience of her brother's presence. It might be a demand for money—it might be in relation to the political objects of his mission, of which Anunda had a deep dread, lest her husband should become an active party, and so be embroiled with the Mahomedan officers of the country. She considered for a moment: but Anunda's was no timid nature. She was not afraid of Radha; and with Tara's happiness at stake, she could risk no ceremony with the sister of him who had evidently caused more than a passing cloud.

"Radha," she said gently, "thou art more than a sister-wife to me. Nay, as a daughter I have trusted to thee the happiness which lay nearest my heart and hers; and I believe thee faithful to it, and that this home and all in it is growing precious to thee."

"To me? Ah, yes, O sister and mother, too! Radha is new to you all," she replied, "but will be true now, very true, and will not fail! O mother, if you could know what it is to me to have a loving home!"

"Then Tara must not be injured—no evil must come to her," said Anunda, interupting her.

"To Tara, mother? We are sisters, who will do her evil?"

"I fear thy brother, Radha—not thee. Hath he said aught to thee?" returned Anunda.

"My brother! O, heed him not, he will soon go," returned Radha, her features expressing distress and agitation, and she already feared the worst.

"Ah, then, it is as I expected—as she dreaded. Radha, this must not be. Hast thou any power over him?"

"None," said the girl, bursting into tears, for what she had most apprehended appeared to have reached her at last—"none. He has been wilful always—to me, to our father when he lived, and to all. Where he goes—who are his companions—what he does—no one knows except our Prince whom he serves, and Tannajee—who came so suddenly that night—whom I showed to you. No, mother, I have no power and no influence. What does he care about me?"

"He must care," said the matron stoutly, "or he must care for me; and yet, for thy sake, I would not provoke him. But, O Radha! when thou hast had a child lying at thy heart—drinking its life from thy breast—climbing about thee—thou wilt understand what a woman can dare for it—what I could dare for Tara! Wilt thou speak to him, or shall I?"

Radha feared her brother. She did not know the extent to which his unscrupulous and profligate mind might carry him, but she had not forgotten his threats. Though she felt assured that, with the protection her husband could afford her, she was now beyond all ordinary harm at his hands, she feared the consequences both to herself and Tara with which he had before threatened her, and she dreaded his violence. Could he have been mad enough to speak to Tara? Could he have sent any insulting message to her? Something must have occurred, and she felt too sick at heart to ask.

"Thou art silent, Radha," continued Anunda; "why?"

"I love Tara; I love him too," she said earnestly, the tears starting to her eyes. "Yes, I will speak to him, even though he should strike me. Mother, I can bear it from him. Can you send me to him?—now, now!—or send for him? If I am to go, let it be at once, for this is a matter in which I cannot hesitate. O dear mother!" she continued, rising and advancing, "I am a child yet to thee. Let me put my head on thy breast for once, and bless me there as thou wouldst Tara: bless me ere I go to him. No, not so, not so; but as Tara lay on thy breast, so would I too, for once."

"Come, Radha!" cried Anunda. "O child! O sister-wife! come; henceforth between thee and me there is no veil. I had longed to draw it away, but thou hast done it now, and I am happy. Yes, henceforth ye are to me as one," she continued, smoothing the soft cheek as it lay at her heart—"new and old, but alike."

"Enough; now I am content," cried the girl, rising and clapping her hands, "and there shall be no fear for Tara. Send some one with me and let me go; he should not come here."

"No, Radha," said Anunda, calling a trusty woman-servant to accompany her, "not here. Go to him, and return soon."

CHAPTER L.

"Is my brother within? has he returned from the temple?" asked Radha of a man sitting in the porch of the house in which Moro Trimmul resided, and, though in another street, was only a few steps distant. "Is he come, Chimna?"

"Yes, lady, he is come," returned the man, who was an old retainer of the family, and had known her from infancy; "but if you take my advice, you will not go to him now: he has eaten nothing, and is in one of his rough angry moods. I did but speak to him as he entered, and got as many curses as will serve me for a month. Why not come another time?"

"Nay, Chimna, but it is an urgent matter, and I must now have speech of him," she replied. "Go, say I am come, and that he must admit me. Begone at once," she continued, seeing him hesitate, "else it will be worse for you."

"I had rather you went yourself," returned the man, "what if he should beat me? But no matter, I will go; perhaps I may not do you much more service, for he speaks of departing."

"Ah, indeed! When?" exclaimed Radha. "He is not ill?"

"Soon, perhaps," replied the man, putting his finger to the side of his nose, as a caution to secrecy, while he stepped across the court to the verandah, "very soon, I think. No, he is not ill, only vexed with something."

Radha's heart beat fast in her bosom. O, if it were but true; and that her brother, alarmed or repentant, no matter which, were about to depart, it would solve all difficulties at once. That very day—to-morrow! It seemed hard to wish him gone; yet there would be peace to Tara and to her mother, which was endangered by his presence. Surely he would see her. Yes; Chimna was now descending the steps of the house, and beckoned to her with a smiling face. She crossed the court at once, followed by the servant.

"He is in the upper room," he said, "and bid thee come alone: perhaps he is not well, for he is lying down, and seems weary. No wonder he was in ill-humour with me, after that long disputation with the Nassuk Brahmun to-day in the temple,—some relation of the Shastree's, I believe, lady."

"Enough, Chimna; take care of my servant till I return," said

Radha. "You can sit here; if I want you I will call;" and so saying she passed through a door into the inner court, and up the steps which led to the apartments above, which were steep and narrow. The door was closed at the top of them, and she knocked before she opened it. Her brother unfastened it inside. "Enter," he said quickly; "it is well thou art come, I was thinking how I could see thee, Radha." Sit down there," and he hastily arranged a few pillows and a travelling mattress for her, "and speak to me;" and at the same time threw himself heavily upon a low bed which was close to the seat he had contrived.

"O, I am weary, Radha," he continued, "very weary. I have no sleep, no rest; I cannot eat, and there is a burning thirst ever with me. I shall die if this lasts long."

"Brother, you are ill," she replied; "this place does not agree with you? Why not go away for a time and change the air? Chimna says you have eaten nothing; why is this? With all there is to do for the master, this is no time to be ill. Is there nothing better for him than lingering here? Surely Tannajee brought news of him?"

"Ay, sister, and there is more," and he pointed to a heap of letters on the floor; "enough to make one tremble for the result of years of toil and strife with the men of Islam. Listen: Maloosray brought word of their preparations at Beejapoor, and they write that to-day or to-morrow Afzool Khan and his son Fazil, with all the forces at Nuldroog and Sholapoor, and many others, will begin a march upon Wye and Purtâbgurh. What can we do?"

"Is this Moro Trimmul, my brother, who is speaking?" said the girl, with some scorn in her tone, and drawing herself up. "I thought he, like Tannajee and the master, could see no hindrance to the cause of the Holy Mother but death. He used to say so in —in—the old times," she added tenderly.

"The old times?" he echoed. "Yes, the old times, when thou hadst a royal lover, girl; not a drivelling book-worm!"

"Hush, Moro," returned Radha sharply; "no more of that. Thou hast buried it in the marriage, and he is kind to me. Why remember it?"

"Is it to be forgotten? Dost thou forget it, Radha?—then, when we brought thee back from him?"

"He never loved me," she returned; "he could not love a mad child; he told me so when he gently put me away."

"Not for the mad child, but for the beautiful girl, would he care; he does care, Radha. O sister, why was this hateful marriage done, so far away from us?"

"Nay, brother, thou knowest best; but I am content—he is very kind to me; and they all love Radha now, even Anunda."

"Radha," said her brother, raising himself on his arms and looking at her intently, and till his eyes seemed to flash with a light glowing beneath them. "Radha, do not lie. If thou art my sister, thy heart is far away among the blue mountains and their deep forests, and with our Prince. If it be not so, the witchcraft of that house hath compassed thee with a spell, as it has me."

"Witchcraft, brother? they do no witchcraft," she replied simply.

"By the Mother, they do," he cried; "feel my hands, feel my head, they are burning, and Tara has set me on fire."

"Moro, thou art ill; this is fever," returned his sister anxiously. "I was like this yesterday, and Anunda gave me some medicine, and I slept, and it passed away. Let me fetch some, or send the woman for it."

"No, no, Radha," he said hoarsely, "this is no fever; this is a spell on me, and I cannot break it. This is the spell Tara wears round her neck, Gunga told me of it. It would not let her speak; it draws me to her, and then puts me away till I burn. O sister, I burn all over, and at night when there is no one with me—O, it is terrible, terrible; and she comes and mocks me, and holds out water and flowers, and then snatches them away. I tell thee she is a witch, a devil, and she has set me on fire. Bring her to me and I will tell her so."

"Brother, dear brother," said the girl, "you are ill, and there is no one to tend you. I will stay; why did you not send for me? why not tell me of this sooner? Now, I will not leave you, you must not be alone."

"Radha, I am not ill," he replied; "I need no tending. Was I ill yesterday, when I overcame the Brahmuns from Punderpoor in the discussion at night, and when I could have said the Ramayun by heart? Was I ill to-day when I strove with the Nassuk Brahmuns in logic? No, girl, I am not ill in body, only at heart. And when she comes to the temple, and goes round the shrine crowned with flowers, clashing the cymbals and singing hymns with the priests, then I see the charm on her bosom, and it sparkles; and I hear her ringing voice, and I grow mad, Radha—mad . . . . and this fever comes on me, and I burn as they do in hell—as I do now. Look!" he cried in a shrill cry of pain, "look, she is there, mocking me now, and pushing me in. . . . . O Tara!" he continued in a plaintive voice, after a pause, stretching out his hands and shutting his eyes, as he turned away, "do not kill me, do not burn me; I kiss your feet, I worship you, beloved! do not harm me!"

"What can I do? what can I do?" cried Radha, wringing her hands. "He will die. Ho, Chimna!"

"Silence, Radha; for your life call no one. I will strike you if you do," he said, raising his arm. "Look, she is gone! she was there—there, even now. I turned away, for her eyes burned me; there was no love in them—none. She came and mocked me, and you are witness of it. Why did she come in the air? She is a spirit—a witch—and it is always thus. There—look——"

Radha looked tremblingly where he pointed. It was impossible not to be infected with the terror and misery of his face and voice. The room had open arches of wood on one side, across which heavy curtains were drawn; but they were partially open, and, looking through them, all she saw was the terraces of the houses of the town gradually descending into the great ravine: the crags and precipices of its further side: with the trees, and gilded spires and pinnacles of the temple between. Beyond these, the rugged mountain and the plain below, hazy with quivering light, and melting into the sky.

"You see nothing, sister?" he said. "No, she is gone now."

"No, Moro, there is nothing there but the town and the temple. O Holy Mother!" continued Radha, stretching out her hands to it, "save him; save my brother! I vow to thee——"

"Make no vows for me, Radha," he said to her, sharply catching her arm; "she is my enemy; I know it. She loves Tara better than me; she will not give her to me. I asked her for Tara long ago; see what has come of it. I have done all the secret rites that her worship enjoins, but she is not content; she mocks me, and when I look at her eyes they glitter with malice. To-day she seemed to glower at me from among the smoke, and Tara was there offering flowers. They both mocked me. Yes, they are devils; but I fear them no more, Radha. May her house be desolate, and her shrine desecrated."

"Hush, brother!" cried the girl, putting her hand before his mouth, to stop what she believed to be horrible and deadly blasphemy. "Hush! what if she heard you? O Mother, gentle Mother, forgive him this madness. I vow to thee——"

"You will make me curse you, Radha," he said, again grasping her arm violently. "Did I not tell you I would have no vows to her, liar and murderess as she is? Yes, I see it now. You, too, are one with them, and are come to mock me; and yet, Radha," he continued, looking at her tenderly, "was this good of you after all I have done for you? O, faithless!"

"Moro," returned Radha, weeping sorely, and sobbing so that she could hardly speak, "I am not faithless. I am true to you, even to death, my brother."

"Good," he said gravely; but again fixing his eyes upon her, so that she could hardly bear his intense gaze. "True? Ah, yes, if all are false, Radha should be true—true to him and to me. Now, listen," he continued, slowly and impressively, "if thou art true, tell Tara I am in fear of her charm; bid her look kindly on me—bid her put it away from her breast. I will kiss her feet; I will daily measure with my body every step she takes round the shrine, so that she give me one kind look,—so that I see that love in her eyes which is burning in me day and night—day and night.

"But that is not all," he resumed, after a pause. "Am I mad? Dost thou think me so for this raving? By the gods, no! Only for her. Let her look to herself. And I say to thee calmly, sister, thou must say all this to-night, else beware! Listen, I have but one desire in life, that is Tara—one object only to live for, that is Tara. I plead nothing, I say nothing, only that I am not mad.

"Now, listen again. You have much to live for—the pleasures of life, the enjoyments of wealth—honour as the wife of Vyas Shastree,—children to come, and your husband's love, with your children's; but remember, Radha, they are all in my hand. A word from me to him, and you are sunk lower than the Moorlees. All this joy will pass from you. He will cast you out, and I will not shelter you. You shall be worse than the vilest, and men shall mock you. By ——" and he swore a horrible curse, "I will do this and more, Radha, if you refuse. Answer me, girl," and he shook her violently and painfully in his passion.

"Moro!" cried his sister, gasping for breath, "listen. I said once before you might kill me if it pleased you, and I bared my breast to you. Now again, if you dare to look at it without shame, it is before you. But, listen to my words, I will do no treachery; no, brother, no treachery. I am of the same blood and the same spirit as yourself, and you well know I could be true and fearless once, and so may God and the Mother help me, I will be fearless now in a better cause. Yes, strike," she continued, as, without speaking, he hastily raised himself, seized a naked dagger that was concealed under his pillow, and brandished it with one hand, while he pressed her down with his knee, and held her forcibly against the wall with the other. "Strike! your blow will be more merciful than your words," and she shut her eyes, expecting the stroke, yet not flinching from it.

"Stay—hold!" cried a shrill woman's voice, as a hasty rustling of silken garments was heard for an instant between the door and the bed, and Moro Trimmul's hand was seized in a powerful grasp; "wouldst thou do murder? Shame on thee, and she thy sister!"

"She is a devil, too, and mocked me," exclaimed the man moodily, but dashing the knife to the ground. "Who let thee in, Gunga? Go, I want thee not—away! tempt me no more, else I will strike!"

"Fear him not, lady," cried the girl, picking up the dagger hastily; "he dare not strike you now, else,"—and her eyes flashed—"else, Moro Trimmul, thou shalt do no more evil: none to me, none to her.

Beware! I have no fear, and no scruple; let her go safely, and I will stay with thee."

"Go, Radha," he said. "Go, sister——"

"I will not go, Moro Trimmul," cried his sister excitedly. "I was not afraid of you when that dagger's point was at my heart. For myself I am not afraid of your threats, or your words. What you can do to me, what you can say of me, I know not. Whatever it be, and this girl is witness, I fear it not. What men would say of the Pundit, who wronged his sister—you know; and how they would revile and spit at you. Say it, sir, and I follow you through Dekhan, through Hind, till I die by your hand. If you make me shameless you shall be shameless with me; but this remember, I warn them all in the house of you,—I warn Tara of you,—and no harm shall come to her, for your honour is dearer to me, than mine to you."

"If thou hast any influence over him," she continued to Gunga; "lead him aright. Thou mayst have saved him a great crime today, for there was blood in his eyes when he kneeled over me with the knife; but better I should have died than harm should have come to them through me. Lead him away from those evil thoughts, and Radha will be grateful to thee all her life, and may often help thee."

"I love you, lady, and honour you," said the girl, reverently touching Radha's feet; "but in this matter I have no power, much as I desire to help you and him; nor, indeed, in any other now,—yet I will do what I can. He loved me once," said the girl, bursting into tears, "before he knew Tara; but that is gone, for she has his love and cares not for it. Now he only curses me and beats me, yet I will not, I cannot leave him, lady. Forgive the poor Moorlee; but it is better for me to bear his wrath than for him to be left alone. Last night he was fearfully excited, and threatened my life, but I escaped. He grows worse towards evening; but fear not, I will not leave him."

"I will come and watch with thee," said Radha, in a whisper, for her brother had again thrown himself on the bed, and covered himself with a sheet, and she feared to excite him; "let me come?"

"It may not be, lady," replied the girl. "If he kill me, what matter? who would miss the Moorlee, or grieve for her? But you, his sister, must not meet this peril; the Holy Mother has already saved you from one terrible danger, and fate is never to be dared twice. Only believe that one as devoted as yourself watches him, and one to whom life is of no account. Go, do not speak to him now. This madness will pass away, and I will come and tell you of him."

. . . .

"Is she gone, Gunga?" said Moro Trimmul to the girl, who, after Radha's departure, had sat down by the bed and was fanning him. "I hear no one speaking to you."

"Yes, I sent her away. I feared for her," she replied.

"It was well done, Gunga, else—else I might have killed her—— Ay, girl," he resumed, after a pause, "I had killed her but for Tara. Why did she come and not stay? why did she take the knife from me?"

"Thou art always raving of that girl like a fool, Moro Trimmul," said Gunga impatiently. "It was I that saved thy sister, else there was blood in thine eyes, and a devil at thy heart; what if thou hadst struck her?"

"She and Tara are one," he said gloomily; "yes, they are one, and thou, too, wilt go to them. Go, Gunga, they will give thee money."

"May dirt fall on their money, and thine too," she replied sulkily. "I want none of it."

"Thou art insolent, girl."

"I am a fool, Moro Trimmul, to bear with thee," she retorted, without moving. The girl's quick perception showed her that any toleration of his bad humour would only increase it, and of life she was utterly reckless. What tie held her to the man who now seemed almost to loathe her, she knew not: a fascination, perhaps, which she could not resist.

He was long silent, again drew the sheet over him, and lay quietly; at length he removed it and sat up.

"Thou art not gone, Gunga?" he said; "why art thou here?"

"I know not," she returned, "except that I am a fool."

"Go," he continued, "they will be wanting thee in the temple."

"I am not going," she replied; "another will take my work. I will not leave thee now."

"Gunga," he resumed, after a moody silence, "is there peace between us?"

"Such peace as thou wilt have," she replied.

"And if I love thee again?"

"Pah!" she cried; "love!—it is a thing to spit upon now. Can love go from one to another, and return as it went? Can a garland of Champa flowers be worn all night, and keep their freshness and fragrance till the morning? Do not men fling them away as refuse?"

"Then, why come to me, girl? why follow me?"

"Thy heart tells thee already," she said, fixing her eyes full on him, "we have one thing only in common now. That girl—I told thee so at the Pâpnâs that day, and I tell thee so again—when I trample that charm of hers under my feet, and her throat with it, I shall be content, and thou art safe. Yes, Moro Trimmul, but for hope of revenge on her, I would have killed thee when thy love went to her. But thou art a coward; I know it; thou wilt do nothing."

"Thou wilt not say so if I carry her off and put her to shame."

"Ah!" cried the girl, rising and standing over him, "is it so? I tell thee, Moro Trimmul, I will follow her and fawn on her like a dog—I will abase myself before her—I will lick the dust from her feet, if that will help thee to do this."

"Listen to what I say," he continued, raising himself on his arm. "I am calm now—quite calm—I burn no longer. I was mad when she—when Radha—came. I thought I had a chance through her; but she defied me, and there is none."

"Women know women best," said the girl. "I told thee so long ago, but I was not believed."

"I believe thee now," he replied; "and we have only ourselves to rely upon. Ah, surely this is a strange calmness which has come over me. It is not before death, Gunga?"

"No, fear not," returned Gunga. "Love is passing into revenge; I know what it is. Yes, thou wilt act now, Moro. Take her hence but for a day, and she is thine for ever, and will become a Moorlee like me—like the rest of us. Enough, Moro Trimmul. No other harm shalt thou do to her than this? Hast thou the spirit—the courage?"

"I will do it," he said gloomily. "That is what I had determined on myself. When can it be done?"

"On the last night of the ceremonies," she said; "I can get the key of the postern, and keep it open unobserved; and as Maloosray and others went that night, so canst thou take Tara; and I have friends among the Ramoosees, who will help us. I am their priestess, and they dare not refuse me. Take us both; I must see her humiliation. O Shakti powers!" she cried, stretching out her arms, "aid me in this. Ye are more powerful than the Mother, and ye hate her. Art thou determined, Moro Trimmul?"

"I will not change," he said; "the illusion is past."

"Swear on my throat and feet, and I will believe thee."

"I swear," he replied, touching her neck.

"Now I will leave thee, Moro," said the girl. "I have no fear for thee; there will be no more delirium with new thoughts."

"I will follow thee to the temple," he replied; "go on before. I dare not stay here alone; she would come to me——"

CHAPTER LI.

Some days have passed at Beejapoor since we were last there, not idly, certainly. A large army had to be prepared for the field, and for a long, difficult, and perhaps hazardous service. The treasury was opened, and the arrears of all troops disbursed; for the men had to provide as well for their own wants as for those of their families during their absence. The condition of the artillery was looked to with particular care, and preparations made for rough roads and rougher service than other parts of the Dekhan afforded. Sivaji's mountains were high and steep, the jungle and forest next to impenetrable, yet Afzool Khan had taken up the "birra," the gage of service, and had determined to bring the rebel bound to the throne of his young King, there to receive death or pardon, as might be most fitting.

But the old Khan was no boaster. He had seen something of that country when, as a younger man, he had governed those provinces; and in his tours through them had shared the hospitality of Shahji, the father of Sivaji, and had been guided by Sivaji himself through many a rough hunting expedition; he therefore remembered enough to adopt precautions in all respects, and, so far as lay in his power, they were made.

That was not a country for the operations of cavalry, and it was therefore more to the infantry and artillery that he trusted: and it would not be wise to weaken the royal forces in and about the capital too much, lest the Moghuls should take advantage of it, and make incursions across the frontier, nay, even attack the capital itself.

His own Paigah, and troops that had been in quarters for the rainy season at his own town of Afzoolpoor:—some of the Wuzeer's Abyssinian levies, which were at Nuldroog,—some bodies of the old Dekhany horse under Alla-ool-Moolk, the Dâgtorays and Bylmees, were particularly selected; and, with some of the best infantry, the army was complete.

Nothing could exceed the spirit and devotion of the troops. In the beautiful Jumma Mosque, where more than five thousand men assembled daily for prayer, the preaching of the Peer, and the other ecclesiastics of that noble edifice—which yet remains as perfect as it was at the period of this history—eloquently set forth the merits of the Jéhâd, or religious war, in the eyes of God and the Prophet; and the certainty of paradise and its houris, to all who, falling by sickness or in battle, would surely enjoy them. Nor was it in the Jumma Mosque only that this fervour existed. In the royal Palace precincts, the city mosques—at the tombs of the ancestors of the Kings—the beauteous Ibrahim Roza, and noble mausoleum of Sultan Mahmood, nothing was left undone by the preachers to make the war popular, and to blacken the character and motives of the rebels. Frequently, indeed, to such a pitch of excitement were men wrought, that it was difficult to restrain them from attacking Hindus indiscriminately in the streets, and, in the expressive language of the Peer, from "making a pyramid of a lakh of heads before the palace gates." But it was no part of the royal policy to allow such religious fury vent at the capital or by the way: suffice it that, at the end of a long and toilsome journey, which would be made light through religious fervour, there would be free licence to slay, and the raid of Afzool Khan would become memorable in the history of the kingdom.

As the camps of the different leaders, too, formed without the walls, on that great plain which encompassed the city, bards and minstrels, in companies or singly, balled-singers, and, above all, troops of dancing women—thronged to them; and day and night, audiences were formed, sometimes in the tents, sometimes in the open air, where the feats of Sivaji and Maloosray were sung in the native Mahratta or Canarese, with verses added for the occasion, urging the faithful to destroy them.

We may be sure that, if the old Khan and Fazil were active in the field, Lurlee and Zyna were no less so in the house. To Lurlee war was familiar. She had been long weary of a monotonous life in the city, varied only by an occasional day's excursion to the royal palaces at Toorweh, the Ibrahim Roza, or to the Khan's own garden, which was without the walls; and she remembered vividly the time when, for months together, the Khan's tent, or a temporary lodging in a village, were her only home, moving hastily or leisurely, as the service required, from place to place, in her palankeen or on horseback, as might be.

Ah! she was young and active then, and with the sharing of a rough bivouac or hurried march,—scanty food, often cooked by herself, a horse-cloth to lie upon, and a shelter contrived with four spears and a sheet thrown over them—and hard fighting to boot,—were her pleasantest memories of the Khan's love and her own happiness. If she were not so young, the old spirit was at last roused; and, day by day, as the preparations went on, the good lady told Zyna of the old wild times, and excited her desire to share in the new expedition.

To Zyna's great joy her father had directed that the whole family was to move. Lurleo was indispensable to the Khan in the field, where, indeed, her truest value was apparent; and Fazil could not be denied the command he had earned by his sagacity and valour. Who, then, could protect Zyna, even did he desire to leave her? True, the royal Bégum had offered a home, and with it her love to the maiden; she should be her little secretary, and write the King's private letters to her father while he was absent. But it could not be: that loving heart would have pined without those whose daily converse had been its life for years, and the invitation was affectionately but respectfully declined.

We may, perhaps, also hint another reason, not more powerful, certainly, than the love of those nearest and dearest to her, but working with it, nevertheless, in no mean degree. Kowas Khan had not suffered by his father's treachery. It was not only that Afzool Khan and Fazil answered for him with their lives and honour; but it had become clear to the King, and to those who had examined the late Wuzeer's correspondence, that the son had been kept ignorant of his father's plans; so, when the period of mourning was past, Kowas Khan had been taken to the royal court by the Khan and his son, and invested with robes of honour. Of the King's participation in the secret of his father's murder Kowas Khan had no knowledge, and could have none. It was believed to have been committed in revenge by some discharged soldiers, and it were better that he died as he had done, than that his treacherous intention should have succeeded, or that the ignominy of a public execution should have followed its detection.

While, therefore, the young man was still residing at the Khan's house with his mother, and other younger members of the family, he renewed his proposals for Zyna, which were heartily seconded by her, and other female relatives. It was, however, no time for such affairs; and with a tacit consent that, when the campaign was over, there should be no more delay in the marriage, Kowas Khan contented himself with being told by Lurlee Khánum—when the worthy dame had retired behind a screen—that, after a strict investigation, she had come to the conclusion that his temperament was fire and Zyna's air, and that, in consequence, their union promised to be felicitous in the highest degree; and that her friend the Moolla agreed with her.

Did our space admit of it, we would tell how friends on both sides met for the betrothal; and how,—there being no time for more lengthened ceremonies,—they stood up and interchanged packets of betel-leaf covered with gold and silver foil. How both sides swore that those they represented should never swerve from the contract; how the first, and hundred and tenth chapters of the Kôrán, were said devoutly by the Moolla and the assembly; and what good things were provided at night by Lurlee Khanum and her trusty cook Kurreema, for those who came to the quiet ceremony. Many were the complaints of Lurlee's female friends, and perhaps Zyna's also, that there was not greater rejoicing; but Afzool Khan made it known that, when the marriage did take place, there should be no stint; and so the neighbours were satisfied for the present, and consoled themselves with hope for the future.

Bulwunt's wounds had proved of less consequence than was supposed at first, and loss of blood had caused the weakness under which he suffered on the night of the scene in the temple. He was now able to move about, and even to ride, and in the ensuing campaign, in a country which he knew thoroughly, his local experience would be of great use. He was not, however, sanguine as to the result. As he expressed it, hunting Sivaji and Maloosray would be like chasing the wind; it would be heard and felt, but never seen. Nevertheless they might be brought to terms, and hereafter become worthy servants of the royal house.

Everything, therefore, being prepared, and the royal astrologers having fixed a fortunate day and hour for the commencement of the march, the whole of the troops were drawn out in battle-array on the plain north of the fort, and the young King bade the leaders God-speed. Descending from his elephant, he embraced the old Khan, his son, and other noblemen and gentlemen of note; and as the royal Nagárás, or kettle-drums, which had been directed to accompany the force, struck up a march, and were answered by those of every body of horse, infantry, and artillery on the field,—the troops at once proceeded to their several destinations, a few miles distant, shouting the war-cries of their several leaders.

It was necessary, however, for the Khan himself, with his son and Kowas Khan, to visit Nuldroog, where a great portion of the army lay, and whence some of it was to accompany him; for though the troops at Beejapoor, which had been under the late Wuzeer, had shown no signs of disaffection, those at the fort were suspected, and their loyalty must be put to the proof ere the army could proceed. Lurlee Khánum and Zyna, therefore, were despatched under guidance and escort of Bulwunt Rao and others, to Sholapoor, to await the Khan's arrival; and with a party of horse lightly equipped, his son Fazil, the Peer—who had declared his intention of witnessing in person the discomfiture of the infidels, and seeing to the religious exercises of the army during its march—and Kowas Khan, Afzool Khan proceeded by the direct road of his own town of Afzoolpoor to the royal fort.

We need not follow their journey, for the country affords nothing interesting or remarkable for description. After passing the town of Almella, they crossed the Bheema, now falling rapidly, and already fordable in some places for horsemen: and Afzoolpoor, lying near the further bank, was safely reached on the third day.

Here the Khan found employment for two days more: for he was in no hurry to leave his own town, and the various matters to which he found he had to attend. His own last resting-place, a lofty, handsome, square building, with a massive dome, and the mosque adjoining it, were all but completed, and their consecration was necessary. This was performed by the Peer, the Moollas of village mosques around, the Kazee of Nuldroog, and the representative of the saint Boorhan Sahib, who lived at the pretty village of Boorhanpoor, some miles to the north, where the saint's tomb had been erected. "It was well," said the old Khan, "to have the place ready; who could tell whether it might not be required soon?" Who could tell indeed? and so the ceremonies were completed.

Nor would the hospitable representative of the Boorhanpoor saint allow the Khan's party to pass his village without entertainment. Parties of leaders of the troops at Nuldroog, now only a few miles distant, came to the festivities, and, in the meeting with them, all apprehensions were removed from the Khan's mind. Swearing on the holy book before the saint's shrine, they declared their fealty to the King, and their attachment to their young master, in terms which could not be mistaken.

CHAPTER LII.

THE Khan was to march early next morning for the fort, but his departure was delayed purposely to allow of the troops to send out parties to perform the ceremony of "Istikbal," or meeting; and, after again partaking of the good Durwaysh's hospitality, the party rode on without interruption.

The road from Boorhanpoor to Nuldroog leads up the pretty and fertile valley of the Boree river, which is skirted by low grassy hills for several miles. Then leaving the river, as the hills grow bolder, it rises gradually through passes among them, and, after several steep and stony ascents, gains a level plateau, from whence the fort and town are distinctly seen below.

Soon after leaving their post, the party began to meet others from the fort, dressed in their gayest and best costumes; and these, having made their salutes to the Khan, rode forward to the front, so that gradually the men in advance swelled to a considerable number, and had all the appearance of an independent body of cavalry. Out of this, wherever the ground afforded room, and was free from ruts and stones, men dashed at speed, wheeling and circling their horses, so that their movements appeared like those of a real skirmish.

When they reached the level plain on the summit of the plateau above the town, the Khan was met by the Killadar, or governor of the fort, the principal officers of the troops, the civil authorities, and others; some on horseback, others on gaily-caparisoned elephants with clashing bells. Both parties dismounting, and the leaders having embraced each other,—the officers presenting the hilts of their swords as Nuzzurs, or offerings to the Khan,—the procession —for it had now become one—moved on slowly in gorgeous array, amidst the firing of matchlocks and camel swivels and welcome guns from the fort; and the appearance of the Khan and his gallant son, as they rode together through the main street and bazar, dressed in rich cloth-of-gold, was a subject of general remark and approbation by all classes. The prospect of a campaign, always pleasant to the soldiers, especially under so renowned a leader as Afzool Khan, increased the general satisfaction of all concerned.

As they passed its first gate, the booming of cannon from the ramparts announced their arrival within the fort, and was answered by guns from the encampment on the heights to the west. Passing the ditch by a causeway, they entered the fausse-braye by a narrow passage, and thence ascending slightly to the main entrance, with its massive flanking bastions of black basalt, the interior was reached—at that time a busy place, crowded with houses and shops in some parts, but in others laid out in open gardens, and spaces where the troops could assemble.

A curious and picturesque spot in many respects is this fort. Built upon a tongue of basalt, which is precipitous on three sides, and of considerable height, it is joined to the level portion of the plateau to the west, on which the town stands, by a neck considerably narrower than the enciente; and on this side a double wall with bastions, and a deep dry ditch, form the defences. Round the edge of the precipices of the hill itself, is a single wall of great strength, with large bastions at intervals; and the river Boree, lying deep in the valley below, washes the base of the hill on two sides, north and east.

To the north, to secure a constant supply of water to the fort, a stupendous dam of masonry has been thrown across the river upwards of seventy feet high, and of proportional thickness, by which the water is held up in the valley, so as to form a pretty lake of the same depth at the dam, which extends above the town. On the other side of this dam is another fort on a smaller knoll, which serves as a *tête-du-pont* to the dam, and completes the fortification.

To the old Khan the place was familiar. He had often taken turns of duty there to watch the frontier, but to Fazil and his friend it was new; and when ceremonies of reception and the introduction of Kowas Khan to the officers of his father's levies, now his own, were finished, the friends accepted the offer of the Killadar to examine the marvels of the place.

The wonderful dam, through the upper sluices of which the stream was precipitated into a deep pool at its foot, in two pretty cataracts; the suite of apartments in the body of the dam itself, over which the river rolled in flood, and fell in a sheet before its windows; and the noble Cavalier at the east end, from the top of which extensive views of the country on all sides were obtained, were duly admired. It was evening when the friends reached the summit of the Cavalier, and they sate there watching the glorious sunset, over town and fort and lake, in which the piles of gold and crimson clouds broken with dark purple, with the sombre masses of fort walls and bastions, and precipices on which they stood, were reflected in its deep waters.

It was not so easy to prepare the troops required there as at the capital; but the Khan was anxious that nothing should be wanting in their equipment, and a few days was required to complete preparations for the field. This delay enabled the chief officers of the country to arrive and pay their respects, and, among others, Pahar

Singh, no longer disguised, but in his proper character as one of the wardens of the frontier marches, attended and did service with a body of picked men, both horse and foot, which rivalled, if they did not surpass, the royal troops in completeness and splendour of appearance.

Very different were the chief and his nephew now, in comparison with the time when we last saw them; and in the noble figure, dressed in light chain armour and cloth-of-gold, riding a superb grey horse, and giving commands to his men, no one could have recognized the old ragged Fakeer and his cry of "Ulla dilâyâ to léonga," which still often rang in the ears of those who had heard it.

The building, which went by the name of the King's Palace, and which was kept for the use of royal officers of rank, or even for royalty itself, should the King have occasion to visit the fort, had been assigned to Afzool Khan and his retinue; and, after the transaction of daily business in one of the public halls of the fort, he retired, after evening prayer, to his apartments, finding relaxation in a game of chess with the priest, who was a stout opponent, or hearing or dictating his public correspondence.

It was the fourth evening after his arrival, after an unusually busy day; the priest was occupied with a sermon in the mosque, and the Khan had retired into one of the rooms of the house, which, being built into part of the fort wall, possessed a projecting oriel window, commanding a view of the whole of the east side of the fort, with its walls and rugged cliffs. By day these precipices did not appear extraordinarily remarkable; but when shrouded in the gloom of evening and night, with the river brawling beneath them in its rocky bed, their height and effect were indefinitely increased, and the murmur of the river below became delightfully soothing.

One corner of this oriel, furnished with cushions, had become the favourite resort of the Khan. Here he had been sitting alone and undisturbed, and occupied with despatches and other papers the whole of the evening; and he was about to retire to rest when an attendant entered, somewhat abruptly.

"I said I was not to be disturbed, Allee," he cried; "what dost thou want?"

"My lord, there is a man without, who says he has urgent business, and he must have speech of you alone. I said it was impossible; but he declared you would be angry with me if you knew he were denied, and that I was to say to you, 'Ulla dilâyâ to léonga,' and you would understand."

"Admit him, instantly," said the Khan, to his servant's astonishment. "Ha, Pahar Singh again! what new work has he now got here for us?"

Muffled closely in a sheet, with his sword under his arm, the chief approached the Khan, and bent lowly before him. "Send that man away, and hear what I have to say," he said; "it is important."

Allee looked at the chief suspiciously, as though he were trusting his master to a dangerous character; but, at a reiteration of the order, he returned to depart.

"Take this weapon with you, friend," said the chief, laughing, "thou art afraid of it, perhaps; not so thy lord,—nor of me. Keep it for me, however, till I come out."

Allee took the sword. "I did not like the look of him," he said to another without, who belonged to the fort. "Who is he?"

"Dost thou not know Pahar Singh?" returned the man; "that is his famous sword Dévi, which has drank many a man's blood; come, let us look at it. There will be something to do, surely, as he is with the Khan."

"I have but a few words to say, Afzool Khan," said Pahar Singh, as the servant retired; "and I can do a good service, if it please you, my lord, to join in it or aid it."

"If it be a service to the King's cause, why not?" said the Khan; "but none of thy blood feuds, Pahar Singh; thou canst not use the royal troops for thine own purposes."

"Nor do I need them, my lord," returned the chief, somewhat stiffly. "I have enough men of my own to answer for those matters; nay, indeed, for this also, if I have your permission; and only that my rascals are somewhat too free of hand to be trusted in a town at night, I had done it myself ere this."

"Thanks, friend, for thy caution," said the Khan, smiling; "we shall know each other better by-and-by. But what is this scheme?"

"When I left you, Khan Sahib, the night of Jehándar Beg's execution," replied the chief, "I had knowledge that Tannajee Maloosray was in the city, and I knew where he was. My people watched every bazar and street during the day, and we had a strong party near the Goruk Imlee trees, thinking he might like to come and see an old friend for the last time; but he kept close, like a bear in his den, till night, and then stole away. My boy and some of my people wanted to catch him in his den; but I knew Tannajee could not be taken alive by mortal, and I wanted to see him sit like Jehándar Beg under the trees, and die like a man; so I took a body of my horse and rode after him towards Tooljapoor, where he was going. We occupied the pass at Hórtee. But he escaped us there, Khan; and hearing afterwards he had gone to Jutt, there appeared to be no use in following him, as he had twenty-five coss start of us. But I was a fool, my lord; and for once Tannajee outwitted me. He went on next day to Tooljapoor; how, I know not. He was seen there in the temple, and he left again that night, no one knows whither."

"To Tooljapoor in one day!" exclaimed the Khan, "no horse alive could do it."

"Ah, my lord, your high-fed beasts would not, but ours can; and Tannajee and his friend Netta Palkur have the best mares in the Dekhan. No matter; he escaped us."

"He was—he is—the very bone and sinew of this rebellion," said the Khan.

"True, as Sivaji Rajah is the spirit; but he left some of the bones behind him at Tooljapoor," returned the chief, with a grim smile; "and I can pick them up for you, my lord, if you will either help me or let me do it alone as best I can; only remember, if the town is plundered, you know the cause, and I am not responsible for the blame."

"That you had better avoid, friend," said the Khan, "you are badly spoken of already. But the bones, good fellow, the bones! who or what are they?"

"Ah! I had forgotten them," continued Pahar Singh. "Well, there is Moro Trimmul, Maloosray's agent and shadow; as wily, and more mischievous. He is still at Tooljapoor, pretending to give recitations,—and they are very good, my lord, in their way,—and to serve at the temple; but I am not sure that one of the Moorlees is not at the bottom of it, and when a man gets into women's hands, he is easily caught. Then there are all those who will assemble there. Have you remarked, my lord, that hardly one of the heads of the old Mahratta families have come to present their Nuzzurs to you?"

"I have remarked it," returned the Khan, "but supposed they were afraid of some demand for forage, or horses, or money, and therefore kept clear of me."

"Not at all," returned the chief, "they have all sworn to aid Sivaji, and Maloosray took an account of their quotas of horse and foot with him to the Rajah."

"Then they met Maloosray?"

"They did, my lord, the night he came to the temple, and here are their names. There are other people, you see, who have ears and eyes besides Maloosray; and only that your Näib at Tooljapoor is an owl, he had seen this conspiracy long ago, while I was too busy to watch it. Better, perhaps, he did not; we can do our work more securely. And now, do you wish to seize this gang of rebels or not? I advise you to do so, because they are strong, and, should there be any difficulties in the West, are capable of making a serious diversion, especially if Maloosray, or even this Brahmun,—who is more of a soldier than a priest,—get among them. These Nimbalkurs and Ghoreparays, my lord, quiet as they look, are heavily supported by the people; and if the Ramoosees rise with them, the country will be in a flame."

"And how dost thou know all this, Pahar Singh?" asked the Khan. "I must have some warranty that it is true."

"Some months ago, my lord," he replied, "this very Moro Trimmul and others canvassed me as to joining Sivaji's band, and offered me whatever terms I pleased to ask. I refused, for I was content as I was."

"That means," remarked the Khan dryly, "that thou wouldst have joined them if there had been anything to be got by it."

"My lord is still incredulous," returned the chief, "and perhaps I deserve doubt till I have given him further proof. But I feel the King's hand on my head still, and his pardon is more to me than promises, of Mahratta, or Moghul either."

"Good!" said the Khan; "it is well said, and I believe thee. But about these rebels; are they still there? and how many may there be of them?"

"They are there, my lord," replied the chief. "I was in the temple last night disguised as a Byragee, with my nephew and four others: we heard the recitations from the Ramayun, which, to Hindus, are very much what the Peer Sahib is saying now in the mosque yonder, and said yesterday at the Eedgah on the plain, when the whole force shouted 'Deen, deen!' and it sounded like thunder. Jey Rao Nimbalkur was there, and some of the Kallays——"

"How many?" said the Khan, impatiently interrupting him; "what care I for their teeth-breaking names?"

"Five hundred perhaps, including followers."

"And is this temple a strong place? Do we require guns?"

"Strong enough to defend if they knew you were coming," returned Pahar Singh, "but for the most part they will be unarmed, and looking at the show. We need only cavalry to surround the town, and no one can escape us. No guns, my lord; they could not be taken up the mountain at night, and ours must be a surprise, else the temple will be dark as midnight."

"Ya Alla! ya Kabiz!" (destroyer of enemies), muttered the Khan to himself, "a rare trap for these Kaffirs—let them die! Good," he continued; "it shall be done; but when? I should march to-morrow for Sholapoor."

"Do so, my lord, and halt at Tandoolwaree; 'tis half way. I will join you there with some of my people the day after to-morrow, and lead you by a pass in the hills which I know of at night, so that we can surround the place unobserved. Take some of your own men and Ibrahim Khan's Abyssinians; they know no fear, and are more certain than the braggart, plundering Dekhanies, who are afraid of the Mother who sits in the glen, though they are Mussulmans."

"What Mother, friend?"

"Only she in the temple; we Hindus call her the 'Mother'; and she, my lord, must not be touched."

"No, no; nor her people, I will see to that," said the Khan.

"And the affair must be kept secret, Khan," he continued.

"It is known to thee and me, Pahar Singh, and to no one else; not even my son shall know of it till we march."

"Now let me depart," said the chief, "and the night after next I will come."

"God willing," replied the Khan, dismissing his strange visitor with a courteous salutation.

CHAPTER LIII.

On her return home, Tara being still asleep, Radha could not conceal from Anunda the agitation which the scene with her brother had caused her. As she reached the inner apartments, she threw herself upon Anunda's neck, and the terror she felt at what she considered a narrow escape from death, found relief in a flood of tears. The particulars of that scene she dared not fully relate: but Anunda gathered enough from her to believe that Moro Trimmul had threatened, if not struck his sister, and that Tara's suspicions were but too deeply founded.

If Anunda had not felt assured of Tara's purity and devotion to the worship of the goddess, in its spiritual sense only, she would have prevented, at all hazards perhaps, her assumption of service as a devotee. It was, she knew, one of the trials to which the girl would be subject so long as her beauty remained, that her public avocation would expose her to the gaze of all classes of people—the most persistent and dangerous libertines, perhaps, being priests of her own sect. But the act of Tara's profession of service was so sudden, so unlooked for, and had been carried out so immediately, that there was no time to consider the consequences.

Now, too, it was impossible to recede. Once she had vowed herself to the dread goddess she dared not retract, nor could any attempt be made, as they believed, to withdraw her without danger. Many instances of such partial service and relinquishment of it, capricious or meditated, had come to her knowledge, which had been followed by sudden death, or, what was worse, loss of reason and raving madness.

Well, therefore, might the sister-wives tremble at the consequences of transgression, even by temporary withdrawal of Tara's service. It was the first thing that Radha counselled; but, under the instances of punishment which she enumerated, Anunda declared it to be impossible. She could not—dare not—expose Tara to such risk, nor herself be the means of it; and, indeed, she was assured that Tara would never agree. Gradually, however, Anunda's naturally cheerful and sanguine spirit took courage.

"We cannot prevent men's eyes wandering to that sweet face," she said to Radha, as she gently waved a fan over Tara, who still slept heavily, "no more than I can prevent them looking at me if they like, or thee, Radha; but we can protect her from insult and shame, and she is too pure to be approached or spoken to. No; he may look as he pleases, but he dare not speak to her: for thy sake, for the sake of his own honour and station as a priest, he dare not; and his looks she shall not fear—I will prevent them."

"Nevertheless," replied Radha, "let her not visit the temple for several days to come, or, if she goes, we will both accompany her. This will give her fresh assurance, and in a few days he will be gone."

Radha, however, knew her brother well—better than Anunda. She knew that, with any scheme against Tara in view, no matter what it might be, she was incapable of watching him so completely as to defeat his intentions; but she could at least be wary, and gain imformation of them, and a small purse of money with which Anunda supplied her, given to Chimna, gained her constant information of her brother's movements, such as she could not otherwise have obtained.

Moro Trimmul, however, to all appearance ceased to pursue Tara. For several days she did not visit the temple. She herself feared collision with him, and kept away. But gradually, a sense of neglect of her daily duty, the loss of the satisfaction which had resulted from it, and the dread of offending the terrible Being in whose exacting service she believed,—wrought on her mind so as to render inaction intolerable.

And no wonder now. Her own small household tasks, which had previously occupied her leisure hours, had been resigned to Radha; the temple service required her presence for the greater part of the morning and afternoon; and her studies, and some needful rest, absorbed the remainder of the day. Now that she remained idle at home, therefore, the time hung heavy on her hands, and she sighed for the occupation and excitement which had become habitual to her; while the yearning to serve "the Mother"—never to be absent from her—grew stronger and stronger day by day, with a fascination she could not resist. Day by day those weird, glowing, eerie eyes seemed to follow her about, seek her in her sleep, and by turns threaten or entreat her.

"Mother," she said at last, and after a few days had passed in restless idleness at home, "I feel that my life here is not what it was. The Mother's eyes follow me, and she sits at my heart day and night. Why dost thou not come to me, Tara? she says; fear not, but come; no one dare harm thee, and I would have thee near me. This she whispers daily when my time of service comes, and I am here and not with her. O mother, I fear no longer; she gives me strength, and I will go. What can he do to me? The dread of him is gone from me."

"We will go with thee, daughter," replied Anunda, "and remain with thee daily. Before us, he dare neither look nor speak; and perhaps, too, thy suspicions were misplaced."

"Perhaps," she replied; "and why should he do me wrong? I should be sorry if I had thought ill of him without a cause."

So they went. The first day Moro Trimmul was not there. On the second they met him, and received his distant and courteous salutation. He did not even come to speak to his sister, and turned away directly. Gunga was present on both occasions; and on the first day Tara was surprised, and perhaps somewhat gratified, by the manner in which she and some of her sisterhood met her; offered her garlands of flowers, even put them into her hands, and tied them like bracelets round her arms, and into her hair.

"You have been ill, sister," said Gunga, deferentially and respectfully, "and we have done your work, and offered flowers for your recovery to the Mother. Ah," she continued, "because we are poor, and not as you are, Tara, do not look coldly upon us; have we not one common Mother, and are we not sisters in her? So think of us, and we will be your slaves and fellow-servants; for she has loved you more than us, and sent you pure among us. We know, too, you are already changed to us, for we have received the daily offerings as you have kindly directed."

Poor Tara, there was no guile in her loving heart which bred or fostered suspicion. What could she think but that those callous minds had relented towards her? and perhaps the very offerings, which she had thoughtlessly made over to the attendant priests, had been the original cause of all their apparent enmity. Day after day the Moorlees' respect seemed to increase; and while her work was rendered lighter, her repugnance to acknowledge them as co-servitors seemed to lessen. With all indeed, except Gunga, the respect was sincere, and the deference unfeigned; but with her, intercourse seemed only to fan the flame of revenge burning at her heart: and while she repressed it with difficulty in public, in private she yielded to it with all the unbridled rancour and jealousy of her nature.

Against Tara, therefore, these evil notions were now, for different reasons, in perpetual and active combination. It was no part of Moro Trimmul's plan to excite further suspicion. Brooding over fancied neglects and slights, as well as revenge for hopelessness of passion, had, as Gunga rightly guessed, mastered the softer feeling of admiration and love for the gentle object of them; and the desire of his life now was, to crush relentlessly and deface the purity which he could not appreciate. His sister, he believed, had kept his counsel, for she had made no further remonstrance; and the first occasion on which Tara came with her father only, and trusted herself to the companionship of the priestesses, was hailed by Gunga and the Brahmun as conducive to their success.

We can believe that the worthy Shastree himself was utterly unconscious of any element of disturbance in his quiet household. He was perfectly satisfied with his new wife, and was even growing to love her dearly. He was not demonstrative—very learned and studious men rarely are so, perhaps; but Radha studied his disposition and his wants, and, without interfering with Anunda's prerogatives, was supplying them unobtrusively and lovingly; and he felt what he could not fail to appreciate—the action of another tender hand about his daily life.

With Moro Trimmul he continued on the best of terms—nay, his love and admiration of the man was much increased. These recitations in the temple, the disputations on logic and law, the evident knowledge which Moro possessed of the more secret rites and mysteries of the Shasters and Tantras, increased the Shastree's respect. If Moro Trimmul would not come to the house as often as he wished, he was at least no stranger in the temple, and in the ceremonies now proceeding, he was of the greatest possible use. He now frequently spoke of his approaching departure, which only depended upon letters he should receive from his Prince; and it was an event which, on every account of private and public intercourse, Vyas Shastree was disposed to regret exceedingly.

CHAPTER LIV.

The night of the Amáwas, or that which immediately precedes the new moon, is necessarily the darkest of every month, and for several days previous to it the sky had been overcast, as it frequently is at the season we write of, though without rain. The ceremonies in the temple would be protracted till, according to the astronomical calculations, the old moon had passed away and the new one begun, which was some time after midnight. The concourse in the town was perhaps greater than usual. Several of the Mahratta chiefs were still there, each with a complement of followers; and others who lived within a day's journey, were arriving one by one, to attend the last series of recitations which would be given until the next full moon. It was understood, also, that this was the last night on which Moro Trimmul would officiate; and his picturesque style of declamation was more attractive than the measured and monotonous manner of the elder Pundits.

By the afternoon, therefore, the main bazar of Tooljapoor had become a very lively scene. The number of people already in the town was increased hourly by the arrival of visitors from the populous villages round about, and even from Darasew, Thair, Baimlee, and others within a day's ride; and as evening drew in, the passes leading to the town from below, and the roads, too, from the level country above, still showed parties,—some on horses, some on ponies, on foot, or on oxen,—pressing forward to be in time for the opening ceremonies, which would commence as the lamps were lighted.

Sweetmeat-sellers—parched rice—and chenna friers, were driving a brisk trade in the bazars, and their booths were crowded with customers receiving their several quantities hot and hot, as they could be prepared. The night would be far advanced ere the whole of the ceremonies were concluded, and, once seated, no one could move. Many a careful dame, therefore, had tied up a bundle of sweet cakes before she left home and carried them on her arm;—others, with less foresight perhaps, were making provision for the night at the stalls we have mentioned:—while flower-sellers were threading garlands of jessamine and môtea blossoms, and, indeed, of many wild flowers, from fields and hedges, in lack of other materials. Sellers of Pân leaves, tobacco and betel-nut—incense-sticks and pastiles—and oil for the lights of the shrine—were all as busy as a throng of eager purchasers could make them.

Among this crowd, the Shastree, with Anunda, Radha, and Tara, were making their way to the temple before the assembly should render the courts impassable. With the Shastree, who was walking before the women, was Moro Trimmul, who had dined at his house, and who was now on his way with him to the recitation. Chimna, two days before, had reported to Radha that her brother was about to leave. He had, the man said, purchased a palankeen and hired a set of bearers for it, and others had been sent on the road to Sattara, so as to form relays for a night's journey: and, except himself, and one or two who were to be mounted, the other servants were to follow. Indeed, intimation of his intended departure had been made that day privately to the Shastree and to his sister by Moro himself.

He was afraid of staying, he said. Afzool Khan had arrived at Nuldroog; the force there was about to march to Sholapoor, and thence westward. If he preceded it, he could travel unnoticed, otherwise it would be impossible to move at all in its rear, or to pass it without making a considerable and inconvenient detour. As danger threatened the Maharaja, he must be present to share it; and he would return as soon as the storm, which was about to burst, had blown over.

It was no more than all had expected and some had hoped for. So long as her brother's presence was a source of no actual uneasiness to Radha, she was thankful to see him, although she feared a renewal of his threats to her as regarded Tara; but since her last interview with him, she had been possessed with a dread which beset her night and day, either that he would do something desperate, as regarded Tara, or that, in revenge for her not having assisted his licentious purpose, he would put his threat, as regarded herself,—whatever it might be,—in execution.

His proposed departure was, therefore, a positive relief, and, in making the communication to her, Moro Trimmul had carefully acted his part. He deplored the recent scene and his own violence. "Tara's love," he said, "was hopeless as it was criminal; and he thanked his sister for having saved his honour in regard to that misplaced affection. Girls who married could not always keep their relatives with them: better indeed it were so, and in her case particularly; for no doubt he had enemies, and were he denounced to Afzool Khan, he should have some difficulty in escaping."

Could any one have doubted all this, or suspected that any sinister motive lay below it? Impossible! It was the literal truth in most respects, and open to no breath of suspicion.

To Anunda, and especially to Tara, the event was one of positive rejoicing. The good matron had, as we have seen, no objection to Moro Trimmul until Tara's suspicion had been aroused; and, secure in the effect of her own precautions, she had become utterly indifferent whether he remained or not. But with Tara it was otherwise; his presence was the only check on her enjoyment of daily life. Were he gone for good, her services, her household love, would be freed from the incubus which had deadened her existence while he remained, and she would be saved from any apprehension for the future. On all these considerations, therefore, the female members of the Shastree's family descended to the temple that night, with joyful and thankful hearts.

We know, however, partly what Moro Trimmul had determined upon, and how he had proposed to execute it. So far as she was concerned, the girl Gunga had never faltered in her plan. The only stipulation she made with Moro Trimmul was, that she should accompany him,—an arrangement to which he was very unwilling to consent. On this point, however, he found her utterly unrelenting. When she saw his desire to be rid of her, she declared that she would not only retire from the affair altogether, but would denounce him to the Shastree and to every Brahmun in Tooljapoor. She defied his threats; and he knew, by previous experience, that no words could turn her from any purpose which she had in view, and without her co-operation the execution of the plan was quite impossible. What she proposed to do he knew not, she would not tell him; but he had provided a stout horse for her which, with his servants and the litter, were to wait in the ravine below the temple. He did not fear pursuit. The Shastree kept no horse. He could not obtain the services of any horsemen from the authorities at night. Who would care for the ravings of a Brahmun, whose daughter, a priestess of the temple, had eloped, as it would be considered, with her lover? True, Ânunda might revenge herself on Radha,—but to that, the Shastree, for his own honour, would hardly consent.

So they descended the steps into the lower court of the temple together; and while Tara, her mother, and the Shastree entered the vestibule to make their salutation to the goddess, Moro Trimmul excused himself on pretence of bringing his books, and went round to the back of the shrine, where, near the wishing-stone,* he found Gunga and several of the priestesses sitting idly on the basement, basking, as it were, in the evening sun then setting. We have said it had been a gloomy day, even now the heavens were overcast: but towards the horizon the clouds were open, and a bright gleam of red light had broken through them and fell upon the temple and sides of the glen in striking brilliancy; while the rich dresses of the girls, and their heavy gold and silver ornaments, glistened and sparkled in the glowing colour.

Gunga had apparently been giving some description of her new gold anklets; for, as Moro Trimmul turned the corner, she had slid down from her seat, and was moving her feet as to produce a faint clashing sound.

"One need not even put on the bells with these," she cried to her friends, "listen how well they will sound to the music, and I shall dance to-night as the processions move round."

As she spoke, the girl swayed round several times, half circling one way, then another, tossing her arms in the air in time with the steps in which she was moving her feet. There was something in the lithe grace of her figure which struck Moro Trimmul as a new charm, and he stopped to watch it for a few moments ere he was noticed. Perhaps the thought she was not observed, perhaps the certainty that she should that night triumph over her rival, had excited Gunga more than usual; for she had thrown into her movements a spirit and beauty,—a majesty of motion,—as it might be called, which was inexpressibly attractive.

"If thou dance like that to-night," cried one of the girls, "thou wilt win back that lover of thine, Gunga. If he were mine I should not quarrel with him. Ah!" she screamed, "there he is: what if he has heard me!" and, sliding hastily from their seats, she, with the rest of her companions, fled round the corner of the building.

* A large stone placed on the rear basement of the temple. Votaries are directed to place a hand on each side of it, and make a wish. If it turns to the right, the wish will be granted; if to the left, otherwise.

Gunga did not move, but covered her face with the end of her garment.

"If I had known——" she said.

"Thou wouldst not have danced so well," he returned, interrupting her. "By Krishna! girl, not even the Gopîs of Muttra danced more lovingly before him than thou didst then in those few turns. Dance like that to-night, and I shall not be able to resist thee."

"It would be a pity to turn thee from Tara now," she said, with scorn, "so I shall not dance at all. Art thou ready?"

"Yes; I have taken leave of them, and prepared everything," he replied. "Chimna will bring the horses and litter into the ravine, and wait near the steps for us. Thou hast the key?"

"Look," she cried, crossing to the door, which was only a few steps distant, and partly opening it, "it is already open, and the key is here in my bodice. We can lock it outside, and throw the key into the bushes. When I beckon to thee, come, for I will entice her here; but if thy heart then fail thee, Moro Pundit, beware——"

He had need in truth to do so; but there was no occasion for threats, they did but provoke him. "Enough," he said, "we must not be seen together here. I will not fail thee."

CHAPTER LV.

Just then, a company of well-equipped horsemen, in number about two hundred, rode into Afzool Khan's camp at Tandoolwaree; and the same gleam of sun, which had broken through the clouds and shone on the temple at Tooljapoor, and upon Gunga as she danced, caught the tips of their long spears,—and sparkled upon matchlock barrels, the bright bosses of their shields, and the steel morion of the leader.

There was no regularity of dress or equipment among the horsemen, but the fine condition and spirit of their horses, and the manner in which they moved, proved them to be accustomed to act together, as the look of the men gave assurance of their being well tried in war. In their front was a man on a piebald horse, over which were slung two large kettledrums, which were occasionally beaten with a sonorous sound by the person who sat behind them: and two men, both round-shouldered, one of whom carried a small green standard, with a white figure of Hunoomán, the monkey god, sewn upon it, rode beside him, one on each side. Pahar Singh was true to his word; and, entering the camp at a time when his arrival would create no particular observation, proceeded to some vacant ground in a field on the west side of it, where, drawing up his men, he bid them dismount, and, without unsaddling their horses, tether them and await his coming.

"What is the uncle about to-night?" said our old friend, Lukshmun, to the kettle-drummer, as the halt was made, "and why do we stop here? He told us we were to go on to Sholapoor, to prepare forage for the Khan's army."

The man laughed. "Ah, brother!" he said, "dost thou not yet understand the uncle's ways? Now, to my perception, as he has come to the west of the camp, we shall have to go east. Home, perhaps, who knows?—the devil,—if this be one of his errands,—as it most likely is. Certain we have something to do out of the common way, else he would not have stayed apart all day nor picked the men and the mares; nor would he have brought you and Rama and the young master. Well, we shall soon see, for he has gone off to the Khan's tents, where a Durbar appears to be going on."

"Yes, he may be waiting for orders," returned the hunchback. "May the Mother give him luck of them;—better luck than we had in that wild ride after Maloosray, when neither mud, nor stones, nor rivers, stopped us; and when we drew breath at the Hórtee pass, you could have heard the mares breathing and snorting a coss off! That was not the way to catch Maloosray! Yes, he had done too much that day; and the blood had got up into his eyes and head," he continued, after a pause, and wagging his head wisely, "but he is cool now; what will he do?"

"Something," said his companion; "what do we care? Now, help me to get these kettles off the mare's back, Lukshmun, else I shall be whipped if he comes and finds them on. Ho, Rama, come and help, brother. What ails thee? art drunk?"

"May thy tongue rot," replied that worthy, dismounting from his mare; "who told thee I was drunk?"

"Well, then, art thou sober? if that please thee better," returned the man, laughing. "But what ails thee? thou hast not spoken a word since we set out."

"No matter, my eyes are blinded with blood," returned Rama sulkily. "What we are to do to-night will be evil. I saw an omen I did not like before we set out, and three hares have crossed us since. Is that good? I tell thee I cannot see in that direction," and he pointed to the west, "for the blood that is in my eyes."

"The sun is bright enough, Rama," said Lukshmun, laughing, "and the liquor was strong, brother. Thou wilt see better by-and-by, when the night falls."

"Peace, ill-born," cried Rama, aiming a blow at him with his spear-shaft; "only thou art my brother I had put it into thee."

"Ill or well born, we came of the same mother," retorted Lukshmun; "as for me, with this hunch on my back, by the gods, thou sayest true. But go to sleep, my friend, and get the blood out of thine eyes; I like it not. He is generally right when he says this," continued Lukshmun to the kettle-drummer. "Yes, we shall have work to do, and some of us may have to sup with the gods to-night. I pray it may not be Rama, for his wife is a devil; and as for his children—cubs of a wolf are easier to manage."

Leaving these worthies to discuss the probabilities of the night, which was also the theme of conversation among the men, we may follow Pahar Singh and his nephew to the Durbar tent; where, seated at its entrance, were Afzool Khan, his son, the Peer, and other officers of the force, enjoying, as it were, the cool breeze of evening; while reports were heard and read, papers signed, and orders given. Carpets had been spread for some: others sat on the bare ground, or on their saddle-cloths, removed for the purpose. All seemed merry, and the Khan's face was beaming with pleasure. He was, in truth, enjoying his old life, and his spirits had risen with it, with the hope, not only that Pahar Singh would not fail him, but in the capture of the chief malcontents of those provinces, that he should strike a deep blow at the root of the widespread Mahratta confederacy.

Pahar Singh and his nephew dismounted, and, advancing, offered the hilts of their swords to the Khan and those near him in succession, and while receiving and replying to their welcome, took their seats among the rest. "Our time will come, Gopal," said the chief; "wait patiently, they will send for us after the evening prayer."

He was right. As the sun set, the assembly broke up. Performing their ablutions, as a priest sang the Azân, or invitation to prayer, they again collected, marshalled by the Peer, who took his seat in front, looking towards Mecca. All present, joined by hundreds of others from the camp, knelt on the ground in ranks, and obeying his movements, rose—bowed themselves—or kneeled, in unison—as the various changes of the Moslem liturgy required. When the service was over, all, wishing each other peace, with the blessing of God and the Prophet, separated for the night.

"Come into my tent," said the Khan to Pahar Singh, "thou art welcome. What of the work?"

"I am ready," he said; "I have two hundred of my best people with me."

"And I am not behind thee; my people are ready also, and wait thy pleasure," replied the Khan.

"Who is this, father?" cried Fazil, who now entered, having remained to speak with some friends. Fazil had not recognized the Fakeer of the King's Durbar, nor the Jogi of the temple; but there was a vague impression on his mind that he had seen the face under other circumstances.

"Pahar Singh, son; dost thou not know him?" he replied.

"A brave youth, the worthy son of a brave sire, may not object to receive the offering of an old soldier," said the chief, putting out his sword-hilt to Fazil, who touched it courteously; "and he shall have his share of the work if he may, Khan Sahib."

"What work? what is this?" whispered Fazil to his father, and taking him a step aside. "Do not trust him—he is one of them—all men say so. He is not true."

"He is as true as I am," replied the Khan. "I have already proved him, and thou wilt know all by-and-by. He has received the King's pardon, and confirmation of all his possessions. Do not doubt him, for he can render important service."

"Enough, father," said Fazil aloud; and, turning to Pahar Singh, "Where you go I will follow; but who will lead us?"

"I will lead one party, and my son here another. Come thou with me, Khan, and send thy son with mine," replied the chief promptly.

"Where are we to go?" asked Fazil.

"We cannot say till we are on the road," said the chief, smiling. "'Thieves,' they say, 'have longer ears than asses.' I have one of my trumpeters here; and when it is time to move, a shrill blast will be blown: till then, eat and make your preparations, as I will mine;" and saluting them, Pahar Singh and his son walked to their horses, and, mounting them, rode away.

"And do we go with them alone, father?" asked Fazil, following the chief with his eyes, and in a tone of apprehension.

"No," said the Khan, "the order I gave for the Paigah and the Abyssinian horse to march to-night to Sholapoor is for this service, and we shall lead them."

"Excellent," cried Fazil joyfully; "then I fear nothing; but who is this Pahar Singh? Surely I have seen him before."

"Certainly, in the Durbar at Nuldroog, when the deed of confirmation was given to him."

"I was not there, father: I heard of it."

"Ah, true! Well, then, dost thou remember the Kullunder Fakeer of the King's Durbar?"

"Protection of God!" cried Fazil; "ay, and the Jogi of the temple. Strange, I thought I had seen those eagle eyes somewhere. I had not forgotten them. Now, father, I will go with him; but tell him not that I was at the temple. He might resent the death of his follower, and recede from us."

"An excellent caution, son; no, he shall never know it."

"What are the Abyssinians getting ready for?" asked the Peer, who came up at that moment. "Some secret service at Sholapoor, as Ibrahim Khan tells me? There is no mutiny, no disaffection, Khan?"

"It is a secret service, my friend," replied Afzool Khan, smiling, "and Fazil and I are going with them; but there is no mutiny, or cause for any, and we do not go to Sholapoor."

"Where, then?" cried the Peer. "Let me come; nay, I will take no denial: whither thou goest I will follow."

"It were better not, Huzrut," replied the Khan; "it will be a rough ride, and perhaps some rough work at the end of it; nevertheless, as thou wilt. Come, sirs, we had need to eat first. Come, Bismilla!"

CHAPTER LVI.

"A DARK night, my lord," cried Pahar Singh, as the Khan and his son, accompanied by the Peer, rode up to a large fire which, kindled by dry thorns from the hedges, sent up a ruddy blaze high in the air as some loose fodder was thrown on it, displaying the tall form of the chief, as he stood there with his nephew and several others, "and ye are welcome; and here are the rest, too," he continued, as the foremost men of the body of cavalry crowded up, the strong light revealing the dark faces of the Abyssinians and the noble horses on which they were mounted. "Bismilla! as ye say, let us mount and depart."

"I have not kept you longer than I could help," said the Khan, "and the men are divided into bodies, as you directed, under their own leaders. With me are some of my people, and the noble Ibrahim Khan himself with his; and I will remain with you as you proposed. The rest of my men go with my son."

"When we get near the place, Khan," said Pahar Singh, "I will give directions. And now, beat the drum, Lukshmun, and do you and Rama look after the guides—you know the road; go on, and beat the drum occasionally to let us know where you are."

"I would it were daylight, father," said Fazil; "it will be no easy matter guiding all those men in the dark."

"Fear not, my lord," cried Pahar Singh, "we shall see better when we are away from those fires, which only blind us. The roads are dry, and your Beejapoor horses don't fear stones. In three hours or more we shall be near the place, then a rest, and some arrangements; and after that you can give your own orders, and we, your servants, can execute them. Come, sirs, we can strike into the road at the end of the field by the trees."

"Shall we have no torch on this unsainted errand?" said the Peer, rather peevishly.

"Huzrut," said Pahar Singh, "this is hardly work for a man of God, and the roads are rough. No; we must manage with what light the sky gives us, for we have to deal with wary people, and 'twere a pity to take the Khan so long a night ride and show him no sport. If you are afraid the road will be too rough, do not come: but ride with the force to-morrow."

"Afraid!" cried the Peer contemptuously. "I, a servant of God, afraid! Astagh-fur-oolla! If there is any work to do, thou shalt see whether a priest cannot strike as hard a blow as a layman. The Khan can bear me witness that wherever he goes I am ever beside him."

"Pardon me," cried the chief, laughing, "I will doubt no longer. I only fear that, in catching thieves, there may be less need for our swords than for contrivance to outwit them."

"And may not we know how, father," cried Fazil, riding to his father's side, as they reached the end of the field, "what this contrivance is, and where we go?"

"To Tooljapoor, my lord," replied Pahar Singh in a low voice, not so as to be heard by the Peer: "a nest of traitors is assembled there, and we need to take them out of it. Keep together, now, I pray ye, gentlemen: I must ride before all for a short distance, and will rejoin ye by-and-by."

"Tooljapoor!" exclaimed the Peer, when Pahar Singh had disappeared, "a nest of idols and thieves, indeed. The haunt of a devil in the shape of an old woman, whom they all worship. I know her, with her red eyes; and when I have seen the idolatrous Kaffirs bow down before her by thousands, I have longed for the sword of our lord the Prophet to be among them. 'Inshalla!' when——"

"Peace, Huzrut," said the Khan, in a soothing tone, interrupting him. "I have promised that the temple and the idol come to no harm, on condition of taking none who are there, and——"

"Well, well, Khan," returned the Peer impatiently. "I am not a Roostum, to slay all the unbelievers myself, or to overturn that abode of devils! Do as thou wilt, friend; do as thou wilt. I will not strike till thou dost—till I hear thy war-cry; after that—'Futteh-i-Nubbee' (Victory to the Prophet) say I!"

"Ameen!" said the Khan dryly, "but I trust there will be no need of it. Come, Fazil, let us turn into the road and keep it, before the main body comes up. Listen," continued the Khan, as they rode on by an open pathway among the fields of tall corn. "His plan is for the town to be surrounded above, and a ravine below to be blocked up. He would give thee the latter work, son, as the people will try to escape thence."

"By the Prophet, an excellent plan," said the priest,—"no better could be devised. A few horsemen across the mouth of the glen will catch all that come out of the temple like fish in a net. I know the place well. No one could get up the sides of that glen at night, —no, not one."

"I would rather go with thee, father," said the young man; "my place is with thee; surely any one could manage below, and if there be danger——"

"There will be no danger, son," he returned: "these people will be caught in their own trap, worshipping their horrible idol, and will be unarmed. I shall keep outside the gates, and watch for the fugitives. Pahar Singh knows the men he wants, and will take his own people and some of the Abyssinians inside. If needs be, we can meet in the temple, but there must be no question in regard to this arrangement, which even the Peer ratifies."

"Surely, my lord," said the priest, "it is the fittest in all respects; and Pahar Singh, considering that he is an infidel and robber, seems a man of some propriety of manner, and is doing our lord the King good service."

"Dost thou remember the cry, 'Ulla dilâyâ to léonga!' and the tall Kullunder who brought the Wuzeer's papers to the Durbar?" asked the Khan; "that was Pahar Singh."

"Ulla dilâyâ to léonga!" exclaimed the priest. "Yes, I remember. 'Puna-i-Khóda!' (protection of God) was that he? Then the night before there was the same cry in the fort as I left the King; could that have been he also? I thought it might have been some drunken Kullunder, as they said it was."

"The night before Khan Mahomed was killed?" cried the Khan and Fazil in a breath.

"Yes; why do you ask?" returned the priest; "it was near morning."

"It was curious enough," said the Khan carelessly, "but those Kullunders are very early; they like to be on foot when the women are grinding at their mills, to get a handful of flour."

"Yes, it was about that time," said the priest unsuspiciously, and the conversation dropped.

It was almost impossible to reunite again; for the road, which was pretty broad and free from stones at first, shrunk to a narrow path, through cornfields on each hand, and it was difficult for more than two to ride abreast with comfort; and sometimes, indeed, that even could not be managed. They passed several villages at irregular intervals, and proceeded without check or halt. Pahar Singh, for the most part, rode in front of his own troop; but returned occasionally to the Khan and his son, who, being between the advanced guard and the main body, were unimpeded by the crowding which elsewhere unavoidably existed.

Whether it was that their eyes had become more accustomed to the darkness, or that the gloom of the first part of the night had relaxed in some respect, it hardly signified; for, without betraying their presence at any distance, there was light enough to distinguish the path; and to follow, without much inconvenience, the men who preceded them. These were, as we know, ignorant of their destination: and most believed it might be Puraindah, or somewhere on the western frontier, where disturbance had occurred.

Those in advance, however, halted at length; and the rushing sound of the trampling of the heavy body of horse, which had continued through the night like a dull hoarse roar behind, gradually grew fainter as the mass of men collected and stood still. The Khan and his son, with the Peer, were speculating as to whether that was to be the place of divergence, when Pahar Singh and his nephew rode up, and at once put an end to the doubt.

"We separate here," he said; "and this, Meah Sahib, is my son who will lead you; you will find him true and intelligent. Do not go to Sindphul," he added to Gopal Singh; "Lukshmun knows the high-road to Rutunjun by Uljapoor, and that will take you close under the pass between Sindphul and the town. Keep in the hollow near the river, and when you hear our shouts above, turn into the ravine, and get up as far as you can. We will give you time before we ourselves move into the temple."

A few words of farewell, as father and son dismounting, embraced each other; a commending of each other to God and the Prophet; and Fazil and his father separated.

The ground on which they had halted was level, and covered with thick corn-fields, which extended, almost unbroken on their left hand, to the south; but on their right, small watercourses and ravines rendered any passage between the road westward and the hills impossible. Where they stood, the hills were low, and a passage or gap in them to the right was pointed out by Pahar Singh as the direction of the main body: in front, they appeared to grow higher, and a bluff termination of one bay, which stood out a dark gloomy mass against the sky, was pointed out by Pahar Singh to the Khan as near the town, and a light which seemed at times to glow in the air about its brow, as the illumination of the town and the temple.

Ibrahim Khan, and several other officers of minor rank, had now joined the group, and in a few words Pahar Singh explained how they were to act. One body would turn to the right close to the town, and guard the roads towards Little Tooljapoor and Bóree; another party would spread to the left, on the plain which led to the top of the pass; the third, which would be commanded by Pahar Singh and Ibrahim Khan, would enter the town and seize the temple gate, where there could be no egress for any one except through it, or the postern below. Up the precipices of the glen, and over the high walls of the temple, escape was impossible.

"Come, sirs," said Pahar Singh, after a delay which, to the Khan, appeared intolerably long; "they are now near enough: follow me;"

and, turning his horse up the pass, the men, taking the direction from those in advance, moved after them as fast as the stony nature of the ascent would allow.

. . . .

It had been a rare night of enjoyment to the crowds assembled in the temple, and attracted by the unusual amount of entertainment, the town itself was nearly deserted by its Hindu inhabitants, who—men, women, and children of all ranks, classes, and ages—had betaken themselves to the lower court, which was as full as it could well be packed: the people sitting in rows, as we have described on a previous occasion, on the ground, or perched upon terraces, the roofs of houses, and upon that of the vestibule.

As the night wore on, and the assembly seemed in no humour to separate, Anunda, foreseeing the confusion which would arise when the ceremonies should conclude with the last procession, had proposed to Tára, as she joined them for a while in their accustomed seat on the roof of the vestibule, to retire before the crush began; but Tara herself was in the highest spirits: she had no fear of Moro Trimmul; he had not so much as saluted her or seemed to notice her. Gunga and the other priestesses had exhibited a flattering deference, assisted her to bring garlands, and danced before her, as the processions passed round the shrine, singling her out as their object of respect—almost of adoration.

Few who had noticed Tara that night—and who did not?—ever forgot the triumphant looks and gestures of the seemingly inspired girl as she moved lightly and gracefully before the priests; or the sweet, thrilling voice, which seemed to rise high above the rest in the solemn hymns and chants of the ceremony. She felt secure in the protection of her father, and even of the other girls, who had besought her to stay till all was concluded; and the last service, more solemn and more meritorious than the preceding, would be at the sacred hour of the moon's change.

"Do thou and Radha go," she said; "it will be well. I cannot leave anything unfinished, else the Mother will be angry, and I shall regret it. I will stay near the shrine, and return with my father."

Anunda did not object, and she and Radha, congratulating themselves upon having left early enough to escape inconvenience, gained the gate of the temple unobserved, and made their way through the deserted streets without interruption. There was no one in the house; all the women-servants were absent at the ceremony. The watchman who guarded the outer door of the house—one of the hereditary Ramoosees of the town—sat with two of his men in the porch, and, when the women came in, asked leave to go and see the last procession, which was readily granted; so they were left alone: but without apprehension.

From the terraced roof they looked out for some time, for the brilliant illumination lighted up the temple spires, and from the large oil-cressets a heavy smoke arose, which, floating above the temple and its glen, caught the glare below, and ascended high into the air; and so still was the town, that the measured cadence of the recitation could be heard, though not the words; while occasionally a burst of music or solemn hymn suddenly broke the silence, which was otherwise oppressive.

Radha heard her brother's voice when his turn came, and listening to it, wept silently. When should she see him again?—would absence cure the madness that now possessed him?

"Weep not, child," said Anunda, throwing her arm around her, and guessing her thoughts; "it is well he goes. When he departs, thou wilt trust us the more, and be dearer unto us."

CHAPTER LVII.

MEANWHILE the rites proceeded, and the recitations. Moro Trimmul was declaiming, with unusually excited gestures and eloquence, the impassioned passages which had been assigned to him, often interrupted by the cries of "Jey Kalee! Jey Toolja!" and the clapping of hands which proceeded from the people whenever a favourite sentiment or allusion to the glorious days of Hindu power occurred in the text. Before concluding his part, which was the last of the night's performance, he had withdrawn to the back of the temple, and beckoned to Gunga, and a brief colloquy passed between them.

There was no faltering in the purposes of either. Gunga had noticed the departure of Anunda and Radha with exultation which she could hardly conceal. She had gone to Tara after she resumed her position at the shrine, touched her feet, and thanked her for remaining. Other priestesses, too, had crowded round her, and, excited as they were, all united in determining that the last procession should be unusually remarkable.

"See," said Gunga, as she came to him, "all is ready. There is no one by the door inside; but try it, and ascertain who are outside. Be thou ready only, and trust to me for the rest. Nay, I will come with thee—look!"

The place was dark, for there was no illumination behind the temple, and by its mass a broad shadow was thrown on the recess in which the door was situated. The girl stepped into it, followed by the Brahmun, and opened the door slightly. A number of dark forms were sitting without on a small terrace, from whence descended a flight of steps into the ravine. One rose. "Wagya!" she said in a low voice.

"I am here, lady," he replied; "is it time?"

"Not yet. When the next procession passes round the corner yonder, come out to look at it; you will not be noticed. Have you the blanket?"

"It is here," he said, holding one up; "and they are all ready yonder," and he pointed to the trees, where there was a dull glow as of the embers of a small fire—"palankeen, horses and all."

"Be careful of her as you carry her out," she continued. "If she is hurt——"

The man laughed. "There is no fear," he said; "she will be carried daintily like a child, and cannot struggle in this."

"Good," she replied; "now be careful, and watch."

"Art thou satisfied?" she continued to Moro Trimmul, who had remained behind the door.

"Yes; thou art true, Gunga. I am true also, and here is the zone; put it on, and let it shame hers," he replied, taking the ornament from underneath his waistcloth where he had concealed it.

"Ah!" she cried, taking it and clasping it round her waist, "thou art——"

"What is that?" he cried, interrupting her and catching her arm; "there is some disturbance without. What can it be? Listen!"

"I will look," she said; "stay thou here."

She turned the corner of the temple, but could proceed no farther. Every one had risen: and there was a wild, struggling, heaving mass of people before her, from among which piercing shrieks of women and children, mingled with hoarse cries of men, were rising fast in a dreadful clamour: while several shots, discharged in quick succession at the gate above, seemed to add to the general terror and confusion.

"They are fighting at the gate!" cried a man near her; and a cry of "the Toorks, the Toorks!" followed in agonizing tones from the women.

Gunga did not hesitate. She, perhaps, of all that crowd, was the most collected. Darting to Moro Trimmul she said hastily, "Do not move—I will bring her;" and so passed round to the back of the temple. As she did so, she met Tara and several other girls, some screaming, others silent from terror, but evidently making for the postern.

"My father! O Gunga, my father!" cried Tara piteously, "come with me, we will find him. Come; I have none but thee, Gunga, who dare seek him; come with me!"

"Yes," she said, "round this way; I saw him a moment ago. Come, we will get down the steps; I know the way up the mountain from below. Come!" cried Gunga with a shriek; and seeing that Tara hesitated, and that people were crowding through the vestibule into the dark portion of the court, and hiding themselves among the cloisters,—she caught her arm and dragged her forward.

Moro Trimmul saw the action, and, unnoticed in the confusion, seized Tara from behind and bore her to the postern. The girl's shrieks seemed to ring high above all others in that horrible tumult, but they were quickly stifled in the blanket thrown over her, while she was borne rapidly down the steps by those stationed there, to whom Moro Trimmul resigned her.

"Thou canst not return, Moro," said Gunga, who had closed and locked the door unobserved and flung away the key; "let us fly for our lives. Hark! they are fighting within, and may follow us."

"O for my sword to strike in once for those poor friends!" cried Moro Trimmul with a groan. "They have been seeking me, and the rest will suffer. What art thou but liar and murderess, O Toolja! that thou dost not protect thy votaries? must they perish in thy very presence?"

"Hush, and come fast," cried Gunga, dragging him down the steps. "Fool, wilt thou die with the rest? Away! mount and ride for thy life; I will bring her after thee."

. . . .

The Khan and his companions, as they had arranged, separated into three bodies as they reached the town; and as they filed off to the right and left in succession, the Khan, with the Peer and others, rode into the gate, and secured it. They had met no one outside the town; inside were a few of the royal soldiery on duty, who, themselves surprised, could have made no opposition, even had the Khan been an enemy.

Down the centre street, which was also empty, except of stragglers coming from the temple, the horsemen poured, now pressing on fast from the rear; and a body of them, dismounting in the centre of the town, rushed forward down the bazar to secure the entrance to the temple. Then some people, who were advancing, saw danger, and hastened to warn those in charge to shut it, turning back with loud shouts, others coming on. A party of the Nimbalkur's men, who were in attendance with their chief's horses, and were around the entrance within, mounted the small bastions at the sides, while others shut the doors.

Those who reached them first were Pahar Singh and Ibrahim Khan, with some of the Abyssinians and other followers, mingled together, each striving to be foremost.

"Open the gate; we mean no harm," cried Pahar Singh in Mahratta; "we are on the King's service, and if you resist, your blood be on your own heads!"

"We will admit no one," cried a voice from the bastion. "Go! ye are robbers, and we will fire on ye."

"I say it again," returned the chief, "we are a thousand men, and I cannot save you if you hesitate. Open the gate!"

There was no reply, but several matchlocks were pointed from the parapet above, which was loopholed.

"Hast thou the axe, Rama?" asked the chief.

"It is here," said the man, drawing a heavy axe-head from his waist: and, coolly fitting a helve to it, lifted it above his head. "Shall I?"

"Strike!" cried Pahar Singh.

Several heavy blows fell on the gate, and a man called out from the bastion, "Desist, or we fire."

But Rama heeded no warning. Again two crashing blows, struck with his full force, had splintered some of the wood-work, and he had uplifted his arm for another, when one of the men at a lower loophole fired. Rama swayed to and fro for a moment, and, falling heavily to the ground, the blood gushed from his mouth in a torrent.

Pahar Singh did not speak, but he gnashed his teeth in fury. Rama, of all his inferior followers, was the one most devoted—and was brave to recklessness. The chief saw that the shot must have been deadly. He might have shared the same fate; but the men without, his own as well as the Abyssinians, returned the fire, and distracted the aim of those within.

"By ——" and the oath was lost in the clamour—he cried, putting his sword between his teeth, seizing the axe, and striking at the door with his whole force, "ye shall die, sons of vile Mahratta mothers. Every one of ye shall howl in hell for that poor fellow."

Blow after blow followed; and as the panel near the lock broke under them, a number of the chief's men and the Abyssinians rushed against the door, which gave way under their combined weight and force, and entrance was effected.

On the noise of the first shouts reaching them, the Khan, the priest, and others, rushed down the street, and arrived at the scene of action. The firing was increasing, and several of the Khan's followers and Abyssinians had fallen. Some were already dead, others wounded; and, wedged as they had been in a mass, every shot had told on them, while those who defended the gate could not be seen. Its being forced, however, changed the feature of the contest; and the Khan, who, in the heat of the excitement, forgot his caution and warning to the men, now shouted his battle-cry; while the priest, struggling in with the rest, cried to the men—"Bismilla!—in the name of God and the Prophet—slay, slay—ye true believers! Heed not death—ye will be martyrs! Let not the Kaffirs live, who have killed the faithful. Send them to hell, to perish with their devil's idols. Kill! kill!"

With such cries, had men of Islam been hounded on by their priests before. Was he to be less? Here, in the very holiest of infidel temples, should the might of Islam be felt.

But, in truth, the men needed but little excitement; what was there before them was enough. Who did not remember that it was a Jéhâd, a war of the faith, which had been preached to them daily? Who did not remember that to slay infidels in war earned the blessing of the Prophet and paradise? So, with Pahar Singh leading them, his sword between his teeth, and striking down men right and left with every blow of his axe, the infuriated soldiery rushed in a body down the steps and into the large court below.

Who can describe the scene? Shrieking women and helpless men strove to fly before them, but in vain; and the bloody work of their enemies, as they pressed forward, hewing with their long sharp weapons at the unresisting masses, was quick and deadly. Pahar Singh saw Nimbalkur and several other chiefs standing resolutely before the entrance to the shrine, sword in hand, awaiting the onset. "Yield," he cried, "your lives will be spared; why shed blood? Jey Rao, be wise, down with your sword;"—and for an instant the parties stood opposite to each other glaring defiance. But bloodshed was not yet to be stayed. Some of the infuriated Abyssinians again dashed into the mass of the people with a shout of "Deen, Deen!" striking indiscriminately at all before them, and the Mahratta chiefs were swept into the temple. As they were followed, Vyas Shastree, who, remembering his old skill in weapons, and unable to control himself, had seized sword and shield and mixed with the rest,—struck at a huge negro who was foremost, and wounded him severely.

"Dog of a Kaffir," cried the man, grinding his teeth, "get thee to hell!" and had not his arm caught that of a fellow-soldier who was near, depriving the cut of its force, Vyas Shastree had spoken no more. As it was, the blow descended upon his bare head,—he fell senseless among the crowd of dead and dying,—and those who entered the temple, trampled over him as one of the slain.

Pahar Singh's object was to save the shrine if possible, but he felt himself helpless against the crowd of Moslems who, headed by the priest, now filled the vestibule, shouting their fanatic cry of "Deen, Deen!" Life was dear to him, dearer than the idol, for which, in truth, he had no particular veneration, though he had dread. "If thou canst not save thyself, Mother," he muttered, "I am not going to die for thee," and, stepping aside, the men of Islam pressed on.

The priest was among the foremost to enter the sanctum, where two old Brahmuns, cowering beside the altar, were instantly slain; and, seizing the necklaces of pearls and precious stones, he tore them away from the neck of the image, with one hand flinging them out among the people, while with the other he overthrew it, and, trampling it underfoot, spat upon the face in scorn and contempt.

If the men in the temple courts, impelled by religious fury, showed no mercy, and, hunting unresisting men and women into dark corners, slew them indiscriminately till the areas were filled with dead and dying, lying in heaps as they had fallen by the sword or had been trampled down; those who had remained outside were, in their turn, no more humane. Under the cry of "Deen, Deen!—for the faith, for the faith!" more cruelty was perpetrated in Tooljapoor than it has ever since forgotten; and daylight revealed a scene of plunder, rapine, and destruction, such as may be conceived—but hardly described.

Anunda and Radha were safe at home, as we have already related; when, after an indistinct murmur, for which she could not account, the shots at the temple gate were suddenly heard; and, looking from the terrace, they saw the confusion in the court commence. Both were brave, but the terror of Anunda for her husband and Tara, was fast paralysing her senses.

"I will die here," she said; "take the wealth and jewels and leave me. Escape as thou canst, Radha; hide thyself, Moro will come and seek thee."

But Radha would not leave her; and, descending to the lower apartments, they sat cowering in their chamber, shivering at every sound, and, having extinguished the light, remained in utter darkness.

"Lady, lady!" cried a man's voice in the outer verandah; "where art thou?"

"It is Jánoo Näik, the Ramoosee," said Anunda in a whisper. "God reward him for coming; he is true; Radha, let us go with him."

"Lady, lady! the house is not safe! come, come," continued the man earnestly; "leave all—my people will guard it—only come. Your honour is more than wealth, and you can only save it by flight."

The terror of violence brought them forth. "Follow me," he said; "here are twenty men to guard the house—no one will molest them."

The women followed silently, sobbing as they went. The Ramoosee led them northwards out of the town to the edge of the great ravine, and descended a steep path, which they knew led to a spring in one of the broad steps or ledges of the mountain, near which was a recess in the rock familiar to both. "Stay here," he said; "no one can see you. I must return: here, I should only betray you."

"At least, take away our ornaments," said Anunda; "we dare not keep them. Keep them thyself, or hide them somewhere;" and the women hastily took off all they wore, and laid them on the ground before him.

Jánoo sat down on his hams, and counted them deliberately. "There are thirteen pieces, large and small, gold and silver together. Yes, they are safe with me. Now, take my blanket, though it be a Mang's; sit in it till daylight. Ye can bathe afterwards and be clean. I will come early if I can, and take ye down the hills to Afsinga, or else send my son."

So saying, and without waiting for a reply, he left them, ascended the path rapidly, and disappeared over the ledge of the mountain; and the women remained, shivering with fright and cold, and listening in terror to the shots, which rose above the confused roar of screams and shouts proceeding from the town.

On the other side, in the ravine, the progress of the band who carried off Tara was but a short one. Struggling vainly with her captors, she found resistance hopeless. Borne in the arms of two men, others held her hands and feet; and over her one of the thick coarse blankets of the common people had been thrown, which prevented cry of any kind. Tara felt that the men were gentle with her, and in spite of her terror, she retained her senses completely. She was aware that she was taken down the steps, and hurried along rapidly at a run; then there was a pause, and she was thrown into—rather than placed in—a palankeen, the doors shut to violently, and kept closed. They were carrying her away. Who could it be but Moro Trimmul, that was to leave that night? Even now her father might hear her screams, and terror lent strength to her voice; but in vain—succour from him was indeed hopeless.

As may be supposed, nothing had prevented the progress of the party under Fazil and Gopal Singh; and the latter, a pleasant companion, had amused the young Khan with anecdotes of his uncle, and of their border life. He knew the ground perfectly, and they soon reached their destination; and while part of his men were drawn up between the rivulet and the pass, and some even ascended the pass itself, he conducted Fazil into the temple glen, which turned to the right out of the main ravine. At its mouth was some level ground, and the horsemen had just occupied it when the attack began above.

It would have been impossible for the bearers of Tara's litter to carry it over that rough path in the dark; and as she had been put into it, a torch was lighted, which was instantly seen by Fazil and Gopal Singh.

"Not a word from any one," cried the latter; "some one is escaping. They cannot get away from us. Now, Meah, be careful."

"Strike, if any one resists," said Fazil to the men about him; "but it is better to take them alive. Look, 'tis a litter—who can it be? Peace, all of you; be silent!"

The gloom of night and some bushes concealed them, and the advancing party saw and suspected nothing. Moro Trimmul was riding in front, Gunga following him. The palankeen was behind with the Ramoosees and servants around it on all sides. The baggage-ponies had already gone on before.

"Stop!" cried Fazil, as he laid hold of the Brahmun, and held his naked sword over him. "Who art thou?—nay, struggle or attempt to escape, and I will kill thee.—A Brahmun? Who art thou?"

Moro Pundit had had no time to dress himself for the journey. His clothes were in the palankeen. Naked to the waist, with his hair streaming about his shoulders, he had come as he had been reciting. He had no weapons, nor means of resistance; and, though a powerful man, was no match for Fazil, who held him like a vice.

"Moro Trimmul, by the gods!" exclaimed Gopal Singh, who recognized him as the light from the torch fell upon him. "Ah, Maharaj!" he added, "you don't know me, but I have seen you before."

"Then we are indeed fortunate, friends," said Fazil joyfully; "and who is in the litter?"

"My wife," said the Brahmun sullenly; "do as ye will with me, but let her and the servants go on."

"Then thou hast married only lately, Pundit?" said Gopal Singh dryly; "thou hadst no wife three days ago. We had as well look at her, at all events, Meah, and prevent her screaming."

"Open the door! release me! release me!" cried Tara from within in piteous accents. "Let me go! let me go! Ah, sirs, for your mothers' honour, release me!"

"Art thou his wife?" asked Fazil, dismounting and opening the door of the palankeen; "if so, fear not, we have no war with women."

"Not so; I am not his wife," cried Tara hastily, disengaging herself from the litter, and throwing herself at Fazil's feet. "O sir, save me! Noble sir, by your mother's, by your sister's honour, save me from him; he would have carried me away. Nay, I will not rise till you tell me you will take me to my father. O return with me and rescue him, else he will be slain! Come, I will lead ye back; he is a priest of the temple!"

"It cannot be, girl," said Fazil, more disturbed by Tara's beauty, and more agitated than he cared to acknowledge to himself. "It cannot be till daylight, and no one will touch your father if he be a Brahmun; so sit in the litter and fear not. And thou art not his wife?" and he pointed to Moro Trimmul.

"O no, my lord," said the girl trembling; "you have been sent by the Holy Mother to deliver me, else he would have carried me away by force. Do not give me to him, I beseech you."

"Fear not," said Fazil; "no harm shall come to thee here. There is more in this matter than we can now find out, friends," he continued to those about him; "but bind that Brahmun on his horse, and tie it to one of your own."

"Ah, sir, I will do that beautifully," cried Lukshmun, "and with his own waistcloth too. But, friends, see that my wife does not run away, while I am busy for the master there—to my mind she is the handsomest of the two."

It was Gunga who, knowing the path, had turned from it when Moro Trimmul met Fazil, and, slipping from her horse, had tried to escape among the bushes; but the quick eye of Lukshmun had detected her, and he had seized and dragged her forward.

"May earth fall on thee, dog!" cried the girl, struggling with him, "foul hunchback as thou art, let me go."

"Not so," he said, "I know thee, Gunga. My lord, she is one of the Moorlees of the Mother up yonder; and are not all women taken in war slaves?"

"Peace," cried Fazil; "sit quiet there, girl; move not, else I will have thee tied. Ah, that will do, friend," he continued, as Lukshmun finished his careful binding up of Moro Trimmul; "you have not hurt him?"

"Master," replied the man, wagging his head, "it is a plan of my own, and while he is helpless to move, he is in no pain. Is it not so, Maharaj? Now sit quiet on your horse, Punditjee, while I look after my wife; she has a noble gold belt, which she has promised me. Is it not so, O lotos-face?"

"My lord," said Gopal Singh, interrupting, "the disturbance above grows worse—had we not as well send the women and others to the rear? If there is any rush this way, they may come to harm."

"A good thought, friend," replied Fazil.

"It is no use," said Gunga, "the door is locked, and the key was thrown away: no one can escape from thence by this road."

So they remained, while the tumult increased to a roar which filled the glen, above which shots were now and then heard; then fell to a dull murmur, and finally seemed to die away in the distant town. The temple lights became dim, and went out one by one, and the ravine grew dark. Then the stars shone out, and after a while dawn broke, and the mountain, and the rugged precipices of the glen and town above, were gradually revealed in the grey light.

CHAPTER LVIII.

A WEARY delay and suspense had been endured till the day broke. Tara had been told, in kind and respectful tones, by the young Khan, whose protection she had claimed, to rest in the palankeen, and he had considerately shut the door to prevent annoyance to her by his men. So she sat undisturbed, but listening to the fearful din from the town and temple, shuddering at every cry and shriek; and when all was at last silent, speculating upon the probable fate of her father, and of her mother and Radha, in a dreamy uncertainty, mingled with extreme terror.

What had happened? That the town had been surrounded by the King's troops there could be no doubt; yet why the violence? Who could the young leader of the party be, by whom she had been arrested, who spoke her own Mahratta tongue so softly and so well? A strange thing, for he was evidently a Mussulman of rank. He had looked so grand and beautiful as the torchlight flashed upon his bright steel morion and silvery coat of mail. She had never seen aught like him before. He might resemble the god Ramchunder, she thought, when he went to battle with the demon Rawun; and she shut her eyes at a vision at once so beautiful and so terrible. Her gentle mind was all confusion, mingled with dreadful and undefined anticipation of misery; yet one thing was clear, she had been saved by that noble youth from Moro Trimmul and Gunga's united design—saved from worse than death.

The torch carried with her palankeen had been extinguished in the surprise, but the torch-bearer had been detained, and she could see him sitting near the litter pouring a drop or two of oil upon it now and then to keep it alight, yet without flaring. Once it did blaze up, and revealed for an instant the faces of the bearers sitting on their hams in a group, and the horsemen with Fazil in his bright armour standing around them; but all were strangers, else she would have spoken again—anything to divert her brooding thoughts and misery.

As the grey light of dawn increased she could see, through the small Venetian blinds of the litter, that the royal horsemen stood in groups at a short distance, all with their swords drawn. One party watched Moro Trimmul, who, tightly swathed in a cotton sheet so that he could not use his arms, sat upon his horse, which was tied to another. Gradually she could see his features, gloomy and stern; savage, indeed, as he writhed in the bandage which he was powerless to remove. Near him, on a strong pony, sat the girl Gunga, covered with a coarse white sheet, which had been thrown over her. A short stout man was holding her pony's head, and his own horse stood beside her. Around were the soldiers, all mounted, and apart from them their young leader, on a powerful white horse, which stood still, tossing its head, and champing its bit occasionally.

Past this figure, upon which her eyes rested wonderingly, as the growing daylight revealed it more fully, she looked up to the glen, and temple, and town, where all was still—a silence she thought like death. The usual sounds of waking life, the music at the temple, which always played as daylight broke, the earliest morning hymns, and clash of cymbals, were all wanting. They were at the mouth of the glen in a small paddock, near an old temple; she knew the place perfectly, and many a time had wandered there with her mother, or, with other girls, in search of flowers, and pieces of frankincense from the ancient trees which grew among some ruined walls. If the service in the temple had not been interrupted, it would have been proceeding at this hour, and the sound would come clearly to the place where they were; but the stillness was not broken. The men about her occasionally conversed in low tones or in whispers, but were for the most part silent.

It was now light enough to move, and the young Khan, calling to the bearers, bade them take up the litter and proceed. They were about to do so, when Tara again renewed her piteous appeal to him.

"O do not take me away!" she cried, "O release me! I can find my way up the mountain. My father was in the temple; my mother and all my people look for me. O noble sir, what am I to you? let me go; by your honour, do not deceive me!"

"Not so, lady," said Fazil, stooping from his horse towards the litter. "It is not fit for thee to go alone after last night's disturbance; and there are rough folk up yonder, for whom I will not answer with one so fair as thou art. No one ever relied in my honour that was deceived. Still trust, lady, and I will see thee safe amongst thy people; fear not."

"O noble sir," said Tara sobbing, "I do trust, I will trust; but O, give me not to him yonder, who is bound. He would have carried me away, and dishonoured me. O sir, you have been my preserver from this danger, and I kiss your feet. My father is Vyas Shastree, the chief priest of the temple, and we are well known. Take me to him, or send for him, and he and my mother will bless you. O noble sir, deceive not a helpless girl!"

"Vyas Shastree!" cried Gopal Singh, who had overheard the latter part of Tara's passionate appeal; "then this, Meah Sahib, is his daughter Tara, the strange new Moorlee; so beautiful that they say she bewitches all men who see her. Art thou not she, O girl? art thou not Tara, the Moorlee? Speak truly."

"I am Tara," she replied, "but no Moorlee. I serve only in the temple."

"It is a lie," cried Gunga sharply; "she is a Moorlee, and one of us; do not believe her. Was she not dancing in the temple when the disturbance began? He carry her off, Meah Sahib?" she cried to Fazil Khan, pointing to Moro Trimmul. "I tell you we had all arranged to go together, and because she is more dainty than I am, he got a palankeen for her."

"Peace, girl," cried Fazil; "be not shameless."

"O noble sir," exclaimed Tara, interrupting him, "heed her not; what matter what she says? only take me to my father, then you will know the truth. Indeed, indeed, I am no Moorlee like her; and forgive me for saying so much, but you are kind, and so I speak."

"Who is this girl?" said Fazil sternly to Moro Trimmul. "What art thou doing with her? Is she Vyas Shastree's daughter?"

"I give no answer; find out for yourself. Why do you ask of me?" replied Moro Trimmul sullenly. "Cut me to pieces, but you get no speech from me."

"It is no use, Meah, asking him," said Gopal Singh; "let us take her up into the town, and see after her people."

"Not yet," returned Fazil. "My father will most likely encamp at that village yonder, among the trees. Let these persons remain here, and we will go and see what they have been doing in the town. Stay thou here, Shêre Khan, with the men. See that no one disturbs this girl; keep the others apart, and wait for us by the trees yonder. Fear not," he continued to Tara; "I will bring news of thy people; keep close within the palankeen, and no one can harm thee;" and so saying, he turned his horse in the direction of the pass.

"Fear not, lady," said Shêre Khan, a fine old soldier; "he will be as good as his word. Ay, look after him; the bravest, gentlest, most faithful master that ever men served under. Yes, trust to his honour; he will not deceive thee, he is too brave and too innocent for that."

For the time it was a sweet assurance to Tara, and one utterly unexpected; for Mussulmans—or Toorks, as the Mahrattas called them—had hitherto been terrible people in her imagination; but the dread for her father lying at her heart had as yet no relief, and her suspense and terror continued.

Leaving Tara with his party below, Fazil Khan, with Gopal Singh, and others, rode up the pass, as soon as the rugged path could be safely traversed. What had happened in the temple? It was clear there had been some fighting—that Fazil had expected from the Mahratta chiefs; they would hardly be taken without resistance, and there was an undefined dread lying at his heart, that if the fanatical spirit of the men had been aroused by the Peer, some evil might have been done to the Hindu people or to the temple. Again and again he regretted that that holy person had not been sent on to Sholapoor with the main body of the force, and blamed himself for not having foreseen mischief.

Fazil Khan by no means shared the grim detestation of Hindus as infidels, in which his father gloried; and he had been no willing listener to the denunciations poured out against them by the Peer and other preachers, in the sermons on the Jéhâd or religious war, which had been preached at the capital and in camp. True, his father and the Peer, as well as others, resented the mingling, under the green banner of the faith, of Mahratta infidels with Moslems; but Fazil knew them to be good and true soldiers; and his friendship for Bulwunt Rao, and experience of his devotion, had changed the young Khan's feelings very materially. Perhaps, also, Bulwunt Rao's character had, in some respects, softened the Khan's dislike of "infidels," "Kaffirs," as he called them; but on occasions, the old fanatical spirit would break through all restraint, and urge him to deeds for which he had but little remorse. Too justly, therefore, Fazil feared this might have been such an occasion.

They gained the summit of the pass as the sun's rays, rising through lines of cloud which hung over the eastern horizon, spread like a rosy fan into the blue and yellow sky above, tinging the lower lines of cloud with tints of scarlet and gold, against which the dark purple masses of mountain stretching into the plain stood out in bold relief. About the space between the town and the edge of the mountain, some of the Abyssinian horsemen were distributed in groups; while further on were other bodies of men, some mounted, others leading their horses up and down. The Nagarchees, or kettle-drummers of each body, were beating the assembly vigorously, and single men were rapidly arriving from other quarters and joining their divisions. Fazil rode on with his companions, looking for somebody he knew, who might give him news of his father, when, from behind a mass of buildings which formed the corner of a street outside the town gate, a cavalcade approached, led by men of his own Paigah, and in the midst of which rode his father, the Peer, and Ibrahim Khan, the leader of the Abyssinians, accompanied by the tall, martial figure of Pahar Singh.

A hearty greeting ensued from all, and Fazil saw that his father and the Peer were flushed with excitement, while in the severe threatening aspect of Pahar Singh, there was an expression which he could not define, which might be either habitual—the result of the night's fatigue, or something more—perhaps grief.

"Come on, my son," cried the Khan cheerily; "we have ordered up provisions for the men, and can rest here in the Gosai's Mutt, before we ride on to Sholapoor, and get some kichéri cooked, which our friend Ibrahim Khan has promised to see after. Inshalla! we sent many a Kaffir to hell last night before his time," he continued, twisting up his moustaches, "and Tooljapoor will long remember firing upon Afzool Khan's men and killing true believers! but we did not get that Brahmun of Sivaji's,—what was his name, Pahar Singh?—though he was there when we came; and that was a pity. M—M—M——"

"Moro Trimmul," said Pahar Singh, interposing.

"Ay, that was it—thanks, friend; and what hast thou done, my son?"

"I have taken him!—that Moro whom ye sought," returned Fazil, "with two women and their servants."

"Now Alla be praised!" cried the Peer, "that he fell into thy hands, Meah, for that crowns our work; and alive?"

"Alive and unhurt, Huzrut."

"Are you sure it is he?" asked Pahar Singh. "There are as many Moro Trimmuls as there are Tannajee Maloosrays!"

"Your nephew says it is. He, and a humpbacked servant or retainer of yours, both knew him," returned Fazil.

"Yes, uncle," cried Gopal Singh, who now joined the group, "it is the true man; but he is sullen, and will not speak. We have left him below, safely bound; Lukshmun is watching him as a dog watches a rat, and there are all the young Khan's men and ours with him."

"Go, bring him up," said Afzool Khan; "let us examine him, and take his statement."

"Good, my lord; my nephew will go for him, if a Hindu may be trusted," said Pahar Singh, as Fazil thought, with a sneer.

"Certainly," replied the Khan, "let him be brought."

"And the women, Meah?" asked Gopal Singh.

"Not yet," he replied; "let the Brahmun come first;" and the young man, turning his horse, galloped towards the pass.

"What women?" asked the Khan carelessly.

"Two who were with him," replied his son. "I will tell you of them afterwards."

The house they were going to was only a few yards distant; Ibrahim Khan rode on, saluting them as he passed, and they dismounted and entered. "Embrace me, son," said the Khan, before he seated himself, "and give thanks to God for the victory. Alla has been merciful, and has——"

"Yes, he has permitted his servants to do vengeance on the infidels," said the Peer, interrupting Afzool Khan; "the idols of Satan have been overthrown, and their altar sprinkled with the blood of their infidel priests."

"Protection of God!" cried Fazil; "the temple has not been harmed, nor its people, I trust? We had no war against priests, father."

"Not the temple, Meah—not the temple," returned the Peer, rubbing his hands together complacently. "It would take a good deal of gunpowder to blow it up, and we have none; but for the rest, the work was well done. Inshalla! they will not be able to renew their devil-worship; and when the King, on whom be peace, gives permission, I—I, Peer Syud Bundagee—will come and destroy this house of idols, and build a mosque upon it; and true believers will be feasted with cow's flesh slain within its precincts. Ul-humd-ul-illa, who hath given us the victory!"

"Father," said the young man gravely, "is it as he says?"

"Even so, my son, and thank God for it; and I have vowed to give a thousand rupees to the work, in memory of the victory," replied Afzool Khan.

Fazil turned away, sick at heart. What evil might not have been done? more, even, than his fears had anticipated.

"And thou hast no congratulation for thy father, Fazil?" asked the Khan, in a tone of disappointment.

"O father, a thousand that thou art safe through last night," cried Fazil, "and——"

"No rejoicing for victory over the infidels?" asked the priest, with a sneer. "Thou hast a rare sympathy with them, I know, Meah Sahib; is this seemly in a Mussulman?"

"Not with rebels, not with the King's enemies," returned Fazil quickly; "but I never warred against priests and women yet, nor did he. What hath been done, father?"

"Well, son," replied the Khan, "they would not let us in after those Mahratta rebels, and Pahar Singh there broke down the door; meanwhile some of our men had been shot, for they fired first, and Huzrut there cried 'Deen, Deen!' and we all rushed in pell-mell and cleared the court; that is all." He said this apologetically, Fazil thought, and feared to tell the rest.

"Will you come with me, Pahar Singh?" said the young man; "you know the place; I would see it."

"Yes, I will come," said the chief, rising, and sighing as he replied; "perhaps it could not be helped, and yet some things were done which will stir Hindu minds sorely throughout the country. Come, Meah Sahib; it is not a pleasant sight, but I will go with you."

"Keep the prisoner till I return, father," continued Fazil; "I would fain hear what he says for himself."

"If thou wilt go, son, return quickly," replied the Khan, "but I had rather thou didst not. What is the use of it? what is done is done;" and Fazil thought his father sighed.

"I would rather see the worst with my own eyes, father," replied Fazil, "than hear lies from others. Come, sir," he added to Pahar Singh, who waited for him, "I attend you."

"He will be vexed at what he finds," said the Khan when Fazil was gone; "and it will distress his young heart. He has never seen the like, and it requires older eyes, like thine and mine, Huzrut, to look on such sights unmoved."

"Ay, true," replied the Peer; "but one or two battle-fields will be enough to cure him, and methinks he is over-tender to infidels. Well, we shall see what he advises about this Brahmun, for he is clear in council. The man ought to die."

"He will not care about the men," said the Khan, musing abstractedly, "but about the women who are dead; and that loving heart of his mother's which she gave him, will be grieved. God knows I would not have had it so."

"Ameen!" said the Peer, "nor I, Khan. But they were only

Kaffirs after all, and did not Feróze Shah, of blessed memory, make a pile of infidels' heads before the gate of Gulburgah fort?"

Afzool Khan did not answer—he appeared ill at ease: and the priest, taking his beads from his waist-band, settled himself on his heels, with his eyes shut, assuming an attitude of complacent meditation on things divine, as they passed rapidly through his fingers.

CHAPTER LIX.

FAZIL and Pahar Singh went out together into the street. The latter led the way through the gate and along the main streets of the town to its centre, where a busy, motley scene now presented itself. The Amil, or local civil officer, was seated in his Kucheri, or hall of audience, surrounded by a crowd of people to whom he was giving orders for flour, grain, butter, sheep, forage, and the other countless necessities of the force which had so suddenly come upon him. They did not pause there, but turned down the main street leading to the temple, the gilded spires and other portions of which appeared at the end of it, the craggy sides of the glen, and, beyond all, the precipices of the Ram Durra, which were veiled in the blue morning vapour.

Now there was no doubt of what had happened. The pavement of the bazar, worn smooth by the naked feet of thousands of pilgrims and devotees in centuries past, was stained with blood which, as they advanced, was still wet and slippery in many places. Already had the town scavengers begun to wash it away, and were pouring vessels of water on the flags and sweeping them with brooms. A few shops only were open for the sale of flour, butter, and groceries, the owners of which sat within, with scared faces, evidently in the direst terror.

"They lay thick here," said Pahar Singh—the first words he had spoken, "but have been removed, and they are burying them yonder, outside, all together—infidels, as your father would say, and true believers. But stay, Meah Sahib, there is one of my poor fellows lying here in a shop. I thought him dead, but he is alive as yet; let us look at him. A poor fellow," he said, repressing a sob; "a poor hunchback, but he was like a dog to me—not a man. Perhaps he may know me now, or he may be dead; let us see."

Pahar Singh turned to the right into a small courtyard, in an open verandah of which several rough-looking men were sitting beside a body laid on the ground, and partly covered with a bloody sheet. They rose as the chief advanced, and saluted him.

"How is he now, Nursinga?" asked Pahar Singh; "will he live? Rama," he continued, bending over the man, whose eyes were evidently glazing fast, "Rama, dost thou know me—the master?"

The man looked vacantly around, hearing the words, smiled, and felt about with his hands, as if to clutch what it was denied him to see. Suddenly, and as the chief put his own hand into that which sought it, the dying eyes brightened, and met those of his master in a scared, wild gaze at first, but one which softened tenderly into a look of rapt affection. He tried to speak, but it was hopeless; to raise himself by drawing his master's hand to him, and clasping that he had in both his own—but in vain. The lips moved, and Pahar Singh bent his head down to listen. The bystanders could hear nothing; but Pahar Singh said in his ear loudly, "Yes, it shall all be done—all; fear not."

It was enough. Perhaps the man might have lingered a while if he had not been excited; but the old chief's words had suddenly rallied the flickering lamp of life. It had sparkled for a moment, and fell back, dull and smouldering, into the socket; the eyes again glazed, and the clasped hands relaxed their grasp, tried once more to recover it, failed, and fell powerless beside him, and the rugged bronzed features were fast growing into the strange majesty of Death.

"It is no use staying," said the chief, drawing away his hand to brush the tears from his eyes, "he will not know me again. Come, Meah; I, too, am growing a fool. See to him, all of you. If his brother come, well and good; if not, bury him decently, and not with the rest."

"Have you any retainer who is loved and trusted as you would trust a faithful hound?" asked Pahar Singh, suddenly turning round as they were walking out of the court. "Ah! I forget, dogs are impure to you Mussulmans," he continued; "forgive me."

"Nay, no forgiveness is needed," replied Fazil. "Yes, I have one as true and faithful to me as that poor fellow was to you."

"What is he?" asked the chief abruptly—"Mussulman or Hindu?"

"Hindu," replied Fazil; "a Mahratta."

"A Mahratta," cried the chief; "one of the enemies of your race? I marvel, and yet am glad. Yes, be true to him and he will never deceive you; he will give his life for you. Only be true, as I have been to mine. Two in a month," he muttered to himself; "one there, one here; my best and truest. What matter, Meah?" he continued aloud; "sooner or later the message reaches us all. Mine might have come last night, yet I am here."

Was this the old Jogi of the temple of Beejapoor? the sordid lover of gold, the pitiless robber and murderer? A strange contradiction in character as in acts; and now, sobbing as he walked out into the street, Fazil could see that tears were wet on his cheek, and glistened on the grizzled moustache where they had fallen.

"He was shot here," said the chief, pausing at the gate, "while breaking it in with his axe, and the shot came from that loophole. When I got in, the man who fired it died with a blow where he sat, so thou wert avenged, my poor hound. But what use is it, Meah, now my slave is gone? Come; you have already seen enough of this misery, and what is below there is worse. Will you go on?"

"Yes, I will go," returned Fazil. "I would know if one Vyas Shastree was slain, with others."

"Vyas Shastree, Meah!" cried the chief. "Why, he was in the temple. I saw him. Ah, the poor Shastree, I hope not, for I knew him well—a learned Brahmun, sir; indeed come, search for him is at least an object."

It was a terrible sight as they advanced. Why dwell on it? Many bodies had been removed, and all the wounded; but many still remained, men and women together, as yet unclaimed, and there was blood everywhere, glistening and drying in the sun. Near the temple porch were several bodies in a heap. Pahar Singh looked at them all narrowly, but the Shastree was not among them. One of the temple attendants was sitting in the vestibule, weeping in stupid grief; the chief shook him roughly, roused him, and he got up.

"Didst thou see Vyas Shastree?" he asked; "was he hurt last night?"

"He was killed," said the man, "there," and he pointed to the entrance. "He was fighting, and a negro killed him. Ere day broke, they took him up and carried him away."

"Dead?" asked Fazil.

"Dead," said the man,—"quite dead; I helped to put him upon the litter they brought for him, and they have burned him by this time."

"And his wife?" asked the chief, "Anunda Bye?"

"Seek her at her house," said the man, turning away. "She was not here, nor Radha Bye either. His daughter Tara was here, but no one knows what became of her."

It was enough. The Shastree was dead. Another man who advanced from behind the shrine said the same, and Fazil need ask no more. He looked around—the place was slippery with blood, and dark, except for a dim lamp in the shrine. He looked in,—the altar was bloody, and the image, its rich clothes torn and dabbled in blood, lay beneath, on its back, as it had fallen. The dim ray of the lamp fell upon it, upon a few gold ornaments still about its neck and arms, and upon the weird ruby eyes, that seemed to him to glow with a fiendish expression of malice.

"Evil spirit," he said, turning away, "if thou art in being among the devils, thou art at least helpless to rise, or to avenge thyself—lie there for ever. Why does the blessed Alla suffer thy abomination?"

"Come away," cried Pahar Singh to the young man. "Faugh! the place is evil; come—go not near the Mother, she may hurt thee."

"Do you believe in her?" asked Fazil.

"I fear her," was the reply; "she is very greedy and very terrible: she takes life for life, and more besides. Come—we will see after these women: I know the Shastree's house."

Life for life, and more besides! Those words came back with a strange vividness upon Fazil's memory in after times. Then, they but excited a shudder of regret at the superstition which suggested them.

"O that I had come up here, instead of going below!" said Fazil to his companion. "Had I but known the place, I would have done so. O my father, why was this done?"

"It could not have been stayed, Meah. As they say in Persian, 'Shooduni-Shooduni'—what is to be, is to be," returned Pahar Singh; "nay, for that matter, why did I bring your father and his men at all? Some of those pig-headed servants of Nimbalkur's began it by shutting the gate, and killing my poor Rama; and after the Peer Sahib's cry of 'Deen, Deen!' you might as well have tried to stop the Beema in flood as the men. All I could do was to save Nimbalkur and others, while the Peer was pulling down the Mother from her altar, and spitting on her. Aha! holy priest! we shall see who is strongest, the Mother or thee. Bless God for it, Meah, that thy father had nothing to do with that; and when the Peer proposed to send for cows to slay there, he would not have it done."

Fazil sighed. It was not that he feared the goddess Mother, though of her power then, as now, there was an undefined dread among Mahomedans, and ceremonies of propitiation, and deprecation of evil, were often performed privately even among the most strict in religious matters; but he dreaded the effect on the Mahratta people at large. No one could know of the true reason of Afzool Khan's advance on the town; the plunder and desecration of the temple would seem to all to have been the actual purpose; and the deed would produce a shudder of execration, he well knew, from one end of Maharástra to the other.

Thus conversing, they reached the upper gate, where one of the men in attendance on the dying retainer met them. The tears on his face needed no speech to explain them. "He is dead," said the man; "he never spoke afterwards."

"My poor fellow!" exclaimed Pahar Singh. "Ah! Meah, the best swordsman, the best rider—hunchback as he was—the best at all his weapons of all that I have; and the truest heart too, rough and faithful. Well, no matter now. Is Lukshmun there?" he continued.

"No, master, he is not. We have sent for him."

"Do not delay. Bury Rama at once. I do but accompany the young Khan; and then the horn will sound. Be quick."

They passed on, turning to the left, into a street which ascended to a higher level in the town. As they proceeded, evidences of plunder and violence were but too visible. Here a patch of blood on the pavement still wet—there portions of cloths,—brass and copper vessels dropped in flight,—doors broken in with axes, and the interior courts of such houses as were entered in dire confusion—women and men alike, weeping and wailing bitterly.

"This is the Shastree's house, Meah," said Pahar Singh; "enter and see."

There was no one in it. They went to the end of the courts, even to that in which was the temple and Tara's garden, all so trim and neat. The body of an Abyssinian was lying among the flowers, and another of a Mahratta near him. The sacred fire was still smouldering on the altar, and Pahar Singh reverently lifted some logs of wood, and put them on it. Here and there about the rooms were splashes of blood and marks of violence, but none of the room doors were open.

"Their property is safe, Meah," said the chief; "but who are alive, and who dead? There is no one here. Let us ask the neighbours."

They inquired of several. One man said that Jánoo Näik and the town Ramoosees had defended the house and beaten off plunderers; but they knew nothing of the women.

"Come," said Pahar Singh to Fazil, "we lose time here. Let us seek Jánoo Näik. I know him. He will be at the Kucheri, and will know;" and they went.

Jánoo was found, but he had no idea of telling Pahar Singh, the robber chief, and a good-looking Mussulman, where he had hidden Anunda and Radha, who, now safely delivered from their night-watch on the ledge of the rock, had been guided by his son at early daylight over the hill to the village of Afsinga, where they were in safety. Jánoo had returned to his post; and if Fazil and Pahar Singh had opened the kitchen door they would have found five of his men in it, who had watched them narrowly, and were on guard over the house.

To their united inquiries Jánoo had but one answer,—the Abyssinians had attacked the house, carried off the women, and murdered them. "Alas, alas!" he said, pretending to weep bitterly, "they had not even Bramhuns' rites. They were flung into the trench without, and buried with the rest. Alas, alas! and so beautiful as they were. Do ye doubt? Look, here are some ornaments of theirs which I am going to give to the Sirkar," and he showed a small bundle tied up in a bloody cloth, the contents of which chinked as he handled it.

"We can do nothing more, Meah," said Pahar Singh.

"My lord, I ate their salt—why should I tell a lie?" he returned, with a real expression of sorrow. "Go and see if they be in their house." "They are after no good," thought Jánoo; "and if I could only find Tara Bye, the Shastree would give me a gold kurra. At any rate, I have prevented them asking more questions, I think."

"Poor girl," thought Fazil, "she is desolate indeed—father, mother, all dead. Had they any relatives here?" he asked of the Ramoosee.

"None, my lord. The Shastree's elder wife came from Wye in the Concan, they say; and the last one, Moro Trimmul's sister, also from thence. Here there is no one; and I would not tell them if there were," he added to himself. "What do they want with them?"

"We had better go, Meah Sahib," said Pahar Singh. "I will but tell Boorhan-oo-deen the Näib to seal up the house of the Shastree, and guard it from plunder, and join thee at thy father's. Do not wait for me."

Fazil went on sadly. The state of the girl whom he had already rescued from violence, affected him deeply. So beautiful, so strangely beautiful to him, unaccustomed to see the higher classes of Hindu women. "O that Zyna was here," he thought. "She might be a sister to her, and soothe away that grief. Who can break to her what has happened?"

As Pahar Singh had predicted, Fazil found his father and the Peer in the act of dismissing the Mahratta sirdars, apparently with respect; for there was a silver bottle of uttar standing upon a salver, and a tray with betel leaves on it, on the floor, in the centre of the room. Ibrahim Khan and several other officers were sitting around, and the priest had apparently relaxed from his devotional position. A servant took up the salver and tray as Fazil entered, and the chiefs prepared to rise at the signal, as did also the Khan.

"Have we leave to depart, Khan Sahib?" said an elderly man, with long white moustaches.

"Depart in peace," replied Afzool Khan. "I think you all understand now, that it happened inadvertently. 'Shooduni-Shooduni,' you know—what was to be, was to be; and what is done, is done. His Majesty shall hear favourably of your visit to me. Inshalla! he will be satisfied; and all intended fines and confiscations will be averted. Only for that Brahmun intriguer ye had been safe. Did the royal troops ever interfere with ye before? Mashalla, no! Ul-humd-ul-illa. No! Astagh-fur-oolla! No! and never will again."

"And the bounty for restoration of the temple, Khan Sahib?" said the old chief inquiringly.

"Ahem! Good. I will see about it; yes, I have no doubt the King will be merciful. Go in peace," said the Khan decidedly; and, saluting them again, they passed out.

"You see they are satisfied, son," said the Khan quickly; "we have told them it could not have been helped, and they agree. Well, what didst thou see? Did Pahar Singh tell thee how they fired first?"

"He did, father! he told me all, and I have seen all. I pray the merciful Alla never to show me such a sight again. O father, how many houses are desolate and in misery which were happy homes last night before we came!"

"Ameen! my son,' returned the Khan, sighing: "yes, we all say so now. Do we not, Huzrut? But they fired first, and what was to be was to be!"

"And the idol was overthrown; that image of the devil's mother," cried the priest grimly. "Didst thou see that, Meah?"

"I did," said Fazil, "and rejoiced, though those devilish red eyes haunt me still."

"I spat on them, Meah, while they glared at me from the ground," said the Peer savagely; "and I, too, see them still, flashing though the priest's blood which gushed out upon them. But what fear, Meah, what fear? What sayeth the holy book, chapter twenty-second? 'Verily the idols which ye provoke, beside God, can never create even a single fly;' no, nor hurt one either, my son. Wherefore there is no fear—no fear; be comforted."

Fazil thought the priest shuddered as he shrugged his shoulders, and, shutting his eyes, settled himself once more on his heels, and began telling his beads with great devoutness. So a general silence fell among them.

CHAPTER LX.

THE silence was oppressive. The Khan was smoking, and the dull, monotonous gurgle of the hookah went on incessantly, almost irritating Fazil, and provoking him to speak again; but his father had shut his eyes, and puffed mechanically, emitting the smoke through his nostrils, and the priest was evidently absorbed in devotional contemplation. Any interruption would be welcome.

"They have brought up the prisoner," said Ibrahim Khan, a strangely silent man, but good soldier, who rarely spoke to any one. "He is now entering the court door; shall he be ordered in?"

"Ay!" said Afzool Khan, "let him be disposed of before our breakfast. That kichéri, Khan Sahib?"

"Inshalla, it will soon be ready; I will go and see to it," he replied; and he got up and went out, as Gopal Singh, Lukshmun, and some others entered. Moro Pundit was bound as before, with a turban round his neck, the end of which was held by Lukshmun with one hand, while the other grasped a heavy naked sabre. The girl Gunga followed them.

Afzool Khan, the priest, and Fazil looked at the Brahmun from head to foot; but he did not quail, or betray any emotion whatever, except that his broad chest was heaving under the bandage, and his hands, which just appeared below it, were tightly clenched.

"This is Moro Trimmul," said Gopal Singh; "we all know him. He used to lodge here with the Gosais, and they are all here to speak to him. Is it not true, O Bawas?" he continued to some of the household who crowded in.

"It is he, my lord, sure enough," cried several of the Gosais in a breath; "it is Moro Trimmul, who lived here."

"Have ye got his papers?" asked the priest.

"They are most likely in the panniers and bags on the ponies," said Gopal Singh, "or in the palankeen. What matter?—here is the man himself."

"Ask him, my son, if he has aught to say. Ask him in his own tongue," said the Khan. "We would not destroy him unheard."

Fazil put the question.

"I did not intend to speak," said Moro Trimmul, "for I am in hands which know no mercy, and I need none. All who take work like mine are prepared to die at any hour. All I ask of ye is to let this girl go; she is a poor Moorlee who was faithful to me. Let her go, Khan Sahib, with the gold I gave her. As for me, as you have slain many innocent Brahmuns, I am not to be spared, for I have done all I needed, and my mission is ended."

"What hast thou done?" asked the priest.

"Thou art a priest of thy faith," answered the man, "I one of mine; what thou dost and wouldst do for thy faith, I would do and have been doing for mine. Does that content thee?"

"Enough!" cried the Khan, "he confesses. What shall we do with him?"

"Let him die, father," said Fazil solemnly. "He was contriving more evil than you know of, as his face tells,—now look at it as I speak,—yes: and he would have done it too. Let him die."

As Fazil spoke, a grey ashy paleness overspread the Brahmun's face, and a shudder passed through him; but he did not answer, and taking, as it were, a long inspiration, drew himself up to his full height, closing his fingers convulsively.

"Fazil," asked his father, "dost thou say death, my son?"

"I do," said Fazil, "in justice for this man's evil deeds, which have brought misery to hundreds, and will yet cause more."

"Shabash," cried the priest, "Ul-humd-ul-illa! there is good stuff in thee yet, Meah. What sayeth the holy book, chapter forty-seven?

'When ye encounter the unbelievers, strike off their heads, until ye have made a great slaughter.' Yes, let him die."

Afzool Khan mused for a while. The priest's quotation was correct, and his own fanaticism confirmed it. Was he, however, so appalled by the recent destruction of innocent Hindu life, that he hesitated as to this one? or was it in regard to the fact that Moro Trimmul was a Brahmun, and the popular objection to putting such men to death being great, that he now hesitated? Both causes probably combined to influence him.

"I am not going to do it, Punditjee," said Lukshmun to Moro Trimmul in a whisper, "because thou art a Brahmun; but there is no harm wishing thee as sharp a sword as this is. See!"

Moro Trimmul looked askance at the hunchback as he would have done at a reptile, and shrank instinctively from him. They saw his eye wander along the edge of the bright blade from hilt to point; but though he shuddered perceptibly, he said nothing.

Afzool Khan took his chin and beard in his hand, leaned his elbow on his knee, looked furtively once or twice under his bushy eyebrows at the priest and Fazil in turn, but did not speak, and again resumed his position. The prisoner's large bright eyes were fixed on him with an intensely inquisitive and earnest expression, and drops of sweat gathered on his brow and temples; but though his life hung on a word, there was no fear visible, and Fazil could not repress admiration of the man's calm bearing and contempt of death.

"It cannot be, Huzrut, yet," said Afzool Khan at length; "we have much to learn from him; and, after all, son, he was but doing his duty truly and faithfully. If I had sent thee on such an errand, or the King had sent thee, wouldst thou not have done the same? Take him away, put irons on him. He must be sent to the King, and judged at Beejapoor."

"Where thou wilt die under the Goruk Imlee tree like Jehándar Beg," said Lukshmun. "Ah, yes, that was a clean stroke of Rama's; and they don't care for Brahmuns there."

At that moment Pahar Singh entered. "Yes, that is the man," he said, looking intently at the Brahmun. Then turning to his follower, "Go, Lukshmun," he said, "they seek thee. Rama is dead, and thou shouldst go and pour the water at his burial."

"Dead!" cried the man, starting back, and dropping the end of the turban. "Dead! O no, master, not Rama!"

"Go, and thou wilt see," said the chief, turning away.

Lukshmun spoke no word. They saw his broad chest heaving, and he gasped for breath. The shock was too sudden and great, and he fell senseless against the wall. In doing so the gold zone which he had hung over his arm rolled away.

"It is mine," said Gunga, picking it up, and clasping it about her waist. "He gave it me, ask him;" and she pointed to the Brahmun; "ask him; and that fellow would have stolen it. May I go?" she continued, addressing the Khan; "I am only a poor Moorlee of the temple; you do not need me."

"Surely," said the Khan, "we want no women. Go!" and she made a humble salutation to him, and turned aside.

"Is he, too, dead?" asked Pahar Singh, turning to Lukshmun. "They were twins, ye see, sirs," he said to the bystanders, "and his spirit may have gone after his brother's."

But it was not so. Lukshmun had fainted, and revived as water was poured down his throat and a man fanned him with a cloth. He looked about him dreamily; then some one raised him up, and led him away.

"And he?" asked Pahar Singh of the Khan, pointing to Moro Trimmul. "Is he to die? what will ye do with him, Khan Sahib?"

"Not yet; he will go to Beejapoor," returned the Khan, "and answer for his deeds to the King."

"It is just," replied the chief; "he has only done what a good servant should do. He tempted me for his master, as I could have tempted him——"

"That is just what I said," said the Khan, interrupting.

"And he took no man's life," continued the chief, "and the law will spare his."

"The law," interrupted the priest scornfully, "the blessed law is not for infidels, save for their destruction. For what is written in chapter forty-seven——"

"Peace," cried the Khan, who dreaded a dispute between them, "let it pass. I have spared him. Take him away—keep him with the standard of the Paigah, and let no man or woman have speech of him; he can cook his own food."

They led Moro Trimmul away. He said nothing; but Fazil saw a smile of triumph, he thought, flash over his grave features. When they looked for the girl Gunga she had gone also, and was not to be seen. Fazil, too, had disappeared. As the Khan's breakfast was brought, the kichéri and kabobs he loved so well, he washed his hands, and waited awhile for Fazil's return; but able to contain himself no longer, drew near to the smoking dish, and crying, "Bismilla!" he, the priest, and those present, after the necessary ablutions, plunged their hands into the pile of rice, and ate heartily.

Fazil could no longer restrain himself. He had promised the girl he had left below the pass, to get news of her people for her; and, taking advantage of Pahar Singh's entrance, and the confusion occasioned by Lukshmun's fall, had slipped out unobserved. It was but a short distance, his horse was still saddled, and he mounted and rode as rapidly as he could down the hill.

The men were where he had left them, under the trees by the rivulet. Shêre Khan was on foot, standing by the palankeen, pointing to the road and to Fazil as he descended. Some of the men were on horseback, others lying in the shade holding their horses' bridles.

As he neared the palankeen, the old man slowly advanced, and Fazil could see there were tears on his furrowed cheek. He saluted the young Khan respectfully, and put his hand on his saddle-bow.

"I never saw grief like hers," he said, "nor such fear, nor misery, at your delay. 'Why did he go?' was all she could say at first—and since I soothed her, she has cried the more—'Why doth he delay?' Once I persuaded her to go and wash her face at the river and drink water, and she did so, and was the better of it. And, O Meah! she is so beautiful! Even our rough men say she is a Peri, not a woman. Speak gently to her, Meah."

Fazil dismounted and walked on. A large space had been left about the palankeen, and no one had intruded upon Tara. Towards the rivulet the doors were open, and she was sitting on the edge of the litter, but with her feet on the ground without, and her face buried in her knees. She did not look up till the young man was close to her; then, with irrepressible emotion, she threw herself at his feet.

"O take me to them!" she cried piteously—"take me to them! they are waiting for me, they are looking for their Tara! O sir, they will not rest, or eat, till they know I am safe. Let me go—take me to them. Why am I detained? I have done no evil!"

"Rise," said Fazil, "rise—I may not touch thee to raise thee up; but Alla has laid a heavy hand on thee, and thou must listen to true words, though they bring thee such affliction as thou hast not known in thy young life."

Tara raised herself to her knees and looked up. O, the misery of those great eyes in which were no tears—red, dry, and glistening: while the sweet features quivered under bewildering anticipations of what was to follow. Fazil could not bear to look on her, and turned away. "Would there were any one else to tell thee but me," he said, "it would be well."

"Speak," she replied calmly, "there is no deceit in your tongue—he whom you left with me says so; he told me you would not deceive me, and this suspense is terrible, do not prolong it—speak. I will listen."

"Nor will I," returned Fazil; "sit down as thou wast, and may God keep thy heart, as I tell thee of thy misery. Yesterday there were a father, a mother, another wife, and thyself, in a happy home. Now three are gone, and thou art here."

He saw her, as he spoke, clutching nervously at her throat, which was heaving convulsively, and trying to swallow; and ere he could complete the sentence she had fallen sideways from her seat against the door of the litter, and lay there, powerless, for an instant. His habitual respect for women would have prevented his touching her, but she was so helpless that he raised her up, and, taking a pillow from the inside of the palankeen, placed it behind her, supporting it with his arm.

Gradually she seemed to recover a little. "Dead," she said gently, "all dead! O Holy Mother, why is this? Why am I not taken too?" and she shuddered, and cowered down, shrinking from him.

Fazil thought the truth might rouse her, and he was right. He dreaded her becoming insensible.

"Yes, so it has pleased God," he said. "Thy father was killed, fighting in the temple; and in the confusion afterwards, robbers attacked the house where your mother was and the other, and they also died."

"No—no, it could not be!" cried Tara, quickly and eagerly. "Jánoo Näik would be there; he would fight for them and protect them."

"Jánoo himself told me this: he told me he saw them dead—two women, very fair, the elder Anunda, and the younger wife, Radha Bye. Some of Jánoo's people are killed in the house, and he could not save them. Thy father?" he continued, as he saw her lips apparently moving, though the word was not spoken. "Yes, two men, priests in the temple, Khundoo Bhópey and Rama Bhópey—I asked their names—who lifted him upon the litter in which he was carried away, said he was dead and already burned. What can I do with thee or for thee now?" he continued. "Speak, and I will do it, lady, truly and faithfully."

"Is it true?" she asked dreamily, and with a rough husky voice, and staring at him with those great scared eyes. "The Bhópeys would not tell lies."

"I swear it by the dead, it is true," replied Fazil. "I have neither rested nor eaten till I found out the truth. Had there been any one, even a servant, I would have sent for thee. Jánoo told me there was no one belonging to thee in the town, no relatives;—and the Brahmuns are all fled. Men say they will not return to a polluted shrine, and Jánoo Näik and others said you had relatives at Wye, where we are going."

"Yes," she said calmly, and as if echoing his words, "there are relatives at Wye. Sukya Bye is there—and—no matter. Yes. I will go there—let me go."

"My mother and sister will be with us," added Fazil, "come to them. Zyna will be a sister to thee, and no harm shall come nigh thee. I would use no force—it must be of thine own free will; but the town yonder is filled with dead and dying, the temple is desolate, there is no one of thy people alive, and thou wouldst die of fear and sorrow. Come with us; Shêre Khan will take care of thee, as of a daughter, till we reach my sister. I will not come nigh thee, but he will tell me of thee. O lady, I am not false! I am a stranger to thee; but Alla threw me in thy path, when else, dishonour was before thee. From that, at least, I saved thee, and thou knowest it."

"Who art thou?" she said gently; "yes, I was saved from worse than death—who saved me?"

"I, Fazil, the son of Afzool Khan of Beejapoor," he said.

"They say Pathans respect women's honour," she returned, rousing herself. "A poor orphan girl will not be without pity in your sight. Ah! sir, I am sorely bewildered now," she continued, beating helplessly with her hands on her lap. "I cannot think or speak, and my heart is dried up; but he told me—that old man—that you were true, and they loved you, all of them!—and so be kind to Tara, and do not deceive her; she will die soon, and go away, and will trouble you no more."

"By Alla! by my sister's honour! I will be true to thee, O lady!" cried Fazil earnestly; "truer than thou canst now think. Enough; when thou art with Zyna thou wilt know all; till then thou wilt not see me. Call the bearers," he continued, to Shêre Khan; "take her on to camp, wherever it is; get guides from the next village yonder. Procure her food by the way, if she will eat. Here are twenty men with the litter; they will take thee into Sholapoor. Hark!" he continued to the men as they approached, "take this palankeen into Sholapoor at once, and ye shall have fifty rupees from Afzool Khan. Fear not, lady!" he said once more to Tara; "thou wilt be Shêre Khan's daughter till thou art with my sister." Then, mounting his horse, he rode rapidly up the pass.

Tara followed his figure with her eyes, and her heart went with them. He was so kind, so gracious, and so beautiful. She could not realize the fact of her sudden misery and desolation, and yet she could not doubt it. As he disappeared behind a turn in the road, the sense of that desolation became more acutely painful. But she had no time for thought. Shêre Khan rode up, bid her shut the doors of the litter, and told her he should not leave it; and a moment afterwards she felt it was taken up, and carried forward at a rapid pace, while the old soldier caracoled by her side, and the horsemen spread themselves around her, to screen as well as to protect the conveyance in which she lay.

CHAPTER LXI.

Fazil Khan rode rapidly up the pass, for he knew his father would await his coming ere he gave the final orders for the march. Truth to say, he was hungry enough, and a breakfast upon Ibrahim Khan's kichéri and kabobs would be very welcome. As he reached the top, a busy scene presented itself. Wherever he looked, little fires were lighted between three large stones, upon which the small cooking-pans used by the men, and carried in their saddle-bags, were placed; and the savoury smells which issued from them, and pervaded the air, proved that the stews and curries within were in very satisfactory progress, and were certainly very provocative of appetite. While one member of a small mess watched the pot, others were kneading dough, or patting out "chupatees" or unleavened cakes, with their hands, and baking them on their "towas" or iron plates. Hundreds of these operations were going on simultaneously in every direction; for the force had a long day's march before it to Sholapoor. There would be no midway halt, and men and horses must alike be fed. Everywhere, too, the merry laugh, the broad joke or banter incidental to camp life, resounded among the rude soldiery, and the cries of sellers of milk, curds, firewood, and fruit, mingled with them pleasantly.

Already was the scene of the night before forgotten. The dead for the most part had been buried out of sight; and if grief and misery sat at the heart of many a household in the town—mourning for relations slain, or property plundered or destroyed,—in the camp without, no such feelings existed among the fierce and fanatical men. A grim satisfaction prevailed at having defiled one of the holiest shrines of the Dekhan, plundered its property, and slain its priests. To all, the night's events had been those of ordinary skirmish and excitement: forgotten with the next petty cares of life, and anticipation of new scenes of adventure,—and possibly of new plunder.

"Where hast thou been, Meah Sahib?" cried one of a knot of his own men, whom he met almost as he reached the plain above the pass. "The Khan Sahib has been searching for thee, and is anxious. Ah! when wilt thou learn caution, and take some of us at least with thee? Remember this is not Beejapoor, and the people are not in good humour after last night. Any fellow with a gun behind one of those rocks——"

"Thanks, friend," said Fazil, interrupting him. "I did but go to Shêre Khan and the rest of them below, and tell them to precede us; but thanks for the caution nevertheless. Now, get ready soon, for I shall not be long away from ye," and he cantered on to the town

Giving directions for a led horse to be accoutred for him, in lieu of that which had carried him through the night, Fazil entered the Mutt where he had left his father, and found him girding himself for the journey.

"Where hast thou been, son? we could not wait; but they have kept the kichéri hot for thee, and the kabobs are good; only they have too much pepper and garlic in them. The Khan's cookery is not refined, my son: not like thy mother's. Inshalla! she will have a famous dish ready for us this evening, for I am going to send on a camel. Hast thou any message?"

Fazil knew by his father's volubility that he was in good humour. The flurried, anxious expression of his face had departed, as well under the influence of a hearty breakfast as owing to the feeling that, under the circumstances, he had really done his best to smooth over the events of the night. It was unfortunate, certainly, that they had happened; but it could not be helped now. A donation from the King would soothe the Brahmuns. So he had again sent for the local Näib, and charged him to assure all of his sympathy and sorrow. Afzool Khan had taken advantage of the Peer's absence to do this, for in his presence he would have feared to commit himself by expression of any consideration for infidels.

"I did but ride down the pass, father," replied Fazil, "to speak with Shêre Khan, and send him on to camp. They will halt by-and-by, and refresh themselves. Yes, truly, something to eat will be welcome; therefore, sit down and rest. We have a long ride before us."

"The camel is ready," said the rider of it, entering. "What are your orders?"

"Write a line from me to thy mother, Fazil," said the Khan, "to say she is to have kichéri and kabobs ready for us, and that we have won a victory with little loss. That will cheer her, and put her in mind of old days, and we shall have a glorious dish. Inshalla! we shall be hungry, son!"

Fazil wrote what was needed to Lurlee, and added, on separate paper, a few lines to Zyna, to take care of Tara on her arrival. There was no time to write her story, but she would hear particulars from Tara herself. "Take this at your best speed," he said to the man. "Give it into the hands of Goolab Daee, and tell her it is for my sister only. You will overtake Shêre Khan by the way. Tell him to stop where he likes, refresh the men and horses, and push on. It is of moment that he should arrive before us, and he is already far beyond Sindphul."

"Good," replied the man; "your orders are on my head and eyes, and shall be done." In a few moments more, the clash of the bells of the animal he rode were heard as he started, and then died away in the distance.

What was best to be done?—to tell his father of Tara's being sent on under escort of the men, or to leave explanation about her till they reached Sholapoor? Fazil thought over this as he ate, and he ate heartily what was brought, and did justice to it; while his father sat and looked on approvingly, or told his son of what had been done to assure the people, and what he would do, in spite of the Peer, to obtain a donation for the temple. "Yes, it will be better to tell him," Fazil thought. "He will not object, as he is in this complacent humour, and we are alone."

"I had no opportunity of speaking, father, before, else I would have told you," he said, after he had washed his hands and sat down.

"What!" interrupted the Khan, who detected a tone of embarrassment in Fazil's voice—"what has happened? Didst thou lose any men? Who is dead?"

"No, no, father, we had no fighting," replied Fazil. "All I had to say was, that I sent the lady we took, with Shêre Khan. She had a palankeen, and the bearers said they would take her to Sholapoor at once. There were twenty of them, and it is only twelve coss."

"A lady, son! Who?" he answered in an indifferent tone.

"A Brahmun girl, father, of rank. She was escaping in a palankeen, and we took her when we took Moro Pundit."

"Indeed! His wife perhaps?"

"No, father; she said not. She has nothing to do with him; but she was in such grief at her people being killed in the town, that I could only make out she had relatives at Wye, and I sent her on under Shêre Khan. As she was richly dressed, and had valuable jewels on her, I feared to send her back, and she was willing to go."

"Poor girl, poor girl," said the Khan, sighing; "and she is young, you say. Alas, alas! to be so soon a widow!"

"Quite young, father—sixteen, perhaps—and very beautiful. O, so beautiful! I never saw one like her before."

"Wonderful!" returned the Khan. "Then she let thee see her? . . . Ah, Pahar Singh, well, so you are already prepared," he exclaimed, as the chief entered the room suddenly, and saluted them. "Have you eaten? Are your people ready? We go on to Sholapoor."

"I am come to bid you farewell, my lord," said the chief. "I have done my work with you for the present. My duty is not with the army, but on the marches; and I hear of a raid by the Golconda people which I must see to. My nephew Gopal Singh would fain have accompanied your son, but I cannot spare him. He is my only stay since—since . . . . no matter. My men would be worse than useless to you, and you will not miss what I could send. Nevertheless, if——"

"No, no," said the Khan, who in truth had dreaded rather than desired Pahar Singh's company, and that of his lawless freebooters; "no, you are better here in your own country, and I have already weakened the force too much at Nuldroog to withdraw you."

"Then we may go, Khan?"

"Certainly; you are honourably dismissed with thanks, and mention will be made of you, when I write, as you deserve."

"I have only one thing to say, Khan Sahib,—and I pray you to pardon my saying it,—and that is, beware of Moro Pundit. Had I been a Mussulman like you, I had not spared him: but as you have done so, it is not for me, a Rajpoot, to be concerned in a Brahmun's death. He is faithful to his cause, and he cannot be true to you."

"He can do no harm, friend," said the Khan, laughing. "I fancy the Nimbalkur and others have had a good lesson, and will keep quiet; and, for the rest, as I am going to scotch the head of the snake, we need not fear if its tail writhes a little; it can do no harm: but I thank you for your caution nevertheless, and you will see to my people of Afzoolpoor and its villages?"

"Surely, Khan Sahib; be under no apprehension—nothing can molest them. Now, put your hand on my head once more, embrace me, and let me go."

"Go," said the Khan, rising and doing as he wished—"go; be careful, friend; remember the royal clemency, and be true."

"Will you come with me for a moment, Meah?" said Pahar Singh, as he disengaged himself from the Khan's embrace.

Fazil got up and followed him. As they emerged from the courtyard into the street, Fazil saw that Gopal Singh and others, ready mounted, awaited their chief, and they saluted him courteously.

"Come hither, Lukshmun," said the chief.

The man was well mounted, and advanced. Fazil saw that his cheeks were wet with tears, and his eyes red and swollen. Hideous as the face now was, there was a dignity of sorrow in it which was not unimpressive.

"Meah," said the chief, "this is a foolish slave of mine, who implores me to send him with you; he wants no pay,—only food and clothes, and forage for his horse. He will be faithful to you in all danger and trial, and knows no fear. When you return from the campaign, send him to me again. Do you accept him?"

"I do, Pahar Singh, and will be to him as you were, that I promise," replied Fazil.

"Then dismount and kiss the young Khan's feet," said the chief.

Lukshmun obeyed him, dismounted, and prostrating himself before Fazil, embraced his knees. He then did the same to his master, lying at his feet, and sobbing bitterly.

"Get up, fool," said the chief kindly, drawing the back of his hand roughly across his eyes. "Go, thou art safer with him than with me, go! Take him, Meah," he continued, putting the man's hand into Fazil's, who raised him up. "Take him; he will be to you the faithful hound he was to me and my boy yonder: we can ill spare him, but, after what has happened, he is better away for a while. And now, sir, we part. Remember what I said to your father, and that while Mahrattas are weak they will be treacherous. I wish you well; in the words of your people, 'Khôda Hafiz.'"

So saying, the chief mounted, caused his spirited horse to execute several caracoles and plunges, and, with his nephew and followers, rode off rapidly to the plain beyond, where the shrill horn and deep drum of his troop were sounding the assembly.

"Had it been thus if you knew me, Pahar Singh?" thought Fazil, as the last of the rough troopers passed round the corner of the buildings to the plain beyond. "Hardly, I think; but it is well as it is, and your goodwill is better than your spite." As he turned round he saw the hunchback beside him. The bridle of his horse was hooked within his left arm; his hands, joined together, were raised to his nose, and he had balanced himself on his left leg, with the sole of the right foot pressed against the calf of the left. His grotesque features were twisted into a curious expression, in which grief and joy struggled for mastery.

"Your name is Lukshmun?" said Fazil.

"My lord, it is; I am your slave now and for ever:—till I die, if you permit me to serve you in my own way."

"And that is?"

"No matter now," said the creature; "you will find out. If I displease you, I will go away of my own accord and give no trouble; if I please you, let me be near you, and that is enough."

"How is this? You talk like a woman."

"Do you know anything of them, master?" replied the man. "Perhaps not; it takes a long life to know them, they say. Do I talk like a woman? Ah no, sir; to me you are the woman who has bewitched me, and I follow you blindly for the sake of the love I have for you, which sits in my heart."

"Since when, friend?" said Fazil, laughing.

"Since last night, when you were kind to that poor Brahmun girl who owes her honour to you, and long before that, of which I will tell you another time. Can I do anything now?"

"Hast thou eaten?"

"Yes; and I have enough here to last me two days," and he pointed to a bundle of cakes tied at his back. "I can give you one if you like, when you are hungry."

"I do not want it—I have eaten," said Fazil. "Can I trust thee already?"

"O, master!" cried the man piteously, as the tears started suddenly to his eyes. "Do not say that! I am a poor hunchback, who cannot say fine words, what is the use of my talking? If you mistrust me, bid me go. I will return to him who gave me to you—better that, than be doubted. Enough, shall I go?"

"No, stay," continued Fazil; "I will trust thee. Tie thy horse there, and give him some fodder from the bundle yonder. . . . That is well. Now go to the Kucheri; say to the Näib, that Fazil Khan Meah wants the bundle of things given to him by Janoo Näik, and he is to give it."

"And what if Jánoo is there, master? he will not allow it."

"That is why I do not go myself," said Fazil; "but if there is any difficulty I will come. Show this as a token, and it will suffice," and he took off his signet-ring.

"I will bring them without this, Meah, and yet I take it. Tell some one to mind the mare, else if she hears the horn she will break her rope;" and the man, throwing his coarse black blanket over him, shambled off at a quick pace towards the town. It was but a short distance. Fazil waited there looking at his own horses which were picketed in the street. He had no desire to rejoin his father, who was quietly smoking within. Fortunately, too, the priest rode up; said he wanted a hookah, dismounted, and went into the Mutt. He would be company enough.

Fazil watched the street narrowly. Had he done right in sending Lukshmun—ought he not to have gone himself? He could yet go if there were refusal, but there might be no occasion. In a little time, less then he had supposed possible, he saw the hunchback coming up the street at a sharp run, and as he reached Fazil, he put into his hand a heavy bundle of what felt like ornaments of gold and silver, tied in a cloth which was spotted with blood.

"Shabash!" cried Fazil, "it was well contrived. How didst thou get them?"

"Jánoo Näik is an ass, and the father of all the asses in Tooljapoor. I know him of old," returned Lukshmun. "He was there sitting like a scared owl on the steps of the Kucheri. 'Come and drink,' says he to me. 'I will,' said I; 'wait, I have a message from the master to deliver.' Then I went in, and said to a Karkoon, 'Give me what Jánoo gave just now, the people are come for it.' He could not go in there, for he is a Mang. 'Take them,' says a Karkoon, opening a box; 'I don't like to touch them, they are bloody.' So I took them out, master, and here they are. As I passed Jánoo, I gave him a rupee, and told him to go to the Kullal's and get some drink ready, while I delivered my message—and he is gone. O, the owl, the owl! he will be drunk by this time; but, master, that man is as true as steel, and put these in trust; they were not loot to him. Wilt thou sell them here? No, not here?"

"Sell them!" cried Fazil, laughing; "no, surely—why?"

"O, the master never does—he always keeps the gold and silver, and buys them at his own valuation; but he gives us a share, nevertheless, and I shall miss mine of last night's work:—better, however, that the women have it."

"Ah! friend, I fear thou wilt have no such luck with me," returned the young man. "That is no loot, however; it will only go to its owner."

"Ah, Meah, I understand now,' said the man quickly. "Yes, for her. Poor child! poor child! and when she sees the blood!—better throw that cloth away, and tie them up in a clean handkerchief."

"No," said Fazil, "keep it. It is evidence of the worst, and she needs to know it; but let us count them. Thirteen, you see, gold and silver; and look, there is blood on these anklets—let it stay. Yes, now I will trust thee."

Just then the Khan and the priest came out of the court, both accoutred for the march.

"I was seeing to the horses, father," said Fazil, in anticipation of his father's remarks, "and questioning this gift of Pahar Singh's; look at him—a strange being, is he not?"

Lukshmun advanced, prostrated himself, kissed the Khan's feet, but said nothing. The priest was acknowledged by a distant but respectful reverence only, and the hunchback seemed to regard him with antipathy.

"Strange enough, son," said the Khan, looking at him from head to foot: "ask thy mother about his horoscope when we get to camp. He may be lucky, after all—these hunchbacks often are so."

"My lord," said Lukshmun pleadingly, joining his hands, "all the Brahmuns like to try their hands on my nativity, and they all say I am lucky. For I am a twin, and they never could make out exactly which of the two was the eldest born; but they believed Rama was, who was always unlucky, and had a bad wife and worse children, and he was shot yesterday; so the bad luck and bad stars —sun and moon, and all—went with him; and now your slave is the luckiest of men, since he is the property of the noble Afzool Khan and his son Fazil. Surely the stars sent him."

"Thou hast a bold tongue," said the priest. "Peace, be silent."

"Ah, Maharaj!" returned the man, "holy men like you and the Brahmuns think too much upon divine glories, to mind what a poor fool like me says. I, too, know my prayers already, and shall become a Mussulman, when I have heard a few more of your reverence's sermons. O, they are wonderful! Bismilla—ir-rahman-ir-raheem!——"

"Come," said the Khan, "they are beating the Nagaras everywhere, and as all are ready, we need not delay." So, mounting their horses, which were being led about, they rode on to the plain where the men were assembling fast, and closing in heavy masses upon their several standards. In a few minutes, the Paigah of Afzool Khan, Moro Pundit being in the midst closely guarded, moved on down the pass, followed by the Abyssinian cavalry; and their bright steel morions, gay scarves, trappings and standards, gleamed in the blazing sunshine. Yet it was not hot enough to be oppressive; a fresh westerly wind had arisen, driving before it large masses of fleecy cloud, which, as they passed, threw broad chequers of light and shade over the plain, rustling among the tall ripe corn, which bowed before it in golden wavy ripples, and refreshing the men who, though few had slept, were as yet unconscious of fatigue under the excitement they had gone through.

The people of the town watched the long line, that, owing to the rough nature of the road, straggled down the pass, with thankful hearts for deliverance from further molestation; and as the last of the men disappeared behind a shoulder of the mountain, a faint shout of "Jey Kalee! Jey Toolja!" rose from a group of men, consisting of the Nimbalkur and other chiefs who were assembling at his house. Others clustered about the edge of the tableland, and when they saw the long line emerge upon the plain beyond the groves and gardens of Sindphul, and heard the loud booming notes of the Nagaras growing fainter in the distance, many a heart breathed a prayer of thanks for deliverance, intermingled with defiance and deep curses on those from whose violence they had suffered.

In the temple a group of priests were sitting about the shrine weeping, and the image of the goddess still lay on its back, the ruby eyes flashing in the glare of the lamps now lighted about it. No one, as yet, dared to touch it, without some preliminary ceremonies of deprecation of her wrath. Within, the blood had been washed away—but without, in the court, it still lay in patches, blackening and cracking in the sun.

CHAPTER LXII.

THERE is nothing, perhaps, more effectual to deaden, if not to relieve recent misery, than the sensation of rapid motion. Leaning back in the palankeen, with the doors now shut, and the fresh breeze blowing refreshingly through the open blinds, Tara felt herself hurried swiftly and smoothly along, while her attention was at once occupied and distracted by the occurrences of the journey. Sindphul, its temple and trees: the lane which was the bed of the rivulet, through which the bearers plashed rapidly: the village gate now shut, and its bastions manned with men to keep out marauders: the long shady narrow lane, overhung with trees;—then, beyond, the plain, covered with rich crops of grain now ripening: the shouts of the men and boys, perched upon their stages in the fields, slinging stones at birds: the song, drawling and monotonous, of the bullock-drivers at the wells,—were all familiar objects and sounds to the desolate girl being carried rapidly by them. Would she ever see them again?

As they passed their own garden, she looked among the trees—perchance she might see Sudba, the old bullock-driver, or Puréshram, the gardener; but there was no one visible, else she had cried out to them. Were they dead, too? Ah! how often had she wandered among the trees there with her mother, and watched the butterflies among the flowers! The bearers stopped to change opposite the wicket gate, and she could see the bright beds of white jessamine, unpicked as yet, and large marigolds, and white and yellow chrysanthemums, which the men were saving for the Dusséra. Who would gather them now? Over them, the same bright yellow and white butterflies were hovering in hundreds, and the fierce green and blue dragonflies chasing each other, or darting here and there, quick as thought, and glistening in the sun. Then she remembered the omen in her garden as she sat spinning, and fell back on the pillow shuddering. It was true. She remembered too that the bird had sat for a while, and twittered a sweet low song. Was he that bird, that noble, gracious youth, who had spoken to her so gently, so kindly? She tried to follow the thread of this thought back, but failed. Her mind was sadly confused and wandering, now reverting to the omen, now to the objects she was passing, and the people they met:—who were they? what doing? whither going?—to the horsemen, the monotonous tramp of whose horses never ceased, some behind, some before, some around her,—fierce, dark-bearded fellows, whose very proximity she would have dreaded before,—who were now guarding her respectfully by his order; while the kind old man, to whose charge she had been specially committed, rode close to the side of the litter, and where the path was narrow, asked her, through the blinds, if she were well, and wanted anything.

Fazil, son of Afzool; she remembered the name. It was strange to Hindu lips, but had a musical cadence, which her memory retained as she repeated it to herself. Fazil, son of Afzool; and he had a sister Zyna. What would she be like? Would she be kind and loving to her? like Radha? Was he not beautiful, and very fair, almost ruddy.

Into all these channels, confused, and whirling her mind hither and thither like dust and straws before the wind, her thoughts wandered dreamily, apparently avoiding the bare, hideous fact that all were dead whom she loved—all who had protected her up to last night. But this would not long be denied its place. It was a horrible reality not as yet fully understood:—which her gentle mind could not grasp.

Dead! who saw them die? They were alive last night,—who had killed them? If she had seen them die, that, indeed, would be surety. No, it was not true. They could not be dead,—they could not have left her so helpless. It was some fraud, some deception. She had not gone far: Sindphul was close by: she would run and sit in the garden, and wait for her mother; and she half-opened the door of the litter. Shêre Khan rode by it, erect and stern, but bowed down to her as the door moved. "Do you want anything, lady?" he said. "Go to sleep; it will rest you."

The voice, kind as it was, dispelled the other thought, and brought back the bitter reality of desolation and the events of the night. How she had been lifted up—and the girl Gunga's laugh of triumph and mockery rang in her ears, and was before her eyes now, as she pressed her hands against them: the rude men who carried her down the steps: the fearful shrieks and din in the temple: the shots and blows, growing fainter as they carried her away: and, above all, the voice of Moro Trimmul, exulting with Gunga that they were safe from death, and had Tara captive. "To Rutunjun first," he had said, "and then——"

"From that worse than death he saved me," she thought, with a shudder. "Fazil saved me—Fazil, son of Afzool—else I were helpless with Moro now. And they were dead—her people, all dead? Yes, the detail Fazil had related was brief and circumstantial. The Bhópeys would not lie—why should they? They were weeping, and had taken him up dead. Her father, a negro had killed him, they said. She felt no hope could come out of this detail. They had lifted him up and put him . . . . No, she could not follow that. That beloved father, dead—disfigured with ghastly wounds!—mother, whom Jánoo had seen dead, and Radha . . . . all? He had said so. How could he—Fazil—know of Jánoo, or the Bhôpeys, her father's dependants, so as to deceive her with names?"

So, round and round, whirling, dashing hither and thither like the motes in a sunbeam, staying nowhere, sometimes utterly blank, the girl's thoughts ministered to her fast growing misery. The hot dry eyes, red and swollen, looked out sometimes vacantly as the bearers changed shoulders. She felt powerless to move, careless as to what became of her. As the reality of the death of all, pressed on her mind occasionally with greater force, she sat up and gasped for breath, and again fell back upon the cushions; then the monotonous cries of the bearers as they shuffled along rapidly, and the dull tramp of the horses, with the sense of motion, were relief from mental agony: and, after a time, she slept.

The action of setting down the litter, awoke her with a start. Under some trees not far from a village gate, there was the small hut of a Fakeer. Shêre Khan was speaking to the old man, and the troopers were dismounting from their horses. Shêre Khan came to her.

"I have sent for the Josee's wife," he said. "The Syn here says she is a kind woman. She will bring you water and something to eat. We rest here while the men get their breakfasts, and the horses are fed. Fear nothing. Open the litter,—it is cool and pleasant in the shade under the trees," and then he left her.

So it was. She opened the door and looked out. A small grove of mango trees, with a smooth green sward below them, and some cattle and goats grazing there in the cool shade; a boy and a girl tending them looked inquisitively at her, and the girl came up shyly and sat down by her.

"Do you want water, lady?" she said. "I am the Josee's daughter, and those are my goats. I will go and tell my mother you want water. You are a Brahmun, are you not?"

Tara patted her head in assent—she could not speak; and the girl ran away, crying to the lad not to let her goats stray.

By-and-by the child and mother returned, and the latter brought a copper vessel of water and a drinking-cup.

"Here is water, lady," she said; "will you get out and wash your face? Surely, I know you," she continued quickly, as Tara turned her face to her. "Where have I seen you?"

"No matter," said Tara, "I do not know you."

"Perhaps not," said the dame drearily. "So many travellers come and go, and . . . . but no matter. Shall I cook anything for you? will you come to our house and bathe?"

"No," said Tara; "they will go on presently; I will stay here."

"Come hither, Ooma," she said to the girl, who was standing apart, and she whispered to her; "go, and come quickly," she added aloud.

"Do not send for any one else," said Tara; "I am well."

"Are you not ill?" said the woman. "Ah, your eyes are red and swollen."

"I have a headache," replied Tara; "it is so hot."

"Yes," said the woman, sitting down, and putting her arm kindly round Tara, and pressing her head against her own bosom,—"yes, you look tired and weary, but it will pass away. Wash your face and hands, and your feet—it will do you good, and refresh you. Put out your feet—so—I will wash them."

The cool water was refreshing as it was poured over her hands and feet; and after the woman had dried them with the end of her saree, she again laid Tara's head against her breast, and patted her as though she were her own child.

"You look so weary," she said; "have you travelled far?"

"From Tooljapoor," Tara replied.

"Is all well there?" asked the woman. It was a common question with no meaning to the asker, but of how much to Tara!

She could not answer, but clung, almost convulsively, to the kind breast on which she had laid her head.

"I see," said the woman; "so young and rich, and yet thou art in sorrow, lady—rest here." And she drew her the more closely to her, and patted her as before. So they sat till the child came back, who brought upon a plate, covered with a handkerchief, a few simple sweetmeats and some parched rice. "Eat, she said, "if ever so little; eat a bit of 'Luddoo,' and drink some water." Tara shook her head, and only nestled the closer to the soft bosom: it was strangely like her mother's.

"Poor thing, poor thing," thought the woman to herself, "what can ail her? Perhaps her husband is unkind. Eat, my rose," she said aloud, "eat this." And she broke off a piece of the cake and put it to Tara's mouth. "I made it myself, and it is quite pure and clean. Eat it; open your mouth." Tara did so mechanically, and she put it in.

Tara tried to eat, but her mouth was dry and hot; she could not swallow, and felt choking. The woman saw it, and rubbed her throat gently. The hardness and constriction seemed to relax, and she was able to swallow what she had taken, and to eat a little more, the woman feeding her.

"Good," she said kindly, "try again by-and-by. O lady, what heavy grief is on you that no tears come? Can I do aught for you?"

"Nothing," said Tara; "only do not leave me while they are absent."

So they sat silently. If Tara could have wept, it had been well; but that blessed relief was not to come yet. She was quiet, however, sitting there, almost stupified, resting her head against the woman's breast, who still patted her. Every now and then the great, sore, hot eyes looked out drearily. Some of the goats and cattle browsed under the trees, others had lain down resting in the shade. There was no sound but a faint rustle of the breeze among the leaves, the dim buzz of flies, and the droning song of a man, at a well in a garden near, singing to his bullocks, and the distant plashing rush of the water as it was emptied from the bag into the cistern.

And so they sat, till one by one the bearers gathered near them, and tied up their hookas on the palankeen as before. Then the horsemen came up, and she heard Shêre Khan asking her if she were ready, and telling the bearers to take up the palankeen. Tara had put the gifts she had received at the shrine under her waistband, and remembered them. As the palankeen was taken up she took them out and put them into the woman's hand, who, expecting perhaps a few copper coins, stood looking at them in amazement.

"May your grief pass from you, and may God be merciful unto you, my child," said the woman. Ere Tara could reply, a bearer had shut the door, and the men ran on with renewed vigour.

Yes, the little change had refreshed her, and she again fell asleep, mercifully: and it was evening, and the shadows were lengthening fast, when she became aware that they approached a large town, passed through a busy bazar crowded with people, then emerged from it; crossed over a bridge, from which a large piece of water was visible on the left hand, and the towers and bastions of a fort washed by it; then the gloom of a deep-arched gateway, and light beyond. A respectably dressed elderly woman, in Mahomedan costume, took hold of the side of the palankeen, and ran along with it a short distance.

"Stop," she cried to the bearers,—"this is the place; put it down and go away."

Then Tara saw several other women advance and hold up a heavy sheet so as to screen her as she got out, and the door was opened; and Goolab, for she it was, speaking a rough dialect of Mahratta, bid her come forth. As she did so, and stood there, Goolab "took the evil off her," as was her custom;* and other women coming forward with plates, on which were coriander and mustard seed, waved them over her. Thus welcomed, Tara now stood waiting a signal to advance; and Goolab, seeing her trembling violently, put her arm round her, looking with wonder at the richness of her apparel and the heavy gold ornaments she wore, her exceeding beauty causing respect and silence even from the loquacious and privileged nurse.

"Enter," said a low sweet voice from within a curtain hanging across a doorway, which was slightly opened.

CHAPTER LXIII.

TARA advanced, still trembling, and clinging to Goolab, and trying to hide her face in the end of her garment; she was only sensible of the same sweet voice, as a girl of great, and to her strange, beauty, took her in her arms, embraced her, and said gently, "Peace be unto you! you are welcome, with the peace and blessing of Alla upon you!" and that another taller and older lady embraced her in like

* Women pass their hands over the person on whom the ceremony is performed from head to foot; then, turning the backs of their hands against their temples, make all their knuckles and finger-joints crack loudly. This is done to avert consequences of Evil Eye.

manner, and said the same. After that for a long while she remembered nothing.

When she recovered, she was lying upon a soft bedding in a small room, near an open window which looked out upon the lake that encircled the fort, glowing with the reflection of piles of sunset-clouds. On what seemed an island in the lake was a Hindu temple, with a high pyramidical roof, around which hung the rich foliage of several magnificent trees, and temple and trees were reflected double in the still water. These were the first objects that met her sight.

Then, turning round, the same young face that she had seen on entering the apartment bent over her, and a soft warm hand was passed over her face, and the ends of the fingers kissed in loving greeting; but the girl did not speak, though a sweet smile spread over her features, and she seemed to beckon with her left hand to another person behind her, whom Tara could not see. Another moment and her deliverer advanced, saluting her respectfully.

Fazil had ridden fast to overtake Tara, but had not succeeded. Twenty men, a light palankeen, and the hope of a liberal reward, had induced the bearers to put out their utmost speed, and they had well redeemed their promise of reaching their destination before sunset; but he had arrived soon after.

"Go away, brother," said Zyna, "do not speak to her now; you have seen that she is safe—that is enough."

"My sister," he replied in Persian, that Tara might not understand, "not so. It will grieve her, and thee too, sorely, but she must know the truth. Do not go away. I will speak to her in her own tongue, and show her these sad memorials which I have brought. It is mercy not to delay in such cases.—Can you listen to me, lady, a few moments?" he continued to Tara; "what I have to tell you is not worse than what you have already heard, but it will confirm it; and truth and reality are ever better than doubt."

"If you please to say it, sir," said Tara, who had arisen directly she saw Fazil approaching, and stood by the window.

"If—if—you saw anything that had belonged to them you would know it, perhaps," said Fazil hesitatingly.

Tara's bosom heaved so that she could not speak. She appeared as if gasping for breath, with the same distressing symptoms as when, in the morning, he had told her first of her bereavement,—and she trembled violently. She could not stand, and crouched down against the wall.

"O, not now, brother! not now," pleaded Zyna, who put her arm round Tara, and was supporting her.

But Fazil was merciless. "It must be," he said. "And now, lady, listen. If you had any doubt, these will remove it. After I left you the second time I went to the Kucheri, for what Jánoo

Näik told me he had left there, and these were given as having belonged to your mother, Anunda Bye, and your stepmother, Radha Bye. Look at them."

As he spoke he untied a bundle he held, and poured the contents at her feet; heavy gold and silver ornaments of some value, and a few rings.

Tara looked at them for a moment. The silver chain anklets, which were her mother's, were dabbled with blood, now dry on them; the gold pair had been made after those on her own feet for Radha's marriage, by her brother Moro. Enough—all were familiar objects. They swam before her eyes—the room seemed whirling round, and, weak as she was, she sank down again utterly unconscious, with Zyna crying over her.

"Let them remain," said Fazil, "she must see them when she recovers, else she will not believe. Show them to her one by one. I dare not stay;" and he left the room.

Tara had not however fainted, but she was gasping for breath, and Zyna called to Goolab to bring a fan, while she opened the casement of the window still more, to let in air. "He said—he said," sobbed Tara, trying to speak; "lady, I cannot speak—I am choking—O! why do I not die? He said——"

"He said you were to look at them all, one by one," said Zyna, trying to check her own sobs and tears. "He is kind. Fazil, my brother, would not give you pain unless it were for good. Look! here they are," and Zyna spread out the ornaments with her own hands, shuddering at the blood upon them.

Tara looked earnestly at Zyna; the eyes were full of misery—so full that Zyna could not bear them—passed her hands over her own, pressing them tightly, then looked away. Tara turned the ornaments vacantly over and over, sighing, and, as it were, catching her breath convulsively. There was one, a ring with a sapphire set in it, with which she knew her mother never parted, for she believed that without it evil would happen to her, and that it had brought prosperity. It used sometimes to be put on the altar when they worshipped Lakshmee, the Goddess of Wealth—else it never left her mother's hand; but it was there. Zyna did not know this then, but she saw Tara's hand tremble very much as she took it up and looked at it carefully. There was a dark stain inside, and Tara put down the ring, gasping, as it were, for breath, then took it up again.

Zyna watched wonderingly, the changing expressions which passed over the beautiful features: first despair; then, as it seemed to her, prayers were murmured in a language she did not understand, and the features appeared to relax, the upturned eyes glistened, there was a look as if of hope or triumph upon the face. She moved closer to Tara, still closer, as she thought she saw tears gathering in the hot eyes. If Tara could only weep it would be well. Zyna passed her left arm round her, and gently drew the girl's head on her own shoulder and bosom; it fell softly there and rested; the hand which held the ring dropped on her lap, beating restlessly; but the other grasped her so that it almost caused pain. Kind nature did not suffer the terrible struggle to continue longer, else Tara had died; and with almost a shriek of pain, her tears burst forth uncontrollably.

"Thank God for it," said Lurlee, who had entered, and was standing over them, and who now passed her hands over Tara, as Goolab had done; "she will be easier for this, and the worst is past: let her weep. The blessing of Alla and the Prophet on thee, my daughter," she said to Tara. "I salute thee with peace! Thou hast entered at a fortunate moment, and there is joy following thy grief. Fear not; thou hast come to those who will be to thee what thou hast lost."

"She will require much care, mother," said Zyna; "feel how she is trembling; I will not leave her. Ah, yes—that is the reason; take away those things, Goolab; wash them and put them by."

Goolab took them up, and with all her choicest epithets of "Poor little rose! my pretty dove! my lily! my own life!" she tried to soothe the girl; but Tara heeded no one. Keeping the ring clutched in her own hand, she hid her face in Zyna's bosom, then suffered her gradually to lay her head down on her knee, and rock it softly. She dared not speak, but tried to look up gratefully, sometimes, and then clung the closer to her gentle nurse.

"Hush," said Zyna, as fresh bursts of tears often occurred, "I know what has happened, and I will not leave thee, Tara; no, never now. And he, my brother, says it too." So they sat and lay —the two girls—long into the night; and gradually, unable to resist the kindness lavished on her, Tara spoke a little, and Zyna encouraged it, and heard wonderingly, Tara's simple tale of trial and sorrow.

That night, too, her future fate was the subject of earnest debate, often approaching the verge of passion, between Afzool Khan, his son, and the priest. What could they do with a Brahmun orphan, a heathen unbeliever who was a captive, and a slave, by the laws of war? Long and earnestly did the priest plead that she should forthwith be sent to the royal harem. So beautiful a slave would be cherished, loved, and have every luxury at her command; she might become the mother of princes, and the head of the state; and Afzool Khan supported this opinion, which was borne out by texts from the law, plausibly quoted by the Peer.

But Fazil opposed them both, gently yet firmly, and at last almost fiercely. "She is my captive, if captive at all," he said; "my slave, taken in war, according to your own texts, Huzrut—and I can release her, or ransom her, or keep her, as I will. She has relatives at Wye, where we are going, and with your permission, father, she can stay with us till then; we will be her safeguard, honourably and truly. After that," he added with some little confusion, "she can act for herself, and of her own free will; but to send her to the palace, to be decked out and noticed for a while, and then flung aside—no, father; better she died, or better still that we now turned her into the street, to shift for herself among her own people."

"That would be inhospitable, son, if no more," returned his father; "well, boy, let her stay, and welcome. No matter," he thought to himself, "if he have his own way in this thing." The Khan was decidedly in good humour. The kichéri, kabobs, and some other dishes which were especial favourites, had been dressed to perfection by Lurlee, and were relished, as they can best be, with the zest insured by a long ride.

Lurlee had met him in good humour, and the stars were in propitious conjunction to welcome his arrival. The lady had nothing but good to say of Tara, whose beauty and sad history had at once deeply impressed her. "What if she be an infidel," she said, "she will make the better true believer. Let her stay with us, O Khan! she shall be a daughter to me," and the lady sighed. "There is nothing unlucky about the period of her arrival, for the sun was in conjunction with Jupiter, and she was born under Venus, she says; and as she is a Brahmun she knows all about her horoscope and the planets; besides, is not this Wednesday, and she arrived between five and six in the evening, under Venus, so that she is born to us under the same planet as she was born to her own parents? Is not that curious? and by-and-by I shall call her Fazila, according to the blessed scheme of nativity sent by the prophets. And listen further, Khan," continued the lady, pausing and examining her book. "Her name now begins with a T, and that stands for Air, and is lucky, because——" and she was nearly saying it aloud, only she checked herself in time, "because," she said to herself, "Fazil's name begins with an F, and that means Fire, and fire and air always agree best, because the one cannot exist apart from the other."

"I don't understand, Lurlee," said the Khan, "how it is. What about fire?"

"Never mind," replied the lady knowingly, "you will find out more by-and-by, Khan! there is a good deal to be done before then."

So Tara escaped another great peril which she knew not of, and remained as an honoured and welcome guest with her new protectors. And in a few days, when Afzool Khan had made the necessary arrangements, his army was ready to move on. These need no detail at our hands, except as concerns two characters in our history who did not accompany it.

The first was Kowas Khan, who, recalled by the King to manage the affairs of his own troops, returned from Sholapoor to the capital. The young man regretted the necessity; for to share a campaign in real service with his friend Fazil, had ever been one of his most cherished plans. The King's order was, however, peremptory, and was obeyed. "When we return," said the old Khan to him as they parted, "the days of mourning will be expired, and thou shalt have thy desire."

With him was sent the Lalla, who, being naturally of an unwarlike nature, rejoiced at the prospect of escaping hardships of no ordinary kind. And was not Kowas Khan the late Wuzeer's son, and nominal Wuzeer himself? He might become actually so, and what a field for advancement was opened to him if this should be! "May your prosperity increase, may you be victorious," he said to the father and son as he took leave of them. "Inshalla! your poor servant will write you news of the city and court, after the true imperial fashion, which is more his vocation than recording battles; only remember that your slave is grateful."

Afzool Khan's army, now organized in all respects, set forward on its march. A few miles only were traversed daily, and it would require a month or more ere they could reach Wye. Sometimes a house was found for the ladies in a village or town near which the forces encamped; but more frequently they were in the Khan's tents, which were infinitely pleasanter. The two girls grew together, the more as the first restraint passed away; and the lady Lurlee and Zyna were never tired of hearing from the lips of the beautiful heathen, the simple story of her life, her widowhood, and her strange rescue from dishonour.

Was Tara happy? Yes; when she thought of what her fate must have been had she not been rescued from Moro Trimmul, or even if Fazil had yielded to her first entreaties, and let her go without inquiry. She knew not then of the further escape from the royal harem which Fazil had secured; but as it was, gratitude to him had already become the main feeling of her life. Of her parents' death she had no doubt whatever now. The other members of the family would have claimed the property and cast her off. Widow and priestess combined, she would have been helpless against the insult and profligacy of men of her own faith, and now she was at least safe. She was grateful, therefore, and, for the most part, happy too.

But often, as she wept bitterly under the old memories of an innocent and happy home, the loving arms of her mother seemed clasped about her once more, and her caresses almost palpably felt, while the glistening eyes of the goddess appeared to follow her, sleeping and waking, with a reproachful look of desertion. In these moments, Tara endured bitter grief; but ever at hand were the gentle remonstrances of her new mother and sister, and to them also were joined those of her deliverer which, in the constant association which grew out of a camp life, she felt becoming more and more powerful day by day.

CHAPTER LXIV.

AMONG the events which passed at Sholapoor after the arrival of the Khan, was the disposition of the prisoner Moro Trimmul. Heavily ironed and closely guarded, he had been brought from Tooljapoor on horseback, his irons loosened from one leg, and, when they were again riveted, he was consigned to the custody of the Khan's own troop. When the fate of the Brahmun hung in a balance, and Fazil, fearing him, and knowing his indefatigable and successful attempts in propagating the political influence of the Mahrattas, had at first urged his execution, then his transmission to Beejapoor,—there was not a dissentient voice in the small council; but at Sholapoor the aspect of affairs had changed: the priest and his father had sent for Moro Trimmul, and examined him in private; and the sullenness of the man had apparently broken down before the threats of being despatched to Beejapoor, and submitted to his fate with the King.

The Khan and the priest were no believers in the honesty of Mahrattas; and at the second of these examinations, the Brahmun was plied with temptation such as was difficult to resist, and to which he yielded with apparent reluctance, but yielded nevertheless. To assist them in speaking with the prisoner (for though the priest spoke Mahratta perfectly well, yet, as a language of infidels, rarely suffered it, as he said, to defile his mouth; and if he did, subjected that organ to an excessive purification at the hour of prayer),—a Brahmun, who belonged to the accountant's department of the state, by name Punto Gopinath, was employed by the Khan. Of this man he knew but little: but he was a good Persian scholar, as well as an intelligent official servant of the kingdom, and the Khan had no doubt of his fidelity.

Nor, indeed, Bulwunt Rao either; who, a bad interpreter himself, had, on all occasions, been allowed to be present, as a check upon the Brahmuns. Both had joined in trying to persuade Moro Trimmul to disclose the intentions of his master, and had always been met with the same answer, that the Prince only desired recognition of his rights, and that when he heard for certain of the march of the force, he would be sure to send ambassadors to explain what had occurred. So it had come to this, that if ambassadors did arrive within a few days, Moro Trimmul was to be confronted with them; otherwise, that he was to be sent back to Beejapoor, to be dealt with as a traitor.

To Bulwunt Rao, whose Mahratta mind was capable of understanding and appreciating an indirect motive of policy, the Khan's determination seemed perfectly reasonable; and if Moro Trimmul could by any means be brought to consent to lead the force through the defiles beyond Wye, some effect upon the Rajah's position might be obtained. If not, who was to do it?

To Fazil, however, the position taken up by his father was so unintelligible, and so unlike his usual straightforward mode of proceeding, that he feared some extraneous agency was at work. It was not so, however: it was simply the power which strong minds exercise over weaker; and by the Brahmun's cool contempt of death, his certainty that Sivaji would beg for terms, and his willingness to assist if he did,—the Khan's suspicions were overcome.

Nor was it strange, perhaps, that after a time the Khan appeared to attach no particular culpability to Moro Trimmul's attempt to carry off Tara. He had explained the act, by her father having tired of her presence in the house as the jealous enemy of his sister, a new and beautiful wife, and had requested him to take her away to Wye, to devote her to one of the temples there. Some little force was, no doubt, necessary; but her father had authorized its being used, to prevent interference by her mother. What did he care about the girl?—as a widow she was impure, and her not having performed the rites of widowhood, placed her beyond the pale of respectability; yes, the Khan might make a Mahomedan of her, send her to the King, or do what he pleased with his slave, he had no concern for her now.

The Khan thought this state of the case on the whole more probable, in all its aspects, than Tara's own story, heard through Lurlee and Zyna. It did not affect her character, which Moro Trimmul spared no words to commend.

So the Brahmun grew into favour; and as he did so, the flattery which he distributed to the Khan and the priest had its effect, in procuring him liberty, first from his irons, and then of speech with Gopinath and other persons of his own sect, who came to converse with one so well known by reputation. The position of all parties continued thus till a few days after the force had left Sholapoor; when, one morning, as the Khan reached the halting-place for the day, the arrival of envoys from the Rajah Sivaji was announced in camp, and without delay they were summoned to the Khan's presence.

We need not follow the negotiations which ensued; we have only to do with those who took part in them. Most of us know, too, what Eastern negotiations are, when weakness is covered by temporizing expedients of falsehood or treachery. So it has been from the first, so it will be to the end. Moro Trimmul had well guessed what his master's policy would be when he laid his fate upon the result; and when he heard from Bulwunt Rao that the envoys had proffered submission, and begged of Afzool Khan to advance and partake of the Rajah's hospitality at Pertabgurh, where the affairs pending in dispute could be amicably discussed, he was satisfied—he could understand what was to come.

His own liberation soon followed. Of what use was it confining an irresponsible agent, when real ambassadors had voluntarily met the Khan, and declared their master's intention to throw himself on the royal clemency? So Moro Trimmul was set free.

His first act was to seek Gunga. So long as he had been kept within the fort at Sholapoor he had heard nothing of her; but the day the force marched, he had seen her, attended by two stout footmen with sword and buckler, riding among the camp followers, as the division of horsemen, under whose charge he was placed, rapidly passed a crowd of them straggling onwards. She had not observed him, he thought, for she made no sign of recognition. It had been otherwise, however; and we must retrace a little this girl's proceedings, in order to comprehend her present position.

Under that strange fascination which often impels women to endure more from men who ill-use them than from those who caress them, she had been unable to remain at Tooljapoor, and after a brief struggle she had yielded to her destiny. When the Khan discharged her, and the temporary insensibility of Lukshmun had procured her the gold zone, which was valuable, the hard, mercenary nature which had grown out of her vocation, rose as a wall between her and Moro Trimmul, and yet but for a moment.

It said to her, "You have got all you can from this man, his fate is evil; you have had many escapes from him, and this is the last. Go! leave him, you could not save his life if you would; the Mussulmans hate him, and will destroy him, or imprison him for life. Enough that you have escaped; go, and be thankful." This was what she thought, as she picked up the zone when it rolled away, fastened it round her waist, and walked out of the room. Where was she to go? She dared not visit the temple. Dead bodies were still lying there, and there was blood about the streets. She went to Annuda's house, and looked into all the courts. She saw the dead negro lying among the flowers, and, horrified at the sight, she started back; and just as some men opened a door and tried to intercept her, she fled away in terror. She dared not trust herself in the quiet parts of the town nor in the camp; for there were many who would have thought little of a stab with a dagger, or open violence, to rid her of the zone and the valuable ornaments she had about her. The bazar, however, was safe, and she might meet some one she knew, and obtain protection.

There were many. Among them Jánoo the Ramoosee, now very tipsy, yet able to recognize her. He knew she was no friend of Anunda's or Tara's, and to her he told the same story as he had done to Fazil. "Dead, all dead!" he cried, as he staggered away—"dishonoured and murdered by the negroes; and they are buried in the hole beyond the well, without the gate. Go and see—go and see."

She went up through the gate idly, and sat down beside the great well. She dared not go beyond it. A large peepul tree hung over it, and a number of Hindu soldiers were cooking under its shade. She asked for a few hot cakes, and they gave them, and she ate them there. Then she wandered into the fields and gardens beyond, and so round to the Pâp-nâs temple, and sat down on the ledge of rock above the little stream, which thence leapt plashing down the precipice, looking over the broad plain, over which the light shadows of fleecy clouds were chasing each other.

Her eyes filled with tears, for there came back to her, hard and depraved as she was, many tender memories of the man whom she had loved passionately;—feared, hated with bitter jealousy, and again loved with that perversity which is part of the fiercest jealousy, and distorts every semblance of truth to serve its own purpose. The scene of Tara's inauguration came back to her memory, and her beauty. "It was not his fault, Mother," she cried out aloud; "it was thine, to send that lotos-faced girl to bewitch him, else he had been true to me, and thou art rightly served for it. He said thou wast a fiend, and feared thee not; nor do I."

Yes, Tara was gone; would the Mussulman boy, so grand, so beautiful, ever give up so lovely a captive? Surely not. "Let him have her," she said: "she will go away, far, far from me and him, and it is well. Yes, it is well, and what have I to do but follow and watch,—follow and watch?"

Then she rose, remembering her store of money in a pot under the fireplace, in a cloister of the temple, where she had lived. Her clothes, her property, would be gone; what matter, if that were safe?

So she rose up and ran lightly along the plain, back to the gate, avoiding the new graves; then passed down the bazar and into the temple court. All the dead had been removed. The scavengers were washing the court, which she crossed rapidly. As she expected, her room had been plundered, all her clothes were gone, but the fireplace had not been disturbed. She closed the door carefully, then sat down for a while with a beating heart, to see whether she were followed or not; no one came,—no one had cared to stop her, though she had been seen. With a small iron bar which lay in a corner, she hastily dug up the clay plastering of the hearth, and took out the brass vessel she had hidden there, which contained her savings; there were upwards of a hundred rupees in it—wealth to her.

Tying these coins carefully into her waistband, she again went out into the court, and proceeded to the temple. "Do not go there," cried a man sweeping; "it is not washed." But she went on.

It was not washed, and was ghastly with dried and clotted blood. She looked into the shrine, to see what had become of the image, venerated, feared, and yet even detested. It lay there as it had fallen. No one had yet dared to touch it, and the wicked eyes still glistened and sparkled in the light of the lamp which had been placed beside it. "Aha!" cried the girl exultingly; "lie there, liar and murdering devil, as he called thee. He did not fear thee, nor do I. Lie there, till they pick thee up; or why dost thou not rise thyself? Up, Mother, up! shall I help thee?" she cried mockingly, as she seized the stone hand; but she dropped it as instantly—it was wet and cold.

As she did so, she fancied the eyes turned spitefully towards her, and a horrible superstitious terror came into her heart when she looked at her hand and saw it was covered with blood. Then she shrieked and fled shuddering, out of the front entrance to the vestibule, across the court, up the steps, staying only for a moment to wash hurriedly in the sacred cistern. Thus she went into the bazar, and sought out a carrier who she knew possessed a strong pony, who agreed to take her to Sholapoor; and, purchasing a heavy, coarse cotton sheet, she wrapped herself in it, and, mingling with the crowd of camp-followers, rode after the force to Sholapoor.

For many days she could get no speech of Moro Trimmul. She had seen him taken to rivulets and wells to bathe, and he had also seen her; but though she daily tried, on one pretence or other, to get near him, she was repulsed. It was enough, however, that she knew where he was.

It was not long after his release ere he discovered her. She did not importune him, and he could hardly resist the devotion which had prompted her to abandon what had been her home and follow his fortunes. He trusted also to induce her, gradually, again to further his designs against Tara, which, now that her parents, and, as he believed, also his own sister, were all dead, appeared more probable of success than before.

If ever this selfish man had felt a pang of real grief in his life, it was when he had heard of his sister's death. Poor Radha! whom he had settled at last so well, when any provision for her had become next to hopeless—Radha, who, with all her faults, was part of his own rugged nature, polished and set in a more beautiful frame. It was impossible not to grieve for her. This was the first impression;

afterwards there ensued an element of rejoicing in it, which daily grew stronger. That he was free—free to act: free from the keen perception and daring opposition of his sister, which, ever protecting Tara as with a shield, had only yielded to violence at the last.

Now Tara was within his reach, and, comparatively speaking, in a far greater measure than before. He knew her to be safe in the family with whom she had obtained protection. Their own high honour and strict respectability were guarantee for this. Knowing her helplessness, Moro Trimmul had but one source of alarm or apprehension: she might allow herself to be converted to the Mahomedan faith, or it might be done without her consent. Then, indeed, there would be no hope.

But, on the other hand, was she not a Brahmun—wonderfully learned for a woman, proud of this learning, and, above all, a self-professed devotee of the goddess?

"No," he thought, "they may attempt conversion, probably will do so, but she will resist it: and yet she should not be too long exposed to a double temptation." Now, therefore, as before, he discussed plans with Gunga as to what means could be employed to separate Tara from her new protectors, and carry her away into the wilds of his native province, where she could be effectually concealed; and his pursuit of the girl grew once more into a fierce and morbid passion, absorbing and deadening all other feelings of his life.

CHAPTER LXV.

"THE gods be praised!" cried Jeyram Bhópey to Wamun Bhut, late in the day after the attack upon the temple. "He has opened his eyes once more. Speak, Vyas Shastree; you are safe amongst friends: the gods be praised, and Toolja Mata, for this mercy, for we little expected to see you live."

"Who are you?" said the Shastree faintly. "I see very dimly, and it appears very dark.—Anunda! Tara!——"

"I, Wamun, speak to you," replied the elder of the two priests, "and this is Jeyram Bhópey. We carried you away, and you are safe in the house of Gunnésh Hurry, Putwari of Sindphul.—Look, friends," he continued, speaking to others without the door of the room, "the Shastree is alive, and hath spoken, and asked for his wife and daughter."

Vyas Shastree was sensible that the room darkened again, as a number of men crowded to the door; but, feeling sick and faint from the exertion of speaking even those few words, thought himself dying, and relapsed again into insensibility.

Very anxiously did all those friends watch around the wounded man; and it was long before he showed any appearance of rallying strength. Night passed, and they hardly expected he would see the day; but still he breathed, and as morning was breaking, a warm moisture took the place of the chill, clammy, deathlike state in which he had remained previously, and then those attending him hoped that he would live.

He had received a fearful wound. Bareheaded as he was in the performance of the ceremonies so rudely interrupted, he had not thought of protecting himself; but, as the Abyssinians advanced, had caught a sword and shield offered him by a man in the crowd, who drew back and fled, and had passed to the front with some others, crying the shout of the goddess, "Jey Kalee!" "Jey Toolja!" and catching blows on the shield rather than returning them. But when a gigantic negro before him was pressing upon the front rank of those who defended the entrance to the vestibule, so heavily that it seemed as if they must give way, the old soldier spirit within the Shastree was stirred, and he struck desperately at the man. Stung by the pain of the wound, the negro instantly returned the blow with a furious cut, which laid open the crown of the Shastree's head from back to front. Well for him that the shield had greatly broken the force of it, or he had died instantly; as it was, the Shastree fell stunned, and was trampled upon by the advancing crowd; and lay there, unconscious, until the early morning.

Then the two friends who had watch him fall, and who, concealed in the recess behind the shrine, had escaped slaughter, came forth and sought for him. They found him under a pile of dead, still breathing, but utterly insensible. It was impossible to take him to his own house, for the gateway and bazar were filled with Abyssinians, and they feared a renewal of slaughter with the dawn; so they lifted the Shastree from the ground, obtained a bedstead from one of the closed archway rooms, put him upon it, and, being joined by several of the Bhópey priests, had broken open the postern by which Tara had been taken away, and carried him at once, unobserved, to Sindphul.

Had Tara remained where she had been first stopped, she must have seen her father borne past her, and would have been saved; but Fazil Khan had sent her palankeen to the trees by the back of the rivulet, about a gunshot's distance from the path, out of sight; and though those who carried the Shastree were challenged by Shêre Khan's horsemen, there was nothing suspicious in the fact of a dead body, for so it seemed, being carried away,—and the little procession had passed unnoticed.

Heera, the barber of Sindphul, was a skilful surgeon, and on his arrival at the house of the Putwari or accountant of the village, the

Shastree's wound was examined. The barber had seldom seen worse, and during the time which had elapsed since he had received it, the Shastree had become weak from loss of blood. So Heera shook his head. Still he did his best: the wound was sewn up skilfully, and a composing poultice of warm leaves and herbs applied to it, while the bruised body was fomented. All night had Heera watched anxiously with the friends about the Shastree, fearing the worst, for he was restless and feverish; but with the morning came refreshing sleep, and the warm moist skin for which the barber had so anxiously looked. Then he said, "If the gods please, the Shastree will live. Let him be kept quiet, and the room darkened."

At first the women of his family were hardly missed. All those who could escape had fled into the fields and gardens around little Tooljapoor, and many into the deep ravine beyond the town, or to adjacent villages. Sindphul was crowded with them, and no one dare return till the Mahomedan force had passed.

The Bhóslay of Sindphul had searched again and again through his village and its hamlets for the Shastree's wives and for Tara, but in vain. He had sent men to look for them in their own house, but they were not there. The place showed the signs of violence we already know of; and the men in charge of it could only hope that Jánoo Näik might account for them.

Jánoo had been sought, therefore, and found in the liquor-seller's shop drinking out his money; and when asked for Anunda and Tara, said, with drunken solemnity, that he had buried them all. The idea had possessed him that this was the safest answer for all questioners, and he held to it the more pertinaciously as his drunkenness increased. It was impossible not to fear that the story might be true; for all had seen Tara in the throng of priests and priestesses, and knew also that Anunda and Radha had been in the temple.

We left them crouching in a niche, as it were, of the rock, overgrown by long pendant creepers and grass, near the little spring, and there they passed the night. At early dawn Jánoo had come to them with his son, and told them that their house had been attacked in the night, and was no safe place for them. It was polluted, moreover, and they could not return to it. That Tara and the Shastree had escaped to Sindphul; that he dare not take them past the force which was guarding the town and pass, and that they must go to Afsinga, where all was quiet. He knew they had friends in a Brahmun's family which resided there, and thither Anunda and Radha suffered themselves to be guided by the boy, while Jánoo, after seeing them safe across the hill, returned to his post.

Weeping bitterly, hardly knowing whether to go on with the lad or to return, at all risks, to Tooljapoor, the two women had yielded to Jánoo's well-intended but mistaken direction. The path was stony and rough, and their naked feet, unused to such places, were sorely bruised and cut in descending the rugged track by which, through the most intricate and gloomy ravines of the hills, they were guided. It was hardly four miles, perhaps, and yet, faint and wretched as they were, the sun was high in the heavens ere they reached their destination, and were kindly received.

They told their story; but what could be done? Who could go to Tooljapoor? The Brahmun to whose house they had betaken themselves was old and feeble, but a student who lived with him, and who had been absent since daylight to obtain information, returned about noon. He had no news of the Shastree or of Tara; but he volunteered to go again to seek them, and did so, returning at night with accounts of a fruitless search. Jánoo, he said, knew nothing of them, and he had found him telling the same story, that he had buried Anunda and Radha out of sight,—and understood—what the faithful but drunken creature had perhaps meant to convey to all inquirers—that they were safely hidden away.

Perhaps Jánoo would not have been absent so long had he been sober; but the excitement and his potations together had been too much for him. When he awoke, having lain down to sleep in the bazar, it was evening, and they were lighting the lamps in the shops. "It is too late now," thought he, "to go across the hills for the Shastree's wives, and they are safer where they are;" so he betook himself to the house. His men were there in charge. The dead negro had been taken out and buried, and some of the blood washed away; but the place was utterly defiled: the sacred fire had gone out, and the whole premises must undergo purification ere they could enter or inhabit it once more. Jánoo shrugged his shoulders—"They cannot live here," he said; "there is the hut in the garden at Sindphul, and I will take them there and hide them in it."

So in the morning, before it was light, he set out from Tooljapoor, and crossed the hills, with two of his men leading two stout ponies for the women, and reached Afsinga before the sun had risen. He brought no tidings of the Shastree; but it was reported generally in the town, he said, that he and Tara were at Sindphul; and, in any case, they must go there and live in the garden till the house could be purified, and fit to be again inhabited. This was scant comfort to Anunda and Radha; but Jánoo said that most families in the town were in the same predicament, that he knew the Shastree and Tara were not among the dead, and probability confirmed the report that they had fled in the confusion, and were safe.

It was hardly four miles to Sindphul by the road at the foot of the hills on the plain; and they set out, after their hospitable hosts had insisted upon their taking an early meal. Anunda would fain have gone by Tooljapoor, but Jánoo overruled it. There was no one there;

they would only sit down and cry at the house door; and if the Shastree were at Sindphul, they would be delayed going to him. Nobody had been disturbed there; and the Bhóslay and the Putwari would advise them for the best in any case.

All these arguments overruled Anunda, and they set out with their guide. They met no one, except a few men watching in their fields by the wayside, who told them all was quiet. Jánoo would not even take them near the pass of Tooljapoor, but, striking across the plain by the Gosai's Mutt, and through the great mango grove, they reached Sindphul unobserved.

It is not a large village, and they were well known there. Passing up the central street, they had greetings from many friends, both men and women. At last they saw their own old gardener sitting weeping at the door of the Putwari's house; and Jánoo, who was leading Anunda's pony, took them thither. They were both sick at heart as they dismounted and entered. The Putwari's wife and his married daughter who lived in the house were kind people, and met them in the outer court. "He is alive," said the dame; "fear not. Heera has dressed the wound, and he has spoken to my husband, and asked for you. We told him we had sent for you, and that you were coming, and, behold, the gods have brought you." Then she led Anunda, weeping, into the inner court, and Radha followed. The men sitting about the door of the apartment got up, and, feeling they had no more to do, went out, all but the old Putwari.

"Vyas Shastree," he said, as the women approached the door, "be comforted; they are safe, and have come to you. Be gentle with him," he added to Anunda; "he is very weak, and Heera says if he is made anxious, or disturbed, fever may come on; therefore, be careful."

It was well meant to give them caution, but at such moments, nature will have its course. The women had existed—since the attack on the temple, and since they had fled with Jánoo—in a state of intense fear and misery which cannot be described; and yet one mercy had accompanied this dread, that they had not fully known what had happened in the temple, and so hope had sustained them. Now, however, there was no doubt; and in a paroxysm of mingled fear and thankfulness, they cast themselves beside the low bed, embracing their husband's feet, and weeping passionately. The Shastree was too weak to speak or move; he could only lift up his hand gently, as if to bless them and welcome them, while a faint but grateful smile spread itself over his pallid features.

For a little time, and as they sat silently beside him ministering to their wants—for Anunda was an unrivalled nurse, and had at once proceeded to arrange many things about him, as he liked—strange to say, they did not miss Tara; but Anunda's mind suddenly misgave her. Her husband, whom her arrival had aroused, had again fallen into a doze, and she went outside to ask for her. The whole court had been left to them, and the door of the outer one was closed. "Tara," she called gently, several times, but there was no reply. She might be asleep, she thought, in one of the rooms which opened into it, and she searched in each in succession. There was no one. Radha joined her. "Where is Tara?" she said. "She should have been with him." True, she should have been with her father, but she was not.

The women turned sick at heart and sat down. A nameless terror seized them, so absorbing, that they could say nothing, but that she was not. Anunda dare not ask. Of the two, Radha was most self-possessed. Looking through the door, she saw the old Putwari's wife sitting outside it, and as if watching the place. She called her in, and the dame saw at a glance what was needed. O the misery of that mother's face! who, after trying to articulate "Tara," which her lips formed, as though she spoke the word, fell forward clasping the knees and feet of her old friend, and groaning in her despair.

"The gods have given thee one precious object, sister, and taken the other," she said. "Be thankful for what is spared thee."

Then Anunda thought Tara was dead, and so did Radha; but the woman resumed—

"And yet, why should I say so, Anunda? We know not; she has not been heard of. Let us wait. Hundreds of our friends fled from the temple and from the town. Many we sheltered here all yesterday till the force passed by; then they returned home. So Tara may be at some village near, and we have men watching at your house and at the temple. The Bhópeys will send intelligence if they get any."

"She is not in the garden?" asked Radha.

"No; we searched there long ago, and in all the gardens. No, she is not here, and you must wait. She was favoured of the Mother, sister, and will not be deserted. At least we know she was not killed."

Anunda was comforted for the moment by this, and the women went and resumed their watch by their husband. It was a relief, perhaps, not to speak—a relief, too, to find, in watching him and ministering to his wants, a diversion from the other care. Sooner or later Tara might come in. Jánoo had at once gone in search of her; the Bhóslay had despatched horsemen to every village around, and there would surely be news of her before nightfall.

But none came that night, nor the next day. The Shastree was not yet aware of Tara's absence; fever had begun—the fever of the wound—and he was unconscious of most things. Sometimes he recognized Anunda, and sometimes called Radha, Tara. It was a blessed thing then that he knew no more. Neither of the women relaxed for a moment in their work, and sat there by the bed, without sleep and without rest, looking for news of Tara; but none came. Messenger after messenger arrived, but with no tidings of her.

Late next day Jánoo returned. He must see Anunda, he said; he had news of importance about Tara, and, so far as he knew, she was not dead.

Anunda went to the man outside; he might not enter because of his impure caste.

Jánoo was a man of few words and scant ceremony, and he blurted out, "Moro Trimmul and Gunga took her away, lady. I was drinking last night with some of our people, who are strangers, and came from a distance, and who were dividing booty: and they said they had carried off a beautiful Moorlee as the disturbance broke out, and put her in a palankeen, and they were paid by Moro Trimmul, the reciter. They treated me and some of my people to liquor, and told us of this as a good piece of business. And I have not stolen them, lady; but the jewels you gave me are gone; they were given to Pahar Singh's hunchback, who came and asked for them in the Kucheri in my name: but Pahar Singh will give them up; or if not, I will burn a corn-stack of his every night till he does."

All this was told rapidly and confusedly. The detail was hardly intelligible; but one great fact came out beyond all others, and if it were true, better Tara were dead—O, far better!

"Wait," said Anunda, "and I will come to thee again;" and she went in and whispered it all to Radha. She saw the girl's face flush and her bosom heave rapidly. "Gunga must have helped him," she said, "else he had not dared it, and I will see to it myself." So they both went out to the Ramoosee, and Radha at once declared she would go with him to the town above, and make inquiries.

She was shrewd and active. Accompanied by Jánoo and two of the Bhóslay's retainers, she soon found the man from whom Jánoo had heard of Tara, and listened to his story. They had known nothing of Moro Trimmul's purpose, he said, till that night of the recitation, or how the girl they took was to be decoyed away, or who she was; but as the disturbance began, she was brought out by him in his arms, and then they took her. Yes, he knew what had become of her. Moro Trimmul had been put in irons by the Mahomedan chief, and Tara had been carried off to Sholapoor. He and his companions had watched the palankeen from the rocks in the ravine where they had hidden themselves, because, if it had been left unguarded, they would have gone to it.

It was clear enough now, therefore, that Tara was gone, not dead.

That would have been grief—bitter grief; but here was more misery than death would have caused. Who had taken their Tara? for what fate was she reserved? They could only think of her beauty as destined for some Mahomedan harem—reserved for a fate worse than death.

It was piteous to see the mother and the sister-wife prostrated under this misery and the state of their husband; and it was with difficulty that Radha was restrained from going at once to Sholapoor after the camp, and endeavouring to trace and reclaim Tara. If she had only done so—if this energetic girl, used to rough ways and rapid journeys, had been allowed to follow out her own plans, what misery might not have been saved to all! Hard she pleaded, that she could not be denied to her brother. She would force from him an account of Tara, and would bring her back.

But Anunda hesitated; and the Shastree, to whom all was told, weak as he was in body, was more than usually vacillating. The Mahomedan camp, full of licentiousness, was no place for a Brahmun girl. "The Shastree must be attended," Anunda said; and, in Tara's absence, he seemed to cling the more fondly to his young wife, and to miss her ministrations if even she was temporarily absent. Finally, the matter was left in the hands of their friends, the Bhóslay and the old Putwari, and they decided that Radha must not go; but a messenger should be sent, who, assisted by friends and Brahmuns at Sholapoor, would do all that was needful or possible.

In truth, all these friends thought that seeking for Tara at all was injudicious. They could not believe, considering her beauty and public vocation as a priestess, that she could have escaped observation, and they had come to the conclusion that her preservation from dishonour was impossible. Better she were dead; or, if alive, reunion was henceforth impossible, for the hard rules of religious faith must exclude her from all assistance and sympathy. These were home truths which, sooner or later, Vyas Shastree himself would acknowledge; and Radha's plan was overruled.

It was some days before an answer came. Communications were necessarily slow when there were only foot messengers to carry them. The Shastree's fever had passed away, and his wound was progressing favourably. Mentally and bodily, he had passed a fearful crisis; but natures like his bow to these calamities rather than break, and there was hope at least in the messenger who had gone, to which they all clung.

Little by little they heard enough to sustain this hope. The Bhóslay's correspondent, a banker in the town of Sholapoor, had spared no pains for the recovery of Vyas Shastree's child; but beyond the fact that in the family of Afzool Khan there was a new Hindu slave, of great beauty, who was carefully secluded in the zenana, he could ascertain nothing; and the inquiries, he wrote, must be continued in camp, for the force had marched, and was now some stages distant, going towards Wye.

Again, after an interval of weary expectation, and the daily endurance of that heavy weight of uncertainty which is so often worse than the bitterest agony of reality, there came fresh news which they could not doubt. A poor Brahmun of Sholapoor, incited by the offer of reward held out by the Shastree's friends, had proceeded to camp, and returned from it direct. They never forgot that evening of his arrival. The Shastree had, meanwhile, been removed to his own house, as soon as it had undergone purification, and lay, weak as yet, but convalescent, in the verandah of the inner court, living, as he said, in sight of the objects most loved by his lost child; and it was almost an occupation to watch dreamily Tara's bright flowers glowing in the sunlight. He was lying there, watching them, as the evening sun declined, and the colour of its light was growing richer as the shadows of the buildings lengthened, and Anunda had just said he must retire to his room; but he was pleading to be allowed to stay, when the man was announced without.

Weary and footsore, Radha and a servant poured water over his feet, and led him in. "There was no bad news," he said; "none, Tara was well." Then they all listened, with grateful hearts and tears of joy, to the man's tale of having discovered her, though he could not get speech of her or send a message to her; but in Afzool Khan's family there was a Brahmun girl called Tara, who was an honoured guest; her people had been killed, they said, and they were taking her to Wye, to her relatives. He had watched several days about the Khan's tents in hope of seeing her, but in vain; for the servants and soldiers, thinking him a spy, had beaten him and driven him off. Day by day the distance back to Tooljapoor grew greater, so he had returned. But there was no doubt; the man described what he had heard distinctly, and they could now trace Tara from the temple to where she then was. She must believe they were all dead, and was going to their relatives at Wye: and she was at least safe from Moro Trimmul, whom the messenger reported to be in close confinement.

Now, for once, there was no indecision or vacillation in the Shastree's mind. He could bear easy travelling in a litter; and Radha should have it by-and-by, when he grew stronger. He would not delay, and they could yet overtake the army at Wye, or soon afterwards. Very little of the household property had been lost, after all; and Anunda's store of money was at last to prove useful. That night, as with thankful hearts they spoke of their lost child, they arranged plans for setting out to reclaim her; and their friends, who crowded about them with congratulations next day, soon completed the necessary arrangements. The third day was a lucky one, according to the planets; and they moved down the pass to Sindphul, followed by many friends, and the good wishes and prayers of all who had known Tara from childhood.

CHAPTER LXVI.

A PLEASANT life was it to Tara. The daily stages of a large army encumbered with heavy materiel are necessarily slow at all times, and the country roads were not as yet dry from the recent rains, so that the force could not hurry on. The Khan himself was in no haste. On the arrival of the Mahratta ambassadors he had received them courteously, and insisted upon their being the guests of the royal camp. They had not much to say, beyond general protestations of attachment. Their master's demands were simple, they knew; but he would treat for them in person when he met the Khan. Meanwhile, supplies for the royal forces were abundant; the stages they arranged were shorter perhaps than the Khan, and especially Fazil, approved of; but they found grain and forage provided everywhere, and the camp bazar had always the appearance of a busy fair.

On his own part, Afzool Khan, yielding to the persuasions of Sivaji's agents, despatched an envoy of his own, the Brahmun Punto Gopináth, to Pertabgurh. Their master's mind, they said, would be relieved by it; and as Sivaji had evinced confidence in sending his own servants unsolicited, so a similar mark of courtesy could hardly be refused. The Khan did not object to it. The Envoy received his instructions, to act as circumstances might require, leaving all points of detail for future arrangement; and Bulwunt Rao was placed in command of the escort which accompanied him. In this capacity he was safe against all local enemies; and he went the more willingly, as he trusted, under this opportunity, to interest the Rajah in his own affairs.

So there was no hurry, and it was a pleasant life. Every day, or nearly so, there was a change; the force moved forward a few miles, or it halted; tents were pitched, thrown down, moved, and again pitched in pleasant places; perhaps in some soft grassy plain spangled with flowers, or in a stubble field with the stacks of ripe grain standing around them. The Khan's Durbar tent was open to all comers, where the leaders of the various bodies of troops met every day for business or ceremonial visits, as it might be: behind it the private tents enclosed by a canvas wall, which afforded a large area. Before all, floated the royal standard, and a place was cleared near it which was appropriated for public prayer. Five times in each day, if the force halted, did the musical chant of invitation to prayer resound from this spot; and as often did the devout among the soldiery assemble there, and perform the stated devotions. Every afternoon the priest and other divines preached to the people; and it was remarked that the sermons on the holy war, though they were continued at intervals, were of quieter character than they used to be at first.

Perhaps the religious zeal of the Peer had relaxed since the slaughter at Tooljapoor, and was satisfied with the fact of the idol having been overthrown and defiled. Perhaps the Khan supposed enough had been done to terrify the Mahratta people, and that the rest would follow upon negotiation.

There was very little change in the daily life: the early march, the halt for the day, the household occupations, and then the pleasant talk with Zyna and Lurlee. Her tales of the Hindu life, and of her home pleasures and occupations, were told again and again by Tara, often with bitter tears, and yet told again and again, and heard by sympathizing friends.

Two different worlds, as it were, were thus brought together. What did the simple Brahmun girl know of the grandeur of Mahomedan nobles, of which only a faint rumour had ever reached her? To her unclean, she would once have shuddered at nearer contact with them, however rich or grand they might be. Now, how different! They had respected her honour, and they also respected her faith; and every day her little cooking-place was arranged, with water brought by a Brahmun for her bath and her drinking, which no one interfered with. Sometimes, Zyna and Lurlee would look on while the little maiden dressed her simple meal, as she had often done at home,—amused, and wondering at her dexterity; and it was not long before the Khan himself was a petitioner for some delicate specimen of her handiwork, which, it was remarked, he ate with infinite relish, and pronounced better even than Kurreema's efforts to the same end.

They procured the girl the books she loved, and eagerly, and with infinite animation, she would read and expound sacred texts, which even the priest admitted contained at least moral and virtuous doctrine. Occasionally, too, he was unable to control himself, and he answered the little preacher from his own books, hurling at her texts translated from the Koran into bad Mahratta; and half angry with, and half amused by, the seeming petulance with which she resisted conversion, allowed her greater liberties, perhaps, than he had ever been known to submit to before from "an infidel."

"See," she would cry, "Huzrut! here are God's holy words to us poor Hindus hundreds of thousands of years old, but yours are, after all, but a few hundreds. Surely the elder has precedence?" If she could translate the beautiful Bhugwat Geeta to him, that book so full of mystic religious doctrine, he could understand her better, she thought; but she had no words that he could comprehend, in which to convey the sense of the noble Sanscrit; and it must be confessed that her general attempts in argument were failures.

Kind Tara! gentle Tara! was any servant ill,—and the cold air and damp earth gave many fevers,—who so ready with knowledge of simples as the Brahmun girl? who so watchful, who so careful? In turn she had tended Lurlee and Zyna, who suffered at first from the change and exposure in camp. Then Fazil grew ill too, and for several days could not ride. She could ride: she had never travelled in a palankeen in her life—her father could not afford one: so she gave up her litter to him, and rode a stout ambling palfrey of the Khan's which was gentle, and a relief on long marches from his heavier war-horse; and old Shêre Khan and his men, her first escort from Tooljapoor, claimed the privilege of guarding her as she rode, rapidly and fearlessly, and managed the active horse with skill and grace.

Once Moro Trimmul saw her riding with this escort of heavily-armed men. She was wrapped in shawls, and had twisted one round her head like a turban, which covered her face all but her eyes. He concealed his own face and person as she passed, but the fact that she was riding with so noble a company to attend on her, disquieted him. "She is growing into favour," he thought, "and is in danger. It is necessary to act before we reach Wye."

Whether Moro Trimmul was in camp or not, she had not thought to inquire. Fazil had told her once, with a very perceptible tone of disappointment, that he had been released, and had gone away. He was never seen in the camp, but, with Sivaji's envoys, put up in villages near where the force might halt. They did not vex her with his tale of her having been taken away under her father's sanction, which Fazil, Lurlee, and Zyna had never believed, and by common consent the name of the Brahmun was never mentioned among them.

Ah, yes, a pleasant time indeed! What more delicious to a young girl's heart than the consciousness of awakening love? Could she help it? did she desire it? Neither, perhaps; but it would come nevertheless: and there would come too, with all the persuasive adjuncts of her own helplessness and dependence, the sense of evident respect in which she was held by Fazil, and his honourable reticence, even of speech with her. So a new life, a new desire for life, was growing within her, and increased day by day. Did she endeavour to check it? Not then; it was too delicious.

Before it, the old home was fading away, the forms of father and mother already becoming dim and shadowy, as belonging to the past. The old temple occupations, the preparation for daily duty, were being supplanted by other feelings, undecided as yet, but ineffably tender. Did she regret that these were growing into definite form in her own heart? Not then. She had no certainty of what she thought, and if any one, even Zyna, had asked her to define what was passing within her, she could not have done so.

O, the wondrous stirring of that new life, shutting out all the old! the gentle growing of an absorbing passion. If Fazil spoke to her, she trembled; but not in fear. She had no fear of him. No matter what he said, she listened, and never replied. When he was ill, she took to him the little soothing potions she had made, and, as he lay tossing with fever, was conscious that they would relieve thirst, and would not be forgotten. She could speak to him then, a word only, perhaps, to tell him to be patient, that he would be relieved if he would be still. Even this was a fearful but an exquisite pleasure.

How often Zyna spoke of her brother! How precious he was to her; how brave he was; how beautiful! Had Tara ever seen any one like him? No; those timid, loving eyes had never looked up to any one before, far less to such a one as Fazil. What did she know? She could only see that there was, in her eyes, the godlike beauty the old poets wrote of Kāmdeo—those soft, loving eyes which sometimes earnestly looked into hers, before which she dare not open her own. If he came into the tent accoutred, blazing with cloth-of-gold and steel armour, she fled at once, and from a distance watched Zyna embrace him, perhaps fasten an amulet upon his arm, or relieve him of his heavy clothing and armour.

If Fazil were absent, Tara and Zyna would often sit and talk of him. Poor little heart! how it fluttered then. She could not tell his sister what rose to her lips, but, as her heart swelled, she felt as if she could do some great thing for him or for Zyna—defend them, or avert evil from them—even if she died herself, it would be welcome. Yes, the old story—the old story!—the telling of which, in all its wondrous forms, will never finish here, or finish, but to be renewed hereafter!

Did Fazil perceive this? Not yet. He had a true gentleman's best safeguard against presumption, an innate modesty in regard to women, which prevented it; and yet . . . . how often he watched the lithe and graceful figure as it passed from his presence on some trifling errand, or the glowing intellectual face as it quivered under the excitement of explaining any portion of one of her old-world books which interested her,—or the quiet, demure expression which gathered over it, as she sometimes brought—for she would allow no-one else to touch the vessels she cooked it in—her little daily con tribution to his father's dinner, and waited apart with folded arms till he had told her, with a pleasant smile or joke, how much he liked it!

"Ah!" said Shêre Khan, after Fazil's first journey in the palankeen, and as he lay, languid and weakened by his fever, in the outer tent where his retainers could attend on him—"whom hast thou sent us, Meah? They tell of Chandnee Begum of the Nizam Shahee's, but who, after all, was one of our royal race,—that she rode with her army of true believers, and fought with her enemies. By Alla! this girl rides so that it is hard to follow her; and we all say, there is that in her eyes which, had she a sword in her hand, nay, without it, would lead us, as only thou, or the Khan could lead us, Meah. Yes, she is a jewel of great price."

And Fazil liked to hear this; he liked to hear old Goolab exhaust her vocabulary of endearment upon Tara, as she sat by him, rubbing his feet when the fever oppressed him; and when, in those feverish dreams which are part of the disorder, strange fancies beset him, the Brahmun girl often became a prominent actor in those unreal scenes of his imagination.

So it grew on. The habits of Eastern people do not admit of those demonstrations and protestations of love which form part of our social habits. But we have no warrant for saying that their feelings are the less ardent or permanent. We think not; and that there, as elsewhere, they progress silently, and are afterwards called into active exercise by occasion and opportunity, and with possibly more energy and passion than among ourselves.

When Lurlee had rallied the Brahmun girl sometimes upon her attachment to her old faith, now, she said, hopeless,—and Zyna, throwing her arms round her as they sat together in the twilight after evening prayer, besought her to give it up—to come to them as a sister, as a daughter,—and pleaded hard for this,—Tara was sorely tried. Whom had she now to look to? whither was she going? If there were some of her mother's relatives at Wye,—and all she knew of them was the surname,—what was she to do? Even were they there, what was she to do? Against her, ever rose up the hard cruel wall of Hindu widowhood; the servitude, the nearly inevitable dishonour among strangers, of her own faith, the hopeless weariness of an unloved and uncared-for life; and so, better death. All this had passed through her mind before, at Tooljapoor, and then there was no alternative. Now?

O, how hard the new young life pleaded—as these thoughts passed through her mind—the certainty of love on the one hand, even as a friend or dependant, and of respect and protection from all evil, even though to minister to the old Khan should be her only occupation. This, and to see Fazil daily—to see Zyna—to be held to that rough old Lurlee's heart—to be the child, for so they called her, of all the servants,—what had the other life to compare with this? Even if she found her people, what had they to offer her but misery? for so it seemed.

And when, one day (Wye was now only a few stages distant), Zyna told her what they wished—what they all spoke of among themselves—what Fazil had proposed to his father,—and how the old Khan had at first gently resisted it, desiring a high connection for his son, and yet had conceded in the end;—when Lurlee came and pleaded too, and told her, and proved to her by the planets and the elements, that she would be fortunate to the house and to Fazil—a loved and honoured wife,—what could she say? The new life now rose up within her vigorous and defiant against all other thoughts; and its blessed shape—definite, honourable, irresistible, and delicious to contemplate—would not be repelled.

"Only give me time," she cried, hiding her burning face in Zyna's bosom—"only give me time! It is so sudden—so unlooked-for." Then she added, after a pause, and looking up sadly, "I am his captive and his slave; not of your people, lady, but a stranger, and an infidel, as the priest says; impure among my own sect, and of no account but for shame and dishonour. As such, I cannot come to a noble house. Ah, do not mock me!"

"They say," returned Zyna, "that the Emperors of Delhi sought brides from among the Rajpoots, and esteemed them as honourable and as noble as themselves; and thou art a Brahmun, Tara, far purer and nobler than they. But no matter: thou art our own Tara, whom Alla hath sent to us, and whom we have received thankfully, for him whose heart no one as yet has touched. Let it be as we all will;" and Tara, at last, said it should be so.

Was she grateful or happy, this desolate girl? O, far beyond either! All those dreamy imaginings which at home, among her books and flowers, had taken no definite shape, now assumed a palpable reality. In her eyes glorious, in her heart Fazil was supremely glorious also. She dared not look at him now, even by stealth; but there was ever a sweet assurance of his presence—of his care—of his thought, which produced a kind of ecstasy, filling her mind with a sublime devotion and innocent passion: often filling her eyes, too, causing a strangely tight feeling at her heart as if she could not breathe, and then a deep sigh as her tears welled over; and she hoped, with an almost delirious joy, that she was to belong to him by-and-by: no matter how far distant it might be,—only to belong to him, and be for ever with him.

And so the time passed to them all. A pleasant life which, day by day, grew to be more absorbing to Tara, and caused indifference to outward occurrences. But had her enemy been idle?

The force marched late one day. Moro Trimmul had ascertained that the litters and followers generally, would not arrive in camp before nightfall. It was dark, for there was no moon; and he laid his plans accordingly. Day and night, he and Gunga, in various disguises, had watched about the Khan's tents, and had tried to get speech of the servants. He dare not come openly, except to the Khan's Durbar, where he heard nothing. He was nearly hopeless of success, when he understood casually that the evening march was determined upon. All the force was not to move; but some only with the Khan, for the sake of convenience of supplies and water. It was a short stage—only four or five miles, and the Khan's tents were to precede the force. He and his family were to remain in a village for the night, and several houses had been cleared for him. Thus much had Gunga picked up, and for once, fortune seemed to favour their designs.

Fazil had recovered, and again rode with his men. Tara, therefore, once more occupied the litter, which was closed, and carried with those of Lurlee and Zyna. Had she continued to ride as she wished, nothing could have happened. As it grew dark Moro Trimmul—with a small body of horsemen which he had detached from the Envoy's and kept about his own person—followed Tara's litter at a distance, and yet so as not to interfere with it. As it grew dark, and they neared the place where they were to stop for the night, he observed that Tara's palankeen was the last: he knew it from the white devices sewn on the red cover; and he dexterously, yet apparently unpremeditatedly, pushed his horsemen between it and the others, in a narrow lane, in which litters, horsemen, and soldiers were much crowded together. Then he stopped his men, pretending there was obstruction in front; and so the litters of Lurlee and Zyna, which were surrounded by footguards and guides as usual, went on for some distance, never missing the one behind.

Moro Trimmul was exultant. At the next turn in the road, his own servants, who had been instructed beforehand, went to the bearers of Tara's litter, pretending to have been seeking them, and, abusing them roundly for their carelessness in remaining behind, bade them come on rapidly. The men followed blindly; they knew they were to go to a village, and here was one; and, pressing forward, they presently reached a house to which they were directed.

"Put down the palankeen. Gosha! Gosha! Murdana! Murdana!" was cried by several voices; and a screen of cloth being stretched, as usual, from the palankeen to the entrance of the court, and the door of the litter opened, Tara emerged from it unsuspiciously: then the door was instantly closed behind her, a thick shawl was thrown round her head which almost stifled her, and she felt herself taken up by powerful arms, and carried rapidly onwards. She struggled violently, but a voice she knew but too well, hissed into her ear through the shawl, "Be quiet, else I will kill you;" and for a moment she lost consciousness.

CHAPTER LXVII.

TARA revived as the shawl was pushed roughly from her head, and the cool air reached her face; in another moment she was set down in a verandah, closed from the outer court by thick woollen curtains, in which a small lamp, placed in a niche, glimmered faintly. There could be no doubt now. Releasing her, Moro Trimmul drew himself up, panting with the exertion of carrying her, and looked at her from head to foot ere he spoke; while Gunga, advancing from a dark corner of the room, and bending lowly with a mock gesture of reverence, touched the ground near her feet, and then retreated a pace so as to see her better.

"Thou hast had powerful friends, Tara," said the Brahmun bitterly, and with a scornful sneer—"very powerful; even the enemy's general and his fair son; but the gods are not with them, but with me. Once, in blood and terror, didst thou escape me; but not now, girl—never more. Now thou art mine, and there is nothing between thee and me; nor sister, nor father, nor mother; only thee, and only me; and thou hast a long account of misery to pay me."

"The holy Moorlee of the goddess forgot her faith and her vow among the cow-slaying infidels; and the Mother hath sent me to bring her back from her dainty lover, who rides in cloth-of-gold and bright armour," said Gunga, with another mock reverence. "Art thou ready, O Moorlee of Toolja Mata? ready to be such as I am, in her service? Come! there is thy master and mine; be content that thou art saved the sin of faithlessness to her. Didst thou think she—the Mother," continued the girl, advancing a step at each word till she was close to Tara, who shrank from her—"the Mother would loose thee from thy vow to be the petted toy of an unclean Toork? O Tara, didst thou think it? Ah, yes! I know thou didst, faithless, when the fair boy's arms were about thee."

"Silence!" cried Tara panting, as these bitter words stung her to the quick. "Silence! thou art shameless, Gunga. O, what have I ever done to harm thee, that thou hast such bitter enmity to me?"

"Thou art beautiful, and I hate thee for that. I hated thee long ago, before thou wast a Moorlee," she replied. "He loved me once, that Moro Trimmul there; now he cries, 'Tara! Tara!' all day long, like a sick child, and will not look on me. Thou wilt hate me because I have taken thee from thy beautiful lover; but, O Tara, more deeply do I hate thee for taking mine from me. Look, he gave me this gold zone. It is as heavy as thine—heavier. That is all I have left—that is all. He will give thee another, by-and-by; not now, but when he has done with thee. Enough! Take her away, Moro Trimmul. I have done thy bidding, and earned the gold. Take her away—far away—ere I repent of this, the worst work of my life, and join her against thee. Go!"

"Gunga! Gunga! go not," cried Tara, seizing her dress. "There is pity in thy heart, let it come out to me. O, leave me not to him, by your mother, by your——"

"Come," cried Moro Trimmul fiercely, casting his arm about her. "This is child's play, come. . . . . Nay, Tara, gently, and it were better for thee—else I will strike thee," he said, under his breath, but with a terrible distinctness, as she struggled violently, shrieking as she did so. "Gunga! the shawl. Quick, girl—lest she be heard without. Quick! Bar the outer door."

It was too late. Several persons, among whom was an elderly Brahmun of sedate and respectable appearance, attended by armed retainers, came up the steps hurriedly and entered the room. Between the noise of Tara's shrieks and his own exertions, Moro Trimmul had not heard them, and with Gunga's aid had forced Tara to the ground, and was endeavouring to tie the shawl about her head, which she was resisting with all her might; but Gunga had succeeded in catching her hands, and Tara was much exhausted. Another instant, and she would have been helplessly in their power; but at this moment Gunga saw the curtain pushed aside, and one of the men enter with his sword drawn; and, loosing Tara, she upset the cruise burning in the niche, and fled into an inner portion of the dark apartment.

"Who art thou?" cried the man, darting forward and seizing Moro Trimmul's arm; "what murder is this thou art doing?"

He had had no time to escape, or even to rise from his kneeling posture to shake off the soldier's grip, and two others also caught him at the same moment; while the elderly man, calling earnestly for a light, raised up Tara, and disengaged her from the shawl which had been thrown about her. "Art thou wounded?" he said.

"By the Holy Mother," cried one of the men with whom Moro Trimmul was struggling violently, "be quiet, else I will drive my knife into thee. Bind him, brothers, he may be armed. Quick!"

At this moment a man bearing a lighted torch came into the court from the street, and ran rapidly up the steps into the room. As the light flashed upon the struggling group of men, the leader of the party recognized Moro Trimmul, and bid his retainers release him. As they did so, Tara, who had partly risen, sank again to the ground, clasping his knees, and crying piteously for protection.

The old Brahmun understood the situation at a glance. "There was another woman here,—seize her!" he exclaimed. She was not, however, to be found. "Peace," he said to Tara, "peace, my daughter; be comforted, no one shall harm thee. Who art thou? What has happened?"

"I am the unhappy daughter of Vyas Shastree of Tooljapoor, who was murdered, and I am an orphan," she cried sobbing. "O, defend me from him; he would have done me violence and dishonour."

"Moro Trimmul," said the old man sadly, "how often hast thou been warned, and what new wickedness is this?—against a Brahmun girl too, and the daughter of the man to whom thy sister was given! O, shame!"

"She is a Moorlee," he replied sulkily, "and has done dishonour to the Mother by living with Mussulmans in camp. It was from them I have rescued her, and would have taken her to Wye, but she resisted. I have done no evil, Pundit, nor intended any."

"Is this true, girl?" asked the Brahmun.

"Quite true, Maharaj," answered Tara, sobbing hysterically, and hardly knowing what she said: "only take me hence, and I will tell thee all; but I am not impure,—I am not defiled,—I have nothing to be ashamed of. O, put your hand on my head, and take me to my people in Wye. Save me, else I shall die; or kill me, rather than let him or the woman come near me. When I am alone with your family I will tell them all."

"Come," said the man, who was Govind Narrayen, the principal envoy of the Rajah Sivaji, and a Brahmun of wealth and high station in the country, best known among the people under the familiar title of Baba Sahib. "I am well known, and I knew and honoured your father, and grieve his death. Come with me, and you shall go on with my people at once to Wye. They leave the camp to avoid the confusion, and will take care of you, and the bearers and palankeen are still in the street.

"As to you, Moro Trimmul," he continued, turning to him, "I reserve my judgment till I have inquired from this girl of what she complains. I bid you, however, beware. The Maharaja is not what he used to be, and will submit to no profligacy now. I take this girl as my daughter, and she is safe against you. Beware!" And so saying, and giving his arm for Tara to lean on, while he partly supported her with the other, he led her out, and once more placed her in the litter, which was taken up and carried forward rapidly.

The Envoy and his escort had also moved with the camp, and he had sent on his family to a stage some miles distant. As he passed through the street of the village where Tara had been set down, the bearers of her litter, who had remained with it, hearing the stifled scream from within the court, and alarmed by the sudden closing and fastening of the door, had stopped Baba Sahib as he went by, and besought him to see whether Tara was not in danger. He had dismounted, some of his men had burst in the court door, and we know the rest.

"Again baffled, O witch that thou art!" cried Moro Pundit, flinging himself on the ground as Tara passed out, and tearing up the clay of the floor in the agony of his passion: "what sent that meddling fool to aid thee? If it had been only that proud boy she loves, ah! I would have slain him and her together. Gunga! Gunga! where art thou? O girl, I burn—I choke! She too is gone, devil that she is. If thou hadst only helped me sooner I had stopped the screams, and no one could have heard them. Gunga! dost thou hear? By——," and he swore a frightful oath, "come hither, or I will come and stab thee: art thou too playing with me? Beware!"

The girl advanced from a dark corner trembling, yet without fear; and as she did so, he raised himself on his arm, and she saw him grasp a knife at his waistband. "Kill me," she said, "if thou wilt; twice I have aided thee, and twice the Mother hath saved her from us. I will have no more of it."

"No more!" cried the Brahmun, starting to his feet, and seizing her arm he shook her roughly—"no more! This from thee? I tell thee we have gone too far to recede. Will that old dotard be quiet? Will he spare my character? Not he. He has been my enemy from the first, supplanted me in my authority, crossed me in every design, and lastly in this.—Why didst thou bungle with the shawl? Coward! witch! devil!"—and he struck her violently on the face with his open hand at each word. "Why didst thou fail me? Go!" and he flung her away from him, so that she tottered and fell heavily against the wall beyond. "Go! may——"

Her fall and agony of mind prevented her hearing the frightful curses which followed. Once before, when his sister had come to him, the paroxysm of passion had been like this, but only once, and yet he had not dared to strike her. She was not stunned, but O, the misery of her mind! She felt her lips were cut, and her mouth was bleeding. The pain of this, the degradation of having been struck, made the girl desperate. If she had had a dagger she would have stabbed Moro or herself. She could see him very dimly, for the place was dark except the faint light which came in from the drawn curtains. She saw that he was sitting, leaning against one of the wooden pillars of the room, rocking himself to and fro. He had drawn his knife, and a faint gleam of the naked blade was seen now and again as he moved. Was she to die, or he? No matter. In a frame of mind like hers death has no terror. It is only the return to consciousness which brings fear with it, and she lay crouching on the ground, but watching him intently. If he moved towards her, she knew she must die; but he did not move, and suddenly the rocking ceased, he seemed to fall heavily to one side, and lay there motionless.

Was he feigning, in order to get her into his power? No, it did not seem so, for he lay still, breathing heavily. She had heard that thick heavy breathing once before, and now recognized it again. Still she was cautious. She rose gently, and stepping lightly forward stood over him, yet near enough to the steps to escape if he moved. The knife had fallen from his hand, and lay beside him. She took it up, and placed it in her own waistband. He was insensible; his turban had partly fallen off, and his face lay towards the light, turned upwards. He could not harm her now,—he was in her power. . . . . The evil spirit within, tugged hard at her heart, and she drew the knife. Then the blood from her lip trickled into her mouth, and the wound smarted and urged on her hand. If he had risen and spoken a word to her, she would have killed him; but as he lay so helpless, the girl's heart once more softened. "It is my death, I know," she said; "let him kill me; I cannot kill him, and this faint will pass away. Now she is gone, he may love me again." Poor fool, to think it!

Then she watched a few moments, and as she sat down by him raised his head into her lap. The face was cold and clammy; was this death? There was no water, else she would sprinkle some on him, but she fanned him with the end of her garment, and after a while he opened his eyes gently. "Gunga!" he said, stretching out his arms, "where art thou, girl? come to me." It was the old tone of kindness, almost sad. Poor fond fool, she did not resist it; and, wiping the blood from her lips, kissed his forehead.

Meanwhile, Tara, sorely shaken in body and mind, had been put into the litter. She heard the bearers ask the old Brahmun whether they were to take her to Afzool Khan's tents; and he had opened the door, and said to her kindly that she had better come to her own people, and that his wife and sister, who knew them, would take charge of her, and be kind to her; that they were at a village some miles further on, and he himself would escort her there.

She was helpless to object: in the first place, she dare not prefer the Mussulman noble's house, as strangers to her faith and to her own people; nor dare she resist a Brahmun of the Envoy's powerful position in whatever he chose to do. She had no alternative, indeed, for he shut the door ere she could reply, the bearers took her forward at a rapid pace, and the night was somewhat advanced, ere she was again set down at the door of a respectable house in a village, and several women-servants, such as are menials in Brahmun families, kindly assisted her to alight, bringing what there was in the palankeen after her.

CHAPTER LXVIII.

It was a house something like their own at Tooljapoor. There was the master's seat, with its flowers and holy text painted on it; the verandah open to the court; the thick curtains between the pillars let down to exclude the night air, which was chill. The room was neat and scrupulously clean. She was once more in a Brahmun's house.

Before Tara sat two women, both elderly. One a stout and matronly figure, with a grave but kind countenance, and grey hair neatly braided, with heavy gold rings round her neck, wrists, and ankles, plainly but richly dressed, indicating rank and wealth; the other evidently a widow, clad in coarse white serge, her head clean shaved, and her wrists, ankles, and neck without any ornaments. She had strong coarse features, much wrinkled, small piercing eyes deep set in her head, and her skin was flaccid and shrivelled. She was the elder sister of the Envoy, and lived with him a life of austere penance and privation, and, as a Hindu widow, was a pattern of scrupulous attention to the rules of her faith. Neither rose to meet her.

Tara advanced and touched their feet in token of reverential submission and salutation. By the lady, whose evident rank had attracted Tara first, the action was received at least without repugnance, and perhaps with interest; but by the other with marked aversion—she drew back her feet as though to prevent pollution, and shrank aside, evidently to avoid contact.

"Thou art welcome, daughter of Vyas Shastree," said the one: "peace be with thee."

"And that gilded thing is called a widow and a Moorlee!" cried the other, with a scornful glance at Tara. "O sister, admit her not! Why has she any hair? Why is she more like a bride than a widow? —a harlot rather than a virtuous woman?"

"I am a widow and an orphan," returned Tara meekly, sinking down and trembling violently, as she addressed the first speaker. "I have been saved from dishonour, lady. O be kind to me! I have no one on earth to protect me now. They are all gone—all—and may God help me!"

"Your mother was one of the Durpeys of Wye, was she not?"

asked the Envoy's wife, whose name was Amba Bye. "Do they know of thee?"

"I do not know, lady," returned Tara; "they have never been to us, nor we to them; but my mother was a Durpey, and used to speak of them."

"Her father lately married that wild sister of Moro Trimmul's, and Sukya Bye is sure to know her," said the widow.

"O, not to her!—not to her!" cried Tara passionately—"do not give me to her? I beseech you by your honour, by your children, lady, by all you love on earth, not to give me to her. Do with me as ye will yourselves, ye are matrons, but——"

"And why not, girl?" asked the widow, interrupting her.

"Peace! Pudma Bye," said her brother, now entering, and seeing that his sister's question had caused pain, "the girl hath had a sore trial; listen to her, ere thou art hard on her. Speak, daughter, let us know from thine own lips how and why thou wast suffering violence from Moro Trimmul."

"From Moro Trimmul!" exclaimed both ladies in a breath.

"Yes, from him did I rescue her, sister, else she had fared badly, I fear," returned the Envoy. "A violent and wicked man,—who must be brought before the council, to prevent further scandal. But speak, daughter,—thy name?"

"Tara."

"Tara: well, fear not. Amba Bye is strict, but kind. Speak truly, we listen."

And Tara told her little story: how she had become a priestess when the goddess called her; what she knew of holy books; how she had been carried off from the temple by Moro Trimmul, and how he had persecuted her before. How she was taken by Fazil Khan, and had been saved by him from the King's harem at Beejapoor. Finally, how they had treated her with honour and respect, and were taking her to her only refuge at Wye.

Ah, it was a sad story now: a glimpse of a heaven of delight now shut out from her for ever! She saw the stony eyes of the grim old widow wandering over her, from her glossy braided hair and the garland of jessamine flowers which Zyna had put into it just before they left camp, to the gold ornaments about her neck which Zyna would have her wear; and, above all, to the silken saree, and the golden anklets which Fazil liked, because the tiny bells to them clashed so musically as she walked. Over and over again, as she told her simple story, and was believed by the Baba Sahib and his wife, did his sister evince decided unbelief and scorn. But at the last her brother rebuked her.

"I rescued her myself from violence," he said, "and what she tells me confirms her whole story. Peace, Pudma! one so helpless and so beautiful should have thy pity, not thy scorn."

"Let her have her head shaved, and be such as I am; let her live with me, and bathe in cold water before dawn; let her say the name of God on her beads a thousand times an hour during the night; let her do menial service," cried the widow rapidly; "and then, if she can do these things, brother, she is a Brahmun widow, and true; else cast her out to the Mussulmans with whom she lived. Art thou ready to do all this, girl?" she continued, stretching out her long skinny flaccid arm, which was naked to the shoulder, and showed that the serge about her was her only garment.

Tara's spirit sank within her. Yes, such as the being before her were Hindu widows—such they would claim her to be. "It were better if I were dead," she groaned—"better if I were dead."

"Better if thou wast dead!" echoed the widow. "Ay, much better. Such as thou art, were better dead than live, in a harlot's guise, to be a disgrace to the faith!"

"Nay, peace, sister," said her brother—"I will have none of this. While she is with us, she is our guest and daughter, and shall be cared for tenderly. Take her away, Amba, and let her rest. I will see Afzool Khan at the Durbar to-morrow, and inquire if what she says be true; but my heart already tells me it is so."

Amba Bye rose and said a few soothing words to Tara as she stood over her and raised her up. "Come," she said, "I will not harm thee—come." And Tara rose and followed her to an inner room. The old lady had perhaps been afraid of her sister-in-law, or she was softened by Tara's beauty and grief, for, as she closed the door, she sat down and took her to her heart, laying her head on her bosom. "Thou art a gentle lamb," she said, stroking her head. "God help thee, child," and Tara clung to the kind heart, and felt, as it were, loving arms once more closed around her.

That night she slept with Amba Bye. Her sleep was at first broken, and full of fearful dreams; but wearied nature and youth in the end obtained their mastery over her, and she sank into a deep slumber,—so deep, that the sun was high in the morning ere she awoke.

It had been a weary time to Zyna, Lurlee, and the Khan's household, and even the Khan and the priest sat up far into the night, speaking of Tara. No one had slept. As to Fazil, he, with Shêre Khan, Lukshmun, and a body of horse, rode round the country for miles, all through the night, seeking Tara. No one dared speak to him, and the men had never seen him so excited before. He and Lukshmun, whose activity even surpassed his own, had stopped every palankeen; every cart or carriage which was covered; every veiled female they could see. Villages had been searched also, but no trace of Tara was found—none; and Fazil returned home dejected and worn out, only, however, to change his horse and the men, and to start once more with Lukshmun, who would not leave him, on an errand equally fruitless. That day (Fazil was still absent) Baba Sahib sought Afzool Khan after the afternoon Durbar, and told him what had happened: how he had rescued Tara, how he had sent her on to Wye with his wife and sister, and how she would be safe in his hands; and he heard in return how she was respected and loved in the Khan's family.

"We cannot allow her, Khan," he said kindly, "to remain with you, much as you have respected her faith. It would be a scandal to Brahmuns, if the daughter of Vyas Shastree were the guest even of Afzool Khan and his household. It is not compatible with her purity or her honour, which, now her father is dead, her people must protect. We—that is, my wife and myself—have charged ourselves with her for the present; and her people, the Durpeys of Wye, are rich and devout,—they will receive and protect her."

Afzool Khan remonstrated as far as possible. Tara had grown to be a familiar and beautiful object to him; but he felt the Brahmun was right, and he must not connect her name with his son's. He dare not mention to Lurlee what had been done, but he told Fazil, when he returned, and so all knew of it.

"At least she is safe and in honourable keeping," said Fazil, when he had heard all, "and for the rest, as God wills. But as for that Brahmun, father, he escaped me once—it may not be again."

"Look!" cried Lurlee to Zyna, who was sitting sobbing bitterly—"look! Had I only been careful, this would never have happened. It was Sunday night, and Saturn ruled from the second hour of the first watch to the end. Could anything be worse? We should not have moved at all. My pearl, my love, she should not have left us! Hai! Hai! May the peace of the Prophet be with her, and the protection of Alla be upon her till we meet again!"

"Ameen! Ameen!" sighed Zyna, but she was not comforted, nor was Fazil.

CHAPTER LXIX.

MAGNIFICENT as is the scenery of the Western Ghauts of India throughout their range, it is nowhere, perhaps, more strikingly beautiful than in the neighbourhood of the great isolated plateau which—rising high above the mountain-ranges around it, and known under the name of Maha-bul-eshwur, from the temple at the source of the sacred river Krishna on its summit—is now the favourite summer retreat and sanatorium of the Bombay Presidency. Trim roads, laid out so as to exhibit the beauties of the scenery to the best advantage—pretty English-looking cottages, with brilliant gardens, and a considerable native town, are now the main features of the place; but at the period of our tale it was uninhabited, except by a few Brahmuns and devotees, who, attracted by the holiness of the spot, congregated around the ancient temple, and occupied the small village beside it. Otherwise the character of the wild scenery is unchanged. From points near the edges of the plateau, where mighty precipices of basalt descend sheer into forests of ever-lasting verdure and luxuriance, the eye ranges over a sea of rugged mountain-tops,—some, scathed and shattered peaks of barren rock—others with extensive flat summits, bounded by naked cliffs which, falling into deep gloomy ravines covered with dense forests, would seem inaccessible to man.

To some readers of our tale, this scenery will be familiar; but to others it is almost impossible to convey by description any adequate idea of its peculiar character, or of the beauty of the ever-changing aërial effects, that vary in aspect almost as the spectator turns from one point to another. Often in early morning, as the sun rises over the lower mists, the naked peaks and precipices, standing apart like islands, glisten with rosy tints, while the mist itself, as yet dense and undisturbed, lies wrapped around their bases, filling every ravine and valley, and glittering like a sea of molten silver.

Again, as the morning breeze rises in the valleys below, this vapour breaks up slowly: circling round the mountain summits, lingering in wreaths among their glens and precipices, and clinging to the forests, until dissipated entirely by the fierce beams of the sun. Then, quivering under the fervid heat, long ridges of rugged valleys are spread out below, and range beyond range melts tenderly into a dim distance of sea and sky, scarcely separated in colour, yet showing the occasional sparkle of a sail like a faint cloud passing on the horizon. Most glorious of all, perhaps, in the evening, when, in the rich colours of the fast-rising vapours, the mountains glow like fire; and peak and precipice, forest and glen, are bathed in gold and crimson light; or, as the light grows dimmer, shrouded in deep purple shadow till they disappear in the gloom which quickly falls on all.

Westward from this great mountain plateau, and divided from it by a broad deep valley clothed with forests, the huge mountain of Pertabgurh rises with precipitous sides out of the woods and ravines below. The top, irregularly level, furnished space for dwelling-houses and magazines, while ample springs of pure water sufficed for the use of a large body of men, by which it could be easily defended. At various periods of time—by the early Mahratta chieftains of the country in remote ages, and afterwards by their Mussulman conquerors—walls and towers had been added to the natural defences of the place, as well as strong gateways, protected by bastions and loopholed traverses, on the only approach to the summit—a rugged pathway, which could hardly be called a road. Under very ordinary defence, the place was perfectly impregnable to all attacks by an enemy from without; and, at the period of our tale, it was held as his capital and choicest stronghold, among many such fastnesses in those mountains, by Sivaji Bhóslay, a man destined to play a conspicuous part in the history of his country and people in particular, and of India at large.

We have already informed the reader, in a somewhat desultory manner perhaps, for we are not writing his history, of the attempts made by Sivaji to establish an independent power; and, by taking advantage of the weakness and distraction of the kingdom of Beejapoor, of which he was a vassal, on the one hand, and of the ambitious designs of the Emperor Aurungzeeb on the other, to raise himself to a position in which he could secure the actual administration, and eventually the sovereignty, of his native wilds.

Hindu history is in all cases unsatisfactory; and that of the early Mahratta chiefs and principalities of the Dekhan eminently so. On the invasion of the Dekhan by Alla-oo-deen, nephew of the then King of Delhi, in A.D. 1294, the fort and city of Deogurh, now Doulatabad, was held by Rajah Ramdeo Jadow, who appeared then to have been prince of the whole country. Whether he was so or not, whether the chiefs of the wild tracts of the Ghauts and provinces lying on the western sea-coast were his tributaries or vassals, or whether they were actually independent of each other, has never been ascertained; but, on the downfall of the princely house of Jadow, no other ruler or chieftain seems to have made any resistance, and the Mahomedans, gathering strength, and founding a kingdom at Gulburgah, in the centre of the Dekhan, gradually subdued the whole tract, establishing garrisons in the wildest parts, fortifying hills not already used as strongholds, and improving the defences of others, in that noble and picturesque style of fortification which now excites our wonder and admiration.

One of the Mahratta families of ancient native nobility, though not of the highest grade, were the Bhóslays. The Jadows, though no longer possessing princely power, had descended into the rank of landed proprietors, or hereditary officers, under the ancient Hindu tenure, of the districts over which their ancestors had once held sway. Under ordinary circumstances, an alliance between the families would have been rejected by the Jadows; but one fell out nevertheless, and after a strange manner.

At the marriage of a mutual friend, Shahji Bhóslay, then a pretty boy, was present with his father, and the head of the family of the Jadows with his daughter, Jeejee, a child younger than the boy

Shahji. The children began to play together, and the girl's father remarked jocosely what a pretty couple they would make. The remark was heard by the boy's father, who claimed it as a promise of betrothal, and, after some discussion, and objection as to disparity of rank, the children were eventually married. From these parents sprung Sivaji, who, with his mother, as remarkable a person in many respects as himself, became the originators and leaders of the renewed independence of the Hindus of the Dekhan.

The women of India, particularly those of the higher classes and families, are invariably the treasuries of family events, and of deeds of departed or existent greatness. Jeejee Bye, an ambitous, perhaps unscrupulous woman, strove hard to excite her husband, Shahji Bhóslay, to exertion in the Hindu cause. She filled his mind with legends of the Jadows' power; she sought out the histories of his own family; she urged him to assert his right to districts in sovereignty of which he was only the official head; and she actively canvassed all the heads of the Mahratta families, with a view to a combined resistance against the Mahomedan powers, then beginning to show symptoms of a final decadence.

And not without effect. Shahji, the servant and vassal of the Emperor of Delhi as of the King of Beejapoor, rebelled in turn against both; was restless and unfaithful, lacking, while a bold, enterprising partisan soldier, the higher qualities which could direct and take advantage of such movements. He was frequently imprisoned, fined, and otherwise punished, but nothing checked his wife's ambition. Left to herself during his long absences and captivities with her young son among their native wilds, surrounded by rude retainers, she turned to him as soon as he could comprehend her plans; and by the mother and son those designs were sketched out which, in respect of utter hopelessness at first, and splendid success afterwards, have few comparisons in the world's history.

As the boy grew up, his immediate retainers joined him in wild enterprises against the Mahomedans, which to the people savoured of madness, but which, as they increased in boldness of design and execution, were believed to be the deeds of one especially protected by the Goddess Bhowani, the tutelar divinity of the Jadow family. His mother, an ardent votary, pretended to be occasionally visited by the goddess in person, and, filled with her divine afflatus, spoke prophecy. Her son believed in her inspiration: and gradually his friends, Maloosray, Palkur, and others, with a superstitious faith, believed also. Undisciplined, often unarmed men of the Mawuls, or mountain valleys above the Ghauts, who were called Mawullees, and of those below the mountains towards the sea, called Hetkurees, joined the young leader: scaled mountain forts, or descended into the plains beyond the valleys, gathering arms and booty, occupying

Moslem garrisons, putting their defenders to the sword, and never relinquishing what they had obtained.

So year after year passed, and the young Sivaji, as he grew stronger, became more daring and enterprising. Originally a few hundreds of half-naked, ill-armed mountain peasants, his forces of Mawullees and Hetkurees at last numbered many thousands of active, determined men. He had possession of some of the strongest mountain forts in the Western Ghauts; he had built, and was building, defences to other isolated and naturally almost inaccessible mountains. He was arming them with cannon purchased by stealth from the Portuguese of Goa, or cast by his own skilful artificers; and as he gained more perfect local strength, he was silently extending his intrigues to all the Mahratta families of ancient Maharastra by agents like Moro Trimmul, and awaiting the time patiently, till all could rise to overthrow the Mussulman governments which held them in subjection.

Had those governments, after the spirit of the earlier Mussulman invaders of the Dekhan, been intolerant of Hindus, denied them privileges of worship, defiled their temples, confiscated their ancestral rights, or otherwise harassed and oppressed them,—it is probable that Shahji's first attempts towards throwing off the Mahomedan yoke would have met with better success. But, on the contrary, there was now little or no oppression or interference with them in any way; and many of the Mahratta chieftains not only held estates in fief for service, but joined the armies of the Mahomedan kings, and fought with them bravely and faithfully. We have ourselves a counterpart of this, in some respects, in the Norman occupation of our own country; inasmuch as, while some Saxon thanes then held themselves aloof, and retired to the management of their own estates, others were found who joined the invaders, or, gradually imitating their manners, became incorporated with them.

That Sivaji's prospects had assumed a more encouraging form than any of his father's, may easily be imagined from the method in which they had been maintained. The Dusséra, or festival of Bhowani, throughout Maharastra, of 1657, the year of which we write, was to show, by a private muster of the people, what forces were available for a general rising; and after that it would be determined how they were to be employed.

We know what the object of Maloosray's mission to Beejapoor had been, and its result. Sivaji had heard already by express from the capital, of the death of the Wuzeer, the discovery of some of his own correspondence by the King, and the acceptance of the gage by Afzool Khan to undertake a campaign against him with a picked army. He had not heard since, nor had Maloosray arrived; but Sivaji knew that Afzool Khan was no laggard in war, and that he must prepare himself to meet the emergency.

A fascination for sacred plays which had possessed him from childhood, was a strange peculiarity of this man's character. As Sivaji grew up, no distance, no personal danger, deterred him from being present at any which could by any possibility be reached. Sometimes openly, and more frequently in a peasant's or common soldier's garb, the young prince, with a few chosen associates, would appear at places where his arrival was incomprehensible, and his disappearance equally abrupt and mysterious. In the latter days, these "Kuthas," as they are termed, became means of assembling his men without attracting suspicion; but his adherents well knew that the most exciting enterprises immediately followed them.

Soon after the arrival of the news from Beejapoor, notice of one to be held at Pertabgurh had been sent through the country, and from the earnestness and celerity with which the orders were circulated from village to village, the people at large were assured of the proximity of some notable event, and hoped, in their own expressive phrase, that, at last, the "fire would light the hills."

With this partial digression, and introduction to the Rajah's play, the day of which had arrived, our history will proceed.

CHAPTER LXX.

From a straggling, irregular village, which could hardly be called a town, nestling in a hollow under the mountain of Pertabgurh, a rude pathway, for it was little else, ascended to the fort above. Very rough, but very lovely, was this road. The forest, or jungle, had been partly cleared away from its sides, but noble trees still hung over it, affording grateful shade as it wound round ravines and shoulders of the mountain in gradual but easy ascent; and the huge broad leaf of the teak tree, the graceful and feathery bamboo, and other masses of luxuriant foliage, rich with great creepers now covered with flowers, which hung from tree to tree in graceful festoons, or clung in dense masses about their tops,—presented endless and beautiful combinations with the bold upper precipices of the mountain itself, and the distant ranges behind it. Farther up, as the air grew fresher in the ascent, and you looked down into deep gloomy dells, or abroad over the valley, or up to the rugged sides of the great mountain beyond,—a subtle blue atmosphere appeared to pervade everything; and this, the peculiar characteristic of those high tropical regions, seemed to increase in depth of colour,—and, without in reality obscuring the features of the scenery, to soften its rugged outlines, and blend its almost savage elements into harmony.

It has been said of natives of India that they are insensible to beauties of natural scenery. We admit that Mussulmans to a great extent are so, but not Hindus, still less Mahrattas, of these glorious mountains. Their sacred books, their ballads, and recited plays, abound with beautiful pictures of natural objects; and, living among combinations of the most glorious forms in nature, peopling every remarkable rock, deep dell, or giant tree with spiritual beings belonging peculiarly to each, who are worshipped with a rude veneration,—insensibility to outward impressions and their influence upon character would be impossible.

So now, at the time we speak of, a numerous company of men on foot were ascending by the pathway already mentioned to the fort, and that light merriment prevailed among them which ever accompanies the enjoyment of fine scenery and pure mountain air, and excites physical capability for the endurance of the heaviest fatigue. Some ran or leaped, as occasional level portions of road occurred; others climbed among the crags and rocks by its side, or, knowing shorter paths to the summit, struck out of the main road, and breasted the steep mountain with a freedom and agility only known to mountaineers.

Keen-eyed, lithe, spare, yet muscular men; low in stature, yet of extraordinary power of endurance; often heavily armed with long matchlock, and its accompaniment of powder-horns, bullet-bags, and other accoutrements tied round the waist,—a long, straight, heavy two-handled sword hanging over the left shoulder, or a smaller curved sabre fastened into the waistband, with a dagger or two, and a broad shield at the back—such were Sivaji's Mawullees. Ordinarily unburdened with much clothing—a pair of drawers fitting tight below the knee, a coarse handkerchief wound about the head, and a black blanket thrown over all, or crossed over the chest, leaving the arms free, sufficed for ordinary purposes; on festival days, however, all were clad in a clean suit of coarse cotton cloth, with a gay turban, and scarf round the waist, and bunches of wild flowers tucked fantastically into the folds of their head-dress.

This was a festival day—for their Rajah had ordered a Kutha; and all knew when this took place that it was the prelude to some raid or foray—some distant expedition in which honour and booty were to be gained—and when the Mawullees would strike in, hard and fierce, on the unsuspecting Moslems. The "Dhunni," or master, as they called him, had been unaccountably quiet for some time past; but to a man they knew he was not idle, and throughout that country, as in more remote provinces, the conviction prevailed that something unusual was to happen—some manifestation of the will of the goddess, whom all feared and most worshipped. There was nothing apparent or tangible; but expectation and excitement prevailed nevertheless.

For several days previously, the usual messengers had run from village to village among the Mawuls or valleys of the ranges near Pertabgurh, giving news of the Kutha. The players had come from Wye, from Sattara, and other towns, and the Rajah's hill-men had been clearing the usual place of celebration, and were now decorating the royal seat, and stage for the players, with green boughs and wild flowers. The little town was already full of people, and others were crowding up the mountain to make their salutation to their beloved prince who, now seated in his hall of audience, surrounded by a few friends, soldiers, and priests, denied no one the privilege sc dearly prized, that of making a "salam" to their Rajah, and receiving one in return.

Up the mountain-side, through the grim gateways, till they emerged upon the irregular plateau at the top, the men poured in a continuous stream. Some singly or in small groups; others in larger companies headed by a pair of "gursees," or pipers, one playing a drone, the other a reed flageolet, very strong and shrill in tone, the combination of which, as well as the wild melodies played, being curiously like bagpipes in effect. Others had with them their village trumpeters; and shrill quivering blasts of their horns, accompanied by the deep monotonous notes of large tambourine drums, not unfrequently arose together or singly from different parts of the ascent, and were answered by the Rajah's horn-blowers stationed on the bastions above the gates, and elsewhere in the towers above the precipices. The fort was full of men, for several thousands were assembled in it: sitting in groups, rambling about the walls, or by the side of springs and wells, untying the bundles of cakes which each man had bound to his back, and making a noonday meal; or proceeding to their chieftain's kitchen, received the daily allowance of meal bread, which was served out without stint to all comers on those occasions, and of which huge piles stood on the kitchen floor ready for distribution.

All the morning Sivaji had sat in his humble hall of audience, surrounded by some of his tried friends, and some Brahmun priests and scribes. No gorgeous palace was this, like that at Beejapoor, but a broad shed made by poles fastened together, and thatched with grass and teak-leaves, decorated gracefully and appropriately with leafy branches and wild flowers. At the upper end was the Rajah's seat, a low dais covered with coarse cotton carpets, on which the "guddee" or royal seat—a velvet pillow covered with gold embroidery, and a seat to match—had been placed temporarily. Below the dais, the leaders of large and small parties of men came—saluted —seated themselves by turns, and got up and departed with the usual salutation, but seldom without notice; and while other men passed quickly by, the chief had a kind word of greeting or reminiscence or salute for every one. Many saw that his features were clouded with care; but the news from the capital concerned no one, and the Kutha to come off that night would, they knew, prove the usual prelude of active service.

Seated as he was amidst a crowd of friends and attendants, the Mahratta Rajah seemed, in the distance, almost contemptible, from his small stature and plain, insignificant appearance. Dressed in ordinary white muslin, the only ornament he wore was the "jika," or jewel for the turban, which sparkled with valuable diamonds. A light red shawl drawn over his shoulders protected him from the somewhat chill wind, and before him lay his terrible sword Bhowani, and the large black shield of rhinoceros hide which he usually wore. A nearer view, however, gave a different impression. Somewhat dark in complexion, with a prominent nose, broad in the nostril; large, soft eyes, small determined mouth and chin; a thin moustache curled up at the ends, and bushy black whiskers shaved on a line with his ear,—formed a countenance at once handsome and intelligent: while his slight figure, apparently more active than strong, evinced, by its lithe movement even while sitting, a power of endurance which was confirmed by the expression of his face.

No one who had once seen the Maharaja ever forgot him. Though now mild in expression, if not sad, most about him had seen and remembered the face in other and wilder moods of excitement: in war, or in the actual hand-to-hand combats, in which he delighted, and from which he could with difficulty be restrained; while the impression that he was an incarnation of divinity, mingled awe with the respect and love which all bore him.

CHAPTER LXXI.

THE morning ceremony was at length over, and, somewhat wearied by it, and by sitting inactive so long, Siviji rose and passed into his private apartments, to which the shed or pavilion was a temporary addition. The rough mountain fortress afforded no royal palaces. A few terraced houses, divided by courts, with some thatched out-offices and stables, stood on an elevated spot near the walls; and the Rajah's favourite retreat was a small vaulted apartment, which joined the fort-wall—indeed, formed portion of it—and from which a small projecting window, placed immediately above one of the deepest precipices, looked out over the valley and mountains, and commanded a view of part of the ascent.

It was a habit of Sivaji's to go to no ceremony, nor return from any, without saluting his mother. Did he ever leave the house or return to it, he touched her feet reverently, while she gave him her blessing. The son's faith in his mother was only equalled by her faith and love for him; and as a pattern of filial piety and devotion, his example is still inculculated upon the Mahratta youth by many a village schoolmaster.

She met him at the threshold of the door, and, as was her wont, passed her hands over his face and neck, kissing the tips of her fingers; while, bowing low, he touched both her feet, then his own eyes and forehead.

"Is Tannajee arrived, son," she asked, "that thou hast broken up the reception so early?"

"No, mother," he said; "but come with me, for my spirit is heavy, and there is a shadow of gloom over me which thou only canst dispel. No, there is no news, and that vexes me."

She followed him into the apartment we have mentioned. A plain cushion had been placed near the window upon a soft mattress, and he flung, rather than seated himself, upon it, and buried his face in his hands, turning away from her.

She sat down by him, and again passed her hand over his face and neck, and kissed her fingers without speaking.

A mother's loving hand! O ye who know it, who possess it as the rude waves of life come breaking one by one against you, be thankful that it is there in its old place, soothing and sustaining like nought else of earthly comfort! Ye who have lost it, never forget how lovingly it used to do its blessed work. In times of anxious trial, perplexity, and sickness most of all,—ye shall feel it still, in the faith which leads ye where it is gone before, and awaits your coming. So, forget it not!—forget it not!

For a while both were silent. The mother knew the feelings which filled her son's mind too well to interfere with their course. Still she sat by him, and patted him occasionally as she used to do when she soothed him to rest as a child. "If he could sleep," she thought, "this gloom would pass away; but it will do so nevertheless."

He lay still, sometimes looking out into the blue air, watching the swallows as they passed and repassed the window in rapid flight to and from their nests, which hung to the ledges of the precipices—or the groups of people ascending and descending the pathway to the gates. Again, burying his face in the cushion, he lay still, and his mother watched, and gently waved the corner of her garment over his head, lest any insect should light on him and disturb him. There was no sound save the dull buzzing of flies in the room, and sometimes the loud monotonous note of a great woodpecker from the depths of the ravine below.

He turned at length, and she knew the crisis was past. "Mother," he said, "hast thou been with the goddess to-day? To me she is dim and mournful; I ask my heart of her designs, but there comes no answer. Is her favour gone from us?"

"Who can tell her purposes, my life?" she replied, "we are only her instruments. O, fail not in heart! If there be troubles, should we not meet them? If she bid us suffer, shall we not suffer? But, O, fail not—doubt not! Remember thy father doubted and failed, and what came of it but weary imprisonment, fine, pain, shame, and failure? O, not so, my son: better thou wast dead, and I with thee, than to doubt and fail."

"The trial will be heavy, mother," he returned. "Here we are safe, and I fear not for thee: but for the rest, the cause is hopeless, and that is what vexes me. Years of stratagem and arrangement are gone with that man's death, and all we have planned is known."

"And if it be known, son, dost thou fear?" she exclaimed. "What has been gained by these communications with a traitor? O son, he who is not faithful to the salt he eats, is untrue to all besides. I—a woman only—and the priests will tell thee not to trust a woman's thoughts or designs—I tell thee I am glad: I rejoice that a trial has come to thee. One hour such as thou hast passed now, with thine own heart to speak to thee, is worth more to the cause than a thousand priests or a lakh of swordsmen. I tell thee I am glad: for such things only can teach thee to trust thyself, and not to look to others."

"And thee, mother?" he said, smiling.

"No, no—not to me," she replied quickly, "except the goddess speaks by my mouth. No, not to me. I am but a woman else, fearful of thee, my son—fearful of the bullet, the sword, the lance, the wild fray of battle—fearful of——"

"Nay, mother," he cried, sitting up and interrupting her, "not of the sword or the battle; there I am safe,—there I fear not. Were I but there now, this heaviness at my heart would pass away. 'Hur, Hur, Mahadeo!' the cry—the shout rings in my ears and urges me on; then there is no time for thought, as now in this silence."

"And it shall ring again, my son," she replied. "Fear not—doubt not, only act: that is all. Wilt thou be like thy father, drifted here and there by every current of rumour like a straw upon the sea? 'Such a one will not join, what can I do? Such a thing threatens, what can I do? This man says this, shall I follow it? That man says the other, shall I follow it?' So he followed as others led; so he acted as others advised. What came of all? only shame, my son. Had he said to all, Do this, they would have done it. O Mother, O Holy Mother," she cried, standing up and lifting her joined hands towards the deep blue sky, "come from thence—come from the air into thy daughter's heart; teach me what to say, how to direct him, or direct him thyself! O Mother, we do all for thy name and honour, and for the faith so long degraded: let us not fail or be shamed!

"Not thus, son," she continued after a pause—"not thus will the spirit come upon me, but in the temple must I watch alone and pray and fast, ere she will disclose herself to me; and I will do so from to-night. Yes, she will be entreated at last. Perhaps," she continued simply, but reverently, "the Mother is in sorrow herself, and needs comfort. No matter, I will entreat her."

"Surely she hath heard already," replied her son after another pause, "for my soul is better for thy words—stronger, mother. Yes, I see how it will be; nor Moro Trimmul, nor Tannajee, nor Palkur, nor any one but myself. I had thought to lay all these matters before the people at the Kutha to-night, but I will not. I will only say we must work for ourselves—against the Emperor, against the King, and most against Afzool Khan. If they will only trust in me—yes, mother, if they will only trust in me—we shall have victory, and I will not disappoint them or you."

"Now, a thousand blessings on thee, Sivaji Bhóslay, for those words," cried his mother, passing her hands over his head. "I have no fear now—none. Go to the Kutha—tell them all that their time is come; and when you cry 'Hur, Hur, Mahadeo!' each shout of theirs in reply will echo the death-cry of a thousand infidels. Now, let me depart, my son; it is well for me to go to the Mother, and sit before her; haply she may come to me. Better to be there, than that a woman should be near thee, when the woman's spirit has passed out of thee."

"Bless me, then, my mother, and go; nor will I stay here long," he replied. "The shadows are even now lengthening in the valleys, and I should have the people collected ere it is dark."

She placed her hands upon his head solemnly: "Thus do I bless thee, my son—more fervently, more resignedly than ever. Go, as she will lead thee in her own time. To all thy people thou wilt not alter, but, to the Moslems, be stone and steel. Trust no one—ask of no one what is to be done, not even of me. Do what is needful, and what thy heart tells thee. Show no mercy, but cut out thine own path with the sword. If thou wilt be great, do these things; if not——: but no, thou wilt be great, my son. She hath told me so; and thou wilt reckon the true beginning of it from that silent watch there, by the window. I go now, but stay not thou here. See, there are none ascending, and even those descending the hill are fewer. Go to them."

He watched her intently as she left him and disappeared behind a curtain, which fell before a door of the apartment leading to the small household temple. An expression of triumph lit up his large dark eyes and expressive features. "She said I must act for myself," he cried aloud. "Yes, mother, I will act for thee first, and then for the people; and there shall be no idle words again—only 'Hur, Hur, Mahadeo!' when the fire is on the hills."

CHAPTER LXXII.

The servants and attendants of the lady awaited her without, and preceded her to the temple, which was situated in a court by itself, —a small unpretending building, which her son had built at her request. The usual priests sat by the shrine, feeding the lamps with oil, and offering flowers and incense for those who needed their services. This, too, had been a busy day for them, for the Rajah's temple had been opened to those who came to the fort; and many a humble offering and donation of copper coins to the priests, from the soldiery, had been the result. The court had now been cleared of all visitors, and the doors shut. As the lady advanced and sat down before the shrine, the priests made the customary libations and offerings, and stood apart, not daring to speak, for her visions of the goddess were well known, and much feared, and this might be the occasion of one of them. So, as she sat down, the priests and her attendants shrank back behind the entrance to the sanctum, and awaited the issue in silence.

Very different from Tara, as she had sunk down in her strange delirium before the shrine at Tooljapoor, the Maha Ranee, as she was called, but more simply and lovingly the "Lady Mother," was perfectly calm and self-possessed. A small, grey-headed, slightly-formed woman, of graceful carriage and shape, which had altered little, if at all, from the best period of her youth: nor, except in her hair, had age apparently told much upon her: for the arms were still as round, the skin of her cheek as soft and downy as ever, and the firm springy tread of the small naked foot showed no decline of vigour. Her son often told her she was yet the most beautiful woman in Maharastra; nor indeed, in the clear golden olive of her skin, in the delicate mould and sweet expressive character of her features, above all, in the soft lustre of her eyes, had she many rivals.

She had seated herself directly before the shrine, on which was a small gold image of the goddess upon a golden pedestal; and the water-vessels, lamps, and other articles of service were also of gold. The full light of the lamps within shone out on her, and glistened on the white silk garment she wore, with its broad crimson and gold border—upon the jewelled bracelets on her arms—and the large pearls about her neck. The end of her saree, heavy with gold thread, had fallen a little aside as she seated herself, and her soft throat, and a little of the crimson silk bodice below, could be seen—enough to show that if the face were calm, the bosom was heaving rapidly, and under the influence of no common emotion. No one dared to speak to her, or interrupt her thoughts or prayers, whatever they might be; and when she seated herself before the shrine in this manner, the priests and attendants knew she expected a "revelation," and had to wait, even though it might be for many hours, for the issue.

When it came, it was with various effect. At times calm, with glistening eyes and throbbing bosom, her hands clenched convulsively, she would speak strange words, which were heard with a mysterious reverence, and recorded by an attendant priest; at others, the result was wild delirium, when they were obliged to hold her, and when the excitement was followed by exhaustion, which remained for days.* Now, however, she sat calmly, her eyes cast down, but raised occasionally with an imploring look to the image, seldom altering her position, and seemingly unconscious of the time which passed.

Long she sat there; the shadows of the mountains lengthened, till only their peaks shone like fire, and then suddenly died out. The moon rose, and the little court was white under her silver beams, and still the lady sat and moved not. The chill night breeze at that elevation had caused an involuntary shiver to pass over her, which her favourite attendant thought was the precursor of the usual affection, but nothing followed; and seeing it was caused by cold, had, apparently unobserved, cast over her a large red shawl, which fell in soft folds round her person. It was far in the night when she arose from that strange vigil; and, dreamily passing her hands over her face and neck as if to arouse herself, sighed, and advancing to the threshold of the shrine, joined her hands together, and bowing reverently before the image, saluted it, and silently turned away.

"Not to-night, Bheemee," she said to a woman who approached her bearing her sandals, and laid them down at the entrance to the temple,—"not to-night. The Mother bids me go; she is sad, and will come another time. Hark! what is what?" and she paused to listen.

A hoarse roar, a cry as though of a wail of thousands of voices, came from all sides at once, floating up the precipices, echoed from the rocks, and reverberating from mountain to mountain. It seemed to those present, who were already filled with superstitious expectation, as if spirits cried out, being invisible, and that some unearthly commotion was in progress around them. In the pure mountain air, still as it was, these sounds seemed to float about them mysteriously,

* A series of very curious and most interesting papers on this subject, by the late Xavier Murphy, Esq., were published some years ago in the "Dublin University Magazine."—M. T.

now dying away, and now returning more faintly than before, till they ceased, or only a confused perception of them remained. The fierce shout or wail, however, occurred but once; what followed was more diffuse and undecided.

"Something has moved the people more than ordinarily, lady," said a priest who advanced from the outer court. "The assembly can be seen from the bastion yonder, and I have been watching it while you were within; if you would look, follow me."

She drew the shawl more closely around her, and went with him through the court to the bastion, which, situated on the edge of an angle of the precipice, commanded a view of the town and valley below. The moon shone clear and bright, else she had looked into a black void; but the air was soft and white, of a tint like opal, as the moon's rays caught the thin vapours now rising. Some thousands of feet below, was a bright spot in a dell, filled with torches, which sent up a dull smoke, while they diffused a bright light on all around. There were many thousands of people there, mostly men, and there was a glitter as of weapons among them, as the masses still heaved and swayed under the influence of some strange excitement. She could make out no particular forms, but she knew that her son sat in the pavilion at the end, and about that there was no movement. As she looked, the shout they had first heard arose more clearly than before—"Hur, Hur, Mahadeo! Dônguras-lavilé Déva!"*

"O Mother," she cried, stretching out her arms to the sky, and then to the dell below, "enough! thou hast heard the prayer of thy daughter: thou wast there with him, not with me. Now I understand, and it is enough. Come, Bheemee, it is cold," she said, after a pause, and in her usual cheerful voice, "thou shouldst have been yonder in the Kutha, girl, and all of you. Well, the next, to-morrow night, will be a better one, and you shall all go, for I will go myself with the Maharaja; come now, they will not return till daylight;" and descending the steps of the bastion, she followed her servants, who preceded her, to the private aparments.

Below, Sivaji had been busy since before sunset. He had descended the mountain on foot, attended by his body-guard, and a large company of the garrison of the fort—a gay procession, as, accompanied by the pipers and horn-blowers of the fortress, it had wound down the rugged pathway in the full glare of the evening sun; and, amidst the shouts of thousands, and a confused and hideous clangour, caused by the independent performances of all the pipers and drummers of the clans assembled—the screaming, quivering notes of the long village horns, the clash of cymbals, and the

* "O Mahadeo! the fire has lit the hills!"—the Mahratta invocation to battle which is used also as the heading to all threatening notices.

deep tones of some of the large brass trumpets belonging to the temple, which had been brought down from the fort,—Sivaji passed on round the village to the spot which had been cleared for the Kutha.

It was a glen from which all wood had long been cleared away, and short crisp grass had grown up in its place, which, moistened by the perpetual drainage of the mountain, was always close and verdant. Near enough to the village to serve as a grazing ground for its cattle, the herbage was kept short by them; and the passage round and round its sides of beasts of all kinds, goats and sheep, cows, bullocks, and buffaloes, had worn them into paths which formed, as it were, a series of steps, rising gradually to the edge of the forest above.

In the midst was a bright green sward, soft and close, and of some extent, and at all times of the year the resort of the village youth for athletic exercises—wrestling, leaping, archery, shooting with the matchlock, or, most favoured of all perhaps, the sword-playing for which the Mahratta soldiery were almost celebrated. A projecting mound, which might have been artificial, and was possibly the partly completed embankment of some intended reservoir, stretched nearly across its mouth, and while its grassy surface afforded seats to many of the spectators, it shut out the valley beyond, from all observers.

At the upper end of the dell, which in shape was a long oval, and slightly raised above the level sward, was the Rajah's seat, a platform of sods and earth, covered with dry grass, and then with carpets from the fort, upon which the Guddee, or seat of state, was placed. Directly the Rajah had retired from the morning ceremony, the cushions had been taken down the mountain and placed on this dais, which afforded room also for many personal friends and priests who attended the ceremony with him.

In the centre of the sward, but near the upper end, was the place for the players. The smoothest portion of turf had been selected, and around it wattled screens were built, made of leafy branches, for entrance and exit, and also to allow of changes of dress, rest during intervals of performance, and the like. The stage, if it might be called one, was bounded by wild plantain trees cut off at the root, and set in the ground so that the broad leaves continued fresh and green; and above these were twined branches of teak with their large rough foliage, bamboos, and other slender trees readily felled and transported, while long masses of flowery creepers had been cut from the forest, and hung from poles at each side above the players' heads in graceful festoons. Inside all this foliage, were huge cressets of iron filled with cotton-seed soaked in oil, and all round the area below, and especially round the Rajah's seat, similar torches had been arranged, which would be lighted as the ceremony began, and illuminate the whole.

Before the stage, there was a small altar of earth, on which brightly polished brass vessels for pouring libations were set out, and above them, upon a silver pedestal, a small silver image of the goddess had been placed for worship.

Early in the afternoon, people had begun to assemble there, and after the Rajah's arrival in the town, a new procession was formed to accompany him to the place. Thousands had rushed on before it; along the valley, over the shoulders of the mountain, and as best they could, so as to secure good places for the sight; and by the time the head of the procession crossed the little brook which bubbled out beneath the mound, and ran leaping and tinkling down the valley, and had entered the glen,—the whole of its sides and the mound had grown into a dense mass of human beings closely packed together. There were comparatively few women; those who sat there were for the most part the Rajah's Mawullees and Hetkurees, armed as if for battle, ready, if needed, to march thence on any enterprise, however distant or desperate.

A clear space had been left for the advancing procession. In front the Rajah's pipers, playing some of the wild mountain melodies, which echoed among the woods and crags above, broken now and then by blasts of horns and trumpets, and the deep monotonous beat of many large tambourine drums, the bearers of which were marshalled by the chief drummer of the fort, who, with his instrument decked with flowers and silken streamers, strutted or leaped in front of all, beating a wild march. Then followed Brahmuns, bareheaded and naked to the waist, carrying bright copper vessels of sacred water, flowers and incense, with holy fire from the temple on the mountain, chanting hymns at intervals. After them, the players and reciters, male and female, in fantastic dresses, wearing gilt tiaras to resemble the costumes seen in carvings of ancient temples, among whom were the jesters or clowns, who bandied bold and free remarks with the crowd, and provoked many a hearty laugh and sharp retort. After these the Rajah's own guard, some with sword and buckler only, others bearing matchlocks with long bright barrels, who marched in rows with somewhat of military organization; then the servants; and last of all Sivaji himself. Slowly the procession passed up the centre; then the leading portions of it dividing on each hand, the Rajah, advancing, mounted the small platform. Ere he seated himself he saluted the assembly, turning to each side of it with his hand raised to his head, and all rose to welcome him with clapping of hands and shouts which made the wooded glen and the precipices above, ring with the joyous sound. Then all subsided into their seats, and the preliminary sacrifices and offerings began.

CHAPTER LXXIII.

We need not describe them. After the sacrifice of several sheep before the altar, to propitiate the goddess in the form of worship peculiar to lower castes, the Brahmuns continued the rest of the ceremonies. Here were the same recitations of religious books, the Shastras and Poorans; the same processions sweeping round the altar with offerings, and hymns chanted by the priests at stated periods; the same invocations of the deity to be present, as we have already seen in the temple at Tooljapoor; and as they proceeded, shadows lengthened, the sun disappeared behind the mountains, and gloom fell rapidly on the glen and its people.

Very soon, however, it was lighted up; men bearing huge copper vessels of oil on their shoulders, went round the area pouring cans full upon the cotton-seed in the iron cressets, and then lighting them, and a blaze arose from each which illuminated a large space around. Gradually the whole were lit; and the effect was as strange as beautiful.

Tier upon tier of closely-wedged human beings, whose white dresses and gay turbans and scarves appeared even brighter by night than by day, arose on all sides, those nearest the light being clearly seen, while the others, rising gradually to the top, were less and less distinct, till they seemed to blend with the fringe of wood above, and disappear in the gloom. Below, about the place of performance, and around the Rajah's seat, the illumination was brightest; and the thick smoke of incense rising from the altar hung over all like a canopy, diffusing its fragrance to the farthest edges of the assembly. Above, the grim mountain precipices hung threateningly over all, fringed at the top by walls and towers, hardly perceptible in the distance, except where they projected against the sky; and on which, and on the woods, as the night advanced, the bright light of the moon fell with a silvery lustre which our northern climate does not know.

To act a Hindu play is by no means so simple a matter as to act an English one. It frequently lasts several days. On this present occasion it would occupy three nights. There was the introduction, the middle, and the catastrophe. There would be pleasant witty interludes of broad farce between the scenes, acted by the clowns in various characters; satires upon Brahmuns, and priests generally, being a favourite subject: upon landlords and tenants: upon servants and masters: upon lovers—merchants—in short, upon all social topics. There would be political satires also; and the Rajah would see himself represented according to the popular belief, whatever it might be, flatteringly or the contrary, and would take the joke good-humouredly.

So the entertainment proceeded. We, who sit for an hour or two with a languid indifference, or real approbation, as it may be, of theatrical representation here, can hardly appreciate the intense absorption of a Mahratta audience at one of their religious plays, where gods and demigods, represented by clever players and singers, engage in earthly struggles of love or war, and evince human sympathies and passions. So hour after hour passed, and Rajah and people alike sat and listened and watched; now to a grand scene from the Mahabarut or Ramayun; now to a merry farce, or description by the "chorus" of what was to come next; now to a plaintive mountain ballad introduced into the general performance.

It was near midnight, perhaps, when a single horseman suddenly turned the corner of the mound, and, entering the area unperceived, where it was not crowded, rode slowly up the centre. His noble horse seemed jaded and weary, for it moved languidly, yet, when it saw the lights and people, raised its head and gave a shrill and prolonged neigh. Its flanks were smoking, and its coat a mass of foam, proving that it had been ridden hard and fast.

The rider's face was tied up, as is customary with Mahratta horsemen; but as he advanced he unwound the scarf about it, and the stern features and flashing eyes of Tannajee Maloosray appeared to all. For an instant he was not recognized, and his advance, indeed, had hardly been noticed at the upper end of the assembly; but some one who saw him cried "Tannajee!" and the name spread from mouth to mouth, rising into a roar of welcome among the people, as the rider struggled on through the crowd which now pressed about him. Dismounting near the altar, Tannajee gave his horse to a servant; and as Sivaji and all about him rose to meet him, he ascended to the royal seat, and was embraced by his prince in a loving greeting. He had been long absent, and was expected; but his sudden arrival alone, and at that time of night, boded strange tidings; and while his arms were yet around his friend, Sivaji anxiously asked what news he had brought.

"Of sorrow, yet of joy, my prince," replied Maloosray, disengaging himself. "I heard the news at Jutt, and I made a vow which only that altar can clear me of, that I would not sit or rest till I had told it to you and to the people.—Rise, all of ye!" he shouted to the assembly in that voice which, clear and sonorous, they had often heard above the wildest din of battle, "and listen to my words!"

They rose to a man instantly, and with a rustling sound: after which, there was perfect silence. Every face of those thousands was turned towards the speaker. Every form, from the highest tiers to the lowest, bent forward in eager expectation of what should follow.

"Listen," he continued, "O beloved prince and people: we have fallen upon evil days, for the goddess, our Mother, has been insulted, and her temple at Tooljapoor desecrated. Yes," he continued, lifting up his hand to stay the cry which was about to break out, "Afzool Khan has cast down the image of Toolja Mata, plundered the temple of its wealth, slain the Brahmuns, and sprinkled the blood of sacred cows over the shrine; and now the altar there, and the Mother, are my witness that I have told this grief to ye truly!"

Then burst forth that strange wild cry which the lady mother had heard above in the fort. Some wept, others shrieked and beat their mouths, or cast their turbans on the ground. Individual cries, no matter whether of grief or revenge, were blended into one common roar from those thousands, which ascended to the sky, and, reverberating from side to side of the glen, went out through the woods,—up the mountain-sides and precipices of the fort,—softened by distance,—yet uniting to produce that unearthly yell or wail which had arrested her as she left the shrine, and caused the watching priests to shudder.

Apparently, the people waited to hear from their prince a confirmation of the news, or intimation of what was to be done; for, at a motion of his hand, they were once more silent, and listening with rapt attention.

"I thought the Holy Mother was in sorrow," he said, "for she has hidden her face from me these many days, and my mother too sought her, but in vain. And now we know the reason. O friends! O people! shall it be so? Shall the Mother's temples be desolate? Not while Sivaji Bhóslay lives, and ye live! Better we died in honour than lived to be pointed at as cowards, while she is unrevenged! Listen," he continued, using the same gestures as Tannajee to keep the people quiet, as he took up the sword lying at his feet. "This, ye all know, is named after the Mother; see!" and he drew it slowly from the scabbard, "she hath a bright and lovely face, but it must be dimmed in Moslem blood: let her drink it freely! So I swear, and so ye will answer to my cry—Hur, Hur, Mahadeo!"

As he spoke he flung the scabbard passionately on the ground, and waved the glittering blade high in the air. Already was men's blood fiercely stirred by his words, and the Rajah's action rendered them almost uncontrollable. Not one of all that assembly who wore a sword was there, that did not draw and wave it as his chieftain had done; and the light flashing from polished weapons, and the frantic shouts of the old war-cry, as men swayed to and fro, still more excited the rude soldiery—"Hur, Hur, Mahadeo! Dônguras-lavilé Déva!"

No wonder that the sound had gone up the lofty mountain, and was the more clearly heard as the Ranee, looking from the tower above, saw far below the heaving masses in the glen, and caught the bright glitter of their weapons.

But there was silence at last. It seemed as if the men expected to be led there and then against their hereditary foes. That, however, was not to be yet. During the clamour, Maloosray had told his chieftain that Afzool Khan's army was on its march, and that means must be taken to oppose it. So the Rajah once again spoke out in those clear ringing tones which were heard by all.

"Not now, my people," he cried—"not now. If we have sworn to revenge the Mother, she will wait her time, and herself deliver this arrogant Moslem into our hands. Then, O my friends, shall she drink infidel blood, and be satisfied to the full. So fear not: if this news is terrible, it is yet good; so let us rejoice that we have the more cause to be united in avenging it. And now sit down once more; and play on, O players! Who shall say that Sivaji Bhóslay and his people were scared from their Kutha by Afzool Khan?"

"That means, my friends," cried Pundree, one of the clowns, after turning a preliminary somersault in the air, then resting his hands on his knees, and wagging his head with mock gravity, "that the master intends to kill the old Khan himself, and that the Mother will eat him. Now, as I am going to eat the sheep that have been killed there, just to save her the trouble, she will be very hungry—very hungry indeed; and if her belly is not filled by Afzool Khan, ye are to kill all his people and satisfy it. Else beware!—No one likes to be hungry, good folks; and I, for one, am always ill-tempered and beat my wife when there is no dinner, or it is badly cooked. I dare say the Mother is much the same, and if she be so, nothing goes right in the world; so see that ye strike hard, my sons, and get plenty of food for her when the master bids ye. Do ye hear? Do ye understand? As for the cooking of it, ye may leave that to the devil; and remember that I, Pundrinath, the son of Boodhenâth, have told ye all this, and will bear witness against ye and Tannajee Maloosray if ye do it not; and so—beware, beware!"

And then, amidst the laughter caused by the quaint speech and actions of the privileged jester, the play proceeded, while Sivaji heard from his friend Maloosray the tale of the Wuzeer's death, the Kótwal's execution, and the sack of Tooljapoor.

It was more than ever evident to Sivaji, that to attempt to oppose Afzool Khan in the field with the men about him, would be madness; but he might be drawn on, by specious promises of submission, into wilds where his cavalry and artillery would be useless, and in those jungles the men then present would be ample against ten thousand Mahomedan infantry.

Then it was determined to send those agents to Afzool Khan's camp with whose arrival there we are already acquainted.

CHAPTER LXXIV.

But the arrival of an Envoy from the Mahomedan General was an event of no small importance to the Rajah Sivaji. In order to further the plan he had conceived, and partly executed, in the despatch of envoys to the Mahomedan camp—it was his object to disarm all suspicion; and while assuming an appearance of insignificance and weakness which should impress upon the mind of a new-comer his insufficiency to make any resistance, the Rajah was making arrangements which, as Maloosray and other friends knew, boded action of no ordinary kind. When the time came, he would act, he said, as the goddess directed. His mother had been silent for many days, and almost constantly sat in the temple before the altar; and it was certain there would be some special revelation. She had spread the end of her garment* before the Mother, and she had never done so, they said, in vain; but she was silent, and so they waited.

Afzool Khan's Envoy had been received with the utmost distinction. When within a few miles of the fort he had been met by a deputation of Brahmuns and inferior military officers, and delayed only long enough to have the necessary astrological calculations made as to a propitious moment for entrance into the town. There, a house was assigned to him: servants of the Rajah appointed to attend on him: and his escort was supplied with forage and food in abundance. Nothing was wanting to give assurance of simple but earnest hospitality.

The day after, an audience of the Rajah was fixed upon. The Envoy was desired to choose his own time; and the astrologer in his suite, with that of the Rajah, having ascertained a lucky conjunction of planets, the Envoy was carried up the mountain-side in a palankeen to the fort-gate, where sheep were sacrificed before him, cannon fired from the ramparts, and the fort pipers, drummers, and horn-blowers, performed a rude and very noisy welcome. Then the men on guard at the gate, with others of the garrison of the fort, formed a street, which reached as far as the Rajah's pavilion; and the palankeen being carried along this, amidst the firing of matchlocks and shouting of the title of the King of Beejapoor by the royal bard and herald in his suite, the Envoy was set down before the same rude pavilion which we have before described, where the Rajah Sivaji awaited him.

To all appearance an insignificant little man, dark, youthful in appearance, with only one ornament in his turban, dressed in the plainest clothes, and without even the gold embroidered cushion on

* *Pulloo fusarné*—the most earnest and humble supplication that a Mahratta woman can make.

which he had been seated on the day of the Kutha. Punto Gopináth wondered much when he remembered the exaggerated accounts of the Prince which were sung in ballads, told by bards and reciters, and were believed by the people. Was this the saviour who was to come? Was this the man who was to rescue the Hindu faith from obloquy, if not from destruction:—protect Brahmuns, foster learning, endow and enrich temples? Above all, was this the man who was to defy the forces of Beejapoor, the fierce Abyssinians, the fiery Dekhanies—the noble park of artillery? There were no troops, no means of offence visible. True, the fort itself was strong, but the garrison was small, and unworthy of consideration in comparison with the thousands who were even now nigh at hand.

These thoughts hurried rapidly through the Envoy's mind as he passed up the street of men, and the Rajah's authorities and higher order of servants, who stood on each side of this approach to the hall itself. Puntojee Gopináth was a big man in every sense of the word. His body was large and corpulent, and he stooped much. His head was wrapped in a white cashmere shawl, which increased its naturally disproportionate size. His features were massive but flaccid, and his cheeks shook, while his head wagged from side to side as he walked. His eyes were large, but red and watery; and the protruding underlip, full, and set in deep lines at the corners, gave him an air of pompous self-sufficiency.

With all this, the Brahmun was a shrewd, astute person. He was vain, and usually confident. Now, however, as he saluted the Rajah, he felt the eyes which scanned him from head to foot had already taken a measure of him, which might be favourable or otherwise. Perhaps it was flattering, perhaps mortifying; he could not say which. They were in any case different eyes to those of his own rulers and officers, who were Mahomedans. Their eyes took things for granted, and he was accustomed to placid acquiescence, or perhaps to occasional fierce bursts of passion, which never affected him. These eyes, on the contrary, were restless and inquisitive, leaving an impression that they had seen and understood hidden thoughts, and would bring them out, lurk where they might.

Perhaps, for the first time in his public life, the Brahmun was disconcerted; but it was no time to show this; and recovering himself, he offered the prescribed salutation, and sinking into the seat pointed out to him, which was beside, but rather in front of the Rajah, with a loud exclamation of Ramchunder! which was his habit—he settled himself on his heels after the most approved courtly fashion, placed his hands gravely upon his knees, twisted up his moustaches, and felt his habitual confidence return.

We need not, perhaps, follow the conference. The Envoy, as instructed, at first took a high tone as to outrages and treason on the part of the Rajah, and of the clemency and wisdom of the sovereign he represented. There should have been no attempts at insurrection, because the cause was hopeless by force, and the royal ear was ever open to suppliants for justice, if timely submission were made.

The Rajah did not reply personally, but this pitiless scrutiny of the Envoy continued without interruption, and the address was answered by Krishnajee Bhaskur, one of his own Brahmun officers, eloquently and yet respectfully:—What had been done? No redress had been given for injury, for extortion, and local oppression. In despair, some retaliation had been made. It was the mountain custom, even by village against village; and did not affect higher relations, which would only become the more firmly consolidated when the cause of quarrel was past. "But," he added, in conclusion, "the details are private matters, and will be discussed better in privacy, and through Afzool Khan alone, does the Rajah wish to have them arranged. What have we here to oppose him? We have no concealments, no means of defence against such a force as his?"

"Indeed, no," said Sivaji, smiling. "An army of elephants has been sent to crush ants' nests, as the proverb hath it; and if the noble Khan will remain, and take charge of the country now under me, I will resign it to him cheerfully, and become his servant. Wilt thou say this to him?"

"Indeed, my prince," returned the Brahmun, putting up his joined hands, "we who were in Beejapoor well know how much Afzool Khan helped your father, when he was confined, in the old Sultan's time; and how much the rigour of his imprisonment was softened by the Khan's kindness. Ah! he is a humane and generous man, and has no personal enmity against you, my lord."

"We will at least put it to the proof," returned the Rajah good-humouredly. "You are witness that you have seen no preparations for defence or resistance, and the sooner he comes the better. We cannot hurry him and the force, but we will at least make preparations for a peaceful entertainment; and if the Khan will accept of our rude mountain hospitality instead of the Jehâd we hear he has been preaching against us, it will be a happy thing for all."

"A happy thing indeed!" said Bulwunt Rao, who, in the suite of the Envoy, had as yet sat silently, and had not been recognized; "and when public affairs are settled, private justice may be done to suppliants like me, who, only for state quarrels, dare not have entered this fort."

"Who art thou, friend?" asked Sivaji; "a suitor to me, and from Beejapoor?—a Mahratta among Moslems? Who art thou?"

"I may not mention my name here, my lord," said Bulwunt Rao, rising, and again saluting the Rajah reverently; "but I can tell it in private. One whom injustice and evil fate have led where he is, and who, only for them, would have been serving you."

"How can I serve thee?" asked the Rajah sharply; "I am not usually hard of access; therefore come to me when thou wilt, and I will hear thee."

"I will come," returned Bulwunt Rao, looking round to all, "and put thee, Sivaji Bhóslay, to the proof. Men vaunt the Rajah's justice," he continued—"he will find much to do for me;" and he sat down again.

An awkward pause ensued in the assembly, which no one seemed inclined to break: and the person who officiated as master of the ceremonies, having observed a signal from the Rajah, brought in flowers, with pân leaves, and distributed them in order of precedence to the Envoy and all his suite. Bulwunt Rao, however, would take nothing.

"If justice is done me," he said, rising again, "my share of flowers will come with it, and will be hung about my neck in honour; if not, they will hang here,"—and he touched his sword-hilt—"better."

"This savours of a threat, sir," said Sivaji, with flashing eyes.

"The meanest will turn against oppression," returned Bulwunt; "and Sivaji Bhóslay has just pleaded this in extenuation of his own acts. I, too, make the same reply, my prince; and when you know my history, you will confess I am no traitor to Mahrattas."

"All are dismissed," said the Rajah, rising; "see that these gentlemen are safely escorted below;" and amidst the confusion which occurred in many persons rising, and as the Durbar broke up, he whispered to the Brahmun who had been spokesman, and who was one of his most confidential servants, "See that the Khan's Envoy be separately accommodated. I must visit him privately to-night, and thou must be with me, Krishnajee; I will come to thee at the first watch."

CHAPTER LXXV.

The Rajah passed into the inner chamber, and found his mother sitting at the window alone, looking over the road which ascended to the fort-gate. He prostrated himself before her, as was his wont, and, sitting down opposite to her in silence, fell apparently into deep thought. She did not interrupt him; but as the trumpet sounded, and a salute of cannon was fired from the ramparts, and the Envoy's procession passed out, and wound down the pass—she saw him following the palankeen with his eyes, while his lips moved gently, as though he spoke to himself. As it disappeared behind a shoulder of the mountain, he turned to her and smiled.

"Mother," he said, "you saw the Khan's Envoy. I expected

some stupid, wrong-headed, supercilious Mussulman, but behold he has sent a Brahmun, and with him a Mahratta, whom we should know, but no one recognizes him. I think the Mother will give both to me, yet you said one only."

"My vision was but of one," she replied, "and it will be enough. Who is the Mahratta?"

"They said his name was Bulwunt Rao, mother, but he did not mention his surname, and no one knew it," returned the Rajah.

"It must be Bulwunt Rao Bhôslay, Tannajee's cousin," replied the lady. "I know of no other Mahratta of good family in Beejapoor. He is a relative of our own."

"Ah!" exclaimed her son, "yes, it must be he; and I have promised him justice, mother; but what of Tannajee?"

"It cannot be, son," she said; "that is a blood feud, and blood only will quench it. Tannajee did but revenge a murder, and you cannot quarrel with him. Let it be; no good will come of it."

"Nevertheless I will try, mother; and if the Brahmun——"

"Fear not," she returned. "If he be a true Brahmun, the goddess hath given him to thee. I will go to her. It is my hour for watching, and I will pray her to guide thee."

Sivaji sat as before, looking out over the rugged mountain-side and the pass, now glowing in the rich tints of an afternoon sun. If he could only get Afzool Khan into his power, and hold him sure as a hostage, he might make his own terms. Would the Brahmun aid him in this? A word from him and the matter was secure. If he could only be persuaded to write, a swift messenger might be sent to the camp, with one of his own officers to guide on the army. Once the troops entered the defiles they were at his mercy. There was no escape—the whole must surrender or be slain; but he well knew the old Afghan would not agree to dishonour, and to separate him from his force was therefore his chief anxiety. As yet the temptation within him had assumed no more definite form; and in respect to the final result, his mother, strange to say, was altogether silent; but she had again taken up the position she had assumed before the shrine for many days past, and his belief in her inspiration was not to be shaken.

Late that night, muffled in a coarse blanket, and accompanied only by the Brahmun before mentioned, and a few attendants, the Rajah descended from the fort by a steep and rugged pathway, which led from a postern directly to the town, and, leaving the men at the gate, they passed rapidly on to the house where the Envoy had been located. It belonged to the Josee or astrologer of the town, in whose science the Rajah had much faith; and, as was usual with him on all occasions of great enterprise, the aspects of the planets had been consulted, and declared to be favourable at the hour at which they had purposely timed their arrival. The Josee met them at the door. "The Pundit is sitting within," he said, "reading, and there is no one with him. I have prepared the writing materials, too, as directed, and they will be brought if you call."

"Wait, then, in the outer court, friends," said the Rajah to his attendants. "This must be done between us alone. Not even thou, Krishnajee, must know what passes between us."

Punto Gopináth was sitting in the inner verandah of the second court of the house, as the Josee had said, reading. He looked up as the old man entered and said, "There is one here from the Rajah, who would speak with you."

"Admit him," was the reply; and Sivaji could see as he entered, that the Brahmun drew towards him a short, heavy dagger-sword, and placed it so that the hilt lay close to his right hand. "Be seated, friend," said the Envoy, "and tell thy business. What doth Sivaji Bhóslay desire of me?"

The Rajah's face was tied up with a handkerchief, which partly concealed his mouth and changed the tone of his voice, and he had passed his hand, covered with white wood-ashes, across his nose, eyes, and forehead, as he entered, which altered the expression of his eyes very considerably. It was evident that he was not recognized.

"Sivaji Bhóslay desires the prosperity and advancement of Brahmuns," replied the Rajah, "and to enrich them is his sole care. He worships them; and would fain have them as powerful as in the days of the ancients, and in this desire thou canst assist."

"I assist! How, friend? I, a Brahmun, am a receiver, not a giver,—and am only a servant to the unclean," he added with a sigh.

"It need not be so, Pundit. The fame of thy learning hath preceded thee, and the Maharaja desires thy friendship and welfare. I am sent to tell thee this."

"What can I do?" said the Envoy restlessly. "What would he have me do? and who art thou to speak thus to me?"

"No matter who I am—I am authorized to speak," replied Sivaji. "Look, here is his ring as my authority. 'Is he a Brahmun,' the Rajah said, 'and come with Moslem followers to sit in my Durbar? Alas, alas! that such should be, that the pure and holy should serve the unclean. This is indeed the age of iron, and of debasement.'"

The Brahmun writhed in his seat. "There are many besides me," he said, "who serve the people of Islam."

"Who serve the destroyers of Toolja Mata, the defilers of her temple, the slayers of Brahmuns, and of sacred kine everywhere! O, shame—shame!" cried the Rajah eagerly.

"I was not at the shrine when the affray took place," said the Brahmun apologetically. "I could not help it."

"Has then a Brahmun's holiness become so debased that he says only, I could not help it?" returned the Rajah. "Is it pleasing to the Mother, think you, that her people should fawn on those whose hands are red in the blood of her votaries?"

"I would fling my service at the feet of Afzool Khan, and even of the Sultan himself, could I but serve with Hindus as I desire to serve," exclaimed the Brahmun.

"The opportunity might be found, friend," answered the Rajah, "if it were truly desired; but proof of fidelity would be required,—would it be given? What is the Maharaja's desire? Dost thou know it?"

"I guess it," said the Brahmun, "for I am not easily deceived by appearances, and I understood his looks to-day, if I mistake not. Could I only speak with him? Canst thou take me to him?"

"I can tell thy message to him," replied the Rajah, "and will deliver it faithfully. He chose me, else I had not dared to come."

The Envoy appeared to hesitate for a moment. "Impossible," he said—"impossible that I could tell another, what Sivaji himself should alone hear; it could not be."

"Dost thou know me, friend?" returned the Rajah, as he untied the handkerchief which concealed his face, and with it wiped the white ashes from his eyes and forehead—"dost thou know me? It is thus that I salute a holy Brahmun;" and he rose and made a lowly reverence, touching the feet of the Envoy respectfully.

The man strove to return it, but was prevented. "It cannot be," continued Sivaji; "here thou art a Brahmun, and I a Sudra. Let it be as I wish. It is for thee to receive the honour, not I."

"What would you have me do, Maharaja?" replied the Envoy, now trembling much. "I have done evil in helping the unclean, and would now expiate it if possible."

"I have had many things in my mind, Pundit," replied the Rajah, "and the Mother sends perplexing thoughts; but one thing is clear to me—she must be avenged."

The man echoed the words—"She must be avenged."

"Yes," continued the Rajah, "day and night, by old and young, rich and poor, man or woman, there is but one cry going up from Maharastra—'Avenge the Mother!' and yet before that force we are powerless."

"Where are the Mawullees? where are the Hetkurees we have heard of, and the gallant Tannajee?" cried the Brahmun excitedly. "What art thou doing, Sivaji Bhóslay? Men say of thee that thy mother holds thee back, else 'the fire should be on the hills.'"

"Good!" returned Sivaji, smiling; "it is as I thought, and there is yet a Brahmun who is true. What dost thou advise?"

"Hark!" said Gopináth, "come nearer. If I bring Afzool Khan and his men within the defiles, will it content thee? If I do this, what wilt thou do for me?"

"I have prepared for that already,—a Jahgeer, a high office, secular or among the priesthood, as thou wilt,—double thy present pay, whatever it be,—an ensign of rank, and—my friendship. Look, Pundit," cried the Rajah, springing closer to him, and drawing a small bright knife from his breast, "it were easy to slay thee,—for my knee is on thy weapon,—and so prevent my proposal being known: but it is not needed. Fear not," he added, for the drops of sweat were standing on the Brahmun's brow, under the terror he felt—"fear not! only be true, and Sivaji Bhóslay will not fail thee. When he has a kingdom thou shalt share its honour."

"Give me time to write," said the man, trembling under conviction of his own treachery and the excess of temptation to which he was exposed; "I will give the letter to-morrow."

"Impossible, Pundit," replied the Rajah: "the messengers are ready without, and they will bear what must be written to the Khan."

"Who will take the letter?"

"The Brahmun who spoke for me this morning; he and some horsemen are now ready."

"But to the Khan himself there must be no harm done," said the Pundit. "To him and his son I owe many kindnesses: for the rest, as thou wilt. Keep the family as hostages."

"As guests yonder," replied the Rajah; "he will be safe, he and his. Shall I send for writing materials? Krishnajee! Sit there," he continued, as his attendant entered; "see that what is written is plain."

And the Envoy wrote in the Persian character, in which he was a proficient, and which the other secretary understood:—

"I have seen the Rajah, his fort, and his people, and there is nothing to apprehend. They are all beneath notice: but in order to settle everything perfectly, and to inspire terror, my lord should advance with all the force, according to the plan devised here, which the bearer, one of the Rajah's secretaries, will explain personally, and which would be tedious to write. In a strictly private interview, which will be arranged, the Rajah Sivaji will throw himself at the feet of the Envoy of the king of kings, and receive the pardon which he desires. More would be beyond respect."

"It is enough," said Sivaji, when this writing was explained to him—"it will have the desired effect. Take this letter, Krishnajee, and set out for camp at once."

"Stay," added the Envoy, "let him accompany my messenger,—the Mahratta officer who spoke so boldly to-day. It were better he went, and he will not refuse duty. Enter that room and close the door, my lord, while I send for him;" and he called to an attendant to summon Bulwunt Rao.

It was not long ere he came in, flushed somewhat, as it seemed, with drink. "Who is this?" he said.

"The Maharaja's Secretary, who will accompany thee to camp. Go at once, if thou art fit, Bulwunt Rao; it is needful that Afzool Khan receive this as soon as may be."

"I am ready, Maharaj, to ride up Pertabgurh," he replied; "and he?"

"I attend you," said the Secretary; "come, we must leave this when the moon rises;" and they went out together.

"Enough," said the Rajah, emerging from his concealment. "Generations hereafter will record how Punto Gopináth served his prince. Fear not—it will be well with thee and thine hereafter."

CHAPTER LXXVI.

THE letter despatched by the Rajah Sivaji, as we have recorded, was received in a few days by the Khan, and its tenor was not doubted. There was nothing in it which could in any degree disturb the Khan's complacency, or awaken suspicion. If he chafed at the idea of a bloodless campaign, and his friend the Peer, in the ardour of his bigotry, sighed at what now promised to be a tame conclusion to an exciting commencement,—Fazil, on the other hand, and with him the commander of the Mahratta contingent in camp, and others who had more sympathy with the people of the country than their elders, rejoiced that it was to be so; and that a valuable ally and confederate was to be secured to the dynasty which they served, by means which appeared at once just, merciful, and binding upon both.

The new Envoy who brought the letter, pleased the Khan and the Peer extremely. In the first place, he spoke the Dekhan court language fluently, and was a fair Persian scholar. He was known to the Khan as having served in a subordinate department when he himself held the administration of Wye, and he gratefully acknowledged—as he reminded the Khan of—former benefits. The first envoys could not communicate with the Khan except through interpreters. True, his son was usually present, or occasionally the holy priest himself, who might be induced to assist; but the Khan would have better liked to manage these Mahratta envoys himself, and now there was the desired opportunity. Day after day, as the army advanced without check, by easy but continuous stages, the new agent was in close attendance, and very frequently, with the others, was summoned to private conferences. Fazil, too, had his share in them, and to every outward appearance no room existed for suspicion of any kind.

They had now entered the Rajah's own jurisdiction, and were treated more as honoured guests than as an invading army. Supplies were provided at every stage, forage was abundant, difficult places in the roads were found cleared for the artillery, and the people met them with goodwill and courtesy, which was as pleasant as unexpected. Any idea of resistance was out of the question. The usual village guards, or here and there a few horsemen in attendance on a local functionary, were all that was seen of the Rajah's forces; and the Khan was amused and gratified with the Envoy's descriptions of how—to attract attention to his affairs—his master had caused the belief to gain ground that he was possessed of an army of vast power.

In short, all the obstructions and dangers which had appeared so great at a distance had passed away; and as the Khan led his troops more and more deeply into the mountainous district, he could not but feel that if they had been opposed in those rugged defiles, the struggle would have been difficult as well as desperate. The enemy would have had a stronger country to retreat upon, and one more easily defended, while, in proportion, the advance to him would have been beset with peril which could hardly be estimated.

Very frequently Fazil asked particulars of the fort of Pertabgurh from Bulwunt Rao, who described it clearly enough,—an ordinary hill fort, with a garrison strong for local purposes, but, after all, only such as Mahratta chiefs and gentry kept about them; strong in their own position, but helpless for offence. Where, then, were the armies which Sivaji was said to possess? Bulwunt Rao, in reply, pointed to the village people, all soldiers, he said, from their youth, and accustomed to arms: but among them there was no symptom of excitement, nor could Bulwunt Rao, suspecting nothing himself, discover any cause for alarm: and so they proceeded.

Meanwhile, the programme of a meeting had been arranged by the agents between the Khan and Sivaji. Both parties had mooted points of etiquette, which could hardly be overcome. The Rajah, as a prince, could not visit the Khan first, nor could Afzool Khan, as the representative of royalty, visit the Rajah; but they could both meet, and the barrier of ceremony once broken, it mattered little what followed. No troops were to be present. Attended each by a single armed follower, the place of meeting was fixed on a level spot at some little distance up the mountain of Pertabgurh, where the Rajah, the Envoy said, had already prepared a pavilion, which would be fitted up for the occasion. If the Khan pleased, he might bring a thousand of his best horse—more, if convenient—to witness the ceremony from below; but only one attendant besides the palankeen-bearers could advance to the conference. Nothing was to be written, and the agent already at the fort would attend the Khan on the one hand, while another of the Rajah's, if possible or needful, would accompany him from above. No objection appeared, and none was made, to these arrangements.

So the army reached its final stage near the village of Jowly, a few miles distant from the fort; and the last preparations were made that night by both parties. The morning would see the Khan set out early accompanied by fifteen hundred chosen horse—some Abyssinian, some Dekhani, others his own retainers,—all picked men; while the remainder of the army should rest from its labour and exertion, which, on account of the rough mountain roads, had been exceedingly great for the last three days.

At Jowly, too, the camp was more than ordinarily pleasant. A plain of some extent, and which for the most part was under cultivation, afforded ample room for all the force. The grassy slopes of the mountains, by which the plain was surrounded, furnished abundant supplies of forage; a brawling stream ran under the hills on one side, and the Rajah's usual supplies of food of all kinds were abundant at moderate prices in a bazar which, consisting of rough sheds and small tents, was located near the village on the other.

Let us see how the night was passed by both parties.

The Khan's tents had been pitched on an even sward which bordered the rivulet, and several fine trees were included in the area enclosed by the canvas walls. Under the shade of these, Zyna and Fazil had sat most part of the day. A few carpets and pillows had been spread there, and the cool fresh mountain air, the brawling murmur of the brook, and the grand and beautiful scenery by which they were surrounded, so different to the bare monotonous undulations of the Dekhan, were in themselves more exciting than it was possible for them to have imagined from any previous description. But the loss of Tara's society was pressing heavily upon both. All they heard daily was, that she was well and among her people, who were taking care of her. She would remain with them at Wye; and as the army returned, she should see Lurlee Khánum and Zyna once more, and take leave of them, for she could not be permitted to sojourn with Mahomedans. This the Envoy had told the Khan and Fazil the day before.

It was a dreary prospect for Fazil, and apparently a hopeless one. Should he ever see that sweet face more? ever hear the music of the gentle voice, at once so timid and yet so reliant? There was no hope that the Brahmuns among whom she had fallen would now give her up voluntarily. It was impossible to think it. Did they know what he had asked and she had half-promised?—would her life be safe even if they did? Hardly so, indeed; or, if safe, would be spared at the price of the disfigurement which awaited her, according to the strict rules of her faith. What they had arranged among themselves, therefore, could not be openly prosecuted; and, in defiance of his father's cautions, and the apparently smooth progress of public affairs, no effort to demand her, or to recover her by force, could be made as yet.

"Let us settle everything with this Mahratta first, and as we return by Wye, we will have the girl, or know why," the stout old Khan used to say; for he had grown to love Tara very dearly, and missed her presence, though in a different manner, as much as any of them. "Fear not, Fazil, the Kafirs shall not possess her."

So Zyna and Fazil had sat most part of the day, revolving over and over again how best Tara might be assisted or rescued, while blaming themselves a thousand times for that neglect of special precautions for her safety which had resulted in her abduction.

"If only Moro Trimmul could be found, and brought once more to account," Fazil said, grinding his teeth, "it would go hard with him;" but he was not to be heard of. The Envoys in camp declared he had at once proceeded to Pertabgurh to clear himself to the Rajah Sivaji and the lady mother, of whom, in particular, he was an especial favourite; but he was not now even there: he had been sent to a distance; where or why it was not known; and it was impossible to trace him. Bulwunt Rao, Lukshmun, and the lad Ashruf, had all been employed in turn as spies, but had failed to discover him—he was not to be heard of.

It was now late, and the lady Lurlee came and joined them before the evening prayer. She had been busy after her own fashion, and as the priest and some others were to dine with the Khan, had prepared several of her most scientific dishes. She had no doubt as to the issue of the morrow's interview. In the first place, who could resist her husband? and were not the planets unusually favourable? She and the priest had compared notes from behind the screen in the tent; and though he laughed at the curious jargon she had collected on the subject, yet, a steadfast believer in astrology himself, had explained to her how peculiarly fortunate the conjunction was to be at the hour cast for the meeting, and she had fully believed it. If Tara had been there, all would have been perfectly happy; but, as Lurlee said, the planets told her it was only, after all, a matter of a few days' delay; and, indeed, perhaps, after to-morrow she might be demanded.

Fazil, however, in spite of these assurances, was not easy; and after he left the tents for the evening prayer, had taken counsel with Lukshmun who, in regard to Tara, had taken the place of Bulwunt

Rao, to whom Fazil dare not intrust his secret. The day she had disappeared, and Fazil's misery was apparent, the hunchback had divined the cause; and a few inquiries in his capacity of spy had confirmed his suspicions.

"I know but of one thing to do, master," he said, as the young man confided to him his dread of violence to the girl—"send me back to Wye, where she is; give me but ever so small a note, and I will deliver it into her own hand; and if I can bring her away, trust to me to do so. I can traverse these forests and mountains by night; I can hide her away or disguise her; and if she be true to thee, she will come. Give me the boy Ashruf, and a little money, and let us go, even now. He is without; call him."

"Ashruf," cried the young Khan to the lad, who was standing near the tent door, and who entered at once; "wilt thou go with Lukshmun?"

"My lord," replied the lad, "he and I have arranged this already. They do not know us here, and he has been teaching me a Mahratta ballad which she knows, and we can sing it in Wye to-morrow. If he had not spoken I should have told you of our plan. My lord, we will bring her away silently, and no one shall be the wiser. Yes, I will go into the fire for my lord, if he will but prove me."

"And Bulwunt Rao?" said Fazil.

"He is in the clouds," replied Lukshmun, "in the hope of getting back the family estate; wind has got into his head, and he is beside himself. To my mind, the Rajah would be far better pleased to have him put out of the way than to favour his pretensions; but Bulwunt says he has been promised 'justice;' and so," added Lukshmun, with a hideous grimace, "he will have his own way, and what is to be is to be; only write the note, master, quick, and let us go; he won't help us."

"Alas!" replied Fazil, "I can only write Persian; but she knows my signature, for she used to see me write it. Stay, however," he continued, unfastening a thin gold ring from his wrist, "she will remember this better, and understand it: take it with ye, and may God speed ye. Go at once! Bring her, if possible, or mark where she is, and we will go, Inshalla! and fetch her."

The priest was chanting the Azân, and Fazil passed out into the usual place of prayer, which was numerously attended. After its close, the Peer, his father, and all who were to stay to dinner, assembled for the repast, which was served immediately. There was no forward movement of tents that night; and the guests sat till a late hour discussing the probable events of the morrow, and the possibility of an early countermarch, at least as far as Wye, where the open country was preferable to their present confined situation among the mountains.

CHAPTER LXXVII.

WAS there equal confidence in the fort? We must now go there, and listen to the midnight consultation, which may be prolonged till daylight; and yet men on the eve of some desperate enterprise for which they have prepared themselves, need more rest, and often sleep more calmly, than at any other period of their existence.

It was the same chamber that we have formerly seen; but the window of the oriel is shut, for the night wind at that height is cold and bleak, and thick, quilted curtains, which have been let fall before it and the doorway, exclude all air. Sivaji, Maloosray, and Palkur are sitting together, but are silent, for the Rajah's mind is troubled.

"If I only knew what she would have me do," he said at length, looking up. "Hast thou prepared all, Tannajee?"

"Master," he replied, "everything is ready. By midnight, or a little later, Moro Trimmul and the rest of the veterans will be in the woods near Jowly, around the camp. Every position has been marked out, and will be silently taken up. Nothing can escape out of that plain, and they will await the signal of the five guns from hence. The Brahmun swears," he continued, after a pause, "that he will take the pretty sister of the young Khan, in revenge for his seduction of the Tooljapoor Moorlee."

"He dare not," said Sivaji quickly. "I have heard that girl was an honoured guest in Afzool Khan's family; the Brahmuns say she was. No, he dare not touch her; and I have warned him not to do so."

Maloosray shrugged his shoulders. "Perhaps," he said; "God knows! but Moro says otherwise. Let it pass; it is not our business; but he will be none the less active to get the whole family into his power."

"And you, Nettajee?" said the Rajah, turning to him.

"There are five thousand of my best Mawullees sleeping in the thickets east of the fort-gate. They will close in behind the Beejapoor people as they pass, and when we hear the horn, I think, master, few will escape—yes," he continued, fixing his large black eyes on the Rajah, and slightly twisting his moustaches, "few will escape."

"O, the blind confidence of these Beejapoor swine!" cried the Rajah, laughing, as he lifted up his hands. "They have neither eyes nor ears, else they had guessed we are not as we seem. But the goddess Mother has blinded and deafened them, and it is as my mother said it would be."

"Where is she?" asked Maloosray; "she should bless us ere we go forth."

"She is in the temple, and uneasy. As the time comes on, they think she will have a visitation," he replied. "Ah! here is some one to tell us. What news, Bheemee?"

"The lady mother is uneasy, Maharaj, and rocking herself to and fro. It is coming on her, and ye should be near to listen."

"Come, friends, let us go," said the Rajah; "on this revelation depends my course to-morrow."

It was but a few steps, and the place is already familiar to us. The low porch and dark vestibule, the small shrine within, from whence a strong light is shining into the gloom, resting sharply upon the figure of the Ranee as she sat before it, not quietly now, as when we saw her once before, but with her shoulders and bosom heaving rapidly, her eyes shut, or if opened for a moment flashing with excitement, her lips trembling and already speckled with foam; and that peculiar sharp, rocking motion of her body, which always preceded the final attack.

The men stood by reverently. No one dared to speak. The attendant Brahmun offered flowers from time to time, and kept up a low chant or incantation, while occasionally he threw grains of coloured rice upon the altar.

Suddenly the lady stretched forth her arms and shrieked wildly. Maloosray would have rushed forward, but Sivaji held him back. "Wait," he said in a low tone, "no one dares to interrupt her; wouldst thou go to death between her and the Mother? She will come—listen."

There was first a low muttering in which nothing could be distinguished; but words at last followed, to them terrible and awful, as, believing in the dread presence of the goddess, the lady poured them forth with gasps.

"O, I thirst! My children were slain—and no one has avenged them. Blood! blood! I thirst. I will drink it! The blood of the cruel—of the cow-slayers! All, all—the old and the young; the old woman and the maiden; the nurse and the child at her breast; all—all—all!" she continued, her voice rising to a scream. "They who love me, kill for me; for I thirst,—for I thirst now, as I did for the blood of the demons," and the voice again sank to a low whisper which was not audible.

These words had come from her by spasms, as it were; painfully, and with much apparent suffering. She shrieked repeatedly as she uttered them, and clutched at the air with a strange convulsive movement of both hands: sometimes as if apparently drawing to her, or again fiercely repelling an object before her. At last she stretched forth her hands and her body, as if following what she saw, and looking vacantly into the space before her with a terrified expression of countenance, the hands fell listlessly on her lap, and her features relaxed into a weary expression, as of one who had endured acute pain. Then she sighed deeply, opened her eyes, looked around, and spoke. "Bheemee, I thirst," she said gently,—"bring me water."

Sivaji alone had remained with his mother and the Brahmun of the temple, who, as she spoke them, recorded the disconnected sentences. The Rajah's companions, fearless before an enemy, were cowards before the dread presence in which they believed.

"Ah, thou art here, son," she said, turning to him. "Did I speak? Surely the Mother was with me," and she sighed deeply, again drawing her hand wearily across her eyes.

"Come and rest, mother," he replied, raising her up and supporting her tenderly. "Come, thou art weary."

"Weary indeed, my son," she said,—"there is no rest for me till all is finished. Come, and I will tell thee everything;" and he followed her into her own apartments, where she lay down. The attendant brought water, and she drank a deep draught.

"What did I say, son?" she continued. "But no matter. It is all blood before me—carnage and victory! Blood!" she cried excitedly, grasping his arm and looking intently into his face. "Art thou ready? ready for victory!—ready to cry 'Jey Kalee! Jey Toolja Mata!'"

"Ready, mother—yes. There is no failing anywhere. The men are at their posts, and the signals have been decided upon. No one will escape us now."

"No one will escape," she echoed,—"no one must escape—no—not one—not even he."

"Ah, mother," cried Sivaji, "not so; surely with pledged honour, soldier to a soldier, and a solemn invitation, it could not be."

"It must be, son," she said gloomily, "else the sacrifice is incomplete and of no avail. Wilt thou risk that for thine own sake—for my sake—for the sake of our faith? I see it all," cried the lady excitedly, "passing before me—a triumph of glory over those defilers of the temples of the gods; thy rapid rise to power; the legions of the hateful Mahomedans trampled in the dust by greater legions of thine own. 'Jey Sivaji Rajah!' shall be cried from Dehli to Raméshwur.* Wilt thou now turn back? wilt thou be forsworn to her—to the Mother who is our life? Wilt thou be as vacillating as thy father? Beware! thou art more committed to her than he—and does she spare backsliders?"

"He is but one to be spared, mother, and that because of my promise," he pleaded.

"I tell thee it cannot be, my son. She will have him—the slayer of the priests—the murderer of hundreds of the people about her shrine. And that priest of his who, as all say, led the slaughter,

* The celebrated Hindu temple in the southern point of India.

cast down her image, and trampled on it! O son, canst thou hesitate? art thou—so firm and true always—now grown weak? have I borne one in travail who is degenerate? Choose then, now—victory and future blessing, or the result which thou knowest, and we all know, if we fail her—the death which must ensue. Both are before thee; choose, boy; I can say no more!" and she turned away her face to the wall.

But she had conquered, for there was no defying her will,—always the mainspring of the Rajah's actions—and, backed by those seemingly divine revelations in which he devoutly believed, he did not resist her.

"Mother," he said, rising and prostrating himself before her, "I know—I feel that the goddess is speaking from thy mouth still. I hear and obey. Bless me, O my mother, and my hand will be strong; put thy hands on my head, and the Mother will guide the blow surely."

"I do bless thee, Sivaji Bhóslay," she returned, placing her hands on his head, "in the name of her who directs us, and with her power I endue thee. Go and fear not, but do her bidding—thou shalt not fail."

He rose. "I will but speak with Maloosray and dismiss them," he said, "and return. Make up a bed for me here, for I would sleep near thee, mother, to-night."

"Get thee to thy post, Nettajee," he said to Palkur, as he met them without; "there is no fear now; victory is with us—she hath said it. Let the men sleep and be ready."

"And what will you do with him—the Khan?" asked Maloosray.

"You will see to-morrow," said Sivaji excitedly. "You will be with me, and will share the danger. This was reserved for you, O well-tried friend!"

"Enough," said Maloosray to Palkur; "let us go, for the master needs rest;" and, saluting him, they departed.

Sivaji returned to his mother. A low bed had been prepared in the room, and she was sitting by it. He took off his upper garment and turban, and, having performed his ablutions, lay down, and she patted him gently, as she used to do when he was a child. He would have spoken, but she would not listen, and he urged her to sleep herself, but she would not leave him; and when the dim light of day broke gently into the chamber, he woke, and found she had not stirred from his side. "Arise," she said, "it is time. Food is prepared for thee. Eat, and go forth to victory!"

He obeyed her; bathed, worshipped earnestly in the temple, and ate heartily. Then he returned to her, and, in the simple words of the old Mahratta Chronicle, "laid his head at his mother's feet, and "besought a blessing. He then arose, put on a steel cap, and "chain armour, which was concealed under a thickly-quilted cotton "gown; and, taking a crooked dagger which he hid under his sleeve, "and the 'tiger's claws'* in his right hand, he girded his loins, and "went out."

CHAPTER LXXVIII.

The morning broke, calm and beautiful. Long before the highest peaks of the mountains blushed under the rosy light which preceded the sunrise, the Khan and Fazil, with Zyna, had risen and performed their morning prayer. The deep booming sound of the kettledrums woke the echoes around, and reverberated from side to side of the valley, retiring to recesses among the glens, and murmuring softly as it died away among the distant peaks and precipices. As yet, the valley was partially filled with mists, which clung to its wooded sides; but as the sun rose, a slight wind sprang up with it, which, breaking through these mists, drove them up the mountain, and displayed the scenery in all its fresh morning beauty, as though a curtain had been suddenly drawn from before it.

Behind them were the stupendous mountains of the Maha-bul-eshwur range; before, at a short distance, and divided from them by a chain of smaller hills, rose up the precipices of Pertabgurh, glittering in the morning light, and crowned by the walls and bastions of the fortress.

Long before daylight the lady Lurlee had risen, and, careful for her husband, had, in conjunction with Kurreema, cooked his favourite dish of kichéri and kabobs. "It was a light breakfast," she said, "and would agree with them better than a heavier repast, and dinner would be ready when they returned." So Afzool Khan, his son, and the priest, ate their early meal, not only in joyful anticipation of a speedy return, but of accomplishing what would result in honour to all concerned.

They remembered afterwards, that as an attendant brought before the Khan the usual mail shirt he wore, and the mail-cap, with its bright steel chains, over which his turban was usually tied when fully accoutred, he laughingly declined both. "They will be very hot and uncomfortable," he said, "and we are not going to fight. No, give me a muslin dress," which he put on. A few words about ordinary household matters to Lurlee, a few cheering sentences to Zyna, as he passed from the inner and private enclosure of the tent, and he went out among the men.

Fazil followed, fully armed and accoutred for riding. There had been a good-humoured strife between Fazil and the priest the night

* A treacherous and deadly weapon, in the shape of tiger's claws, which, fitted on the fingers, shuts into the hand.

before, as to who should be the one armed follower to accompany his father, and he had chosen the priest. "Fazil was too young yet," he said, "to enter into grave political discussions with wily Mahrattas, and would be better with the escort." So the soldier-priest, like the Khan, discarding the steel cap, gauntlets, and quilted armour in which he usually accoutred himself—appeared, like Afzool Khan, in the plain muslin dress of his order; and having tied up his waist with a shawl, and thrown another over his shoulders, stuck a light court sword into his waist-band, which he pressed down on his hips with a jaunty air, and called merrily to Fazil, to see how peacefully he was attired.

The escort awaited them in the camp, and the spirited horses of fifteen hundred gallant cavaliers were neighing and tossing their heads as Afzool Khan, Fazil, and the priest rode up. "Forward!" cried the Khan cheerily; and as the kettledrums beat a march, the several officers saluted their commander, and, wheeling up their men, led them by the road pointed out by the Brahmuns and guides in the direction of Pertabgurh.

At that time, single men, who looked like shepherds tending sheep, and who were standing on crests of the hills, or crouching so as not to be seen, passed a signal that the Khan and his party had set out. It was still early, and the time when, of all others perhaps, armies such as the Khan's, were most defenceless. Many, roused for a while by the assembly and departure of the escort, had gone to sleep again; others, sitting over embers of fires, were smoking, preparing to cook their morning repast, or were attending to their horses, or in the bazar purchasing the materials for their day's meal. The camp was watched from the woods around by thousands of armed men, who, silently and utterly unobserved, crept over the crests of the hills, and lay down in the thick brushwood which fringed the plain.

As the Khan's retinue neared the fort, parties of armed men, apparently stationed by the roadside to salute him as he passed, closed up in rear of the escort; and others, moving parallel to them in the thickets, joined with them unseen. Quickly, too, men with axes felled large trees, which were thrown down so as to cross the road, and interlaced their branches so as to be utterly impassable for horsemen; and all these preparations went on in both places silently, methodically, and with a grim surety of success, imparting a confidence which all who remembered it afterwards attributed to the direction of the goddess whom they worshipped. As it was said then, as it is still said, and sung in many a ballad, "not a man's hand failed, not a foot stumbled."

At the gate of the fort the Khan dismounted from his horse, and entered his palankeen. Before he did so, however, he embraced his son, and bid him be careful of the men, and that no one entered the town or gave offence. He could see, looking up, the thatched pavilion on the little level shoulder of the mountain, and pointed to it cheerfully. "It is not far to go, Huzrut," he said to the Peer, "I may as well walk with these good friends," and he pointed to the Brahmuns who attended him. But Fazil would not allow it, nor the Peer either. "You must go in state," they said, "as the representative of the King ought to do," and he then took his seat in the litter.

"Khóda Hafiz—may God protect you, father!" said Fazil, as he bent his head into the palankeen, when the bearers took it up; "come back happily, and do not delay!"

"Inshalla!" said the Khan smilingly, "fear not, I will not delay, and thou canst watch me up yonder." So he went on, the priest's hand leaning upon the edge of the litter as he walked by its side.

On through the town, from the terraced houses of which, crowds of women looked down on the little procession, and men, mostly unarmed, or unremarkable in any case, saluted them, or regarded them with clownish curiosity. No one could see that the court of every house behind, was filled with armed men thirsting for blood, and awaiting the signal to attack.

The Khan's agent, Puntojee Gopináth, being a fat man, had left word at the gate which defended the entrance of the road to the fort, that he had preceded the Khan, and would await him at the pavilion. He had seen no one since the night before, and he knew only that the Khan would come to meet the Rajah. That was all he had stipulated for, and his part was performed. He believed that Sivaji would seize Afzool Khan, and hold him a hostage for the fulfilment of all his demands; and the line of argument in his own mind was, that if the Khan resisted, and was hurt in the fray which might ensue, it was no concern of his. But he did not know the Rajah's intention, nor did the Rajah's two Brahmuns who had ascended with him; and they all three now sat down together upon the knoll, waiting the coming of Afzool Khan from below, and the Rajah from above.

As the agreement had specified, except one each, there were to be no armed men: no other people were present but one, who seemed to be a labourer, who was tying up a rough mat to the side of the pavilion to keep out the wind and sun. Gopináth looked from time to time up the mountain-road, and again down to the town, speculating upon the cause of delay in the Rajah's coming; and the others told him he would not leave the fort till the Khan had arrived below, and showed him a figure standing upon the edge of the large bastion which overhung the precipice above, relieved sharply against the clear sky, which was fronting towards the quarter by which the Khan's retinue should come, and apparently giving signals to others behind him.

"Your master is coming," said the Secretary, "they see him from above;" and, almost as he spoke, the bright glinting of steel caps and lance-heads, with a confused mass of horsemen, appeared on the road to the fort, among the trees, and they sat and watched them come on. Then the force halted in the open space before the outer gate, where the Khan's little procession formed, and entered the town. After that, the houses and the trees of the mountain-side concealed them. How beautiful was the scene!

The wind had died away, and the sun shone with a blaze of heat unknown elsewhere, striking down among those moist narrow valleys with a power which would have been painful, but for the cool refreshing air by which it was tempered. The distant mountains glowed under the effect of the trembling exhalations, which, rising now unseen, tempered the colours of the distance to that tender blue and grey which melts into the tint of the sky. The rugged precipices above were softened in effect; and the heavy masses of foliage, festoons of creepers, and the dense woods, rich in colour, combined to enhance the wonderful beauty of the spot. There was perfect silence, except the occasional monotonous drumming notes of woodpeckers in the glens, and the shrill chirrup of tree-crickets which occasionally broke out and was again silent.

In a few minutes, the shouts of the Khan's palankeen-bearers were heard below, and the litter suddenly emerged from a turn in the road, being pushed on by the combined efforts of the men. The Brahmun's heart bounded when he saw the figure of the priest beside the litter, holding to it, and pressing up the ascent vigorously. "Will he escape?" he said mentally; "the Mother forbid it,—let her take him!" A few more steps, and the palankeen was at the knoll; it was set down, and the Khan's shoes being placed for him by a bearer, he put his feet into them and got out, speaking to the priest, who was panting with his exertion.

"Is he not here, Puntojee?" cried the Khan to the Brahmun, who saluted him respectfully.

"No, my lord, not yet. Ah! look," he continued, as he turned towards the pass, "there are two men on the path, and that one, the smallest, is he."

The men coming down appeared to hesitate, and waved their hands, as if warning off some one.

"It is the bearers," said one of Sivaji's Secretaries. "The Rajah is timid, and fears the crowd he sees."

The Khan laughed. "Good," he said to the men. "Go away; sit down yonder in the shade. You will be called when I want you;" and as they got up and retired, the two men advanced slowly and cautiously down the pathway.

Afzool Khan went forward a few paces as Sivají and Maloosray came up. "You are welcome, Rajah Sahib. Embrace me," he said to Sivaji. "Let there be no doubt between us;" and he stretched forth his arms in the usual manner.

Sivaji stooped to the embrace; and as the Khan's arms were laid upon his shoulders, and he was thus unprotected, struck the sharp deadly tiger's-claw dagger deeply into his bowels, seconding the blow with one from the other dagger which he had concealed in his left hand.

Afzool Khan reeled and staggered under the deadly wounds. "Dog of a Kafir!" he cried, pressing one hand to the wound, while he drew the sword he wore with the other, and endeavoured to attack the Rajah. Alas! what use now were those feeble blows against concealed armour? Faint and sick, the Khan reeled hither and thither, striking vainly against the Rajah, who, with the terrible sword now in his hand, and crying the national shout of "Hur, Hur, Mahadeo!" rained blow upon blow on his defenceless enemy. It was an unequal strife, soon finished. Falling heavily, Afzool Khan died almost as he reached the earth.

Meanwhile, Maloosray had attacked the priest with all his force and skill, but the Peer was a good swordsman, and for a short time held his ground. Neither spoke, except in muttered curses, as blows were struck; but Tannajee Maloosray had no equal in his weapon, and as he cried to the Rajah, who was advancing to his aid, to keep back—the priest, distracted by the assault of another enemy, received his death-blow, and sank to the ground.

"Jey Kalee!" shouted both. "Now, blow loud and shrill, Gunnoo, for thy life," continued the Rajah, "and thou shalt have a collar of gold."

The man who had appeared to be a labourer, seized his horn, which had been concealed in the grass, and blew a long note, with a shrill quivering flourish at the close, which resounded through the air, and echoed among the mountains; and thrice repeated the signal.

Then a great puff of smoke, followed by a report which thundered through the valley, burst from the bastion above. Those who were looking from the fort, and the Rajah himself, who ran to the edge of the knoll, saw the wreaths of fire which burst from the thickets about the plain where the Mahomedan cavalry stood, and a sharp irregular crash of matchlock shots came up from below, and continued. Hundreds died at every volley, and there were writhing, struggling masses of horses and men on the plain—loose horses careering about; and some men still mounted, strove to pierce the barriers which had been made on every side, crowded on each other, and, falling fast, became inextricable. Soon, too, the Mawullees, under Nettajee Palkur, emerged sword in hand from their ambush, and attacked those who survived. Some escaped; but of the fifteen hundred men who had ridden there in their pride that morning, few lived to tell the tale.

. . . .

Moro Trimmul had taken up his position over night on a hill overlooking the main camp of Afzool Khan's army. A few boughs placed together formed a cover and screen on a high knoll, which commanded a view of the camp beneath, and of the summit of the fort whence his signal was to come. He sat there watching, and observed the force below, careless, without a guard, without weapons—the men sitting idly, wandering about, or cooking, as it might be. Every moment seemed interminable; and the eyes of those who looked with him were strained towards the fort.

"One," he cried at last, as the first puff of bright smoke burst from the bastion—"two—three—four—five! Enough. It is complete, my friends. Now, cry 'Hur, Hur, Mahadeo!' and upon them. Spare no one! Come, friends, let us sack the Khan's tents first, where I have some work of my own to do."

"Beware," said an elderly officer, who stood near him—"beware, Moro Pundit, of the master, if thou disobey him in this. He will suffer no insult to the women."

"Tooh!" cried Moro Trimmul, spitting contemptously, "I am a Brahmun, and he dare not interfere with me. Come!"

Ten thousand throats were crying the battle-cry of the Hetkurees, as they burst from the thickets upon the bewildered army. Why follow them? In a few hours there was a smell of blood ascending to the sky, and vultures—scenting it from their resting-places on the precipices of the mountains, and from their soaring stations in the clouds—were fast descending upon the plain in hideous flocks.

Shortly after the Khan had left—he could scarcely have reached the fort—two figures, a man and a boy, ran rapidly across the camp at their utmost speed towards the Khan's tents—they were the hunchback and Ashruf. When Fazil had dismissed them, the night before, they had taken the read to Wye; and immediately beyond the confines of the camp, where the road ascended a rocky pass, had been seized by the Mahratta pickets posted there. In vain they urged they were but Dekhan ballad-singers; they were not released. "Ye shall sing for us to-morrow," they said, "when we have made the sacrifice, the ballads of the goddess at Tooljapoor;" and, bound together, they lay by the tree where the party of men was stationed. There they heard all, but were helpless.

"Ah, masters," said Lukshmun, as daylight broke, "unbind us; we are stiff with the cold; we will not run away; and I will sing you the morning hymn of the goddess, as the Brahmuns sing it at Tooljapoor. See, my arms are swelled, and the boy's too."

"Loose him, brother," said one of the men, "we shall soon now have the signal. Wait you here," he added, as Lukshmun finished the chant, "and we will fill your pouches with Beejapoor rupees when we come back."

"Alas!" said the hunchback, with a rueful face, "this little brother came from Wye last night, to say my elder brother, Rama, was dead. Good sirs, let me go and bury him," and he began to sob bitterly.

"Let them go, Nowla," said another of the men; "they will be only in our way; we can't stop to guard them."

"My blessings on ye, gentlemen! Only let us go now, and we will come to you and sing congratulations when you have won the victory," said Lukshmun humbly.

"Go," said the men, "but do not return to camp, else we will slay you if we see you there."

"They will die, or worse," said the hunchback, whispering to Ashruf, "for Moro Trimmul is the leader here. Come, let us save the Khan's wife and the lady Zyna," and they turned into the jungle in the direction of the camp.

The boy was bold and quick-witted. As they ran on, "I can get into the zenana," he said, "under the tent wall, and perhaps we can make them change clothes, and fly—but if they stay?"

"I will get the ponies ready," replied the other, and they ran the faster over the plain, unperceived.

They reached the tents, and the boy entered as he said. Who would believe them? Zyna heard the tale with sickening dread, and Lurlee, assured by the others, at first disbelieved him, and threatened him with stripes. The women-servants crowded around, and some began to shriek, and were with difficulty pacified; others mocked him and turned away. Still the boy urged: and the hunchback, desperate, and dreading the delay, now found his way into the enclosure, and prostrated himself before them.

"I know the country," he said: "fly! take what jewels you can carry, and come. God be with them, lady!" he continued, as Zyna and Lurlee cried aloud for their husband and brother—"God be with them! they are mounted and will escape, and we may yet meet; but stay not here, else ye will die, or be dishonoured, and the Khan will kill me."

Then another voice was heard without, shouting. It was Shêre Khan, who had been left in charge of the private camp. "Go!" he cried, "I see men moving in the woods, and there is confusion and treachery." And others said the same. Then, too, they heard the five guns of the fort, and there broke from the mountains around a hoarse roar of voices, "Hur, Hur, Mahadeo!"

This decided them. A hurried change of clothes, some coarse garments thrown over them, and the ponies being led within the enclosure, the ladies were lifted on them and carried out. O, to see the stupid misery of those women! Hitherto secluded, they could understand nothing; they had no power to resist; and why they should be taken out among men, when the shouts and screams of the camp were growing wilder every moment, they could not understand. So they wrung their hands in speechless terror.

"Come with the ladies, Shêre Khan," cried Lukshmun; "come, save thyself, old man!"

"No," he replied sadly; "my time is come, and the sherbet of death will be sweet. Go thou, and all of ye who can," he added to those who had gathered with the women. "Quick! quick! else it will be too late."

The shouts of "Hur, Hur, Mahadeo!" were already mingling on the confines of the camp with the battle-cries of the Moslems, who had rallied in small parties, and the flood of attack was there stayed for a little: this saved the fugitives. Close by the enclosure of tent walls ran the rivulet, and its banks were high and covered with brushwood on the sides, which concealed the party. Lukshmun, with a true freebooter's instinct, led Zyna's pony down the bank, accompanied by some of the terrified women-servants, and Lurlee followed. So they proceeded at a rapid pace down the stream, meeting no one, and concealed from view.

They heard the hideous din of shouts, screams, and shots increase behind them, but it gradually softened with distance, and in a little time Lukshmun turned up the sandy bed of a tributary brook, on the sides of which the jungle was thicker, while the bed was narrower and more tortuous; and, bidding every one tread only in the shallow stream which flowed in the midst, in order to afford no traces of footsteps, he hurried on, still leading Zyna's pony by the bridle. "Fear not, lady," he said confidently,—"the worst is past, and God will be merciful; fear not."

In the camp there was but a short resistance. On the one hand, the desperate valour of the mountain soldiery, the certainty of plunder, revenge for Tooljapoor, and the example of Moro Trimmul and other leaders; and on the other, the helpless, disorganized, bewildered mass before them, rendered the assault irresistible. The first attacking bodies were succeeded by mass upon mass of fresh assailants from all quarters, and these successive tides of men surged resistlessly across the camp, overwhelming all.

When Moro Trimmul and his party reached the Khan's tents, they found no one. The tracks of the ponies, where they had descended the bank, were, however, visible, and were taken up by his followers, who dashed forward like bloodhounds on a scent. "Away after them, Kakrey!" cried the Brahmun to a subordinate officer. "Thou art a better tracker than I. Bring them to me,—then," he added to himself, "Fazil Khan, we will see who wins the game,—you or I."

CHAPTER LXXIX.

THE ambassador's family, with whom Tara had received protection, had arrived at Pertabgurh the day before the events related in the last chapter. At Wye some traces of her mother's family, the Durpeys, had been found, but they were now residing at or near Poona: it would require several days to communicate with them; and a much longer period for them, or any one of them, to come for Tara and take her away. Meanwhile, therefore, there was no resource but to stay where she was, and to endure, what was daily becoming more and more insupportable.

Personally, Govind Rao, the Envoy, was kind to her, and continually renewed his offers of assistance and protection; but from his sister, the widow Pudma Bye, Tara had to endure insult and ill-usage, from which the Envoy's wife was unable to save her. Few, indeed, in the house, chose to risk the bitterness of Pudma's tongue, or the virulence of her spite. Her brother even feared her, and avoided her as much as possible.

So she employed herself in ascetic penances and religious exercises, fasted long and often, and mortified herself in various ingenious ways, with a view to establishing a character for sanctity which should make her famous. As might be supposed, she, the general distributor of the family alms, had many friends among the priestly Brahmuns, who attended the house and partook of her brother's charity; and it was an object with many, by flattering her vanity, to make those alms as large as possible, and to induce her to undertake ceremonies which could not be performed without priestly aid, and, necessarily, money.

The chief of these priests was one Wittul Shastree, an elderly man of grave aspect, but with a hard expression of countenance, which might proceed from austerity or avarice, or both combined. He was the agent or commissary of the prince superior of the Brahmuns of the province, and held authority sufficient for the disposal of cases of heretical error, misconduct as to caste affairs, and other matters of religious discipline. On grave occasions of ceremony he directed these proceedings, and, in virtue of his office, was in proportion feared by all who might by any possibility come under his influence or power.

Tara's presence in the family could not be kept a secret. The fact of a widow existing there who wore silken garments and jewels, and who had not her head shaved, was an infringement of caste discipline which required prompt investigation; and as the Envoy arrived at the fort, the Shastree betook himself to Pudma Bye, as well to receive the donations which were his due since she had been absent, as to make inquiry.

The Envoy himself was absent at the Rajah's Kucheri. Amba Bye was busy arranging her house after her long absence, and Tara was assisting her with an alacrity and intelligence which at once surprised and gratified her. On her own part, the worthy good-natured dame was not slow in evincing warm affection: which had arisen out of the helpless condition of Tara on the one hand, and the loving confidence which she had displayed on the first evening of their companionship.

Ah! it was a cruel struggle for the poor girl. Perhaps we, who belong to another creed and faith, can hardly estimate it. And yet the springs and motives of human action have parallels so close everywhere, that we can at least follow the events which had to be endured, alike without aid, and without sympathy.

Poor Tara! could she deny herself the secret contemplation of the noble youth who, she knew, was her lover? Could she forget the sweet companionship of Zyna, the rough but loving caresses of the Khan's wife, and the hearty greeting of the Khan himself? Alas, no! it was impossible, and yet all these were in direct antagonism with her own creed, with the people of her own faith. What had she been taught to believe, but that Brahmuns were the gods of the earth —divine emanations, incapable of sin, and only resting here for a while in expiation of the errors of former births, till they were absorbed again into divinity, as a drop of rain-water in the sea, or as the sparks falling back into the fire!

She herself was a Brahmun of the highest rank and caste: the very idea of a Mussulman should have been abhorrent and repellant to her. Was it so? Alas, no! She, an orphan as she believed herself, had felt her sorrow soothed, and her honour powerfully protected: she had been received into loving communion with a noble family: she could not help contrasting their soft polished manners with the rude homely speech and rough demeanour of those with whom she now was—far ruder among those mountains, than even among the people of her own town.

Again, and far above all, that portion of the old old story which she had heard and believed, when she knew herself to be beloved, would not be forgotten. It lay at her heart, rankling sometimes and chafing, because so impossible—and again was remembered in a sweet confidence which, though more impossible, was yet inexpressibly soothing. "He will remember me—he now thinks of me," she would say to herself in the lonely night, when ofttimes a bitter cry was rung from her, which no one knew of; "and he would take me away if he could—ah yes! he would have done it—if he could."

From the first moment antipathy was conceived against Tara by Pudma Bye, that virtuous lady had continued to brood over it with increasing dislike to her. She had tried to excite in her brother abhorrence for Tara's condition; and, failing that, in Amba Bye, with whom she had as little success. Both believed Tara to be a priestess of the goddess whom they feared. The Envoy had tested her knowledge of sacred books, which was nearly equal to his own, for he did not pretend, he said, to be a scholar; and in several disputations with other Brahmuns who, attracted by the news of Tara's learning, had come to hear her read and recite what she knew, she had acquitted herself with favourable impressions upon all. But the woman's hatred of the girl's beauty, and her ascetic austerity, which would have made Tara like herself, could not be controlled; and, under the influence of the Shastree, was likely to have full scope.

But Wittul Shastree could not restrain himself; and, unable to get speech of the master and mistress of the house, Pudma Bye was resorted to—a willing communicator of all that she herself thought, all that she had said and argued, and all that she had heard of Tara's sojourn with the impure Mussulmans. As for herself, she did not, she said, believe Tara's story of Moro Trimmul's outrage; she, on the contrary, believed what he said, that it was a meritorious attempt to withdraw her from a scandalous position—scandalous alike to herself and to the faith.

The Shastree's mind was at once made up as to his course. There had been several offensive stories current in regard to young widows lately, and not without reason: and they had escaped his punishment. This at least was sure—the Envoy dare not deny, and could not evade his power; and if Tara appealed to the Rajah himself, it would be on a point of caste discipline with which he—Rajah though he was—would not dare to interfere.

"Let us hear her first," he said to the lady, as, having listened to Pudma Bye's account of Tara, he sat in the outer verandah of the house the morning after their arrival, while Tara was within; "wilt thou call her, daughter? we should not judge unheard."

Poor Tara's heart failed her sadly when Pudma called her. She clung to Amba Bye instinctively, trembling as she saw the priest sitting without, and protested against meeting him. "He is a stranger to me; what have I to do with him?" she said. "Let me go away. I am not his to be questioned, but the Mother's at Tooljapoor."

"Go," whispered Amba Bye to her; "he is all-powerful here,—over the Rajah, over my husband, over all. Go, tell him the truth. I will not leave thee. Go, Tara."

"Wilt thou now screen her, sister?" cried Pudma Bye, in a shrill voice, and stretching out her bare skinny arms to Tara. "Is her shame to be our shame—we that have no spot or stain upon us?

2 G

If thou art bewitched, I, that perform the nine penances daily, should not be exposed to this! Come, girl! it is pollution to touch thee—nevertheless, come, else I will drag thee to him."

"Go!" cried Amba, frightened at the other's voice of threat and scorn combined, of which she had had long and sad experience in the house. "I dare not keep thee now,—she is terrible. Go, Tara, and answer what they ask thee. Say the truth and the Mother will hear thee. O, that my lord were here! O, that he were here!" and she sat down, sobbing and wringing her hands helplessly.

"Come," cried Pudma, as, seizing Tara by the arm, she pulled her forward. "Art thou a child, to be ashamed,—thou that art a Moorlee?"

Tara's limbs trembled so that she could hardly move.

"Ah, Mother," she prayed silently, "I am not false to thee yet; let me not be tried more than I can bear. I will go, even to death, but not to shame. O Mother, not to shame! Let me go, lady," she continued to Pudma Bye, "I will follow thee."

She did so, and, bending down submissively before the priest, stood up with her hands joined in an attitude of supplication. For a moment the stern man's features relaxed into an expression almost of kindness, certainly of extreme interest. The youth of the girl, her gentle grace, the sad but beautiful expression of her face—above all, its purity of expression—sent conviction to his heart that there was no room for calumny, none even for suspicion.

Pudma saw the hesitation, and, herself resolute, resumed rapidly and passionately—

"Is that a figure to be a widow and a priestess—that thing with a golden zone, and necklaces and ear-rings, and a silken garment like a harlot? Is that a widow who daily combs her hair, braids it, puts sweet flowers and oils into it, decking it for a lover? O Shastree, is that what a virtuous widow should be? Is that a condition of penance and austere privation whereby to inherit life eternal?"

The Shastree's features changed rapidly. "It cannot be," he said; "such adornment and beauty is not of a virtuous woman. Now I believe thee, sister, and thy brother must be spoken to. He cannot keep a thing so offensive in his house, and be among us."

"Hear me, my lord," said Tara, appealing to him piteously. "I am pure—I have done no evil—I am an orphan and a Moorlee, but not as others; such as I am, the holy Bhartee Swami, whom I have served hitherto, hath made me. Write to him if you will——"

"What is this?" said Govind Rao, who entered at the moment, interrupting her; "what art thou asking of her, friend? Let her alone; she is my care."

"Look," returned the other, rising, "if thou art satisfied to have one like that remaining in thy house, the Swami must know of it, and there will be a fine, and shame will come to thee among the council. If she be a widow, let her be treated as widows should be. If——"

"If I am a Moorlee of the goddess, as ye call me," said Tara, interposing, "I am already shameless in your eyes, and no widow: let me go. No Moorlee is asked what she does, or what she wears. The Mother will not have those near her who are disfigured, and I cannot break the vow I have made to her; she would destroy me."

Panting and excited, flushed with the desperation of her speech, Tara stood erect, with her eyes flashing, her glowing beauty exciting the involuntary admiration of the men, and the virulent hatred of the woman who sat with them.

"See, brother!" cried Pudma Bye, "look at the witch—look at her glowing eyes. It was by these shameless eyes that she won men's hearts at Tooljapoor. Beware! beware of yourselves, lest ye too fall! Ah!" she continued with a scream, "put her away—kill her; but let her not go—Brahmun as she is—to the cow-slayers!"

"Peace," said her brother; "why this spite, Pudma? what hath she done to thee? Peace, and begone to the inner rooms. Begone!" he cried in a louder tone, and stamping his foot, "begone! Dost thou not hear?"

"I hear," she replied doggedly; "but I will not go, unless the Shastree bid me. Choose now between us: send me out of thy house to thy shame, and keep her, to thy worse shame; or send her away. There can be no compromise between good and evil, shame and dishonour."

"She speaks truly, friend," said the Shastree mildly. "It must be done. How do we know she is a priestess?"

Tara had not entirely lost the presence of mind which she naturally possessed, though she found it failing rapidly. "Put me to the proof," she said quickly,—"the proof. If there be a temple of the Mother's here, let me sit in it before her a night and a day—haply she may come to her child, as she did at Tooljapoor. Ye can watch me too, there. If she come not—then she hath abandoned me, and ye can kill me if ye please, sirs; better ye did so, for I am indeed friendless."

"Not so," cried the widow; "thou hast friends, Tara, many and powerful—myself the greatest of all; but—not as thou art. Choose!"

"I have chosen, lady," said the girl sadly. "Take me to the temple now—even now,—and leave me there. A vessel of water is enough, and a woman to watch me at night, if ye will not watch yourselves. I have already eaten, and want no food. I would go to the Mother."

"It is some device, brother," said Pudma suspiciously; "some device to fly, to escape, or——"

He smiled and shook his head. "It requires a braver heart than a girl's to face the mountain-paths alone at night among the bears and the panthers, sister, and nought but a bird could escape down the precipices. Why these unjust suspicions? Art thou ready, Tara? If so, follow me, and thou too, Shastree; we will settle this matter at once. There is no one now in the Rajah's temple. He has already paid his devotions, and is preparing to meet the Khan. Come, the ordinary priests are there, and there is no fear of her. Come, Tara, fear not. If thou art true, the Mother will defend thee. Dost thou trust her, girl?"

"Take me to her," she replied. "I have no refuge but with her. I am ready." Then she turned to embrace Amba Bye, who now entered sobbing, and fell upon her neck.

"I will come to thee by-and-by," she whispered. "It is but a step, and I will watch with thee at night. I have a vow to pay to the Mother. Go with my husband."

We know the place already. It was where Sivaji's mother had sat. A few words to the attendant priest by Govind Rao and the Shastree, explained the ordeal to which Tara had voluntarily subjected herself, and she was permitted to approach the shrine and make her obeisance and offerings. They watched her, and saw that she did her office as one used to the duty; and when it was finished, she went before the shrine, sat down, and began to chant the morning hymn of the goddess in low and sweet tones, rocking herself to and fro.

"There can be no doubt of this, Shastree," said Govind Rao,—"she is what she tells us."

"She may be," he replied, "but till the goddess comes into her and speaks by her mouth, she may not be fully believed. Let us leave her," and they went.

Tara grew absorbed in her devotion: she noticed no one. By-and-by a gun was fired from a tower near her, and four others followed. Then a pause ensued, and the priest fed the lamps with fresh oil, tinkled the bell on the shrine, and poured libations to the image, renewing these ceremonies with much earnestness. Tara scarcely noticed them, for though it was broad noonday without, it was dusk within the closed vestibule. By-and-by a girl, bearing a tray of lighted lamps, and garlands of flowers, entered, but so that her face could not be seen, and, delivering some to the priest, began a ceremony herself, which was strangely familiar; and as Tara turned her head for an instant, she saw that it was Gunga, and that she herself was recognized.

Gunga clapped her hands with joy. "At last," she cried excitedly, "at last! See, I am worshipping for the victory which he has gained by this time. Hush! thou wilt see Zyna here presently.

Moro will bring her captive; then there will be three with him—I, and thou, and she. Ha, ha, ha! a merry three, girl. Dost thou hear, O Tara?" But some strange chill had struck at Tara's heart, and, sinking down on the floor, for a time she was insensible.

CHAPTER LXXX.

GUNGA'S appearance is easily explained. On his arrival at Pertabgurh Moro Trimmul had been sent to bring up some of the Rajah's Hetkurees from the Concan, the tract below the mountains next the sea, and he had besought the post of honour in the ensuing attack upon the Mussulman camp, which had been granted to him.

In this he had two motives: the one, personal distinction, and the desire of retaliation for Tooljapoor, which was shared commonly with all Brahmuns; and, secondly, and probably most urgent, the desire of revenge upon Fazil Khan, and, if possible, the capture of his sister and family. That either Afzool Khan or his son would survive the fight, he did not think possible, or if they escaped death, and were captured, that they would be spared.

Of the Rajah's intentions in regard to the Khan, he had no idea; and when Maloosray and Palkur were with their prince on the night preceding the Khan's visit to the fort, Moro Trimmul was in company with his own men, placing them in positions in the woods, ready to obey the signal which had been communicated to him. Gunga, therefore, had been sent on to the fort under charge of his servants, and directed not only to have the house swept and prepared, but, as the guns were fired from the fort, to offer sacrifice for him in the temple, and await his coming.

"Dost thou know her?" asked the Brahmun priest of Gunga, when he heard her speak to Tara, and observed the effect of her address.

"Know her?—Yes, Maharaj," returned Gunga, "she is a Moorlee of the temple at Tooljapoor, and I am another,—that's why I know her."

"It is curious," said the man, musing. "There, raise her up till my wife comes; we have had charge of her given to us, and she is to watch here to see if the Mother comes to her to prove herself what she says she is. Did she ever prophesy?"

"The Mother came to her once," replied Gunga, "when she was made a Moorlee; but I never saw her come afterwards. If she would be a true priestess, she perhaps would come; but she is only half a one at heart, and that's why trouble follows her."

"What trouble?" asked the priest.

"O, her father and mother are dead, killed in the fight at Tooljapoor, and she is here, among strangers, with no one to help her; is not that trouble enough, Maharaj?" replied the girl. "And she is so beautiful, too; they say she is a witch, and steals men's hearts, and throws them away; but I don't know that she is—she is only beautiful—look at her."

"Ah, that's the worst I have heard yet," said the man, musing.

"Yes, but she is pure, quite pure, sir," returned Gunga earnestly, "not like me and the rest of us; and we envied her, and I hated her; but I don't hate her now, and when she wakes I will tell her so. Tara, Tara! wake! She is not dead, sir, is she?" continued the girl dreamily, pushing away Tara's hair from her face, and looking into her eyes: "she does not answer me. O, speak to her!"

"No, she is alive," replied the Brahmun, feeling her hand and forehead. "Wait, I will bring some water."

"Would she were dead—dead ere he came," Gunga muttered to herself. "He will not spare her now—ah me! not now: and in the heat and confusion of victory, who will care for her? All those she loved last, too, are dead—all gone—and that fair boy with the rest! Ah me, better she died! Tara, drink! here is water!"

A woman came with a brass vessel full, and helped Gunga to raise her up, while she poured some into her mouth, and sprinkled her face gently. They saw Tara heave a great sigh; and presently, as the woman fanned her with the end of her garment, she awoke and looked dreamily around her—first to the woman, then to Gunga, against whom she was reclining. Her first impulse was to rise, but in the attempt she sank down again, and buried her face in her hands.

"Why art thou here?" she cried piteously. "O Gunga, go! leave me." She did not yet comprehend what had been said of victory, for she made no allusion to it.

"No, Tara, not now," said the girl—"not now. I will tell thee why. Go," she continued to the woman. "You are kind. Go now. I have that to say to my sister which no one must hear. Go! We are priestesses, and will serve the Mother in our own fashion. But if I need shelter for her, wilt thou give it?"

"Ah," replied the dame, "we are poor people, and can do little; but the Maha Ranee is kind and just—I will speak to her."

"True," replied Gunga absently; "if needs be, I will come to thee again—now, go. Tara!" she continued, stretching out her hands to her imploringly when the woman had gone out—"O Tara, look up! look up, and see if I be like what I was;—cast me not away now, for we are both in the like misery! O Mother!" she cried to the image on the altar, "bid her speak to me, ere it be too late;—bid her trust to me, and save herself! Tara, behold I kiss your feet; trust me now, as I swear on them not to fail you. No, no, never, never more—never more, except in death. See what I do!"

She arose, went to the shrine, and prostrated herself before it on her face, so that her hands embraced the feet of the image. "O, kill me, Mother—O, kill me, Mother!" Tara heard her cry, in a passionate burst of weeping; "kill me, if thou wilt, for touching thee, who am not worthy; but hear me, and help me to save Tara. She is thy child. O, let me save her for thee. I will,—I will, if thou wilt bid her trust me, for I am not lying now. I am true to thee and to her!"

The words were almost inarticulate, and gasped or sobbed, rather than spoken. They fell strangely on Tara's ears as Gunga still moaned rather than spoke. "Mother—O Mother, I am true, I am not lying; bid her trust me! bid her trust me!"

It was impossible to resist them. Tara rose and went across the vestibule to her. "Gunga," she said, "get up, I am here: what wouldst thou of me?"

The girl arose, put away the dishevelled hair from her face, and again bowed before Tara, embracing her knees. She was not repulsed this time. The priest had watched the scene wonderingly—he could not understand it. Tara was standing beside the door of the shrine, the light from within streaming out upon her. Her slight figure was drawn up to its full height, and her beautiful features were calm—almost sublime in their expression. Lying at her feet, and clasping them, was the other girl, still moaning in apparent agony.

"She hath done some terrible crime," thought the Brahmun, "and the other will intercede for her."

"O Tara—O Tara," cried Gunga piteously, "I dare not look up to thee now; all my shame is rushing back into my heart; my words and my touch are alike pollution to thee! O Tara, I dare not ask forgiveness—I who have wronged thee so foully. Speak, for time passes quickly, and they will be here—wilt thou trust me now? O Mother, Mother! what can I do? what can I say to make her trust me—to make her forgive me?"

"Look up, Gunga," said Tara, sitting down, and gently parting the hair on the girl's forehead, "what hast thou done? It was he, not thou; see, I forgive thee freely."

"O yes, it was he, not I," she cried,—"I resisted, and he used to beat me. Yes, he beat me cruelly only yesterday, when he left me, and then it came into my heart to save thee! Yes, the Mother told me—I know it now—to come here, and I have found thee. Listen!" she continued, rising, and looking hurriedly about her. "There is no one near—all are gone. Come! come! we are not seen;—come at once,—do not delay: we can escape during the confusion. Hark!

they are fighting below—come! I tell thee the tigers and the bears on the mountain, are better for me and thee than they. Dost thou not hear?"

"It is the men firing for the Khan's arrival," said Tara gently; "there is no fighting. Who should fight?"

"Ah no," cried Gunga, "they are attacked,—the Khan is already killed. I heard it as I came in—they are all dead or dying. O Tara, I tell thee that no one will escape,—no, not one. Hark! the din increases, and thou art here: alas! alas! O Mother! tell it to her," she exclaimed, with passionate gesticulation, to the senseless image before them—"tell it to her—she will not believe me—Tara, dost thou not hear?"

Just then, an eddy, perhaps, of the mountain-wind, brought up to them from the deep valley below, a hoarse, confused din of shouts, shots, and conflict. It could not be mistaken. Tara had heard it once at Tooljapoor, but this was far more tremendous.

"Come!" again shrieked Gunga, seizing her arm, and dragging her away—"come! It is our last chance for life—do not throw it away. We can get out and hide among the bushes; and I will never leave thee, Tara, never."

But she spoke to one now wellnigh bereft of sense. The Khan killed, the rest attacked, and the fierce turmoil of the fight coming up stronger and stronger, till the fretted roof of the temple seemed filled with the sound, overpowered Tara; for at last, the hideous truth seemed to flash upon her, as she sat down and buried her face in her lap in an attitude of mute despair; but Gunga would not let her rest.

"Ah, I am believed now," she cried wildly: "listen! Moro Trimmul, with thousands upon thousands, has attacked the camp, and he swore to me to bring the Khan's wife and daughter hither. O Tara! will he spare them? He swore he would not, and he beat me when I pleaded for them. Look! here are bruises on me. I tell thee he will not spare them or you. Come!"

"I will die here,—I will not go from the Mother, Gunga," replied Tara. "I am her child now—only hers: let her do with me as she wills, I will not go. Save thyself, care not for me," and she arose and prostrated herself before the shrine. "O Mother," she cried piteously, "I will not leave thee again. Death or life, what matters it to me? let it be as thou wilt. I have promised not to leave thee, and I am here waiting." Then rising, she seated herself as she was used to do before the shrine, and spoke no more.

"I can at least die with thee, Tara; I will not leave thee," said Gunga. "Whatever comes, let it come to us both; I am as ready to die as thou art—I will not go."

They sat there long. The sun declined, and the evening was

drawing in. Once only Gunga had gone out to see whether she could gain any intelligence, and had returned saying the doors of the temple enclosure were shut. The Brahmun priest had disappeared like the rest, but there were shouts as if of victory which rung through the building in bursts, evidently growing nearer. Tara seemed not to hear them. It might be that utter despair possessed her, or, as Gunga hoped, that some manifestation of the goddess was about to take place. She scarcely moved now, but when the shouts grew louder she shuddered, and drew the end of her garment more closely around her as if she were cold.

It was thus that the Maha Ranee, Sivaji's mother, found her and Gunga as she entered with her attendants for the evening prayer and worship, and to give thanks for the victory.

As the lady had approached the temple, the attendant priest told her of Tara, and why she had been left there by the Shastree and Govind Rao, and the tale had excited her curiosity, if not her compassion.

"She is sitting there before the Mother," he said, "and does not speak. Perhaps she will answer you, lady, but it seems as though a fit were coming on her. I will tell her at least that you have come," and, stepping forward, he advanced to Tara and whispered in her ear.

The Maha Ranee followed, and paused as she entered the vestibule. The light shone full upon Tara, and her expression of deep misery could not be mistaken. Long afterwards, the first sight of that pale, wan, despairing face recurred to the lady with pain, and she never forgot the look of hopeless grief which Tara had first turned upon her.

"There is no inspiration in that face," said the lady to the priest,—"none. It seems to me the Mother hath forsaken her. Of what is she accused?"

"She was taken from the Mussulman chief, we hear," said the Brahmun, "and was to have become a Mussulmani. They say, too, she is a sorceress, and does evil with her eyes; but Govind Rao placed her here, and knows about her."

"I fear her not," cried the Ranee, with flashing eyes. "Who is she, that she dare sit in my presence? Put her out! Away with thee, wench!" she continued to Tara, "get thee hence! If thou art forsworn, begone! The Mother hath drunk blood to-day, and will not spare thee! Take her away, Bheemee—she is an offence to us."

"Get up, girl," said Bheemee roughly, as she advanced, followed by several other women—"get up; dost thou not hear? else we will cast thee out."

Gunga came forward boldly. "Do not touch or hurt her," she

said: "I fear she is not now in her right mind. If I may take her, I will look after her. Get up, Tara," she whispered in her ear: "come, we will go and hide ourselves. Come, for thy life, come!" and she tried to lift her up and drag her away.

But Tara could not rise; her limbs seemed paralysed by grief or terror, and she did not evidently understand what had occurred. Not noticing the Maha Ranee, she disengaged herself from Gunga, and once more stretched out her arms to the shrine before her, and cried in piteous tones which affected many around her to tears, "O Mother, I will not leave thee: do with me as thou wilt, even to death!" and so lay moaning.

"Send for Govind Rao and Wittul Shastree, lady," said the old Brahmun priest, who was sobbing and wiping his eyes: "they know of her, and you will hear about her from them."

"Good," replied the Ranee, already softened, "let them be brought instantly,—they are without. We will await their coming."

Some little time elapsed, and others assembled. No one knew what was going to happen. After a while Tara seemed to regain sense and to remember why she was there, for she sat up, and they saw her lips moving as if in prayer. As the trumpets sounded the setting of the first watch at sunset, and the great kettledrums and pipes played the evening music in the Nobut Khana above the gate, the Brahmun priests entered with the usual offerings, and began to chant one of the evening hymns of praise, as they moved round the shrine in time with the faint clash of the silver cymbals, which one of them carried. Then, timidly and faintly at first, but increasing in power as she sang, Tara joined the chant. It was an emotion which she could not restrain, and which not even the sense of desolation and dull misery which had overwhelmed her, could repress. She was unconscious of the effect it produced upon those who listened to her, as her full rich voice rose above the hoarse and unmusical chant of the priests; but as it gradually ceased, and the sound died away in the recesses of the temple, it affected many of those who heard it to tears, and was never forgotten.

"No wonder," said the Ranee, who had listened to the hymn with emotion which she hardly chose to acknowledge,—"no wonder they say she is a sorceress. See, she has no fear—no perception of what is to happen, or who are around her. That is not natural; it is magic, and may not be looked upon."

"Lady," said Wittul Shastree, who, with Govind Rao and the other Brahmuns, now approached her, "we attend you; what are your commands?"

"We doubt the girl yonder, and they tell us she is dangerous, and a sorceress; we would have her removed ere we render sacrifice for victory," she replied; "but the priests tell us she is there by your order. Is it so?"

"By her own will," said the Shastree; "not our orders. We would have made her over to the council for chastisement and discipline, because, as a priestess of Kalee, she hath been residing among the Moslems; but she claimed ordeal and sanctuary with the goddess, and we sent her here. Has any vision appeared to her?" he asked of the attendant priest.

"None," replied the man. "They have been talking together, she and the girl beside her, who wanted her to get up and go away; but she has not stirred since the five guns were fired, and she was told of the victory."

"I will ask her again what she wishes, lady," said Govind Rao, "but better than I, Moro Trimmul should do it, who, we hear, has married his sister to her father. He, too, is without with the Rajah; they have just come up into the fort."

"Let him be called," replied the lady, "and keep out other strangers. Be ye all seated, sirs," she continued to the Brahmuns who had accompanied the Shastree, "while this inquiry lasts."

CHAPTER LXXXI.

THE inner part of the vestibule was not large,—a square room, supported upon massive stone pillars at the corners, with a slightly raised dais all round; and as the Brahmuns entered and took their seats, Tara could not avoid noticing them, and appeared more conscious of surrounding occurrences than before. Thinking she would rise, Gunga approached to assist her, but Tara motioned her away. "My time is not yet come," she said; "I will not go;" and again she drew her garment about her, and resumed her silent position.

But not for long. There was a sudden movement among those without, and a way was cleared for one who came in rapidly.

"Who wants me here?" cried a strong manly voice, apparently hoarse from shouting. "A girl! what girl? Let me pass."

As he strode in through the men who were sitting behind, Tara turned her head, and suddenly beheld her enemy.

She rose at once, excited and defiant, so noble in her manner, so expressive in her abhorrence, that Moro Trimmul shrank back a step, abashed.

"Begone!" she cried, stamping her foot. "There is the Mother; not a second time shalt thou take me from her. My fathers," she cried, appealing to all around, "he would twice have dishonoured me, and I have been saved. Now I am under your protection, O, give me not to him! Take me to the mother of the Rajah; she will protect me."

"She is here," said the Shastree, stepping forward; "and thy fate shall be decided before her. Fear not, daughter."

"Friends," said Moro Trimmul, looking round, "have care for my honour! Twice have I rescued her from shame. Once when she was escaping from Tooljapoor; once in separating her from those who have been slain. Give her to me, for her shame to be hidden away for ever."

"I will not go; I will not go!" cried Tara, entering the door of the shrine, and clasping the feet of the image. "Kill me if ye will, here,—I am ready; but I will not go with him."

"I claim them both, sirs," cried Moro Trimmul passionately; "her, and her sister Moorlee yonder. Beware, all of ye, how ye interfere with the family honour of a respectable man. I will brook it from no one, not even from Sivaji Bhóslay himself! Have I won a victory to-day at the Mother's command, and am I to be disgraced and humbled before her, by a deranged girl and doting priests, ere it is closed? Come forth, Tara!" he called, in a hoarse voice—"come forth, else I will tear thee thence. Away with her," he cried to two of his attendants, who had seized Gunga, and were holding her fast—"away with her to my house, and bind her there; I will bring the other. Now, friends, beware who stays me, for, by the gods, he dies, be he who he may!" and he drew his sword, and was advancing, when the Shastree stepped before him.

"Madman," he cried, stretching forth his hands; "forbear! put up thy weapon,—no one here dreads it. We are Brahmuns, as thou art! Fear not," he continued to Tara, who had stood up also by the altar, and was trembling violently, but not with terror. "Fear not; thou art under the protection of the council, and he dare not interfere with thee."

"Fool and dotard," exclaimed Moro Trimmul under his breath, and from between his clenched teeth, "I will settle with thee for this, one day yet. As ye will, sirs," he continued bitterly, looking round and panting as he dropped his sword's point. "My honour is in the hands of a priest's council at last, not in my own keeping, and I am helpless; but hasten what ye have to do, for I will not leave ye till ye have decided in regard to her. Look at her—harlot and witch, sorceress and devil—who hath already destroyed men's souls,—will ye believe the Mother protects such as she is?"

"Let it be so," said the Shastree. "Tara, art thou willing to abide the night, as the issue of the ordeal suggested by thyself, to wait her coming? If so, we will stay here with thee."

"Mother," she said in a low voice, turning to the altar, and joining her hands in supplication before the image—"Mother, if I am thy child, tell me what to say to them; or, if thou wilt, let me be another sacrifice to thee, and it will be well. Mother,—O Toolja Mata! dost thou hear?—Tara is ready before thee—ready to come!"

Low as the words were spoken, they were heard by all; and remembering the events of the day, and believing in the power of the goddess, it was expected the girl would fall and die where she was, on the solemn invocation; but it was not so. For a few moments she stood gazing intently at the image, without altering her position of supplication; then she smiled, her hands dropped, and she turned at once and faced the assembly. Not even in her first office as priestess had her beauty been more glorious—the expression of her features more sublime.

"O priests and elders," she said calmly and simply, in her sweet musical voice, "hear my last words: I am an orphan and a widow, I have no one left on earth to protect me,—not one. To be in danger of that man's evil designs, is to die hourly. Did he succeed as he has tried, it would be to live in shame; now I can die in purity. The Mother calls me; she will not come to me, though I have asked her. She is far from me, yet she beckons to me; look, there!" and she stretched forth her hand to the roof—"she calls me, and I come, pure, and purified by fire. Now listen, all ye Brahmuns; I am true and pure, and I am sutee henceforth. When ye will, and where ye will, I am sutee; and on his head be curses, and the vengeance of Kalee, who forbids it. Let me die in the fire, and I am happy! What she puts into my mouth, I say to you truly. Let no one forbid it."

No one spoke, no one answered. The people before her rose as one man. Many trembled, some wept, and women screamed aloud; but Tara stood there unmoved, her bosom heaving rapidly, and the glowing beauty and rapture of her face unchanged.

"Jey Kalee! Jey Toolja Mata!" exclaimed the Shastree; "let it be as she says, brothers. Henceforth she is sutee, and we accept the sacrifice, for the Mother hath said it by her lips. Ah, the ordeal is fulfilled indeed, and to the honour of her votary! Fear not," he said, "daughter: by this act is thy husband delivered from hell; and all thou hast suffered in this life is sanctified unto thee. Bring flowers, bring garlands," he cried to the people; "crown her here at the altar, and let her be worshipped."

"Tara, Tara!" cried a husky voice close to her, entreatingly; "Tara, what hast thou done? Art thou mad? O girl, why hast thou doomed thyself? Come, there is yet time: come with me!"

"Begone!" cried the girl, interrupting him; "I spurn thee, Moro Trimmul, before all these elders: false and cruel as thou art, I am at last beyond thy reach!"

"Come away, Moro," said Maloosray roughly, who had just

entered, and dragged him backwards with one hand, while he seized his sword and wrested it from him with the other; "art thou a child? dost thou fight with priests and women? Come with me; the Rajah calls thee." The Brahmun struggled to be free, but Tannajee's powerful arms were about him, in which he was borne away, helpless to resist.

Not in her first admission to the office she had held, not in the holiest of ceremonies at which she had before assisted, was greater honour ever done to Tara than now. Bedecked with garlands, with incense burnt before her, the priests present formed themselves into a procession, and, chanting hymns of praise, led her round and round the shrine. The temple court and its precincts were now filled with people, who took up the shouts of victory—"Jey Kalee! Jey Toolja Mata!" and as she passed onwards, throwing handfuls of flowers among them, all who could reach her, touched her garments reverently, or prostrated themselves before her, with frantic cries for blessings. And so they led her on.

How many sweet memories crowded into Tara's mind now, and urged her on. There was no fear, no irresolution—father, mother, Zyna, Fazil—all dead, as she thought, and a fierce and ruthless enemy persecuting her to the last. All she could think on was, that she was free, that no one could harm her now. Had they then led her to death, she would have gone, singing the hymns triumphantly.

. . . .

Late that night Moro Trimmul returned to his place of residence. Long before, when Sivaji's power was in its infancy, and the young men had taken procession of the mountain-built fort, and led their bands forth to plunder and destroy the Mahomedan villages around, Moro Trimmul had fitted up a hollow bastion on one of the angles of the precipice—in which the builder had left a small room and anteroom—as his place of shelter. The inside was rudely plastered with clay; and a sleeping-place, also of clay, had been raised from the floor, on which was placed a mattress and pillow. In the face of the bastion a small oriel window had been built, which had a balcony projecting from the wall, large enough for two people to sit in. Seated there, you looked down a dizzy depth upon the forest below; but on all sides the precipices, the woods, and their deep glens, and the varied mountains beyond, formed a combination of glorious beauty, which there, above all other places in the mountain fortress, was most deeply felt.

Thither had Gunga been taken by the Brahmun's servants on the morning of the battle. He had charged them to have the place swept and newly plastered with clay, and Gunga, with having it done as he wished. On its completion, she had gone into the temple to worship for him in the exercise of her vocation, as the signal was to be given, which they all told her of. She knew of his design. He had charged her to watch Tara, and, if she saw her, to give him information of her actions. He had told her that he should bring Fazil's sister to the fort, for he felt sure she could not escape him. Herself, Zyna, and Tara should be confronted at last. How long should the latter elude him? For the Khan, Gunga cared nothing; for Zyna and Fazil as little—they were Mussulmans, and must perish, —but for Tara!

Ah yes, strange indeed, perhaps, yet not unnatural, had been the revulsion. The jealousy which had urged Gunga to hate the girl, and assist in plots for her ruin, had strangely altered to love. Twice had Moro Trimmul been foiled; twice he had fallen savagely upon her, and beaten her cruelly. We know when he did when Tara was last rescued, and how Gunga, relenting, had not then abandoned him. But it had not ended there. The fierce rage of disappointment had broken out again and again, and he had vented it upon her brutally. She had borne this patiently at the time; but she had now sworn to herself, in the temple of the goddess at Wye, not only to lend herself no more to Moro Trimmul's design, but had formed the resolution to assist Tara to escape—to carry her off by mountain paths; and she knew that if they could once enter the forest near the fort, they were safe.

Day by day, as these thoughts passed through Gunga's mind, the love for Tara grew stronger, till it became an absorbing passion. Would she but trust her—would she but believe her—they might yet again see their beloved Tooljapoor, and she would work out her forgiveness by devotion. It was not too late, she thought: but . . . .

We have already told how she met her in the temple: but it is impossible to describe her despair at her failure to induce Tara to escape, or when the man she dreaded, bid his servants seize and bind her. If she could have remained with Tara—only near her . . . .

Alas! it was too late now. She had scarcely been carried, shrieking, from the temple, by the servants of Moro Trimmul, when another man followed, and said Tara had become a Sutee, and was to be burnt next day beside the tank in the fort. Then Gunga felt the heroism of the girl's resolution. At least Moro Trimmul could not injure her; she would soon be beyond reach of his persecution. It was well—yes, it was well. She could at least see her die; and then? . . . .

The desire of death sat hard at her heart. At first she shuddered at it; but once it had entered, it abode there and grew stronger. If Moro Trimmul cast her off now, it would be but to be haunted by the memory of the girl she had wronged so cruelly, and the love for whom, and the despair of whose forgiveness, had pursued her night and day—night and day: but it seemed to have reached her at last. "Yes, she touched me kindly," she said to herself; "she parted the hair from my face as a sister would have done: ere she spoke to me she forgave me: and I will see her die, decked in flowers, as a holy and pure sacrifice. I will worship her as she goes to death, and then I will follow her. O Tara, there, not here, I may be forgiven before the Mother."

Moro Trimmul's servants had taken Gunga, and literally obeyed the orders they had received; bound her with one of her own garments, lest she should do herself or them injury, and laid her gently upon the couch in the inner room. How long she had lain there she had no idea; but, as the time passed, it only confirmed her resolution. She would die, no matter how. There was nothing definite in her mind, but that she would die: a dull despair blunting every faculty —a reality of determination before which her very senses seemed to refuse office.

She heard Moro Trimmul ask without where she was, and the servant answered that she was within, lying on the couch. A small lamp had been lighted and placed in a niche; and as he entered and stood over her, she feigned sleep. She felt him unfasten the bandage round her arms, and then he dragged her roughly to her feet.

"Devil!" he cried, "this is thy doing, and she is gone. Lost! O Tara, how beautiful thou wast in living death!" he continued, apostrophizing her, "speaking thy own death-sentence—as I listened, I could have died for thee."

"Thou art a coward, Moro Trimmul," cried the girl, scornfully and desperately; "thou darest neither die thyself, nor kill me. Thou die with Tara? she would spit at thee, as I do."

He struck her brutally to the ground with his clenched hand. "Lie there, witch! devil!" he cried. "Thou hast been the cause of all this; alone, I could have done it. Thou and she are one now, else why didst thou not decoy her here? Did I not tell thee to do so? Speak!" and he pushed her with his foot as she lay.

She arose. "Moro Trimmul," she said calmly, but with desperation in her voice, "may the Mother forgive me what I have done with thee against Tara; that is all I pray now. Between me and thee all is ended, long since. Let me go. I will serve thee no longer, I spit at thee and defy thee; and in the Rajah's court, before every image of Kalee in the Dekhan, if I live, I will sing thy shame and her honour. Let me go out!"

She saw him set his teeth, as his eyes flashed with a wicked glare, draw a knife from his waistband, and spring at her. The glitter of that knife was the last thing, perhaps, of which she was conscious, except that she seized the hand that held it, instinctively, and then came a struggle for life. But only a brief one. A weak girl, before a powerful man, could not endure long,—sickened, too, as she was by his previous blow. Back—back, he forced her to the window, which was open; on the little balcony without, they swayed to and fro fearfully for a moment; but he wrenched his hand free by a desperate effort, and, striking her one heavy blow with the knife, where he knew not,—as the body dropped heavily in his arms, he pushed it forth into the dark air. He did not hear it fall, though he listened; but in the morning, the vultures, which lived on pinnacles of the precipices, were seen descending in hundreds to their hideous feast below.

CHAPTER LXXXII.

FAZIL KHAN had followed the progress of his father up the mountain-side with intense interest. The little pavilion on the knoll, the group of Brahmuns already there, and the open and nearly level spot which had been selected as the place of meeting, were distinctly visible from where he stood with Bulwunt Rao, and a few other of his trusty associates and retainers. Around, the horsemen—now mostly dismounted—were dispersed in picturesque groups, talking together or lying lazily upon the soft sward holding their horses' bridles, and shading their eyes from the sun.

In the town through which his father had gone, there appeared no stir. A few men were lounging about the gate, and upon the bastion near it, and thus were looking out upon the Moslem horsemen apparently in idle curiosity. The gate was open, and the towns-people, and women with jars of water on their heads, were passing to and fro unconcernedly as usual. There was nothing to excite suspicion or apprehension, except in the mode of reception of his father, and the strange, unusual proposition, that the first interview should be on the mountain-side, and alone; but Bulwunt Rao had explained this characteristically, and with a fair show of reason, and Fazil, though uneasy, was obliged to be content: there was no remedy now.

So the Khan's progress in his palankeen had been watched with intense anxiety as he ascended the rugged pathway. At times the bearers could be seen, and the priest holding the side of the litter to help himself along: again the thick foliage, and turns in the road, hid them from view. At length Fazil saw the Brahmuns on the knoll rise and advance a few steps, and the palankeen emerge upon the open space, where it was set down; and his father got out, adjusted his turban and shawl, and stood with the rest. Then the bearers and the priest moved a little aside; and as the two men from above appeared, his father advanced to meet them, and embraced one.

It was but for a moment, and the fatal result was at once apparent.

With a cry of horror, which aroused many around him who had not been watching the proceedings above, Fazil saw his father reel and fall, rise again, as his sword flashed in the air, and with the Peer maintain the unequal combat we have already described. No sound reached those below; they could only see the flashing of the weapons in the sun, and the struggle of the combatants. Involuntarily, Fazil urged on his horse. Alas! of what avail now? Others had been watching as well as he; and the blast of the horn, which rose shrill and quivering as the Khan fell, was answered by volleys of matchlock shots from the woods around. The gates of the town were shut, and the walls and bastions manned as thickly as men could stand on then, whose fire on the horsemen below was hot and deadly.

The effect of the surprise upon the helpless cavaliers need not be detailed. Panic-stricken, and hemmed in on every side, they rode hither and thither, vainly seeking places of egress through the woods, or by the way they came, and were shot down in scores either where they stood, or as they gathered in groups and charged hither and thither in the vain attempt to reach a foe. Among these, Fazil Khan, with Bulwunt Rao and some others, had kept together; and, in the emergency, Bulwunt's clear perception, not only of the danger, but the best means of extrication from it, saved his young master. On the first perception of his father's fate, Fazil had seen that it was impossible to give help. The town and its walls stood between him and the ascent to the fort, and were utterly impassable. His next idea, in his grief and desperation, was to die with his men as martyrs to the faith; and he was about to dismount, and take his chance on foot, when Bulwunt stopped him.

"No, Meah," he cried, "not while there is hope. They who will be helpless indeed without you, will need you yonder in camp. If it must be, I will die with you, but not now. Follow me, and we will soon join them."

Well was it for Fazil Khan that in his retainer he possessed equally, a devoted friend and one who had known the country as a youth. In his recent visit to the fort, Bulwunt Rao had explored some of his old haunts. One pathway, lying near that by which they had come, was hardly visible from the plain, but if it could be gained, it opened out afterwards into a long glade, which joined the main-road below. It might be guarded, and they could but fight their way through it or fall. Certainly it was better than the way they had come, before which, from the deadly fire maintained there, the horsemen had already fallen in a heap.

"Look," continued Bulwunt Rao, pointing to the entrance to the main-road, "there is no hope there. They have been at their old trick of felling trees across it, and no horse can pass. The Abys sinians have fallen in a heap, and if we try, we shall but follow them. We need not be martyrs yet, Meah," he laughed cheerfully. "Now, set your teeth, my sons," he continued to the men around, "and follow me. We may not all get through; but, Bismilla! come, and let God take whom he pleases."

There might have been fifty men; and others, as many more perhaps,—as they saw these ride together in a desperate race in one direction,—joined them. Bulwunt Rao and Fazil were leading; and as they approached what seemed a portion of impervious wood, Fazil's heart failed him for a moment. "You are wrong, Bulwunt Rao," he cried. "We cannot get through this—let us turn."

"Madman!" exclaimed the other, seizing the bridle of his horse. "By your mother and sister, I swear I am right! Follow me, my children," he shouted, looking back, while he again urged his horse to its utmost speed; "we are near now."

He was right. A portion of the jungle jutted out beyond the rest, and made a slight shoulder, as it were, behind which was the path. As they turned round the corner, they saw a body of foot-soldiers drawn up across it; but ere these could raise their matchlocks to fire, the impetuous horsemen were among them, trampling some down, and hewing fiercely at others with their long Spanish swords.* The attack was irresistible, and, the first line of men forced, they encountered no others. Straggling shots were fired at them from the sides of the mountain, but without effect; and after riding nearly a mile down the glade at the same speed, the pathway turned into the main-road, and they heard the din of the fight die away behind them. Of the fifteen hundred gallant cavaliers who had ridden that morning from the camp at Jowly, they were the only survivors.

While Nettajee Palkur was finishing his bloody work on those who remained after Fazil Khan's escape, by closing up the pathway, and attacking from all sides at once, such of the horsemen as remained in the field,—Moro Trimmul was busy with his part of the general slaughter; and as the fugitives rode on, the din of the fight behind growing fainter as they proceeded, they were met by that of the greater work in front,—more furious, and more terrible.

Yet they pressed on, until, reaching a rising-ground which overlooked the field, they could see it all in its hideous reality. The Mahrattas had seized the Beejapoor guns, and that point of defence no longer remained to the Mahomedans. Thousands of the enemy's foot-men, in compact masses, were charging disordered groups of men huddled together, who made a vain resistance. Great numbers

* The Portuguese of Goa used to import large quantities of Spanish and Genoa sword-blades. They were held in high estimation at Beejapoor, and they are still often to be met with in the country. The Rajah Sivaji's famous sword Bhowani, with which he killed Afzool Khan, is a Genoa blade of the first water.

of horses were careering madly about, but, for the most part, the troop-horses were still at their pickets, and were now protected by the Mahrattas. It was evident that the surprise had been as complete and irretrievable as at the fort.

Casting his eyes round this field, in sickening apprehension—indeed, in almost hopeless despair—the young Khan looked towards the tents where he had left his sister and Lurlee. The tents were standing, but the outer enclosure walls were thrown down, and a crowd of followers and soldiers were apparently struggling together in the plunder of what they contained. The place was apart from the field itself, and Fazil pointed to it; he could not speak.

The men with him had had no time for thought. From the moment the Khan had died at Pertabgurh till they drew rein on the eminence over the camp, they had ridden for life. But the worst was now evident; and what they had hoped to find, was gone. The conviction that all their companions,—those whom they had loved in life, were dead, at once fell upon their hearts; and Bulwunt Rao, and many another rough veteran, burst into passionate weeping.

Fazil appeared calm, but it was the calm of desperation and of misery. "Why do you weep, friends?" he said. "They are all dead; why should we live? Death is better than dishonour! Come and see—Bismilla!"—and he turned his horse's head in the direction of the tents.

None thought of the risk. "Bismilla!" shouted the men, as, with teeth hard set for a last struggle in life, they rode a mad race to their old camp. Near it they passed many a familiar face lying upturned to the sun; and, hewing their way through a crowd of plunderers which were upon the area that had been covered by the Khan's tents, Fazil saw that their walls were torn down, and that no one remained; and in the bed of the rivulet which, lying low, screened them from observation, they drew rein. In his misery Fazil would have dismounted, and again sought death on foot, but Bulwunt Rao saw the intention, and prevented it, as he had done before.

"No, no, Meah," he said roughly; "you are our master now; and as the gods have enabled me to save you once to-day, so we will all try again. If they you sought have been taken, they are in honourable safety with the Rajah: if they are dead, there is no help but in submission to God's will."

A shout from several of the men caused Fazil to look round. He saw some persons running towards the party who had emerged from the thick jungle on the other side of the stream. They were grooms who had hidden themselves.

One of them clasped Fazil's knees. "They are safe," he cried; "Meah, they are gone this way with the hunchback and Ashruf, who would not let us follow lest we should be seen. They went down the river; and see! here are their tracks. Come!"

What need to speak more now? The new interest absorbed all other considerations. Several of the grooms were good trackers, and the hoof-marks of the two ponies could not be mistaken. They knew them well.

Late in the afternoon—often bewildered in deep silent forests, often thrown out, often despairing of success, often passing hard rocky ground where Fazil could see no tracks whatever, but where Bulwunt Rao and the trackers held their way with confidence, a small group of people were discovered, from a knoll where the trackers stood for a time uncertain, sitting near a large banian tree, on the bank of a mountain stream.

At a little distance, too, from them, sat a few men armed with matchlocks, who were apparently guarding the rest.

Fazil and the scouts approached, cautiously leading his horse; and the first greeting was a rough one from the guards, who raised their guns to fire; but the next, a frantic cry of welcome from the hunchback and Ashruf, who ran forward and prostrated themselves before him.

"O Meah, they are safe—they are safe!" cried Lukshmun, rising first. "Come and see," he cried, bursting into tears; "and the gods have sent thee."

Hearing his cry, Goolab rushed forward, clasping his knees, and, unable to speak, was sobbing passionately.

Yes, they were safe—Lurlee and Zyna. A rude bower of leafy branches had been hastily made, with a screen of boughs twisted into stakes in front; and so concealed were they by the thick brushwood, apart from the grassy glade, that the little commotion which Fazil's coming had caused, had not been heard by them. Having dismounted, and preceded by old Goolab, who, in her uncontrollable joy, now ran before, screaming the news of his arrival, he entered the enclosure—and the two desolate women, whose utter despair nothing as yet had soothed or alleviated, fell upon his neck and wept aloud.

How long they sat into the night they could not tell. Kakrey, the Mahratta officer who had followed the party by Moro Trimmul's order, had overtaken them; and, touched by the beauty and sorrow of the women, had not molested them. The nearest Mahomedan garrison was Kurrar, a town at some distance; but he had engaged to guide and protect them thither, and the reward promised by Lurlee was at once confirmed, and even enhanced by Fazil. Kakrey had already told them that the Khan's escape was impossible; and they were thus prepared for the sad news which Fazil brought.

Kakrey decidedly objected, however, to Fazil's horsemen, and even to Lukshmun and Ashruf; they were strangers, and would be inevitably suspected. Fazil and his men must take another road, he said; and the ladies must submit to hardships among mountain villages and rough tracks for some days. They had no other chance of escape but in disguise, and alone with him. He had already procured rough food and coarse clothes, and there was little time for rest; ere the morning he must take them away.

Poor Lurlee! All night while Fazil sat there, she had pored over the book of astrological diagrams in a hopeless puzzle of mind. Why should she have been mistaken? Why should her husband have died who had left her so hopeful in the morning? Were they all wrong? was all this, the faith of her life, false?

It seemed so; but one thing was at least certain, that Tara's nature and Fazil's were alike; and she appeared, in spite of her grief, to return to this discovery with a peculiar zest. "I am not wrong," she said, "in this; look!"—but we will spare the detail. She was too much bewildered by far, to understand as yet the loss that had befallen her, nor was she at all convinced that she was a widow. No, the stars could not be wrong; and for all they could say, she only believed the more that the Khan would return. "Who had seen him die?"

Fazil was convinced of Kakrey's good faith. Bulwunt Rao unhesitatingly answered for him. They were neighbours, and had been boys together. Fazil's promises of reward were too profuse to have aught in competition with them. It was hard to persuade Zyna that he must leave her again; but as they were situated, they could not remain together, and must separate. For Fazil would not leave his men, and he determined, with Bulwunt and the hunchback, to hover as long as possible about the vicinity of Wye. He might be joined by other fugitives, he might rescue many of his people, and even make head against the enemy; above all, perhaps he might get news of Tara, and assist her. He should avoid the Mahratta horse, and with a guide like Bulwunt Rao, and one of Kakrey's followers, who volunteered to accompany him, he could either conceal himself or advance as needful.

So, with many tears, and almost despairing, Lurlee and Zyna, dressed as peasant women in the coarsest clothes, left him ere morning dawned. Lurlee was not remarkable; but the fair skin and beautiful features of Zyna were often objects of wondering interest and admiration among the mountain peasantry, as they journeyed on.

. . . .

Three days afterwards, Fazil and his men, who had been joined by other stragglers on foot and on horseback, were lying during the day in the place of concealment which had been chosen by Kakrey's follower, and approved of by Bulwunt Rao and the hunchback. In the depth of the jungle near Wye, there was a large banian tree, planted by a small temple now deserted, because of some evil repute. The tree had flourished while the temple had decayed, and was large enough, with its offsets, to have sheltered thousands. The outside boughs trailed on the ground, screening everything within, where the bare, gaunt branches, and the naked roots falling from them, rose high into the air, covered above with a thick foliage. A bright rill sparkled past the tree; grass was abundant on the hill-sides, and a liberal price for grain had induced some villagers near, to supply the men's wants for a few days. Every day, the hunchback and the boy Ashruf, disguising themselves as mendicants, had sung ballads in the town of Wye, in order to gain information of passing events.

They were lying concealed in this hiding-place when, in the afternoon of the third day, the hunchback broke in upon Fazil and some others sitting together. "Bid them all go away," he cried excitedly; "I have strange news, Meah, for thee,—for thine ear only."

The men rose and went to a distance. "Can it be of his father?" they said.

No, it was not of him; he was beyond all hope now, and his bloody head festering in the sun above the gate of Pertabgurh.

"Meah," said the man, in a low voice, "Tara the Moorlee is alive, but they are going to burn her to-morrow; and I saw them taking wood to the river-side to make the pile. They say the goddess came to her at Pertabgurh, and told her, before the Rajah, to be a Sutee, and he is going to make a great show of her to the people. I waited till I saw her come into Wye in a palankeen, and I would have told her you were here, but I could not get near her for the crowd—they were throwing flowers upon her. The people do not know her name, but I knew her: it is Tara. O Meah, you will not let the Brahmuns do this!"

"By Alla and the Prophet, no!" cried the young man, starting to his feet. "Dost thou know the place?"

"I—I can lead a Duróra on the house," said Lukshmun hesitatingly. "God forgive me, it is not the first I have led, and I observed it all before I left."

"Where is Bulwunt Rao? Call him."

"He is asleep," replied Lukshmun; "I will go and bring him."

"Meah wants you; come," he said to Bulwunt Rao, after waking him; and when he joined Fazil, all was told him; and the three men consulted long and earnestly as to how the girl might be rescued.

"O, were but Rama and a score of Pahar Singh's Ramoosees here," said Lukshmun, "we could go and bring her to you to-night, without waking her; but your Mussulmans would make but a poor hand of that work."

So, after discussing the subject in every way, there seemed no chance of success but in an effort to carry her off from the pile itself. The attempt might succeed or fail; but the men who would undertake it were at least desperate, and to abandon the girl to her fate without endeavouring to rescue her, was not to be thought of. In any case, they must leave their hiding-place on the morrow, or starve. A long march might take them at once beyond the disturbed country; and they were not, in their present mood, likely to falter in their project.

Tara! Her name aroused a thousand sweet memories. The day after the interview with the Rajah, she was to have been demanded as a subject of their King; and, in the Rajah's apparently submissive mood, Fazil had anticipated no refusal. What had happened to place her in the situation in which she was, he could not conjecture; but Bulwunt Rao and Lukshmun understood at once that she was the victim of Brahmun intrigues excited by Moro Trimmul, and rejoiced in the prospect of frustrating his intentions. Finally, the whole project was explained to the men; and in their hearty acquiescence, and in the excitement of a new and desperate action, the young Khan lay down that night, and, for the first time since the slaughter, slept soundly.

CHAPTER LXXXIII.

MEANWHILE, the Shastree, Anunda, and Radha, were pressing on as fast as the nature of their travelling would allow. The Shastree had a palankeen, for he was still weak, and the women rode; but as he gained strength, he was able to ride in turn.

At first their stages were necessarily short, with frequent halts; but as they proceeded, they had increased the daily distance; and the news of the action at Pertabgurh, which had spread over the country with incredible rapidity, made them more and more anxious to reach Wye, and ascertain Tara's fate. All attempts to trace her on the road were fruitless. The army had passed, but in the confusion attendant upon its progress, individuals could not be traced or distinguished.

At the last stage before Wye they found the village where they rested in much excitement. It was understood that a Sutee would take place in the town the next day; and though it was not known who the person was, the certainty that such a ceremony would occur was beyond question; and it was evident that people from all the country round would attend it.

Anunda had not been at Wye since her youth. Her parents, who had resided there, were long since dead, and she knew, vaguely only, of some distant relatives. The Shastree, however, in his professional expeditions, had frequently visited the town which, from the number of Brahmun families residing there, was then, as it still is, the seat of much learning, and, from its many temples on the bank of the Krishna river, esteemed sacred.

The chief priest of one of those temples, Vishnu Pundit, was an old friend and antagonist in scientific and literary discussions, and Vyas Shastree knew he was sure of a hearty welcome, even if his coming were not formally announced. But considering that his wives might be an inconvenience, he had sent a note on by a messenger, who had engaged to deliver it by daylight at furthest; and as they set out for their last march, it was in hopeful, perhaps joyful anticipation of news of Tara, by which their long suspense would be ended.

Mingling with the parties, therefore, which thronged the roads to the town, and hearing many speculations as to the nature of the Sutee, but nothing definite, the travellers passed on as rapidly as possible; and a fairer scene than the bed of the sacred stream, with its hundreds of bathers in the sparkling waters, the temples on its banks, and the broad flights of steps leading to the river, could hardly be imagined; but there was one object in particular upon which all their interest centred. In the middle of a broad bed of sand near the stream, some men were already piling logs of wood into a square mass, and pouring oil on them; fixing tall poles at the sides, and hanging garlands of flowers and wreaths of leaves to them. The pile was large, and would soon be completed for the sacrifice.

Vyas Shastree rode to the spot, and inquired of the men—they were Brahmun priests—for whom the preparations were being made. They did not know, they said,—it was a state matter. When the Sutee came there to die, she would be seen. Meanwhile she was at Vishnu Pundit's house, and he might go and see her, and worship her, as others were doing.

At Vishnu Pundit's house! The place to which he was going! Certainly, then, he should see the woman, whoever she might be, that was to be burned. "Had her husband died, then, last night?" he asked. If he had, the Pundit's house must be impure, and he must look elsewhere for lodgings.

"No; the Sutee was in pursuance of a vow," they said,—"not an ordinary one, and an effigy would be burned with her."

The Shastree was puzzled, and rode on, musing much at the strangeness of the act, and unable to account for it satisfactorily. Such sacrifices, from such motives, were no doubt meritorious, but they were uncommon.

He was not far distant now from their destination, and, joining Anunda, who, riding a stout ambling pony, was forcing her way through the crowd, followed by the litter in which sat Radha, he bade her come on leisurely, and himself urged his horse forward as quickly as the crowded streets would allow, to his friend's house. Vishnu Pundit himself was standing at the door of the outer court opening into the street, across which some men were tying garlands of green leaves and flowers. Seeing the Shastree advancing, he came to him, and, assisting him to dismount, embraced him warmly.

"I received your note," he said; "but I have had no time to reply to it. I have no room for you, old friend, owing to the Sutee whom the Maharaja has sent to me—that is, not till to-morrow; but meanwhile my neighbour the Josee gives you one of the courts of his house. Take the ladies there," he added to an attendant, "as they arrive. But do you, Vyas Shastree, come with me. I must speak with you alone. Ah, we had mourned you dead—yet how wonderful it is that you are here, and to-day, too! Come, I have much to say to you that is strange—most strange."

The Shastree followed him curiously into an inner court—one like that in his own house at Tooljapoor, where he taught his pupils. Numbers of people were pressing through the outer court, bearing offerings for worship; but in the place they went to, they were alone, and the Pundit closed the door.

"Vyas Shastree," he said, looking at him intently as they sat down, and speaking with irrepressible concern and grief in his voice, "O friend! O dear old friend! I have dark news for thee to-day. Alas! and woe to me that I have to tell it! Hast thou a daughter named Tara?"

"I have come to seek her—followed her thus far—what of her?" replied the Shastree, sickening with apprehension—"what of her?"

"She was a priestess of Toolja Mata at Tooljapoor, was she not?" asked the Pundit.

"She was so, friend, and the Mussulmans carried her off. But they spared her honour! O, say they spared her honour!" he exclaimed piteously, and stretching forth his hands.

"She was an honoured guest with them, friend, and would that—— O, how shall I say the rest?" he thought,—"how explain this misery? Alas, what evil fate hath sent him to-day!"

"Thou art keeping something from me," said the Shastree, striving to be calm. "If—if Tara—my daughter—— What is it, O friend? we have suffered much suspense, much anxiety:—for her sake have taken this weary journey; and we hoped to have found her here among friends, perhaps with thee. What hast thou to say of her? Did they not give her up, as we heard they would? Have—they——"

"Yes, she is here," returned the Pundit hesitatingly, and turning away his head in a vain attempt to repress his tears. "She—she—is a widow, is she not?" he asked.

Then the truth flashed upon the wretched father with fearful rapidity. That crowd of people; that hideous pile of logs: the preparations and rejoicing were for her death—for Tara's, and after all he was too late to save her! O, if he had only hurried on,—if he had only left home sooner! But thought now had no definite form. It was a confused and conflicting chaos, utterly uncontrollable. "Where have ye put her?" he asked, in a low husky voice, as, with a sickening pressure at his heart, his features assumed the haggard expression of weary age.

"Friend," said the Pundit, passing his arm around him and trying to raise him up, "come and see. Such poor honour as we can do to her on earth while she is with us, we have already done and will continue. Come and see. Arise! If thou art a true Brahmun, hear this, like a god on earth as thou art, and believe it for her eternal glory. How few are chosen for this sacrifice! true jewels only are they—pure gold, to be purified in the fire!"

"In the fire," he echoed dreamily—rising, and supporting himself against a pillar in the room with a hopeless gesture of despair—"in the fire!—I tell thee, Vishnu Pundit," he added presently, "it cannot be: who has wrought this cruelty upon her? Who has done it? Of her own act and will it could not have been; but if the council have dared to—to——"

"She thought you dead—you, her mother, and your new wife," replied the Pundit, interrupting him. "She was suffering hopeless persecution and insult; and in the temple at Pertabgurh she stood before the Mother's image, and declared herself sutee before the Brahmuns. Could we recall the words? I was present. Had it been my own daughter I had been thankful. O Shastree! it was her glory!"

Vyas Shastree could not reply. "Let me see her and hear it from her own lips," was all he could utter at all intelligibly.

"Certainly, if thou wilt," replied the Pundit; "she is ready to go even now, but the hour is not come. And yet, Vyas Shastree, beware; would it not be better she believed you all dead, and so died happily looking for you, than, seeing you alive, be shaken in her determination? Will not the love of life come out of this, and rise defiant to all convictions? Alas! alas! my friend, it is not for me to come between your love and her mother's and that poor child; but beware! she cannot retract now and live, otherwise than in dishonour and infamy; and hereafter you will cry in agony to the goddess Mother, she had better have died—and will be guilty of sin in having shaken her faith if she live. Did you refuse when she was called before?——"

The Shastree groaned, and his breath came as it were in broken gasps. He was trembling violently. "I—I—must see her," he said. "Let her decide;" and, unable to stand, he again sat down.

"Drink some water, Vyas Shastree; it will refresh you," said the Pundit, bringing a vessel full from the end of the apartment.

"No, no, friend," he replied, putting it away, "I will not eat or drink till this is past, if it is to be. Let us go. I am no less a

Brahmun than thyself. If the Mother whom she serves has spoken to her, it is well—she will go to her. My child! O my child!" cried the miserable man in his agony. "O Mother, what hath she done for this to come to her—she, so pure, to need the sacrifice of fire! O Toolja Mata, was it needed? Come, Shastree, I am ready now," he continued, after a pause. "Do not delay."

The Pundit said nothing. He again passed his arm round his friend to support him, and, leading him to a door in the further end of the room, opened it. A small court intervened between the place where they stood and a larger one beyond, the door of which was open, and showed a crowd of people, mostly women, struggling to approach some object beyond. All had garlands of flowers in their hands, and vessels wherewith to pour libations. Suddenly there was a shrill piercing scream; and the crowd swayed to and fro, retreating backwards before some priests who were putting the people out.

"What can have happened?" cried the Pundit, hastening on. "Come quickly."

Vyas Shastree felt instinctively that Anunda had seen Tara, and he rapidly followed his friend. As he entered the next court, he saw at a glance all he yearned for—all that he most dreaded to see.

A bower, as it were, of trellis-work, had been fitted up in the large apartment of the Pundit's house which was raised slightly from the ground, and it was covered with heavy garlands of green leaves and flowers, as though for a bridal. In the narrow doorway of this bower stood a slight female figure, richly dressed in a bright crimson silk dress, striving to put away the arm of a Brahmun priest,—who was preventing her from stepping forth,—and struggling with him. The face was full of horror and misery, and the eyes flashing with excitement and despair. Before her, without, lay an elderly woman senseless on the ground, supported by a girl and several other women who were weeping bitterly. Tara, Anunda, Radha!—how had they met? Alone, he could have met Tara firmly, but with them? Not now, however, did the Shastree's heart fail: no matter what followed, honour or dishonour, he would not leave his child. Darting forward past the Pundit, pushing aside some women, who, screaming senselessly, would not be put out,—Vyas Shastree leaped upon the basement of the room, and, dragging away the Brahmun priest, stood by his child. "Tara, O my life! O my child!" he cried passionately, "come forth, come to us!"

It was the effort of an instant only, for the attendant priests had seized him and drawn him back forcibly, while they held him up. "Thou canst not touch her now without defilement," one said, who knew him. "She is sutee, O Vyas Shastree, and pure from thy touch, even; she is bathed and dressed for the sacrifice."

"Tara, Tara!" gasped the unhappy man, not heeding the words.

"Tara, come forth—come; I, thy father, call thee! O my child, do not delay; come, we will go away—far away, to the Mother——"

To the Mother! Perhaps if he had not said this, Tara would have been unable to repress those last fearful yearnings to life which now tore her heart; but the echo fell on her own spirit heavily and irrepressively. To the Mother! Yes, in her great misery, all she could see in her mental agony—what she saw in the temple at Pertabgurh,—all that she had dwelt upon since,—were the glowing ruby eyes of the Mother far away at Tooljapoor, glittering, as she thought, in glad anticipation of her coming. The same Brahmun priest who was preventing her egress when her mother appeared, had again crossed his arms before the door. As she saw her father advance, Tara staggered back affrighted; it was as though he had risen from the dead; and at his despairing cry the girl could not have restrained herself, had not the echo of his last words fallen on a heart which, though wellnigh dead to life, had rallied for a while to its purest affections;—but only for a while.

"Thou canst not move hence," said the Brahmun priest. "Cry 'Jey Toolja! Jey Kalee!' O Tara! thou wilt not now deny the Mother!—all else is dead to thee."

No, she could not deny her now—she would not. With that strange light in her eyes—that seemingly supernatural force in her actions, which the people thought the emanation of divinity, Tara's spirit was rallied by the priest's words. "Jey Toolja Mata!" she cried, stretching her arms into the air; "I am true, O Mother! I am true; and even these shall not keep me from thee now!"

Strange enthusiasm! stranger fortitude, which, having no terror of a horrible death, has carried on its votaries even to the flames with a constancy and devotion worthy of a nobler fate! In other cases, earthly love—the desire to free a beloved object from the pains of suffering for life's errors, and insure final and perfect rest to its immortal spirit—or a gratification of the all-absorbing grief which looks on present death as the only remedy for despairing sorrow—might exist; but here was no such incentive. The spiritual portion of the girl's nature was alone concerned in the question; and that, once excited by position and circumstance, had insured a more perfect observance of her vow than earthly passion.

A strange enthusiasm indeed! Ah yes,—from the period to which we can trace it in a dim legendary superstition of the past, through the two thousand years since the Greek philosopher stood on the banks of Indus and Ganges and recorded it, to the time when it was made to cease under the stern power of a purer creed—how many have died, alike self-devoted, alike calm, alike fearless! Women with ordinary affections, ordinary habits of life, suddenly lifted up into a sublimity of position,—even to death,—by an influence they were unable to repress or control—barbarous and superstitious if you will, but sublime.

Tara had conquered. Her father hung upon her words with an absorbing reverential fear, as the last sound of them died away and was drowned in the shouts of "Jey Toolja Mata!" which burst from the Brahmuns around, and were taken up by the people without, whose frantic efforts to gain entrance were redoubled. He had heard her doom from her own lips, and, believing in the inspiration which prompted them, his head fell on his bosom; then the men, feeling his frame relax, let him go, and he fell prostrate before his child and worshipped her.

They had removed Anunda into an inner room, and her senses had rallied under the care paid to her. As he rose with a despairing gesture, and turned away from his child, the Shastree sought Anunda. "There is no hope," he said, "wife—none. It is her own act, and the Mother takes her. She is doomed, and I saw it in her eyes. It is enough that we have come to see it; she is already gone far beyond us, and we dare not recall her."

He closed the door, and within were Radha, Anunda, and himself. What he said to them—how he consoled them, no one ever knew; but after a while they came forth, bathed and purified themselves, and went and sat silently near their daughter.

Now, they looked at her calm, glorious beauty as she sat within the bower, decked for the sacrifice, with heavy wreaths of jessamine flowers about her head, and rich golden ornaments about her person, —their faith, cruel as it was, bid them rejoice. No more contumely now, no more reproach, no more sin, no more persecution. Her little history was told them by Vishnu Pundit, and believed. Tara was pure, and if the Mother had called her—even through the fire—she must go.

So they sat listening to her, as she recited those passages from the Holy Books which her father loved, relative to humble and yet glorious martyrs like herself,—men and women who had undergone the trial, and were at last free. Sometimes she spoke to them calmly—told them how she wished her ornaments to be disposed of—what charitable donations were to be given in her name—what messages were to be delivered to her friends, and the servants who had tended her; but she never spoke of the past, nor alluded to her parents, as though she had believed them dead. She never mentioned Afzool Khan or his family; she shed no tear, nor did any human weakness appear to mingle with the rapt devotion which it was evident filled her mind, and absorbed every other faculty.

So they sat—the girl within, the father and mother and Radha without, the bower—their eyes blinded by tears, their voices choked with sobs. Tara bid them not to weep; but that emotion could not be denied. No one dared to intrude upon that last terrible severing of earthly ties. And so the priests chanted, and the shadows fell eastwards, and lengthened.

CHAPTER LXXXIV.

After a while, they heard the sound of drums and cymbals, and of the rude Mahratta pipes, advancing up the street, playing a wailing, mournful air, and the musicians stopped at the door of the outer court. The people within fell back, and made a lane of egress, and Tara rose and came forth from the bower. Once she prostrated herself before her father and mother, and those with her saw a shiver—whether of grief, despair, or terror, who could say—pass through her body; but she recovered herself quickly, and as she stood on the upper step of the basement, she asked for flowers, and, throwing handfuls among the crowd, descended the steps into the court.

Then slowly on through the people, who worshipped her as she passed; and out of the court into the street, where an open litter, such a one as she had sat in when they made her a priestess of the temple at Tooljapoor, awaited her. Carried in this, as in a triumphant procession, and with baskets full of flowers before her, she threw them among the crowd. As she proceeded through the streets, shouts from the people around her, and from those on house-tops, trees, and terraces, were redoubled; many women shricked, and most prayed aloud for the Sutee. The clash of the music increased, and the march played was one of victory; while companies of Brahmuns, bare-headed, joined the procession, singing and chanting the hymns of death. So, on through the town, past the holy temples, and into the river bed, where thousands awaited her, and set up a hoarse shouting as they saw her first. What was the first honour of life as a priestess, to this glory of its death?

She reached the pile, now covered with fluttering pennons, and streamers,—orange, white, and crimson,—and thousands of garlands, which the people had hung or thrown upon it as votive offerings since the morning,—and the litter was set down for her to alight. It was with difficulty the crowd was kept back so as to form a space round the pile which would admit of her passing in procession; but it was cleared at last by the Brahmuns, and the people hung back awestruck and staring at the beauty of the victim.

Tara looked at the pile; but there was that strange ecstasy glowing in her eyes which appeared to have rendered her unconcious of its purport, or of all else about her. Sometimes she cast up her eyes with a strange bright smile, and nodded as if she were saying, as perhaps she did, "I come, I come." Again she looked round her dreamily. The roar of the people's voices, the clash of cymbals, the shrill screams of the pipes and horns, the hoarse braying of trumpets, and the continuous beating of deep-toned drums, were around her, drowning the sound of words, and the bitter sobs and low shrieks of her mother and Radha at her side. Her father's spirit seemed to have risen to the need of the occasion, for he stood near her joining the solemn chant, which blended with, and softened, the rude music.

As she stood, the Brahmuns worshipped her, and poured libations before her and on her feet, touched her forehead with sacred colour, and put fresh garlands over her neck. Then the last procession was formed, in which she would walk round the pile thrice, and ascend it, as her last act of ceremonial observance. Now, and before she had to take off her ornaments, she turned her full gaze on it, and they thought, who were watching her, that she seemed to comprehend its purpose. A huge platform of logs, black with oil and grease that had been poured upon them, strewed with camphor and frankincense, which had been scattered lavishly by the people in their votive offerings, and smeared with red powder. A rude step had been made for Tara to ascend by, and on the summit some bright cloths were laid as a bed, where she might recline, upon which a small effigy of a man, rudely conceived and dressed, had been placed. Her marriage-bed in the spiritual sense of the sacrifice, on which, through fire, she would be united to her husband. The whole was garish, hideous, and cruel. Face to face with death so horrible, so imminent, the girl seemed to shiver and gasp suddenly, and sank down swooning.

Vishnu Pundit, and another old Brahmun, raised her up. "It must not be," they said to each other in a whisper; "she must not fail now, else shame will come upon us."

Moro Trimmul was near her also, and had been one to seize her mechanically as she was falling. To him the scene was like some mocking phantasy, which held him enthralled, while it urged him to action. Since he had murdered Gunga, his evil spirit had known no rest; no sleep had come to him, except in snatches more horrible than the reality of waking. Again and again he had felt the rush of the girl's warm blood upon his hands, and the senseless body falling from his arms into the black void of air, to be no more seen or heard of—and had started up in abject fear. Day or night, it was the same; —the short struggle, the frantic efforts of the girl for life, his own maddened exertions to destroy her, were being acted over and over again. Every moment of his life was full of them; and nothing else, do what he might, go where he would, came instead. He had eaten opium in large quantities, but it only made the reality of this hideous vision more palpable, and exaggerated all its details. He had busied himself deeply in the arrangements consequent upon the victory and the distribution of plunder, but with no effect. Haunted by Gunga's murder on the one hand, by Tara's determination to die as Sutee on the other, the remonstrances of Maloosray and other friends only irritated him the more. They had endeavoured to restrain him from going to Wye to see her burned, but with no result—he had broken from them, and ridden over alone that morning.

Soon after he arrived, he heard that Vyas Shastree and his sister were already there, and he had sought her, and in his former desperate manner, threatened and persuaded in turn. It might be that, having experience of these threats, Radha no longer feared them, or that the position she now occupied was so utterly hopeless as regarded Tara, that even he must see that it was useless to persecute her further. As a last resource, he had proposed to some of his own men, desperate and licentious as himself, to attack the procession, and carry Tara away; but, hardened as they were, the sacrilege of violently abducting a Sutee, was an impossible crime against their faith, and his proposal had been rejected.

He was there, therefore, alone. He had bathed and performed the needful ceremonies with the other Brahmuns, and the thought that he should at least see Tara die, came, for the time, like sweet revenge into his heart, feeding his evil passions and sustaining them. Devils both, Tara and Gunga, witches and sorceresses. What matter if both died horrible deaths? it was the penalty of their crimes; and in such thoughts a momentary consolation was offered by the mocking fiend at his heart, to be whirled away to the chaos of despair, in which Gunga seemed writhing in her blood, and Tara tossing her arms in the agony of the fire.

Thus he had walked with her, almost beside her, from the house, through the streets, to the pile by the river-side. In the litter, surrounded by chanting priests, she was unapproachable; but, sinking to the earth helpless before him, she seemed once more fated to be his prey.

"Tara, Tara," he whispered quickly and sharply in her ear, as, helping her to rise, he passed his arm under her. "Come, O beloved! save thyself, even now—even now. I can do it. Come, O beloved!"

The words and his hot breath on her cheek roused the girl more completely than aught else could have done. She did not speak, but she arose, strong and defiant, and, shaking him off, pushed him away so violently from her, that he staggered and fell backwards.

. . . .

For some time past, a body of horsemen, with their faces tied up, after the fashion of Mahratta cavaliers, the housings of their horses weather-stained, and their arms rusty and unpolished, had moved about the bed of the river and the bank beyond, and as the procession advanced to the pile, pressed on nearer to the crowd. It might be a hundred men or more; and the leader, who was a Mahratta, spoke cheerfully to the people who addressed him, and told them of his pursuit of the Mussulmans, and the raid they had done into the Beejapoor country, from which they were only now returning in time to see the show before they went home to the fort.

Our old friend Bulwunt Rao had become spokesman and ostensible leader; and the hunchback rode with him, and bandied words with the bystanders freely, but in good humour. With them, too, was Fazil Khan, who joined heartily in the rough jokes which were passing—many, at his own expense of ragged clothes, rusty arms, and gaunt features: and thus the band pressed on to the very skirts of the crowd, as if to see the Sutee, but actually to take up the position necessary for their adventure. During the day they had passed several bodies of Mahratta horse, but had been taken for a similar party, and had as yet been unchallenged; and in the crowd, their bold confident demeanour, and the ready replies given to all questions, with the certainty among the people that every Moslem soldier had perished at Pertabgurh, or was a prisoner, prevented any suspicion of their real character.

Bulwunt Rao had seen Sutee rites before. They had watched the procession issue from the town, and he knew Tara would alight from the litter when she arrived at the pile. As she did so—as the litter was carried aside, and before the procession around the pile was formed—they had determined to ride in upon the crowd and bear her away. They had no fear of the result; there was not a doubt among them. They knew that every horseman in the town would be present there, unarmed and on foot, and that miles would be passed by them ere pursuit could be made. Their old hiding-place was not known, and beyond was open country; and if a long ride by night, what fear?—the horses were fresh and well fed.

"Be ready, Meah," said Bulwunt Rao, in a low voice. "See, they are clearing a space around the pile for her to walk. Holy Krishna! how beautiful she is! 'Jey Kalee! Jey Toolja Mata!'" he shouted with the crowd. Then turning to the hunchback, he bade him go round the rear of the party and see they all kept together. "As one man, Lukshmun, when they hear our shout, let them follow."

So they advanced nearer and nearer, and the crowd on foot, unable to resist the pressure of the horses, gave way before them. The sword of every man was loosened in its sheath, and a few of the rear men, who had matchlocks with lighted matches slung over their backs, unslung them, and held them on their saddlebows ready for use. If any one had noticed Fazil Khan, they would have seen him smoothing a cushion, as it were, of cloths upon the pommel of his saddle, while he wakened his horse with an occasional touch of his leg, and kept him excited for a sudden rush.

He moved up close to Bulwunt Rao. "If I fall, dear friend, in this," he said, "tell them how it was, and take the men to them. Do not wait for me; let them do with me as they list."

Bulwunt Rao smiled. "Fear not, Meah," he replied. "Ride thou in to her, and trust to us for the rest."

Fazil's teeth were hard set, and his heart throbbed quick; but he was calm and cool. It was no time for chance work, and there must not be any mistake now. He felt his sword was loose in the sheath, and smiled to himself. The men had orders not to strike unarmed people; but if any resisted, there would be some revenge for Pertabgurh he thought, and, looking round, saw the rough faces of his followers in thick array behind him, holding in their horses as though for a race.

They saw Tara alight. Fazil was not a stone's-throw distant, and perhaps she might see him, but she did not. He was not in her thoughts now; the agony of relinquishing him had passed from her in the despair of life long ago. They saw her suddenly sink down, and Vishnu Pundit and Moro Trimmul stoop to raise her up.

"Bismilla! Futteh-i-nubbee!" cried the young Khan, as, pressing his horse's flanks, the animal bounded forward. "Bismilla, brothers, Ya Alla! Ya Alla!"

"Ya Alla! Ya Alla!" shouted the rest behind, as they too gave their horses the rein, and all dashed forward furiously.

Some men with poles and sticks struck at Fazil, Bulwunt, and Lukshmun, as they came on first, but none there had arms. It was as Tara, watching the effect of her effort against Moro Trimmul, stood apart, with flashing eyes and heaving bosom—belonging for the moment to the world she had abjured—that the hoarse shout of the horsemen fell upon her ear. She looked at them for a moment; she saw people go down before them, trampled, shrieking, under foot, and the weapons flashing in the sunlight. Then two men stopped for an instant—she was between them: both stooped towards her at the same moment, and one threw himself off his horse, and lifted her to the other's saddle.

As it was done, a man sprang at Fazil's horse's bridle, with a frantic execration, caught it, and jerked it violently. The noble beast, urged on—for Fazil saw the danger—partly reared, but was held down by the bridle; else it had fared ill perhaps with the young man—for Tara was not sensible now, and he could only hold her up with difficulty—had not Lukshmun been nigh.

"I never kill Brahmuns," he said through his teeth, "but thou art a devil;" and he struck at Moro Trimmul's bare neck with all his force. As the wretched man sank to the earth under the terrible wound, the hunchback sprang to his horse, clambered upon it like a cat, and flourishing his bloody sword, though he struck no one, rode by Fazil's side onwards, unharmed.

No one opposed them; the action was too sudden and too desperate. The crowd, also, was not so thick towards the river, and gave way before them; and, dashing through the shallow ford, the horses throwing up the bright water in a cloud of sparkling drops, they galloped up the bank, and even then, were beyond pursuit. A few of the matchlock-men, firing their pieces over the heads of the crowd beyond, shook them in defiance, as they turned to ride after their party; and a few shots in return, the balls of which sang shrilly in the air over their heads, were fired after them by people in the throng with harmless effect.

It was long ere the party drew rein, and no one spoke. Tara lay easily, supported on the cushion by Fazil's arms, and he watched anxiously for signs of returning consciousness. It came at last, as he felt her cling to him, and she looked up to his face, as they crossed a small streamlet leisurely, with a pleading look which could not be mistaken.

"Ah, fear not," he said; "fear not, beloved! Thou art safe now; and that hideous pageant is far behind. Didst thou think, Tara, I would leave thee to die that frightful death without an effort?"

The beauteous eyes opened again, and closed softly as the tears welled from them. The rapt glittering expression of religious enthusiasm had passed away, and left the world coming back fast into them, with all its tender interests and love, a thousandfold more powerful than before.

That night, another pile was lighted by the river-side, and a corpse, never removed from the spot where it fell, was burned upon it; but the pile of the Sutee remained, grim and black, and the garlands of flowers had withered in the next day's sun ere it was dismantled.

There were a thousand rumours current in the town for some days as to who could have done so bold a deed, but no one guessed the truth. Had Moro Trimmul lived, he could have told; but he had never spoken after the hunchback's sturdy death-blow. So the people believed that some of the starving Beejapoor cavalry, wandering about, had determined to attack the people collected for the Sutee, and plunder them of what they could; and that the rich ornaments which the Sutee herself had worn attracted their attention, and they had carried her off for them.

Some days afterwards, too, near a spot where the fugitives had rested for a while, the remains of a young woman, so much torn by wild beasts as to be unrecognizable, with some shreds of silken garments about them, were found by the village people. It was clear that a murder had been done, and the circumstances under which Tara had disappeared, rendered it probable that these remains were hers. So they were taken into Wye: and the miserable parents, believing them to be their daughter's, had them burned by the river-side in all honour and respect, and thenceforth believed her dead. They did not leave Wye immediately. The excitement and fatigue had exhausted the Shastree, who required rest; and the ceremonies consequent on Tara's death, and necessary purification, occupied some days; so Vishnu Pundit's persuasions prevailed, and they remained with him.

CHAPTER LXXXV.

KHUNDOJEE KAKREY performed his promise faithfully. By secret mountain paths known to few, and through the dense forests of the tract which lies between Pertabgurh and Kurrar, on the right bank of the Krishna, the Mahratta guided his charge safely, and with as much comfort as the nature of the journey would admit of. The two women maintained their disguise of peasants, and Zyna's ability to speak Mahratta, as well as Lurlee's to speak Canarese, assisted in aiding the deception. By night Kakrey sought shelter of villages where he seemed to be well known, for a decent house was always ready for them to sleep in, the best delicacies of country farmhouses cooked for them: and frequently, not only the matron of the house, but other women of the village, attended to bathe them, and otherwise minister to their comfort.

But for all this, those days were remembered as a time of bitter grief and sore trial; the more difficult for Zyna to endure, because Lurlee could not be brought to believe that her husband was dead, and preserved throughout, a demeanour of hope, if not, indeed, of actual joy. "No one saw him die," she would say, "his body was not buried by them. They dare not say he is dead, and I will hear no more of it. When we are at Kurrar he will return, and we will go home together." Again and again, too, were the astrological diagrams consulted: but the lady was unable to find any error in them, and for the present they were to her far more conclusive than the report she had heard from Fazil, and it was a happy thing for her, perhaps, that the delusion lasted even as far as the town to which they were journeying.

With Zyna, however, there was no delusion. She had at once believed her brother's report. Kakrey, too, had told her that there was no hope of her father's existence. Of Tara's fate he knew nothing. Mourning for him, therefore, and in miserable anxiety about her brother, Zyna had had to endure a twofold trial, which her naturally buoyant disposition and innate piety only, enabled her to sustain. Possibly, too, had she remained in one place it would have been more severe; but the daily movement—in a manner before unexperienced by her—the sense of freedom from restraint in the wild country they traversed, the beautiful and, to her, wonderful mountains, forests, and natural objects of all kinds, which, brought up as she had been in the seclusion of a zenana, she had had no chance of seeing before—served to divert her mind from the terrible reality of her loss, to fill it with hope, and to render the sense of danger they incurred in their escape to be blunted by the excitement of perpetual change.

Of the servants who had escaped with them, and who joined Fazil's party, Goolab alone remained to attend the ladies by permission of their guide. She had been divested of every particle of Mahomedan attire, and, dressed in a coarse Mahratta saree, with a dab of red colour smeared on her forehead, and mounted upon a small ambling bullock, passed readily for a Mahratta farmer's wife. In this ride, the old woman was in her element; now guiding the docile animal she rode, beside Lurlee, now beside Zyna, cheering them on when they were fatigued, and often dismounting and supporting them in places where the ponies hesitated and had to be carefully led. Unless near a mountain village, their guide, Kakrey, seldom approached them; he was generally in advance with some of his men, while others remained behind, guarding the rear. When in motion, the party was made to resemble, as far as possible, the appearance of people journeying upon a pilgrimage, and small orange flags, carried by several of the men, and fastened to the pommels of the women's saddles, assisted and maintained the deception.

It was on the afternoon of the fourth day that, emerging from a rugged pass in the mountains, they saw below them part of the wide plain of the Dekhan, the blue waters of the Krishna river sparkling in the sun, and the town, which they had hitherto only hoped to reach. Great numbers of white tents were pitched upon the plain near the fort, showing the presence of a considerable force, and the royal standard fluttered lazily in the evening breeze from its highest tower. It was a pleasant scene of quiet soft beauty, and seemed a true resting-place for the now weary and almost exhausted travellers. The last march had been a longer one than usual; for some of the way they had passed through village lands, in regard to the people of which Kakrey was not without apprehension; the country was becoming more open, and the danger of detection greater; nevertheless, he had guided them safely and truly, as he had promised.

It had been no easy matter to sustain the lady Lurlee that afternoon. All the confidence she had displayed hitherto, false as it was, seemed to have suddenly deserted her as she drew nigh to her destination; and while they rested during the hottest part of the day, under some cool shade by the side of a rivulet, Zyna saw that the old diagrams were laid aside for once with a heavy sigh, and seemed to afford no comfort. She thought the evident weariness might be the result of a longer and rougher ride than usual, and tried to soothe Lurlee. "Only a few coss more, mother," she said, "and we are safe with our own people: do not fail now, when the end is so near!"

"It matters not—what is the use of it?" replied Lurlee—"who will care for us, now they are gone from us?"

"The Blessed Alla, and the Prophet, and the saints," answered Zyna devoutly, "and there is Fazil too——"

"He could not love me, now that Tara is not with me," returned Lurlee, interrupting Zyna.

"Tara, mother?"

"Yes, his soul will be gone away to her and to his father, Zyna. He is dead," replied Lurlee, sighing. "I know it now. All day long the old man's face has been before me, gashed and bloody, and I think," she said, passing her hand across her eyes, "that I am not deceived now—no, not now."

"We shall know the best or worst soon, mother; but Fazil could not have been deceived," replied Zyna.

"And thou hast not wept, Zyna! O hard heart! Was he nothing to thee? It is the old who cannot weep—the old like me."

Zyna's tears were falling fast, but she checked them. "I would not grieve thee, mother, needlessly," she said; "when Fazil comes, he will tell us all."

"If I could see her, the daughter the good Alla gave me, Zyna—the girl who softened my heart—and give her to him—it would be enough! but they took her away, and she, too, is dead! Once," she continued mysteriously, after a pause, and catching Zyna's arm,—"once since we were out in these wilds, she came to me in a dream, and mocked me. She said she was going to die, and go to her Mother, but she would come to see me first. Ah, she was very beautiful, Zyna, and smiled lovingly upon me in her old way. Now, when she said that, it must have been near morning, when we were asleep in the village where they gave us milk to drink, and about the third watch of the night; but I cannot understand what planet ruled the hour. Ah me! I used once to do so, but the more I look at the tables now, the more I fail."

"Trust in Alla, mother, not in them," replied Zyna.

"I have no trust in them," muttered Lurlee gloomily—"none now in anything; all have failed me, and she most of all. O Tara! why didst thou go? O my child, my child, whom Alla gave me when I had none, and when thy mother died. Alas! why was I mocked, Zyna? why did Alla take him too, who loved me, and leave me here? O daughter, this is unjust oppression, this——"

"Hush, mother! else Alla will hear thee, and be angry, and the saints too; and can any one resist fate? O mother, be patient!" said Zyna soothingly. "Only for their help we had not escaped the slaughter, and worse—dishonour; and yet we are here, and our friends now are not far off."

"Your friends and Fazil's, girl!" she returned tartly. "I have been of small account enough already among ye, and am not likely to improve."

"Do not speak bitter words, mother, I beseech you," cried Zyna entreatingly. "We are your children—indeed we are, and will never leave you. If Fazil lives——"

"Peace!" rejoined the lady, interrupting her, "do not let falsehood come into thy mouth, girl. Enough for me that Tara is not, and thou art."

Zyna could never reply to Lurlee's caustic speeches, least of all under the pressure of their mutual bereavement; and as they sat there they broke forth from time to time from her without tear or sob—old grievances—old jealousies—old allegations of neglect. Matters which Zyna had utterly forgotten, seemed to have rushed back on the lady's memory like a flood. They were hard to endure; and yet not so hard, Zyna thought, as the false confidence, the fearful mockery of truth and reality, which had lasted till then—that disbelief in her father's death for which she could not account.

"Ah, if Tara can only be rescued from them, there may be some natural revulsion yet," thought the girl; and yet what hope of that? She could not deceive herself into a belief that Tara would be given up, or that she could escape from her family; perhaps, on second thoughts, she would not desire it—but if it could be so? And amidst such conflicting thoughts, and the endurance of Lurlee's dogged, desperate state of mind, the afternoon's journey into Kurrar, though the last, was indescribably more miserable than any which had preceded it.

They descended the pass, and were once more on level ground. "Hence to Beejapoor," said Goolab cheerily, as she was leading Lurlee's pony down the last steep descent, "there are no mountains —a child might ride thither without trouble. Keep a good heart, therefore, O my Khánum! trust in Alla, and the Prophet, and the blessed Peer Khaderi, and thou wilt see it. I vow Fatehas to the shrine, and to feed——"

"They are liars like thyself," retorted Lurlee savagely: "peace, for a prating old fool as thou art! Did not the planets tell me

Afzool Khan was alive, and now men say he is dead! After that, can I believe? O woman, thou art mad—so keep thy tongue silent!"

Goolab thought her mistress mad—perhaps she was so in some degree. Excitement, grief as yet without vent, and heavy fatigue in a blazing sun to one unaccustomed to exposure, might easily cause temporary delirium, and it was with difficulty that she supported her mistress upon her pony over the ground which intervened from the bottom of the pass to the town. Shiverings had come on, and it was evident that the poor lady might be seriously indisposed.

Several of Kakrey's Mahratta foot-soldiers, who had guarded them, had run on to secure a lodging of some kind, and the travellers were met at the town gate by one who had returned to wait for the approaching party, and he guided them on. Other parties had reached the camp from the fatal field, and more were still coming in daily, so that the arrival of the travellers was unnoticed, and from their disguise their persons and rank were quite unknown. To those who saw them pass, they appeared women of the country who had made a long journey that day, and were utterly wearied; for Lurlee, closely muffled, was supported by Goolab, who walked by her side, with her arm thrown round her waist; and Zyna, even more entirely concealed from observation, leaned forward, supporting herself on her arm, as if hardly able to maintain her place on the saddle. Kakrey and his followers had closed round them so as to protect them from the jostling of the people in the narrow street and crowded bazar of the town, and all cheered the ladies by the assurance that the house secured for the night was a good one, which belonged to a respectable Mahomedan merchant, who had given part of it without hesitation on hearing for whom it was needed. It is doubtful, indeed, whether either of them could have supported their fatigue much longer.*

CHAPTER LXXXVI.

A FEW steps further on, and Kakrey turned the ponies into a side street, and stopped at the handsome gateway of a respectable house. The steps up to the entrance being easy, the active mountain animals scrambled up them in turn, and their riders were thus taken at once into the first court. Then, when the gates were closed, Goolab lifted them from their seats; and the men, who had remained without, took possession of the guard-room inside the first archway, which, while

* Khundojee Kakrey's escort of the ladies of Afzool Khan's family to Kurrar became known to Sivaji, and he was tried and beheaded for—as it was esteemed—the act of treason.—*Mahratta Chronicle.*

it afforded ample accommodation, enabled them to continue their protection to the last.

Once more in private, and their mufflings removed, and as Goolab led Lurlee into the second court, they were met by a lady of middle age, who, attended by several servants, advanced and saluted them cordially, yet with a peculiar reverence.

"The wife and daughter of Afzool Khan are welcome to our poor house. O lady! why did you not advise me of your coming?"

"Who art thou?" asked Lurlee faintly, "and who told thee of us?"

"My husband was at his office in the bazar," replied the lady, "and some men came asking for shelter for noble travellers who were very weary. He asked who they were, and was told of you. O lady, your steps are fortunate, and Alla hath led you here to do us honour. Many benefits hath my lord received from the noble Khan, and there is much to repay—very much."

"Have you hot water for a bath, lady?" cried Goolab, interrupting her, "and some decent clothes instead of these, and some food that noble ladies can eat? They will be better than fine words. Alas! that for the last four days we have eaten dry parched pease, dry bread, garlic, and porridge—unblessed food, O lady; and my mistress, you see, is ill of it, and talking to her won't cure her!"

"Fear not," replied the dame, smiling; "we have had scant notice, yet we may do something," and she was as good as her word. Hot water to bathe with, was quickly prepared, and clean refreshing clothes; and the rubbings and kneadings of several young girls relieved their weary aching limbs. Soft cushions were put down to lie on; and there was a hospitable, grateful hostess ministering to every want. Even Lurlee's churlish humour was already softened by the attention paid to her; and she remembered, with satisfaction, in spite of her late disbelief, that the day was Thursday, and that, as she entered the house between five and six in the afternoon, the hour was ruled by Mercury, and was propitious.

About the same time, a body of horsemen—there might have been from two to three hundred of them—were approaching the town from the other side, through the camp which spread out irregularly among the fields and gardens. Their horses neighed frequently as they passed tents where others were picketed, seemingly envious of their rest and comfort; and the appearance of the whole party, jaded and wayworn, indicated a long weary march in a hot sun that day, which had now come to a close.

As they passed the first tents, the men loitering by the wayside asked carelessly who they were, and being told, followed them eagerly; while the news that one remnant of the noble host which had been so treacherously destroyed at Purtabgurh had arrived, traversed the camp before them. As men of the Paigah of Afzool

Khan were recognized, many a rough heart swelled, many an eye filled with tears, as the horsemen proceeded: while crowds followed them, greeting old friends who had escaped, or tendering their respectful salutations to the young Khan, and congratulating him on his escape.

Bulwunt Rao and the hunchback were in front, and as they neared the town urged their horses on. "Wait for us at the gate; we will not be long, and will bring the water," cried the latter; and when Fazil reached it, a litter—which had been rudely constructed of a bed-frame and stout bamboo poles, covered with some coarse sheets—by which he had been riding, was set down. The men who had carried it were exhausted, and as they placed it on the ground, lay down themselves at a little distance.

Fazil dismounted and approached it. "Tara!" he said, "Tara! art thou asleep? We have arrived, and there is now no more fatigue or danger. O Tara, awake!"

The girl turned mechanically towards him, but did not seem to recognize him; her eyes were much glazed, and her lips cracked and parched. "Water," she said faintly.

"Alas! I dare not give it thee, Tara," he replied. "O my life—O beloved, look up! wait but till they return, and all will be well!"

She shook her head, and a smile, very sad and sweet, seemed to pass over her face, but she did not speak. Fazil looked out among the people passing to and fro; perhaps there might be a Brahmun among them, who could give her a few drops of water to moisten her mouth, but he saw none. How wearily the time seemed to pass! With what impatience did he watch the gate whence Lukshmun or Bulwunt Rao, on their double errand, should return; and with what misery did he look upon the poor girl, lying in heavy fever, without the means of relieving her! How he longed for his sister or Lurlee! but it might be days ere they arrived, and till then he must trust her to strangers.

It had been a weary day, indeed—a day of intense anxiety to all who accompanied him. Under the excitement of release from imminent death, and in the rapid ride of the afternoon of her rescue, Tara had borne the fatigue wonderfully; and as night set in, and they took some hurried rest among the corn-fields of a village, Fazil hoped that she would sleep, and be refreshed against the morrow; but it was not to be so. During the night the girl began to speak incoherently at times, and it was evident that she suffered from high fever. Still they must proceed; there was no delaying there. The tracks of his party were distinct, and a force of the enemy's horse might yet overtake them and destroy them if they tarried.

So, after feeding their horses on green corn-stalks, and themselves obtaining a rough meal from the green heads of corn roasted in a fire, they again set forth. They had no other food, for they dare not stay to cook it, and they had avoided villages as likely to expose themselves to collision with the surly people. Once or twice, straggling parties of cavalry had been met; but they had passed without notice, and the farther they proceeded, the less chance there was of interruption. So far all was well; but Tara grew worse, and could no longer sit the horse on which she had been placed; so, in a village which was passed, a litter was contrived, a drink of milk obtained, and the party again set forward. Finally, they had arrived safely at Kurrar; but Tara now knew no one, she could not be roused to speak, and lay moaning piteously, as if in pain.

"When she gets water it will refresh her," thought Fazil, as he sat helplessly by her, praying, in his own simple fashion, that God would be good to him and spare her. "Weariness and the terror of death have caused this," he said to himself, "and rest alone can cure it."

At last Lukshmun returned with a Brahmun and some water, and the man, looking into the litter, shook his head hopelessly.

"She is dying," he said; "let her be taken out and placed on the ground, that her spirit may depart easily."

Fazil flung him away angrily. "She shall not die," he cried passionately; "give her the water—as much as she will drink." But it was of little avail,—she scarcely swallowed any, and motioned the man away with her head impatiently.

Then came Bulwunt Rao. "I had much ado to find the merchant," he said, "and when I did, he told me strange guests were already with him, and that he could not find room for a Brahmun woman. Nevertheless he yielded at last, and we are to go. I rode by the house. The porch was full of men, so we must seek shelter elsewhere. The merchant said he would meet you at the door of the house, but he does not yet know who you are. I did not tell him. I only said you were a nobleman of Beejapoor."

"And why did you not tell him?" cried Fazil, with some impatience; "he owed my father a thousand benefits."

"So much the better, Meah," returned Bulwunt, "and he looks as though he would repay them. Come, it is close by."

The bearers again took up the litter and carried it on. Fazil accompanied it on foot, holding the side; and at the same door which we have already described, stood a pleasant-looking man, dressed in flowing Arab robes and a green turban, and several servants behind him,—who saluted Fazil courteously as he stood aside for the litter to go by.

"Meer Jemal-oo-deen, if thou art he," said Fazil, "will have forgotten one whom he knew long ago."

"I have forgotten your face," returned the man, "yet you are welcome, and the peace of the Prophet be upon you. Who are you?"

"Fazil, the son of Afzool Khan," was the reply.

"O, great joy! O, thanks be to Alla!" cried the man, lifting up his hands, "and blessed be the saints and the Prophet who have sent thee. Embrace me, and come in quickly, for thy mother and sister have also been brought to us, and are safe within."

"Then she will live! they will save her!" cried the young man excitedly. "They will save her! O Meer Sahib, where are they?"

"Within, in the zenana," replied the merchant. "Sorely exhausted, I hear, but already better; and she?" and he pointed to the litter.

"No matter, sir," said Fazil, advancing; "all will be told you hereafter. She is much to them; but she is grievously shaken, and we lose time. She cannot speak, and is burning with fever."

"Ah, is it so? Then let her be carried in," and he clapped his hands. "Take that litter within at once," he said to the women who came; "then see to the lady who is in it."

Four stout women took up the litter, carried it into the inner court, and set it down.

Lurlee and Zyna were lying in an inner room, the door of which was open, and from whence the entrance to the court could be seen. "What can they be bringing in?" said Lurlee, as she saw the end of the strange litter entering the door. "A man following, too! Begone!" she screamed violently, hiding her face under the sheet; "begone! this place is private."

"Mother," cried Fazil, who heard her voice but did not see her; "it is I; and here is Tara. Come, O Zyna; where art thou? Come quickly to her."

O delicious joy! Lurlee, forgetting all her previous troubles, sprang from the bed on which she had been lying languidly, and Zyna followed; and they fell upon his neck with low whimpering cries, like dogs when they have found a lost master. Where was fatigue now?

Tara! It was far in the night ere consciousness returned to her. "No matter, Alla hath sent her again to us," said Goolab, whose ideas were always of the most practical description; "she is ours now, and we will bathe her." And some Brahmun women, who lived hard by, came and assisted. So, ere morning broke, Tara was lying on Lurlee's bosom sobbing gently: and, with her loving arms wound round her recovered treasure, Zyna was sobbing too.

CHAPTER LXXXVII.

SOME three weeks after the events recorded in the last chapter, Zyna and Lurlee were sitting near the foot of the bed on which Tara was lying, and two Brahmun women—widows, as appeared from their shaven heads and coarse serge garments—sat on each side of it. One was fanning her gently. The bed was very low, hardly a foot from the ground, so that the women were seated on the floor, leaning against its frame. They had watched all night in pairs by turns, and the dawn was just about to break; but a small lamp, in a niche of the wall, threw a faint light over the room and the verandah beyond, and fell upon a figure lying there, covered in a sheet, which appeared, from its measured breathing, to be asleep. All four women were weeping silently, and their faces had that worn, haggard expression which is consequent upon long and continuous watching.

"When did he say he would come again?" asked Lurlee of one of the women in a whisper.

"They will both be here at dawn," said the woman addressed; "but they said they could do nothing now, unless she rallies of herself: medicine cannot help her; and still she sleeps."

"Look," said Zyna, with a tone of awe in her low voice, "if you can see her breathe. I have been watching for some time, and I cannot see the sheet over her move as it used to do. Mother! mother! she is not gone from us!"

"No, daughter," returned Lurlee, "she lives still, but she is near to death, fearfully near, and is in the hands of Alla. If she wake up restless, as she was before, we must put her on the floor, that the spirit may pass easily; but, as it is, we may yet hope, for there is rest now after her weariness, and she hath not asked for water all night. You have given her none, have you?" she asked of the women.

"No, lady," replied the elder of the two; "none since she went to sleep. It is near dawn, and if the soul had to pass it would be restless to go; yet she sleeps. We cannot move her, nor is there need; she breathes as gently as a child. Look!"

The woman took the lamp from the niche in the wall, and, shading it with her hand, yet so as to suffer a little light to fall on Tara's face, looked at it earnestly. "She smiles," she said in a whisper; "behold, lady, but do not rise, else it might wake her."

Lurlee and Zyna leaned forward and regarded her anxiously. Yes, the lips, though blistered with the parching heat of fever, seemed fuller and redder, and, as the sweet mouth was partly open, the light fell upon moisture on the white pearly teeth which glistened brightly. The cheeks were not so wan and sunken, and the eyes, instead of being partly open, with a dull glassy stare which, except when they flashed in delirium, had been their only expression for several days past, were now closed entirely, and the long eyelashes rested peacefully, as it were, on the cheek. One hand had been placed under her head, and the other lay across her bosom. Her breathing could scarcely be seen, and yet, if they looked intently, the arm across the bosom heaved slightly now and then, and as it were without excitement.

"It may be the flush of life which precedes death," said the woman; "yet then they do not often smile, nor dream. See, she is smiling again."

"Ah, there is no death in that smile, daughter! Look! O blessed saints, pray for her! O Prophet of God, she will be thy child soon; intercede for her, and have her spared! O holy Syud Geesoo Duraz! I vow a golden coverlet for thy tomb, and Fatehas to a thousand poor mendicants, if she be saved!" cried Lurlee, with clasped hands and streaming eyes. "O, give her to me! All have children but me, and this one strange child I took into my heart when ye sent her, and she abode there. O, take her not—take her not from me! What use would she be to ye now in her young life? Wilt thou not pray too, Zyna, for her?"

"Mother, I have prayed," replied Zyna earnestly. "Fazil hath prayed. We have vowed Fatehas to all the shrines, and to the holy Saint at Allund. Mother! I will send my gold anklets and her zone to the shrine there, if she but live, and will give her others."

So they watched and prayed, and saw the smile playing gently and sweetly over Tara's mouth and eyes. Was it to hear the whisper of the Angel of Death? It might be so, and then the last dread change would follow; the eyes would glaze and sink, the breathing become shorter and more difficult, and they must take her up and lay her down on the ground to die. Would it be so?

For many days Tara had lain between life and death. The great excitement she had passed through—during which her mind, strung by despair and superstitious belief, had sustained her—had passed away suddenly, and left its never-failing result in the utter prostration both of mental and physical power; and the exposure she had been subjected to in that wild night-ride from Wye, with the succeeding days of heat and fatigue, in the midst of constant alarm, had combined to produce severe fever. As she was lifted from the litter the evening she arrived by the women, she was entirely unconscious; but in Lurlee she had at once a skilful and loving nurse, and after a while she had recovered sufficiently to distinguish with whom she was, and to feel that the hideous insecurity of her life—nay, the imminent peril of a horrible and violent death—had passed away.

But after that short period of blissful recognition, and with the sound of Lurlee and Zyna's passionately endearing welcomes in her ears, unconsciousness had returned, and she knew no more for many days. The burning fever, accompanied by low delirium, continued without intermission. Happily her mind retained its last pleasant impressions most vividly: and from time to time, Lurlee and Zyna heard her murmur to herself more of her deep love for Fazil than she would ever have dared to tell them, and they listened wonderingly to the strange mingling of his name with those of gods and demigods of her own faith, and to the impassioned expressions which broke from her in that wild, perhaps poetic, language, with which, from her own studies and her father's recitals, she had become familiar.

The doctors of the town were early summoned; and there was an old Gosai, known to the merchant's wife, who lived in a village near, whose repute for curing cases of fever was very great, and who was sent for, when the doctors' period of nine days' illness had elapsed without any relief. He declared the fever would last three weeks: and that, on the twenty-first day, or thereabouts, Tara would either live or die, for the disease was dangerous and difficult to subdue, but—he would do his best. So they sat and watched her day and night; life now seemingly trembling on her lips, and yet again rallying within her, and giving hope when otherwise there was none.

Now, too, under the long sleep, her features had relaxed; the skin had lost its unnatural tension and dryness, and a soft smile was there which looked like life; and still they prayed and made vows.

"No," said the woman, holding the lamp and watching Tara, "it is not death, lady—not yet. There is no change; and see, the smile, faint as it is, does not pass away. Surely there are sweet thoughts below it—thoughts, perhaps, of life. Let us wait and pray."

And still they sat, and, after their own fashion, humbly prayed too; and the morning broke, and Fazil, who, wearied by watching, lay outside, arose, performed his ablutions, and, with Zyna, spread their carpets, and performed the morning service. Then he watched in turn; and the doctors came, looked at the sleeping girl, and one of them gently put his hand on her pulse and felt it, and smiled, and nodded his head approvingly. "There is life in it," he said gently, "but it is very feeble. Wait till she wakes—that is the crisis of life or of death; but, perhaps—God knows—it may be life."

It may be life! Ah, yes! Many who read these pages will remember like scenes; watching the fluttering spirit of one most beloved—parent, or wife, or child—with an intense and wondering earnestness of misery or of hope, mingled with prayer: incoherent perhaps—no matter—yet going straight from the heart, up to Him in whose hands are the issues of life and of death, to be dealt with as He pleased. Is there none of this among the people we write of? Why not as much as among ourselves? The same motives exist there as here, the same deep ties of affection, the same interests, and the same hopes and fears—often, indeed, more powerful as belonging to minds more impetuous, and less regulated by conventional forms. Then the hope is greater, the agony of bereavement more bitter, and the suspense between the final issue, perhaps, more unendurable.

So they sat around her. The kind, hospitable merchant's wife, with whom they still resided, came forth from her own court of the house, and, smiling as she saw Tara, bid them be of good cheer. No one spoke afterwards, but they watched the tranquil face; and the expressions still varying upon it, under the thoughts passing within, gave increasing hope of life.

It had been a sore struggle; but life at last was suffered to triumph over death. From the time when the weary tossing to and fro ceased, and the parched lips refused to speak even incoherently, and the deathlike sleep began, the exhausted frame had been gathering strength. More than a night, and nearly a day, had passed in hope and fear alternately to them, but in rest to Tara; and as the shadows were falling long towards the east, the sweet eyes opened to the full, and looked around.

They could see but dimly at first; but they read in the faces which at once turned towards her, now the most precious on earth, the assurance of that love, of which, as her spirit hovered on the threshold of the unknown eternal land, she had been permitted to dream. There was no fever now in those soft eyes—no glare, no glassy brightness: but dewy, and their deep brown and violet shaded by the long lashes, into an expression of dreamy languor—they seemed more beautiful by far than they had ever appeared before, and Fazil thought, as his creed suggested, that those of a Houri of the blessed Paradise, or a Peri angel of the air, could not be more lovely. None of them could speak then; but the tears were falling fast from their eyes in great and irrepressible emotion, as they stretched forth their arms to welcome Tara to life.

"My child! my life!" cried Lurlee, sobbing, who was the first to find utterance. "Now, God hath given thee to me again, and I will never leave thee—never. O, do not speak; it is enough that we see thee come back to us, more precious, and more beloved than ever!"

Tara attempted to reply, but was too feeble. They saw her lips moving, but no words could be heard. She tried to stretch forth her hand to Zyna, but she could not lift it. Zyna saw the attempt, and threw her arm round her. "Not now, beloved," she said—"not now. Lie still and rest; we are all near thee, and will not go away."

So more days passed, and Tara grew stronger, though slowly. The shock to mind and body had been very heavy, and needed long rest and much care; but she was in tender hands, and gradually, but surely, they saw progression to convalescence, and were thankful. Lurlee could not restrain her pious gratitude; and Friday after

Friday, the poor of the town, Hindus as well as Mahomedans, received a munificent dole of food and money, and rejoiced at the widow's profuse charity.

Dear reader, if you have ever recovered from such an illness as befell Tara, you will remember, vividly and gratefully, the pleasant languor, the perfect rest, and the sensation of growing strength of life,—amid its weakness, such as you cannot estimate till you attempt to act for yourself. You long to speak, but your tongue refuses words; you long to rise and help yourself, but your members as yet decline office. If you can turn yourself about as you lie, it is all that is possible. Then, if you are ministered to by loving hands, and you hear sweet familiar voices around you, how often has your heart swelled, and run over at your eyes, silently, and in very weakness, as you have abandoned yourself to their sweet influences! How powerfully the new life which God has given you, grows under their ever-present care! Sometimes you can hardly bear the excess of joy, and tremble lest it should suddenly cease; and again, you find periods of rest possessing you—dreamy unrealities—incomplete perceptions—even vacuity, which is not sleep, nor yet waking—and still with all, a consciousness of increasing strength which will not be denied.

It was so with Tara. No one spoke much to her, she could not bear it, nor could she reply; but if Zyna sat by her, or Lurlee, and held her hand, it was enough for reality; and morning and evening Fazil was admitted to see her, and to satisfy himself that she was gaining ground. The past was never alluded to by any of them. At first she had only a dim and broken remembrance of it, as of some great ill-usage or suffering. As she grew stronger, the detail became more distinct: and they often saw her shudder, and draw the end of her garment or the coverlet over her face, as if to hide it from observation, or to shut out some terrible sight from her view. Yet to herself there was an unreality about the whole, which she could neither comprehend, nor account for. Most of all about her parents: were they indeed alive, or was their sudden appearance on the day of the Sutee, a reality, or a trick of imagination—was all she retained in her mind one of the hideous dreams of her illness rather than a fact? Who was to tell her the truth?

All that Fazil had heard from the hunchback, he had told to Tara as they rested here and there in their escape; but her own mind was then in that state of terror and confusion that she could tell him nothing, nor, indeed, could she find courage to speak to him at all. Long before, when they had been together in camp, she had never dared to answer him. It was enough for her that he spoke, and that she listened. Her mind, as he rode with her that night before him—for he would trust her to no one—was sorely unhinged. That she had escaped death she knew; that she was with him she knew also:

that she feared pursuit, and might be taken and burned alive, was an absorbing terror, which shut out the shame of her flight; and it was perhaps a happy circumstance that the fever, which had so long affected her brain, shut out all realities till she was stronger, and calmer to bear them.

CHAPTER LXXXVIII.

DAY by day, as strength returned to Tara, remembrance returned also. It might have been with abhorrence of her present position—with dread of her broken vows—with terror of the Mother's vengeance, and with a sense of her own pollution as an escaped Sutee—which would have utterly overwhelmed her with remorse, and forbidden recovery at all; and in such a case, death would have been welcome. We will not say that there was no revulsion of feeling: it would have been unnatural in one with so fine an intellect as Tara possessed, had there been no struggle. Perhaps the new life to which she awakened, after the illness she had undergone, had blunted the perceptions of the old; perhaps, as Zyna and Lurlee told her, that it was her destiny, which she could not resist; and that, if she were to have died, as her creed had determined, could Fazil have prevented it?—would she have been delivered at all? Had she not already undergone the pains of death in preparation for it, and been delivered from them?

Then Lurlee again brought forth her books, and went over all her old calculations, and there were the priest's also with them, all tending to the same point. If her faith had been shaken for a time, in the fact that Afzool Khan had died, when the planets showed that he should be victorious, might there not have been some mistake? Here at least there was none; none in the restoration of her child, as she called Tara, from death to life—none in her having been rescued from the evil idolaters and Kafirs, to be newly born into the true faith, acceptable to Alla and the Prophet. All this was very plain and incontrovertible.

Could Tara deny it? It was not clear that she even attempted to do so: and ever nigh her, were anxious pleaders against any justification of the rites of her own faith, from the most horrible consummation of which, she could not possibly have escaped. "Even your father and mother could not have saved you had they desired it," argued Zyna, "from dying in the fire before them: they would have seen you burned, and shouted 'Jey Kalee!' with the rest, to drown the scream of your dying agony; but they would not have relented." No; Tara's heart told her they would not have relented, and she must have perished, but for Fazil.

And when he pleaded?—It was long before he attempted it; but it was at last irrepressible. More than his sister and Lurlee, he knew what struggle would ensue in Tara's heart if she were called upon too suddenly to renounce her own faith; for he had lived, young as he still was, more in the world. On this point, he had as yet forborne to address her at all. But such love as his for the deserted girl, must be spoken by himself. Lurlee and Zyna had told him all they had said, and it seemed strange to both that he was silent; but he had judged rightly. What the girl could bear from them, could not have been endured from him till her bodily strength assisted her mind to bear it, and he waited his opportunity.

It was the first time she had ever mentioned her own affairs; almost the only time she had spoken freely at all. She had reverted to the past, to the day of the attack on Tooljapoor, and to Fazil's recovery of her mother's ornaments; for the Brahmun women had bathed her that day, and she had performed some simple ceremonies of her faith for purification after her illness, and charitable gifts had been distributed by Fazil and Lurlee on her behalf. So she had suffered Zyna to twist a garland of flowers into her hair as she used to do in camp, and to put on her some of the old ornaments which, while she was yet decked for the Sutee, had been brought away with her: and when Fazil, who had been absent all day in the camp, returned before sunset for the evening prayer, he found her talking earnestly with his sister.

Still pale, but only showing the traces of illness in the purity of her colour, Tara had perhaps never looked more lovely than in the resumption of some of her former richness and elegance of costume; and as Fazil entered the court, for the moment unobserved by her and Zyna, who were seated together, he stopped involuntarily to regard her.

Tara would have fled when they saw him, but Zyna would not have it so.

"Look," she said, "brother, is she not like herself once more? See how I have decked her for her sacrifice of thanks to-day! Surely all that is past is as a dream, and Tara is again what she was the evening she was taken away from us. Is she not, brother? She is not changed?"

"Yes," he said, "changed, I think, in spirit in her new life, as we had hoped—that is all! Tara, sit down: we will all remain together, and you must hear me now, with Zyna as witness.

"There is nothing new to say," he continued, after a pause—"nothing. It is only the old tale, once told before, when you believed it: and it is not changed, only confirmed. Ah! we have both been tried since; and if out of that trial you have come, like me, strengthened, then there is no doubt. Tara! in the deadly struggle by that hideous pile, with the crash of music, and frantic screams of the people in your ears, even then your heart bore witness to me that I was true. Am I false now?"

"O no, no, no!" cried the girl, throwing herself uncontrollably at his feet, after her old Hindu fashion. "Not false, not false! You are my lord and my saviour, and I worship you! I will be your slave, your servant, for my life, and Zyna knows it; but consider——"

"Not thus, beloved," he said, gravely but kindly stooping and raising her up, "will I hear that, but so, face to face. There is no shame in it now—none; for it is our destiny, Tara: let it be as honoured as, methinks, it is loved. Sit there and listen." And Zyna put her arm round her, and they sat down together side by side.

"I have to say hard words, perhaps, Tara," he continued, "but you must hear them. In saving you from death by fire, I have brought you into a living death from your own faith; for you are an outcast now, as you know—you cannot return to it. You could not be received as a Brahmun, nor would any other caste assist you. Shaven, denied shelter, and even water, by the very mother who bore you—if she live—you must herd with the vilest, and enter that condition of abject dishonour and profligacy which Moro Trimmul intended for you, and from which God—your God as well as mine, Tara—has now delivered you. There is nothing else for you that I can see but death, and that is now gone from you, and will not return. Could you escape this, Tara? Is this a life for you?"

He saw the girl shudder violently, and bury her burning face in Zyna's bosom; while Zyna, drawing her to herself more closely, said gently, "Listen, listen; is he speaking the truth? You do not answer, O beloved!"

Tara could not reply, but she clung to Zyna the more closely.

"Or instead," continued Fazil, "there is, what was said once before, in presence of my honoured father—peace be with him!—which I now repeat, and Alla and the Prophet, who sent me to you, and you to me, are witness of its truth,—that all of honour, all of wealth, all of love and respect that I possess, I will share with you as my wife, till I die. You are not of us, nor of our creed: no matter, we can admit you honourably to both. It is no disgrace to quit the blood-stained belief of Hinduism to join the glorious ranks of the true believers; but a blessed gain, for which, out of all these trials, Alla hath preordained you. Enough, O Tara: before Him, your God and mine, and before Zyna, answer to me truly and freely, once and for ever. He is witness that there is no constraint upon you."

Could she resist that earnest manly pleading—she, already won long ago? she who, in all her trial, had carried about in her heart that image of glory and beauty, which she could only compare with the heroes and demigods of her own sacred poems—her highest standard,—and who, in putting it away, had done so, only to die in that horrible, calm despair, which preceded voluntary immolation? It was impossible!

As she sat there, and as he ceased speaking, there rushed through her mind a sudden flood of old memories which, had the love she bore for him been weak, or less deeply rooted than it was, had swept it away as the torrent sweeps dry straws from its bed, and they are seen no more. Father, mother, Radha, the old pleasant memories of Tooljapoor, and the old people; a happy childhood, a joyous budding into womanhood without care. Next, her service to the goddess, and all that had come of it—terror, desperation, and living death. She could not serve her now, even did she desire it; and she could not see the image as before, nor the weird ruby eyes which used to follow her, and seemed to glint into her very heart. She remembered the fierce Brahmun, her foe—the glittering fly which she had seen in her little garden—and trembling, clung more closely to the breast on which she was lying; and, last of all, the hideous pile of black logs, the crash of gongs and drums, the shouts of the people, the fluttering pennons, the torches blazing around her to light her to death, and the agony of two women as they beheld it all, and of an aged man who had come to her and caused her once more to fear——

It takes long to write this; but all, ay more, rushed through the girl's heart as a strong flood in a moment, tossing and whirling fiercely: yet it shook nothing there. How true was it that, in that long unconsciousness and delirium, the old life had passed away, and the new one came with other obligations to be fulfilled. She was weeping passionately while Fazil was speaking, but when the rush of thought came, it was with awe, which repressed other emotion, and was succeeded by calm, inexpressibly sweet and assuring. Yes, love for him had resisted the fury of passion in its last attempt, and she could not control it now. Zyna felt her arms withdrawn from about her, and Tara, covering her burning face, on which the tears were glistening, with her garment, bent down before him, not in prostration, as before, but kneeling and bowing her head reverently, as she joined her hands in an attitude of supplication.

"Do with me as thou wilt, my lord," she said gently; "my life is thine, and I am thine henceforth till I die. I am helpless now—do not forsake me; and God and Zyna are witness that I pledge my troth to thee, freely and humbly. I have no fear—none! it is past now!"

"Shabash! Shabash! Tara," cried Zyna exultingly, clapping her hands; "now thou art ours indeed. See, mother," she continued, turning round and looking up, as Lurlee entered, "he asked her, and she has agreed; and you are witness of it as well as I."

"I am witness," said the lady; "I have heard all, and I am

content. Alla and the Prophet have answered my prayers. Ah! I shall have a precious child to give to thee, Fazil, ere long."

"Put her hands into mine, mother," he replied. "It will feel real, that she is to belong to me hereafter: it will be an earnest of the end."

"It is not one of the orthodox customs, Fazil," said the lady, gravely and hesitatingly: "and I never saw it done at any betrothment; nevertheless, wait an instant—I will return directly."

She did so, while they sat as before, bearing a silver salver—on which there were some pieces of sugar-candy, and seated herself by them.

"Thou art still a Brahmun," she said to Tara, "but thou wilt take one of these from thy mother? There," she continued, as she put a piece into each of their mouths, repeating the blessing, "Bismilla! It is done; ye cannot go back. There should be rejoicing, and music, and feasting; but,—Bismilla! it is done, and ye cannot retract. O children! O children! she cried, bursting into a flood of tears, "I am a widow, and have suffered sore bereavement; but ye are the light of my eyes and the only joy of my heart now! Here are her hands, Fazil," and she took up Tara's, and put them into his—"thine, boy, till the end!"

Fazil stooped his head, and put his forehead upon them; they were not withdrawn, and he fancied that the slender fingers closed on his confidently;—was it fancy?

"They should know of it, if they live," said Tara hesitatingly, and with a gasp in her throat; "methinks they do live, mother, and that I saw them—there—at Wye—my father and mother; but it is all confused now, and it may have been a dream during my illness."

"O no!" cried the lady, "let them not come between us now, if they live; but they are not alive, Tara."

"Perhaps not," she said, with a sigh; "nevertheless, if my lord would send some one and ask. They would be found in Vishnu Pundit's house at Wye; and if they are dead——"

"Surely," said Fazil, interrupting her, "I will send Lukshmun even now. If they are there, they should come on at once; there is no fear. Could you not send a letter, or a token, Tara?"

"I will write," she replied; "and here is a ring of my mother's that she loved dearly; it would have been burned with me! Let them take it; and if my lord would write, too, to say—to say—I am alive, it would be enough."

"It shall be done at once," he said, rising; "O mother, surely thy science told thee this would be a happy day!"

"See!" exclaimed the lady triumphantly, taking her tablets from her bodice, "you mock the planets sometimes, son, but see; while you were speaking I looked. Is not this Wednesday? and, see, here is

Venus ruling the hour as you sat and plighted your faith! O children, this cannot be wrong, for the sun is just setting, and the work is finished."

As she spoke, the last gleam of its rays, as it sank in a glory of gold and crimson, flashed into the apartment, lighting up the girls' radiant faces, and sparkling upon their rich dresses and golden ornaments.

"Beautiful as thou art, Tara," continued Lurlee, "thou wilt be lovelier still when we deck thee as his bride; and so may the blessing of thy new mother rest upon thee, and the evil I take from thee now,"—and she passed her hands over the girl from head to foot,—"depart to thine enemies!"

"Ameen! Ameen!" cried Zyna, as Tara, falling upon her neck, again wept silently those tears of joy which she had with difficulty repressed.

CHAPTER LXXXIX.

"WELL sung!" cried the young Khan cheerfully, and joining in the general applause which followed a pretty Mahratta ballad which the hunchback and Ashruf had just sung, to the accompaniment of a lute played by the former and a small tenor drum by the latter—"well sung! Where did ye learn that?" he continued, advancing from the entrance to the court where he had paused as he came out. "It is something new."

The men, who were seated or lounging about the entrance hall to the house, rose and saluted Fazil. It was evident at a glance to Bulwunt Rao that something had occurred to remove the sad expression which his lord's face had worn so long; for it had given place to one radiant with joy, and he exclaimed cheerily,—

"Thanks be to the gods! it is gone at last, Meah! Never, since we rode together to Pertabgurh, have any of us seen a smile on your face that was worth looking at, or one which was not followed by a sigh, as much as to regret it had ever been there; so I cry, with thanks to the gods, the grief is gone at last. What say you, brothers? look at him; did I speak truly?"

Amidst the hearty responses to this congratulation by his retainers, Fazil Khan sat down among them, and the hunchback and Ashruf, stepping forward, assumed the positions of professional ballad-singers, and saluted him.

"Shall we sing it again, Meah?" asked Lukshmun; "you did not hear it all. 'Tis a fancy of my own, about a damsel waiting for her lover, who passes her by with another, and so she goes and weeps."

"And we have all been crying over it, Meah," added Bulwunt Rao; "'tis so sad a tune too—so plaintive."

"But as I am not in a crying mood, friend," returned Fazil, laughing, "it would hardly suit me now, so another time—meanwhile there is something to be done which is urgent."

"Are we to meet a new army, and take our revenge, Meah?" cried several of the men. "Ah, we know the country now, and should not fall into another trap like the first."

"No, no, friends," said the young man sadly, "there is no such good news as that; 'tis but a private matter of my own, which our ballad-singers may help, perhaps."

"We, Meah?" exclaimed the hunchback; "thou well knowest, that if we were bidden to leap into the flames for thee, we would not hesitate. Speak, that we may hear and do."

"It is somewhat private, friends," said the young man, looking around. "If I might be alone with these and our old friend for a little, no one may take offence; you will know all by-and-by."

"Surely not," cried several, rising and going out, followed by the rest.

"Stay, Bulwunt Rao," said Fazil, putting his hand on his arm, "your counsel may be of use;" and when they were alone, he continued, "She will not be content unless she sees her father and mother; and she declares they are at Wye, and came to her the day she was to be burned."

"Impossible!" cried Lukshmun; "they are dead, and this must be some device of the Evil One—of that old Mother on the hill there, who wants to get her back; and she has sent spirits in their guise to mock her. She does such things very often, Meah Sahib, and I don't like to hear of this."

"Well, they must be substantial spirits," returned Fazil, laughing, "for she told us that she had heard them speak, and that she thought her father had lifted her up once. They must be alive."

Lukshmun shook his head. "I did not see him, or hear of him, at Wye," he said; "and as I know them well, I should have recognized him and his wife anywhere. And, about the witches—if I were to tell you what I know about the Mother's devices," he continued solemnly, wagging his head, "I should not be believed. Nevertheless——"

"Nevertheless," said Fazil, interrupting him, "thou art to go and see—thou and Ashruf. Wilt thou go, lad, if he is afraid of the witches?"

"To the death," cried the boy cheerfully; while Lukshmun, leaping up into the air, turned a somersault, and came down where he stood. "Go!" he said; "yes, Meah. I have a spell against the Mother and all sorcery, and his majesty the devil to boot, which

Pahar Singh taught me. Where are we to go, Meah, and when?"

"Now," replied Fazil; "take two of the ponies and ride straight to Wye. Her parents will be found in the house of Vishnu Pundit, or he will direct you to them. If they are gone home, or to Poona, or anywhere else, they must be followed up and brought back; and they will come when that ring is given to her mother—so she says."

"They may need money," said the man, musing. "Brahmuns never move without coin. Something for expenses, is the first thing they ask of one. Is it not true? Nevertheless, Vyas Shastree is rich enough. O yes, he knows me, and I can get into Vishnu Pundit's house, too. Come, lad, we must put on the Byragee's dresses."

Ashruf followed him. While they were absent, Fazil wrote the letter they were to take, which ran as follows:—

"*To the respectable and learned in the Véds and Shastras, Vyas Shastree, of Tooljapoor, who is kind to his friends;*

"*From Fazil, son of Afzool Khan, with greetings, and the peace and salutation of God; and after wishing you health and prosperity—*

"*You are to know that your daughter Tara is here, with my mother and sister, in honour and health; but she hath been ill unto death, and being, by God's favour, restored to life, wishes to see you and her mother urgently, and sends a token, by which you may be assured she is here.*

"*You will learn more from the bearer, my servant, who is to be trusted; and I pray you to lose no time in setting out, for we await your coming. I have sent money for your expenses by him, which you are to be pleased to use freely.*"

The hunchback and Ashruf reappeared after a while in their new costume, which was that of Jogies, or religious mendicants of that part of the country. Orange-coloured turbans and garments, purposely torn and ragged, yet withal scrupulously clean; large strings of wooden beads about their necks, wrists, and ankles; black blankets, to keep out cold or heat, thrown over their shoulders after a graceful and picturesque fashion; and the lute and small drum they had used before. The faces of both were smeared with whiting, and the broad trident of Vishnu was drawn in red and white paint upon their foreheads. The hunchback would perhaps have been known by his figure; but Ashruf, from the smart Mussulman boy, gaily dressed as became his master's favourite attendant, was utterly transformed, and could not possibly have been recognized.

"Shabash!" cried Bulwunt Rao and Fazil involuntarily; "it is complete—no one could know you."

"Except by this hunched back of mine," said Lukshmun, "I would wager that I went anywhere as anybody you please, Meah,—from the holiest Synd down to the lowest Kullunder—from the Secretary of Ramdas Swami himself, to what I am now,—and was not discovered. Hindu or Mussulman, 'tis all the same—only I must have a religious garb on, Meah Sahib: for my mind, you see, having that turn naturally, I am most at home in one. Did any one suspect us when we sang ballads in the ambush at Jowly, and found out what Moro Trimmul wanted to do? or in Wye, when we saw Tara? O Meah! this is a joyful errand, for I shall pay a rupee to a Brahmun, and get bathed in the river—just where they were going to burn Tara Bye—to wash away my sins, and be absolved from shedding a Brahmun's blood. The gods forgive me if I killed him!"

"I hope you did," returned Fazil, laughing: "and now, here is a purse of gold, tie it round you, and use what is needed; and here are the letters which are to be put into Vyas Shastree's own hand. If he cannot get mine read, this ring and her letter will be enough. If they are gone to Poona, or back to Tooljapoor, send Ashruf back to me, and go on thyself."

"To the top of Mount Méru, or the lowest deep of Nurruk," cried Lukshmun, snapping his fingers. "Fear not; we will bring them, lad—won't we? and, master, if I have to go on, and can send thee a letter by a sure hand, may I take on my son here? I cannot sing ballads without him."

"Ah yes, my lord!" pleaded the lad, joining his hands, "to bring them to her."

"Good," said Fazil; "I trust you both. Go, and be discreet, and God's blessing and mine be with you."

"And now, my lord," said the hunchback, "let us sing one ballad before we depart—one that she must know well: it will give her hope. Go and tell her that some singers are here who know the ballads of the Bala Ghaut, and will sing her one. She will recognize the tune, for I have heard her father sing it, and they say he wrote it for her, for her name is in it. We shall sing it before Vishnu Pundit's door at Wye."

"As thou wilt," replied Fazil; "I will tell her;" and he arose and went to the inner court door. "Do not follow me," he said to them —"she can hear from hence, and there are women within—it is private."

Fazil had watched Tara as the prelude began, and he beckoned her to the door. "Come and listen," he said; "they are singers of your own country, and I have brought them to sing a ballad to you." She arose, and Zyna followed her.

The hunchback and Ashruf stood at the doorway without, and, after a short prelude, sang, as nearly as we can translate it, as follows:—

1.

"Fast her tears fell—faster, faster,
As the days pass slowly by,
And her heart is sorely laden
With the dreary, hopeless sigh.
O that cruel, ceaseless sighing!
Weary tears which sadly fell,
All unheeded as she wept them
Daily by the garden well.

2.

"Mother! Mother! oft she pleaded,
Toolja Mata! hear my vow!
Hear thy daughter's cry of sorrow—
Why shouldst thou forsake me now?
Not less thine, O Mother holy!
If my lover come to me;
If he come, a golden necklace
We, thy children, vow to thee!

3.

"As she went for water daily,
Raised alone the pitcher still,
She repeats the prayer and promise,
As with tears her soft eyes fill!
The goddess watched the weary maiden,
And her daily burthen borne;
'Faithful,' she cries, 'in earthly sorrow,
Daughter true, no longer mourn!'

4.

"Then next morn, with anklets tinkling,
The maiden tripped, and ceased to sigh;
As she stooped to raise the pitcher—
Light she felt it lifted high.
And sweet words he whispers to her—
'Tara, all thy sorrow's past!
Faith and hope have won thy lover.'
And the vow?—'Twas paid at last."

It was one of those plaintive Mahratta airs, at once so musical and tender, and whose character is so original, as to deserve the rank of national music. How often Tara had heard it! Her father had written the words, and composed the air, to amuse her when she used to be sad; but she had no lover—no one then to take the burden, to help to lift the pitcher, which was so heavy! Ah yes! she remembered it well, and that her father had said afterwards, it should not be sung in the house because it made her sadder, for there could be no lover.

So she listened, and the melody seemed to strike some new and tender chords in her memory, which as yet had been untouched; and they looked at her wonderingly, and in silence, as the features softened into a smile, and the eyes gradually filled with tears, which flowed as from a fountain within, and rolled silently down her cheeks. As the vow was named, they saw her hand rise to her neck and unclasp the heavy gold necklace she wore, and when the last words were sung she put it into Fazil's hands.

"Let the Mother have it," she said, "as our vow—she is not angry with me. You will not deny this, my lord, to Tara?"

Before they could answer her, a strange brightness seemed to come over her face and eyes, as she looked upward as if following a vision. "It is enough," she said gently, after a silence which they did not break; "the Mother is not angry with me—it is accepted, and I am free; for when the trial came, she says, and Gunga called me, I did not leave her."

They did not understand then, to what she alluded; but it was evident that the excited spirit had again wandered into the past, and had returned, more at peace than before.

"Yes," said Fazil, "as thou wilt, beloved—thy vow shall be truly paid, at last."

CHAPTER XC.

On the second morning Fazil's messengers reached Wye, without interruption, tethered their ponies in the courtyard of a temple, where they obtained shelter, and set about the work they had to do without loss of time. Taking their instruments, they wandered into the bazar, and sang their ballads to willing listeners; for the hunchback was a master of his art, and had a willing and skilful pupil in the boy.

"Wast thou not in the camp at Jowly?" said a man coming up to Lukshmun, "and this lad too, before we attacked the Toorks,—and we let thee go? Ah yes, and you promised to sing the hymn of the goddess at Tooljapoor, and did not return when we were victorious! Ill for you, for you would have had a share of the gold. By the Mother! you shall sing it now. Come with me!"

"Not so," said Lukshmun; "we are engaged to sing at Vishnu Pundit's house—where is it?—and shall be free in the evening only and if thou canst direct me to one Moro Trimmul, a Brahmun, and let me go now, we will sing an hour at night for as many as you choose to bring to the temple of Ballajee, where we have put up, and take what you have to give us."

"Moro Trimmul!" cried the man laughing, "thou wouldst have to go deep into hell for him. Where hast thou been, friend, that his fate did not come to thine ears?"

"I was afraid," replied the hunchback; "I fear fighting, sir; and if a drawn weapon is flashed in my face, I faint. So we ran away from Jowly—did we not, my son? and have been travelling about the country ever since, getting what we can. But what of the Brahmun, sir? was he killed in the fight at Jowly?"

"No, no—not there," replied the man; "but he is dead, nevertheless. Some one cut him down the day the Sutee was carried off."

"Ah yes, I have heard of that, sir; the people have strange stories about it; but who carried her off? and who killed the Brahmun? A Brahmun slain! O the impiety!" continued Lukshmun devoutly; "think of that, my son! A holy Brahmun!"

"I don't know; I was not there," replied the man; "we were still out at Jowly, or it would not have happened: but they said some of Afzool Khan's men, who were starving, made a Duróra on the Sutee, and carried her off; as to Moro Trimmul, he was no loss—a bad man, my friend, though a Brahmun. They might have spared the girl, however, for all the use she was to the Brahmuns afterwards. I wonder no one kept her, for she was very lovely, they say."

"O sir," cried the hunchback innocently; "and did she not live? Who killed her?"

"They say not," he replied; "and that the cruel men killed her for the ornaments she wore. There was a woman's corpse found some days afterwards on their track, and the remains were brought here, and her father was told of it. They say he went mad after that, for he believed they were his child's. He married Moro Trimmul's sister, you know. Ah, it is a curious story altogether."

"Indeed," returned Lukshmun simply; "I should like to hear it all. If I sing for you to-night will you tell it to me?"

"A bargain!" cried the man joyfully; "come to us without fail; we are a jovial lot, and there may be good liquor, and some of the dancers too. I will come for thee. 'Faith, the story of the Moorlee's murder by Moro Trimmul is as good as a scene in a play."

"What Moorlee?"

"O, the Tooljapoor girl, Gunga, who was with him. They found her body under the window of his room at Pertabgurh, hanging in the trees below the precipice, and so the whole came out; but he was dead before then. One of those dare-devil Mussulmans had killed him, and they took some of the Sutee wood, and burnt him there, by the river."

"Ai Bhugwân! O Lord, forgive me for having slain the Brahmun," ejaculated the hunchback to himself; "and I did it too. Well, I can't help hitting hard when I do hit; and truly he had murdered some one, it appears, so it was only justice after all. Yes, sir," he continued, "I understand. And the Sutee's father?—her name was T—T—T——"

"Tara," said the man; "and her father is Vyas Shastree of Tooljapoor. He is better now, and I saw him a while ago sitting by the porch of Vishnu Pundit's door, weak, but better; people pity him very much. Now I must go. You will not forget?"

"No," said the hunchback; "you will find me at the temple after the lamps are lighted; till then we must sing about the streets. Come, my son. Let us hurry on, boy," continued Lukshmun. "I know the house. Do not pretend to notice any one; we will sing the ballad of the Vow, after the first invocation."

They passed on rapidly: up a few cross streets and alleys, till they reached that in which was the house that they sought. In the covered alcove, beside the outer door, sat several Brahmuns, apparently talking together; one elderly man, covered with a sheet, was reading.

Lukshmun and Ashruf began to sing their ballads at the doors of every house as they advanced, and women from within, came out and gave them handfuls of flour or rice, which were dropped into the bag which Lukshmun carried. Gradually, as they came nearer, the hunchback changed the songs to those of his own country, Canarese and Mahratta in turn, and he was sure there must be some, with which the Shastree was familiar.

Yes, it was he, reading, while the others sat near him, and conversed among themselves; thinner than when the hunchback had last seen him, and looking weak, yet still remarkable and unmistakable. Once or twice the Shastree had looked up at the singers, not so as to seem to care about their performance, but as if a familiar sound had reached him. Now, however, it came to the turn of the Pundit's house, and the hunchback and Ashruf stopped before it.

"Go on," said one of the Brahmuns impatiently; "you have been bawling all down the street, disturbing our meditations, and the Shastree there is weak. Go on, and make no noise."

"Maharaj," said Lukshmun, humbly putting up his hands, "we are under a vow, made before the Holy Mother at Tooljapoor" ("May she forgive me for telling the lie!" he thought parenthetically), "to sing before every house in Wye, and bring her what we get; 'tis a good work, learned sirs, and we are poor people,—do not hinder us; 'tis a long way to go, and we are weary. Let us sing you a ballad for our vow, or only a verse, else we cannot go on."

"Make haste then," said the first spokesman impatiently.

Lukshmun returned the lute; and as he played the prelude which Tara had heard, he saw Vyas Shastree, who had not noticed him, look up. His large eyes were opened to the full, and he leaned forward with an expression of intense curiosity. Then the singers broke at once into the ballad:—

"Fast her tears fell—faster, faster,
As the days pass slowly by."

"Hold!" he exclaimed, waving his hand; "who are ye? and whence come ye?"

"From Tooljapoor, O Pundit," said the hunchback humbly.

"Who taught you that ballad?"

"No one taught it me. I heard it, and have remembered it. They say one Vyas Shastree composed it. Maybe you have heard of him, sir. He had a daughter named Tara. She was a Moorlee. I have heard they are all dead now."

"Ye belong to Tooljapoor?"

"No, Maharaj; I am from near Allund—a long way from this; but the vow I made is for" ("The gods forgive me if I tell another lie!" he said inwardly)—"for a—child—O kind sir; if the Mother will send me one. Your worship speaks Canarese?"

"Yes," said the Shastree, replying in that language; "who art thou?"

"Do they understand it?" asked the hunchback.

"No," he replied, "none but my wife, and she only a little. Why dost thou ask?"

"Can I go into the court? I know all the ballad, and can sing it sweetly for the women; they always like it," returned Lukshmun. "Will you listen, Maharaj? 'tis not very long;" and as they went in, they sang on more loudly and confidently than before. Some women of the house came and looked at them, and listened, and among them were Anunda and Radha. The hunchback looked from the Shastree to his elder wife, and saw the tears falling from both their eyes; at last the Shastree rose and went in to her, and when Anunda saw him, she burst into bitter weeping.

"Grieve not for one at rest," Lukshmun heard him say; "at rest in the peace which was denied her here. Yet the old ballad moves me strongly, wife. Come hither," he cried to the singers; "take this for the sake of . . . . No matter now; I am Vyas Shastree, and what strange chance hath sent you I know not, but take this," and he offered money.

"The gods be thanked! No; not from you," exclaimed Lukshmun, in Canarese. "Come aside," he continued in the same tongue, "for I have that to tell you and her, which will give you new life and strength. Listen," and he whispered in the Shastree's ear; "Tara lives, well and in honour. I bear a token and a letter which she hath sent you. Come, and I will give it; 'tis for her mother, and this letter for thee," and he took it from a fold in his turban.

"Anunda! O wife!" cried the Shastree, trembling and gasping

for breath, as he leaned on her, opening the letter. "She lives—our Tara. Come—he knows of her; see her own writing, the holiest and most secret Muntra I taught her; she hath written it."

"Away with ye!" cried Radha to the other women about, "this is not for your ears;" and the group were left alone; for Radha, advancing, shut the door of the court, and stood there with them.

"Do ye know this?" asked Lukshmun, when he had disengaged the ring from his inner garment. "Lady, it was to be given to thee, if thou art her mother! She is well who gave it to me, three days ago."

Her mother! Who could doubt it who saw Anunda then? The piece of gold spoke a thousand loving greetings to her. She laughed and cried by turns. She could speak nothing intelligibly. She kissed it rapturously, and hugged it close to her bosom, then looked at it till the tears rained from her eyes, and again did the same. A new life! a new daughter! born again, as it were. Anunda could not believe it.

"Thou art mocking us," she said at last, as a revulsion of feeling appeared to possess her. "This was among the jewels given to Jânoo Näik, when . . . . she never got it."

"True," replied Lukshmun, "and she has the rest," and he enumerated them; "and here is a letter about her from my master, with whom she is. Listen to me, I can tell you better than that writing."

Listen? ah yes, to the sweetest tale they had ever heard, did they listen for hours. The Brahmuns at the door wondered, and the people from within came and looked and wondered too, why the Jogies sat here talking to the Shastree—but still they sat. Once, for a moment, the Shastree's cruel belief rose up against him, and forbade him to see an outcast; but nature asserted its own. "They dare not meddle with me," he thought, "and we cannot be as she is. But no matter, we will go to her, wife; yes, we will go to-morrow. Get the things ready. Thou wilt guide us, friend?"

"And guard ye, too, with our lives," said Lukshmun. "Yes, to-morrow early, we will set out."

And so next day Vishnu Pundit and his friends marvelled that the Shastree and his family left them so suddenly, and knew not why they went, or whither.

CHAPTER XCI.

We need not relate how the hunchback was washed clean from his sins, how he and his companion entertained those who came to them that night, nor how he resisted their temptations to stay and sing to others, who, they told him, would load him with gold. Those he was taking to his master were more precious than gold; and the same anxiety to present them to him in safety, was shared equally by Fazil and by Tara while awaiting their arrival.

Five days,—two to go and three to return—perhaps more; never had time appeared so interminable to those who remained at Kurrar: never had journey appeared so wearisome to the Shastree. The spirit within him was strong and earnest, but he had suffered much; and, till roused by the hunchback's tidings, Anunda and Radha feared that he had sunk into that lethargic apathy which often precedes death. He could not be awakened from it. Had Tara died a Sutee, it might have been endured. Excitement and religious enthusiasm, even the glory of the voluntary sacrifice, would have deadened nature for a while, at least, in both her parents; but the attack upon the sacred procession, though but one had died in it, by, as they supposed, lawless robbers—and the subsequent murder, as they believed, of their child—had produced a revulsion which, to the Shastree, had wellnigh proved fatal, and for many days those about him gave up hope of life. The remains, as they supposed, of Tara had, as we know, been brought in, and burned by the riverside with all due ceremony; and after the period of mourning and impurity had passed, the Shastree and his wives were to have set out on their return home. Still, however, they lingered; for the climate had not agreed with Anunda, who had, in her turn, fallen ill with fever, and they could not travel.

During this period, they had heard from friends much of what had befallen Tara: and yet not all of Moro Trimmul's share in her misfortunes. The only person who could have told them truly was Gunga, and she was dead. Radha had her own suspicions of her brother; but beyond his wild attempt on the day of the Sutee, to induce her to put Tara into his power, she had not seen him; and his violent death, while it affected her mournfully, ended her anxieties ere the murder of Gunga was discovered.

It was with difficulty that the impatience of the Shastree and Anunda could be restrained. They reached and passed Sattara the first day, and would fain have travelled by relays of men without resting, but the hunchback and Bulwunt Rao, when they joined him, would not hear of increased exertion. "I will write by a speedy messenger that you are safe," he said; "but if I do not bring you in well to them, my lord will be angry, therefore submit yourselves to necessity,"—as, indeed, they were obliged to do.

Of his master's intentions, the hunchback had said nothing. Who was he, to know anything about them? The lady Tara was in honour as a guest; that was all he knew. Yes, his master had carried her off. Could he know that one who had been his guest, and had truly eaten of his salt, was to be burned alive, and not make an effort to save her? and she was still a Brahmun, and had Brahmun women attending upon her.

But Bulwunt Rao, who waited their coming at a village on the road with an escort of the Paigah, had no such discretion, and told what he believed—that Fazil and Tara had been privately betrothed. The lady Lurlee, he said, had one day distributed suger-candy and pân to all the household, and to the mosque and other holy places in the town: and some had been sent to him on a silver salver covered with a cloth of brocade. What did that mean? And when the Shastree remonstrated, with a natural horror, at the idea of a Brahmun girl marrying a Mussulman, Bulwunt Rao replied curtly—

"What could you do with her, Shastree, if you had her? You see she is no longer a Brahmun, but an outcast. You could not even give her water; and the two old Brahmun women who attended her in her illness, and the one who now waits on her, will have to be purified with plenty of ceremonies—and plenty to pay for them, too, will be needed; but do not care for that, Shastree, my lord is very wealthy. So, you see, we must give her up as a Hindu, and even let her go into the other faith."

The Shastree would groan at these home truths, but could reply nothing. As to his wife, she rejoiced heartily, and had no misgiving. The expression of a mother's nature would not be denied to Anunda; for there is no mother with the experience of a life's love grown into her heart, who does not rejoice in the thought of a wife's useful happiness to her daughter, and in the expectation of its fruits! All that had been done to soothe Tara, to distract her mind, to fill up the vacant place there with other interests—learning, religious exercise, and devotion to the service of the goddess—had been tried in turn, and were, as Anunda felt, but a mockery.

Possibly, most probably, indeed, under other circumstances, Tara's pure mind would eventually have taken refuge in asceticism, and those severe penances, in which the woman who had persecuted her at Pertabgurh, had grown to take delight; but, knowing the too frequent condition of the indulgence of lawless love by women situated like her daughter, and exposed to the same temptations, Anunda had often trembled for her safety; and yet owned to herself that, to doubt her, was profanation.

No, she could not object. Had she been simply asked the question previously, as a proud Brahmun woman, she must have refused. Now, circumstances had put that far beyond her reach. To object, would not retard the final issue, or influence it in any way; but to consent joyfully, would add so much, and so supremely to Tara's happiness, that opposition quickly grew to be an impossibility in the good lady's mind: and before she came to the end of the first day's journey, Fazil himself could not have desired a warmer advocate.

A good deal of this fell out from being left to herself. Palankeens had been hired; and as the three travellers were carried on singly for hours together, each had fallen into the train of thought most congenial. Radha had certainly no voice in the matter, but was delighted. Anunda, between joy for her recovered child, and her new prospects of an honourable life, had been wellnigh beside herself at first, and the quiet soothing motion of the litter was of all things the best, perhaps, to calm her, and bring her practical mind into perception of the true realities of the position. "We have mourned her as dead," she said to herself, "we have performed all the ceremonies, and distributed all the charities necessary for the occasion; now she is alive after all, and born again into a new faith; so the death which we believed in, was a type of what was to be fulfilled. I see it all now," she said to herself, "and so it has been ordered for her without the pain of burning. Strange, my husband does not see this, but I will tell it to him when we arrive."

And so she did. Radha, too, caught up this tone of argument as best suited to her husband's mind, and the two women agreeing, left him little to say. It did not appear he had anything to urge or to object. "This is some punishment for her sins in an earlier life," he said to Anunda; "and 'tis well it is no worse."

Anunda and Radha could not see the punishment, except that Tara would have to eat unclean things; otherwise, what was left to be desired?

If this was their deliberate opinion at the close of the first day's march,—the second day, and the quiet jogging motion of the litters, the change of air and scene, and the peace which had settled gradually into their hearts, had much more than confirmed it. Whatever there was of objection, was dealt with on the first evening; and on the second, as they rested for the night, impatience to see their child once more, an irrepressible yearning to place her happiness beyond doubt, or chance of mishap, had driven out all other feeling. So, on the third morning, as they entered their litters for the day's journey, and knew they would reach Kurrar before sunset, Anunda, who laughed and cried by turns in a strange manner, as she dressed their morning meal herself before they set out, saw, with a thankful heart, that the heavy care which had sat on her husband's spirit for so long had passed away, and his old placid, benign expression, had taken its place.

That afternoon, as the sun's rays lengthened, and were filled with that golden radiance which clothed the meanest objects with glory, and lighted up the town and fort, and the camp beyond,—the little procession of the three palankeens, and the small body of horsemen, approached the town gate. Bulwunt Rao had timed their arrival to suit the lady Lurlee's desire, for the astrological tables had been once more consulted, and the Moollas of several mosques had been obliged to declare the most fortunate hour for the entry of the party into the town. Messengers, too, had met them, enjoining care in this respect; and Bulwunt Rao and the hunchback were both relieved by the appearance of a last emissary at the gate to express approval of their arrangements and to urge them on.

No need of hastening now. The bearers themselves were in hurry enough; for Bulwunt Rao's promise had been liberal, and they had kept the horsemen at a brisk canter for the last few miles of the journey. Now, therefore, shouting and hallooing to each other, the men who carried the litters, rushed through the gate of the town, and up the main street at their utmost speed; and there was a race between the three sets, in which Anunda's were victorious, and clamoured for largesse as they set down her palankeen before the door of the kind merchant's house where Tara still was. Much the good lady had deliberated in her mind whether she could ever be touched by Tara without pollution, and whether it could be avoided; and we believe we are correct in saying that she had determined, if it were to cost her half, or all the money she had left in the banker's hands at Tooljapoor, she did not care, but she must hold her child once more to her heart.

Could she have repressed it? Ah no! a very outcast in shame, in misery, in misfortune—no matter had it been so—the loving mother's heart would still have been open, as her arms, to receive her child; but in Tara's renewed life, as it were, in joy and in honour, what signified the temporary impurity of contact with one only impure by the hard rules of their sect? Anunda trembled very much, and scarcely knew how she got out of the litter; but as she emerged, a figure she could hardly see for the tears which blurred her sight, and which seemed to swim before her, bowed down and kissed her feet, was raised up, and, falling on her neck, wept aloud. Then it was strained to her heart with a face buried in her bosom which dare not look up, till her father and Radha entered, and Tara, prostrating herself before him, clung to his knees sobbing. With him, too, some scruple about touching her had remained; but his emotion on sight of her could not be resisted, and he raised her up and blessed her as of old. I do not think any of them could speak, and if they did say anything, it was not intelligible enough to be recorded, and is better imagined.

Then Anunda sat down, for she was very dizzy: and Tara saw the loving arms stretched out, and went and lay down in them on the soft bosom in her old place, and hid her face there, and felt her mother's tears fall hot and fast upon it, while her own were wiped away by the dear hands that had often wiped them before. By-and-by she looked up, and her mother saw in the clear soft eye, in the ineffable expression of her countenance, that all trouble and anxiety was past. No more excitement now, false and mocking, even though sustained by religious fervour; and the peaceful calm which had grown upon the face since her recovery, was a new expression to her mother, which she felt could not change again.

Then Lurlee came with Zyna presently, when the Shastree had been sent away, and, putting Tara aside, Anunda arose and bowed before her, kissing her feet, and embracing her knees. "She is thy child now, lady," she said; "take a mother's thanks and gratitude for her honour and her life. In our simple Hindu fashion, we know no other salutation, else it would be given."

"Nay, not to me, but to Alla, who hath preserved her—not we," replied Lurlee. "Noble ye are, though of another faith. Let us embrace as sisters, to whom our mutual God hath given one daughter."

"It must be done, sooner or later," said Anunda to herself, as she withdrew from Lurlee's arms, "and better at once. Come hither, Tara: see how soon I give thee away, my child, after I have recovered thee. Wilt thou forgive me? Take her, lady," she continued, putting Tara into Lurlee's arms; "thou art more her mother now, than I. She hath been born to thee in a new life; be it as thou wilt unto her."

"I take her," replied Lurlee, "as she is given, freely and truly. I had no child, lady, and often had prayed for one, and Alla and the Prophet gave her to me long ago, before all this misery, and when my lord lived, who would have rejoiced with us to see this day had he been spared. Yes, believing you dead, we took her to be our child, he and I. Now you have given her to me, and the gift is precious and is accepted: but I will not take it yet; we are proceeding home, and you will come with us,—we will travel together. When we arrive, I will receive her; till then, let her remain with you; as yet she is pure from us——"

"Yes, mother, I am pure, I have transgressed nothing," said Tara gently. "I know," she continued, interrupting Anunda, "I am not as before; but you can give me what I need till—till . . . . and there is no help for it now." Anunda and the Shastree did not object, and so it was settled among them.

How much they had to learn of each other's acts! Nor was it till Tara told all, and they understood what the infamy of Moro Trimmul's conduct had been, that they felt the true honour of Fazil's character, or the deep loving kindness of the lady Lurlee and his sister. A grateful subject was this, now that she could speak unreservedly with Radha and her mother, and Tara had to repeat her tale again and again to willing ears. Sometimes her father, too, listened wonderingly; and there was no part of it upon which he dwelt with more pride, even to rapture, than Tara's simple relation of the ordeal, and her devotion of herself to a cruel death rather than to dishonour.

"A true Brahmun thou," he would say, passing his hand over her head as she read him the old lessons, "and thou wilt not forget these, nor the Mother. If thou hadst failed, even to death, she had not released thee from thy vow. As it is, see, she would not be denied a life! He used to scoff at her, and she drank his blood—not thine, my faithful child, not thine—and gave thee a new life, which will be happy. Yes, the Khánum's skill in astrology is good, for my own calculations confirm her results, and, comparing his scheme of nativity with thine, Tara, there is no discordance." But, nevertheless, the fact of Fazil's being born a Moslem and Tara a Hindu, often puzzled Vyas Shastree more than his science could explain, or than he cared to acknowledge.

CHAPTER XCII.

There were many cogent reasons, public as well as private, why Fazil Khan's presence in Beejapoor was urgently required. Soon after his arrival at Kurrar, he had received the King's letter of condolence on his father's loss, with confirmation of all his estates and privileges, and with them a private letter in the King's own writing, urging him to come on without delay. The full effect of the destruction of the army had as yet, perhaps, hardly been felt, and the means of retrieving the disaster, or repelling the invasion which was likely to follow, were difficult to devise. As usual, the royal counsels were much distracted; but, young as he was, the character which Fazil Khan had acquired among the soldiery during the few short months of this campaign had raised him already to a rank far beyond that of his contemporaries, and even many of his elders. Only for Tara's long illness he would have proceeded to Beejapoor immediately after his arrival at Kurrar, and left the duty of collecting the fugitives to others; but that had rendered delay unavoidable, and all those who had escaped slaughter had joined him. On the other hand, Kowas Khan wrote that his preparations for the fulfilment of his marriage-contract were complete, and protested against further delay: and when the days of mourning for his father should expire, Fazil had no valid excuse for procrastination. In this the lady Lurlee agreed perfectly, and her idea of a double marriage in the family was by no means unacceptable.

In truth that long-desired event much occupied the good lady's thoughts, almost, indeed, engrossing them. What preparations would not have to be made! and all by her. There were Zyna's clothes and Tara's to be put in hand immediately; there were stores of flour, and butter, and spices, and sugar to be laid in, flocks of sheep to come from Afzoolpoor, all the dancing women in Beejapoor to be engaged, fireworks to be made, and sweetmeats without end. All the new bridal ornaments had to be designed and executed, and this was no easy matter. Inshalla! however, she was determined it should all be done; and when Lurlee Khánum took anything into her head, there was less difficulty, perhaps, in doing it, than with others who talked more.

They did not tarry now. An express was sent to the capital that they had determined to leave Kurrar on the ensuing Monday, and Lurlee was more than ever particular that on this, their last voluntary journey, all that could be done to insure its being propitious, should be observed. They were to travel south-eastward, and Monday was the sixth day of the month, so that the mysterious "Murdan-ool-Ghyb" (the invisible being) was behind them, as he ought to be. The old tablets showed, too, that Venus ruled the hour before noon, which was a very convenient time for starting, because everyone would have bathed and eaten, and they could travel on till evening without difficulty. Now, too, the weather was cool, nay, the air was positively cold in the early mornings, when exposure to it was not wholesome, and all their preparations were made accordingly. As they were about to enter their litters, the good lady made both the girls and Fazil look at themselves in a glass, which was the crowning ceremony of all; and we believe that there never were merrier faces, or a journey begun in truer hope, and with more thankful hearts.

True, Lurlee missed the familiar countenance which, though sometimes it used to look kindly on her, and sometimes was impatient, was in the main a loving one—sadly,—very sadly; and as the city grew nigh, she had a dread, shared by Zyna and her brother, that the first days in the old house would be inexpressibly painful. So, also, when remembrances of the dear old Khan came over her, the good lady would weep plentifully and be the better of it; and Goolab and the cook Kurreema, who, having escaped the Mahrattas, rejoined her mistress at Kurrar, and had shared all her trials, were ever ready with pithy consolations, and practical expectations of the blessings in store for her which, indeed, she was well inclined to believe.

We may say, too, as perhaps hardly unnatural, that Zyna's approaching marriage was by no means terrible in contemplation: and the eagerness of her betrothed to have it concluded, gave earnest of the happiness which she hoped for, indeed felt assured of. We feel that we do not know much of this young man, and that, if it had fallen to his lot to accompany the Khan's army, he might have become a prominent character in this history, and displayed that devotion for Zyna and his friend Fazil, which we believe he really possessed. But after all, perhaps, it was better as it was. Who can say, for instance, whether he would have escaped the bloody field at Jowly, or the massacre in the ambush at Pertabgurh,—or the deadly fever of the forests and jungles, which had destroyed so many who had escaped the sword?

We have no doubt, too, had the lady Lurlee set herself to work to find out astrological reasons why he did not accompany the Khan, that they would have been discoverable: but as she had agreed with her husband that, for the present, he was better away, so she had left these mysteries unsolved, and the issue to the young man had been favourable. Not only had his house been put in order in all respects, and the ceremonies after his father's death completed, but those preparations begun in which Zyna was so deeply interested, and of which our friend the Lalla, who, as we know, had been attached to the young nobleman by Afzool Khan as secretary, wrote minute and eloquent accounts.

According to him, never had such preparations been made: while the accomplished scribe exhausted the Gulistan, the Mejnoon-i-Leila, and other love-stories, for the choicest couplets to adorn his letters, he not unfrequently composed other verses himself. Most frequently, too, in the bold rough hand which Kowas Khan wrote, there would be a postscript to say Fazil (which meant Zyna) was only to believe him as devoted as ever in all respects; and whenever Fazil gave these epistles to his sister to read, and directed especial notice to the postscripts, we are strongly inclined to consider that she found them by far their most acceptable portions. Under the constitution of Mussulman society, even had her lover been in camp, he could have seen nothing of Zyna, and she would have been in stricter seclusion from him, perhaps, than others. As she was content to take him upon hearsay, and to trust, like all her people, to after-life with him, to know him as a lover and husband too, we do not see what business we have to discuss the matter at all in this narrative.

So the journey was soon over, and little more than a hundred miles, with a light equipage, was quickly traversed. Lurlee had written to her old friend, the Moolla of the ward in which they lived, to send a special messenger to inform her at what hour it would be lucky to enter the house with two expectant brides in company; and that worthy, in conjunction with other friends, had duly solved this knotty question: and sent a return express to meet them at the last halting-place, wherein all the particulars were duly disclosed, and, we need not say, most scrupulously observed.

Fazil had wished to ride on several stages in advance and get to court, where the King looked anxiously for his coming; but Lurlee would not hear of it. "Who could tell," she said, "what might not result from so incautious a proceeding? They had met with great misfortune, which was happily past; were they to risk more? No; she was positive;" and we believe fully, that they were all much too happy together, to wrangle with her.

Fazil saw Tara daily; and she and Zyna were little troubled by Lurlee, who was now busied in consultations with her domestic advisers, which appeared to be delightfully interminable. Every now and then, however, she would come into the tent where they sat—for Zyna was teaching Tara the pretty embroidery-work she practised herself—and, looking at Tara and saying nothing, would pass her hands over her, and press them against her temples, to remove evil, and then go away smiling.

Ah yes, she was very precious now. If Zyna or Tara laughingly asked how much evil could have accumulated in those short intervals, the good lady would shake her head, and once shocked Zyna by saying, that she should not think even, of Tara's beauty, lest it should altogether depart. We believe, however, that Zyna did not fear such a catastrophe. It was growing much too palpable and real to be doubted, or to be in danger of fading away: and became only the greater when, as Zyna looked at it, and whispered something which was probably a secret between the girls, though Anunda guessed it as she sat with them, Tara covered her face, or hid it in Zyna's neck, or in her mother's bosom.

But the first few days after they arrived—in spite of congratulations of friends—of kind messages from the palace—of piles of Nuzzurs, or offerings of various kinds—were melancholy ones to all, yet tempered with grateful acknowledgements of providential care. Immediately on arrival, the requisite offerings were despatched to all the holy places of the neighbourhood and the city itself, as they had before arranged. The old Moolla, as almoner, collected a strange tribe of vagrant Fakeers, who were fed to repletion in the large courtyards; and the Shastree and Anunda made their offerings after their own fashion, at Hindu temples.

The journey, and the constant association with Lurlee and Zyna, had done much to reconcile Anunda to Mussulman ways; and, perhaps, in such matters women are more facile than men, for she was prepared for the evidences of wealth and rank which she saw on her arrival; but her husband and Fazil did not make much progress. The simple Hindu priest could not bring himself to be on an equality with the young Moslem noble; but he admitted the respect of Fazil for him gratefully, and a sincere affection sprang up between them out of it, which, if undemonstrative, was not the less permanent.

All Vyas Shastree now wished for, was the unavoidable termination. Till it took place he was not in his proper position. Few, if any, Brahmuns knew the history of Tara in the capital; but he did not feel justified, being impure, in visiting members of his own sect, till he had performed expiatory ceremonies, and so, with his wives, kept himself secluded in a court of the house specially allotted to him, and the garden we know of, the shade and quiet of which suited him. Radha, too, required rest and care; and so a month passed, for Lurlee would not be hurried. She had much on hand, she said, and must do it after her own fashion; and no one interfered with her and her assistants.

Perhaps we need not follow the good lady to the end of it; but as all matters of this kind, when loving care directs them, have an inevitably happy conclusion, so we are bound to relate that nothing was wanting here. Tara said that Zyna's marriage might be as splendid as it could be made, and suited to the rank and condition of two noble houses; but with her it should be different, and so it was. If there was a shade of disappointment upon the old lady's brow, because the son of Afzool Khan was not married with the same splendour as the son of the late Wuzeer, who had no family to boast of, it passed away when Fazil himself declared it could not be otherwise, and the wistful pleading face of Tara confirmed it.

So, as part of the magnificent ceremony which united Zyna to her betrothed—the like of which had not been seen in Beejapoor for years—Tara was admitted to the Moslem faith, and the blessing of God and the peace of the Prophet said over her as she repeated the new creed, received her new name of Ayésha, and was received into her new home. Then the chief Kazee, who had conducted the prayers, blessed all, and cried with a loud voice, solemnly—

"O Lord God! grant that such love may live between these couples, thy servants, as was between Adam and Eve, Abraham and Sara, Moses and Sufoora, his highness Mahomed—on whom be peace—and Ayésha. Ameen and ameen!" and all the assembly repeated solemnly, "Ameen and ameen!"

Some of the old Khan's friends wondered, some sneered, some blamed the young man's choice, but more congratulated him; for, as they said, "though she was once an infidel, she is now a true believer; and, after all, was he not free to choose what would best insure his own honour and happiness?" We are bound to record, however, that those matrons who, being privileged friends and guests, were indulged with a sight of the bride's beautiful face—as Tara's veil was raised from amidst the cloud of gauze and silver tissue in which it was enveloped—did not wonder at all that it had been irresistible; and there might have been some envious also, regretting that daughters of their own had lost their chance in the choice which Fazil had made. So, to prevent any evil consequences, Lurlee, with her own hands, waved over Tara's head in succession, tray after tray of lighted lamps and certain condiments which would infallibly avert evil glances, and ended by passing her hands over the bride and blessing her. "Mayst thou be fruitful," she said, embracing her, "and remain, with beauty undiminished, the joy of thy lord; and may his love for thee increase till it is fulfilled and perfected in Paradise. So be thou blessed, O my daughter, altogether!"

Even more fervently did her mother bless Tara. Although Annnda had cheerfully taken part in those portions of the ceremonies that were possible without clashing with the observances of her own faith, yet for the most part they were strange, and she had felt out of place. But she and her husband were thankful they had witnessed all to the close—thankful that Tara had been with them to the last. Henceforth their lives must be divided, but there was an assurance of honour and protection to their child which soothed the inevitable separation, and filled their hearts with hope and trust.

Long she sat alone with them, and they spoke of the future calmly and joyfully. There had been no misgiving from the first; and while they could not, if they would, have recalled Tara to their own faith, they saw in her future life as much of true happiness as they could have wished for. So they blessed her; and after their own simple fashion put her hands into Fazil's: and he took her from them, and, touching their necks, vowed to be faithful, and they believed him.

"They have given thee to me, O beloved," Fazil said to Tara, as her parents departed on their journey homewards. "Now fear not. As sacred to me as my vow before the priest, was the last vow to them. Fear not now, Ayésha!"

"I would rather be Tara to thee, my lord, for ever," she said shyly. "The little maiden who, once rescued by thee from dishonour, has lived in thy heart since then, cannot change to thee, even in name."

"Be it so," he replied. "To thy new people be Ayésha; to me, Tara—so be witness, my God and thy God—evermore!"

CHAPTER XCIII.

EPILOGUE.

PERHAPS I ought to have told my fair readers more of the particulars of this double marriage, but I am afraid they would have found them as tiresome in the relation, as Zyna and Tara did in actual sufferance of the nine days of their continuance. We can at least imagine that, with unlimited means, the jewels and trousseaux provided for both brides by the lady Lurlee (and these things are as indispensable there as here) were—perfection. And we may also state thus much in confidence, that particular friends were admitted to private views of them. The young to be envious: the old to be congratulatory—

envious too, perhaps, who knows?—for such things happen there as well as here. Then, as marriage gifts were presented by friends, there were trays upon trays from the Queen to both of jewels, brocades, and muslins, which need not be specified; and the royal lady availed herself of her privilege to see the brides, and put sugar-candy into both their mouths, wondering at Tara's beauty, and heartily wishing them both God-speed on their life's journey.

Did not also the poets of the city write verses, and the singers sing them; and are they not sung there to this day? Were there not poor folk fed by hundreds, Hindus as well as Mussulmans, and clothed too? and was there one of the sixteen hundred mosques in the city, where alms and thank-offerings were not distributed in proportion to their importance? "No one else remained to be married," said the lady Lurlee, when she had collected all the poor couples she could hear of, given them clothes, and had them married with her children. And, Mashalla! of what had been done, she was in nowise ashamed. No, indeed; and plenteous were the congratulations and blessings showered upon her, and upon them all, by high and low.

Vyas Shastree, Anunda, and Radha, remained long enough to see Tara reconciled to her new station in life, and to appreciate how irresistibly charming the quiet natural dignity of the Brahmun girl became, among the new society into which her destiny had thrown her. But, beloved as she was by many a sincere friend among her new faith—as years passed, the devotion borne to her by the retainers of the house, the farmers on her husband's vast estates, and the poor everywhere, was most affecting to witness, and increased with time; and her parents heard with joy and pride, far away in their own home, of the bounty of the good lady, Ayésha Khánum.

They left their daughter, then, at peace; and her last connection with the temple, where her father served, and where she was long remembered, was the presentation to the shrine, of the necklace she had vowed to it, which was taken there in solemn procession, and hung round the neck of the image. Some time afterwards, and when all expiatory ceremonies were completed, Radha's first child was born—a son, which Anunda adopted as her own: and in her care for it, found love and occupation to fill her heart and her time, and to supply, in some part, Tara's absence.

Mother and daughter met, however, frequently. No entire year elapsed without a reunion, and in the course of time came children too, who climbed in turn about the good dame's lap and called her grandmother. Then her heart clave to them—strangers though they were in faith—and after her own simple fashion she lived much among them during the latter years of a tranquil and happy life. Sometimes the Shastree came with her to Beejapoor, but not often.

Fazil Khan lived in stormy times and bore his part in them. The destruction of the force under his father's command had not only been a sore loss to the King's army, both in *matériel* and in men,* but a vital blow at the very existence of the kingdom and of the Mussulman power in India. Treacherously as it had been gained, the Rajah Sivaji did not slumber on his victory. His people were assured it had been suggested by divine counsel, and carried out by divine aid, and that their prince thenceforth was an incarnation of divinity. He, perhaps aided by his mother, believed this of himself, propagated the belief, and acted upon the effect of it. He was everywhere active and persevering: now invading the kingdom of Beejapoor, plundering up to the gates of the capital, and inflicting rapid and terrible blows in all directions: now attacking the Moghul posts and forts, and extending his authority until, though professing subservience to both, he became virtually independent equally of Dehli and Beejapoor, and finally assumed the state and insignia of a sovereign.

Fazil Khan had not long concluded his marriage ceremonies, ere he was called upon to take the command of part of a new army, with which the King took the field in person. Tara would not leave him, and shared the fatigue and peril of the new campaign in a manner which called forth the lady Lurlee's warmest approbation. She had not been more, she said, to his father than Tara was to his son, and she always contrasted her practical usefulness and endurance, with the behaviour of other ladies who could not leave luxurious palaces, and the state and splendour which had greater charms for them, than the rough vicissitudes of camp life.

For a time the royal forces succeeded in checking the Mahratta incursions and restoring tranquillity on the borders, and Fazil Khan continued, like his father, to render service as a commander whenever he was called upon; but he could not be induced to take office in the administration, and as disquiet and intrigue at the capital became more formidable, retired for the most part to his estate of Afzoolpoor, near the Bheema river, and usually lived there, visiting Beejapoor only on occasions of ceremony. He never married again, as the law would have allowed, and at his death was buried beside his wife in the mausoleum which his father had built at Afzoolpoor, and where such of the remains of the old Khan as could be afterwards recovered, had been deposited. The mausoleum still exists as perfect as when built, and on the several anniversaries of their deaths, flowers are strewn by the Mussulman priests of the town and by the people over their graves, and prayers are said for the repose of their souls in Paradise.

We have said that the Mussulmans of India received their first

* The loss of the Beejapoor army at Jowly was 4000 horses, with all the guns, elephants, camels, *matériel*, and treasure of the army.

material check in the massacre at Pertabgurh, and we state this advisedly. That event, in 1657, led as directly to their ruin, and the steady rise of the Mahrattas, as did the English victory of Plassey, in 1757, to the destruction of both. For though, by the conquests and subversion of all the independent Mussulman kingdoms of the Dekhan by Aurungzeeb, the empire of Dehli culminated to its highest splendour,—it was not maintained: and rapidly fell to pieces under the effects of disastrous civil wars on the one hand, and the increasing power of the Mahrattas on the other. In 1689, Beejapoor was again attacked by the Moghul armies under the Emperor in person, and, surrendering by capitulation, ceased to be an independent kingdom. The rest is matter of general history, with which this particular chronicle has no concern.

Sivaji died in 1680, after a life which was a stirring romance from first to last, but not before the power he had aroused and created had become for the present invincible—fulfilling his mother's prophecy, that the Hindu war-cry, "Hur, Hur, Mahadeo!" should be shouted in victory throughout the land of Hind, in triumph to the goddess who led it on, from Dehli to Raméshwur.

It was singular that Kowas Khan, with his father's tragical fate fresh in his memory, should have been unable to resist the same temptations to treason and treachery. Though he had ceased them for a while, the Emperor Aurungzeeb renewed his intrigues at Beejapoor; for Kowas Khan, who became regent of the State after the King Ali Adil Shah's death, entered into negotiations with the Moghul general, Khan Jehán, who commanded in the adjoining provinces, to give a daughter of the royal house in marriage to a son of the Emperor's, and as the price of this, to hold the kingdom of Beejapoor himself in dependence, which had been his father's aim also. The plot was discovered, however, and Kowas Khan was assassinated in 1675, eighteen years after the events we have recorded.

Some of his lineal descendants still survive, and the memory of the lady Zyna and of her beauty lives among them. There is a noble mausoleum on the west side of the town of Suggur, in the province of Shorapoor, which, at the period of which we write, belonged to this family. It was begun by the "Wuzeer" of Beejapoor, and finished by his son Kowas Khan: and in it the remains of the lady Zyna and her husband rest, under the care of their descendants, who, now reduced in circumstances, have preserved a small village with its lands, which adjoins the tomb, as the only remnant of the once princely estates which were held by their ancestors; and the revenues of this village, which had originally been assigned in payment of oil for the mausoleum, are now their only support. They are, however, most respectable. The soubriquet of Wuzeer is still attached to them; and the head of the family, Sofee Sahib, still preserves much of the "aristocratic" dignity of descent. The family palace at Beejapoor, though deserted, is still standing, and is, or was, one of the very few private buildings there of which the roof is entire. Perhaps by this time, however, its owner may have been unable to resist the price he could obtain for its massive teak timbers. The roof may have been sold, and the handsome rooms and courts left open, to decay rapidly under the influence of the seasons.

A few words in relation to some other characters in our history, and we have done.

Pahar Singh did not long maintain his promise of abstinence from violence. It had become, together with avarice, the ruling passion of his character, and led him on, after a while, to fresh outrages; and though pardoned by the King again and again, in memory of his strange services, it was impossible, in the end, to overlook the daring character of his proceedings, and his occupation of royal territories. Nor was it long before Kowas Khan discovered the active share the robber chief had taken in his father's murder; and though the King's acquiescence in that deed was more surmised than ascertained, the fact of his being acquainted with Pahar Singh's part in it was not afterwards denied. On an occasion, therefore, when, by a more than usually serious outrage, the King's pardon had been absolutely withdrawn, his reduction and punishment became unavoidable,—Kowas Khan led an army against the castle of Itga, Pahar Singh was slain in its defence, his estates confiscated, and the castle and its walls blown up.

His nephew escaped, but returned to the village to live as a farmer under reduced circumstances. When Aurungzeeb conquered the country, he became again "Hazaree," or commander of a thousand, and the title remained with his descendants, who, however, never abandoned lawless courses. Long afterwards, a descendant, also named Pahar Singh, became a leader of Dekhan Pindarees, or freebooters, after the Mahratta war of 1818-19, and when that crime was no longer practicable, took to a minor practice of it in highway robbery. In 1828-29, the family were found to be largely connected with Dacoity and Thuggee, and the leading members of it were tried, convicted of both crimes, and sentenced to various terms of imprisonment, during which their head, Pahar Singh, died.

Persevering to the last, the other members, on their release, again took to highway robbery on horseback, and for a brief period were the terror of certain districts in the Dekhan, extending their operations, too, to distant points; but they were gradually hunted down,* and the last six were brought to justice by the writer of this chronicle in 1850, and sentenced to penal servitude for life. One

* They were apprehended by the author, committed to the Zillah court of Sholapoor, and there tried by the judge.

member only of the family survives free, and, as late as 1860, was a private in the police of the —— district.

Our friend the Lalla, who played a conspicuous part in the early portion of this history, became a prosperous and wealthy man; but the question of his honesty remained an open one. He sent for his family, and settled at Beejapoor, and his talents gained him lucrative employment in the state. He remained attached to Kowas Khan, whom he is believed to have corrupted; and, finally, as the kingdom was on the point of dissolution, he is said to have made peace with his old master, the Emperor Aurungzeeb, by materially assisting his designs, and tampering with the nobility and officers of the state previous to the last investment of the city. He probably returned to Dehli with the royal camp, for no traces of his family are to be found in Beejapoor.

Bulwunt Rao remained as he was, the leader of a troop of his own horses in the Paigah, or household forces of Fazil Khan. When his cousin and hereditary enemy, Tannajee Maloosray, was killed in that famous escalade of Singhur, near Poona, which has furnished the subject of many a Mahratta ballad, Bulwunt Rao went to Sivaji, and the circumstances he related being well remembered, he obtained substantial justice in the restoration of his hereditary property. Sivaji offered him service, which was respectfully declined, and the motives for refusal being appreciated, he was honourably dismissed. He married among his kinsfolk, and his wife, a practical woman, kept his house well. It is questionable, however, whether his habits were ever reclaimed, and he died before the dissolution of the Beejapoor kingdom. His wife, finding the care of the troop-horses irksome, sold them, returned with her children to the family estate, and settled there, and their descendants are now connected with many of the noble families of the Dekhan.

The hunchback, Lukshmun, after his return home, took to Itga all that he had saved, together with a heavy purse of gold which Fazil Khan had given him, which he buried immediately on his arrival. Somehow or other, however, the fact of this gold being possessed by him, got wind, and the idea of a mere retainer possessing gold at all, was too much to be endured by his avaricious master, who demanded to see it. We are sorry to record, that the poor fellow was obliged to submit to some rough torture, which was more than he could bear, ere he would surrender it; but Lukshmun always supposed that it was by the desertion of his master at Tooljapoor, rather than by the possession of the gold, that evil eyes fell upon him; and perhaps he was right. The gold was given up to his chief, and by it the last link between them was broken; and profiting by Pahar Singh's temporary absence, Lukshmun, taking his wife and children with him, left Itga one day, and returned to Afzoolpoor, where Fazil

Khan's retainers were stationed, and was protected by them. Pahar Singh threatened to burn the town if he were not given up; but Fazil Khan paid what was demanded for him, and he remained.

Years afterwards, and as his lord's children grew up, the hunchback was their especial favourite. He taught the eldest boys athletic exercises, the use of their weapons, and riding; and as long as any girl was allowed to go out of the private apartments, he carried her about in his arms, told charming fairy stories, and manufactured playthings—his dolls, being of all, the most hideous, and most delightful. Nor was there any greater treat to the children possible, than when their mother sometimes, and especially on certain anniversaries, sent for the hunchback and Ashruf, now a stout cavalier in the household troop, and having seated them outside a screen, made them sing ballads again as they did once long ago; and of all their store, "The Vow of the Necklace," was ever the greatest favourite with the children, because their mother's name was mentioned in it. With her, because—well, no matter: we know why, long since, and 'tis now an old story.

Many years before them, and in all honour among her children, as she always called them, the lady Lurlee passed away. She never gave up astrology, and found perpetual occupation in discovering lucky days for her grandchildren's wants, and for all sorts of household observances. Not a tooth could be cut, or any ailment of childhood exist and pass away, without appropriate ceremonials of thanksgiving, in the discovery of proper times for which, the old lady was held to be especially skilful. Nor in these only. Was she not the authority of the neighbourhood for ascertaining lucky marriages, for deciding the proper colours for proper days of her grandchildren's dresses; and did not she keep the cords of all their birthdays, and tie the knots in each as the anniversaries returned? Was she not the undisputed director of all such household family matters, and the universal referee on them by all her acquaintance?

Her affection for Zyna and her children remained to the last, though she never cordially liked Kowas Khan, or forgave him for being the son of one who had been a slave. But her love for her own child, Tara—the child whom God had sent her—transcended that for Zyna. It filled her heart, and overflowed upon her grandchildren, who loved her dearly, and did with her pretty much what they pleased. After Kowas Khan's death she went to Zyna, and lived with her till her son was old enough to protect his mother; then she settled finally into the place she held with Tara and her children; and when she breathed her last, her head lay on Tara's bosom—resting peacefully.

With her outward conversion to a strange faith, did Tara forget the old? No, it was impossible. Though her studious disposition enabled her to master enough Arabic, under her husband's teaching, to understand the daily prayers, and some simple ceremonials, yet the grand old Hindu hymns of the Védas, and other devotional portions of the Shastras, especially the Bhugwat Geeta, were never forgotten; and when the purport of them was explained to her husband, he did not object to her reading them. She could not either, change her frugal mode of living; and, to her death, never overcame her natural repugnance to animal food. In this respect also, her husband indulged her; though perhaps the lady Lurlee thought it a sad dereliction of orthodox observances in general, which could only be overcome on the festivals of the Nowroz or the Bukreed, or other occasions of religious ceremonial.

When Tara was dying, and the Moollas without were chanting the service for her departing soul, her eyes seemed once to flash with a bright radiance, and her husband and children, who were around her, heard her say gently, "I come, O Mother," and repeat some Sanscrit words. The priests, jealous of her perfect conversion, would have it, that she alluded to Miriam, the Mother of Jesus of Nazareth, for there could be no other Mother. It might, indeed, be so, for she seemed of late to have taken a peculiar delight and interest in this history, especially since some Christian monks from Goa, who had established a mission* at the town of Chittapoor, only a few miles distant, had come to beg alms of her, and had told her of the purer faith of Christ, and his loving mother Mary. It might have been that she spoke of this; or, more probable perhaps, that her spirit, trembling on the brink of the unknown world, had wandered back into the old days of her trials and deliverances, once, ere it departed.

* The mission still exists, and is visited periodically by priests from Goa. There are, or were, about seventy Christians in it who, with an affecting simplicity, preserve their faith in purity. They are shepherds, weavers, and distillers.

GLOSSARY.

A.

Alla, God.
Alla-hu-Akbur, God is victorious!
Alkab, honorary titles prefixed to letters according to rank.
Amān, mercy.
Ameen, amen.
Ashruffees, gold coins—mohurs.
Astagh-fur-oolla, exclamation of abhorrence—God forbid!

B.

Bābool, mimosa.
Beebee, lady.
Bismilla, in God's name!
Bhugwān, an appellation of the Divinity.
Bhugwat Geeta, a devotional episode of the Mahabharut.
Bhuttote, Thug designation for strangler.
Bukreed, Mussulman festival in commemoration of the offering up of Isaac.
Bunij, Thug designation for a victim.
Burr, the banian tree.
Burkhast, dismissal of an assembly.
Bye, Mahratta term for lady.
Byragee, one of the Hindu sects of devotees.

C.

Chenna, a kind of pulse—"gram."
Cheyla, a disciple.
Chóbdar, mace-bearer.
Coss, two miles.
Coss bur, about two miles.

D.

Daee, a nurse.
Dallal, a broker.
Darógha, a superintendent.
Dévi, the goddess Bhowani.
Dhotee, a man's waistcloth.
Dooputta, a scarf.
Duffadar, subordinate officer (military).
Durbar, a court assembly.
Duróra, gang robbery with violence.

F.

Fateha, thank-offering.

G.

Ganja, hemp leaves cured for smoking.
Ghee, boiled butter.
Gooroo, spiritual teacher.
Gopis, the nymphs of Muttra.
Goruk Imlee, Adansonia Gigantea.
Gosai or *Gosavee*, a sect of Hindu devotees, who are sometimes bankers.
Gosha! Murdhana! Private! cried out by their attendants when Mussulman ladies leave their houses.
Gowra (Canarese), head authority of a village.

H.

Hai, Hai! alas, alas!
Hookum, order, direction.
Hoondee, bill of exchange.
Humeana, waist-belt to carry money.
Hur, Hur, Mahadeo! the Mahratta war-cry—invocation to Mahadeo.
Hurkara, a messenger.
Huzrut, prince—my lord.

I.

Inshalla, please God!

J.

Jehád, religious war—crusade.
Jemadar, military officer (captain).
Jo Hookum, respectful affirmative—"as ordered."
Josee, astrologer.
Jowan, a young man, applied generally to soldiers.
Jungum, priest of the Lingayet sect.

Junum-Putr, literally, birth letter—"horoscope at birth."
Junwah, the sacred thread of a Brahmun.

K.

Kabob, piece of meat fried or roasted.
Kafir, infidel.
Kāmdeo, the Indian Cupid.
Kasee, Benares.
Kazee, Mahomedan law officer.
Khayet, one of the Hindu castes, usually scribes.
Khilwut, private apartments.
Khóda Hafiz, God protect you!
Khódawund, my lord.
Khundoba, an incarnation of Siva.
Kichéri, rice and pulse boiled together.
Kótwal, magistrate of a town or bazar.
Kowl, deed of protection and assurance.
Kucheri, court-house.
Kullal, publican, spirit seller.
Kullundur, a sect of fakeers—"calendars."
Kurra, a ring for the wrist.
Kurreem, kind, merciful.

L.

Lakh, one hundred thousand.
Lóta, a drinking vessel.
Luddoo, a sweetmeat made of sugar, milk, and flour rolled into balls.
Lownee, a Mahratta ballad.

M.

Máma, a confidential female attendant.
Máhá, great.
Mang, a low caste of Hindus in the Dekhan.
Máta, mother.
Meah, respectful title of the eldest son of a Mussulman family.
Mirdha, court usher or attendant.
Mobaruk-bád, congratulation.
Moolla, Mussulman priest.
Motee, pearl.
Mudd, the line drawn above an address to a superior.
Muezzin, the caller to prayer.
Mudud Khana, a shop where intoxicating drugs are prepared and used.
Mutsuddee, a clerk or scribe.
Mutt, a monastery.

N.

Náib, agent, deputy.
Näik, a title used by chiefs of the lower tribes.
Nagara, large kettle-drum.
Narayun, a Hindu epithet for the divinity.
Nobut, honorary band of music.
Nobut Khana, the place where the Nobut plays.
Now Ratree, the nine nights before the Dusséra festival.
Nowroz, Mussulman New Year's Day.
Nullah, a watercourse—rivulet.
Nummo Narayun! salutation to a Gosai.
Numascar! a respectful Hindu salutation to a Brahmun.
Nurruk, Hades.
Nuzzur, offering to a superior

P.

Pacheese, twenty-five, a game like backgammon.
Padshah, king—emperor.
Paigah, household troops.
Palkee, an open litter.
Pán, betel-leaf.
Patel, chief authority of a village.
Peepul, Ficus Religiosa.
Phoolka, a light kind of bread—a "scone."
Pooree, a kind of light pancake.
Pundit, a learned Brahmun.
Purméshwar, a Hindu epithet for the divinity.
Putwaree, a village registrar and accountant.

R.

Ràm, an ancient king of Oudh, esteemed an incarnation of Vishnu.
Rámchunder, an epithet of divinity.
Raméshwar, a celebrated Hindu shrine near Cape Comorin.
Ramoosee, one of the lower tribes in the Dekhan.

S.

Sahib, sir.
Saree, a woman's garment in one piece.

Seeta, the wife of "Ram."
Serái, a traveller's resting-house.
Shabash, well done!
Shastree, a Brahmun learned in the Shastras.
Sheea, a heterodox Mussulman—follower of Ali.
Sheernee, rice and milk for thank-offerings.
Shookr, thanks.
Shookr Ulla, thanks to God!
Shukti, secret worship of Hindu demons, the rites of which are horrible.
Shytan, the devil.
Sirkar, the Government: authority.
Sonar, a goldsmith.
Soobhán-Ulla, praise to God!
Soonnee, an orthodox Mussulman.
Sowaree, retinue.
Sree Mata, Holy Mother.
Sree Swami, Holy Lord.
Sudra, the lowest of the four divisions of Hindus.
Sutee, chaste, faithful.
Syn, respectful epithet of a fakeer.

T.

Toba, for shame!
Tusleemât, the three obeisances to persons of high rank.

U.

Ul-humd-ul-illa, praise be to God!

V.

Vina, a large lute or guitar with frets.

Y.

Ya Alla kureem, O merciful God.
Ya Khubeer-o, O giver of information!—one of the ninety-nine attributes of God.

Z.

Zemindar, a land-holder.